LIVING WITH THE GODS

'The first condition of human goodness is something to love; the second, something to reverence.'

GEORGE ELIOT

'Religion is an attempt to find meaning in events, not a theory that tries to explain the universe.'

JOHN GRAY

'Religious beliefs are not universal truths, but community truths, and they guide lives rather than describe facts. They express what it means to belong to a community and to owe allegiance to its values.'

DON CUPITT

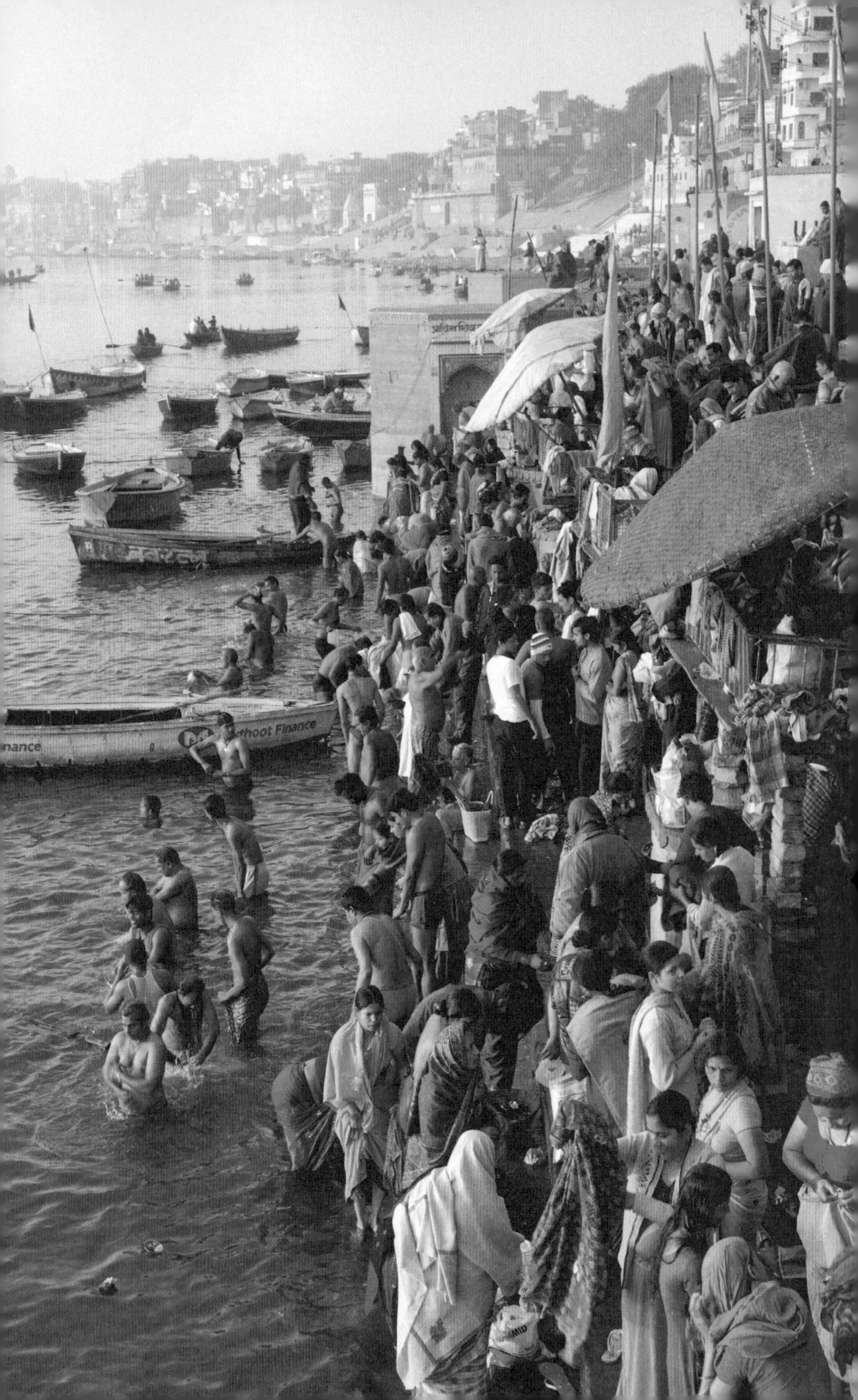

nance
thoot Finance

Neil MacGregor

Living with the Gods

ON BELIEFS AND PEOPLES

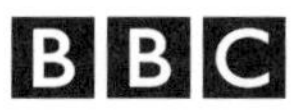

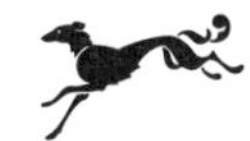

The British Museum

Alfred A. Knopf
New York
2018

FOR PAUL KOBRAK,

companion through earth and air, fire and water

THIS IS A BORZOI BOOK
PUBLISHED BY ALFRED A. KNOPF

www.aaknopf.com

By arrangement with the BBC and the British Museum

LCCN: 2018030942 (hardcover); ISBN: 9780525521464 (hardcover)
ISBN: 9780525521471 (ebook)

Front-of-jacket image: Nose and lips of Akhenaten, c. 1353–1336 BC. The Metropolitan Museum of Art, New York. Purchase, Edward S. Harkness Gift, 1926 (26.7.1395)

Manufactured in Germany
First United States Edition

Frontispiece: Sunrise at the Harischandra Ghat at Varanasi on the Ganges, with bathers facing the rising sun (see p. 39)

CONTENTS

PART FOUR

The Power of Images

PART FIVE

One God or Many

PART SIX

Powers Earthly and Divine

INTRODUCTION
BELIEVING AND BELONGING

Living with the Gods is about one of the central facts of human existence: that every known society shares a set of beliefs and assumptions – a faith, an ideology, a religion – that goes far beyond the life of the individual, and is an essential part of a shared identity. Such beliefs have a unique power to define – and to divide – peoples, and are a driving force in the politics of many parts of the world today. Sometimes they are secular, most obviously in the case of nationalism, but throughout history they have most often been, in the widest sense, religious. This book is emphatically not a history of religion, nor an argument in favour of faith, still less a defence of any particular system of belief. Looking across history and around the globe, it interrogates objects, places and human activities to try to understand what shared religious beliefs can mean in the public life of a community or a nation, how they shape the relationship between the individual and the state, and how they have become a crucial contributor to who we are. For in deciding how we live with our gods we also decide how to live with each other.

Belief is back

After the end of the Second World War the Western world basked for decades in a prosperity without precedent in history. The United States offered most of its citizens – and its immigrants –

what appeared to be endlessly rising standards of living. In 1957, the Prime Minister, Harold Macmillan, famously told the British public that they had 'never had it so good'. They agreed, and he comfortably won the next election. Across Western Europe and North America, economic growth was the norm: peace had on the whole led to plenty.

In the rest of the world, the Soviet Union and the United States were locked in bitter conflict, sometimes military, always ideological, competing to win new recruits for their preferred systems of Marxist state communism or liberal democratic capitalism. As both are essentially economic propositions, the debate increasingly and unsurprisingly centred not on their very different notions of freedom and social justice, but on which system could provide the greater material benefits for its society.

There is a striking example of this elision – equation – of ideals with their material outcomes on the US dollar bill, or, more precisely, on two dollar bills. Even though most of its population was Christian, the United States had been founded on the explicit basis, enshrined in the Constitution, that the new nation should not have an established religion. But in 1956, in an effort to distinguish itself even more sharply from the atheist Soviet Union, Congress resolved to make greater public use of the long-familiar motto 'In God We Trust'. In a gesture rich in unintended symbolism, it was decided that the words should appear not on public buildings or on the flag, but on the national currency. They have been printed on dollar bills ever since, and on the ten-dollar bill they hover protectively over the US Treasury itself. The ironic phrase the 'Almighty Dollar' had been circulating since the nineteenth century, warning against the conflation of God and Mammon. Now, however, one of the defining American beliefs was to be expressed on the most revered manifestation of its success: its money.

On the face of it, it might seem that the new wording on the

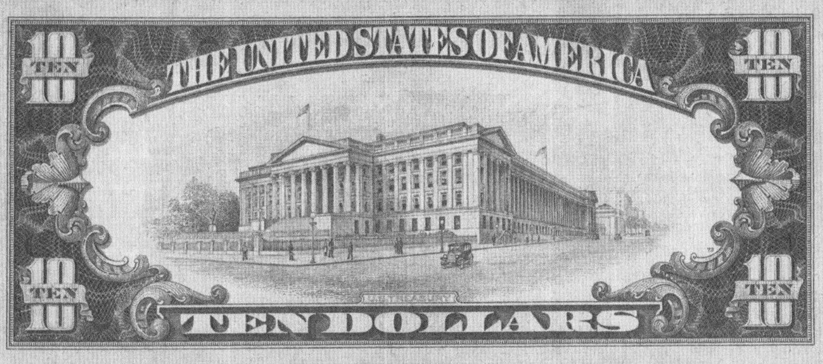

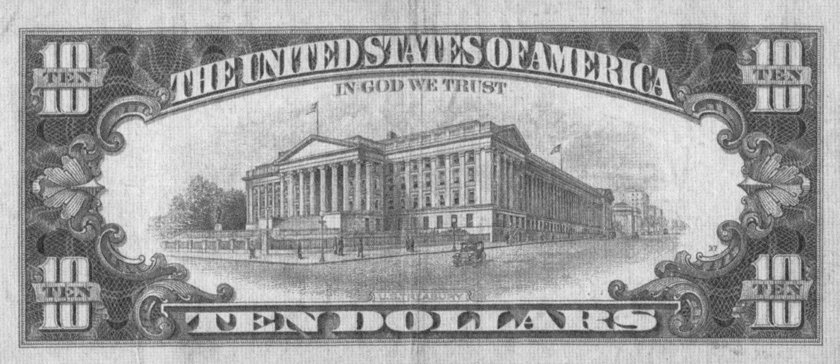

The ten-dollar bill, showing the US Treasury, before and after 1956

dollar bills was an assertion of the supremacy of God in the US political system, a twentieth-century American version of the letters *DG – Dei Gratia*, 'By the Grace of God' – which accompany the portrait of the sovereign on British currency, or the Qur'anic texts on the coinage of many Islamic states. In fact, it was almost the reverse.

This striking combination of the financial and the spiritual, far from being a step towards theocracy in Washington, was symptomatic of a wider change in the balance between ethics and economics. On both sides of the Atlantic, the role of organized religion in public and private realms alike was receding. Society was becoming increasingly secular – more swiftly in Europe – and fewer and fewer were attending traditional religious services. The 'revolutionaries' of 1968 argued in terms of economic injustice that hardly mentioned God, let alone putting their trust in him. After the collapse of Communism in the Soviet Union at the end of the 1980s, the consensus almost everywhere was clear. The battle of ideologies was over: capitalism had won, communism had failed, religion had withered, and if there was a faith – a set of assumptions shared by almost everybody – it was now in material well-being. As Bill Clinton memorably put it in the US presidential election campaign of 1992: 'It's the economy, stupid.' Few disagreed; and, like Macmillan before him, Clinton was elected leader of his country.

Twenty-five years later, to the surprise or bewilderment of the prosperous West, organized religion is, all around the world, once again politically centre stage. To an extent rarely seen in Europe since the seventeenth century, faith now shapes large parts of the global public debate. The competitive materialisms of the Cold War have been replaced. The whole of the Middle East is caught up in murderous conflicts that are articulated and fought not in economic but in religious terms. The politics of Pakistan and Israel, both founded as explicitly secular states, are increasingly confessional. In Indonesia and Nigeria, Myanmar and Egypt, communities are attacked and individuals killed on the pretext that the practice of their faith makes them aliens in their own country. India, whose constitution enshrines the state's equidistance from all religions, is convulsed by calls for the government to assert an explicitly Hindu identity, with grave consequences for Indians who are Muslims or Christians (Chapter 25). In many countries, not least the United States, immigration policy – effectively the case against immigrants – is often framed in the language of religion. Even in largely agnostic Europe, the Bavarian

Prime Minister urges the presence of the cross in official buildings as the marker of a Catholic Bavarian identity, and the French government bans the public wearing of the full-face *burqa* (Chapter 28). In Switzerland a referendum is held to ban the building of minarets (Chapter 9), while thousands march regularly in Dresden to protest against alleged 'Islamization'. The most populous state on earth, China, claims that its national interests, the very integrity of the state, are threatened by the exiled spiritual leader of Tibetan Buddhists, the Dalai Lama, a man whose only power is the faith he embodies.

The Islamic revolution in Iran in 1979, deeply shocking to the secular world, and which at the time appeared to be pushing against the tide of history, now seems instead to have been the harbinger of its turning. After decades of humiliating intervention by the British and the Americans, Iranian politicians found in religion a way of defining and asserting the country's identity. Many since then have followed the same path. In a way that could hardly have been imagined sixty years ago, the reassuring politics

The difficulties of faith in the public realm. Watched over by police, French Muslims pray in the street in Clichy on the outskirts of Paris, in protest at the closure of their unauthorized place of worship, March 2017.

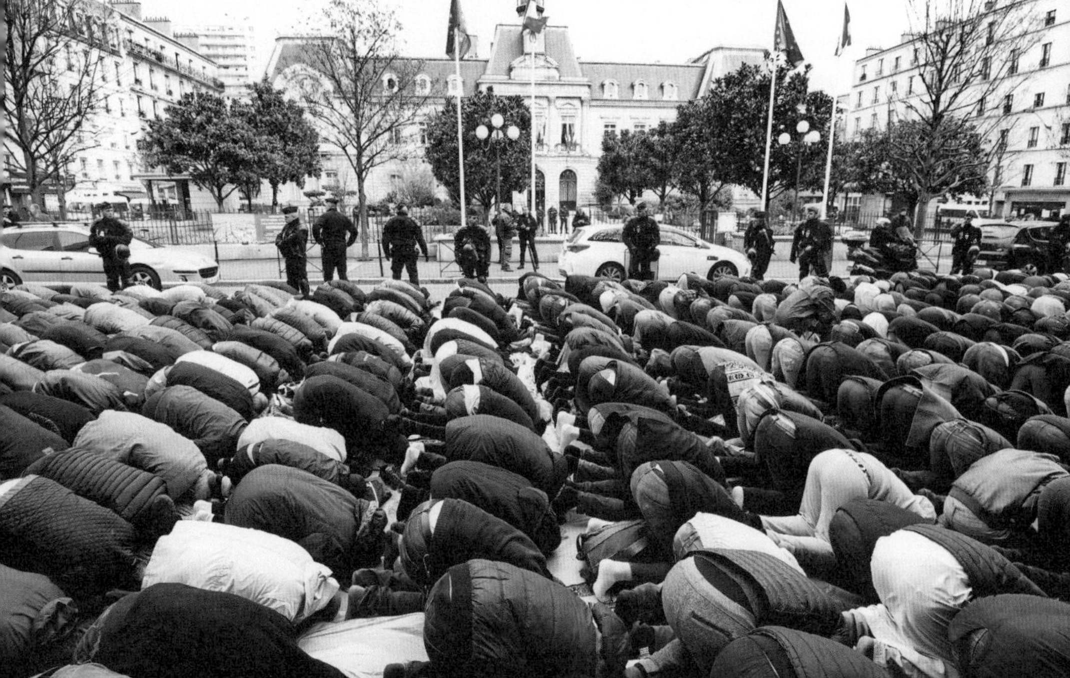

of prosperity has in many parts of the world been replaced by the rhetoric and politics, often violent, of identity articulated through belief. One of the arguments of *Living with the Gods* is that this should not surprise us, because it is in fact a return to the prevalent pattern of human societies.

Living in stories

'We tell ourselves stories in order to live.' Joan Didion's famous sentence opens a collection of essays she wrote around her experiences in the secular America of the 1970s. It is not a reflection on religion, but it speaks to exactly that compelling need which we all have, for stories that order our memories and hopes, and give shape and meaning to our individual and collective lives.

We begin where the oldest surviving evidence begins, in the caves of Europe at the end of the Ice Age. We shall see in Chapter 1 that a society with a belief in something beyond itself, a narrative that goes beyond the immediate and beyond the self, seems better equipped to confront threats to its existence, to survive and to flourish. At the beginning of the twentieth century, the French sociologist Émile Durkheim argued that without such overarching stories, what he called 'an idea that it constructs of itself', there can in fact be no society. Those stories, the ideals they illustrate and the ceremonies in which they are enacted constituted for Durkheim the essential elements of any system of communal belief: and, in a sense, the stories *are* the society. If, for whatever reason, we lose or forget them, in a very real way we, collectively, no longer exist.

Systems of belief almost always contain a narrative of how the physical world was created, how the people came to be in it, and how they and all living things should inhabit it. But the stories and associated rituals usually go far beyond that. They tell members of the group how they ought to behave to one another, and crucially they also address the future – those aspects of the society that will endure as succeeding generations perish and pass. They embrace the living, the dead and those still to be born, in one continuing story of belonging.

The most powerful and most sustaining of any society's stories are the work of generations. They are repeated, adapted and transmitted, absorbed into everyday life, ritualized and internalized to such a degree that we are often hardly aware that we are still surrounded by the tales of distant ancestors. They give us our particular place in a pattern which can be observed but not fully understood – and they do it almost without our knowing it. It is a process we can witness every day as we – and others – repeat that most familiar of sequences, the days of the week.

Living in time

Sunday, Monday, Tuesday, Wednesday, Thursday, Friday, Saturday. The idea of dividing the cycle of the moon into four seven-day weeks may have begun in ancient Babylon. In its familiar modern form, it probably derives from a Jewish model, echoing the story of the Creation as told in Genesis, in which God, having made the world in six days, rested on the seventh – and ordered humanity and their animals to do likewise. In consequence, every week connects us to the beginning of time itself, as its days plot the round of our work and our leisure, the recurrent rhythm of our existence. But they do more, and what that is will depend on our language and our beliefs. The names that we give the weekdays in English are an inherited meditation on the cycles of time, as we observe the pattern of the sun, the moon and the planets circling above us; and the story they tell is for English-speakers only, for nobody else's week is quite the same as ours.

Sunday, Monday – it begins with the sun and the moon, which we see virtually every day, and whose separate movements mark the months and the years. After them, in most of Western Europe, come the days of the easily visible planets. In the Romance languages, this is obvious to all: Mars – *martedì/mardi*; Mercury – *mercoledì/mercredi*; Jupiter (Jove) – *giovedì/jeudi*; Venus – *venerdì/vendredi*. The order may surprise modern astronomers, but it is the sequence that the Romans followed and that they left behind them. In England, somewhere around the seventh century, the planets tethered to the exotic gods of Rome were renamed for the equivalent northern gods, and it is their Anglo-Saxon names – Tiw, Woden, Thor and Frige – that distinguish the days for English-speakers on Tuesday, Wednesday, Thursday and Friday. On Saturday, these homely Anglo-Saxon gods are, however, joined by Saturn, the one Roman immigrant who stubbornly retained his Latin name, making our week, like our language itself, a peculiar German–Latin hybrid.

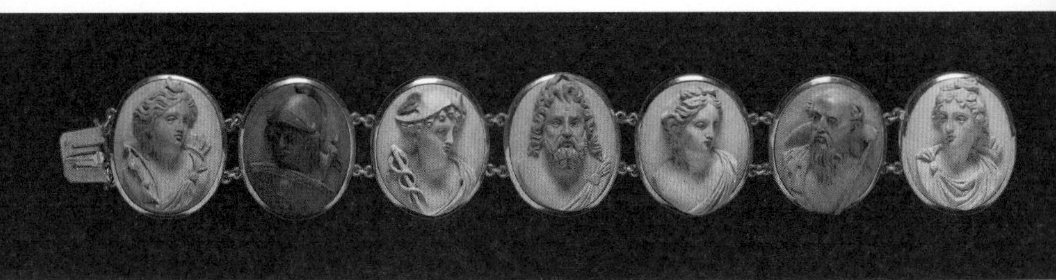

Moon-day to Sun-day. The Roman gods of the English days of the week, on a mid-nineteenth-century Italian cameo bracelet

Encompassing the different cycles of sun, moon and the five planets, every week thus implies not just a long span of many years, but also the company of many gods and the vastness of space itself. In the names of our days is the entire solar system, the time–space continuum as it was known in the ancient Mediterranean world and transmitted to the north of Europe. The turn of the week is – in English – a concise cosmological history, in which we still live every day with the gods of our ancestors and our conquerors, inhabiting an ancient but stable structure of time.

This huge embrace of the week is pleasingly visible, and surprisingly portable, in a splendid nineteenth-century Italian cameo bracelet, where the sun and moon flank the planets in their due sequence, all carved in relief and rendered in characteristic Roman mode. But although the bracelet was made in Italy, it makes sense only in English: because the English weekend is very different from the one in Southern Europe. In Italian (and in French and the other Romance languages), after Friday there is no Saturn's day. Instead, the week shifts into a different religious world, and the fifth of the pagan gods gives way to the Sabbath of the single God of the Jews – *sabato* and *samedi*. And after the Jewish Sabbath comes not the day of the sun, but *domenica* or *dimanche*: it is the day of *dominus*, the Lord. In Latin Europe the weekend is not about the pattern of movement in the skies, but about how we should worship on earth. Thus the days of the week give time a shape, placing the everyday routine of our single lives in a pattern both of cosmic harmony and of social order.

The seven-day week is now a global phenomenon, but the different names for its days everywhere tell a series of local stories, depending on custom and language. Most of the Europe that was shaped by the Roman Catholic church retained the pagan Roman planetary gods, even though long supplanted, and the Romance languages added to them the Jewish and Christian holy days. But in Eastern Europe and the Middle East the Greek Orthodox church rejected those displaced pagan gods – and their planets – entirely. It chose instead to stay with the radically different tradition of the Jews, a model later adopted also by the Muslims. For all of these, the week has a clear centre: the one and only God, and the day principally devoted to his worship – Friday, Saturday or Sunday as appropriate for Muslims, Jews or Christians. The days in between have no pagan or cosmic resonances, but are simply numbered in sequence – the day after, or the second day, the third day, and so on. So the turn of the week in Hebrew, Russian or

Arabic, to venture no further afield, tells a story quite different from ours: a narrative of the active practice of faith and of rigorous monotheism, of one single god around whom alone the pattern of our lives is to be ordered – a god who emphatically does not share time with the gods of the heathens (Chapter 22).

To name the days of the week is, for most of the world, to declare, consciously or unconsciously, the religious history of your particular community. It is why the anti-religious French revolutionaries, eager to devise a calendar which, like the metric system, the whole world could use, concluded that the only way forward was simply to abolish the week altogether (Chapter 29) and move to a decimal system of days. It was logical, and they believed it should be universal. Yet here too, after a handful of years, the old gods returned.

Naming weekdays may be complex, but cultures diverge even more sharply, and far more bitterly, when it comes to numbering the years. Where to begin counting? When did time – or, more precisely, when did *our* story – start? For the Jews, that meant Jehovah's creation of the world, for the Romans the foundation of their city – in each case a perfect demonstration of their view of their place in world history. But for others it was the moment when the world began a second time, and all things were made new. For Christians that is the birth of Jesus; for Muslims it is when the Prophet moved from Mecca to Medina and the community of the faithful took shape. Imperial China began counting the years afresh with every new reign. For French Revolutionaries the establishment of the Republic and of new institutions of the state made 1792 Year One. In Aztec Mexico the sequence had neither beginning nor end, but moved in complex, endlessly repeating fifty-two-year cycles. There is in short no universal story: numbering the years, like naming the days, conveys each particular society's idea of what it is and of its own special place in time.

The expanding power of Europe and America over the last two

centuries has led (or compelled) most of the world to divide historical time as they do, into the years Before Christ and Anno Domini, the year of Our Lord. Many, despite their own very different beliefs, agree to use the same numbering, but understandably baulk at using the letters BC and AD, which endorse (or at least acknowledge) an exclusively Christian narrative. They prefer instead the neutral notion, increasingly popular since the late nineteenth century, of a Common Era, which retains the Christian chronology, dating events from the supposed date of the birth of Jesus, but relabelled as CE or BCE.

The idea of the Common Era is an ingenious and largely successful attempt to find a narrative framework which, irrespective of language, culture or religion, can embrace all humanity. But it is a rare example. Perhaps it is possible only because two (or, in the case of Iran, three) calendars can happily co-exist, each to be used for different purposes (Chapter 29), an ecumenical, even bilingual, view of time. Most conflicts between our local and global narratives have not proved so easy to resolve.

The limits of language

The familiar example of the days of the week and the calendar touch on many of the topics we shall be discussing in loftier contexts later in the book. They show with wonderful clarity the astonishing longevity of belief patterns once established, and the extent to which rituals of worship in many – perhaps most – societies structure the rhythms of life.

In *Living with the Gods* we shall be looking not at the life of monastic retreat, or private spirituality, at what individuals believe, or the abstract theological truth of religious ideas, which must be unknowable except to devotees. We shall be looking instead at what whole societies believe and do. It is a way of addressing religion – as practice rather than doctrine – that may seem foreign to those brought up with the idea that belief is based on divinely inspired texts held to contain absolute truths, from which religious authority ultimately derives. If there is one image that sums up that view of organized religion in the West, it would surely be Moses on Mount Sinai receiving, directly from God, the Ten Commandments: one all-powerful, all-controlling God, handing down a text, written in unchangeable stone, which sets out clear and immutable doctrine about how we should worship him, and what we should (but mostly should not) do.

Needless to say, that is a reductive caricature, as any Jew, Christian or Muslim would quickly point out. Moses on Mount Sinai is, for all three traditions, only one part of a much larger story, which embraces millennia of contact with God, many other divinely inspired texts, many other kinds of social practices, and constantly evolving interpretations of the Hebrew scriptures, the Gospels and the Qur'an (Chapter 20). Nevertheless, literal, fundamentalist readings of those texts are still a major cause of violent disagreement between groups of Muslims, Christians and Jews.

The Abrahamic faiths really are unusual, and not just in their belief in a single God. Most faiths of the world for most of history have not had texts that claimed such unique status – if they had texts at all. Even fewer have any notion of a central authority, which, like the Vatican, might define a corpus of doctrine which adherents are required to believe. Hindus and Buddhists of course have many texts, but none that has self-evident primacy, and so the meanings accorded to them and the practices around them vary enormously from place to place. The Greeks and Romans, rigorous in so much else, had virtually nothing that we would regard as a statement of faith: their notion of religion was essentially something that citizens did. A view of faith systems that concentrated on doctrines and texts alone would be a sadly limited exercise.

It is in any case often difficult to say what specific beliefs people would, if pressed, affirm. We can, however, observe their

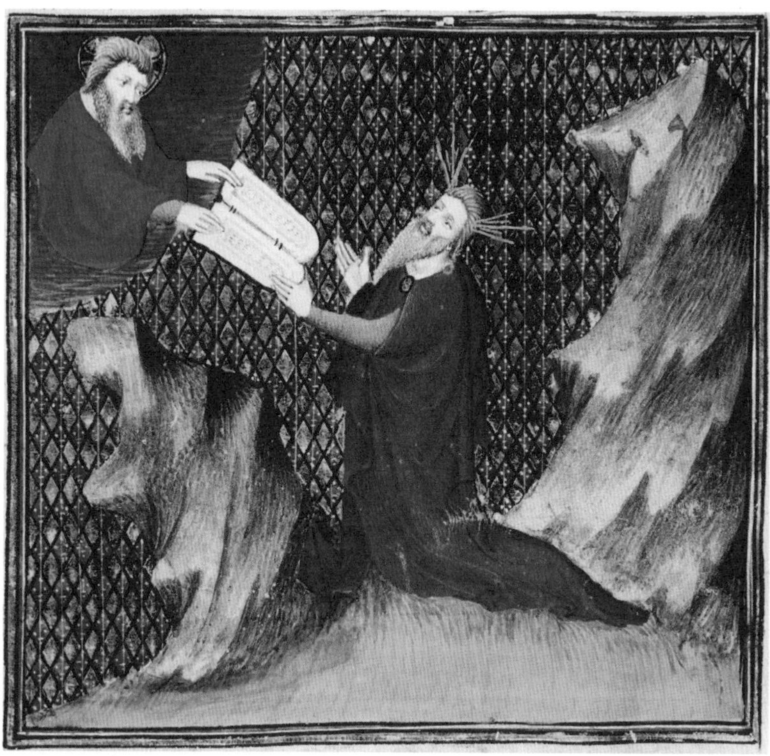

The laws of life and faith, handed down from God to Moses, in an early fifteenth-century French manuscript illumination

actions, the ceremonies large and small that express their beliefs, and which, regularly repeated, shape a life and a community. So the book focuses on those significant ceremonies, on the things that people use in them, and the places where they perform them. I have chosen sites where large numbers gather for sacrifice, pilgrimage or ritual celebrations, over as wide a geographic span as possible. The objects come almost entirely from the collection of the British Museum, but that is hardly a restriction, as it covers the globe and ranges from the earliest human societies to the present day and enables us to embark on a worldwide journey through the material and social manifestations of belief.

The great advantage of this approach is that objects and places allow us to address on an equal footing the large global religions and much smaller belief systems that are embedded in one particular landscape (Chapter 23); practices tightly controlled by king or clergy, and those, like the festival of Christmas or the cult of Our Lady of Guadalupe (Chapters 15 and 16), where the laity play an unscripted, pivotal role; religions that disappeared long ago and those that still flourish. They also let us consider forms of belief and behaviour not usually regarded as religious, such as state atheism, or the cult of the national leader.

There is another advantage too. In a world of several thousand different tongues, the silence of objects allows us into territory difficult to enter in other ways. Our bracelet of the days of the week, which is English-speaking and cannot be translated into Italian (let alone Arabic) without losing much of its meaning, powerfully demonstrates the profound links between language and belief. It is not just that together they are the most powerful forces in forging the identity of any community. The words in which we can talk about faith or religion are themselves inevitably shaped by – and in most cases limited to – our own habits and forms of thought. For obvious historical reasons, European languages are at ease with the notion of the single God of the Abrahamic tradition, or the classical gods of Greece and Rome. But beyond that, in Mesopotamia, India or Japan, for example, Europeans struggle to cope with unfamiliar, disconcertingly fluid ideas of the divine. When we try to find words to match the understanding of landscape that shapes the lives of people in Vanuatu or of Aboriginal Australians (Chapter 23), it quickly becomes clear that we simply do not have a vocabulary for ideas which are central to the lives of these communities, but which we have never encountered. 'Animate beings' and 'animated landscape' have an arid, abstract ring to them, far removed from the immediacy of the everyday experience itself. 'Spirits', which is probably the best we can do, sounds fey, and risks conjuring notions of table-tapping. All we can do, when we venture in our own language into the thought worlds of others, is to acknowledge our inadequacy: we are discussing matters for which we do not have the words.

This approach through objects, places and activities is inherently and necessarily fragmentary. It cannot in any way amount to a narrative history of faith. But it can, I hope, offer access, often refreshingly direct, into some of the different ways that societies have found of imagining and inhabiting their place in the world.

Who are 'we'?

Another of the central arguments of *Living with the Gods* is that religion addresses many of the same defining questions as politics. How does a society organize itself in order to survive? What sacrifices can society properly demand of the individual in the service of a greater good? Above all, who is included in the community that we call 'we'? The narratives of faith can create uniquely powerful symbols of solidarity. In the fire of the Parsis (Chapter 2) or in the statues of the goddess Durga (Chapter 17), every part of the community – rich and poor, weak and strong, living and dead – is represented and honoured. Few political units have found metaphors so emotionally compelling for a society in which everybody is included.

Religious beliefs have also of course been consciously manipulated by rulers and priests across the millennia to exclude parts of society – faith being used in the service of political oppression. The supreme example is the Nazi murdering of the Jews. We shall look here at the less familiar seventeenth-century persecution of Christians in Japan and Huguenots in France, in each case designed to define and to eliminate those who were not to be considered as 'we' by a powerful central state (Chapter 28). But those same faith structures can also be the refuge and the strength of the oppressed. The history of the Jews (Chapter 27) after the destruction of the Temple in Jerusalem and the campaigns of Hadrian, or the survival as a community of the enslaved African Americans (Chapter 10), can be explained only in terms of a set of beliefs which sustain when other supports have fallen away. In such circumstances religion offers an architecture of meaning in which people may find shelter and hope. And if it is not provided by those in power, those without power will often find ways of creating it for themselves, like the Mexican workers struggling for better conditions in the United States (Chapter 16). In each case, in politics and religion alike, people are defining their identity.

The thinkers of the European Enlightenment, among them the drafters of the US Constitution, hoped that, if they could separate organized religion from the government of society, they would banish for ever the spectre of religious wars. In that aim, they were by and large successful. Yet they perhaps addressed the symptom rather than the cause: the human need for belonging, and for a story to sustain it in which everybody has a part. The shared narratives of faith, uniting and inspiring, dividing and excluding, were quickly replaced by the no less strengthening and no less destructive myths of nationalism. It seems that Durkheim may have been right, and that what we venerate is often an imagined ideal form of society itself. Do we have such a notion of what our society should be today? In recent decades, as nation states have been enfeebled by economic globalization or, in parts of the Middle East and Africa, have collapsed entirely, religion has become an ever more significant marker of identity. Narratives of faith and the sense of belonging which they can offer are more attractive, more powerful and more dangerous than a generation ago.

The Enlightenment philosophers thought they had discovered how to accommodate different religious communities peacefully in one political structure: tolerance mixed with secularism. The Romans had achieved a remarkable degree of inter-faith harmony, by the elegant device of inviting the gods of the peoples they conquered into the Roman pantheon (Chapter 21): most were happy to accept the invitation and a new, expanded sense of imperial identity was the result. But such a relaxed and porous approach to faith was based on public rituals of worship, not a fixed doctrine of belief, and it is hardly open to the text-based monotheisms, with their single jealous god.

World-wide adoption of the Common Era calendar is a relatively trivial example of an agreement – generally acknowledged but hardly discussed – which established a universal commonality without denying individual identities. Is it possible now for humanity to find a pluralist global narrative, a set of assumptions and aspirations, which might embrace – and be embraced by – everybody in our hyper-connected and ever more fragile world? It is a question of life and death for the vastly increasing numbers of migrants in many parts of the globe (Chapter 30). 'Who are "we"?' is the great political question of our time, and it is essentially about what we believe.

PART ONE

Our Place in the Pattern

These first five chapters look at stories from four continents told by communities to articulate their understanding of the cosmos, and their place in it. These are stories of animals and plants, of fire, water, light and the seasons. They offer explanations of the way people experience the world, and the role all living things play in the repeating patterns of nature. Societies inhabit these cosmological narratives, daily and annual, and so conduct a constant dialogue between a particular community and the great scheme of things. The rituals associated with these stories affirm these understandings and, as they do so, greatly strengthen the identity of the community.

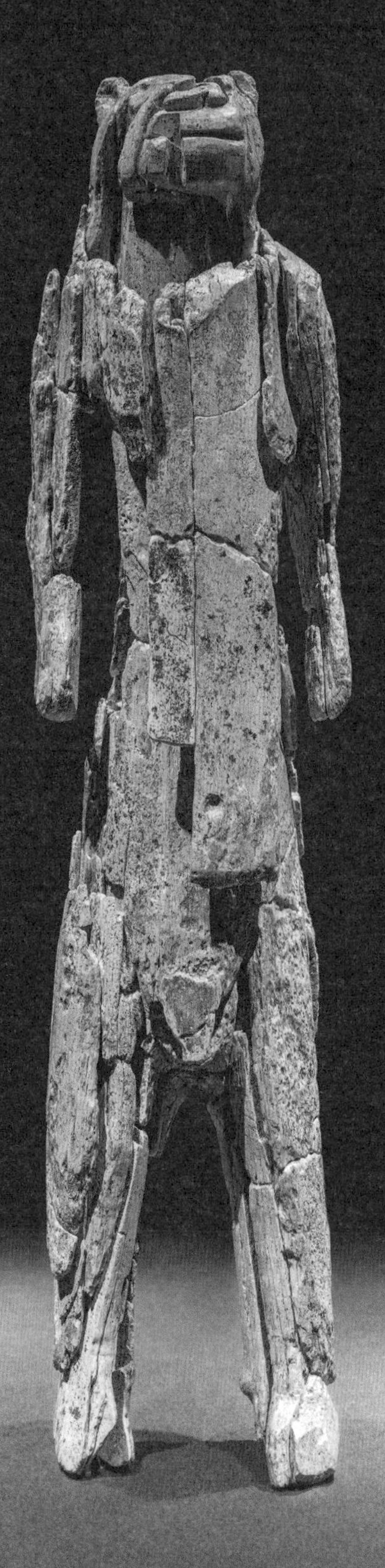

1

THE BEGINNINGS OF BELIEF

On 25 August 1939 two men were excavating at the back of Stadel cave in the Hohlenstein cliff, not far from Ulm in south-west Germany. The area, just north of the Danube, was known to contain remarkable material from the Ice Age, and it was hoped that this cave might yield some new finds. It was the last day of the dig: as everybody knew, war was about to break out. Both men – the anatomist Robert Wetzel and the geologist Otto Völzing – had received their call-up papers for the German army.

As Wetzel and Völzing were preparing to pack away their tools, they made a discovery. Forty metres in, in a further, smaller cave, they found many tiny fragments of mammoth ivory which looked as though they had been worked by human hands. But there was no time to examine the fragments, or to begin to work out what they were or what they might mean. They were packed away with other material from the excavation, and put into temporary storage, and the two men went off to war.

Wetzel briefly noted in a local scientific journal in 1941 that he and Völzing had made a 'sensational' find, but for thirty years no one really knew what they had discovered. The finds from the

The Lion Man of Ulm, made from mammoth ivory 40,000 years ago, the earliest-known representation of something beyond human experience

dig lay in crates housed first at Tübingen University, then in an air raid shelter in Ulm, before finally reaching the city museum there. The task of sorting and publishing the material from the cave excavation of thirty years previously was eventually given to its curator, Joachim Hahn, in 1969.

Within just a few days, something remarkable happened. Hahn and two colleagues realized that 200 or so of the mammoth ivory fragments could be put together to form a standing figure, around thirty centimetres in height. What was more, this figure was human – but not entirely so. In its incomplete state, Hahn thought it might be part bear. But with the incorporation of more fragments discovered some years later, the full pattern finally became clear. This was indeed a human body, but with the head of a lion. He quickly became known as *der Löwenmensch*, 'the Lion Man'.

Legs apart, arms a little out from his sides, he stands upright, perhaps on tiptoe, leaning slightly forward: a macho, somewhat aggressive pose. The calves, carefully shaped, are clearly human, and the navel is just where it ought to be on a model of a man. The upper body is slender, more feline, but on top of it are strong shoulders and an extraordinary head.

Jill Cook is the British Museum's expert in deep history:

This is the head of a cave lion, common in Ice Age Europe, and bigger than the modern African lion. The head is looking at us with a powerful, direct gaze. The mouth seems almost to smile. The ears are cocked, and inside them you can see the small opening for the auditory canal. When you look in detail at the back, you can see behind the ear little furrows, formed where the muscles contract to turn the ear in order to listen. This is not a human being wearing a mask. This is a creature, albeit a creature that cannot exist. And he is attentive, he is listening, he is watching.

Radiocarbon dating indicates that the Lion Man is around 40,000 years old, which means it was made towards the end of the last

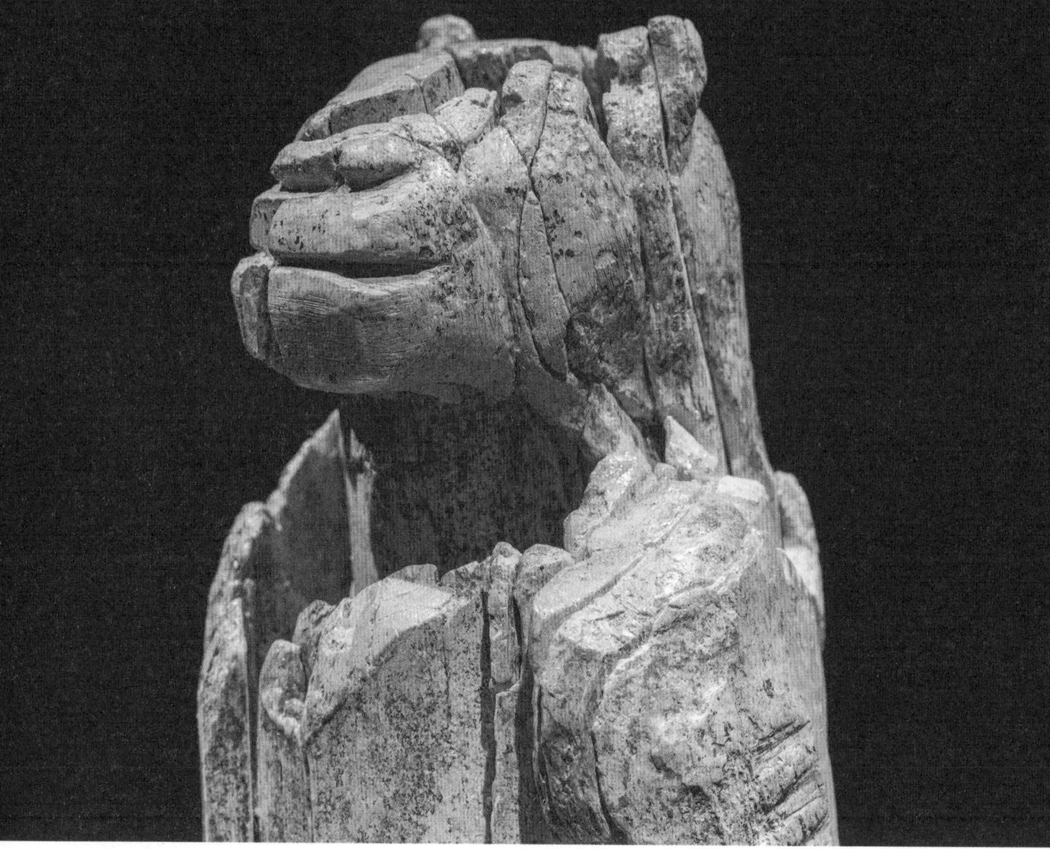

The head of the Lion Man, listening and watching

Ice Age, a dating supported by information gathered from other material found in the area. If that is indeed the case, as seems probable, then this small sculpture holds a unique place in human history. It is not just a supreme representation of two closely observed species: it is by some margin the oldest evidence yet found of the human mind giving physical form to something which can never have been seen. For the first time that we know of, a combination which could exist only in the imagination, an abstraction, has here been made physically graspable. Nature has been re-imagined and reshaped, the boundary between human and animal dissolved. The Lion Man represents a cognitive leap to a world beyond nature, and beyond human experience.

The precarious and dangerous world of those who made the Lion Man was one of very low temperatures – in Europe, around 12°C lower than today – and long cold winters. If they survived infancy, average life expectancy was probably little more than thirty years. In the short summers, there would be plants and berries to eat, but essentially they could survive only by hunting, using a range of stone tools to kill, strip and scrape their prey. They were dependent on animals for fat and meat to cook on their fires, and for furs and skins to provide clothing. Compared to these animals, humans were poorly provided with teeth or claws, were smaller than bears or mammoths, unable to run as fast as wolves, and no match at all for the greatest of all their predators, the lion. It can hardly be an accident that our sculpture combines the tusk of the largest animal they knew with the head of the fiercest – and the body of the only one capable of imaginative thought about the world they all inhabited.

The more closely you look at the Lion Man, the more it is clear that this is very far from being the result of an idle hour or two of whimsical whittling. The stance and posture of the figure suggest deep knowledge of ivory as a material – in particular the tusks of a young mammoth, from which the figure was made. Most of all, the precision of detail supposes highly developed technical skills, mastery of many different tools and a serious investment of time. As Jill Cook explains:

You can see the curvature of the tusk along its whole length, cleverly used to give the impression of a figure leaning attentively forward. The sculptor also knew how to take advantage of the cavity in the centre of a tusk to achieve the broad, masculine separation of the legs, and how to exploit the close grain of the ivory to achieve the meticulous details of the head. The Lion Man can only have been made by an accomplished sculptor, who had already carved many pieces, and who knew the material inside out. It is an entirely original, technically very difficult, artistically brilliant

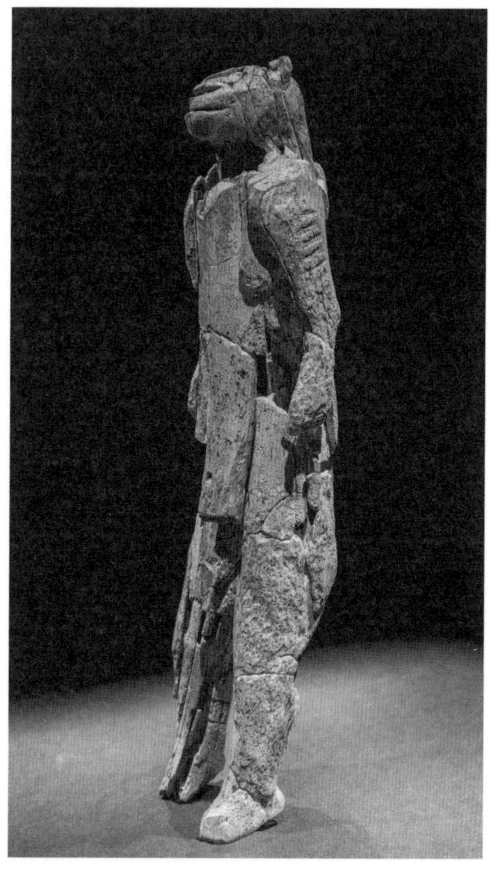
The Lion Man, showing the curve of the mammoth tusk from which it was carved

work, with a sense of power and spirit to it, which for me makes it a masterpiece.

It was made using a number of different stone tools, and would have required a great deal of very close, demanding work. For example, trying to separate the arms from the body using a small stone saw would have taken many hours of repetitive action and intense focus. From experiments using similar tools we can calculate that it would have required at least 400 hours of work. And as Jill Cook says, it is quite obvious, from the level of skill deployed, that this cannot have been the first work of the sculptor who made it.

That last observation raises a key question. This was a small community, probably only a few dozen people, certainly not more than a few hundred. Their primary concern must have been getting and bringing in food, making clothing, keeping the fire going, protecting their children from predators, and so on. Yet they allowed someone of great ability to spend a lot of time away from such tasks, acquiring and exercising the skills needed to make the Lion Man. Why would a community make such a huge investment in order to produce an object which could play no part in its physical survival? Jill Cook gives her view:

I think it is probably more about the community's psychological survival, something that strengthens the sense of themselves as a group. We do not know whether the Lion Man was a deity, a spriritual experience, a being from a creation story or an avatar used to negotiate with the forces of nature. But it is an object that makes sense only if it is part of a story, what we might now call a myth. There must have been a narrative or a ritual to accompany the statue that would explain its appearance and its meaning. What that story was, of course, we can now only guess. It was about humans and animals obviously – but presumably it was also about something beyond ourselves, beyond nature, which can somehow help to strengthen a community and enable it to overcome dangers and difficulties.

We know that at this time the people in the area were also making and listening to music. A variety of flutes, for example, have been found, some made of bird bones, which were already hollow, others much more complex and carved from ivory, which would again

A bird-bone flute found in the Ulm region, contemporary with the Lion Man

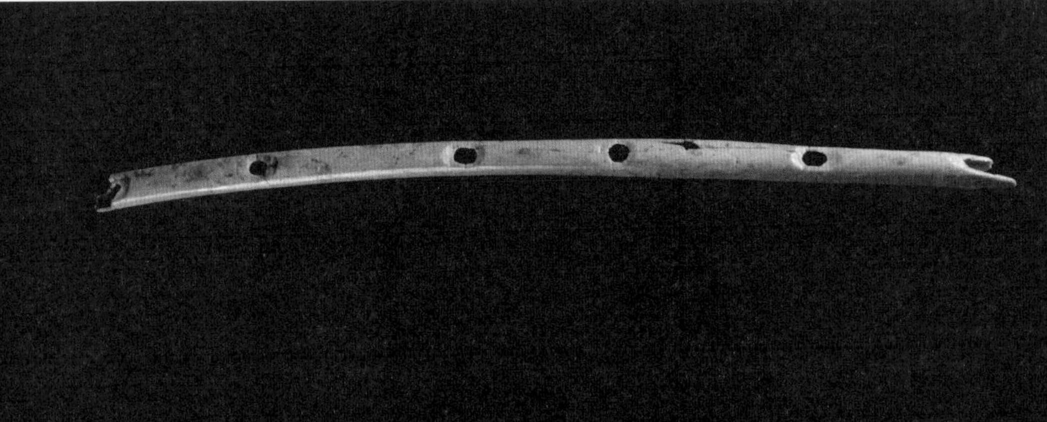

require a large investment of skill and time. We have also found a little figure who is clearly dancing. All these objects are about shared social activity, but also about transporting you into another realm, and that may well link to the purpose of the Lion Man.

There are two important recently discovered details about the physical condition of the statue. Dr Kurt Wehrberger, the scholar at the Ulm Museum now responsible for the Lion Man, reports that examination by digital microscope has revealed that the mouth – and only the mouth – has been infiltrated by an organic substance, which may be blood. Its presence suggests some sort of ceremonial ritual in which the lion's mouth played a part.

Perhaps even more importantly, it can also be seen that the irregularities you would expect to find on the surface of mammoth ivory are not present: they have been smoothed away as a consequence of prolonged handling. Dr Wehrberger thinks that the Lion Man must have been held by many people over many years, possibly even over several generations. Made by an individual, this figure was shared by the group over a long period of time. Jill Cook imagines the scene:

I think we can visualize them sitting round the fire, which will keep them warm and keep the wild animals away, listening to the sound of a flute, looking at the magic that the flames create, handling the statue, telling stories of this composite creature as an avatar who could link them to unseen spirits, either benevolent or dangerous. Tales of the visible world, but also of worlds that transcend it, to which the Lion Man, as a transformed fantastical being, could give access – not as an individual experience, but as something in which all could share.

The people in the cave who handled the Lion Man were human beings very like us. They were the same species as we are – *Homo sapiens* – and had essentially the same brains as we do. They – we

– had emerged in Africa, and by around 60,000 years ago seem to have spread out rapidly, reaching Asia, Europe, Australia and eventually America. Earlier hominids had been making tools and hunting animals for well over a million years, but these people were, in one crucial respect, different.

Clive Gamble, Professor of Archaeology at the University of Southampton, is an expert in early human development:

Imagination is at the core of it. The thing that really singles us out is how our brains work, our ability to go beyond the here and now. What we do very well is thinking ahead, into the future, beyond our individual lives, as well as into the past. That lets us embark on long journeys – the speed with which Homo sapiens inhabits the earth is astonishing. We can construct myths and legends. We can inhabit other worlds and make great imaginative leaps, bringing together things which do not occur in nature, as in the Lion Man. That is a really new and dynamic departure.

For Clive Gamble, it is these sorts of imaginative leaps that are necessary to establish a view of our place in the cosmos, and of how we relate to other animals. They allow us to imagine other people – the community – continuing to exist when we no longer do, to develop a belief in an afterlife, to create symbols, ceremonies and rituals.

Those beliefs – whatever we call them – would not be something special and separate, but an integral part of social life, pervading all activities. And it is not just about their own immediate group. I think that belief systems at this stage could have been almost as important as having enough people to defend your territory, or even controlling a food supply: because shared beliefs would have allowed people to connect across social universes much larger than the local group. They would share with others a particular understanding of the world, and the symbols or rituals that could

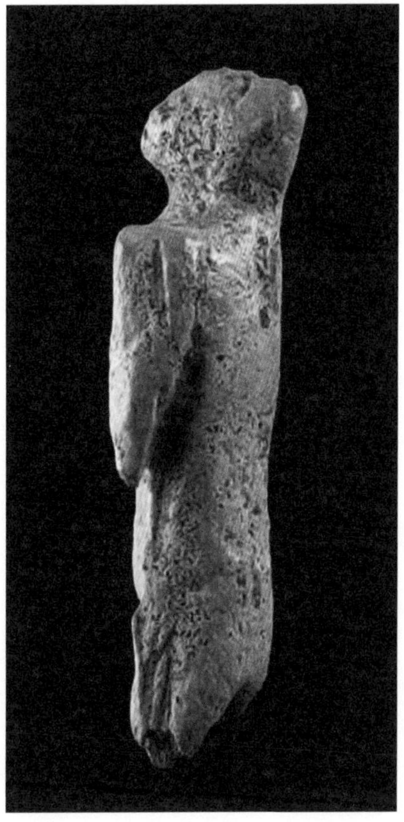

The 'little Lion Man', also from the Ulm region, between 31,000 and 33,000 years ago

be used to articulate it. And that would give them some sort of kinship – a kind of community – over a much larger area than was ever possible before.

Supporting this last suggestion – that belief systems and practices might have been shared over a wide area, and drawn people together across considerable distances – is the discovery of at least one other statue of a Lion Man in the region. In recent years the cave where the Lion Man was found has been re-excavated by Professor Joachim Kind of Tübingen University. It is spacious, roughly rectangular, about forty metres deep and ten metres wide, not unlike a chilly village hall. It would always have been very cold, because it faces north. Professor Kind believes that this cave, which never sees the sun, is not a place where people would have chosen to live. Near its mouth is a fireplace, clearly much used, but where there are surprisingly few remains of stone tools, bones and so forth, the normal residue of human habitation – far fewer than in most caves of the area. This appears to have been a place where people did not permanently live, but occasionally gathered.

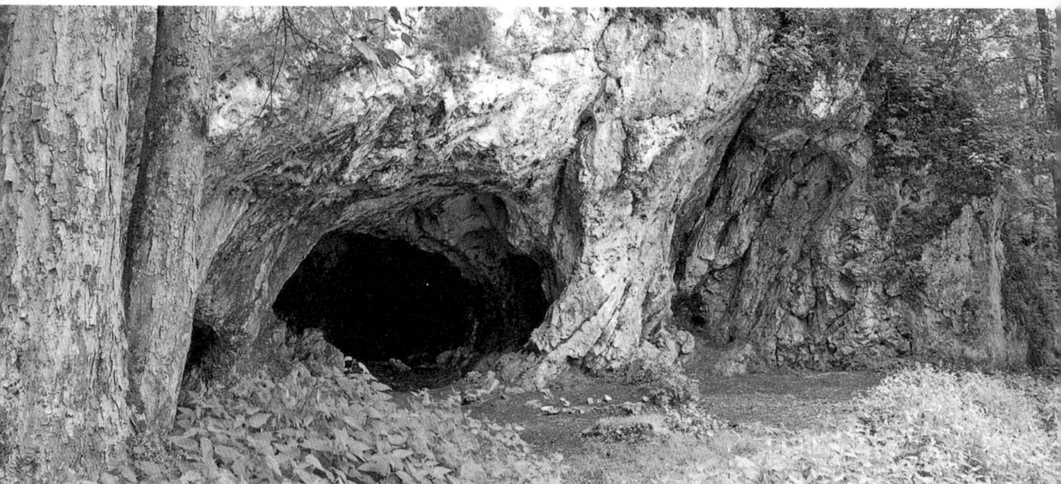

The Hohlenstein cave where Robert Wetzel and Otto Völzing found the fragments of the Lion Man in 1939

Professor Kind thinks the main cave was used by groups who came from a wide area, for relatively short periods of time, probably to take part in ceremonies.

In the smaller cave at the back, where the fragments were excavated, the recent digs have revealed nothing at all connected with daily life, but instead objects of a different sort: the teeth of Arctic foxes, wolf and deer, pierced so they could be suspended and worn with little ivory pendants and a cache of trimmed reindeer antlers. Like the Lion Man, these are objects of no practical use, but it is easy to imagine them being deployed in rituals. Professor Kind thinks that this inner cave was a special area where activities of some kind connected with the Lion Man may have taken place, and where the ritual objects were stored. He thinks one might almost use the word 'sanctuary', and call it a holy place.

We shall never be sure what the Lion Man meant to those people on the edge of survival, who sacrificed so many hours to bring it into being. But we do know that they had minds, and that they were capable of complexity, so it may not be impossible to imagine what they were doing and thinking. Like everything to do with deep history, much is speculative, and is adjusted as new evidence emerges. The best hypothesis is that the people of the Lion Man made a great work of art, constructed a narrative linking the natural and supernatural worlds, and enacted that narrative ceremonially with a wider community. This is something that all human societies have done: searching for patterns, and then composing stories and rituals about them, which put us – all of us – in our cosmic place. You could say that it is when a group agrees on how the fragments of this great puzzle fit together that you have a community: that *Homo sapiens* is also *Homo religiosus*, where the search is not for *my* place in the cosmos, but for *our* place, and where believing is closely connected with belonging.

Though the Lion Man seems to have been kept at the back of the Stadel cave, there is only one place where his story could have been told. It is the place of visions, the place where stories have always been told: round the flickering, magical, warming and dangerous fire. That is the subject of the next chapter.

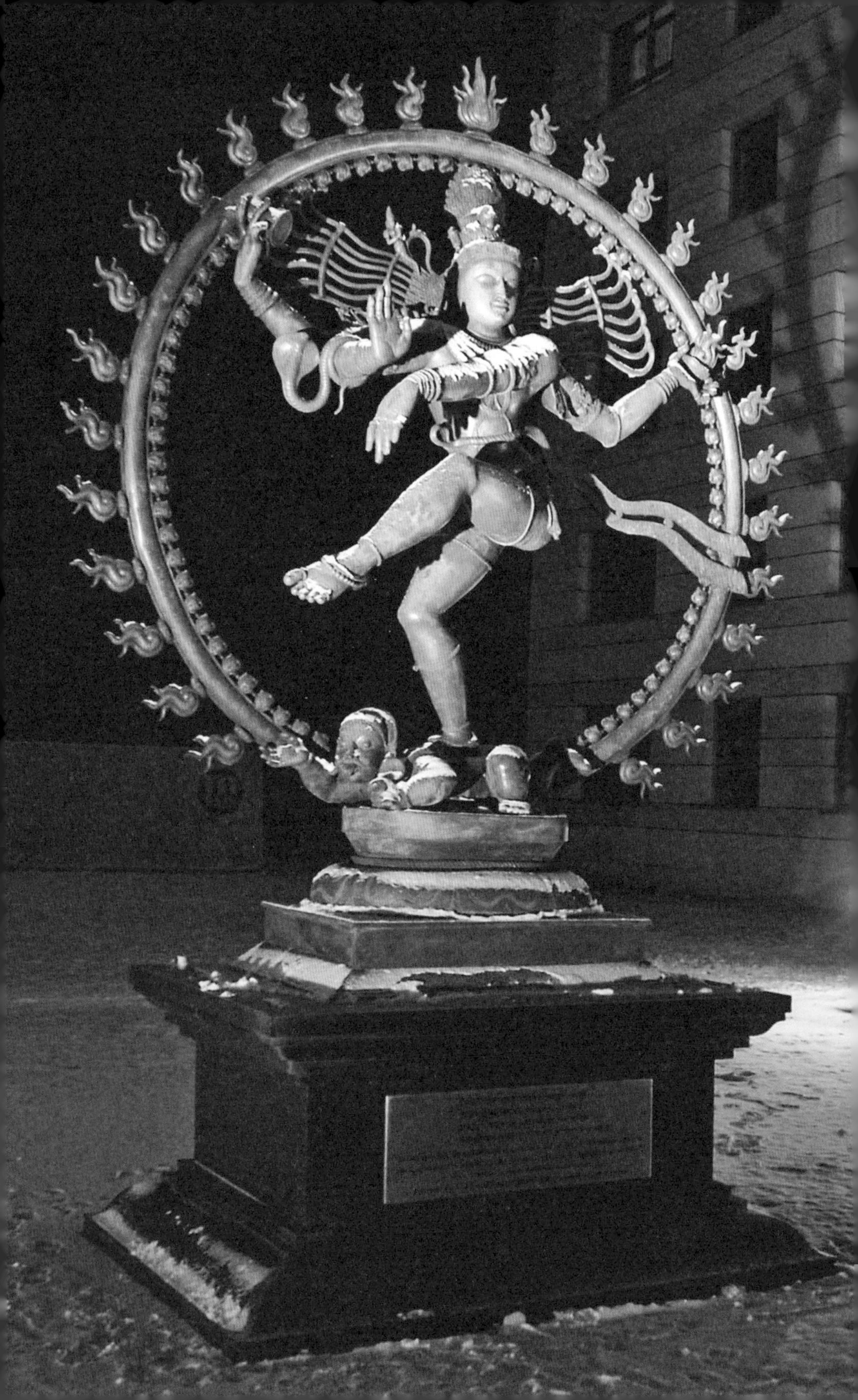

2
FIRE AND STATE

Outside the headquarters of CERN, the European Centre for Nuclear Research, near Geneva, the Hindu god Shiva dances in a perpetual circle of fire. Many visitors to this place of rational scientific inquiry are disconcerted to be greeted by the statue of a god. But nothing could be more appropriate than this god in this place, and not only because India has long worked closely with CERN on many projects: in Hindu tradition Shiva's fire creates and sustains us, yet it also destroys us. Like nuclear energy, fire ultimately eludes human understanding or human control.

It is not, of course, just the Hindu tradition which finds the divine in the dangerous flickering of fire. Prometheus in classical mythology had to steal it from the gods themselves to allow humans to use it for their purposes. For the Jews, Moses encountered god in the flames of the burning bush, and for Christians the Holy Spirit came upon the apostles in tongues of fire. Visible yet ungraspable, powerful but immaterial, fire is for many societies the most obvious, intrinsic emblem of the divine.

It is also profoundly human. Indeed it has been argued that it is fire that made human society possible. Once our remote ancestors

Shiva dancing the Cosmic Dance of destruction and renewal, a gift from the Indian Government to CERN, on the laboratory campus near Geneva

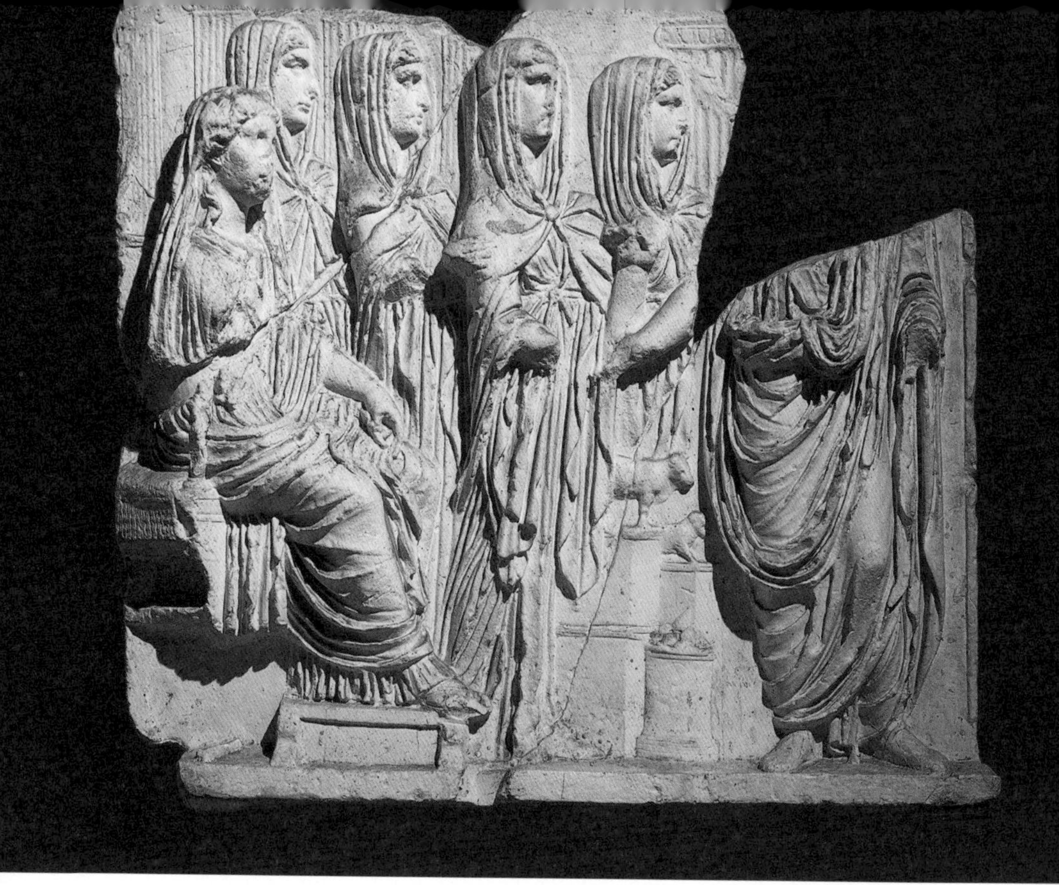

The goddess Vesta, seated with her head covered, and four Vestal Virgins. Roman, first century CE

learned how to use it, probably around a million years ago, it not only provided heat and safety, while keeping dangerous animals at bay; it was round the fire that the community cooked and ate. Cooked food allowed more calories and protein to be consumed, and, over tens of thousands of years, for human brains to grow. And as the community sat round the fire, they shared their stories. Fire as the focus of society: the idea ought not to surprise, for 'focus' is the Latin for hearth, and every time we use the word, we pay unconscious tribute to the incomparable gathering power of fire. The community that imagines itself gathered round a fire may be a family, a village or even a nation. For two of the greatest empires in history – Rome and Persia – fire became, in radically different ways, the divine emblem of the essential unity of the state.

The two empires that in the third century CE fought for dominance in the Middle East today face each other in the British Museum coin room: from Persia, a gold image, about the size of a ten-pence piece, showing a Zoroastrian fire-altar with two male attendants. From Rome a dark bronze coin, with a view of the temple of Vesta, and, in it, a group of the famous Vestal Virgins.

Vesta was for the Romans the virgin goddess of fire, protectoress of the peace of home and hearth. She was a completely domestic goddess. Unlike other goddesses such as Venus or Juno, there are no rollicking tales of her amorous or military adventures: she simply stayed at home, by the fireside, keeping the household safe. Yet in one sense she was the most important deity in Rome. Unlike the others, she had for most of Roman history only one temple, in the heart of the Forum, and, unusually, it had no statue of the presiding goddess: Vesta was to be found only in the perpetual flame of her hearth. But that hearth, her temple, was the hearth of the whole city and of the empire, and their success and survival

The rounded Temple of Vesta in the centre of the Roman Forum – the 'hearth of the empire'

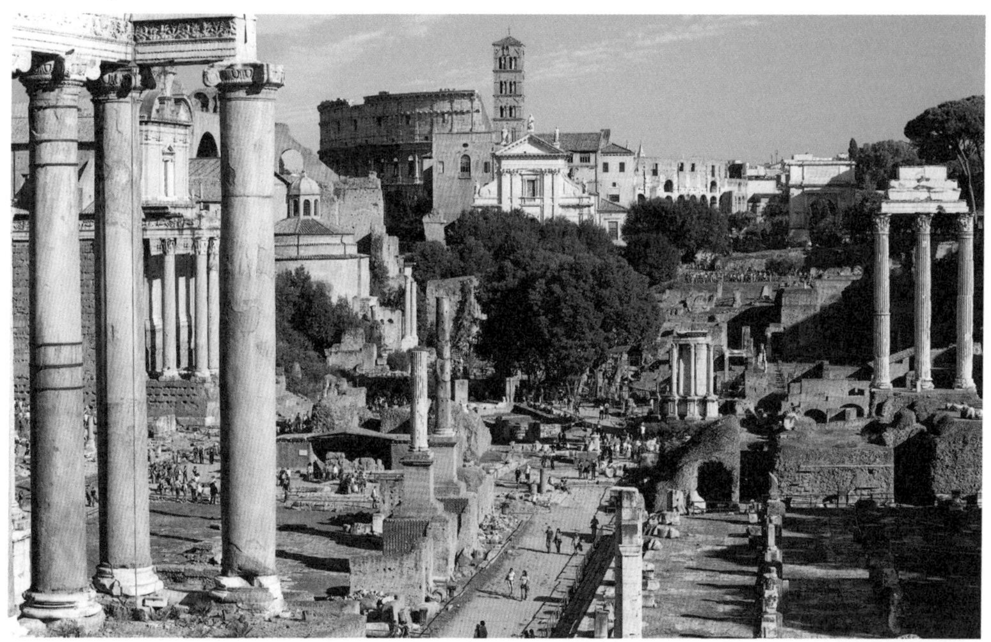

ultimately depended on Vesta's flame. The domestic fire of Vesta was the central symbol of the Roman state. Her flame had to be kept perpetually burning, and in consequence it required constant and specialized attention.

We can see this clearly on our coin, struck sometime around the year 200 CE. On one side there is a round temple, with the words *Vesta Mater* – Mother Vesta. The virgin goddess – it is a paradox found in many societies – is also the quintessential mother figure. There is, as usual, no image of the goddess, but on either side of the flaming cauldron stand three women. These, explains Mary Beard, Professor of Classics at the University of Cambridge, are the Vestal Virgins:

They were the priestesses of Vesta, and they had one absolutely central job: tending the sacred flame of the city. In the middle of the Roman Forum, in the Temple of Vesta, was the hearth that we see on this coin. It was supposed to be kept burning permanently, and the job of the Vestal Virgins, as the priestesses of the goddess Vesta, was quite simply to keep that fire alight.

A fire of this spiritual and political significance could be properly tended only by the irreproachably pure young girls selected specially for the purpose – there were generally six of them – who throughout their time of service must remain virginal. Mary Beard continues:

If the fire ever went out, it was a sign that the established relationship between the Romans and their gods had been disrupted. And when that kind of disruption occurred, you had to do something to put it right. The finger of suspicion might well be pointed at one of these priestesses – with the doubt that she was no longer a virgin.

The punishment for a Vestal Virgin convicted of such a failing was a fearful death – being buried alive. The sentence was, we know,

Black bronze Roman coin, *c.*200 CE, showing the Temple of Vesta with six Vestal Virgins (*above*) and a bust of the empress Julia Domna draped (*below*)

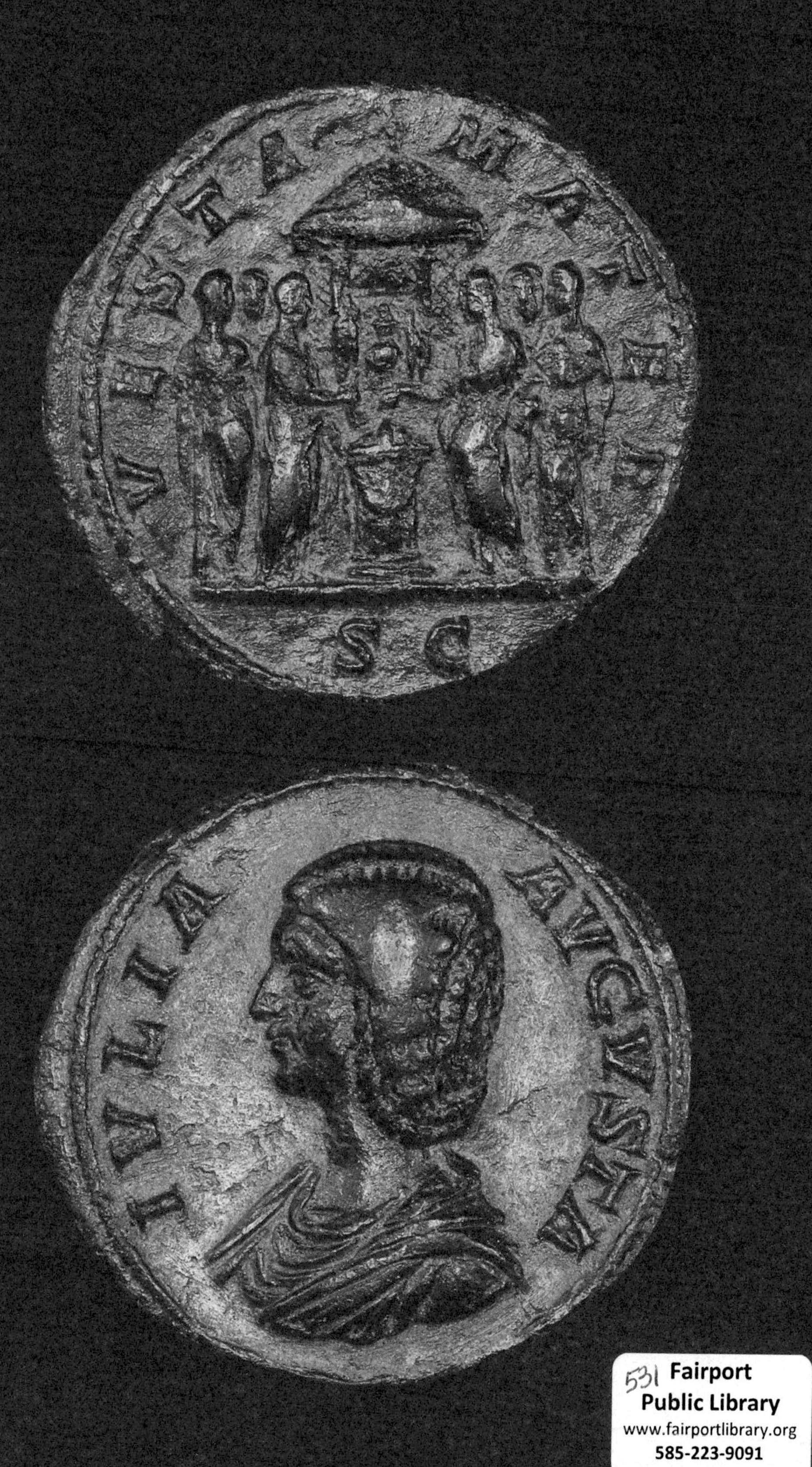
VESTA MATER
S C
IVLIA AVGVSTA

occasionally carried out. So why would anyone want a job like this? Mary Beard explains that one of the reasons was the status that it conferred:

Like almost all Roman priesthoods, this was an elite job. But it was very unusual because it was a female elite job, which guaranteed the Vestal and her family a place at the very heart of Roman religion – and so at the very heart of the Roman political world too, because this temple and this hearth lay right at the centre of Roman public space. These women had many privileges – they got the best seats at the theatre, and so on – because although they were tending a fire, they were not just guarding a barbecue. They were guarding and looking after something which stood for Rome itself.

The specifically female nature of this link between the temple of Vesta and the very idea of the state becomes clear when we turn the coin over. Here you see not, as you would expect, the emperor, but the bust of a woman, with the inscription *Iulia Augusta*: this is Julia Domna, wife of Emperor Septimius Severus, who ruled from 193 to 211. The emperors had established a second temple of Vesta in the imperial palace, so the empress is here being advertised as fulfilling the Roman womanly ideal: tending to the hearth of both family and state. By being linked to the fire of Vesta, she can claim to share some of the high political responsibilities of a Vestal Virgin, while also being the mother of the nation.

As Mary Beard points out, this rare example of female power in the otherwise overwhelmingly male world of Roman politics had a long and fascinating after-life:

Vestal Virgins have remained powerful symbols in the cultural and political imagination of the West. You find later European aristocratic and monarchical women trying to pick up on some of their unique kind of authority – on this quintessentially Roman version of what female power could be.

Not surprisingly, one of the canniest manipulators of this useful bit of history was Elizabeth I of England. As the Virgin Queen, whose legitimacy had been denied by the Roman Catholic church, Elizabeth must have relished the opportunity to show herself heir to an even older Roman institution, and one that affirmed the central role of an unmarried woman in the great affairs of the nation. One

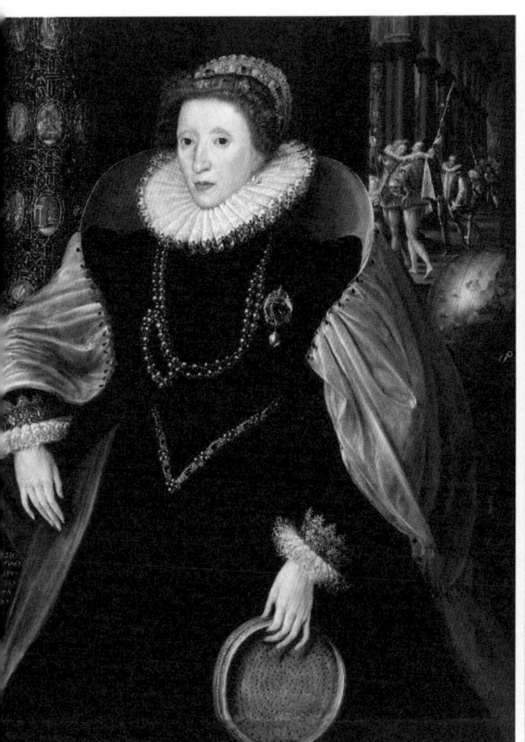

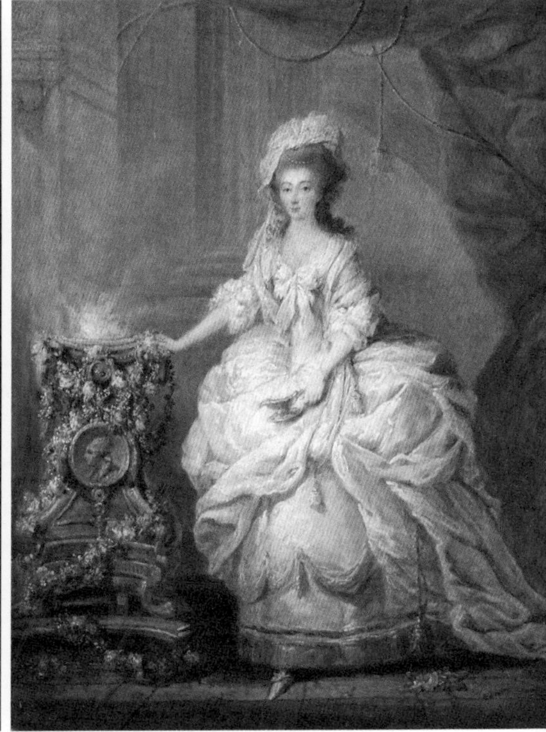

Elizabeth I of England holding the sieve of a Vestal Virgin, 1583, by Quentin Massys the Younger (*left*) and *Marie Antoinette of France as a Vestal*, circle of Jacques-Fabien Gautier d'Agoty (*right*)

falsely accused Roman Vestal had proved her virginity by carrying water in a sieve: so in this portrait (and there is more than one such picture) Elizabeth too carries a sieve, affirming both her virginity and her unique fitness to guarantee the survival of the state. (It must have been a pleasing reflection for Elizabeth that while Mary

Queen of Scots might be the Catholic candidate for the throne, nobody would ever associate her with chastity.) Two centuries later, as Marie Antoinette of France tried to assert her role as model wife and mother, with a proper place in the political sphere, she too had herself painted as a Vestal. Understandably, she discards the sieve of virginity and is shown standing by the sacred fire, the emblem of the nation, to which she will devote herself. Here were two women, like the empress Julia Domna hundreds of years before them, showing they could be trusted with that most civic, even existential of tasks: tending the flame of the state.

There is a last, pleasingly democratic chapter to this tale of the astonishing longevity of the idea of the sacred hearth – from the first autumn of the Great War. It very quickly became clear that to wage a conflict on this scale, not just the fighting men, but the whole population would have to be engaged. In October 1914, the Welsh composer Ivor Novello set one of the First World War's most enduringly popular patriotic songs:

Keep the Home Fires Burning,
While your hearts are yearning,
Though your lads are far away
They dream of home.

Every woman in Britain in 1914 – a state that, like ancient Rome, allowed most women virtually no political role – was now summoned, as wife, mother or sister, to do her bit to save the state by tending the flame. Every hearth was, like the temple of Vesta, the hearth of the nation.

One of the other great superpowers of the third century, and the only one with which Rome had serious foreign policy relations, was the Sasanian Empire in neighbouring Persia (modern Iran). And here too fire played a central role as the focus of the community. But the femininity of Rome's sacred hearth was exchanged in Persia for an idea of holy fire which is male from start to finish.

The Sasanian Empire, controlling most of the territory between the River Indus and modern Egypt – and sometimes very much more – endured for roughly 400 years, from around 230 CE until the Islamic invasions of 650. It was effectively Rome's only rival, and more than a match militarily: in 260 the Roman emperor Valerian was not just defeated by the Persian forces, but humiliatingly taken prisoner by them.

The predominant faith of the Sasanians was Zoroastrianism, a monotheistic code of ethics and rituals based on the teachings of the prophet Zoroaster – better known in Europe as Zarathustra – who may have lived around 1000 BCE. It is centred on the worship of one invisible supreme being, Ahura Mazda, the Wise Lord, who requires of his followers truth, good thoughts, good words and good deeds: the consequence will be a just society. Ahura Mazda may not be seen, but one of the ways he may in some measure be apprehended is through fire. Purifying and immaterial, warming but destructive, the sacred fire of the Zoroastrians is not an object of worship in itself, but the focus of utmost reverence, serving to help those near it to concentrate on the purity of god and his truth.

Our gold dinar from the Sasanian Empire, struck between 273 and 276, clearly demonstrates the central political significance of this holy fire. On one side is the Sasanian Shah, with long flowing locks, wearing crown and diadem. He is Bahram I, who eventually negotiated with his counterpart in Rome a peace settlement in Syria: in 274 CE, Persian envoys processed through the streets of Rome, not as captives but as honoured guests in the Triumph of Emperor Aurelian. On the other side of our coin, two armed male attendants, elegant and elongated, lean on their tall staffs and respectfully look away from a central altar, on which the fire of Ahura Mazda burns. As in Rome, religious and political power meet and merge in a flame.

But the Iranian fire is radically different from the Roman one.

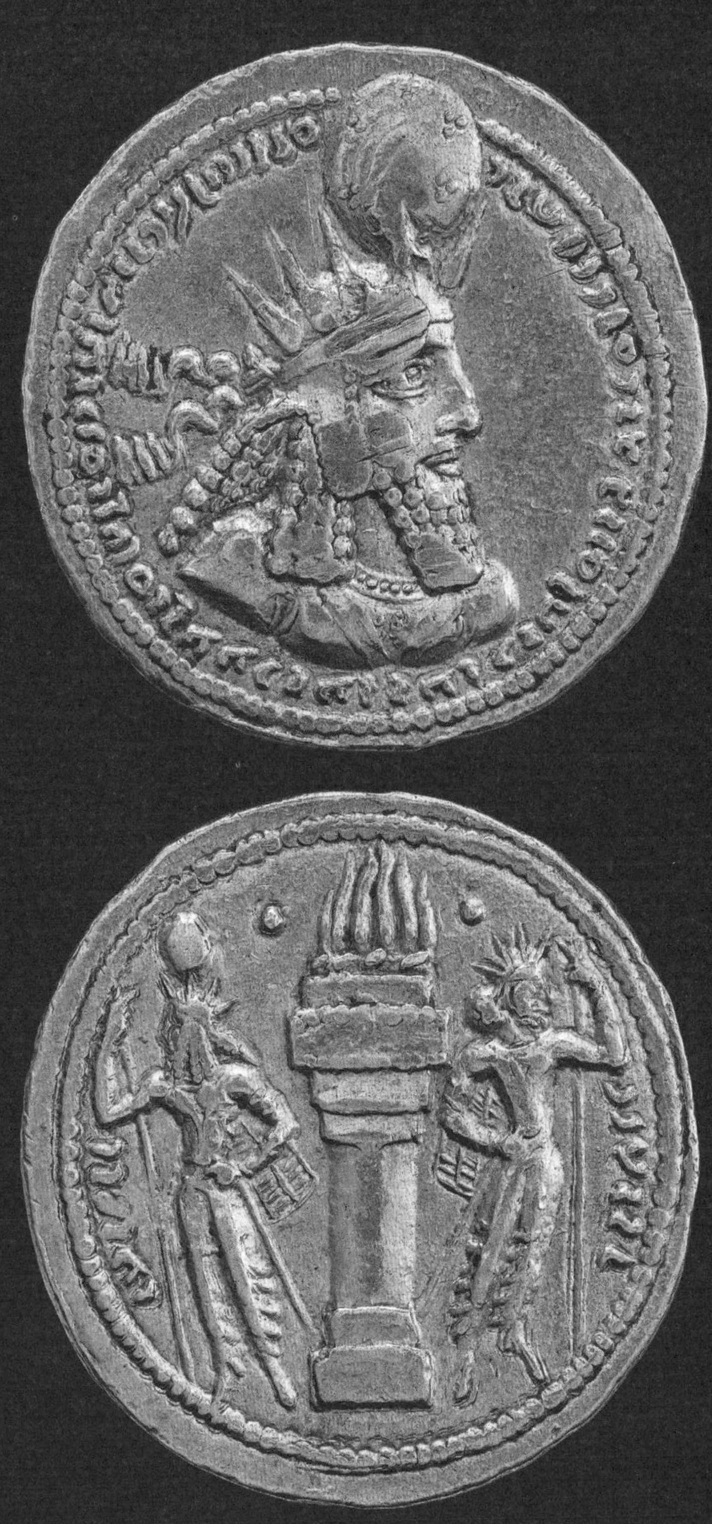

Where Vesta's single hearth stands symbolically for the whole Roman state, the highest form of Zoroastrian fire comes – literally, physically – from every part of its community. In a brilliantly conceived ritual, Zoroastrian priests take and combine different kinds of fire, from the hearths of bakers and metal-workers, priests and warriors, and so on: in all, fires from fourteen sectors of the community, combined and purified, until the whole of society is emblematically brought together in one shared flame. But to achieve the sacred fire, two further fires are needed. First, from a cremation pyre, so that the dead are joined to the living in reverence of Ahura Mazda; and lastly lightning, fire from the sky, binding earth to heaven. The whole process of constructing such a fire may take over two years and can require as many as thirty-two priests. The result is a sacred flame, known as Atash Behram, the fire of victory, to which everyone has symbolically contributed, a powerful emblem of a united society, linking past and present, human and divine. The fire we see on the back of Bahram I's golden dinar is a tour de force of social theology.

The Sasanian Empire, with Zoroastrianism as its state religion, continued to flourish, while in Western Europe Rome stumbled, and for the three centuries after our coin Persian culture shaped much of the Middle East. But in the 640s, in the face of the Arab invasions, the empire collapsed with astonishing speed, and Islam became the new religion of the state. The sacred fire did not, however, disappear: it moved.

A group of Zoroastrians fled from Iran to settle in Gujarat in north-west India. Coming from Persia, they were known as Parsis, and, although small in number, the community still plays a significant part in modern India, especially in the commercial capital, Mumbai. According to tradition, the Parsis brought with them from Iran ash from a sacred fire, and in their new home set

Gold dinar of the Sasanian shah Bahram I, *c.*275 CE, with Bahram wearing a radiate crown (*above*), and a Zoroastrian fire altar with two armed attendants (*below*)

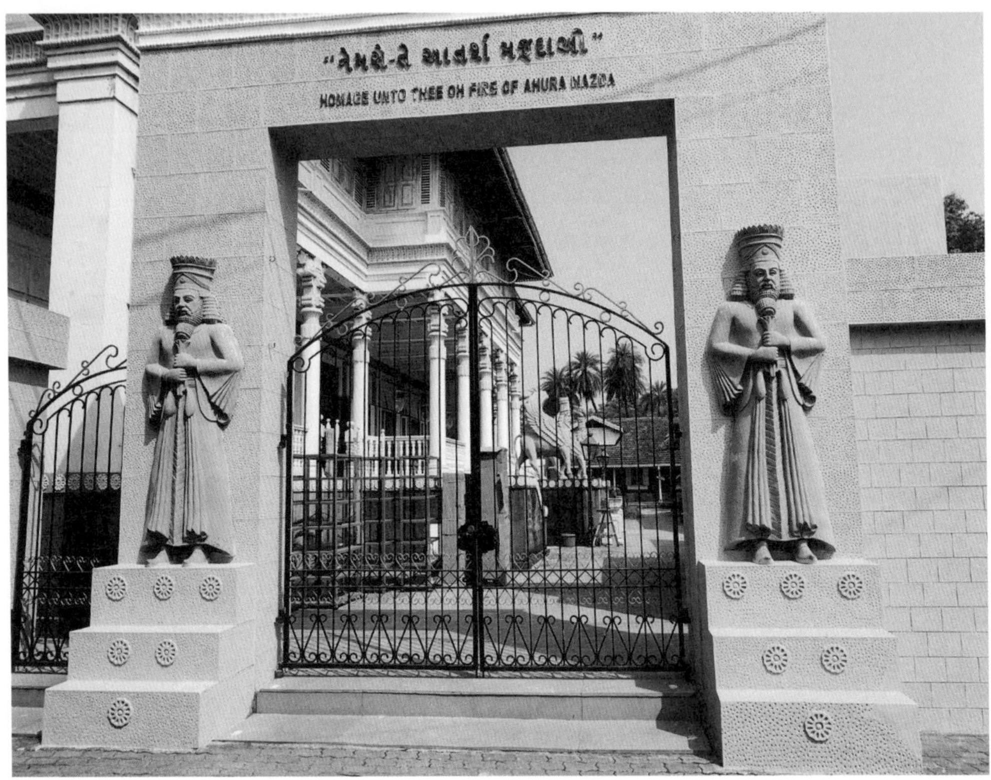

Entrance to the Zoroastrian fire temple, the Iranshah, at Udwada, in Gujarat. The fire is said to have been burning for over a millennium.

about consecrating, and then tending, a new holy flame. It is said that this flame has been unextinguished since 721, and it burns today in Udwada, in Gujarat.

When you visit this remote, rather run-down seaside town a few hours' drive north of Mumbai, in many ways reminiscent of a faded English coastal resort, it comes as something of a shock to see outside the Parsi fire-temple the sign 'Iranshah', announcing that this is the abode of a monarch, the king of Iran. As the high priest explains:

We always call fire 'king', or 'shah'. The name Iranshah was given to it because after we left Iran, when we came to India as refugees, we knew that we would not be able to establish our kingdom here. There would be no physical, political king: instead the sacred fire became our king.

This, then, is a spiritual rather than a political kingdom, at the centre of which stands a sovereign in exile, a sacred fire, that continues its ancient purpose. The high priest goes on:

People say that we are fire worshippers, but we are not. Instead, fire is a medium through which we try to relate ourselves to Ahura Mazda, the Lord of Wisdom. Without fire, people can't survive. Without heat, people can't survive. Fire is everything.

The important thing is to live your life in such a way that you bring out the best in your spirit. If your thoughts are good, your words will become good. And if your thoughts and words are good, your deeds will become good. That is our religion.

Non-Zoroastrians are never permitted to enter the precinct of the Iranshah, or to see the Atash Bahram, the sacred fire. It really is treated very much like a king. In the centre of a square, railed-off precinct stands the dais for the silver urn which holds the flame. Overhead – as above a throne – hangs a silver crown, and above that a silver canopy. On the wall behind hang shield and swords: the Iranshah, the king of Iran, as befits his royal

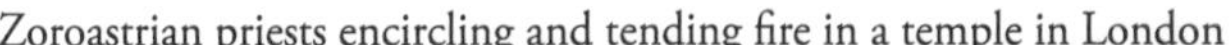

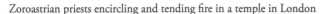

Zoroastrian priests encircling and tending fire in a temple in London

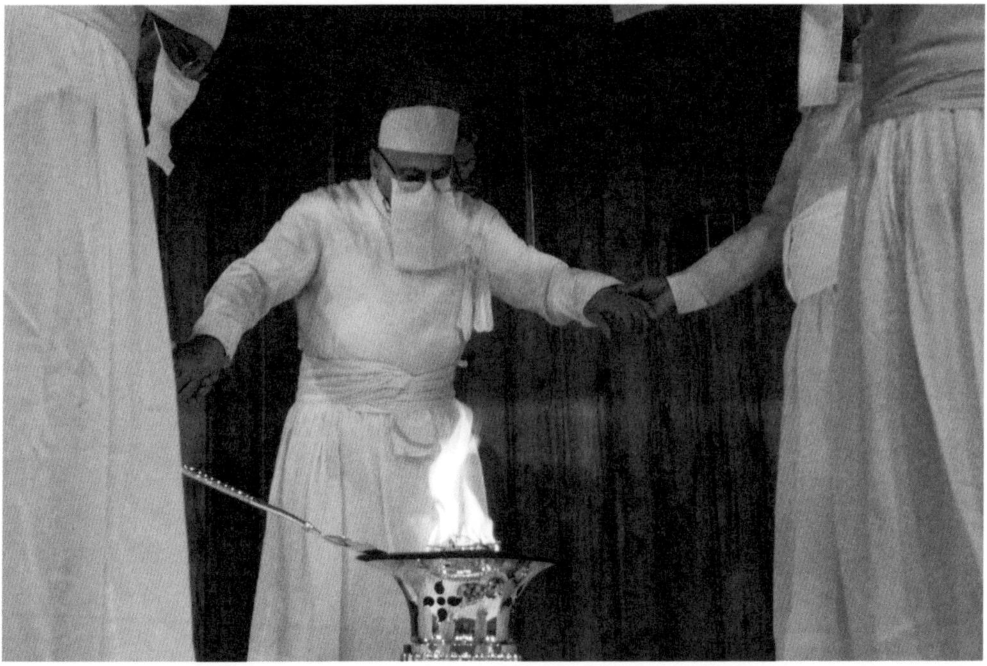

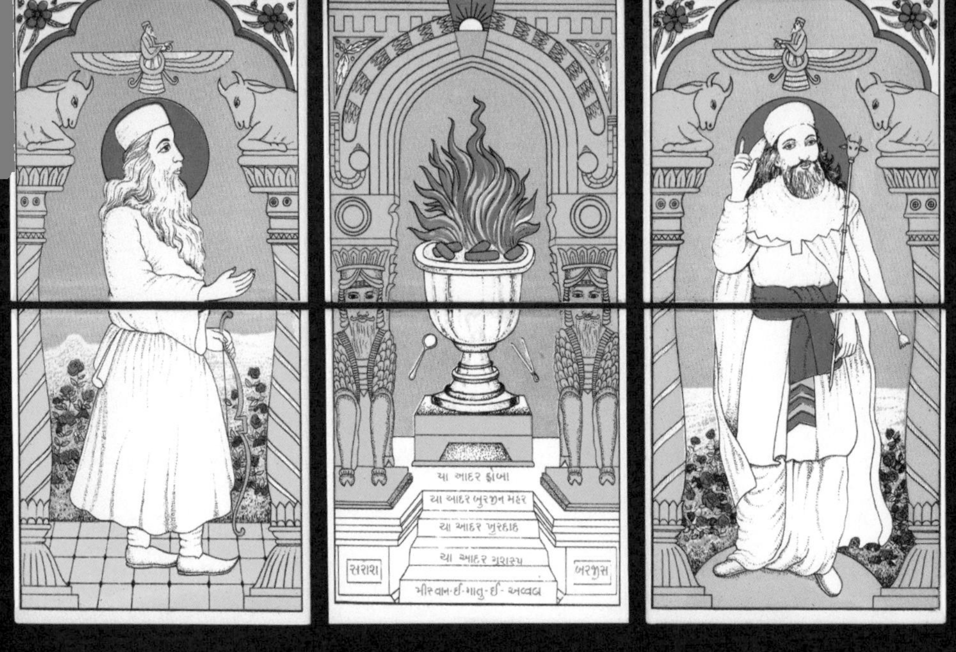

A set of six glazed ceramic tiles, made in Mumbai in the 1980s showing the sacred fire of the Parsis, with the tongs and ladle used for tending it. On the right is Zoroaster, on the left is the shah Lohrasp, traditionally believed to have been his patron. The architectural framework is clearly inspired by the ancient Persian capital, Persepolis.

status, has his canopy, his guards and his throne. This sovereign fire is, as in all Zoroastrian fire-temples, carefully kept burning by priests, dressed in the purity of white, who wear masks to avoid inadvertently polluting the flames, which they feed with sandalwood and other noble aromatic woods offered by the faithful.

But here the similarities to a conventional court end, because in front of this fire, in which all society is symbolically present, all society stands equal before Ahura Mazda. The high priest tells us:

When people come to pay their respects, there are no separate corners for men and women, for the rich and the poor, for the different strata of society. This is a universal community, drawn from across society. The main aim of this fire is to be communal and peaceful, with every class of society gathered around it. That is its basic purpose.

A particularly striking illustration of the possibilities of Parsi fire as the rallying point of the community was given a few years after the British left south Yemen in 1967. As the Parsis who had followed the British there in the nineteenth century began to move out, many of them to Mumbai, there were concerns about what would happen to the holy Atash Bahram fire, housed in the city of Aden, if there was nobody to tend it. In 1976, after much religious debate and international diplomacy, a Boeing 707 was specially kitted out to be able to carry a live fire. The plane was crewed only by Parsis, and it was sent to Aden by Air India, a company founded by a Parsi family, the Tatas. The Holy Atash landed safely in what was then Bombay. A migrant fire for a migrant community had once again moved on.

For Parsis, as for all Zoroastrians, fire still plays essentially the same religious and social role as it has throughout the centuries. In Rome, reverence for Vesta proved impressively resilient in the face of the Christianization of the empire, after Constantine's conversion around 312: it was a symbol too deeply embedded in the mind, and the heart, of the people to be quickly cast aside, and for some decades even Christian emperors continued to honour and support the cult. But in 391 Emperor Theodosius ordered the closure of the temple in the Forum, and Vesta's flame was finally extinguished. The last Vestal Virgin stood down in 394. Only a generation later, the Goths sacked Rome.

If Vesta's flame has long been dead, its distant daughter is nonetheless burning brightly – in a state which has ostentatiously shorn itself of all religious identity, but still venerates a sacred fire. Under the Arc de Triomphe in Paris burns a flame of ultimate national significance, which is tended daily by a group dedicated to ensure that it never dies. First lit on 11 November 1923, and

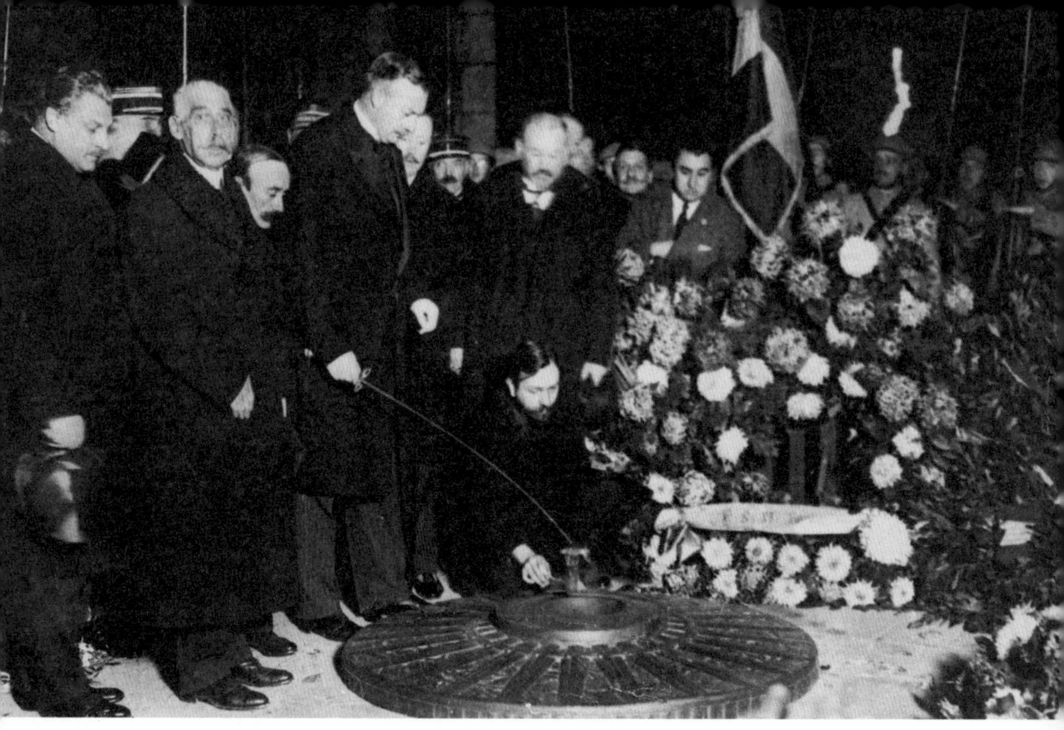

Inauguration of *La Flamme de la Nation* by General Maginot, 11 November 1923

inaugurated by the Minister of War, General Maginot, it honours an unknown soldier of the First World War. Significantly, the association set up to look after it refers to it officially as *La Flamme de la Nation*, the 'Flame of the Nation', explaining that it not only honours the dead, but embodies the state's confidence in its future. Like the fire of Vesta and the Atash Bahram, it must never go out. In a startling survival of a deeply embedded ritual, every evening, at 6.30 p.m. a small group performs the public ceremony of *Le Ravivage de la Flamme*, 'the Keeping Alive of the Flame' – former soldiers and schoolchildren together doing the duty of Vestal Virgins.

As in Rome, the French flame quickly came to be seen as a symbol of national identity, uniting everybody in the nation, and the daily tending of it became so charged with meaning that it continued even under the German occupation in the Second World War. The first official public ceremony of the new President Macron in 2017 was to join his predecessor in paying tribute in front of *La Flamme de la Nation*.

*

The spirit of any community is hard to pin down and define, but there is, I think, a disconcerting aptness in this identification of the flourishing of a society with the survival of an insubstantial, flickering flame. Just as any fire will perish if it is not carefully tended and fed, so the institutions of a society will crumble if not constantly repaired and renewed. There is perhaps in the cult of the flame, as embodying the life of the state, a symbolic recognition of the fragility of all political institutions, and our obligation to be vigilant in keeping them in good repair.

Alongside fire lies a second element, also mysterious, essential to our survival, and also perilously difficult to manage – like fire with the potential for great destruction, but also for purity and new life. We shall encounter it next, as we find out how nature and faith, in their deepest patterns, seem not just to flame but to flow.

French President Emmanuel Macron lights the flame at the Tomb of the Unknown Soldier at the Arc de Triomphe, immediately after his formal inauguration, 14 May 2017.

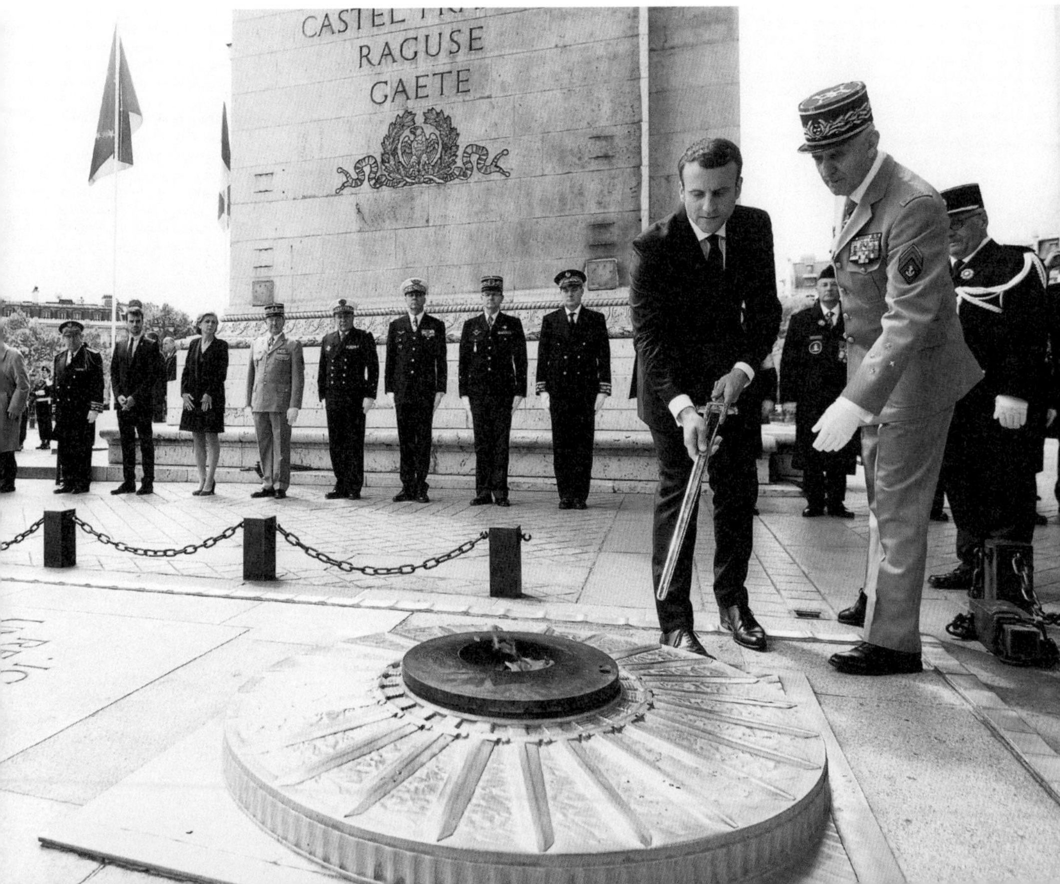

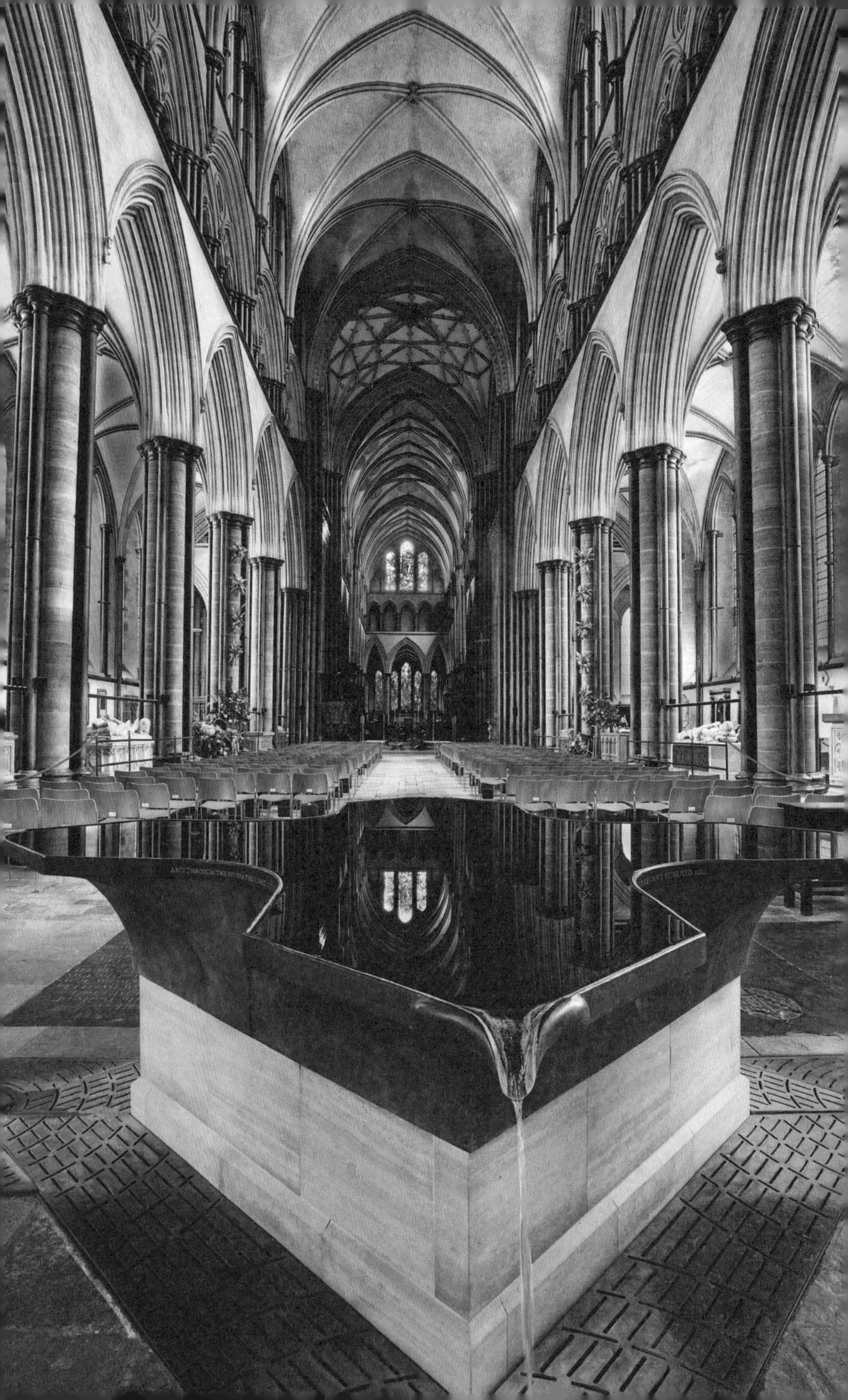
AND THROUGH THE RIVERS

3

WATER OF LIFE AND DEATH

Entering Salisbury Cathedral today from the great west door, the first thing you encounter in the nave is water. It is a baptismal font, or, rather, a fountain, a broad bronze basin in the shape of a cross, brimming with water which pours unceasingly from each of its four arms: on the surface mysteriously still, yet constantly overflowing in its promise of renewal.

There is great significance in having water at the entrance to this cathedral, for in Christian theology the water of baptism serves as the door through which every Christian enters not just the faith but the whole Christian community, past, present and future. For the Bishop of Salisbury, Nicholas Holtam, the baptismal waters are the very 'water of life' itself:

They purify us. It's about the journey to the Promised Land, passing through the waters of the Red Sea. We come out the other side of the font, as it were, and into the nave of the cathedral, where the community gathers to celebrate the Eucharist. We're called individually, but we gather together. And this is about the whole church, not just this cathedral. Becoming a Christian, you are baptized into the worldwide church so that, belonging here, you belong in all times and all places.

The baptismal font near the great west door of Salisbury Cathedral

It is of course not only in places of Christian worship that you are likely to be greeted by water. 'You who are faithful!' enjoins the Qur'an, 'When you undertake ritual worship, then wash your faces, your hands to the elbows, rub your heads, and your legs to the ankles.' The need to wash before prayer, before the individual joins the community in the face of God, has determined the architecture of the great mosques, where substantial spaces for ablutions have to be accommodated, and the provision of fountains and baths has helped to shape the urban geography of the Islamic world.

Water to prepare the body for the activity of the spirit, water that readies humans for a new relationship with the world: it is an idea that chimes so strongly with everyday experience that it is, unsurprisingly, central to many faiths. In modern Judaism, as in ancient Egypt and in classical Greece – indeed all round the world – water plays a central role in religious practice, cleansing both body and spirit, and helping define the community. Sometimes water from a particular source is especially revered. Muslim pilgrims to Mecca will try to bring back in special bottles water from the Zamzam spring (see Chapter 14), which at God's command started flowing to slake the thirst of Hagar and Ishmael: it is kept for special moments, and may be pressed to the lips of the dying. For Jews and Christians the waters of the River Jordan, in which the prophet Elisha ordered Naaman to bathe and be cured of his leprosy, and in which Jesus was baptized by John the Baptist, have a particular significance. The British monarchy to this day uses Jordan water for royal baptisms. Roman Catholics all over Europe accord special properties to water carried home from Lourdes. But for no faith does water, and a particular water, play such a significant role as for Hindus.

In a South Indian painting of around 1900, in front of a row of improbably coloured trees, we see four people standing in a river, which is here rendered as a two-dimensional ribbon of vivid blue, inhabited by a crocodile, a turtle and fishes. The three figures on the right, a man and woman with a child between, are being addressed by a blue, diabolic figure on the left: clearly two worlds are in uncomfortable dialogue. The composition and style are simple and bold, some might say crude, which is to be expected, because this is just one of a set of sixty paintings designed to accompany a popular story-telling performance, not unlike a puppet theatre, somewhere between public entertainment and community worship. The story it tells, found in the Mahabharata and other Hindu scriptures, is one of India's best known morality tales, still popular today.

Its main character, the legendary King Harischandra, was famed across India for always telling the truth and keeping his word, no matter the cost. The plot has echoes of the story of Abraham and Isaac, and perhaps even more of Job. As a test, played out in front of the gods, the rich and powerful Harischandra is stripped of power and wealth, and subjected to dreadful ordeals to see whether his integrity can be broken. Our painting shows a critical moment in the narrative. Harischandra and his family have come on pilgrimage to the city of Varanasi, to bathe in the holy waters of the Ganges, which is where we see them. But, even here, an evil emissary, the blue figure on the left, pursues them with threats. In order to honour a promise to pay a large sum of money, the king will soon have to sell his wife and only son into slavery, and himself to work as a lowly attendant at a cremation site on the banks of the river. At the very moment when – rather than fail to keep his word – he is about to kill his wife and cremate his son, the gods restore both of them to him, and invite him to take his place among the divinely blessed. Goodness is rewarded and all ends well. Gandhi claimed that this story, which he heard as a child, did much to strengthen his belief in the absolute power of truthful integrity.

Over: South Indian painting, from around 1900, showing the story of King Harischandra with his wife and son bathing in the Ganges at Varanasi

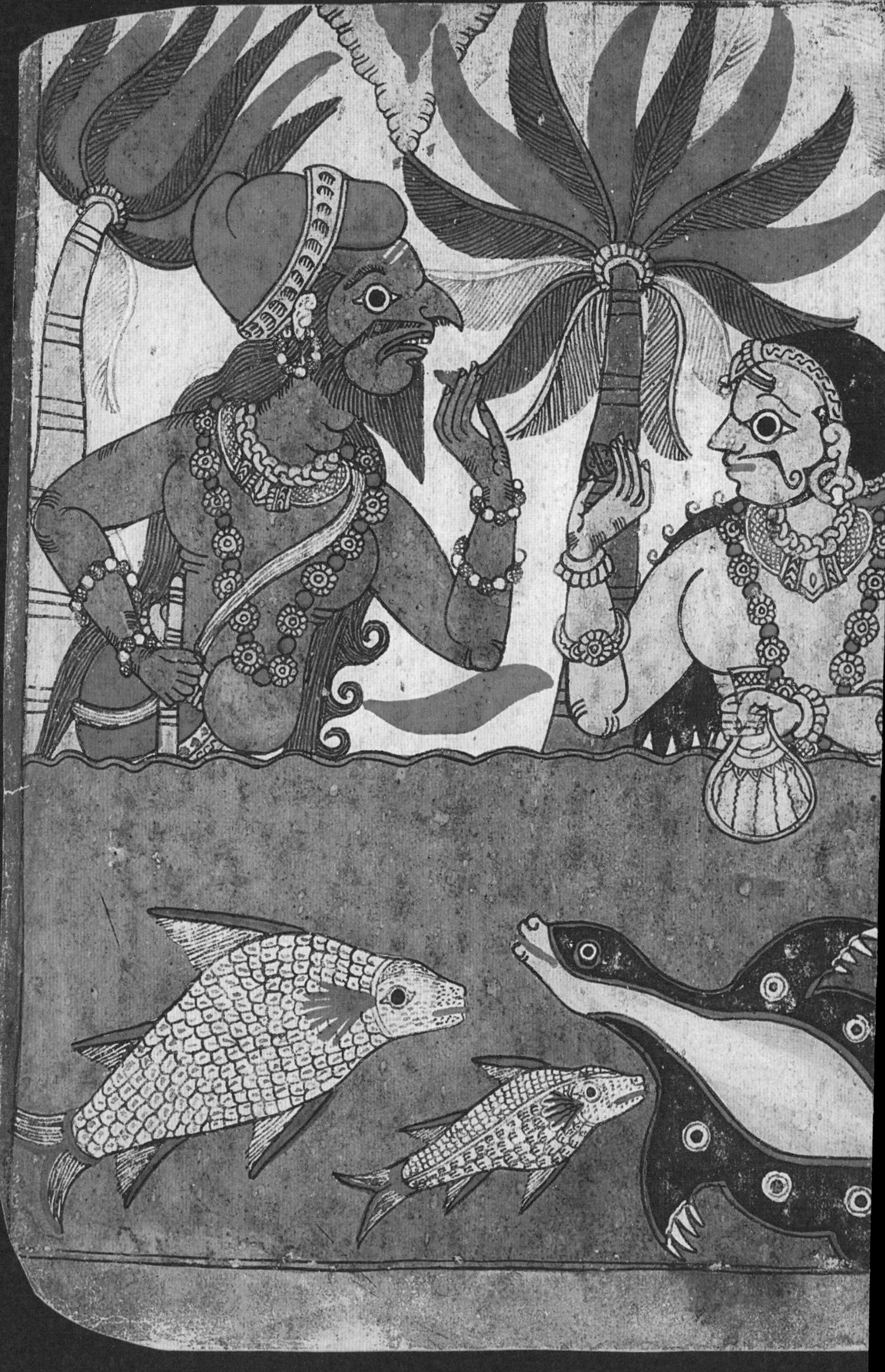

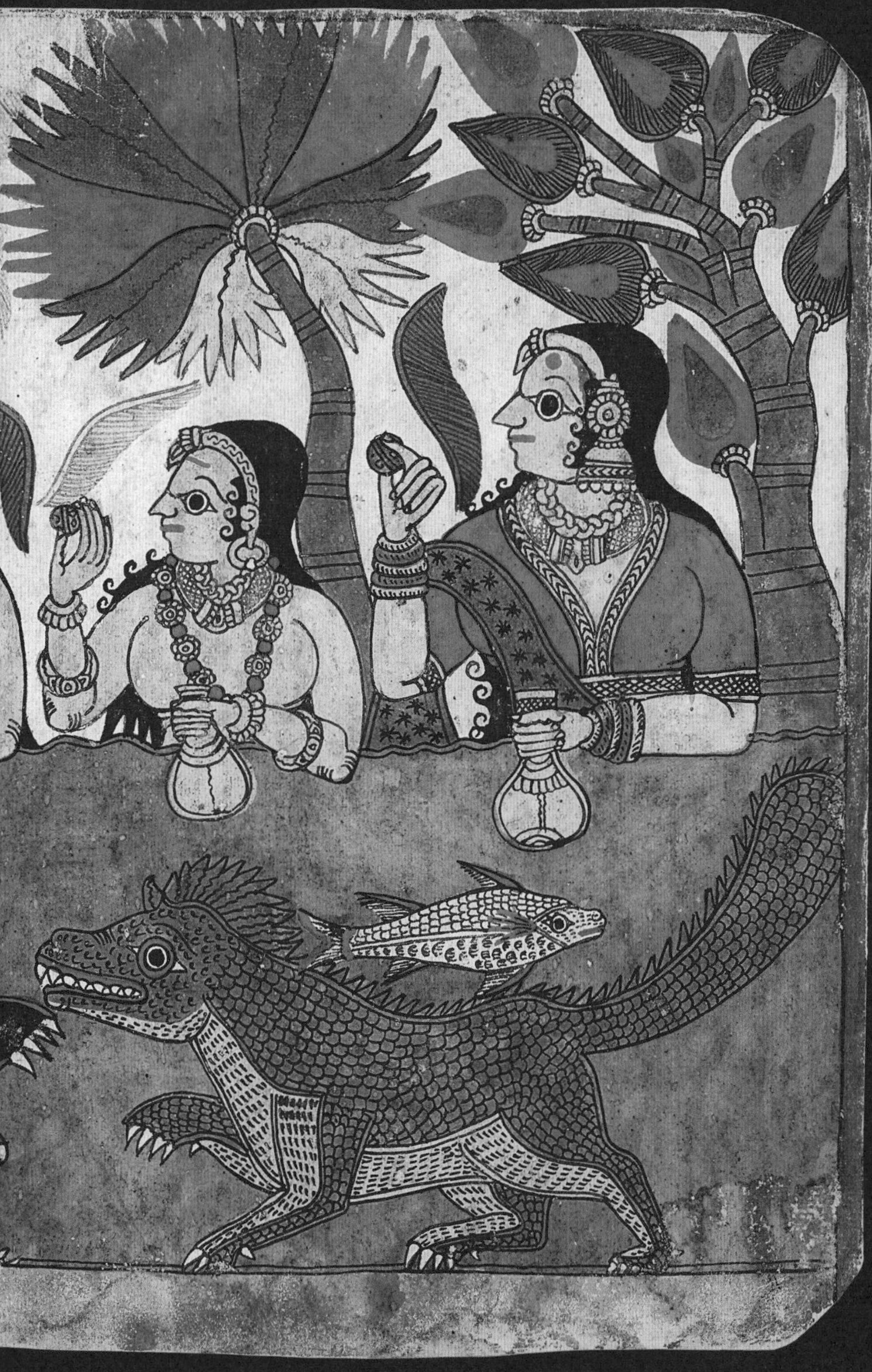

It is no surprise that the climax of the story, the ultimate conflict of good and evil, of life and death, takes place by the Ganges in Varanasi, because the water depicted in this painting is like no other. Every morning there, you can see people standing, like Harischandra and his family, waist-deep in the Ganges. Facing the rising sun, they take the water of the river in their hands, hold it up, and reverently pour it back. And they do it because this river, says Diana Eck, Professor of Comparative Religion and Indian Studies at Harvard University, is the 'river of heaven':

The Ganges is said to flow originally across the sky and in the heavens, in the form of the Milky Way, before coming to earth on India's northern plains for the salvation of the souls of men and women. So the Ganges is actually a liquid form of the goddess Ganga. The river – the goddess – opens a channel of communication and of communion between heaven and earth. One could say that the Ganges descended to earth long ago, but in the powerful religious imagination of the Hindus, it continues to descend from heaven even now.

The water of this river which links earth to heaven, which is the goddess herself in liquid form, is revered by all Hindus, and those who make pilgrimage to the river usually want to take some of it home with them, just as Muslims do with the waters of Zamzam spring or Christians with those of the Jordan. To do so they have for centuries bought brass or copper jars – there are several in the collection of the British Museum – similar in shape to the three shown in our painting. But those who could carried more away with them; for possessing Ganges water in bulk has long indicated particularly high status.

The seventeenth-century Frenchman Jean-Baptiste Tavernier, who travelled widely in India, tells of Ganges water 'brought from a great distance' being drunk at a Hindu wedding: 'for each of

Sunrise at the Harischandra Ghat at Varanasi on the Ganges, with bathers facing the rising sun

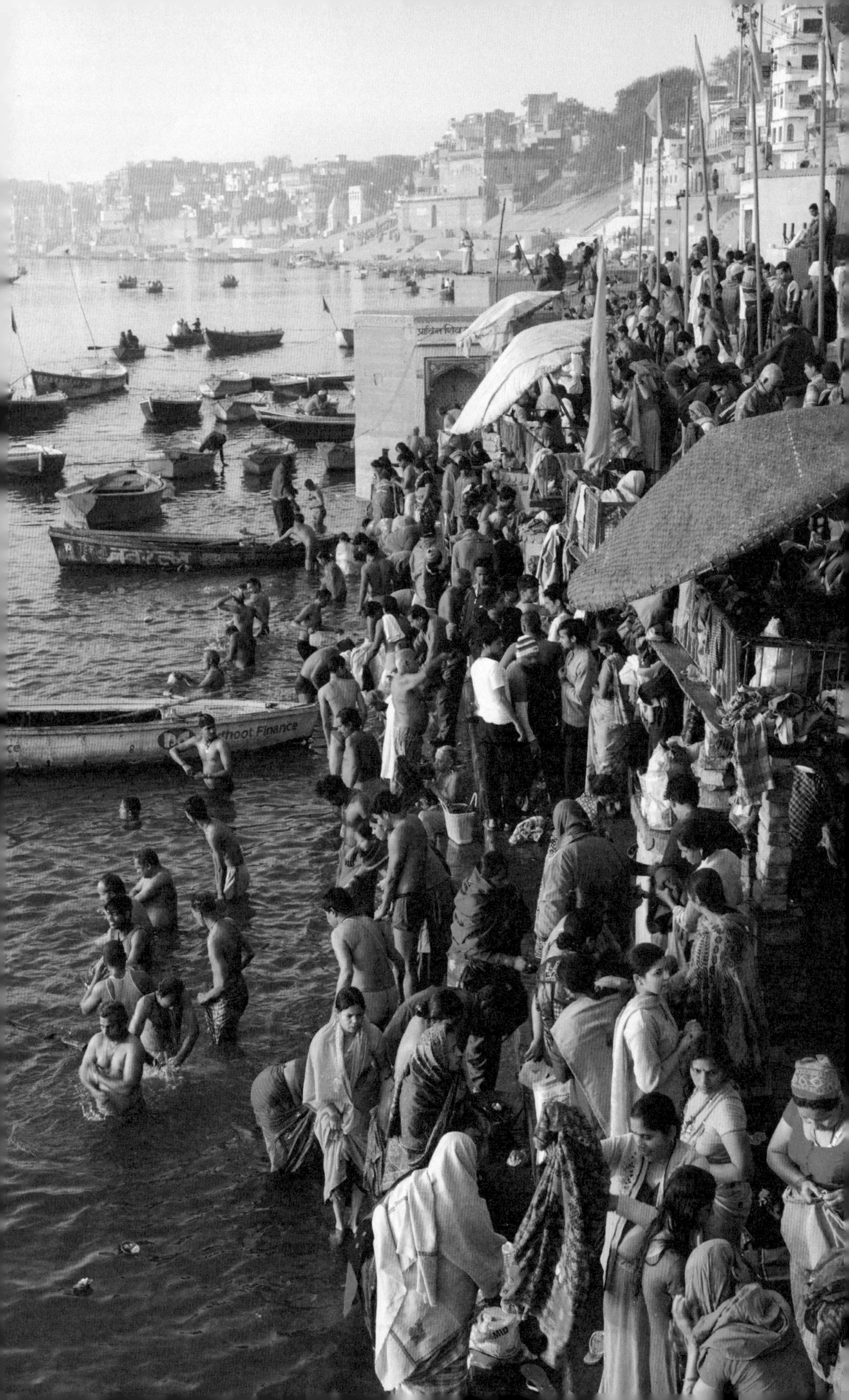
thoot Finance

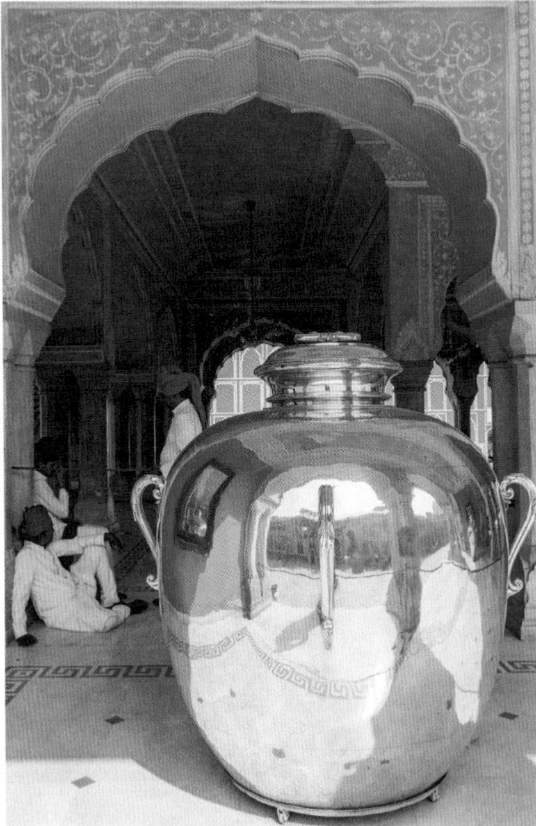

One of the huge silver vessels made for the Maharajah of Jaipur to carry Ganges water to London, where he attended the coronation of Edward VII in 1902

the guests three or four cupfuls are poured out, and the more of it the bridegroom gives, so he is esteemed the more generous and magnificent'. The Mughal emperor Akbar, the contemporary of Elizabeth I of England, even though a Muslim, saw unique virtue in the Ganges water which his Hindu subjects so revered: 'His Majesty,' reported Abul Fazl, 'calls this source of life the water of immortality … Both at home and on his travels, he drinks Ganga water. Trustworthy persons, stationed on the banks of the river, dispatch the water in sealed jars.'

Akbar's example was followed for centuries by the grandest of India's rulers, few among them grander than the Maharajahs of Jaipur. So when in 1902 the then Maharajah was invited to London for the coronation of the new emperor of India, Edward VII, he arranged to take with him an ample supply of Ganges water. The result, which can still be seen today in the City Palace in Jaipur, are believed to be the two largest silver objects ever made. The enormous urns stand five foot three inches tall and weigh 345 kilograms. Each one of them can hold more than 2,000 litres of water: to get at it, you need a ladder and a ladle. These are vessels entirely worthy of their princely owner and their precious content.

It is somewhat anti-climactic to have to report that a modern Maharajah would have no need of such splendid silver jars. He could now arrange to have the water of Ganga delivered to him in London – or anywhere else – simply by ordering it online.

Ganga is poured from the heavens by the creator god, Brahma. Her turbulence is tamed as she falls through the hair on the head of Shiva, the god who – as we saw in Chapter 2 – destroys,

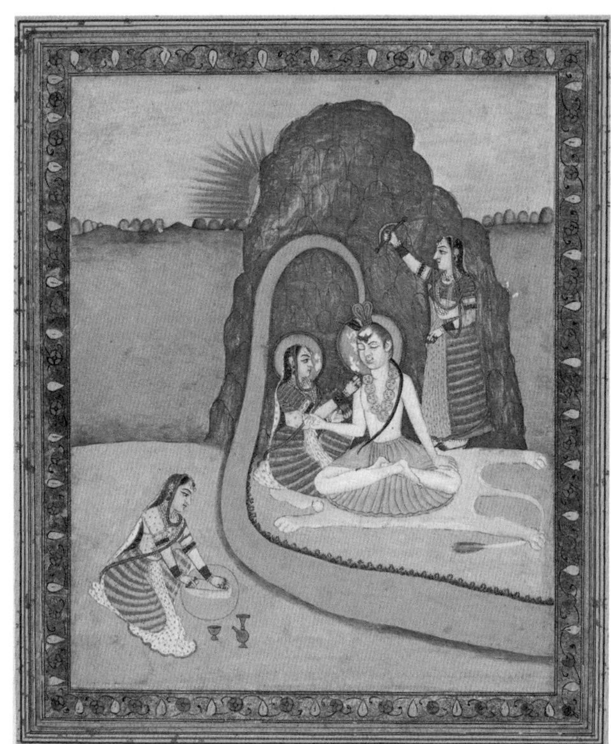

The River Ganga flows quietened from the hair of the god Shiva, in this gouache in the Jaipur style from around 1750

transforms and re-creates. And then finally she comes crashing and tumbling into our world as the life-giving River Ganges, running from the Himalayas, south and east to the Bay of Bengal.

When she reaches Varanasi, however, the ever-changing Ganga turns north towards the fixed, unchanging Pole Star, back towards the place of her birth and her ultimate home. This makes Varanasi a *tirtha*, a crossing point, a place where two worlds meet, where heaven and earth are close. In such a place a transition from one to the other is particularly auspicious, and can most readily be enacted. So to bathe in the Ganges here, to cup its water in your hands and to let it fall again, to reverence the river with offerings of fire or rose petals, is to draw especially close to the gods. Diana Eck describes how:

What is accomplished by bathing in the Ganges is a kind of purity. It might simply be the purity of taking a bath every day, but it is also a washing away of what we might refer to as sin, or of those things that are polluting to us. And it also accomplishes the act of worship. When the water is taken up into one's cupped hands and poured back into the river as an offering it is a form of worship. And Ganges is a place for worship on an enormous scale: it just so happens that this particular cathedral is a river.

It was to worship and bathe in the 'cathedral' of the Ganges that Harischandra and his family came as pilgrims to Varanasi. That our painting showing the scene, however, comes from south India, well over a thousand miles away is, for Diana Eck, not at all surprising. She argues that it is precisely such religious narratives and practices, widely diffused across the sub-continent over millennia, that have created what she calls the 'sacred geography of India'.

India has a long narrative tradition of what constitutes the land in which people dwell. It's told in story, in pilgrimage and in ritual. So the sense of this being a land in which people have a shared sense of belonging is very old. Most of all, it is the rivers that matter. They really are the temples of India. Long before there were temples constructed, the rivers were seen as sacred, and that continues in the daily rites of bathing that you see in a place like Varanasi. But Ganga is present not only in the waters that flow across this particular riverbed in north India, the Ganges. She is part of sacred waters wherever they are. One can bathe in Ganga almost anywhere in India.

For the non-Hindu, this is perhaps the river's most remarkable quality. It flows, as everybody can see, through India's north-eastern plain. But it is present – spiritually – in all the great rivers of India. Myths and legends tell how the water of Ganga is miraculously channelled into the major rivers of the west and the south of the country, turning them too in some measure into Gangas, binding the whole of the sub-continent together in this sacred geography, a shared reverence for Ganga, which is everywhere expressed through ritual and pilgrimage and stories told in all the languages of India. Thus the water of the Ganges has played a significant part in shaping the idea and the identity of India long before the era of the nation state.

The waters of Varanasi, however, do more than just cleanse you physically and spiritually, helping you to lead a better life. As Devdutt Pattanaik, one of India's leading religious commentators, explains, they also offer you the perfect death:

South is the direction of death. The river dies in the south, so in India most of the crematoria are on the southern side of villages. The north, on the other hand, with the never moving, unchanging Pole Star, is the land of immortality. So when the river turns north, as it does at Varanasi, that stretch of water acquires special significance. This is the city of Shiva, the god who enables you to conquer death and enter rebirth, or to escape from the cycle of birth and death altogether. This is what makes Varanasi a place where

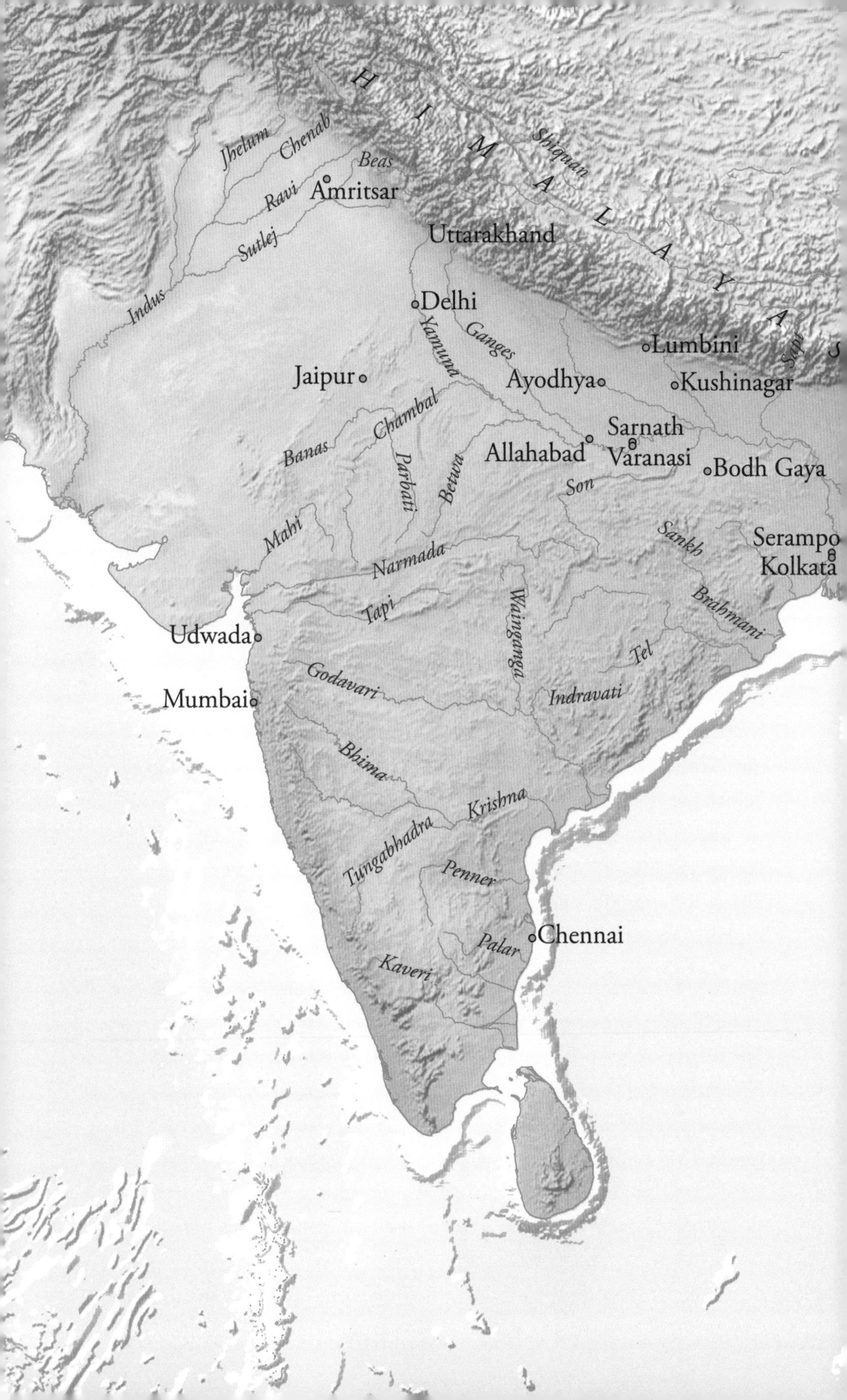

H I M A L A Y A
Shiquan
Jhelum
Chenab
Beas
Amritsar
Ravi
Sutlej
Uttarakhand
Indus
Delhi
Yamuna
Ganges
Lumbini
Jaipur
Ayodhya
Kushinagar
Chambal
Sarnath
Allahabad
Varanasi
Banas
Parbati
Betwa
Bodh Gaya
Son
Sankh
Serampo
Kolkata
Mahi
Narmada
Brahmani
Waingangа
Tapi
Udwada
Tel
Godavari
Indravati
Mumbai
Bhima
Krishna
Tungabhadra
Penner
Chennai
Palar
Kaveri

people want to die. If I die here, I shall either be reborn quickly or I shall not be reborn at all, and so shall reach the blessed land which is free of both birth and death.

For Hindus, if you are cremated on the banks of the river at Varanasi, or if your ashes are brought there and surrendered to the Ganges at this special *tirtha*, you may at last be freed from the burden of the cycle of reincarnation: your soul will be liberated from all bodily constraints and can be reunited at last in everlasting tranquillity with the creator spirit.

This is why the river at Varanasi is lined with its famous cremation ghats, platforms to which bodies are brought all day, to be placed on the funeral pyres whose warmth you can feel as you pass at any time from dawn till dusk. One of the most sought after is still today called the Harischandra Ghat, where it is believed that the admirable king in our painting worked so humbly and behaved so honourably that he was at last rewarded by the gods.

Funeral pyres at the Harischandra Ghat at Varanasi

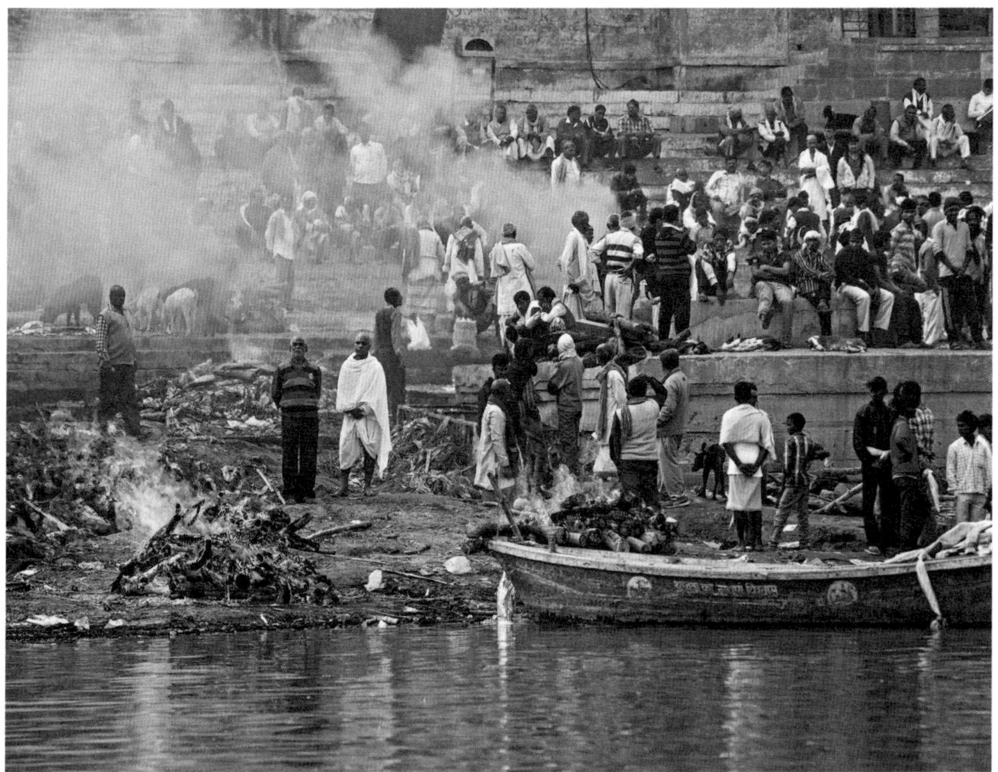

Although this is a place of death, of the obliteration of the body, there is little sign of mourning around the ghats – perhaps because everyone knows that soon all will be resolved by Ganga.

In the British Museum, you can find a striking illustration of the wide reach of this river's power. It is a modest black-and-white engraving, and it too shows clothed people standing waist-deep in the Ganges. But here something very different is going on. A young Hindu man wearing a white dhoti stands with his eyes cast modestly downwards. Behind him, enveloping him with one arm while the other gestures towards the heavens, stands an Englishman from Derby, in full academic dress. We are witnessing an outdoor christening, in which the water of the Ganges is not now the binding element of India's sacred geography but, as the Bishop of Salisbury explained, the initiation into a global Christian community through baptism. We cannot see from the print whether crowds are gathered on the banks of the river to witness the British Baptist missionary William Ward do his work, but a powerful demonstration effect was clearly intended. The print, published in 1821, has echoes, clearly conscious, of famous images of the baptism of Jesus by John in the River Jordan. Less subtly, the strident language of an English Baptist magazine of the day explains what is at issue: 'Surely they need Christianity, who have … no better Saviour than the Ganges, no other expectation in death than that of transmigrating into the body of some reptile.'

The engraving is a vivid representation of the religious consequences of imperial conquest. As missionaries followed the expansion of British commercial and military power in India, the two cultures increasingly came into conflict, to the great irritation of the British civil authorities. Though successful conversions were rare, they worried about the political consequences for British rule of the missionaries' assault on deeply held Indian beliefs. As we can see here, the sacred elements of one faith could become an

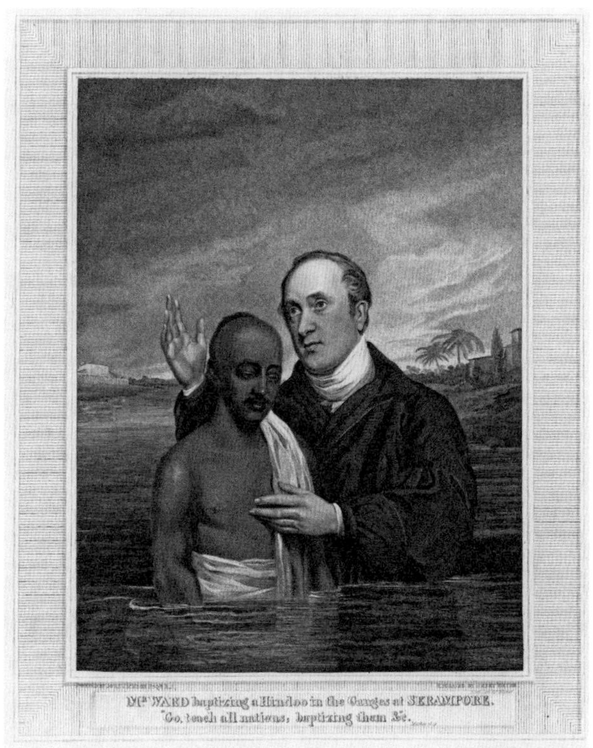

Mr WARD baptizing a Hindoo in the Ganges at SERAMPORE.
'Go, teach all nations, baptizing them &c.

The Baptist missionary William Ward baptizing a 'Hindoo' in the Ganges at Serampore, 1821

exquisitely apposite point of attack by the other in the struggle for the conquest of souls. As the baptism proceeds, light begins to shine over an India long 'dark'.

But Devdutt Pattanaik reads the print quite differently, and in a much more relaxed manner:

Most Hindus would see no problem at all in being baptized and yet still following their temple rituals. There is no idea of conversion – of leaving a belief behind you. You just include another god, who might be helpful; and another ritual is always welcome. I see here a gentle Brahmin, wondering what this strange man is doing. The reverend, on the other hand, is trying to say that he has managed to get Brahmins on his side, and that eventually all Hindus will come into the fold.

Hinduism always exasperated and bewildered the West,

because they just didn't know how to make sense of its fluidity. At one time when the Indian penal code was being designed, the British colonial authorities wanted to find something for Indians to swear on as they testified. The Bible was used in Europe, but what should Hindus use? One answer the British came up with was: holy Ganges water. But, of course, in India no one looks at Ganges water in that way, so Indians would take the vow, and think nothing of it. You can imagine the British bureaucrats tearing their hair out – how were they to govern this strange country?

There is much about Ganga which still perplexes Europeans, especially watching the thousands of faithful who not only bathe in its waters, but drink them. Viewed from the steps of the ghats at Varanasi, they look, to say the least, uninviting. There is a fair amount of detritus – vegetable matter, plastic bags and worse – floating by, not to mention the other forms of pollution that cannot be seen. For many years, this dimension of the river has been ignored by the authorities of the Indian state. But as Diana Eck points out, that is now starting to change:

The high court of Uttarakhand in North India, where the Ganges and its sister river the Yamuna rise, declared early in 2017 that rivers have rights. They can be considered indeed as having the same rights as persons, so people can be punished for polluting them. It's a fascinating thing: this is the first time that a court in India has given personhood to a river, both to the Ganges and to the Yamuna.

And it makes sense. The rivers of India, I think, are more important than most of the temples. So the fact that India does not have free-flowing, pure rivers is astonishing. They really should have a higher level of water quality than any rivers in the world because of the way they are used so intensively as ritual theatres. The purity and the health and the cleanliness of these rivers is not only a question of pollution in an age of rampant disease. This is a theological issue as well, and a very important one. We're talking, after all, about the flowing waters of the body of the goddess.

The court's judgment was subsequently reversed on appeal, but the debate about the rivers' personhood can nonetheless be seen as a remarkable modern, secular engagement with an ancient Hindu belief.

The story of Ganga, the goddess who is one river and yet many spread across the sub-continent, is one of those points in religious life where the literal, the symbolic, and the metaphorical powerfully converge to shape the imagination of a people. Our popular, brightly coloured illustration of Harischandra, designed to accompany public story-telling, is a small but emblematic part of a centuries-old process that has contributed to the moulding not just of a religious community, but of the identity of India.

The first Prime Minister of independent India, Jawaharlal Nehru, stated in his will that he did not believe in religious ceremonies and wanted none around his cremation. But then this thorough-going unbeliever, who had ensured that the constitution of modern India would be resolutely secular, went on:

The Ganga, especially, is the river of India, beloved of her people, round which are intertwined her racial memories, her hopes and fears, her victories and her defeats ... the Ganga has been to me a symbol and a memory of the past of India, running into the present and flowing on to the great ocean of the future ... And as my last homage to India's cultural inheritance, I am making this request that a handful of my ashes be thrown into the Ganga at Allahabad, to be carried into the great ocean that washes India's shore.

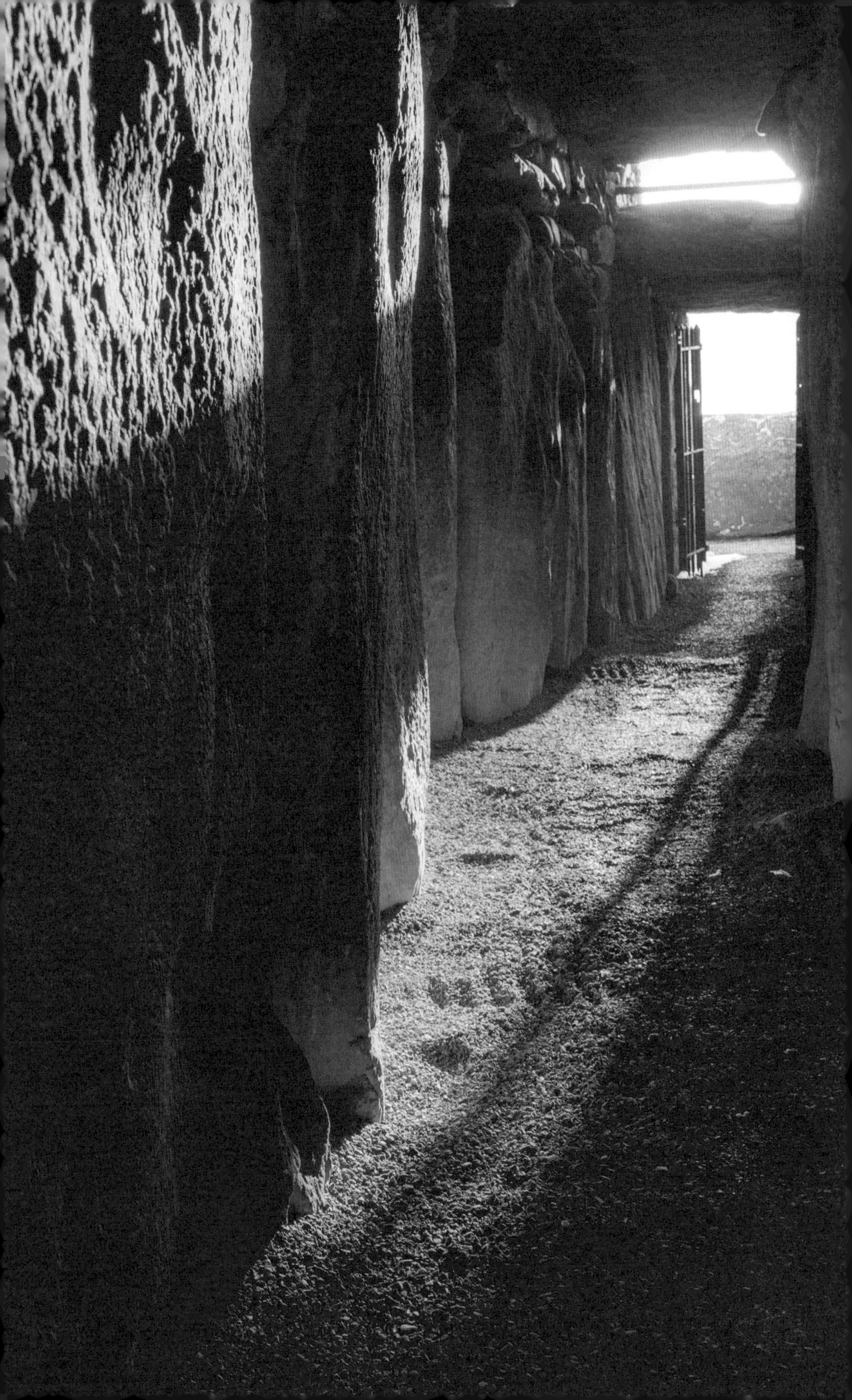

4

THE RETURN OF THE LIGHT

At Newgrange, about thirty miles north of Dublin, there is a dark stone vault, deep inside a manmade hillside, a structure older than Stonehenge, or than the pyramids in Egypt. Inside, it is dry, and cold, and so dark that you can hardly see anyone else standing in it with you. But this is no ordinary darkness: it was created for a purpose.

People began waiting in the darkness of Newgrange over 5,000 years ago, waiting for something both essential for life and beyond comprehension: the first light of the rising sun, as it begins once again to move north after the winter solstice. It is the cosmic promise, given in the depth of winter, that light and warmth will return and new crops will grow. We have so forgotten our dependence on the seasons that perhaps the closest we can now come to experiencing the anxious anticipation of our ancestors is when we wait not for some*thing* – but for some*one*. The experience is deeply personal, and there is no reassuring sense that what we are waiting and hoping for will happen. At Newgrange it always has.

Every year, at precisely 8.58 on the morning of 21 December – cloud cover permitting – a shaft of direct sunlight hits an opening

The rising sun enters the underground tomb at Newgrange, Ireland, on the morning of the winter solstice.

above the entrance to this stone age structure, then moves, concentrated into a golden beam about fifteen centimetres wide, along a passage lined with great megaliths, until it penetrates the vaulted chamber deep inside the mound, lighting the back-stone of the space where the dead were once buried. For seventeen minutes, this narrow sunbeam illuminates the underground tomb. The light of the sun comes to the dead. Heaven and earth are linked. From this moment on, the sun will be nearer, the days will be longer, and new life will begin. This huge stone structure was devised, aligned and built for those seventeen ineffable minutes.

The tomb at Newgrange is obviously a great architectural achievement. Close observation determined its setting, skilled calculation its construction. But it is also an epic act of stage management, a triumph of sensory manipulation. As the sunbeam moves along the passage, it is impossible not to feel that the light is coming to seek *you* out in the darkness, to find you and to change you.

*

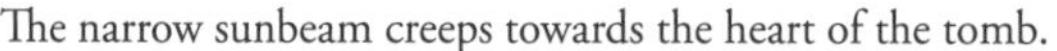

The narrow sunbeam creeps towards the heart of the tomb.

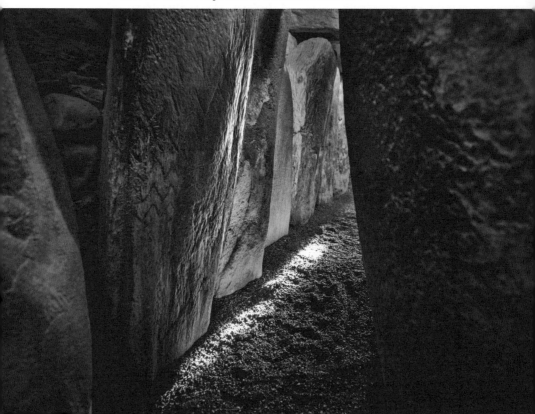

In English to this day we refer to mid-winter as 'the dead of winter', and for most of history that was no mere poetic conceit, but a lethal reality. Until well into the twentieth century, European mortality rates increased substantially in the winter months. For early farming communities anywhere between Ireland and Japan, every winter brought the same existential challenges. Would there be enough food and fuel to enable the community to survive, as the plants died, birds and animals migrated, and the cold set in? How many people would perish before those that survived saw the annual miracle of the crops returning to life? Individual lives would surely end, but if the sun returned, the community would go on.

The pivot of this cycle of death and life, the very moment of transition, is the mid-winter solstice. So it is not surprising that Newgrange is only one, spectacular, example of many buildings across Eurasia – including the megalithic tombs of Gavr'inis at Carnac in Brittany, or the temple of Ggantija on Gozo – that are aligned to the first rays of the returning sun, on which farming communities everywhere knew their survival depended.

We cannot know with certainty what beliefs or rituals led to the making of Newgrange, but all experts agree that there must have been both. Walking into the heart of this circular manmade mound feels like making a short journey into the mystery of life and death. On the east side is a narrow mouth, about a metre wide, leading into a passageway just big enough for one person to pass through at a time, a tunnel roofed and lined with massive stones, which sometimes jut into your path so that you have to stoop and squeeze your way through until, after nearly twenty metres of stumbling, you come out into a wide chamber. There, ten courses of large flat step-stones laid one on top of another rise and converge to form a corbelled pyramidal roof, an astonishing six metres high. In three small recesses off the chamber are large stone basins to hold the bones and ashes of the dead. You are now standing under 100,000 tons of stone, and the structure is essentially intact. Five thousand years after it was constructed, this chamber is still entirely watertight.

Clare Tuffy of the Irish Government's Office of Public Works, who is a specialist in the history of the site, sees this as very significant:

Professor Michael O'Kelly, who excavated Newgrange in the 1960s, thought you would not go to so much trouble to keep a tomb dry if it was just a place for dead bones; but if that was where the spirits of your revered ancestors continued to live, then it would be important that the roof was watertight. It would be not so much a tomb as a house for the dead, a place where they lived on. It is easy to conclude that the beam of sunlight entering the underground chamber was contrived to reassure the spirits of the dead that nothing in nature ends in darkness and death, that there is always rebirth. Perhaps the sunbeam was also the pathway for the recently dead to join the spirits that had gone before.

We imagine 5,000 years ago that not everybody went inside,

Aerial view of Newgrange showing the monumental scale of the manmade mound and the entrance

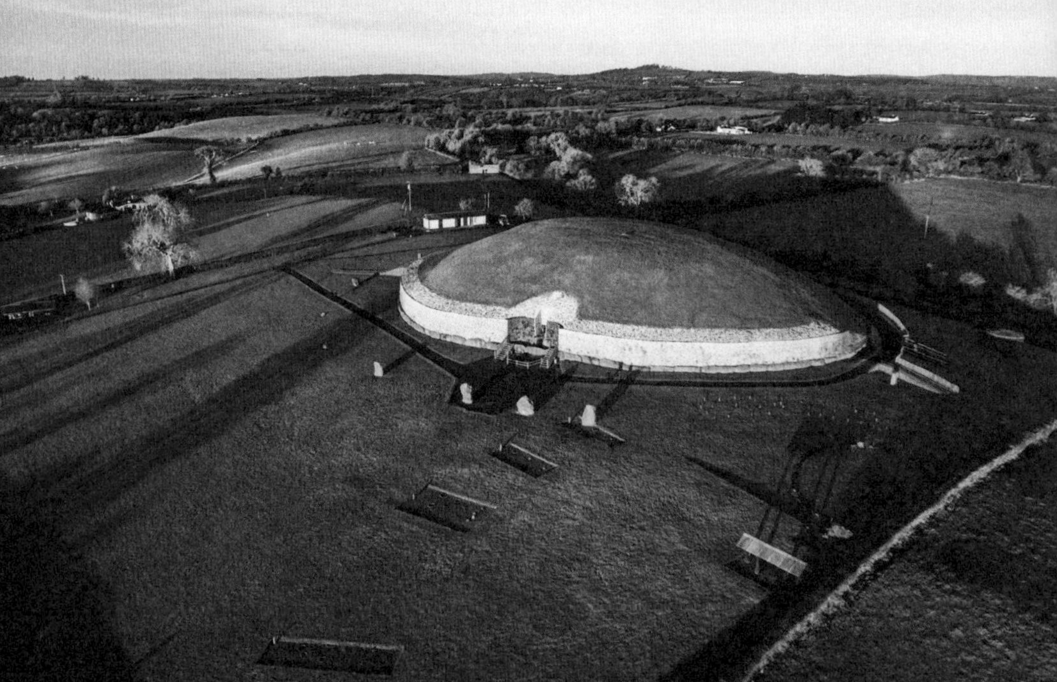

that there would have been special people – perhaps a kind of priest – whose job it was to communicate with the spirits of the ancestors. Perhaps they had a role in seeing them safely reborn, or perhaps the spirits had a message for the people at that time of year. For them, the solstice may have been a time when the barriers between life and death faded.

We can only speculate about the nature of those beliefs – although there can be little doubt that some complex structure of faith and ritual must lie behind the making of Newgrange – and the communal achievement which this building represents is beyond question. From the outside, the scale of the monument, and of the effort required to make it, is breath-taking. Sitting high above the River Boyne, it commands views over the rich farming land of the surrounding country and other smaller monuments nearby. The entire area within the bend of the river has been reshaped to serve as a theatre for rituals now lost, a prodigious imposition of human ingenuity on the landscape.

Newgrange itself is about eighty-five metres in diameter and nearly fourteen metres high. The dome of the mound is covered with grass, but all around the base are long grey stone slabs, ninety-seven of them, laid end to end, and each weighing up to five tons. Like the hundreds of huge stones that make up the passage and the chamber, all were brought from the coast and hauled or rolled up the hill. Hardly less striking are the tens of thousands of smaller white stones of sparkling quartz now reassembled to form a retaining wall around the entrance. Every one of these came from the Wicklow mountains over forty miles to the south. Beyond this tremendous physical achievement lies an equally impressive intellectual one. Newgrange could not have been built without many years being spent observing the sky and the sun, then marking the land, so that everything was perfectly aligned. This is clearly the creation of a highly organized community, one with enough people and agricultural surplus to devote a huge and impressively

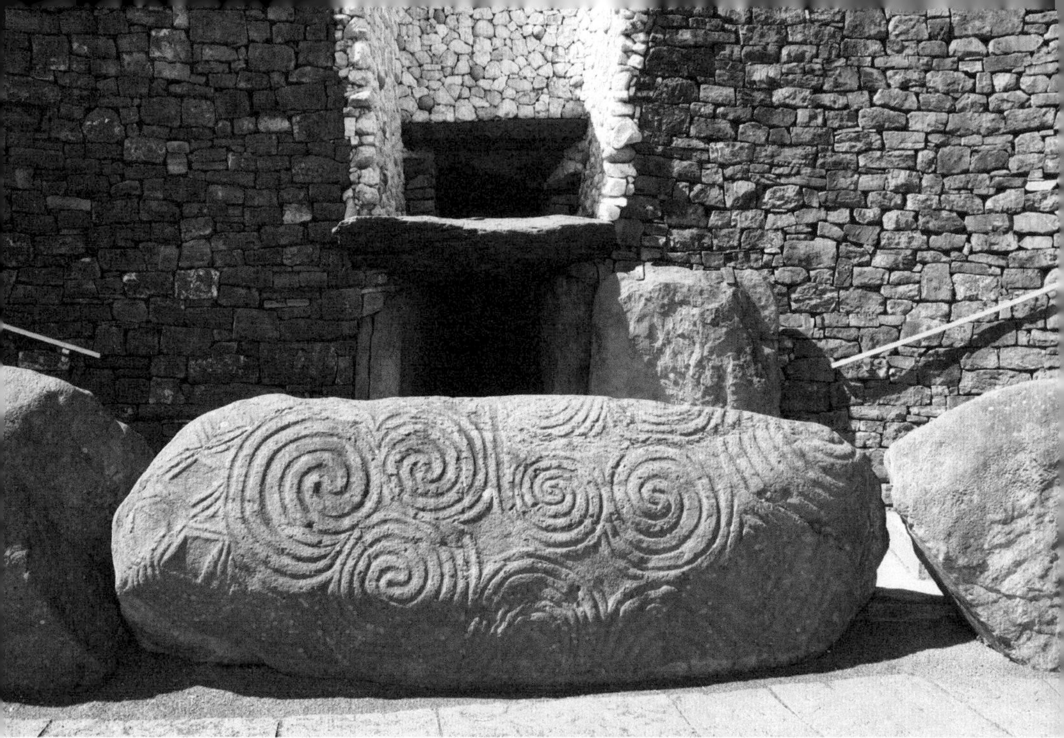

The gigantic patterned stone across the entrance at Newgrange

skilled labour force, possibly over several generations, to constructing such an extraordinary monument. Newgrange represents the same phenomenon as the Lion Man, but on a far greater scale: the investment of critical resources for existential rather than material advantage. Clare Tuffy describes the technical challenges:

The people who lived here 5,000 years ago are our direct ancestors. They were already farming in the valley for over a thousand years before they started building megalithic tombs. They began on a fairly small scale, but then something happened – we don't know what – and they started building really huge monuments like Newgrange.

I imagine they had cadres of specialists. They had practised astronomical observers. They clearly had expertise in engineering and geology, because the stones they used on the outside of the monument are extremely hard-wearing: they knew which stones would last better than others.

The larger stones were mostly quarried over twenty miles

away, likely carried on rafts along the coast and then up the River Boyne. But to walk from the banks of the river to the top of the hill where Newgrange is, even with your arms free, takes twenty minutes. They were transporting these huge megaliths, probably rolling them up the hill. They must have had expert groups planning the transport of the large stones. And all this highly technical knowledge probably had to be transferred to the next generation. Their lives were much shorter than ours, so a monument like Newgrange is unlikely to have been built in a single lifetime.

Although its builders have left us no records, Newgrange articulates with rare poetic power the pattern within which any agricultural community in Europe or Asia must live and die. The golden shaft of the sun entering and warming the dead in the winter earth is a compelling manifestation of the struggle to bring into harmony the life and death of the individual, the cycle of the seasons, and the continuing life of the farming community. The cost of that struggle must have been immense, demanding extraordinary resources. It can only have been a response to awesome religious beliefs, enshrined in complex rituals, and perhaps the terrifying visions of seers.

Emerging from the Newgrange passage tomb on the morning of the solstice, you walk straight out into the rising sun, and into a festive din of people greeting the return of the light with the liveliness and laughter it deserves. There are dancing, singing and the banging of drums. It could almost be a re-enactment of a scene regularly played out at the same moment of the year on the island which flanks the eastern side of the Eurasian landmass as Ireland flanks the west. In Japan too a group gathers at the solstice to celebrate and cajole the absent sun.

Over: The winter solstice in Japan. Woodblock print (1830) by Utagawa Hiroshige, showing the attempt to lure the Japanese sun goddess Amaterasu out of her cave

花開耶姫なり父の尊姫を
幸して一夜に妊娠れたまひしを
深く疑ひ玉へば姫無戸室に入
誓て曰妾娠める子もし神の胤
ならずんば焦亡び天孫のならば
火も害ふこと能はじと茅を積
火を放ち焼給ふに火炎の中より
生れ給ふに御名をひこほ
ほでみのみことゝ申たてまつる
龍宮城より豊玉姫を娶て
皇子をまうく
第五鸕鷀草葺不合尊なり
豊玉姫の妹玉依姫を妃とし
て四柱の彦神をまうけたま
ふ是までを地神五代と
いふなり

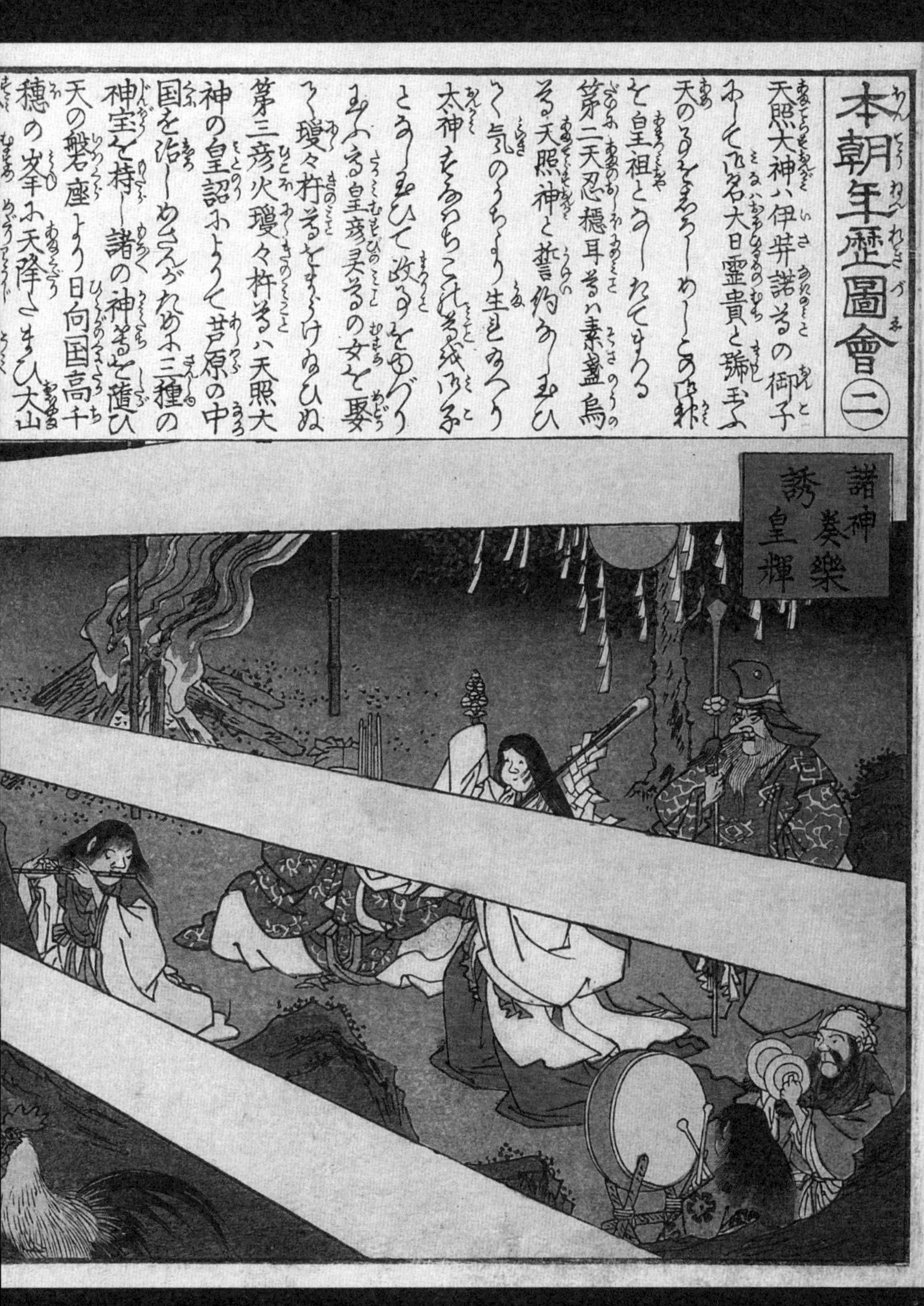
本朝年歴圖會 二
天照大神ハ伊弉諾尊の御子
にして又の名大日霊貴と称ふ
天の下をしろしめしたまふ
を皇祖と称したてまつる
第二天忍穂耳尊ハ素盞烏
尊天照神と誓約したまひ
て気のうちより生れたまへり
太神詔ありて是を我子
とし給ひて政事をゆづり
給ふ高皇産霊尊の女を娶
て瓊々杵尊を生ませたまひぬ
第三彦火瓊々杵尊ハ天照大
神の皇詔によりて葦原の中
国を治しめさんがため三種の
神宝を持し諸の神等を随ひ
天の磐座より日向国高千
穂の峯に天降させ給ひ大山
諸神奏楽
誘皇輝

We can see them doing it in a woodblock print by Utagawa Hiroshige (1797–1858) now in the British Museum. But the Japanese way of imagining the winter solstice drama of death and life is radically and fascinatingly different from that of the prehistoric Irish, and this time, as you can see, we have a text. Here the sun is doing something very strange: it is not streaming *into* a narrow, stony fissure, as contrived by the builders of Newgrange. It is streaming *out*. On the left-hand side of the print, beams of pale sunlight pour from a cave into a world outside that has gone so dark that a fire has had to be lit. Dr Christopher Harding of the University of Edinburgh, a cultural historian of Japan, explains:

The Japanese sun goddess, Amaterasu, has had a big argument with her brother. And she's hidden herself away in this cave, plunging the world into darkness. Outside, a group of gods and goddesses are doing everything they can think of to try to lure her out. Drums are banged, cymbals are crashed, a flute is played. A cock has even been brought along to try to crow her out. But none of this has worked.

Now, a mirror has been placed on a tree and a goddess has got up to perform what is in effect a dirty dance. Everyone watching bursts into laughter, and Amaterasu creeps towards the edge of the cave, eager to find out what all the fuss is about.

'I've just plunged the world into darkness,' she says, 'so why are you lot all laughing?' 'Because there's a new goddess out here,' comes the reply, 'who's even more magnificent than you are.' Amaterasu thinks, 'Surely not', and creeps closer and closer to the mouth of the cave. Just as she looks out, she will see herself in the mirror; for a moment she will be startled, because she's never seen her own image before. Another god, who has just crept up to the mouth of the cave – the Strong-Armed Man of Heaven – will then grab her by the hand and pull her out. And the sun will be brought back to give her life-giving light to the world.

This story, of a cave pulsating with the light of the sulking sun, is told in Japan's earliest written work, a chronicle called the *Kojiki*, completed in 712 CE. In our image, the dancing goddess Ama no Uzume – the Goddess of Mirth and Dawn – is shown fully robed. But in the original telling, she stands on an upturned tub, half-naked, to perform the bawdy, comical dance that finally captures Amaterasu's attention. Christopher Harding comments on this difference:

From a Western point of view, we think of gods and goddesses largely in terms of solemnity, piety and respect. But here, it's all about dance and play and laughter – that's how you bring the light back in the middle of winter. It seems to us wrong, almost sacrilegious. But in Japan there's a sense that religion doesn't have always to be po-faced. There's no reason why piety and playfulness cannot go hand in hand when dealing with the divine.

Although we don't have a text to explain what happened at Newgrange as we do with this story of Amaterasu, in both cases we can be reasonably sure that what is going on is a powerful fusion of the religious and the political. The building of Newgrange clearly took vision, direction and co-ordination of the sort that needs strong leadership and competent administration. And at the time that the Amaterasu story was written down in eighth-century Japan, the country was starting to come together politically, its leaders staking a claim not only to earthly power, but to divine ancestry. The imperial family of Japan to this day claims to be descended from Amaterasu, the sun goddess herself: the good ruler, it is implied, like the returning sun, is essential for the stability and prosperity of the people. (Lesser, priestly families trace their ancestry back to some of the deities we can see standing outside the cave.) A ritual based on the scene shown in the Hiroshige print was for centuries performed not just at the winter solstice, but when the emperor was ill and his spirit needed reviving. And

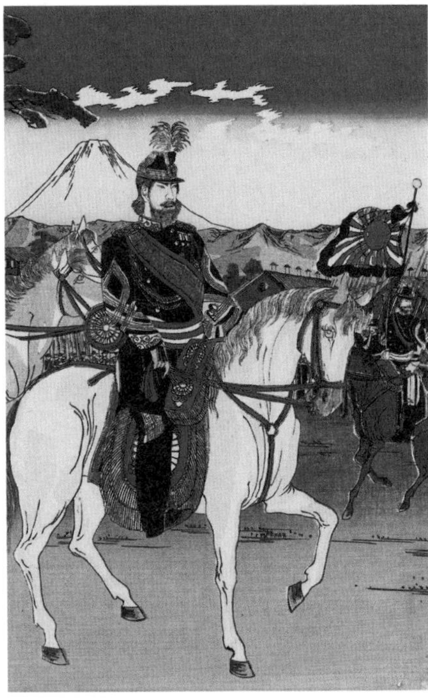

The emperor of Japan at a military review in 1887, with the flag of the Rising Sun, by then a Japanese national symbol

the mirror of Amaterasu is now part of the imperial regalia, still preserved, though never to be seen, at the goddess's shrine at Ise. The sun of Amaterasu still casts a long shadow in modern Japan.

The centrality of the emperor in Japanese life has waxed and waned over the centuries. As Christopher Harding explains, following the Meiji Restoration in 1868 a modernizing Japan, trying after centuries of isolation to emulate the West, but wanting to escape its political and cultural clutches, breathed new life into this old fusion of light and life, of the nation, the winter solstice sun and the emperor:

If you look at the Hiroshige image, made around 1830, you are immediately struck by the sun's rays emanating from the top left-hand side. If you think about that, you can see that it is almost the basis of modern Japan's national flag: the red disc radiating beams of light. In the late nineteenth century, a new set of leaders took over in Japan and they wanted to use the emperor as a focal point for people's loyalties, trying to knit their new country together. So they toured him around the country, reminding people of who he was – because for centuries he had been hidden away in Kyoto. Most importantly, they advertised his divine lineage and at the same time Japan adopted, as one of its main flags, the rising sun.

To a Western mind, the myth of Amaterasu is impossibly strange, yet its purpose, like that of Newgrange, is immediately comprehensible. To everybody, whether East or West, the power of the sun's returning is fundamental to existence. It demonstrates quite literally that, for nature if not for the individual, there is life after death.

The myths and rituals of the winter solstice are still deeply embedded in Japanese national consciousness, and they seem to be making something of a revival in Ireland. Newgrange is now Ireland's favourite national monument, attracting ever larger numbers of visitors – an aspect, some suggest, of a search for a new Irish identity, transcending centuries-old religious divides.

With all the greatest mysteries, the last word should be with the poets. In December 1999, Seamus Heaney stood inside the stone chamber at Newgrange and witnessed the last solstice of the millennium. His poem 'A Dream of Solstice' seizes the magic of the winter solstice, the waiting for a new beginning, the watching:

> *for an eastern dazzle*
> *To send first light like share-shine in a furrow*
>
> *Steadily deeper, farther available,*
> *Creeping along the floor of the passage grave*
> *To backstone and capstone, to hold its candle*
>
> *Inside the cosmic hill. Who dares say 'love'*
> *At this cold coming? Who would not dare say it?*

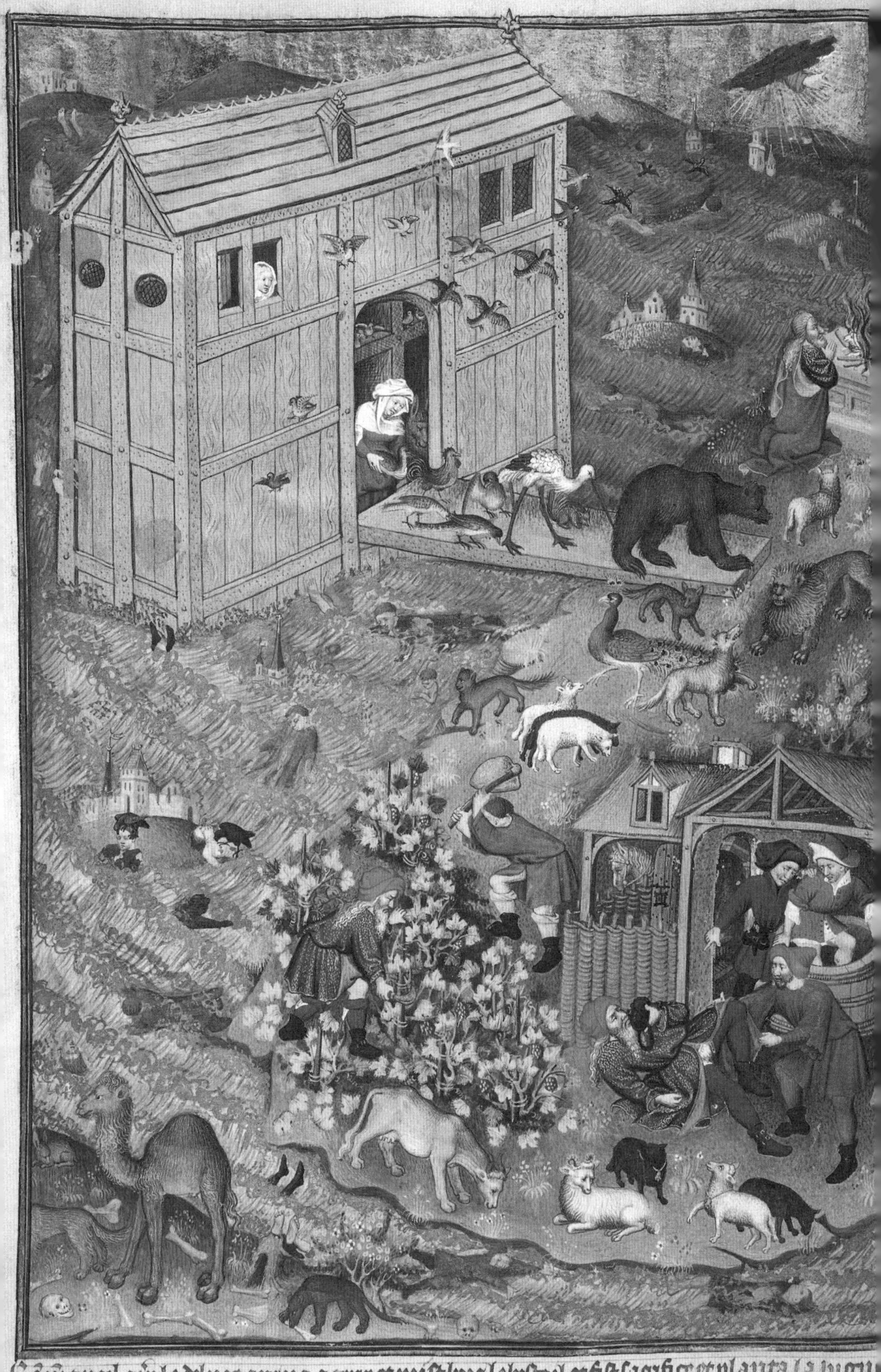

Cōm̄t noel ap̄s le deluge arriua a terre et mist hors le bestail et fist sacrifice et planta la vign

5

HARVEST AND HOMAGE

If there is one scene from the Hebrew scriptures that young children today are likely to recognize, it must surely be the story from Genesis of the animals, two by two, entering Noah's Ark. It is an enchanting myth derived from a cataclysmic event: a single family rescuing the animals of the world from destruction in the great flood – humans and animals literally all in the same boat.

But when the flood subsided, and they all got out of the boat, the relationship between the shipmates became less cosy. We can see the moment in the miniature from the *Bedford Hours*, painted in Paris around 1420–30. The successive phases of the story are shown together. The bodies of the drowned still float on the surface of the receding waters, as submerged towns and buildings (among them a playfully anachronistic church) begin to reappear. Mrs Noah is helping the poultry onto the gangplank, sheep have begun to graze, the camel is heading for the desert, and the bear and the lion are preparing to prowl. While the last animals are still disembarking, Noah and his family have begun farming and planting vines – and Noah's sons have not only trampled out

The animals leaving the Ark, from the *Bedford Hours*

the grapes, but already found their father shamefully drunk. What we see here is the new divinely ordained agricultural order of the world: livestock and wild animals, crops and vines, seedtime and harvest, all organized for the benefit of mankind. It was the world familiar to all Europeans in the fifteenth century, and indeed to most Europeans until the twentieth.

On the right-hand side, Noah makes his thanks-offering sacrifice to God, whose hand appears from the clouds. At this point, Genesis tells us, God speaks to Noah, setting out the future relationship between humans, animals and plants in the clearest terms. In the first chapter of Genesis, at the moment of creation, God had quite simply given humankind 'dominion' – over everything. What that means is now spelt out in much greater detail. 'And the dread of you shall be upon every beast of the earth, and upon every fowl of the air, upon all that moveth upon the earth and upon all the fishes of the sea; into your hand are they delivered. Every living thing shall be meat for you; even as the green herb, have I given you all things.'

This biblical idea of dominion, of a literally god-given right to do with every living thing as we please, to kill or harvest anything for our sustenance, has had great influence on how Western civilization uses and abuses the natural world. In many ways it appears merely to describe the experience of modern city-dwellers, now comprising more than half the population of the planet, living far from the plants or animals we eat, in an environment overwhelmingly composed of things made by us or existing only for our benefit.

Yet in this regard the Judaeo-Christian tradition is unusual. Most belief systems urge a more complex, reciprocal relationship between us and the living world, whereby we have obligations to the animals and plants which sustain us, and dominion is tempered by an awareness of dependence.

*

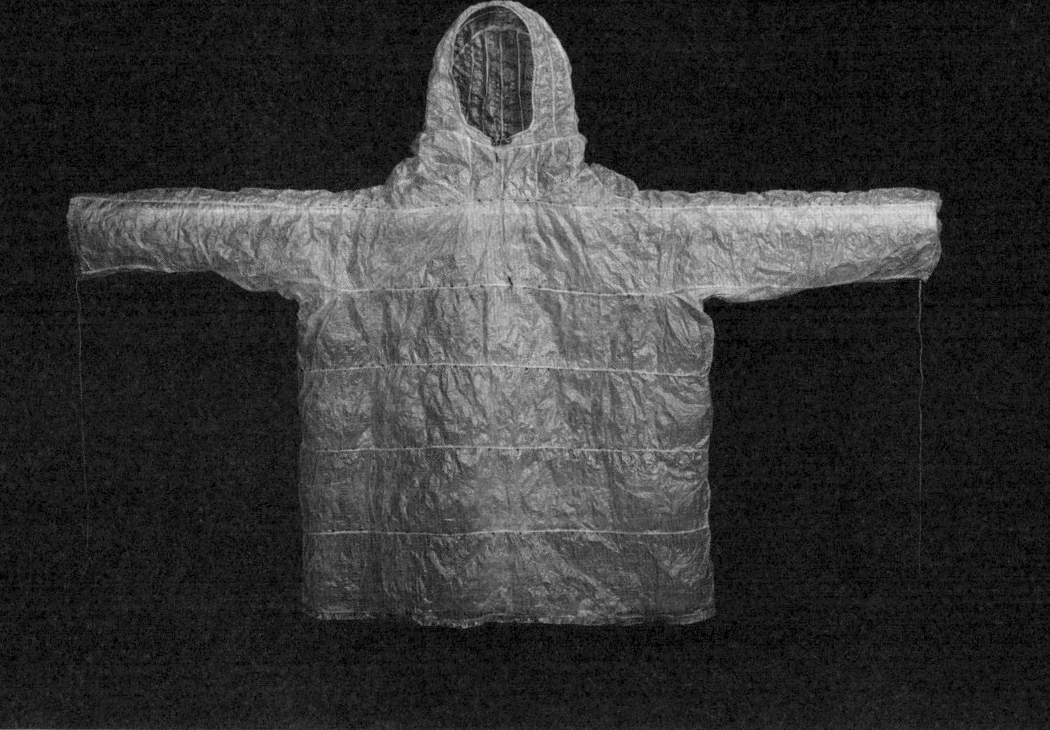

Seal-gut parka made in south-west Alaska by Flora Nanuk, in the late nineteenth century

It might seem strange to consider that more complex relationship by first looking at an anorak. This loose-fitting parka, sewn from horizontal strips of transparent material, is the perfect garment to keep out rain and wind. It looks as though it could be a more effective, indigenous version of the plastic rain-capes that you see on summer tourists as they walk round wet European cities. Totally wind- and water-tight, it was made by a Yup'ik woman, Flora Nanuk of Hooper Bay in south-west Alaska, to wear when she went out picking berries during the brief Arctic summer.

It is made from the animal on which, above all others, the Yup'ik people depend for their survival: the seal. The body of the parka is composed of bearded-seal intestine, scraped inside and out, blown up, dried, cut lengthwise into extended strips, then stitched together. The armpits are made out of parts of a seal's colon for extra resilience. In autumn, the Yup'ik people have

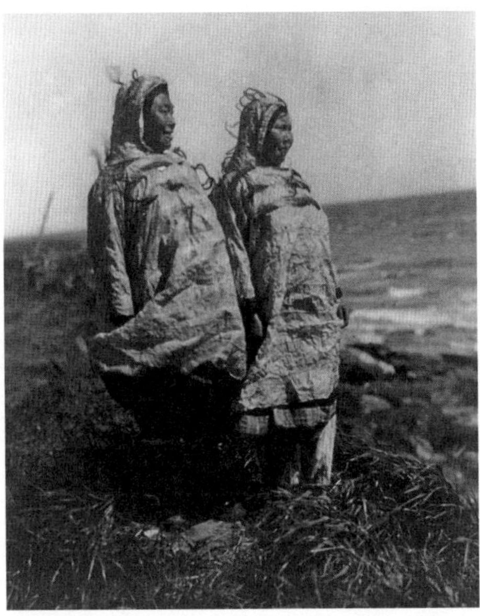

Alaskan women wearing seal-gut parkas, 1929

traditionally gone inland to hunt caribou for meat and skins. The most important season for food, however, is the long, frozen spring that follows winter, when seal can be stalked across temporary sea-ice. Their flesh, skin and intestine crucially provide both clothing and nutrition. Their fat is rendered into oil and served as a condiment with meals; historically it was also used as fuel for cooking, heating and lighting during the long Arctic winter. But seals also play another, less expected, role in the winter life of the community. Amber Lincoln is the curator of the North American collections at the British Museum:

The winter months were largely cold and dark, with oceans and rivers in great measure frozen over. While people in western Alaska travelled and camped widely during the summer and autumn, the darkest months compelled them to stay inside. Men would gather and repair tools, mend and make nets. Women would make and repair clothes. These winter months were also the season when the whole community could come together, with time to conduct ceremonies and celebrations.

To these ceremonies, people invited the spirits of the animals that had been harvested throughout the year, and celebrated them. In a way, they were thanking them for giving their lives for the nourishment of Yup'ik people. The animals who had been taken were honoured with dancing and storytelling and good food, so that other animals would decide to give themselves up to hunters in the coming year.

Among these animal spirit guests were of course the seals, especially at the Bladder Festival, one of the most important winter celebrations. The soul of a seal was thought to reside in its bladder: so when a seal was hunted, and the body cut up, the bladder was preserved. It was given a place of honour during the festival and then released back into the sea through a hole in the ice: the soul could thus return to the sea, and so, it was hoped, encourage other seals to visit the next season. It is a potent ritual, publicly honouring the animal that you needed to kill, on whose death indeed

The Yup'ik people celebrating with sealskin drums in the depths of the Alaskan winter, *c.*1914

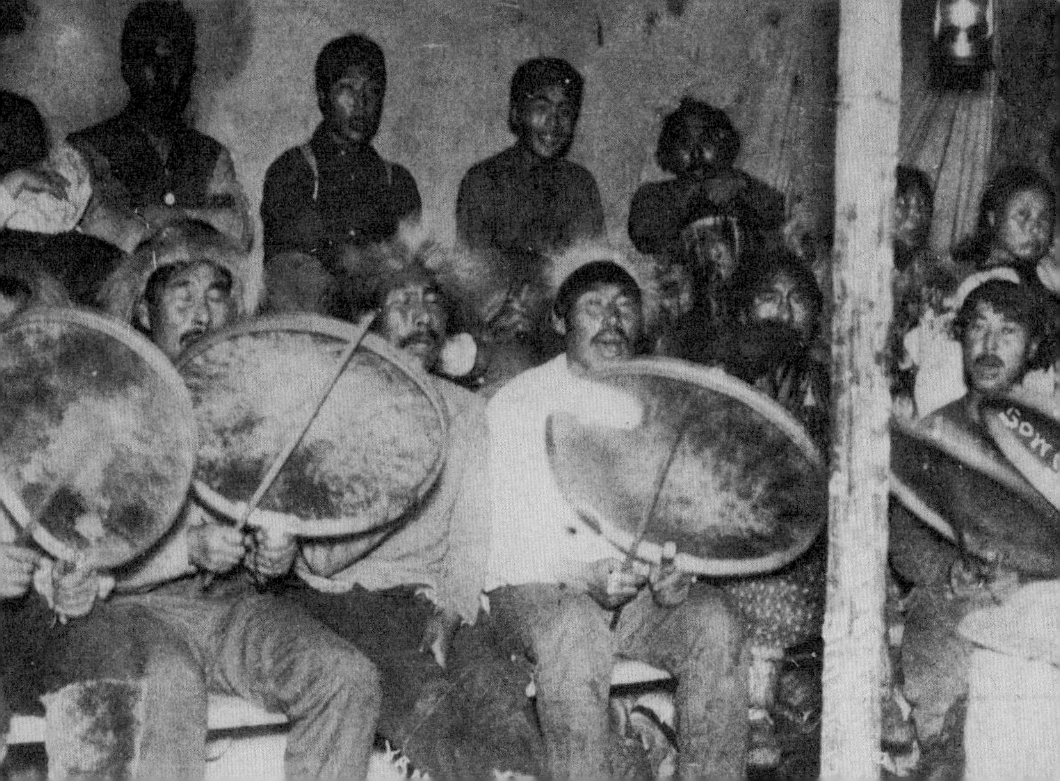

your life depends: harvest and homage going hand in hand. Amber Lincoln explains further:

The way you treat animals matters at every stage: you offer a seal you have killed a drink of water, so that its soul will not be thirsty. Those animals, it is believed, will then go off and tell others how well they were treated. This shows us that in the Yup'ik hunting relationship, agency ultimately lies not with the hunters, but with the animals. They would consent to let themselves be taken by hunters who were respectful, who paid attention to their needs.

The thinking behind this practice, asserting a respectful, entirely equal partnership between animals and humans, where the animals have real agency, is almost impossible for a highly urbanized society to grasp. Most foreign to us is perhaps its assumption of such close inter-connectedness and mutual obligation. The duties of humans, however, go far beyond merely respecting the living, or tending the dying, animal: as Amber Lincoln describes, how its body is used after death will also have long consequences:

You take good care of their hide. You properly dispose of their bones. You use all parts of the animal because they are aware, even after you hunt them. Other animals have awareness, too, so this relationship is really reciprocal.

This parka is therefore much more than just a means of keeping out the cold and the rain. It is an expression also of that obligation to use every part of the seal's body, not just because they are all useful, but as a mark of respect to the dead animal. In the British Museum, as well as the parka, are harpoons made of seal bone, drums of seal stomach, seal fur clothing and decorations playfully made out of seal whiskers. Of course, these are evidence of a frugal, resourceful society, but they are also a community's way of acknowledging and honouring the gift of a life.

The bond between humans and animals is so intimate that they must be treated as far as possible on the understanding that they and we are in a real sense members of the same community. This view, Amber Lincoln explains, is mirrored in patterns of everyday behaviour, even in the conventions of courteous conversation:

I've been at Game Meetings, which is where Alaskan state agencies come together with hunters, to talk about how many animals can be harvested. Yup'ik people always remind the officials that the animals under discussion are paying attention to us, may be able to hear us. 'Please, talk nicely. Don't necessarily use their name. You don't need to say "bear" ten times. You can use a different word.'

Their world view was and largely continues to be that animals, and indeed landscape features and plants, are aware. That's how Yup'ik people describe it – we might use the word sentient. And this awareness includes the ability to respond to human thought and human action. So Yup'ik people try to think good thoughts, respectful thoughts, to one another and towards the world.

Every part of the seal's body is used, to make harpoons, drums and boots.

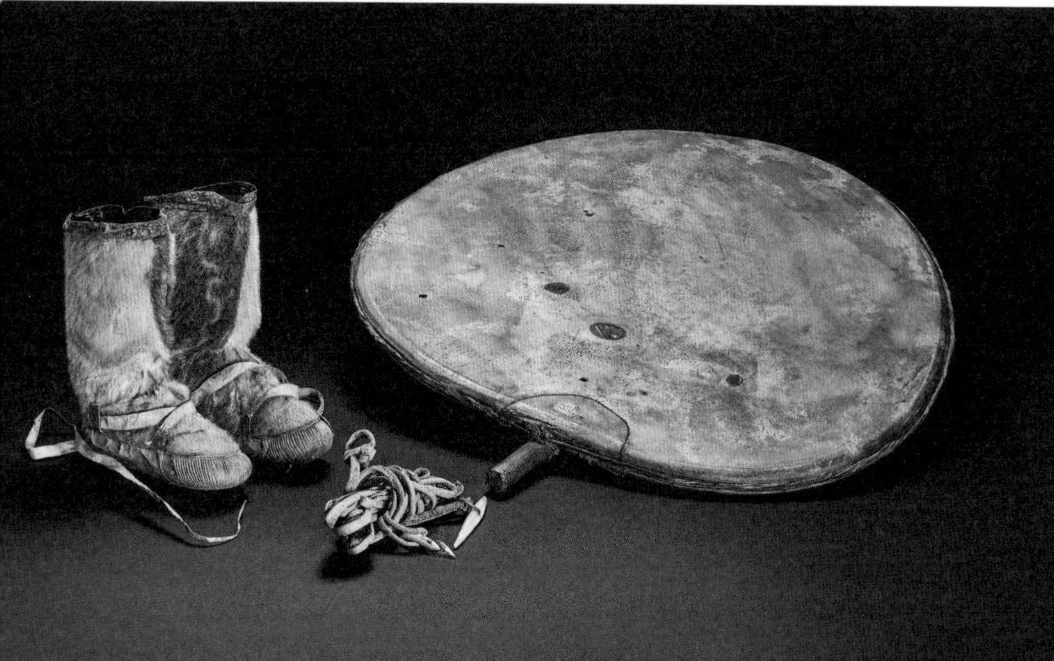

The notion that our relationship with the natural world is essentially reciprocal, that it constantly requires balancing gestures from the human side, Amber Lincoln elaborates, finds expression in every part of Yup'ik life:

Massive amounts of driftwood float down the rivers, and people in western Alaska traditionally benefited greatly from it. It was a huge resource. Even today they collect it. There are very specific, distinct kinds of driftwood that were used for house building, for boats, for mask making, for all the different parts of their material culture. There is a sense that this gift of wood should be used only for its proper purposes – the purpose for which it was given. So if, for example, instead of using the wooden masks that they make, Yup'ik decide to sell them, then they will burn an equivalent, balancing amount of wood.

There is of course no text that sets out the Yup'ik view of the place of humans in the cosmos. But their habits of belief and behaviour tell not of dominion but of a constant dialogue between living things that goes beyond any individual life.

In a world used to industrial farming and battery hens, we may struggle with the concept that sustaining a proper balance in our relationship with nature demands not just respect, but reciprocity too. Yet it is an idea that is central to agricultural as well as hunting societies, and it lies at the heart of many of the religious practices of ancient Egypt. The Alaskan rivers brought much-needed wood, but the Nile was the precondition of almost the entire food supply. And here too, as among the Yup'ik people, mutuality and ritual were necessary to keep the cosmic scheme in balance.

For the people of ancient Egypt, living in a region with some

Opposite, top: 'The fields laugh': barley ripening on an Egyptian painted limestone relief, *c.*1340 BCE. *Opposite below*: 'The gods' offering descends': harvest after the Nile flood. Egyptian tomb painting, *c.*1250 BCE

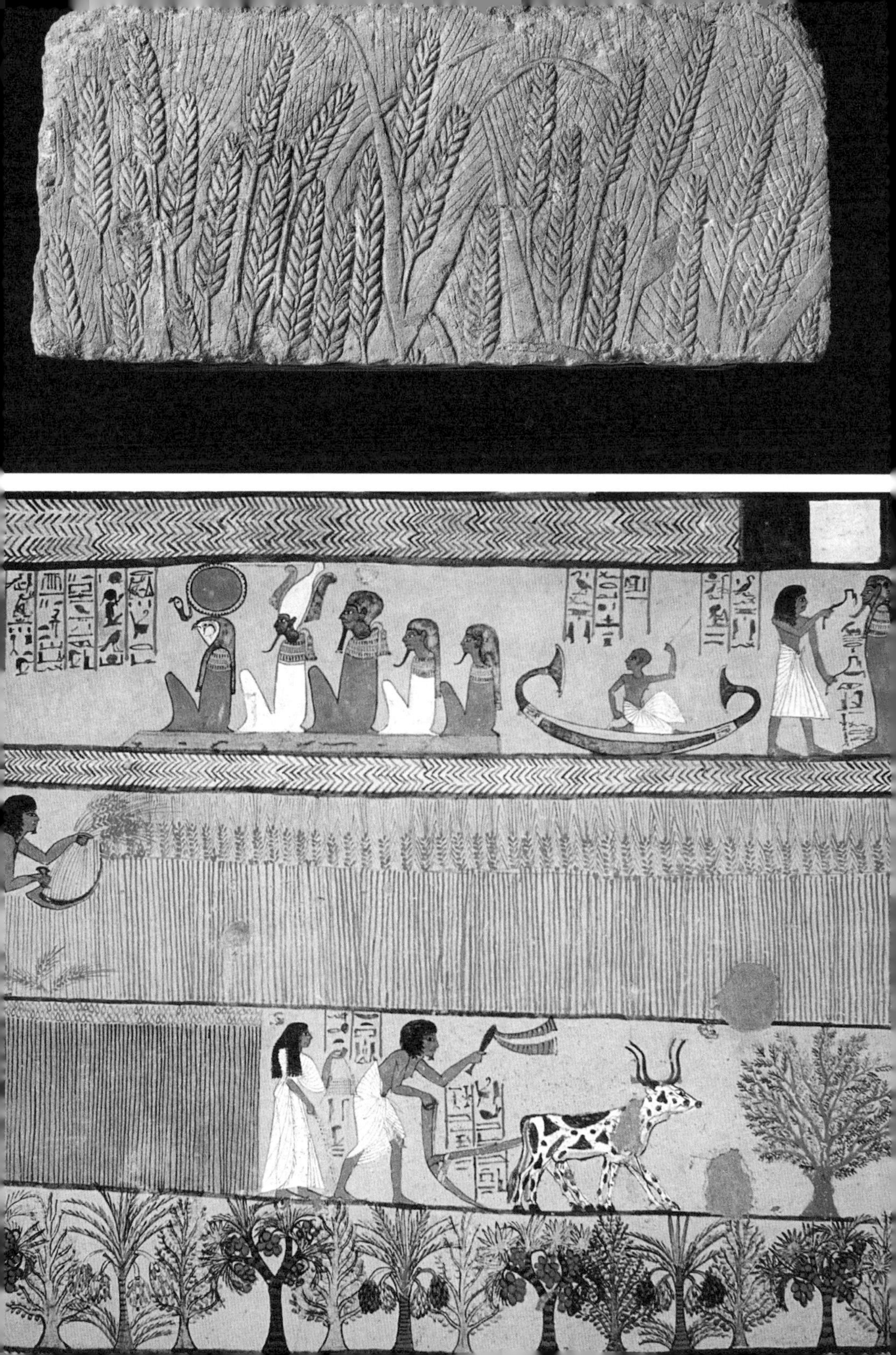

of the lowest rainfall in the world, the Nile was an essential source of life. Each year, monsoon rains falling to the far south, on to the highlands of what is now Ethiopia, raised the water levels of the river. A much-needed flood would follow, peaking between July and September. At this point – in the words of an ancient Egyptian text – 'the fields laugh … the god's offering descends, the visage of the people is bright'.

'The god's offering' was the exceptionally fertile black silt left behind by the receding waters, in which farmers could plant their crops. The kingdom of Egypt was so reliant for survival on this seasonal flood that it emerged around 3000 BCE as an almost entirely linear state ranged along the great river and its banks. Yet things could easily go wrong. Settlements and precious land were sometimes destroyed when the waters ran too high. And when they did not run high enough, there was famine. In the Hebrew scriptures, Joseph proves his worth to Pharaoh by storing surpluses in the seven fat years so that Egypt can survive the seven lean years which follow them. Everything hinged on the proper balance of nature.

This dependence was so profound that it went beyond being a matter of life or death. It became a matter of life *and* death: and the god represented in a small brown figure now in the British Museum played the key role in ensuring that the proper balance was maintained. But, unusually for a god, he did not 'preside' over that process: he was caught up in it himself. He too lived and died. John Taylor is the British Museum's curator of Egyptian funerary artefacts:

Made between 700 and 300 BCE, this little statuette, is about thirty centimetres high. It represents a mummified human figure. The head, made of beeswax, has gilded lines accentuating the eyebrows above full, oval eyes; but the body is completely shrouded in linen wrappings, so you can't see the limbs. You can, however, see that he has a prominent erect penis, bulging forwards at the front; and he is wearing a crown.

Corn mummy figure of Osiris, *c.*700–300 BCE

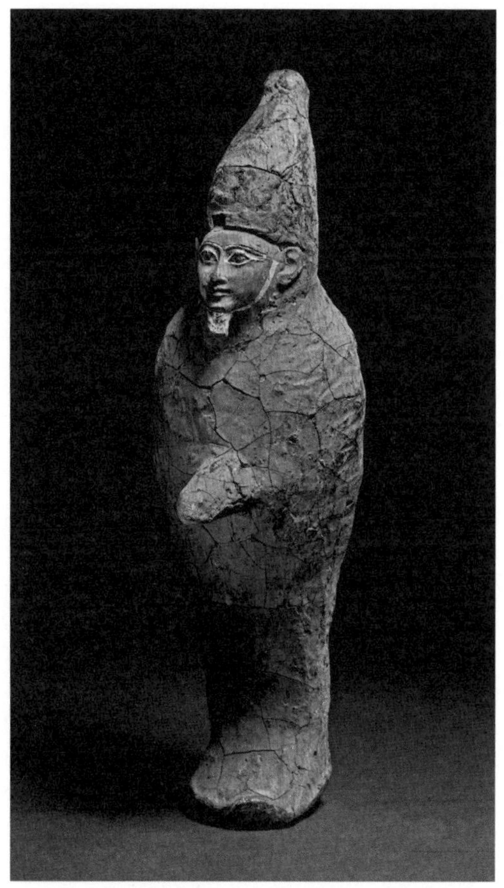

This is an image of Osiris, a king and a god, who died, was mummified and came back to life. The erect penis is to show that he is fertile, capable even after death of producing new life.

According to Egyptian mythology, Osiris was in the distant past a particularly beneficial king, who taught the Egyptians agriculture, gave them laws and civilized them. But his jealous brother killed him, and Osiris's body was cut into pieces and scattered throughout Egypt.

His wife, Isis, collected the pieces together and had him reconstituted as a physical being and mummified. He was then brought back to life but continued as the ruler of the underworld, the kingdom of the dead. The core of the Osiris myth is the idea of a god who embodies the whole of Egypt, who dies and returns to life, and so gives to everybody the hope of new life.

That mystical idea is given powerful physical expression in our little statue. For if we could unwrap these dry, cracked bandages, we would find underneath not just more earth and beeswax. We would find something else entirely: corn, ready to germinate inside this body from seeds planted within it. This single small figure holds in it the image of death and the sprouting of new life. Figures like this one were at the centre of a great celebration held in Egypt every year during the fourth month of the flood, as the waters were falling back, exposing the fertile silt below which would soon be planted, as John Taylor goes on to describe:

The purpose of little figures like this one is to provide hope for the future, that the crops will grow and that life will continue. They are made for the festival of Khoiak, a name derived from the apt Egyptian term ka-her-ka, 'sustenance upon sustenance', just before the new season's planting began. The priests gather grain seeds from the riverbank, mix them with earth, beeswax and other ingredients, and mould them into a mummy-shaped figure of Osiris like this one: which is why they are known as corn mummies.

These small figures then pass through a number of rituals and are carried in ceremonial processions, witnessed by large numbers of people. Eventually they are brought to a sacred place, where they are stored safely and kept throughout the year, until the next Khoiak festival. At that point the process is repeated. The old corn mummy is buried with fitting ceremony, a new figure is made to replace it, new seeds placed inside it, and the cycle continues.

The purpose of this festival is to ensure that this fertilization of the land and the production of food will continue in perpetuity. And part of that ritual involves making these special images

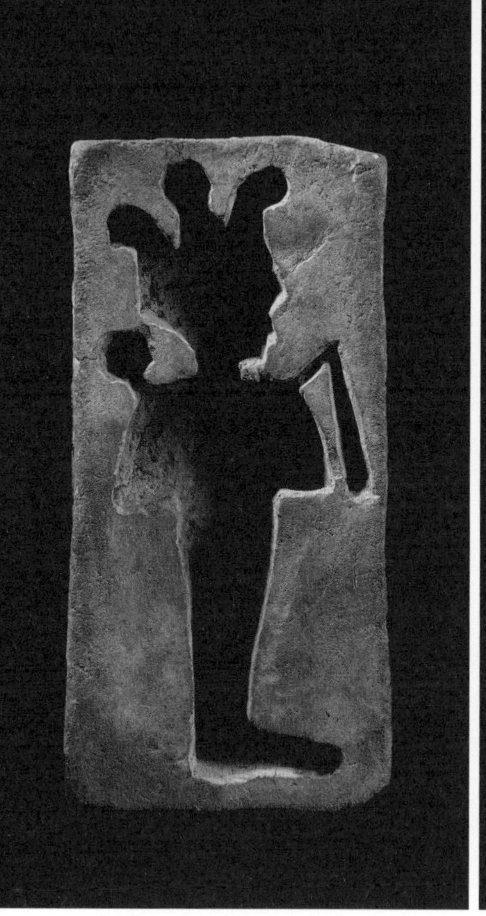

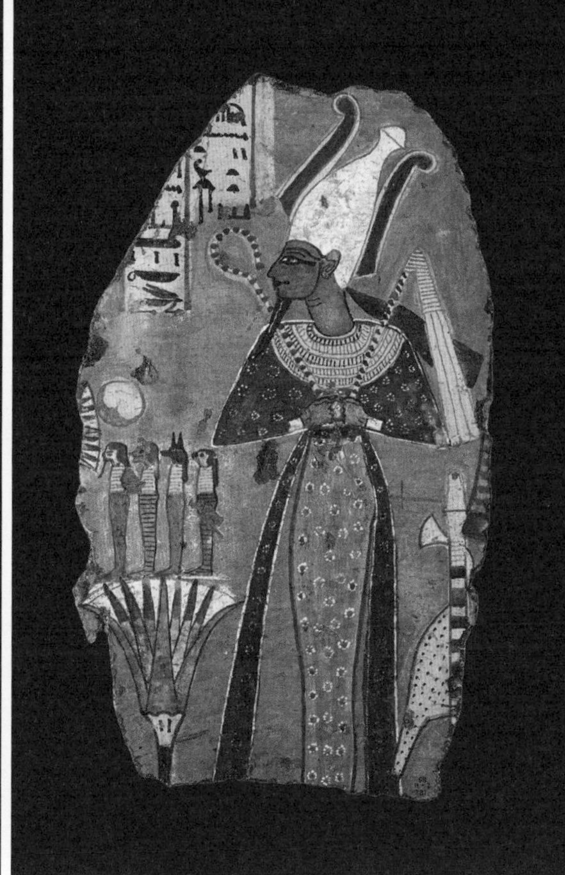

An Osiris-shaped mould in which seeds were planted in an Egyptian tomb (*left*).
A wall painting showing Osiris, ruler of the Egyptian underworld, in splendour (*right*)

of Osiris: within the body of the god you plant the kernel from which will spring new crops and new life.

This was an all-encompassing celebration, then, of the seasonal cycle. Osiris lives, dies and lives again. The fertility of the land returns so that Egypt can eat, and Egypt itself is renewed.

It might be tempting to look at a figure like the corn mummy of Osiris, and the rituals that went with it, and imagine a people hoping to twist nature's arm. But that would not be quite right. We would be getting trapped, I think, in our own modern Western conception of nature: that it is outside us, and that it should somehow be made to conform to our desires. Rather, it seems to many scholars that we are dealing here with a seasonal ritual that is not so much about humans exerting power *over* gods or nature, but working *with* them, playing their allotted part to help keep the system in balance and functioning as it ought: collaboration rather than manipulation. John Taylor describes this interaction:

In all aspects of ancient Egyptian life and religion, there was an awareness of a greater power, something beyond ordinary human agency. Egyptians clearly believed that they had to interact with this power so that the world as they knew it could continue and life could go on. Because his dismembered corpse had been distributed throughout the country, the body of Osiris is seen as a metaphor for the whole of Egypt. The cycle of his life is linked very closely to that of the Egyptian year, and is firmly integrated into the daily routines of the people. Only thus can the divine power of the gods bring new life.

These complex ideas and rituals, meticulously detailed in texts, are profoundly political. The link between them and the continued existence of the Egyptian state itself is apparent from the placing in royal tombs – Tutankhamun's among them – of a wooden mould in the shape of Osiris. Within it was earth with barley seeds. In the darkness of the tomb lay the promise of new crops and new life for both king and people.

The parka and the corn mummy appear to come from thought-worlds far removed from each other, and even more remote from our own. Osiris is for most people today a god irrecoverably dead, his reconstitution and resurrection as alien an idea as the soul of a seal journeying in its bladder to speak to its fellows. But both Alaskan and Egyptian societies, in very different circumstances, evolved narratives to acknowledge with humility their dependence on the natural world. In consequence, both could devise actions to engage the whole community in husbanding it. Most of the modern world is now struggling to do either.

PART TWO

Believing Together

In the previous section, we looked at the stories societies tell which make their lives meaningful and give them their place in the patterns of the natural world. In this section, we look at how the transient existence of each single life is woven into the much longer time-span of the community as a whole – how one life meshes with many across the generations. We shall look at ceremonies of induction and initiation, at activities such as prayer and song that bind us together – and at the great disruptions of birth and death.

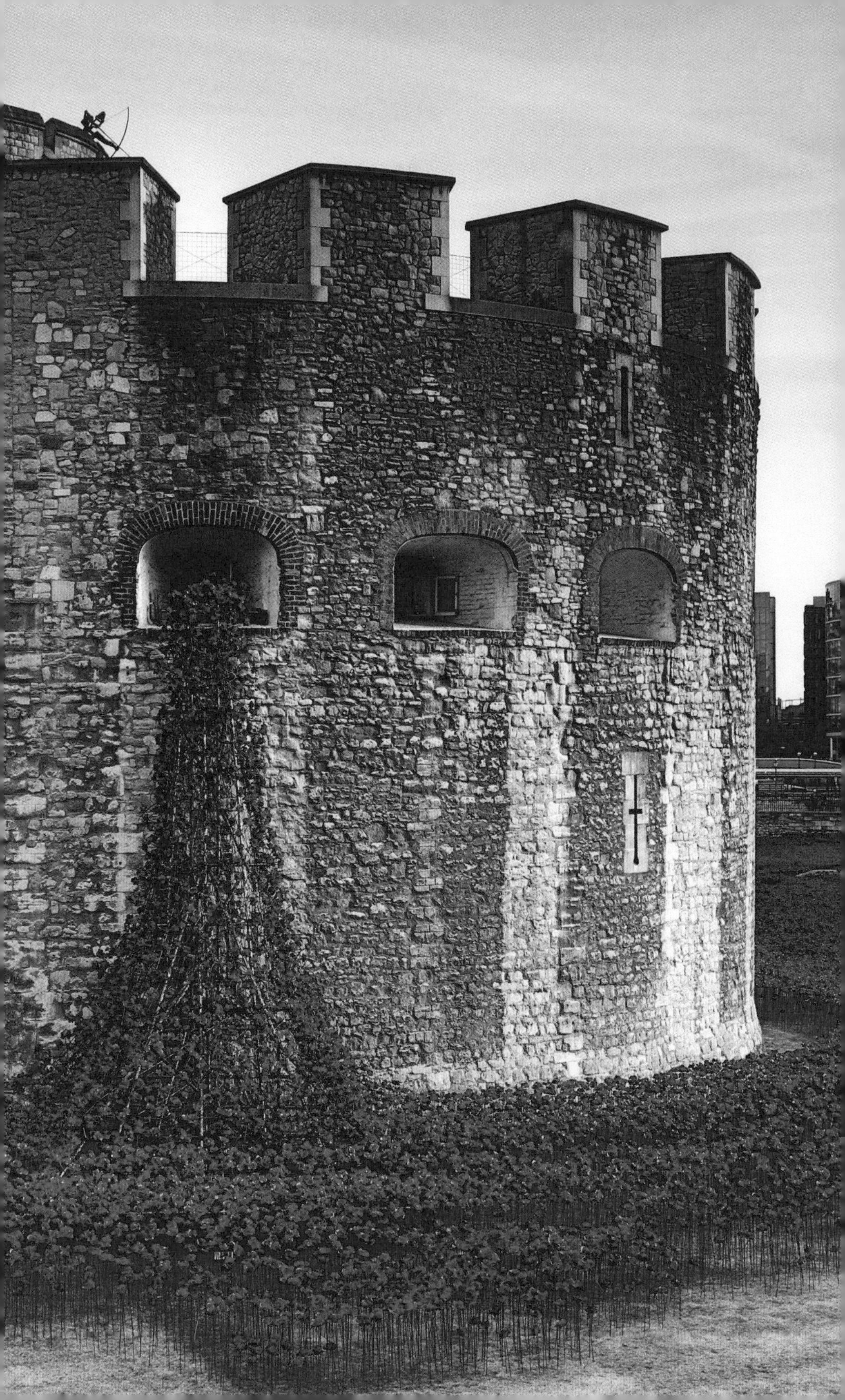

6
LIVING WITH THE DEAD

Let us begin at the end. Is there life of some kind for human beings after they die? Most societies for most of history have believed that there is. If we share that belief, other questions, which are as old as humanity itself, necessarily follow. How do the living stay in touch with the dead? Do they need our help? Or is it we who need their help? And, if so, how do we ask for it? Are the dead and the living bound, for a while at least, in a network of reciprocal obligations? We are used to asking how societies look after the vulnerable, the weak and the old. But on the whole we have lost the habit of asking how they look after what is possibly the most demanding – and for many the most helpful – group of all: the dead.

Once the rituals of burial and mourning are completed, it remains to be decided what the proper relationship between us and our ancestors should be. In medieval England, as across the whole of Catholic Europe, the position was clear. The community of the Christian faithful comprised both the living and the dead, two parts of the same body; and offering prayers and masses for the souls of the dead was one of the central duties of the living. Every congregation, every parishioner, played the part in this process

Blood Swept Lands and Seas of Red by Paul Cummins and Tom Piper, at the Tower of London, 2014

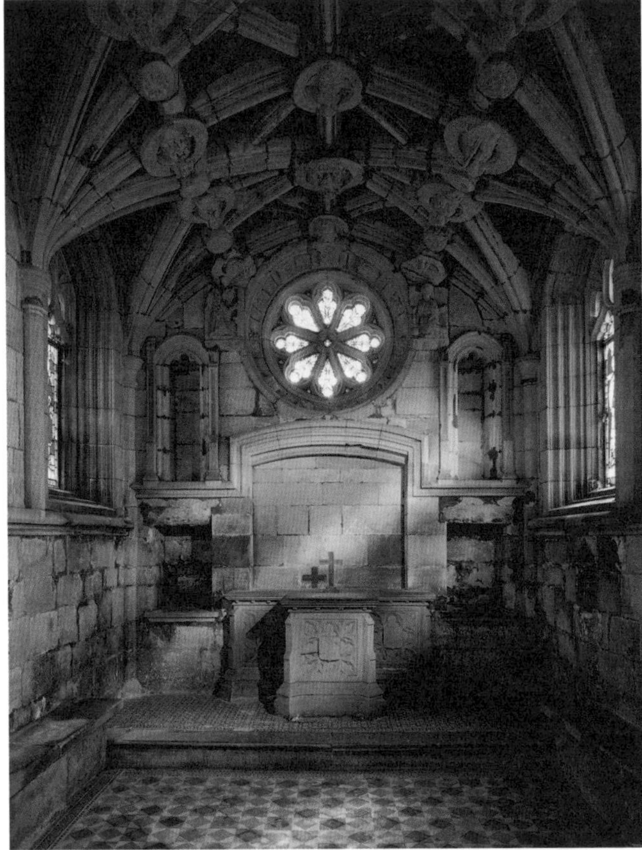

Medieval England prays for the souls of the dead: the Percy chantry at Tynemouth Priory

that their means allowed. Elaborate chapels and chantries – indeed, in Oxford a whole magnificent college, All Souls – were built to house these ceremonies of intercession, which were designed to speed the souls of the departed through the pains of purgatory, and to secure for them, as swiftly as possible, the prize of salvation and a place in heaven. Vast legacies were left by the wealthy so that their souls, and those of their family, might be prayed for in perpetuity. The necessary rituals required the labour of enormous numbers of people – not least the priests needed to celebrate the masses. In England 500 years ago, the dead were major employers.

It was a pattern abruptly and brutally broken at the

Reformation. Most Protestant theologians rejected the very idea of purgatory, where sins were to be expiated by long suffering, and so necessarily abandoned the notion that rapid release from it could be procured by prayer or by payment. Masses for the souls of the dead were abolished. The endowments that funded them were liquidated or confiscated. In Protestant Europe the living could, by the middle of the sixteenth century, do little to help the dead, from whom they were now separated by a seemingly unbridgeable gulf. The change in doctrine transformed the duties of the clergy and the economics of the church, and hugely enriched rulers and their favoured leading subjects. No less important, it reordered the relationship between present and past.

*

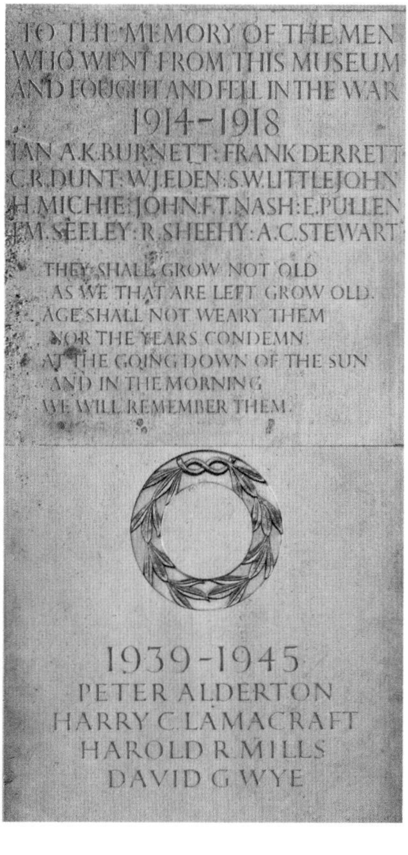

'They Shall Grow Not Old' – the memorial at the entrance to the British Museum remembering staff who died in two world wars

It is not evident what kind of connection we in Britain today have with the dead. Most of the millions who visit the British Museum every year come up the front steps to the main entrance. Few notice, as they move though the classical columns of the portico, that they pass on their right a memorial to Museum staff who died in two world wars (see p. 83). Their names are carved into the Portland stone, along with the familiar words, 'At the going down of the sun and in the morning we will remember them.' It is a pattern found in public buildings across the country. In schools and railway stations, in corporate offices and clubs, usually somewhere near the entrance, the names of those who died in the two world wars are written in stone, with the same exhortation to all who enter: to remember them. It is less and less clear how many do so – and even less clearly articulated, is why they should.

Once inside the Museum, however, visitors soon encounter completely different ways of imagining and conducting the relationship between the living and the dead: not praying for them, not merely remembering them, but conversing with them on a regular basis – and not just as spirits, but in person, with the ancestors themselves physically present.

Jago Cooper, head of the Americas section at the Museum, has in his charge a number of bundles wrapped in dull brown cloth, each one a metre or so long, carefully packaged and tied.

These are mummy bundles from Peru, containing the remains of ancestors of the people that live there today. Inside each bundle is a mummified body, meticulously prepared and wrapped in textiles. It is a practice which went on for more than 6,000 years in Peru and northern Chile, and it enabled these ancestors to play a posthumous role in society completely different from any that we in Europe could imagine for our forebears – or for ourselves.

Because of the arid desert conditions which preserve dead bodies naturally, the practice of making mummies was widespread not

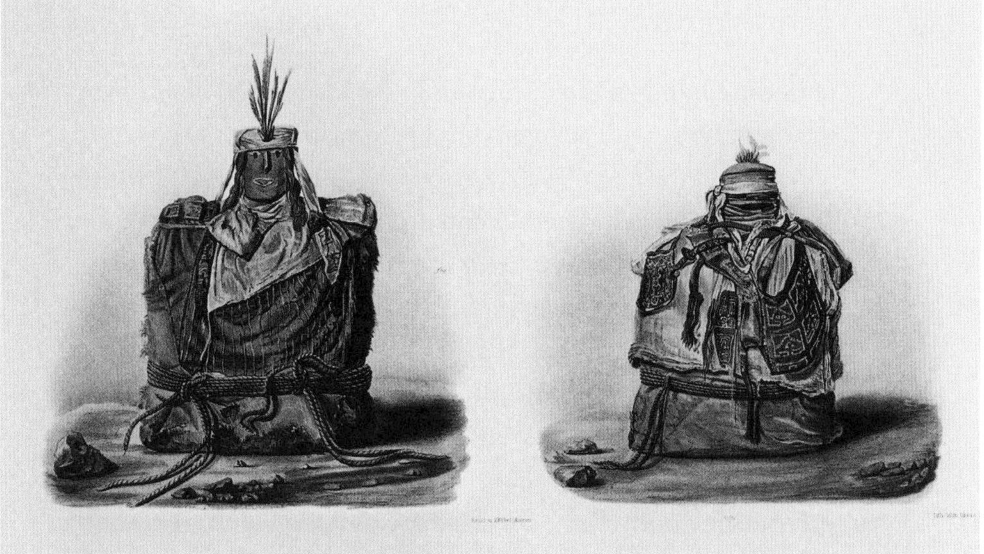

Peruvian mummy bundles topped with a 'portrait' of the ancestor, as illustrated in the 1880s

just in Peru, but throughout the Andes, and it appears to be at least as old as the much better-known tradition in Egypt. After death, the soft tissue would be removed and the body usually placed in a crouching position before being wrapped. The ancestors in the British Museum bundles were probably mummified some time around 1500, not long before the practice ceased as a result of the Spanish conquests. The textiles have faded to a dull brown, but it is just possible to see that the blankets were once brightly striped, with an elaborate fringed edge: the pattern and colouring would have indicated both the status of the dead (inevitably only the elites were preserved) and the region from which they came. In addition, many of the mummy bundles had painted faces – schematized portraits – attached to them, so that when they were sat upright, there could be no doubt that these were still in a sense real people, honoured as individuals long after their death.

In this book we are looking mostly at objects, and what they can tell us about belief. But these mummy bundles are categorically not objects. They are dead people – the Museum tries to treat them with the respect paid to them by the Peruvians themselves until the coming of the Europeans in the 1520s. In ancient Egypt, the mummies, equipped with all the necessaries for the after-life, remained in their tombs, perhaps visited at intervals by members of their families who might come to feast with them or to make offerings. Peruvian mummies by contrast had an altogether livelier after-life. Preserved in caves or on high mountains, wrapped in their gaily coloured blankets made of cotton or alpaca wool, they would be taken out by their descendants on special occasions, paraded through the streets, and for a time brought back, almost as returning VIPs, into a society of which they were still very much a part. There they had a continuing, and significant, role to play in the affairs of state. First, in Jago Cooper's words, they established the credentials of the ruling class:

To have your distinguished ancestor with you at the table during an important meeting was to proclaim your lineage and your ancestry: descent from them by direct bloodline was the basis of your own claim to power. You were heir not just to that person, but to their wisdom, power and authority. That continuing connection to ancestral knowledge was a fundamental building block of elites within the Inca Empire, where leaders would consult their ancestors directly as they made important political decisions.

The role of the mummies thus went far beyond merely demonstrating the status of their descendants. Sitting among the living, their experience and judgement could be invoked. Jago Cooper describes how they also added, by their very presence, a quite different understanding of the dimension of time:

For us, when our ancestors die they are in the past and our descendants are in the future. For the Inca and many cultures of the Americas, the thinking was – and often still is – fundamentally different. For them all time is together: the present, future and past exist concurrently, are always running in parallel, and it is possible, with skill, or sometimes in a trance, to move between the different times, and to draw on the insights that all three can offer. The mummy bundles of the ancestors would be brought into the room to contribute the wisdom of the past to the conversation. But also in the room, and part of the debate, would be the spirits of descendants not yet born. They too would help shape political decisions, in which they had such a large stake.

It is as though the bodies of Gladstone and Disraeli were occasionally brought out to sit round the Cabinet table in London, to remind ministers of both the weight of history and the claims of the future. Bringing the mummy bundles from the tomb to the council chamber gave uniquely physical expression to a compelling political idea – one best articulated not by a scholar of Peruvian history, but by the eighteenth-century political theorist Edmund Burke, in his *Reflections on the Revolution in France*: 'Society is ... a partnership in every virtue, and in all perfection. As the ends of such a partnership cannot be obtained in many generations, it becomes a partnership not only between those who are living, but between those who are living, those who are dead, and those who are to be born.' Burke's idea would have resonated as strongly with pre-Reformation Europeans as with pre-Columbian Peruvians.

It is therefore all the more surprising that this Peruvian practice of close contact with the bodies of the dead so deeply disconcerted the Spaniards when they encountered it. The Roman Catholic Mass is still celebrated every day over the physical remains of the dead. Every altar – even a portable altar-stone – should contain within it the relics of a saint, ideally of a martyr who died bearing witness to the faith. In the presence of (part of) the body of a saint the Mass will be said, and beside that physical body part worshippers will stand in prayer before God. In the Catholic church saints long dead are asked to help with every aspect of daily life, and to intercede with God for mercy on the souls of the departed. Sometimes their preserved bodies are still carried in procession,

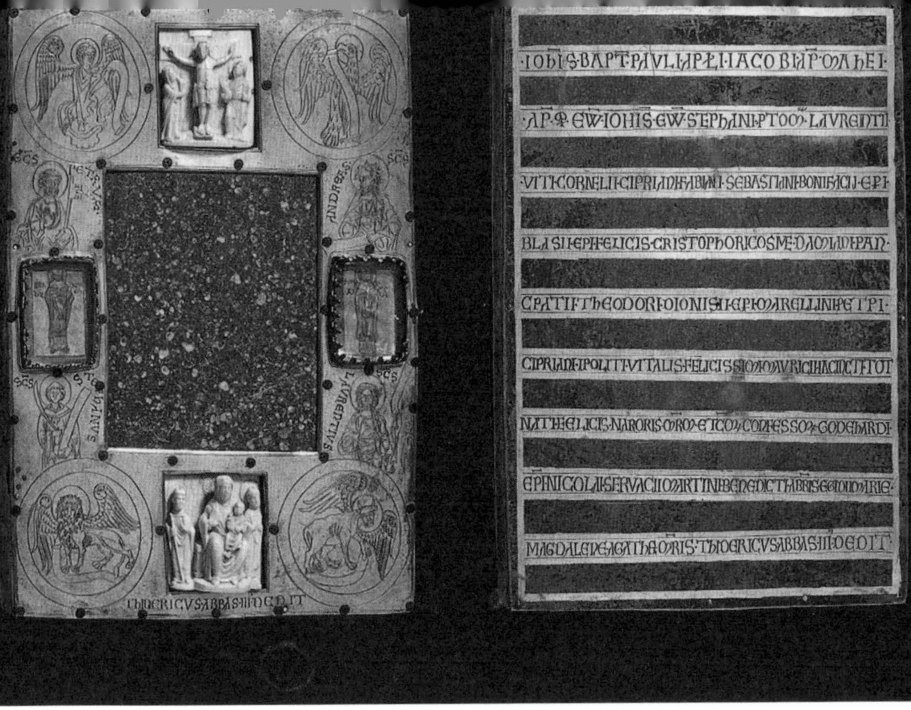

Saying Mass over the bodies of the dead: German portable altar, around 1200. On the back are the names of the saints whose relics, each carefully labelled (*below*), are contained in the cavity behind the altar-stone.

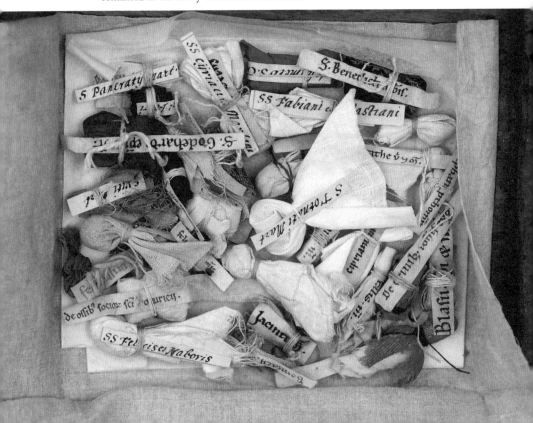

very like those of the Peruvian ancestors. This idea, that the world of the dead constantly intersects with our own, is found around the globe: from Mexico's Day of the Dead to Japan's Bon festival, families gather every year – in cemeteries or elsewhere – to eat, drink and be very merry with deceased relatives. Death is a division within, not a boundary of, the community. In China, where death changes relationships but does not dissolve them, an annual, domestic reunion with the ancestors has for centuries been a central family ritual. The bodies of the dead are not physically present, as in Peru, but their spirits are, and they come to dwell – for a time – in likenesses made specially to receive them: the whole history of portrait painting in China is inextricably linked to images made to serve in these ritual dialogues with the ancestors.

In the British Museum is a pair of paintings created for precisely this purpose: two 'ancestor portraits', painted on silk hanging scrolls, from the Ming dynasty – probably around 1600. A man and a woman, each seated on a wooden chair which is almost covered by their deep red robes, stare out from a background of plain dull gold. Each scroll is over two metres high – these dead ancestors are unquestionably larger than life. They are, however, anything but life-like: the faces are impassive, devoid of any emotional or psychological responses.

Jan Stuart is Curator of Chinese Art at the Freer–Sackler Galleries in Washington:

People wanted a portrait that would reproduce the heaven-endowed quality of a face, which would record the enduringly significant facial features, not as seen or encountered in any particular moment – so not frowning or smiling, not by daylight or by night. That is why there is no light or shade: these are intended

Over: Ming dynasty ancestor portraits. The man wears a prominent badge that indicates his rank – or perhaps that of a descendant.

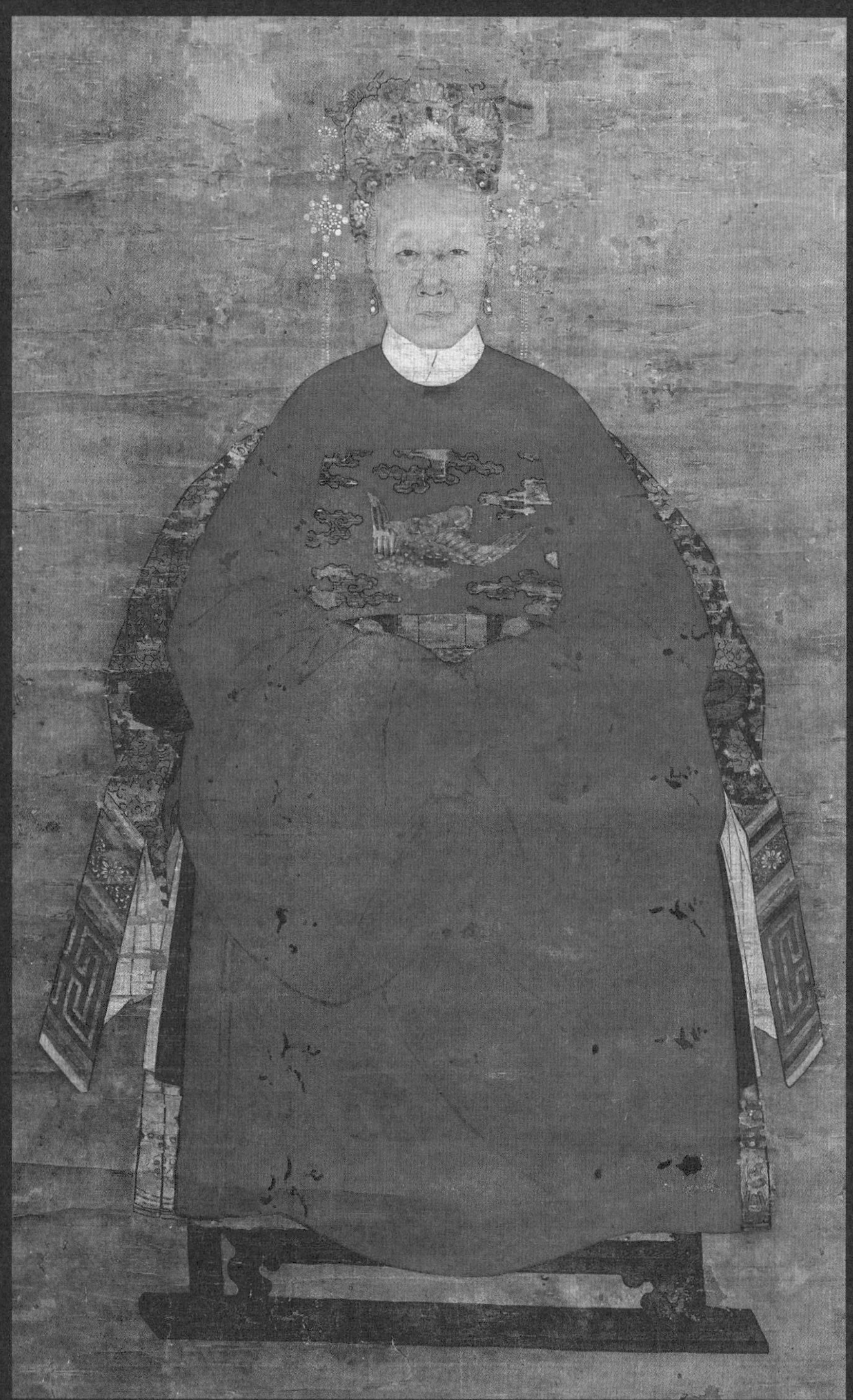

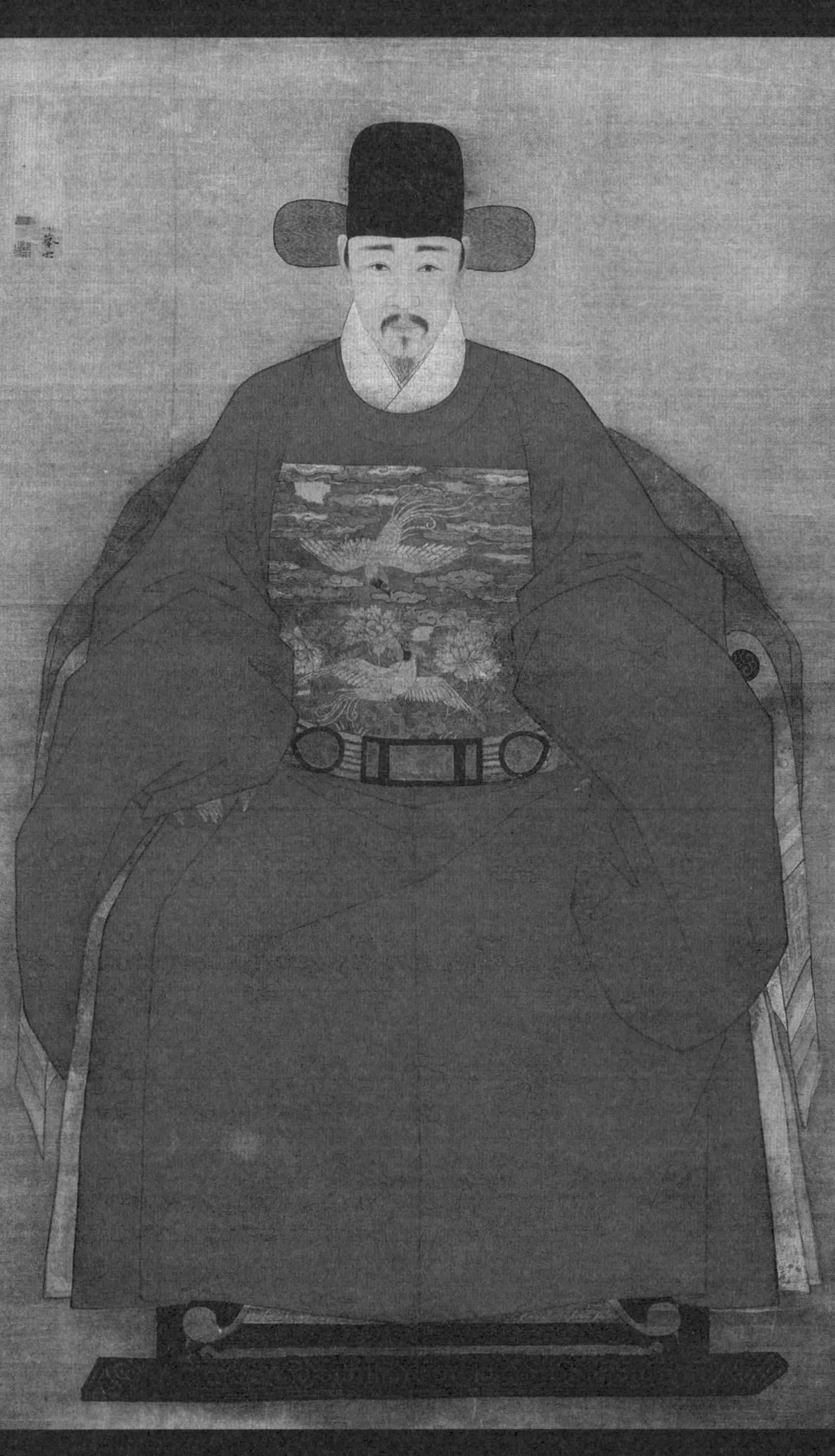

to be timeless faces. The two portraits may well have been done after death, possibly by an artist who had never even seen the sitters. Often, artists would use physiognomy charts – not unlike our police identikit sketches, designed to put together a likeness and a personality. They showed how to draw high cheek bones, for example, and thus indicate that a person's personality was full of power. Certain kinds of eyebrows would reveal intelligence. These charts showed classic facial characteristics – and what they told us about the person who possessed them.

Veneration was principally owed to the portrait of the father, but families would often request a portrait of the mother as well. They would be hung together, with the husband's portrait always to the east of his wife's – the place of greater honour. The similarity in scale and dress in these two portraits might suggest that these were husband and wife. But the fact that their chairs are different (the man's is decorated in lacquer, the woman's is of wood) indicates that they are probably unconnected, and that they were paired only much later in order to appeal to Western collectors – a marriage made not in heaven but by a dealer, for the art market. Yet whether singly or together, these portraits were made, as Jan Stuart describes, to enable the people they represented to play a role in the lives of their descendants for centuries after their death:

Portraits like these were brought out for specific occasions, of which the Chinese New Year is the most important. Lighted candles and burning incense would be placed below them, along with offerings of fruit and wine. Then the chief descendant, the oldest son, along with other family members, would pay obeisance to the portraits. They would kneel down and knock their heads on the floor in front of them, so that the deceased parent or grandparent would know that they were being honoured, that the family was still connected to them and would make sure that the departed souls were properly cared for.

People would have been well aware of what could happen if they failed in their duties towards paintings like these ones, and the people they represented. Ancestral spirits remained benign as long as they were cared for appropriately, and from time to time they would take up residence in these portraits to receive offerings. Decades, even centuries later, they would recognize themselves in the painting – hence the care taken to secure the timeless elements of their likeness – and so would know which one to inhabit. The man in our portrait has on his chest a panel of splendid embroidery, clearly a badge of rank. Fascinatingly, however, it may not be his own rank. Ancestors remained so closely identified with their descendants that if a son or grandson got a promotion in, say, the

Giving thanks in front of a portrait of an ancestor, in a painting by Yin Tang of around 1500

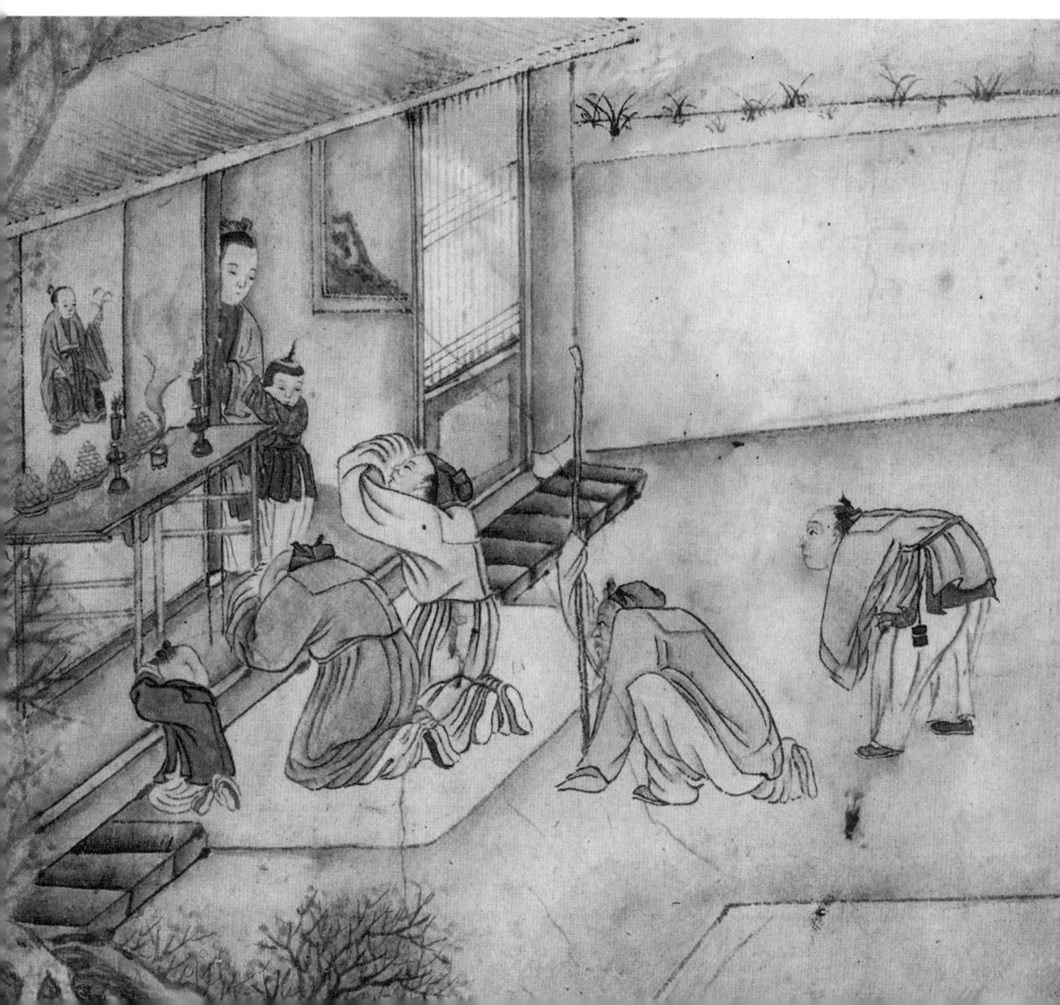

imperial civil service, the ancestor would – posthumously – also be promoted. A new portrait would be painted: a close copy of the first, but now featuring insignia of the higher rank, and the older portrait would be ritually burned.

Ancestors not properly venerated could wreak havoc, causing illness or financial failure. On the other hand, if treated with proper reverence and allowed to share in the family's continuing successes, they would bring good fortune to their descendants – from the birth of sons to long life and increasing wealth. After the annual ceremonies, portraits would be rolled up and carefully stored – which is why these paintings are in such good condition. Not until four or five generations had passed did a person's relative become a 'distant ancestor', their spirit no longer requiring offerings of food and wine, their portrait no longer needing to be displayed. Only then could portraits properly be sold, as probably happened to these two in the course of the nineteenth century. Among other consequences of Mao Tse-tung's 'One Child' policy is a widespread worry among those now old that there may be no one in the future to pay proper honour to their spirit.

China's Communist leaders, especially during the Cultural Revolution, tried hard to suppress traditional religion, including the veneration of ancestors, which they viewed as a counter-revolutionary activity. But, in recent years, the Chinese dead have been making a comeback, and the ancient practices have been resumed. Many mainland Chinese, in common with the worldwide diaspora, today bring themselves at certain times of the year into the presence of their ancestors.

In doing so, they mostly use digital photographs – updating a portrait tradition that stretches back over 2,000 years. The offerings have been updated too, going beyond the traditional fruit and wine. Paper models of computers, cars and refrigerators, of luxury goods of all sorts, even of wi-fi routers, are now burned, so that the smoke will carry the necessary item to the spirit of the

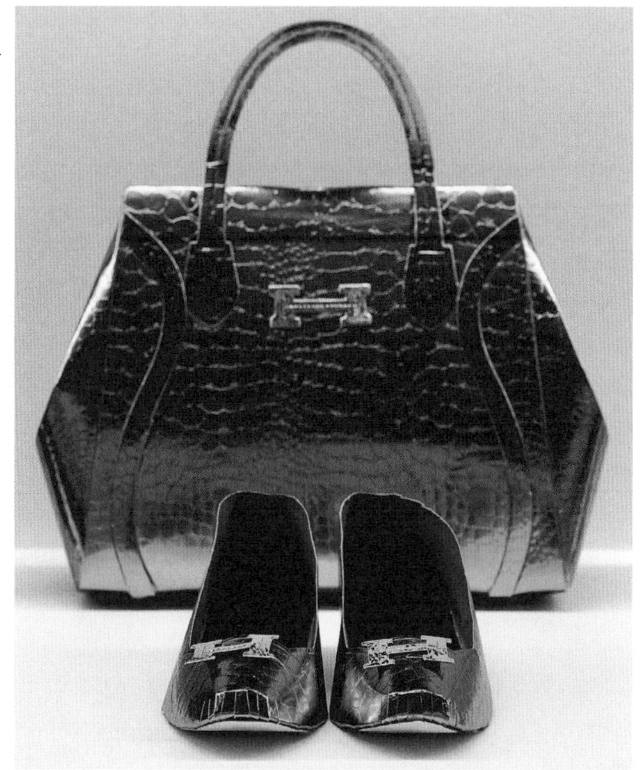
Modern gifts for the fashion-conscious ancestor: paper versions of luxury goods are burned to ensure that the dead have only the best.

deceased. The ancient ritual is very much alive: an essential part of looking after the dead is keeping them in touch with the changes of modern life.

When our pair of Chinese ancestor portraits arrived at the British Museum in the 1920s, the Curator of Oriental Prints and Drawings was Laurence Binyon, a pioneering authority on the art of the East. Binyon is now better known as a poet, and it is his words, from 'For the Fallen', written in 1914, that are carved on the war memorial beside the Museum's main entrance – and on countless other memorials across the country. They are lines which are heard and repeated every year on Remembrance Sunday, at the heart of our most public and solemn act of national remembrance at the Cenotaph in Whitehall:

At the going down of the sun and in the morning
We will remember them.

The nation pauses to remember, to honour the courage of those who died in battle, and to pay tribute to their sacrifice. But beyond that? To borrow the Chinese phrase, they have for most people now become 'distant ancestors'. Only the very old can remember alive those who died in the Second World War, and we no longer ask them to play any part in our continuing communal life, neither sharing the joys nor shaping the decisions of the society they died defending. Other European countries remember with a clearer purpose: to reinforce or to change the behaviour of their citizens. In Russia, the triumphant celebrations of the dead of the Great Patriotic War 1941–5 play a key part in strengthening national (many would say nationalist) fervour; and in France the regular reanimation of *La Flamme de la Nation* under the Arc de Triomphe (Chapter 2) is a calculated exercise in the renewal of patriotic spirit. Germany by contrast dwells on the crime and folly that led to war, and uses remembrance to urge the present not to repeat the terrible mistakes of the past. For both France and Germany, reconciliation between former enemies is paramount in the rhetoric of commemoration.

In comparison, what underlies the British remembrance is less certain, and appears to have changed in recent decades. Paradoxically, as the memory of the war dead as individuals has faded, the sales of poppies and the number of commemorative events have steadily increased. It is as though remembering has itself become an object of nostalgia, that there is a desire to recapture the intense emotion and the sense of purpose with which previous generations mourned and commemorated a great moment of national history. In 2014, to mark the centenary of the outbreak of the First World War, a spectacular installation of 888,246 ceramic poppies – one for each soldier of the British Empire who died in the conflict – spilled into the moat of the Tower of London. *Blood*

Swept Lands and Seas of Red (p. 80) was a magnificent and moving sight, as the iconic building itself appeared to shed its life-blood in an unstaunchable flow. Yet appeals to extend the display were rejected on the basis that its transience was an essential part of the artistic conception. It was essentially – supremely – an aesthetic event, designed to touch the emotions, but not to endure. Our national commemoration, unlike that of other countries, does not demand that the lives lost should determine and change our behaviour, or inform the decisions we make in the present. We remember our dead, but we no longer live with them.

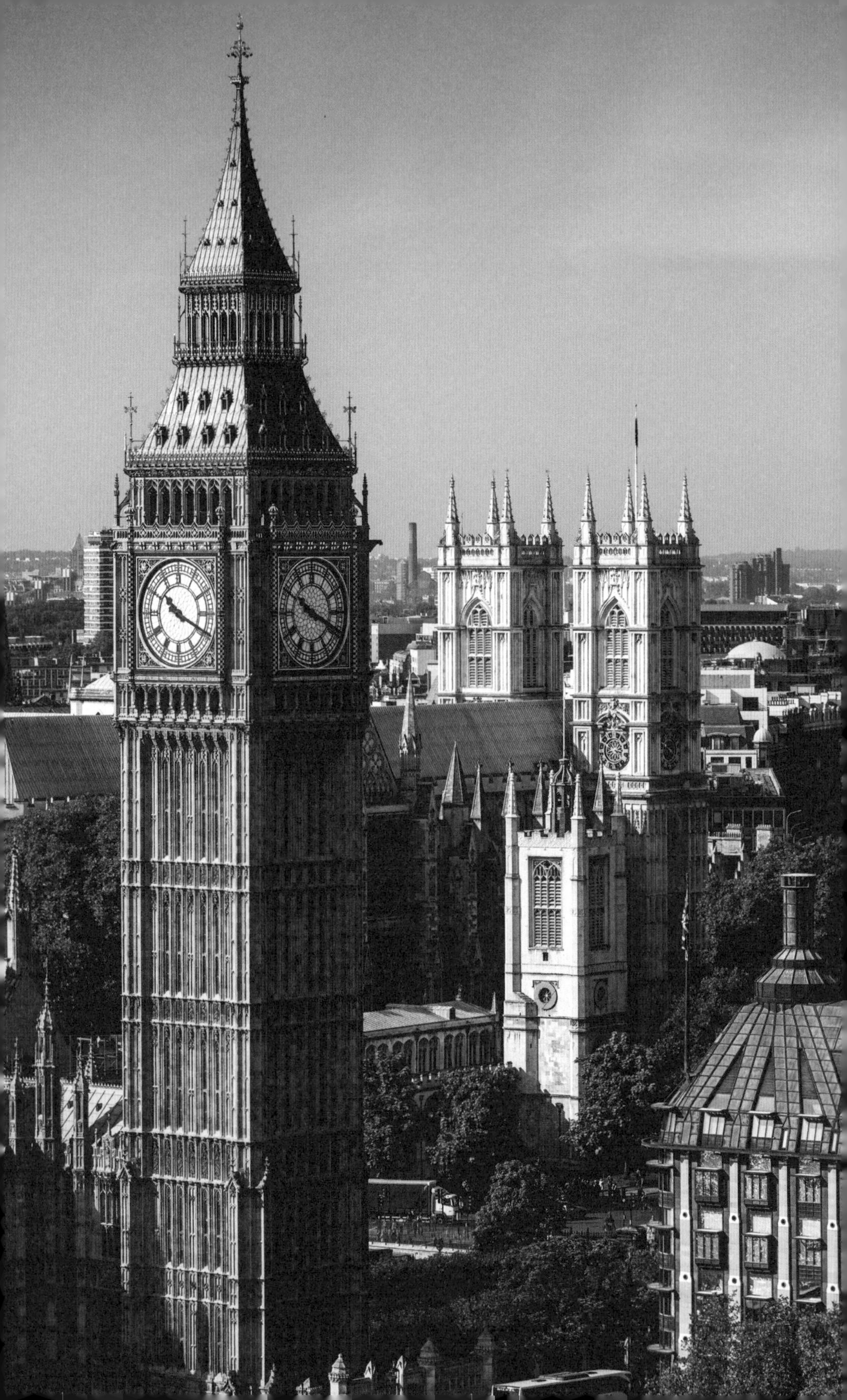

7

BIRTH AND THE BODY

A short walk down Whitehall, past Downing Street and the Foreign Office, the Cenotaph and the Treasury, and into Parliament Square, leads to the religious and political heart of the British state. On the left stand the Houses of Parliament, the Palace of Westminster and the Elizabeth Tower, which houses Big Ben; on the right Westminster Abbey, where for over 1,000 years the monarch has been crowned and divinely invested with temporal authority (Chapter 26). Nestling modestly between the two, and often scarcely noticed by the crowds of sightseers, is the one building in this group not dedicated to the exercise or the display of power: the parish church of St Margaret. But in a sense what both its famous neighbours represent, religion and politics, begins here. This church is dedicated to Saint Margaret of Antioch, patron saint of women in childbirth.

Holy Margaret, Mothers pray to thee for an easy birth, when their term comes. Thou art merciful to them ... they bear witness to their safe delivery ...

Since the twelfth century (these words are from a Latin hymn of around 1520), pregnant women have been praying to Saint

St Margaret's, Westminster, with the blue sun-dial clock-face on its tower, set between the Houses of Parliament and Westminster Abbey

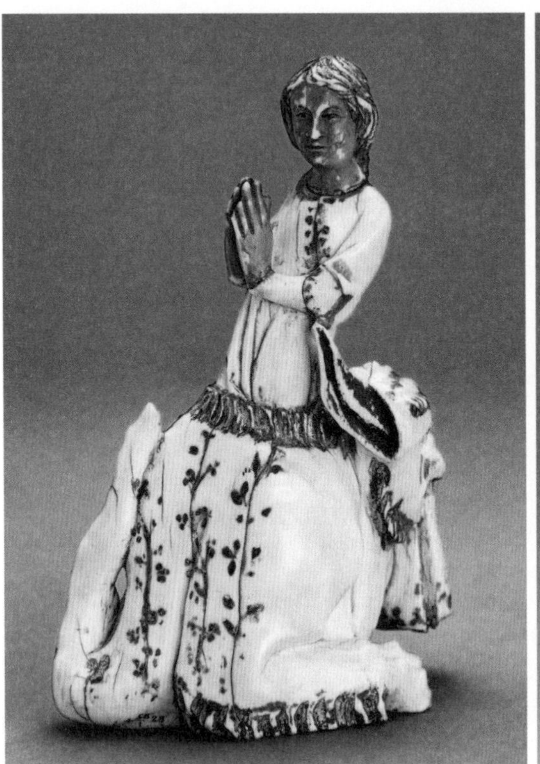
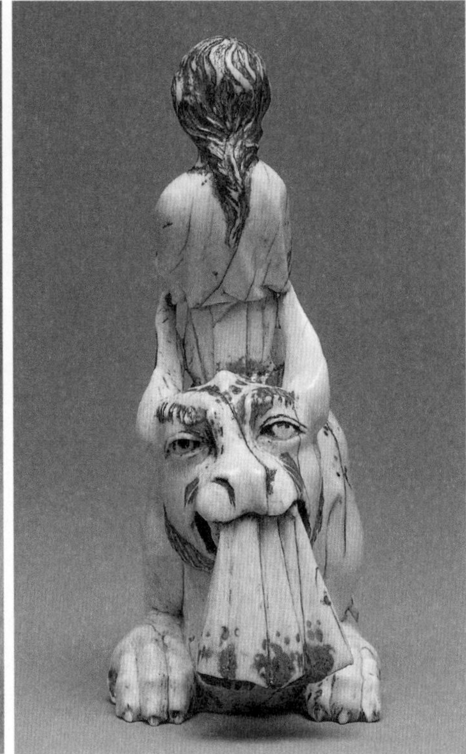

Saint Margaret miraculously bursts from the back of the dragon that has just swallowed her, in a mid-fourteenth-century gilded ivory statue made in Paris (*left*). Still chewing Saint Margaret's skirts, the dragon realizes the saint herself has escaped (*right*).

Margaret of Antioch for the safe delivery for their child. The prayers were often recited in front of a devotional image, like the little sculpture of gilded polychrome ivory now in the British Museum. Carved and painted in Paris some time around 1350, clearly for a wealthy patron, and standing about twenty centimetres high, it shows the saint with her hands clasped in prayer. She is rising up in triumph. Her upper body curves elegantly backwards – a constraint of the elephant tusk from which she has been sculpted – as she bursts forth from the hunched body of a beast, upwards and out, through its back. The beast is actually a rather weary-looking dragon – the devil in animal form – and it is munching listlessly on Margaret's gilt-edged robes, which are still hanging out of its mouth, as the saint it has not even finished swallowing escapes uneaten and entirely unscathed.

Although the quality of the carving is high and the state of conservation generally good, close inspection reveals that the fingertips on Margaret's right hand are not original. She was probably once holding a crucifix, because according to legend she was rescued from death by invoking the saving power of the Cross. This split the dragon's body apart – and with one bound, the saint was free. She went on to exorcise demons with great success, converting hundreds to Christianity in the process. When eventually she was beheaded, her reluctant executioner fell dead beside her, as her head was carried to heaven by a flight of angels. Even more important for posterity than Margaret's victories over devils through the Cross was her swift emergence from the dragon's miraculously opened body. By an analogy not especially flattering to women in labour, she became associated with safe and rapid delivery in childbirth, the protectoress who would bring both mother and baby unscathed through the ordeal. As the saint had burst from the dragon, the child would spring from the womb.

Margaret's career as a saint is an unusual one. She was alleged to have been martyred in the great persecutions of the emperors Diocletian and Maximian around 300, but from as early as the fifth century the church questioned not just her famous encounter with the dragon, but her very existence. In the mid-490s, Pope Gelasius I declared her probably apocryphal; and even the *Golden Legend*, the popular medieval anthology of saints' lives and achievements – a work which records the most startling miracles in credulous, deadpan prose – explicitly rejected the story of the dragon. Yet the public appeal of the saint and of her miracle was simply too strong to be quashed. Not for the only time (see Chapter 16) the scholarly scruples of the clergy were overwhelmed by the wishes of the laity. Margaret prevailed. Where George had conquered his dragon by force, Margaret had escaped hers by quiet womanly piety, and this female dragon-tamer (the dragon, being a manifestation of the devil, naturally survived his side of the encounter) became one of medieval Europe's most popular saints. She was taken as a model for, and asked to help with, every part of a young woman's life.

Margaret, the chorus of mothers quickly enters thy temples; every year they bring sacred gifts; they teach their unmarried daughters to visit from an early age and praise thee.

Throughout Christendom her name was given to many girls, among them the daughters of kings and princes. In England alone there are today well over 200 churches dedicated to Saint Margaret of Antioch.

Our ivory sculpture – possibly once owned by the French royal household – is the luxury Parisian expression of a Europe-wide cult that was found in every class. In Germany, she was one of the fourteen 'holy helpers', those indispensable saints who could always be relied on in moments of greatest need. In the 1420s, hers was one of the 'voices' that spoke to the simple village girl in Lorraine, Joan of Arc, as she dreamt of rescuing France from the English. And just a few years later, in 1434, she appeared in an affluent Italian bedroom in Bruges: we can see her emerging from a miniature wooden dragon on top of the bench beside the bed in Jan van Eyck's *Arnolfini Portrait*. Margaret is clearly visible over Mrs Arnolfini's shoulder, to reassure her that she will be on hand, by the bed, when the moment to give birth comes. Women in labour had Margaret's life story read aloud to them to ensure an easy delivery. A fragment of her girdle, with which she reportedly bound the dragon and led it captive, was one of the most prized relics of the Abbey of Saint-Germain-des-Prés in Paris. It was carried in great solemnity to be laid on the stomach of the queens of France when they were in labour. There could be no clearer demonstration of the high politics of birth. The body of the queen is an affair of state. The succession to the throne is even today a matter of national concern in the United Kingdom. But royal

Emerging from a winged dragon, Saint Margaret stands protectively beside the bed in Bruges in Jan van Eyck's *Arnolfini Portrait* of 1434.

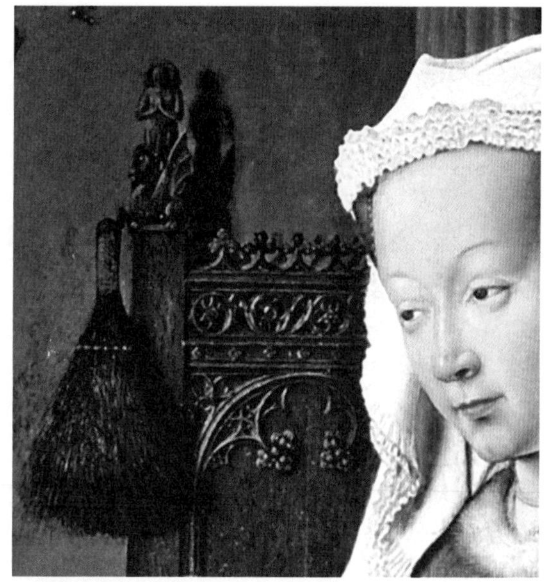

births are merely the supreme expression of a universal truth: that all society claims a stake, and a responsibility, in the birth of a child. Under Saint Margaret's protection in Paris so great a king as Louis XIV came safely into the world. It is no surprise that in London her church is so close to the seat of political power.

As might be expected, almost every human society has devised comparable prayers and rituals – ceremonies that involve many people beyond the woman herself – to help both mother and baby safely through childbirth. But in a moment of such peril it is not enough merely to pray in aid of the forces of good. The powers of evil must be warded off, and they are always on the prowl – recognized and dreaded long before Margaret and her dragon, and still thought by many to be present and dangerous today.

She is fierce, she is raging, she is a goddess, she is dazzling,
she is a she-wolf, the daughter of Anu
Her feet are like those of Anzu, her hands are soiled
Her face is like the face of a mighty lion.

This is Lamashtu, daughter of Anu, greatest of the gods. She is the bringer of miscarriage, infant death and stillbirth, the 'extinguisher of life' in ancient Mesopotamia. Lamashtu was known to slip into the house of a pregnant woman, try to tap her seven times on the stomach, and so kill the baby inside her. Alternatively, she would kidnap the unborn or newborn child. Unlike other demons, who operated mostly under divine command, she acted on her own initiative, delivering evil unpredictably, and for its own sake. Just how terrifying Lamashtu was is clear from a rectangular stone amulet in the British Museum, about the size of a mobile phone. It was carved in Babylonia or Assyria over 2,500 years ago, and looking at it is still a spine-chilling experience.

Five times the size of the donkey she stands on, Lamashtu rears up at us. She has a snarling lion's head, grasps an enormous snake in each hand, and is suckling, one at each breast, a jackal and a wild pig. Ominously, her donkey has broken into a trot – Lamashtu is on the way to pay her visit to a woman in labour, which is why the amulet should very quickly be turned over. On the other side is a magical incantation, an extract from a much longer ritual text, which, if recited, will stop her in her tracks and frighten her away. Over sixty such amulets are known to have survived, so they must have been widespread, presumably purchased from a temple or shrine. Revealingly the texts on them range from immaculately scripted incantations to crude attempts at writing: it is clear that around 700 BCE every part of Mesopotamian society sought protection from Lamashtu. Throughout the ancient Mediterranean, Lamashtu had many similar sisters. The Hebrew Lilith, the Greek Lamia and the Roman Strix were all bearers of random misfortune, especially to unborn and newborn children, and were mostly connected with animals of the night. All had to be repelled, by rituals and incantations similar to those used against Lamashtu. In the Mediterranean world today, the sinister goddesses are no longer named, but even in devoutly Islamic and

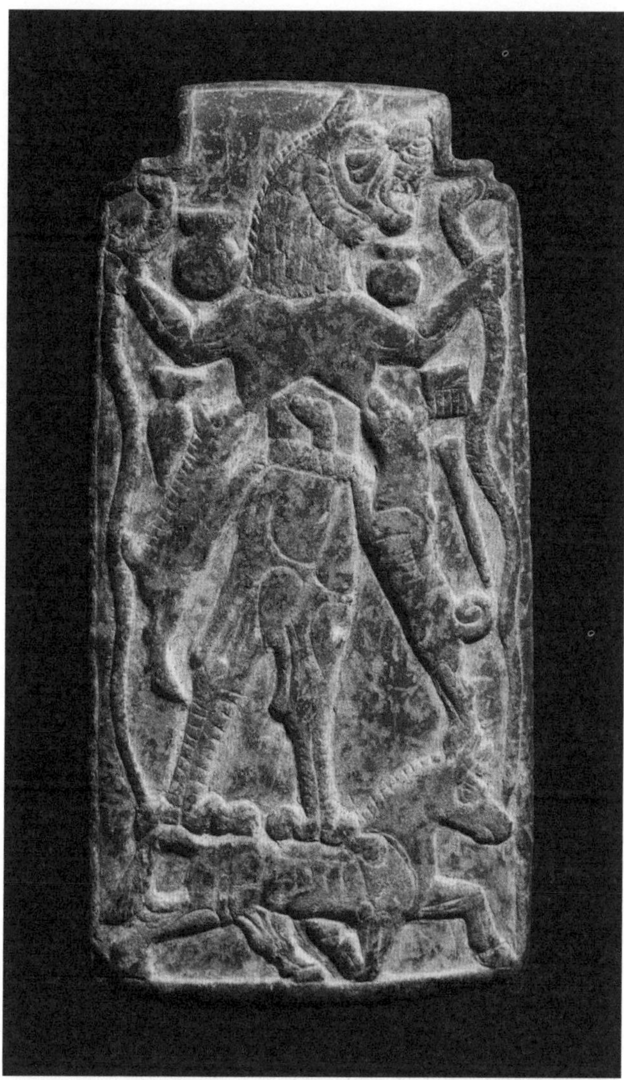

Lamashtu, extinguisher of life in ancient Mesopotamia, sets off on her donkey. Portable stone amulet from 800–550 BCE

Christian societies there is a deep and widespread fear of the Evil Eye – a malign and unpredictable force, likely especially to strike pregnant women or infant children. Protection is indispensable, and so amulets to ward it off are frequently attached to clothes and bed coverings. An Albanian cradle cloth of the 1950s from the Catholic region of Mirdita is a typical example: on the red chequered wool a black cross has been sewn, but to it have been

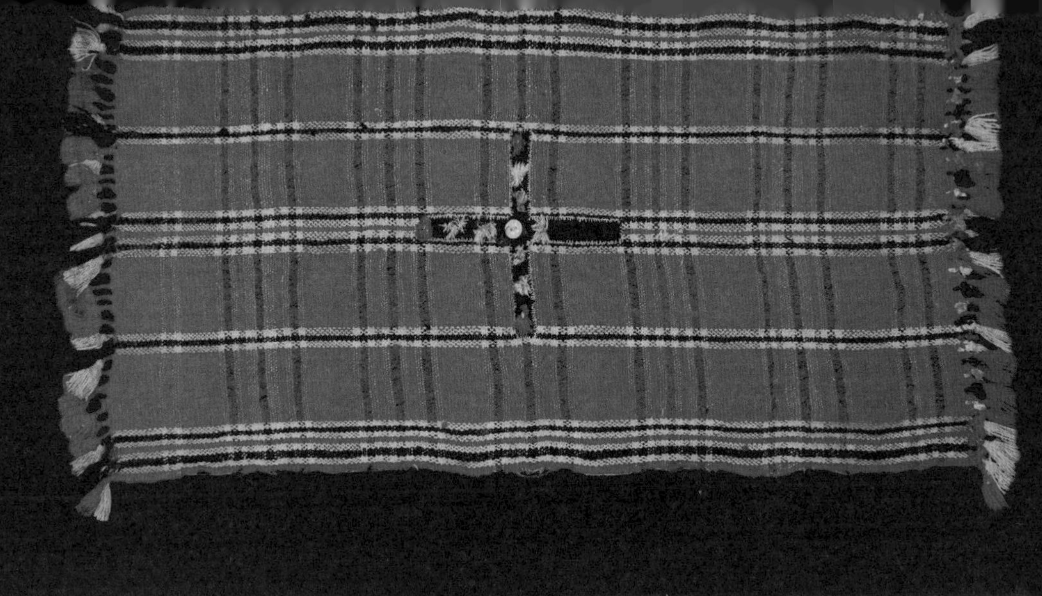

Albanian cradle cloth of the 1950s with the cross and yellow button to ward off the Evil Eye

added tufts of coloured silk on the arms, and in the centre a bright yellow plastic button. Both serve to distract and deflect evil spirits. The Christian cross has taken on the added pagan role of amulet against Lamashtu's successor, the Evil Eye.

In the twenty-first century, most of us are more likely to rely on modern obstetrics than a spell carved in cuneiform script to keep Lamashtu and her ilk at bay. Rather than invoking Saint Margaret, we tend to place our faith in the expertise and technology of the maternity ward. Or do we? In many countries, the most modern science is still often accompanied by traditional religious customs and practices. As with the medieval survival of the cult of Margaret, the needs and wishes of the laity are stronger than the well-founded medical opinions of the learned. In childbirth, all sources of help have to be invoked.

In Japan, where expectant mothers enjoy ready access to some of the world's most advanced biomedical technology, obstetric clinics also frequently sell traditional 'pregnancy sashes'. These are of no proven medical value, but offer a protection against misfortune which is deeply rooted in popular belief. Dr Aya Homei, a specialist in the history of Japanese medicine at the University of Manchester, explains:

Women in Japan commonly wear a pregnancy sash after the fifth month – traditionally after a so-called quickening, when you first feel the baby move in the womb. The custom is that you start wearing it over your stomach on what is a 'dog day' according to the Chinese zodiac, because a dog is supposed to have a very easy birth. Nowadays you can get a pregnancy sash anywhere – you can even just buy it in a department store. But after buying it, women go to a shrine and get a stamp put on it there – to indicate that this sash has been blessed.

It is impossible not to be struck by the parallel with Saint Margaret's girdle – in this case open to everybody and not just to the queens of France and other powerful Parisians. Nevertheless, it is a surprising survival. Most Japanese now define themselves as being *mushūkyō* – 'of no religion' – and see their society as one of the most technologically advanced in the world. Yet these same people take their pregnancy sashes, known to be medically ineffectual, to be blessed at Shinto shrines and Buddhist temples, which also thrive on selling and blessing *omamori* – amulets, which appear to offer pregnant women very much the same kind of protection as prayers to Saint Margaret, or as amulets against Lamashtu. *Omamori* are usually bought in a small crisply designed plastic pouch, about the size of a playing card. Inside is a piece of tightly woven cloth, in white and salmon pink, packaged with a small sheet of paper: the printed Japanese text reads '*anzan omamori*': 'protection for a safe birth'. As Aya Homei explains, many women carry an amulet like this with them all the way through their pregnancy. But it is a charm with a limited shelf life:

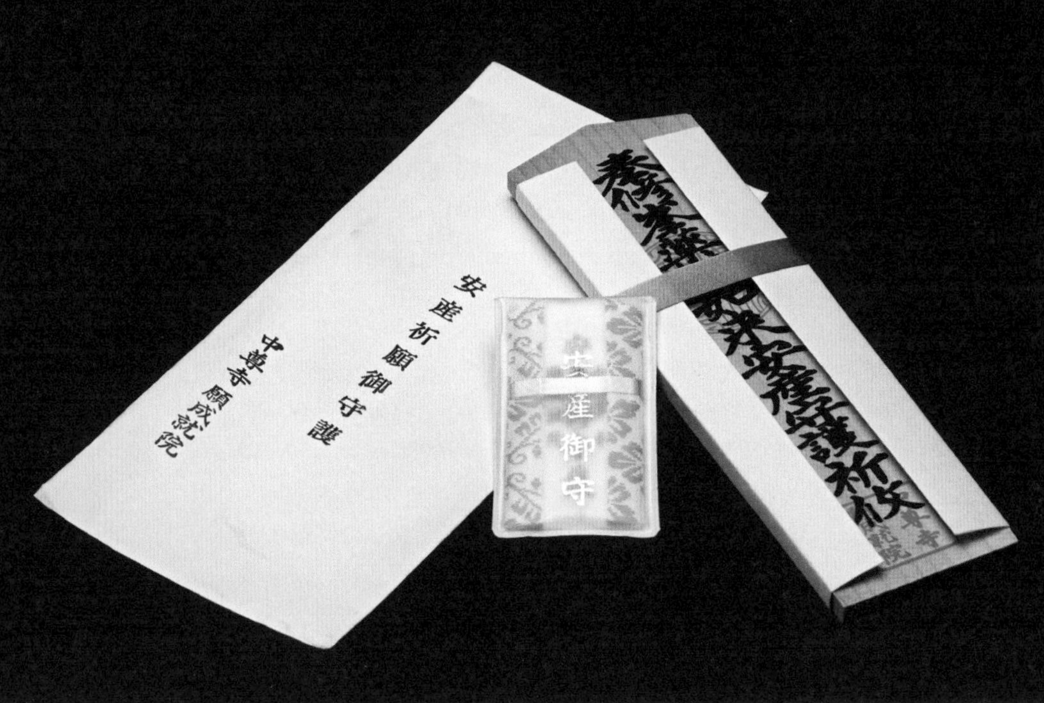

Modern Japanese amulets made of wood, cloth and paper to protect women during pregnancy

Omamori are often compared to a kind of electric battery: meaning that the blessing, or the force which protects you, will after a while run out. The recommendation is that you should not reuse the same omamori for subsequent pregnancies: you should keep buying a new one for the second, third or fourth babies. And the convention is, that after you have been safely delivered, you should bring the omamori back to the shrine where you bought it, and report to the deity that yes, I had a good birth – thank you very much.

An amulet bought and blessed in a holy place to protect the mother through pregnancy and childbirth, and then a journey of thanksgiving to the shrine for a safe delivery – it is a pattern that would be familiar in many countries, it would have surprised nobody in medieval Europe, and it demonstrates that in Japan medicalization has by no means removed the desire for religious help.

*

There is, however, one aspect of the treatment of mother and child in which traditional Japanese religion diverges sharply from the global norm, and seems – to the Western observer at least – to have moved with great originality: abortion. Aya Homei talks about the evolution over the last few decades of a particular, and particularly Japanese, ceremonial ritual:

It is a form of memorial service performed at Buddhist temples which is intended to mitigate the pain and suffering inflicted on the large numbers of infants who could not come into this world, who were not born, because of stillbirth, miscarriage or abortion. Interestingly it is a relatively recent invention, devised by doctors and midwives co-operating with Buddhist priests. It became prevalent only in the 1970s, when abortion started being so widely practised that it was effectively used as a form of birth control.

Those who have made the choice to have an abortion bring offerings to the temple, in the belief and hope that the Bodhisattva Jizo, patron deity of children and lost travellers, will look after the child who will not now be born. After the service, the parents place toys and sweets around a stone statue of the Bodhisattva in a cemetery within the temple precinct – making them powerfully poignant places. This new memorial service is a Buddhist phenomenon, and it appears to reflect a view now widely held in Japanese society: that although a potential human life is being denied, the decision to abort is neither a legal issue nor a matter for the public realm, but essentially a private and spiritual one.

In Europe and America, by sharp contrast, abortion has in the decades since the 1970s been at the centre of an acrimonious, often violent, debate about the politics of the female body. It is a debate – a political conflict – in which religion has played a large part, and especially the imperatives which religion has traditionally carried with it. Is the unborn child already a member of the

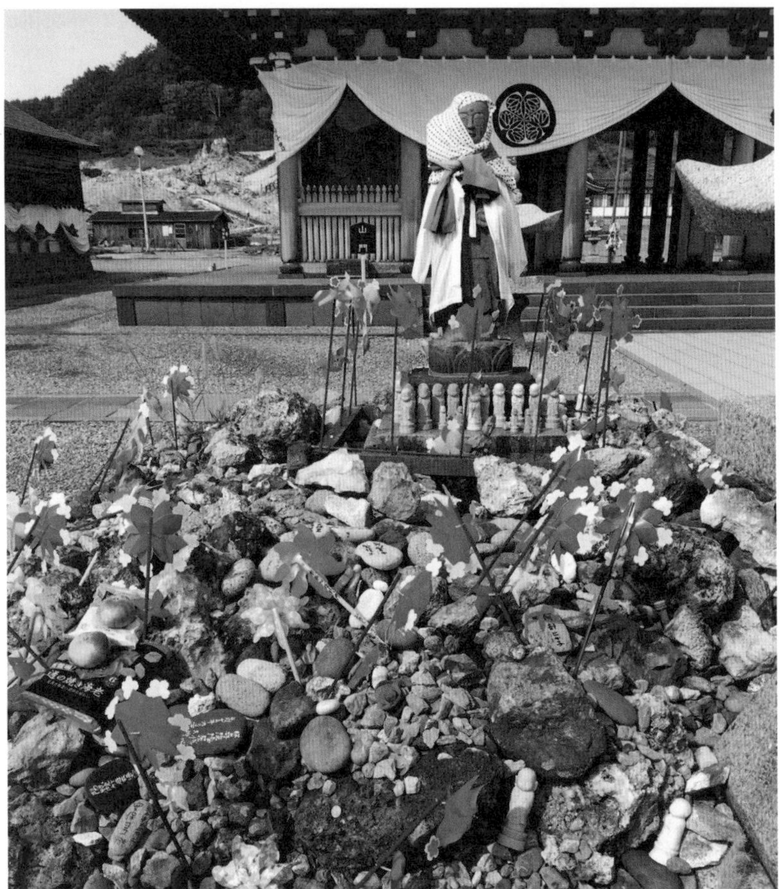

Toys for children not born, on a cairn at a Buddhist temple in north Japan

community, and so deserving of its protection? Should the political power, which has in almost all times and places meant the power of men, have the right to make decisions about the bodies of women who bear children? Should the individual woman have the right to decide all such questions for herself? Francesca Stavrakopoulou, Professor of Hebrew Bible and Ancient Religion at the University of Exeter, argues that these issues have been greatly complicated by the teachings of the Abrahamic faiths:

Ultimately, it comes down to a notion of a hierarchy of bodies. Within all three of the major monotheistic religions, male bodies are better than female bodies. It was Adam whom God created first, and made in his own image. Male bodies do not automatically become impure once a month. So there is a sense in which – in this tradition – to be male is to be more like God, and to have a female body is to be somehow deficient, and in need of purification.

Judaism, Christianity and Islam have all for centuries taken the view that human fertility, and in particular children, are gifts from God, something to be nurtured and pursued as one of the main purposes of life. So right from the moment of puberty, a woman's body is already in a sense claimed by the wider community. To disrupt the process of having children is to do wrong to the society and to God.

And that takes us back to St Margaret's, Westminster. It is perhaps today more appropriate than ever that this lovely late-Gothic church should be located here, in the public space between religion and political power; for both are spheres in which women, a century after their political emancipation began, are still struggling for a fully equal role. Saint Margaret is an emblem of female power, exercised differently, but no less effectually than the male aggression with which Saint George tackled his dragon. There are few areas today in which women more want to exercise that power than in challenging and changing male attitudes to the female body. We are still a long way in Europe from any agreed view on how to balance the rights of the woman and the claims of the community in this area of supreme importance for all, but of unique difficulty and danger for the mother. We are even further from consensus on the legal or religious status of the unborn. Here the Japanese approach still seems to be an exception. Can we imagine a day when in St Margaret's, or any other church, there will be a ceremony for children not allowed to be born, and outside the church a garden with their toys?

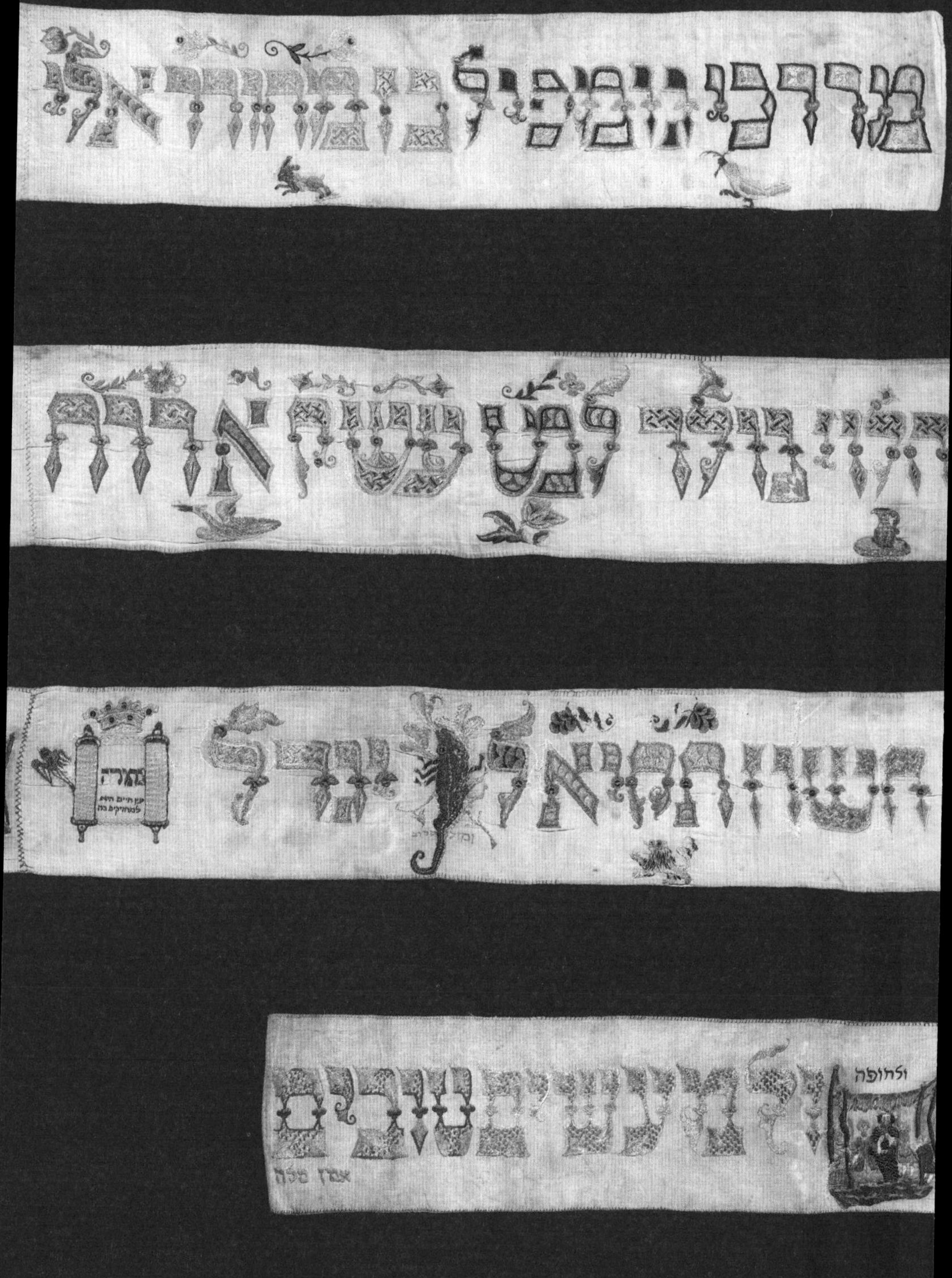

תורה
עץ חיים היא
למחזיקים בה
ולחופה
אמן סלה

8

A PLACE IN TRADITION

On 31 October 1750, in a Jewish community somewhere in Germany, at the full moon, on the eve of the Sabbath, Mordechai Gompel was born. That is all we know of his life, and all we are ever likely to know. Yet we can say with great precision what those who cared for him in his first months hoped and prayed his life would be, because they set down those hopes and prayers in an engaging – and extremely well-preserved – piece of needlework. It is a strip of linen embroidered with coloured silks, about seventeen centimetres high and three metres long. It would have been presented to the synagogue in thanksgiving for Mordechai's birth, for use as a binder to tie the scrolls of the Torah, the first five books of the Hebrew Bible. The scrolls would be rolled up, bound with a strip like this and then stored in the Ark, from which they would be ceremonially taken out so that extracts could be read every week to the congregation (Chapter 20). It is not known how or when this binder came to the British Museum, but it was probably once attached to a manuscript Torah scroll now in the British Library.

Beverley Nenk, responsible for the Judaica Collection at the Museum, sets out what we may infer of its earlier history:

The Torah binder of Mordechai Gompel, Germany, 1750. The four pieces of the original circumcision cloth are now sewn together in one long strip. The Hebrew script reads from right to left.

Originally it would have been a square or rectangular piece of linen, used to swaddle the baby boy during the ceremony of his circumcision, when he was eight days old. After the circumcision, it would have been cut into four strips and sewn together – you can see the joins quite clearly. And then, traditionally, the women of the household, the mother and the sisters, would have embroidered it. From the style of the sewing we can say that it must have been made in Germany, but it is impossible to be more specific. They have used brightly coloured silks, which are still vivid, and enlivened them with sequins of silver-plated copper. Inevitably these have now tarnished, and we can't clean the silver without damaging the cloth, but originally they would have sparkled and looked very beautiful.

This elegant piece of needlework lays out the ideal life of an eighteenth-century Jewish boy – a life in which the religious and the social are indistinguishable – and defines his identity in the context of thousands of years of Jewish tradition. Through the ceremony of circumcision, when the cloth was wrapped around him, he was made heir to the ancient covenant between the Jews and their God, and was bound by the law of Moses. Almost as important, Beverley Nenk tells us, he was given his name:

Written in Hebrew, to be read from right to left, the first words we see are the baby's name, Mordechai Gompel. Then comes the father's name, Eli ha-Levi. Underneath are a little pitcher and basin, the symbols of the Levis, who traditionally washed the hands of the priests in the Temple. Next we read that he was born to good luck, to 'mazel', an abbreviation for 'mazel tov', on the eve of the holy Sabbath, on the full moon and under a good constellation – you can see an exquisitely detailed Scorpio. Then it has the date in the Jewish calendar, which equates to 31 October 1750.

This is Mordechai's inheritance – individual, familial and cosmic, his story up to his eighth day, when his circumcision takes place.

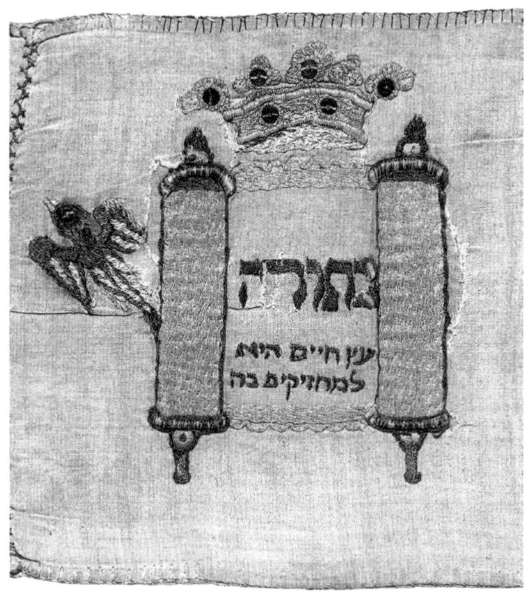

The scrolls of the law from which Mordechai Gompel will read

It is followed by prayers for his future role in society. The first thing asked for is that he may grow up to study the Torah, and the words are accompanied by a small image of the scroll of the law, with above it a crown, and below it the traditional description: 'This is a tree of life to those who hold it fast.' Learning to read or chant the Hebrew of the Torah in the synagogue, which usually requires long preparation (Chapter 20), is the indispensable task which must be performed – today, as in the eighteenth century – before a boy can take his place as a full member of the Jewish community. Traditionally the Bar Mitzvah – becoming a 'son of the law' – is celebrated at the age of thirteen. From then on, the boy may be called upon to read from the Torah in the synagogue, he may be counted as one of the ten adults that make up a minyan, a prayer quorum, and he has, in religious law, the right to own property and to testify. These new rights are accompanied by new obligations: he now has the duty to follow the precepts of the law, and he himself – no longer his father – is henceforth accountable for his actions. He also becomes responsible for the community as a whole. In a ceremony still widely practised in Jewish communities around the world, the boy has, in the presence of the congregation, become a man, a responsible adult.

Our embroidery may well have been given to the synagogue specifically to tie the scroll from which Mordechai Gompel read at his Bar Mitzvah and from which he would read in the future, the cloth of his infant circumcision literally binding his life as a man to the law that will govern it. Immediately following comes the hope that he will pass under the *chupah*, the wedding canopy: marriage and parenthood are among the duties that the new adult will be expected to fulfil. Beverley Nenk describes how this is the only point in the embroidery where the human figure appears:

There's a beautiful and moving vignette of a couple getting married under a canopy, wearing exquisite eighteenth-century clothes. They are standing under the ceremonial canopy while the Rabbi marries and blesses them, looking for all the world like figures from a Mozart opera set not in the seraglio but the ghetto in Frankfurt or Hamburg.

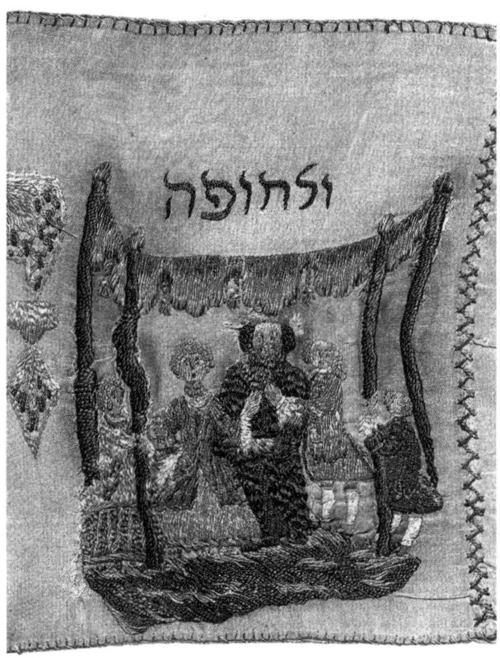

A traditional Jewish wedding canopy, *chupah*, under which he will marry

Now that he is able to play his full part in the prayer life of the synagogue and is happily married, ideally with children, says Beverley Nenk, Mordechai's parents have only one thing more to wish:

The scroll concludes with a prayer for a third blessing, which is 've'ma'asim tovim': that he may do good deeds throughout the whole of his life. Then, at the very end, are the words: 'Amen Selah', So be it.

'So be it.' Mordechai Gompel's scroll presents a crystal-clear view of what was expected from him as a member of his society, and of the stages by which he would play his part in it. It was a life framed in terms of duties to be fulfilled, and – characteristically for the Abrahamic faiths and for the Europe of his day – it was a life to be led by a man, but embroidered by (no doubt several) women.

In many reformed Jewish synagogues today, however, there is much greater equality between the sexes. Girls become Bat Mitzvah, daughters of the law, also around the age of twelve or thirteen. Like their brothers they too learn to read the Hebrew text of the Torah in the synagogue, and so assume publicly a new role with greater personal responsibility. In spite of growing secularization, the ceremony remains extremely popular with both girls and boys. Abe and Rebecca Dein, a brother and sister who live in north-west London, both found in it a powerful affirmation of their new, adult, identity and of a very old tradition. For Rebecca Dein:

It was so important for me, because that was the time when I became a Jewish woman. It was nerve-racking, because everyone was looking at me and it was so quiet. I'd never even touched the Torah before, but I'd worked very hard for that moment. After I had finished reading my passage everyone smiled at me and said: 'Mazel Tov' – I was now part of them, and I was with them. I just felt so good. I felt that now I was one of the community.

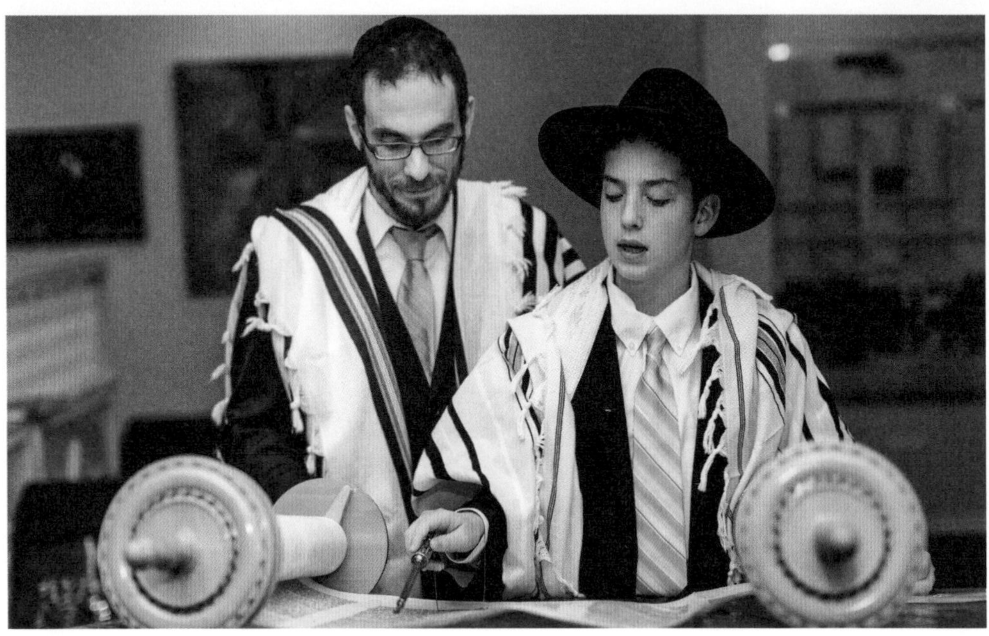

A boy preparing for his Bar Mitzvah learns to read the Torah scroll using a *yad* (Chapter 20)

For her brother, Abe Dein, there was a similar exhilaration in being received into the adult community, but above all a great sense of taking his place in a long continuum:

It was very important that ancestors before me had done this. The Bar Mitzvah has been around in the Jewish tradition for centuries and centuries. I don't believe in God myself, but I really love Jewish culture. It's a tradition you would want to carry on, because everyone has done it before you. Practising and memorizing my 'parsha', which is a section of the Torah, was a lot of work. When I finished, I looked up, and everyone was smiling. And I felt, yes, I've done it. It was ... well it was a coming of age.

One of the striking things about the Jewish Bar and Bat Mitzvah ceremonies is how unusual they now seem in an increasingly secular Western world. Not so long ago many communities' hopes for, and expectations of, their young – even if never given such explicit visual form – would have been just as clear as those embroidered on Mordechai Gompel's Torah binder.

*

In the last chapter we saw how bringing a child safely into the world, and getting it healthily through its early years, has always been fraught with worry and danger. Once the perils of infancy have been safely navigated comes the biggest challenge of all: parents – and the wider community – need to prepare the child for the world he or she will live in. Socializing a child is such a long process that it usually leaves few objects behind which document it succinctly. But there is one such physical record, as eloquent in its own way as the Torah binder, from a very different kind of community and from the other side of the world. It looks at first sight like a small bunch of dried flowers. It is light brown, about twenty centimetres long and nearly 200 years old. It comes from Vanuatu, and was the first object to enter the British Museum from Melanesia, the vast area of the Pacific that runs from New Guinea to Fiji. It was donated in 1831 by George Bennett, a surgeon on board the *Sophia*, a ship that had been chartered in Sydney for the purpose of

The bundle of bound hair collected by George Bennett in Vanuatu around 1830

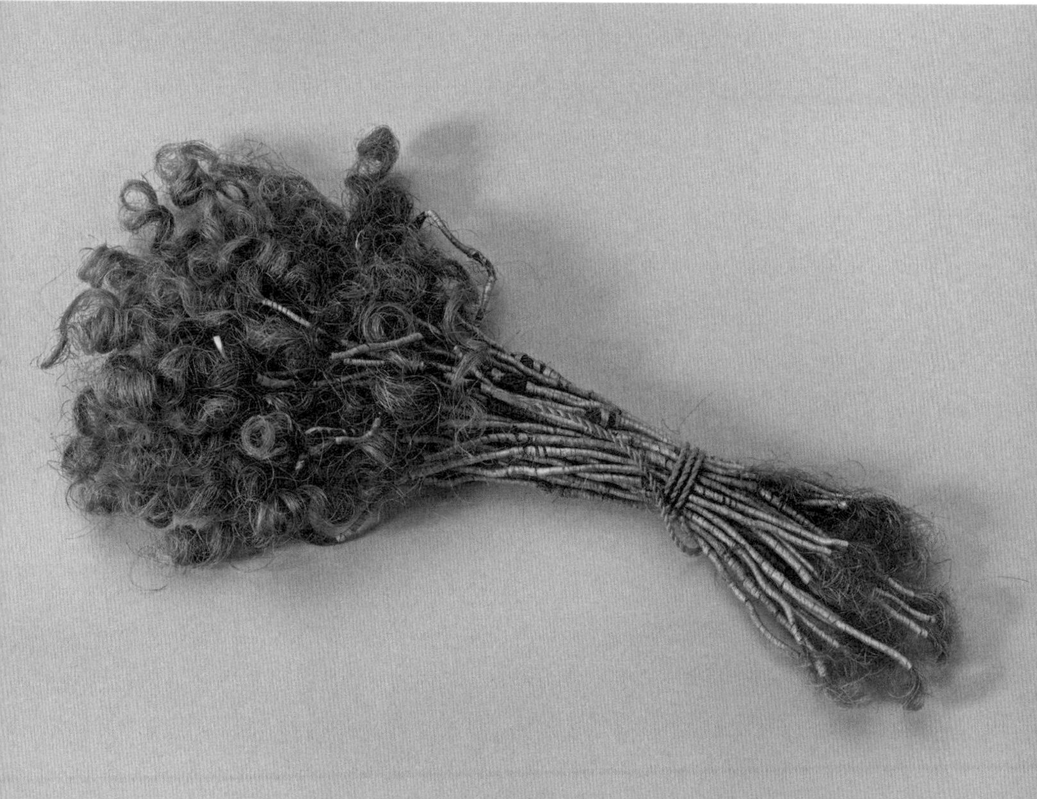

collecting sandalwood from southern Vanuatu. The Museum register soberly recorded its arrival as a 'Tuft of the hair of a male inhabitant of Tanna, one of the New Hebrides Group, as worn by the natives'.

This bundle of carefully plaited human hair was indeed 'as worn by the natives', but it was, and is, much more than that. It is the record of a long process of instruction, literally the binding into a young man of all that he needs to know to take his place in society as an adult. And it is a process still carried out on the island of Tanna in the Republic of Vanuatu. In the years after boys reach puberty, and as they are growing to maturity, senior men bind their hair at regular intervals with leaf-fibre, shaping it into something like dreadlocks. While they are binding, they tell the boys important traditional knowledge about the world, what its history is, how to behave to your kin, how to conduct yourself in life.

Sam Posan, a fieldworker at the Vanuatu Cultural Centre, who comes from the island of Tanna, where George Bennett collected our bundle of hair, describes how this course of education for life is organized:

You circumcise the boy first. Then you fasten his hair. And you teach him everything, about the world, about how to behave. You are fastening tightly all the things you are telling him – binding them into his head. Then two or three months later you both come back and you ask the boy questions, to see if he still remembers what you taught him or not. You will meet again and bind his hair again, and tell him once more the things he's forgotten. You will fill his head. And when his bound hair reaches the bottom of his back, the old people say – then he will be a man.

It seems that George Bennett arrived at a moment when one young man had just completed this long course of induction: at that point the bound hair is cut off, to mark the boy's move into adulthood. It seems rarely to be kept, and to have no particular value,

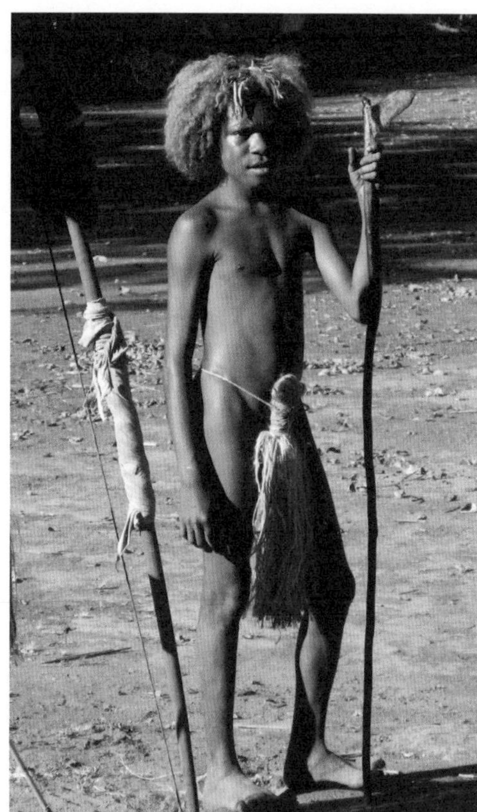
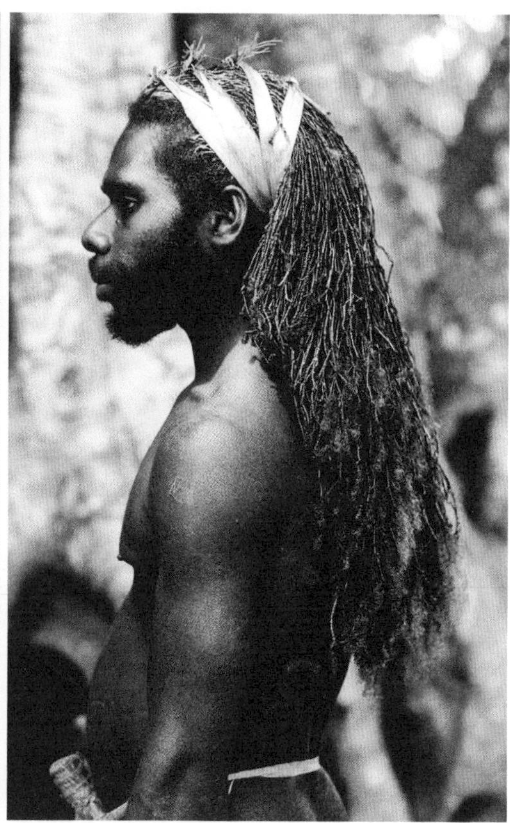

Stories and knowledge are progressively bound into the hair of young men in Tanna, Vanuatu. The process takes several years.

even to the new adult himself. But when, a few years ago, some men from Vanuatu visited the Museum, they recognized at once what the cut, bound hair was, remarking: 'this is our university'.

Sam Posan explains that if a man lives according to what he is taught as his hair is being bound, then the stages of wisdom through which he will pass can be marked off on the fingers of one hand:

You begin with your little finger, which is you when you are a child, and you don't know anything about the world. Then you grow a bit bigger, you reach the next finger: you ask and ask, and the old people tell you everything. Then it comes to the time of the tall middle finger, when you learn to do everything, when the spirit of the things that you are doing comes into you. Then you go down again to the next finger, and that's when you teach the children.

When you are old, and have white hair, then you come down to the last finger, to the thumb. You sit down like a stone in its proper place. Young people have their knives and if the knives get blunt, they come and sharpen them on your stone. They can ask the old person everything, and he will tell them everything, because he has walked through those experiences.

This is life in Vanuatu articulated as a five-finger exercise – with rights and obligations set out as clearly as in the Torah binder, and with a comparable focus on continuity and tradition. As with many societies across the world, there can be great comfort in knowing so securely where you stand, both within your own life and in the community. Like all structures, however, while they support, they also constrict. In the first place you must accept someone else's definition of who you are, as a man or a woman, and for a woman that will in most societies usually mean a subordinate role.

Professor Linda Woodhead, of the University of Lancaster, has made a special study of these rites of passage and initiation:

Because men in most societies have a higher status and more of a public role, the ritual of boys' initiations is more public and more gruelling. Masculinity is generally more about public display, so a public initiation ritual is the way you are presented as a man in that society. Of course, women are also initiated into many different traditions by other women, but the rituals are likely to be more domestic and private, with less ceremonial.

Modern Western society hardly lacks for rites of passage – from the school prom, to the first holidays with friends, or descending into muddy, drunken, chaos at music festivals. But we have moved away from a model of elders initiating children into an adult world – children joining their parents in a new role, after an intergenerational transfer of wisdom. The traditional twenty-first birthday party thrown by parents for friends and family, coming with the right to vote and to be given 'the key of the door' – classic markers of adulthood in the public and private spheres – has now largely faded away. Instead, the young initiate each other into adult worlds of their own – with joyous baptisms of beer, song and dance.

Linda Woodhead thinks that this development is the inevitable consequence of technological advance, but also of the increasing insistence on choice and individual rights in preference to patterns of convention and obligation:

Something is happening in our society, which has to do with the speeding-up of change. Those rituals where you are initiated into a set wisdom, a fixed body of learning which is passed on across the generations – all that stops making sense when things are changing so rapidly that a teenager already knows a lot more than their parents about critically important things like digital technology. That disrupts the old pattern of the handing down of knowledge. I think as a society we're grappling with the problem of how the values which are enduring and do not change can be transmitted.

We also now have greatly widened access to any kind of cultural good that might be wanted. There's much more room for choice, for thinking about the kind of person you want to be and the kind of gang you want to belong to. We want to choose the kind of rituals that will go along with becoming what we have individually decided to become. We are a liberal society. We want choice. We don't want our future handed down to us.

It is an enormous change. The embroidered Torah binder. The plaited hair from Vanuatu. Your place in a tradition. Your responsibilities as well as your rights. These are precious visions of life, framed for individuals by their community. Offered a blank piece of linen, now, and asked to sketch out our hopes for our children, we would surely wish them health and happiness. But what else? I suspect that most parents today would say that it was not up to them – that their children must make their own way and their own choices. It would be a very difficult thing to ask of any child, to devise the narrative of their own Torah embroidery, or to bind the knowledge they need into their own hair. But Linda Woodhead argues that even if the rituals of initiation into adulthood have largely disappeared, Western society has been so deeply shaped by its long Christian traditions that it perhaps no longer requires them:

We remain a very morally coherent society. You can see it clearly, for example, when we have collective tragedies. What immediately resurfaces are the traditional Christian values – love, solidarity, caring for one another, standing up against evil: in spite of the decline of the church, all those things remain deeply embedded. There is enormous moral consensus.

Of course many other faiths also proclaim these values. For Linda Woodhead, their persistence suggests that even in consumerist, multi-cultural Europe, there appears still to be a secure ethical framework within which young adults – perhaps now more freely than ever before – can make the choices that will shape their lives, not as society has determined, but as they wish them to be.

9
LET US PRAY

O God, to whom all hearts be open, all desires known, and from whom no secrets are hid … (Book of Common Prayer)

I show you sorrow, and the ending of sorrow (Buddha)

In the name of Allah, in the name of God, the Most Gracious, the Most Merciful … (Qur'an)

O Great Spirit, whose voice I hear in the winds … (Native American prayer)

Holy Mary, Mother of God, pray for us now and in the hour of our death … (Roman Catholic liturgy)

Hear, O Israel: the Lord our God, the Lord is One (Torah)

At the beginning of the twentieth century, it was one of the most popular pictures in Europe and America. In a field, in the evening twilight, a man and a woman pause from the back-breaking work of harvesting potatoes, and stand in silent prayer. Millet's *L'Angélus*, a celebration of traditional rural piety, was painted in 1857, and rapidly became an icon of French Catholic identity,

Over: Jean-François Millet's *L'Angélus* painted in 1857 was widely reproduced. This engraving was printed in 1881.

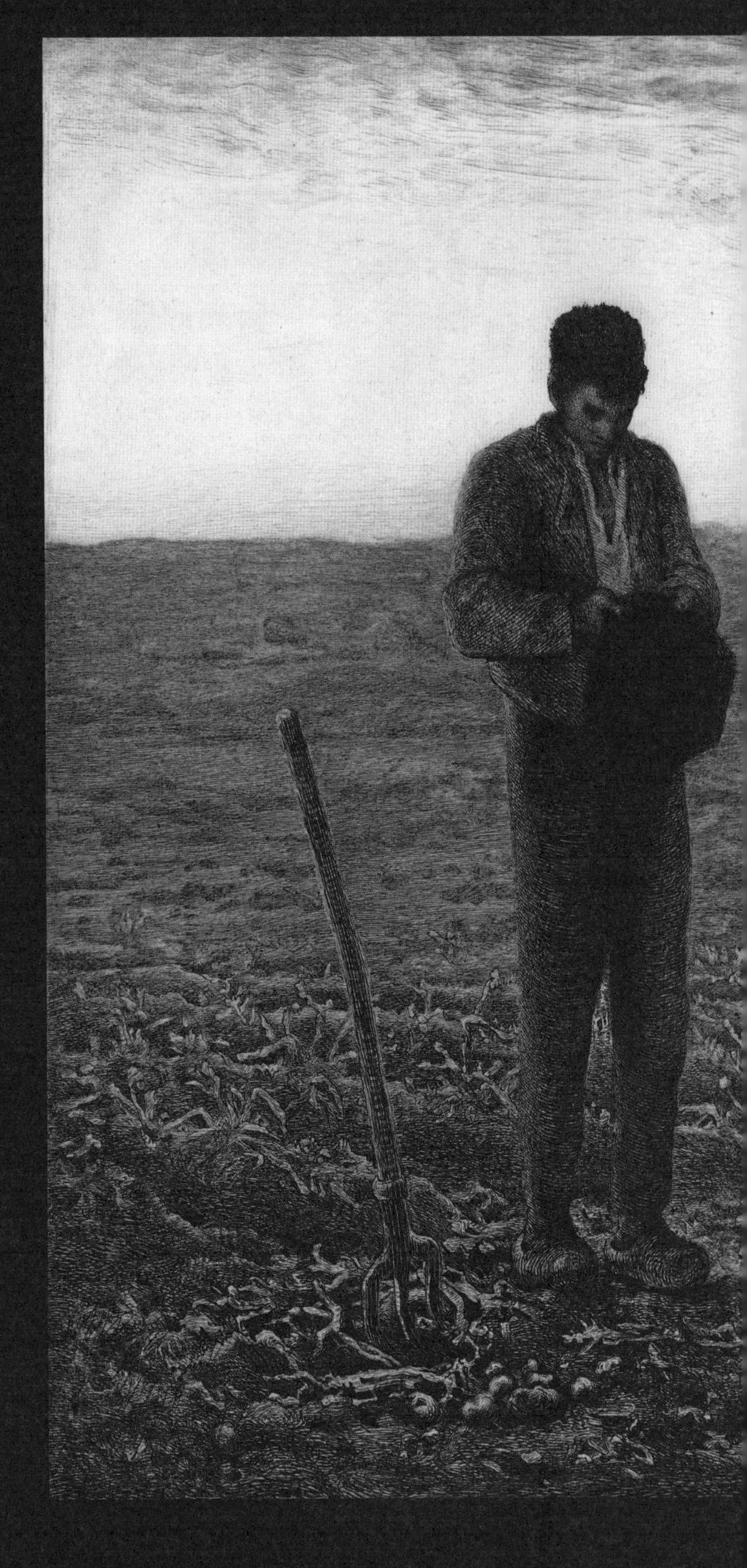

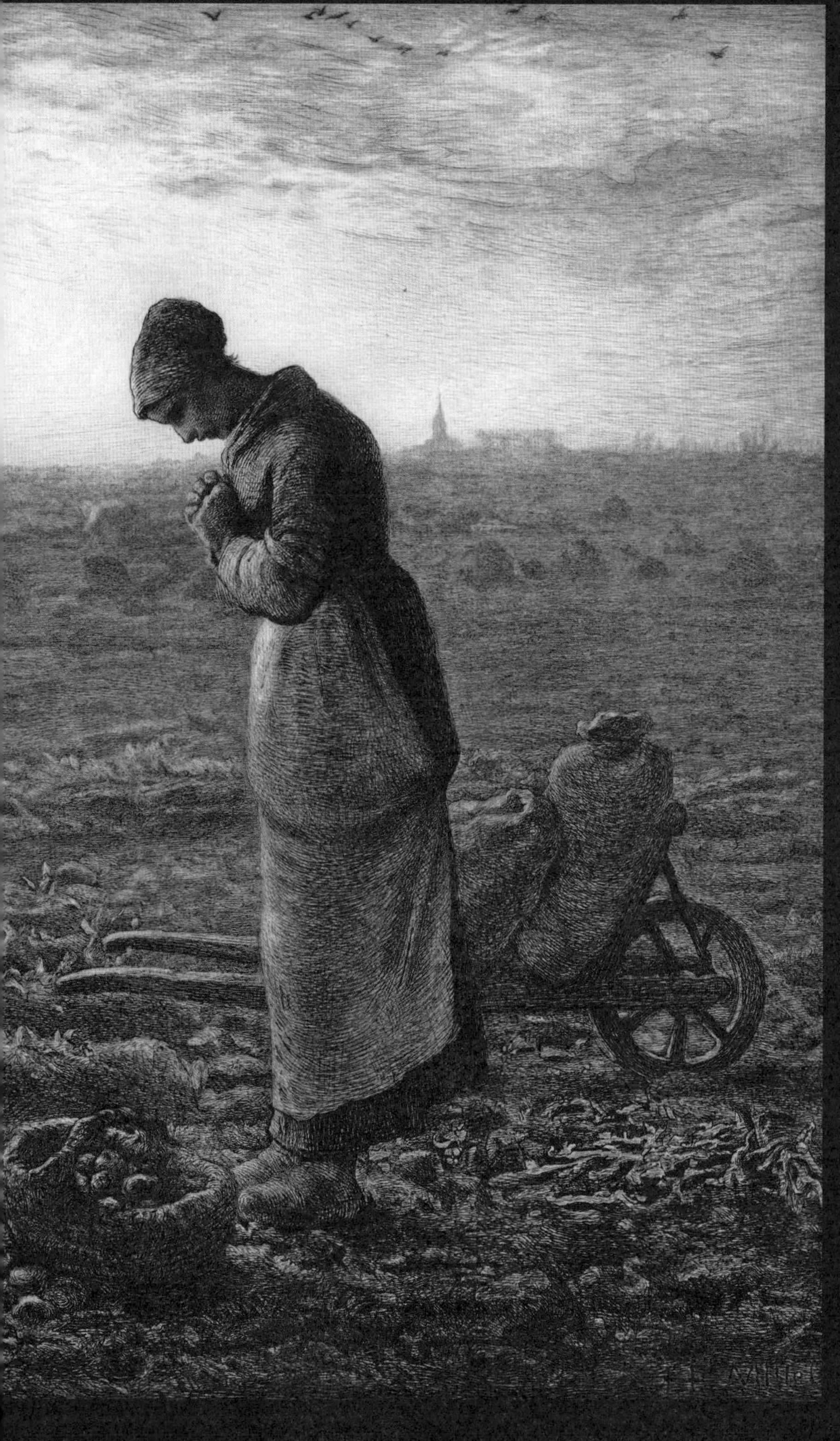

reproduced in thousands of engravings like this one and in countless cheaper photographic versions. To national dismay, it was swiftly bought by an American, and then in 1890 acquired by a patriotic French collector for an enormous sum – 750 times the original price – and carried back to Paris in triumph. It hangs today in the Musée d'Orsay.

In the engraving you can see clearly the spire of the village church, where the bell has just been rung. It reminds everybody to stop their work for a moment and say the Angelus prayer, which invokes the angel who announced the birth of Jesus to the Virgin Mary, and who prays for all sinners. The Angelus bell did not – does not – call people to church: it calls them to stay where they are, but to redirect their thoughts away from their immediate everyday concerns and towards God. It is a public summons to a private act.

It is easy to see why this image of rural peace had such a powerful appeal for people living in the new industrial towns and cities, where factory work never stopped: by the time our engraving was produced in 1881, the tradition of the Angelus, indeed the very idea that you might be allowed to stop to pray in the middle of the day's work, was to most Europeans living in cities at best a memory. But Millet's picture struck another, perhaps even deeper, nostalgic chord. In the anti-clerical politics of the French Third Republic, which ultimately led to the complete separation of church and state in 1905, it spoke reassuringly of another France, as it had claimed to be before the Revolution of 1789 – a nation united and defined by its devotion to the Catholic faith (see Chapter 28). It is surely no coincidence that in another country that until recently defined itself in very similar terms – Ireland – the Angelus bell (in spite now of considerable public protests) still rings, on national radio at twelve noon and on national television at six in the evening.

In a similar way for millions of Muslims in Europe and beyond, the sound of the muezzin is also a regular, familiar part of life. Five times a day, Muslims everywhere pause for a few minutes, just like the Christian peasants in *L'Angélus*. They suspend the business at hand, focus their thoughts on God, and, wherever they may be in the world, all turn towards Mecca to perform the *salah*: the Islamic prayer ritual of reciting, standing, bowing, prostrating and sitting.

Much prayer of course takes place in the context of the weekly gatherings in synagogue, church or mosque. So it may seem odd, in a book concerned above all with belief as a communal enterprise, to concentrate here on an activity so highly personal as private prayer – each soul's individual and complex quest for what the Anglican priest and poet George Herbert with sublime simplicity called 'something understood'. Since this usually involves putting aside the obligations of everyday life for a little while, prayer may seem – from the outside, at least – to be a form of social withdrawal. But as the Angelus and the Islamic call to prayer demonstrate, what appears to be the most highly individualized of spiritual activities can also be a profoundly communal act.

We shall return to that paradox at the end of this chapter, but I want to begin with the more practical problem of how people prepare themselves to pray, especially when they are not gathered in a place of worship. Almost all religious traditions address this question of how to pray alone. It is a task with which most people need help, if only to overcome some of the unavoidable consequences of our humanity – that we have restless bodies and highly active minds, not quickly quietened; a desire for control and security, not easily relinquished; and a sense of our inner world as an enclosed space, into which it is rarely straightforward to allow the divine to intrude. So, how do those who wish to pray settle themselves? And, once settled, how do they then open themselves, so that they can not only speak, but listen?

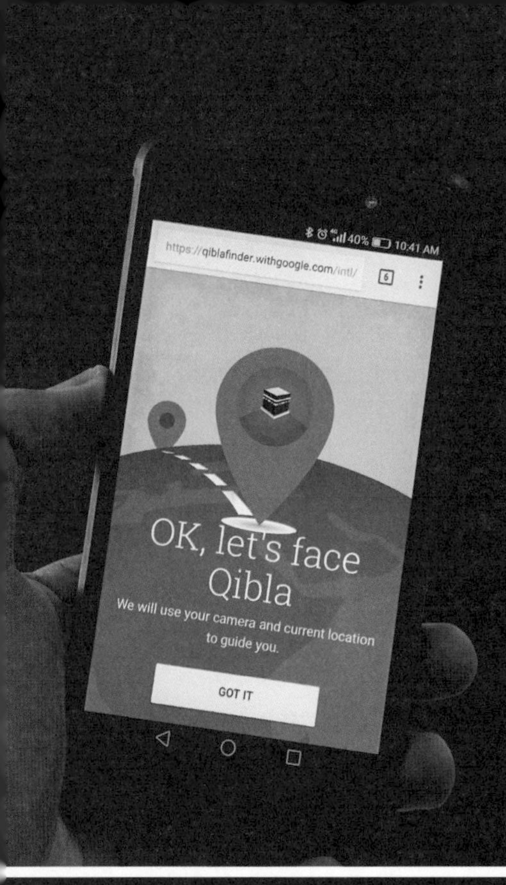
https://qiblafinder.withgoogle.com/intl/
10:41 AM
OK, let's face Qibla
We will use your camera and current location to guide you.
GOT IT

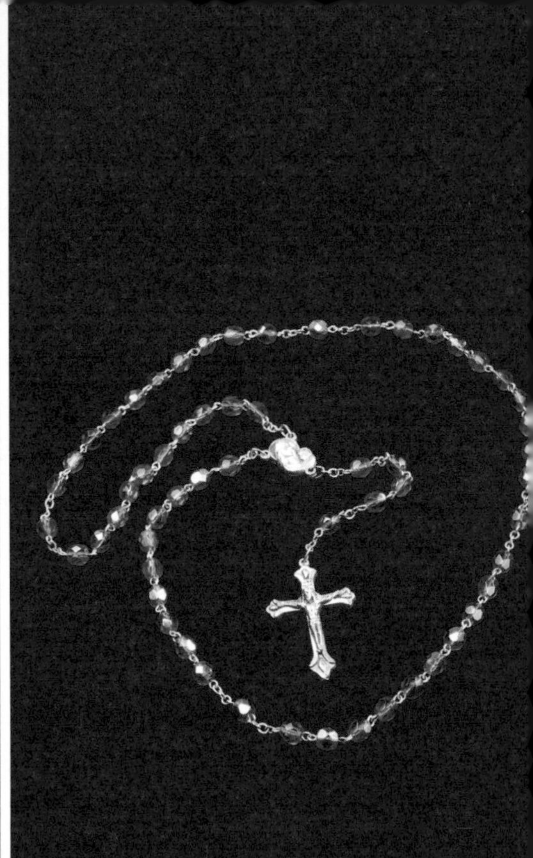

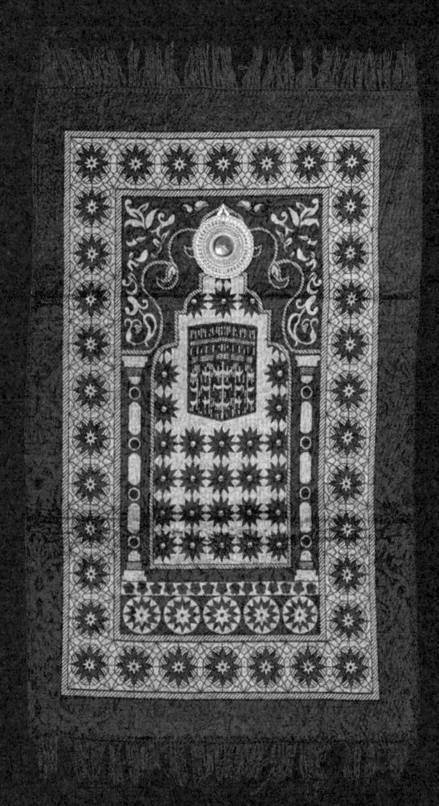

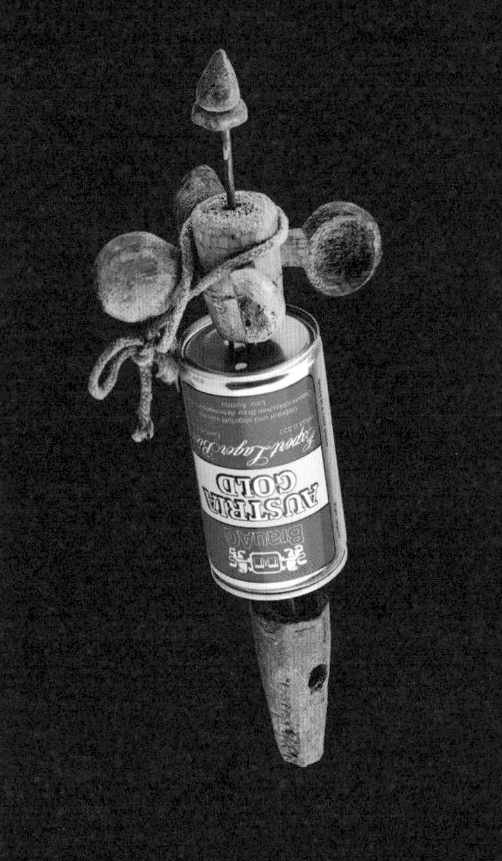
AUSTRIA GOLD
BrauAG

The best way to disconnect from our physical surroundings seems counter-intuitively often to be to focus on our physical body – our posture, our breathing – and then to use objects, such as prayer beads that we can touch and tell. It is those material objects that help, for a moment, to leave the material world behind. Some of them are beautiful and precious works of art made of box-wood and crystal, ivory and precious stones. But most physical aids to prayer have little aesthetic or commercial value – indeed some, like the Buddhist prayer-wheel designed to repeat mantras and prayers perpetually, can be made out of ostentatiously recycled materials that rejoice in their very ordinariness. Objects like these matter far less for what they are than for what they do.

For a Muslim preparing to pray, there is always one pressing question: how to know where to turn in order to face Mecca? To find *qibla* – the right direction – you need a *qibla*-indicator, and there are few more stylish than the one made out of ivory and gold in Istanbul in 1582 or 1583, now in the British Museum. It is circular, and looks like a slightly oversized powder compact. Under the lid, the lower disc is essentially a compass and a sundial rolled into one. Painted in the middle is a black cube, ringed with a red fence: it represents the Kaaba, the sacred building linked to Abraham

Opposite: Aids to modern prayer: (*clockwise from top left*) *qibla*-indicator app on a smartphone; Catholic rosary beads; Buddhist prayer wheel from Kashmir made from a beer can; Islamic prayer mat from Saudi Arabia

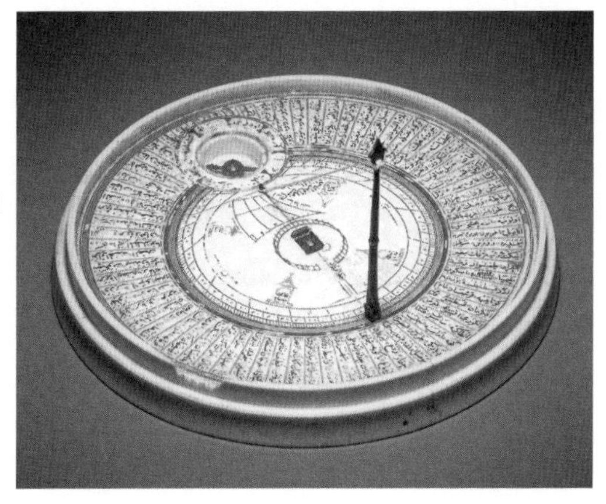

Right: Ivory *qibla*-indicator with sundial, made in Istanbul in the late sixteenth century

and Muhammad, that stands at the centre of the Great Mosque in Mecca (see Chapter 14). The compass shows you *where* to turn to face both Mecca and the Kaaba, while the little golden sundial tells you *when*: if there is no muezzin within earshot, it will tell you the time for your daily prayers.

Dr Afifi al-Akiti from the Oxford Centre for Islamic Studies explains:

Once you know you are facing in the right direction, you next make sure that you are in the right frame of mind. You clean yourself physically, and then perform the ritual ablution – what Muslims call Wudu. Then you go on to your prayer mat. Essentially you want to try to create a sacred space. It's a bit like Aladdin going on to the magic carpet. You are the pilot, going through all the instruments to make sure you have done all the pre-flight checks. And once you are ready, then you can take off into prayer.

I think it is important to remember that for most prayers, the direction is not particularly significant. The Koran says: 'to God belongs the east and the west, and no matter which way you turn you shall find the presence of God'. The famous theologian Al-Rumi said: 'I looked in temples, churches and mosques but I found the divine within my heart.' So the direction itself is important only for this form of regular daily prayer called the salah, the formal liturgical prayer designed to give a sense of unity. But the internal prayer itself has to take place within your heart. It is not bounded by time or space.

Dr al-Akiti, like all Muslims, has his *qibla*-indicator and his prayer mat to orient his body and direct his prayer, although modern technology means that many Muslims now have an app on their smartphone that tells them immediately which way to face.

For Sri Lankan Buddhists, as Sarah Shaw from the Oxford Centre for Buddhist Studies describes, the helpful object to settle the spirit and focus contemplation is more likely to be a small

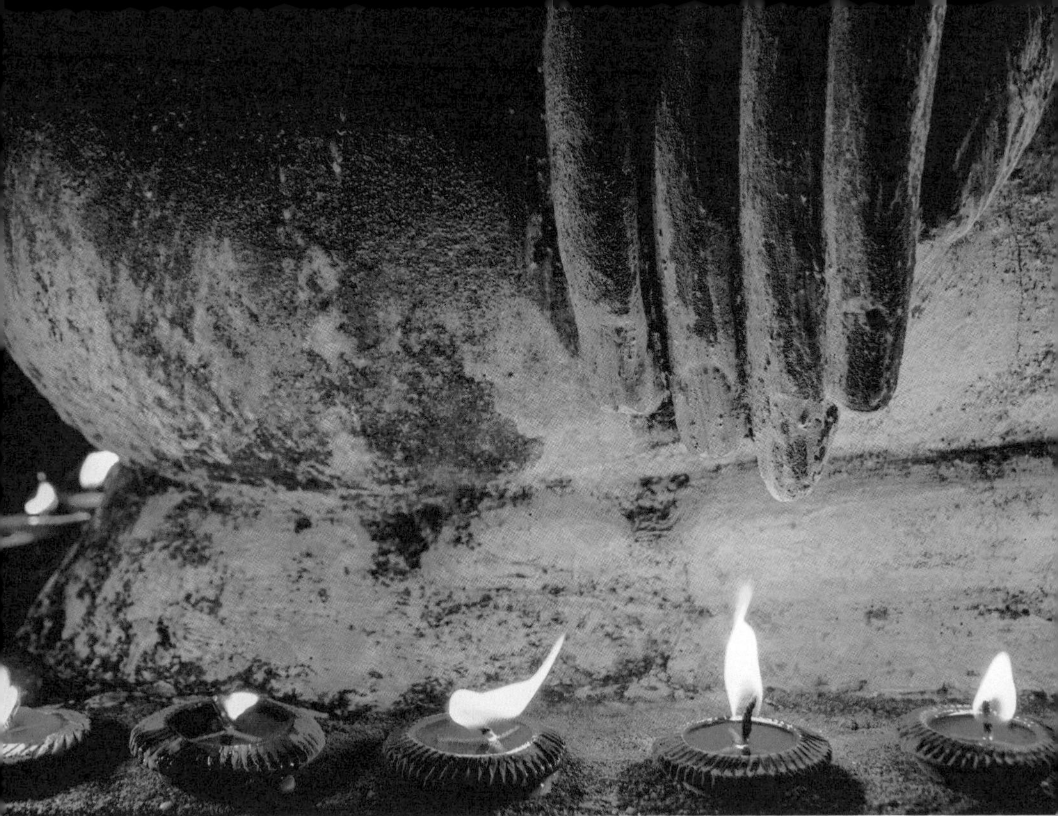

Butter lamps burn beside the hand of the Buddha.

pottery bowl that costs just a few rupees, and can serve as a lamp: lighting this is a way of paying respect to the statue of the Buddha, as representative of the fully awakened mind. To activate it requires only some butter or coconut oil and a few strips of torn cotton:

If you tear a little bit of cotton and twist it in opposite directions, then at some point the tension in the middle becomes so strong that it makes a kink in the cotton and becomes a wick, which will last for a long time. In Sri Lanka, they say that a wick like this, formed by such tension, is an embodiment of the middle way of the Buddha, the middle point between two extremes – and so a pointer to enlightenment. Lighting the lamp is a profound ritual, earthing, tranquillizing and very satisfying, as rituals often are. Symbolically, it is of course the light that dispels spiritual darkness.

This paying of respects at the outset of prayer involves what Buddhists call 'taking refuge': you must first of all put yourself under divine protection. It is an idea found also in Muslim prayers, which often open with the words 'In the Name of Allah, the Most Gracious, the Most Merciful'. And Brother Timothy Radcliffe, a Dominican monk and theologian, tells us how there is a comparable process at the outset of Roman Catholic prayer:

We begin by making the sign of the Cross in the name of the Father, the Son and the Holy Spirit. That is placing ourselves inside Christ. Christ isn't just somebody that you address, He is somebody you inhabit, in whom you are at home. Then it is very important that your body be well placed. We are animals, rational animals, and so it's very important, if we are to pray, that our bodies should be well rooted, well seated, breathing well. When you read books of theology, it's often so abstract. In fact it is about getting down to earth, to our physical body as it lives and breathes.

Once the body is settled, the next impediment to concentrated prayer is the wandering human mind. For Sarah Shaw, as for Timothy Radcliffe, breathing is the starting point: we can manage our breathing consciously, but we can also relax and simply let breathing happen:

This is actually necessary for meditation, necessary if the mind is to be fully engaged in thought. It is often compared to a bee going to a flower: it knows where it wants to go, but it also needs to circle around and get to know the flower again and again and again and again. When you repeat a chant or a little mantra, you're simply allowing that very discursive, dispersed part of the mind to come together, to unify, and to settle on one object. So I find chanting very helpful, because that part of my mind which is always engaged during the day – like a bee buzzing everywhere – has a chance to settle on just one flower.

But as anyone who has attempted it will attest, reaching and sustaining this kind of focus is a great deal more difficult than it might sound. So it is perhaps not surprising that most faiths have developed repetitive forms of prayer, part of whose point is to assist the journey into concentrated stillness.

It is often, according to Timothy Radcliffe, a journey sustained by stringed beads or rosaries:

I think in Islam, Buddhism and Christianity, you find at some moment there is the presence of beads: we tell our beads, we count our beads. It's a very tactile act, accompanying the process of moving through prayer. I think as bodily beings we need physical practices like these which penetrate the whole of us.

In the early centuries of Christianity, prayer was thoroughly physical, as with prayer rituals in Islam today. People stood, they bowed, they prostrated themselves, they genuflected, just as Muslims still do. But in the sixteenth century prayer seems to have become more mental, more abstract. The Puritans banned all dancing and singing, and we lost a lot of that bodily dynamism of our prayer, which Muslims – I think wisely – have retained. In the Catholic church this is something we are now trying to recover.

Passing from one bead to another, we pray with our fingers and our body. The rosary helps calm the spirit by repetition: the beads lead you through the cycle of life, in ten Hail Marys, which begin by addressing her at the moment she conceives Jesus, and end by asking her to pray for us in the hour of our death. And then there is a larger bead, for the Our Father. The repetition of the familiar prayers is a very effective way of letting go of the worries of the moment.

Dr al-Akiti finds a very similar practice – with a very similar intent – in many Islamic traditions:

In some circles you can hear just a single syllable – hoo, hoo, hoo, hoo – which is to be recited a hundred or a thousand times, to help you to meditate. According to the Qur'anic tradition it is only through remembering God and meditating that you find peace and contentment of heart.

This kind of repetitive prayer can be performed anywhere, in private or in public. It may be done alone, or in informal groups, and crucially it needs no priest or imam to direct it. It is an activity of the laity. Yet in both the Christian and Islamic traditions, what is striking about the regularly repeated individual prayers – of the rosary or of the *salah* – is that they are never about the individual: they define the person praying as unequivocally a member of a community. When single Muslims pray, they unite with Muslims in every place, as all turn towards Mecca. The two peasants in the fields in Millet's *L'Angélus* are joining everybody in the village praying at the same moment. The opening words of the Lord's Prayer are not 'My Father' but 'Our Father', and 'we' and 'us' continue all the way through: there is no 'I'. Only God is singular. However we do it – whether we kneel, sit, stand or prostrate ourselves– it is 'we' who pray. As in almost all religious rituals, to connect with God is also to join more fully with each other.

Yet at the same time as binding communities together, the public call to private prayer can also drive them apart. The Angelus in France in the late nineteenth century, as in modern Ireland, came to be seen as a symbol of a national identity which was consciously – and, to many, controversially – Catholic. In central Europe today, strident arguments about European cultural identity have crystallized around the competing sounds of the traditional church bell and the muezzin's call to prayer, which some feel proclaims Islam in an intrusive and unacceptably public way. The underlying question: is Europe an essentially Christian civilization, or not? In Germany, the Pegida movement protests against the Islamization of the West; in France, Islamic prayer in the street

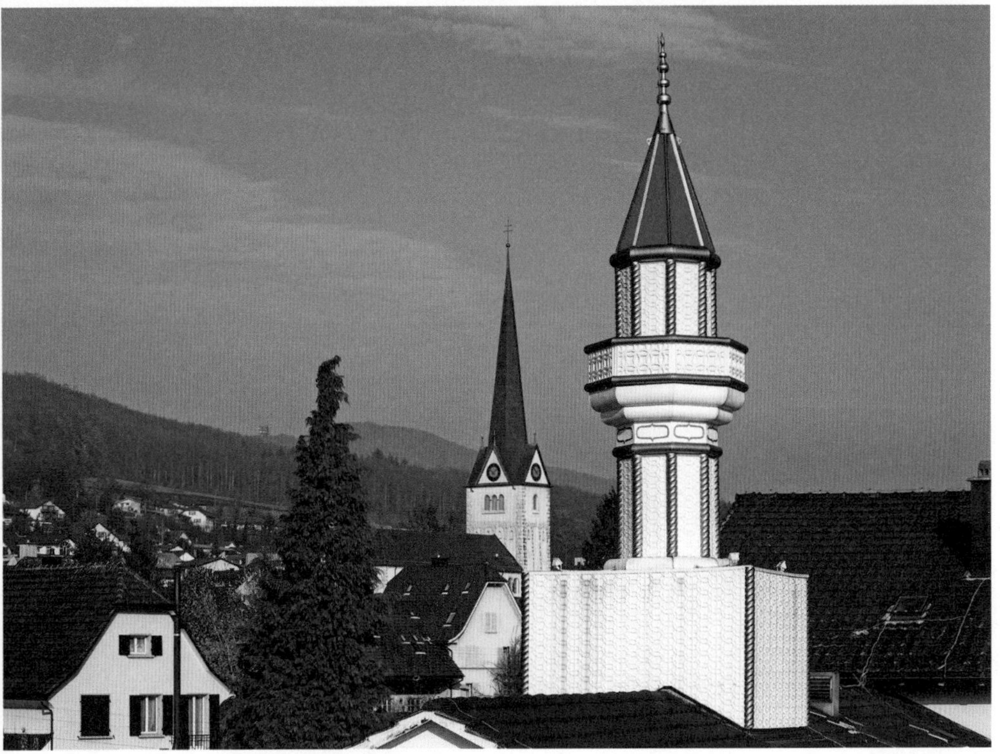

The controversial construction of minarets such as this one in Wangen, Switzerland, led to a federal referendum in 2009.

is forbidden (Chapter 28); and in 2009 in Switzerland, a majority voted in a federal referendum to ban the construction of all new minarets. But it is not only historically Christian lands which seek to defend their traditional identities. Saudi Arabia, for example, does not allow the building of Christian churches, even less the ringing of church bells or praying in public. Prayer, the most intimate spiritual activity, can when practised communally be an explosive political topic.

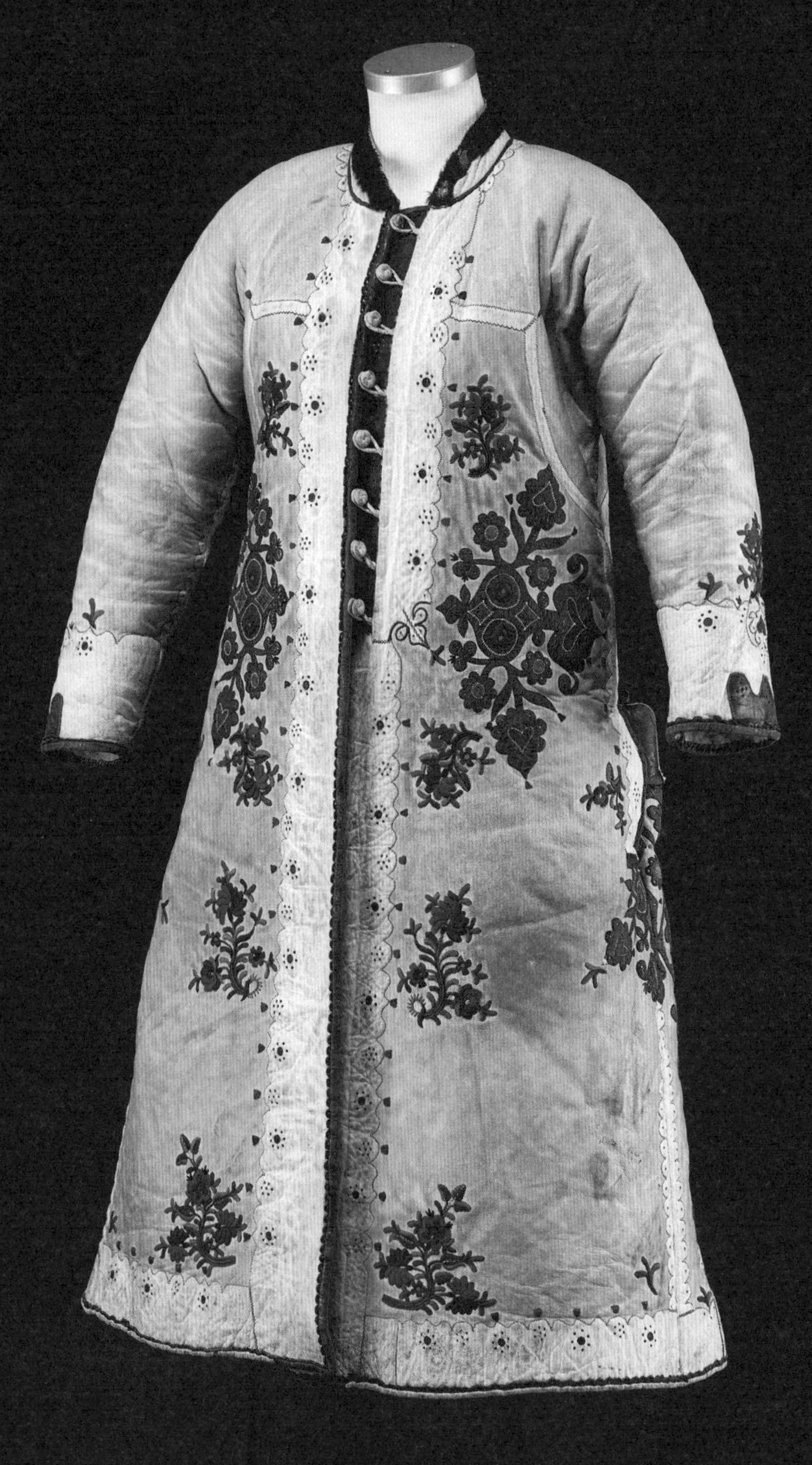

10

THE POWER OF SONG

The Protestant Sunday has had a bad press. Instead of being the welcome day of rest and relaxation, it became for centuries synonymous with enforced abstention from even the most harmless pleasures. But there is one Protestant Sunday habit, often overlooked, which certainly involves celebration and enjoyment, which binds people together with unusual power, has had a huge impact on Western culture, and is in no danger of being banned: community hymn singing, or, more precisely, the phenomenon of a community defining itself by singing a hymn.

In the world before and beyond the Abrahamic religions, 'community worship' has usually meant those few times a year when everybody came together for festivals linked to changing seasons, major sacrifices, or similar ceremonies (Chapter 15). But for the rest of the year, sacred places – temples, shrines or groves – would normally be visited only by smaller groups of priests or devotees, carrying out regular, perhaps daily rituals and activities. Individuals might visit with some frequency, but the whole community came together only rarely.

And then – really quite recently – all that changed. The rise of

A magnificent Lutheran *Kirchenpelz* made in Transylvania in the late nineteenth century

Christianity and Islam as truly global religions brought to much of the world the Jewish pattern of a *weekly* cycle of worship focused on a communal gathering. It is a model of human activity designed to replicate God's as related in the Book of Genesis – his creation of the world in six days, and his rest from his labours on the seventh. Friday evening, moving into Saturday, is the Jewish Shabbat, or Sabbath, when many Jews will refrain from all work, and go to synagogue. Every Friday just after noon, Muslims come together for congregational prayer, as enjoined in the Qur'an: the Arabic for Friday means simply 'day of assembly'. And Sunday is, for most Christians, 'the Lord's Day' – and that means church. These weekly gatherings bring people out of their homes, and into a shared space where in worship they affirm their one-ness as a community before God. Great pains are taken, in all three traditions, to mark this transition from ordinary life into time set aside for the faithful to present themselves to God and to each other.

One of the most obvious ways to show that on this day the focus of life has changed is to dress up, to don what in the Christian world used to be called your 'Sunday best'. And few Sunday bests could be better than one now in the British Museum. It is a *Kirchenpelz* – literally, a 'church fur' – a sheepskin coat made in the late nineteenth century in Transylvania, then part of Hungary, now western Romania. Its wearer was a member of the German-speaking Saxon community, which had settled there as farmer immigrants around 1200, and had retained a very distinct identity ever since. It is by far the most spectacular object in the British Museum that speaks of a Lutheran identity.

Inside, the fleece is wonderfully warm; on the outside, appliquéd on to the sheepskin are patterns of deep-red and pale-cream leather, complemented by fine embroidery in red, green, purple, blue and pink. This is a joyful, colourful virtuoso piece of art and design – as well as being a sturdy overcoat to wear against the cold Transylvanian weather.

Both women and men would wear a *Kirchenpelz* like this to church. They were objects of considerable value, and were given to mark some special occasion, such as confirmation or marriage. But this kind of Sunday best was about more than just looking respectable in the pews. To wear a coat like this was to proclaim public allegiance to the Lutheran church, identity as a Transylvanian Saxon and membership of a particular German-speaking community which, though much reduced in numbers, still survives in Romania today.

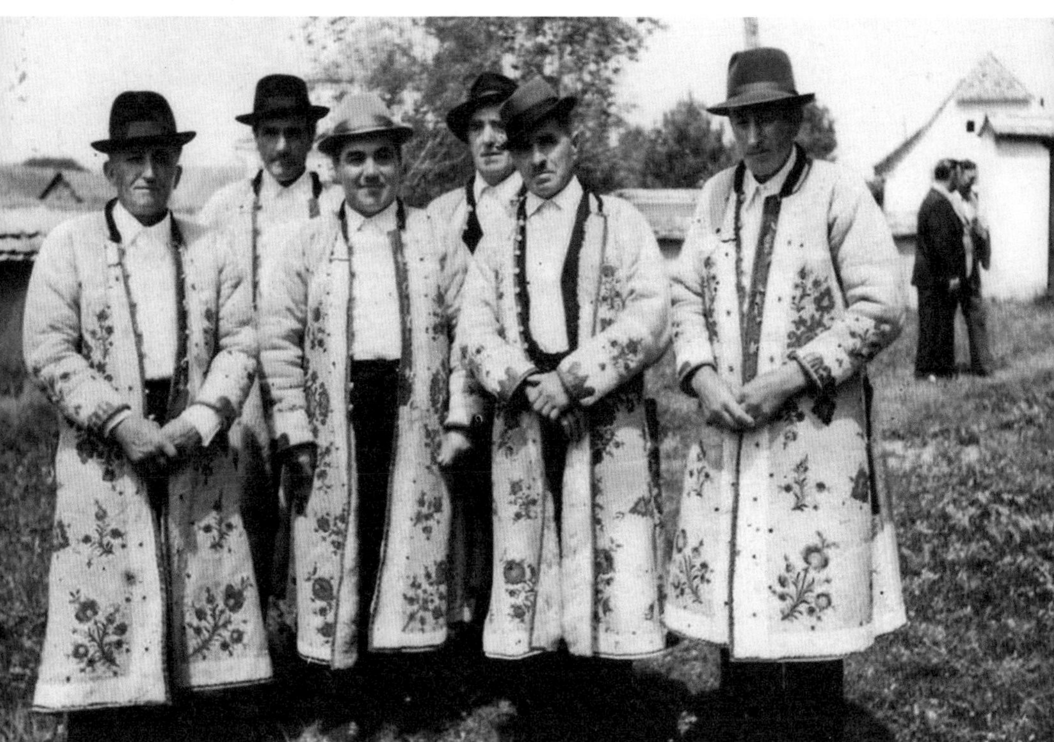

Sunday best: Saxon Transylvanians wearing their *Kirchenpelz* in Brașov, Romania, 1983

Even more significant than wearing this *Kirchenpelz* in church, however, is what its owner would be doing there; and for Lutheran congregations in Transylvania, as for Lutherans everywhere, that has always meant singing. It was one of Martin Luther's great insights that few things bring disparate people more quickly and effectively together than sharing a song they all know by heart.

John Butt is a conductor and organist, and Gardiner Professor of Music at the University of Glasgow:

The regular way of worshipping for a Lutheran, from the sixteenth century right up to the present day, is through chorales: choral hymns of a kind inaugurated by Luther himself. These lay out not just elements of dogma and of faith; they also form the entire skeleton of a service as congregational hymns, often introduced by the organ, to set the mood or spirit of the song.

Luther did not of course invent hymns and communal singing, but he transformed them and made them central to worship as never before. Before the Reformation, religious music tended to be sung by trained specialists, the congregation mostly remaining silent. Texts for music, as for the entire liturgy, were almost exclusively in Latin. Lay people were not exactly passive, but their participation was limited by their understanding of the language, and worship was shaped and mediated by professionals, both religious and musical. As Luther's understanding of Christian teaching changed, his idea of what weekly worship could and should be changed with it. John Butt continues:

Luther proclaimed the doctrine of the priesthood of all believers: that the special sacrament of priesthood is not the exclusive prerogative of an elite priestly class, but of everyone who has faith. That had the almost magical effect of creating individual responsibility for one's own faith (which alone will bring salvation); but along with this came a new sense of communal responsibility, that the congregation has to work together to help everyone advance in faith. A Lutheran chorale reflects this, and nurtures it, by bringing the individual and the community together in a very potent way. Luther realized that singing songs together, whether spiritual or secular, created a profound communitarian resonance, a sense

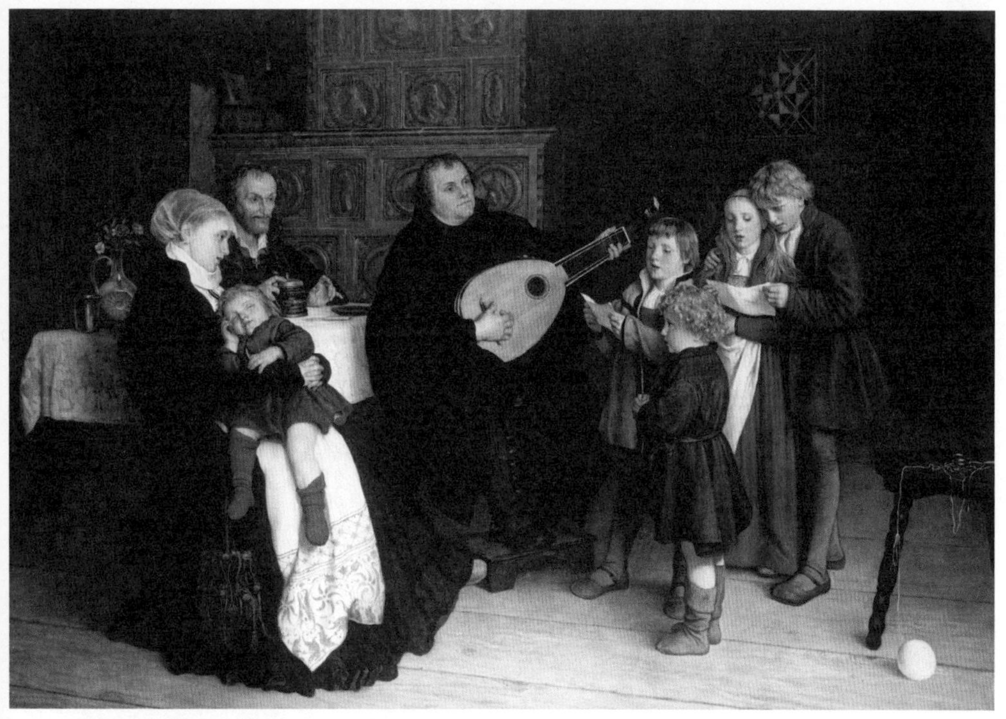

Music as part of the legend of Luther: Gustav Spangenberg's 1866 painting imagines the great reformer strumming while his children sing.

of belonging, and he quickly began to develop this as he moved further away from the Catholic church.

Luther effectively created modern German by translating the Bible into straightforward language that would be comprehensible to people from every part of the German-speaking world. He wanted them not only to understand and speak the word of God, but to be able to sing it: so he began writing hymns and music for the new congregations. '*So predigt Gott das Evangelium auch durch die Musik*,' he told his followers: God also preaches the gospel through music. In 1524, just seven years after his famous ninety-five theses had triggered the Reformation, he published the First Lutheran Hymnal. It contained eight songs, so is often referred to as the *Achtliederbuch*. Four of the eight were by Luther himself, among them his paraphrase of Psalm 130, '*De Profundis*': *Aus tiefer Not schrei ich zu Dir* – 'Out of the depths have I called unto thee'. The hymnal was so popular that later the same year he published another, this

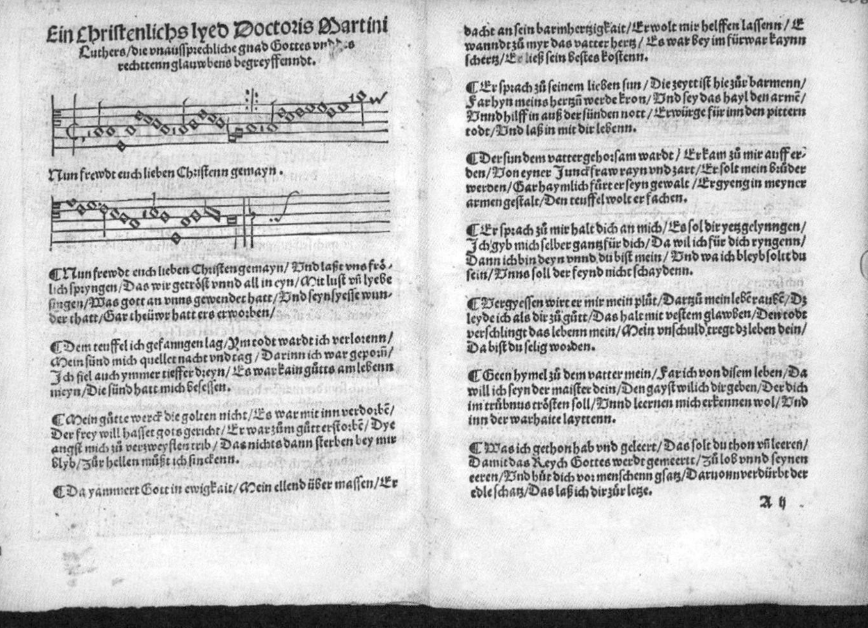

Ein Christenlichs lyed Doctoris Martini Luthers/die vnaussprechliche gnad Gottes vnd des rechttenn glauwbens begreyffenndt.

Nun frewdt euch lieben Christenn gemayn.

¶ Nun frewdt euch lieben Christen gemayn/ Vnd laßt vns frölich sprynngen/ Das wir getröst vnnd all in eyn/ Mit lust vñ lyebe singen/ Was gott an vnns gewendet hatt/ Vnd seyn sysse wunder thatt/ Gar theüwr hatt ers erworben/

¶ Dem teuffel ich gefanngen lag/ Ym todt wardt ich verlorenn/ Mein sünd mich quellet nacht vnd tag/ Darinn ich war geporñ/ Ich fiel auch ymmer tieffer dreyn/ Es war kain gütts am lebenn meyn/ Die sünd hatt mich besessen.

¶ Mein gütte werck die golten nicht/ Es war mit inn verdorbẽ/ Der frey will hasset gots gericht/ Er war zům gütt erstorbẽ/ Dye angst mich zů verzweyflen trib/ Das nichts dann sterben bey mir blyb/ Zůr hellen müßt ich sinckenn.

¶ Da yammert Gott in ewigkait/ Mein ellend über massen/ Er dacht an sein barmhertzigkait/ Er wolt mir helffen lassenn/ Er wanndt zů myr das vatter hertz/ Es war bey im fürwar kaynn schertz/ Er ließ sein bestes kostenn.

¶ Er sprach zů seinem lieben sun/ Die zeytt ist hie zůr barmenn/ Far hyn meins hertzů werde kron/ Vnd sey das hayl den armẽ/ Vnnd hilff in auß der sünden nott/ Erwürge für inn den pittern todt/ Vnd laß in mit dir lebenn.

¶ Der sun dem vatter gehorsam wardt/ Er kam zů mir auff erden/ Von eyner Junckfraw rayn vnd zart/ Er solt mein brůder werden/ Gar haymlich fürt er seyn gewalt/ Er gyeng in meyner armen gestalt/ Den teuffel wolt er fachen.

¶ Er sprach zů mir halt dich an mich/ Es sol dir yetz gelynngen/ Ich gyb mich selber gantz für dich/ Da wil ich für dich ryngenn/ Dann ich bin deyn vnnd du bist mein/ Vnd wa ich bleyb solt du sein/ Vnns soll der feynd nicht schaydenn.

¶ Vergyessen wirt er mir mein plůt/ Dartzů mein lebẽ raubẽ/ Dz leyde ich als dir zů gütt/ Das halt mit vestem glawben/ Den todt verschlingt das lebenn mein/ Mein vnschuld tregt dz leben dein/ Da bist du selig worden.

¶ Geen hymel zů dem vatter mein/ Far ich von disem leben/ Da will ich seyn der maister dein/ Den gayst wil ich dir geben/ Der dich im trübnus trösten soll/ Vnnd leernen mich erkennen wol/ Vnd inn der warhait layttenn.

¶ Was ich gethon hab vnd geleert/ Das solt du thon vñ leeren/ Damit das Reych Gottes werdt gemeert/ Zů lob vnnd seynen eeren/ Vnd hüt dich vor menschenn gsatz/ Daruonn verdürbt der edle schatz/ Das laß ich dir zůr letze.

A ij

Luther's first hymnal, the 1524 *Achtliederbuch*

time with twenty-six songs. Passages from scripture, and reflections on them, were turned into rhyming verse, then set to tunes easy for everybody to sing and to remember. These new 'Protestants' could take possession of the Bible not just as a book to read in their own language, but as songs which even the barely literate could understand and carry around in their heads and hearts. Chorales were recited from watchtowers and sung in the street. In a profoundly new way, the word of God had been given to the people. It is well known that the success of the Reformation was due in part to the printing press; for John Butt, it was also in part due to the power of song:

Rhyming, of course, is a very important way of memorizing, getting certain texts into your head – to such an extent that sometimes you can't even get rid of them. Luther took the standard prose texts of the Order of the Mass in Latin, and turned them into rhymes that had a ring and a resonance to them. He was very good not just at doing this himself but at encouraging others to adapt existing melodies so that they took on a wonderful rhyming shape. In fact, one could argue that the Lutheran chorale lies behind much of the development of Western musical phraseology for centuries afterwards. It is a revolution in one sense, even if it is continuity in another. Pre-existing hymns and songs were sometimes used, but Luther completely reformatted them. Many people outside Lutheranism were envious of the way he somehow managed to create this community feeling of shared faith, in a way that other Christian denominations, at least in Luther's time, were not achieving.

The importance of all this in strengthening the resolve of the early Protestant congregations, and in attracting new members to join them, can hardly be doubted. Social psychologists have long recognized the importance for the cohesion of communities, and for the enhanced well-being of individuals, of the kind of activity that Luther was developing, involving frequent participation by the entire group. Steve Reicher is Professor of Social Psychology at the University of St Andrews:

Physical synchrony is very powerful in producing psychological synchrony. The more we are together in a bodily sense, the more that facilitates being together in a psychological sense, producing a sense of shared identity. Singing, chanting, standing, marching are all absolutely critical in producing a sense of 'we-ness'.

You could even say that the people who take part in these activities become part of my extended self. That shared identity utterly transforms our social relations. It moves them towards intimacy. When we have shared identity, we begin to stop seeing people as 'others'. They're like us, they're of us, they're with us. We trust and co-operate with them more. We help them, we support them more.

This is of course an insight common to many religions, as indeed for armies everywhere. It is, for many Muslims, a powerful aspect of Friday prayer, as large numbers stand, kneel, move and pray at the same time (Chapter 9). Every totalitarian regime has used marching, singing and synchronized movement – many people acting as one – to rouse participants and spectators alike to a confident conviction of shared purpose.

It is easy to see what this strengthened sense of community would have meant in the Germany of the 1520s and 1530s for those small groups of Lutherans directly challenging the authority of their local ruler, the Roman Catholic church or the emperor himself. John Butt adds yet a further dimension, suggesting that the very act of singing is likely also to alter an individual's mental and physical state, leading to a heightened receptivity:

Going back to the sixteenth century, we know that congregational worship and singing could be very emotional. People were moved to tears by musical experience, whether they were singing themselves or hearing someone else. When you are singing, your breathing changes. You are sometimes short of breath, and you sometimes have more oxygen than normal. You experience a sort of buzz, a change in your physiology which goes beyond the resonance of the music.

Because group singing helps believers to internalize the scriptures, moves them profoundly and builds congregational solidarity, it is no surprise that the Lutheran model of musical settings for rhyming vernacular texts was enthusiastically adopted by most other Protestant churches. It was taken up with particular verve by the more extreme Reformers, who liked to emphasize the Biblical basis of their worship by singing only the Psalms. Believed to have been written by King David himself, these ancient Hebrew poems were now rendered into German and French and English as easily remembered rhyming verse. Singing

A rare first edition of the Bay Psalm Book, designed for congregational singing among early Massachusetts Protestants. Most copies were used to destruction.

THE

VVHOLE BOOKE OF PSALMES

Faithfully

TRANSLATED *into* ENGLISH

Metre.

Whereunto is prefixed a discourse declaring not only the lawfullnes, but also the necessity of the heavenly Ordinance of singing Scripture Psalmes in the Churches of God.

Coll. III.

Let the word of God dwell plenteously in you, in all wisdome, teaching and exhorting one another in Psalmes, Himnes, and spirituall Songs, singing to the Lord with grace in your hearts.

Iames V.

If any be afflicted, let him pray, and if any be merry let him sing psalmes.

Imprinted

1640

the Psalms in your own language quickly became the badge of a new Reformed religious identity, individual groups identifying themselves with particular translations and the accompanying tunes.

It was a supremely successful strategy. Across northern Europe and North America, Protestants of all sorts sang themselves into new and resilient communities that survive to this day, and none more so than the Puritan English settlers who in the 1630s sailed to Boston with the Massachusetts Bay Company. These religious refugees were as erudite as they were pious: the basis of Harvard University was established in 1636 and two years later it was equipped with a printing press. The scholarly clergy of the young colony soon provided a new version of the Psalms in English, impeccably accurate in translation, set to stirring tunes, and reassuringly different from anything sung by other settlers. The Bay Psalm Book, the first book to be printed in British North America, appeared in 1640. It defined and united Boston Protestants for well over a hundred years. In November 2013 a first edition became the most expensive printed book in the world.

Anglicans, Methodists and Baptists in due course followed the Lutheran example, and in the nineteenth century the Catholic church too recognized the power of communal song, making vernacular hymns part of its liturgy. But it was above all African-Americans who enriched and transformed the pattern, combining European hymns with long African musical traditions to create songs with an incomparable intensity that forged and sustained a sense of community among slaves: the black spirituals.

One eighteenth-century English hymn demonstrates what this combination of simple language, rhyme and music can achieve in very different contexts: 'Amazing Grace'. The words were written in 1772 for the poor, and poorly educated, parishioners of Olney, Buckinghamshire, by the local Anglican curate, John Newton.

Amazing grace! how sweet the sound
That saved a wretch like me.
I once was lost, but now am found,
Was blind, but now I see.

Newton brings together a number of familiar biblical references (the parable of the prodigal son, the good shepherd seeking the lost sheep, Christ healing the blind) and puts them into rhythmic, rhyming verse. Only a single word, significantly the first, is of more than one syllable. The theology – the wondrous redemption of sinful humanity by divine grace alone – is impeccably Lutheran and instantly graspable: scripture and doctrine in four short lines.

About seventy years later, in the late 1840s, these lines were matched to the traditional melody 'New Britain', and published with a simplified musical notation in hymn books across the United States. The impact, especially among the barely literate populations of the south, was great. There it had a very specific resonance: before his conversion and ordination, Newton had been a slave-trader. He talked openly of his early sinful state, and later joined Wilberforce in the campaign to abolish the Atlantic slave trade. In Harriet Beecher Stowe's anti-slavery novel *Uncle Tom's Cabin*, published in 1852, the hero slave, Uncle Tom, at his moment of supreme suffering, sings verses of Newton's hymn to

'Amazing Grace' set to the tune 'New Britain', 1847

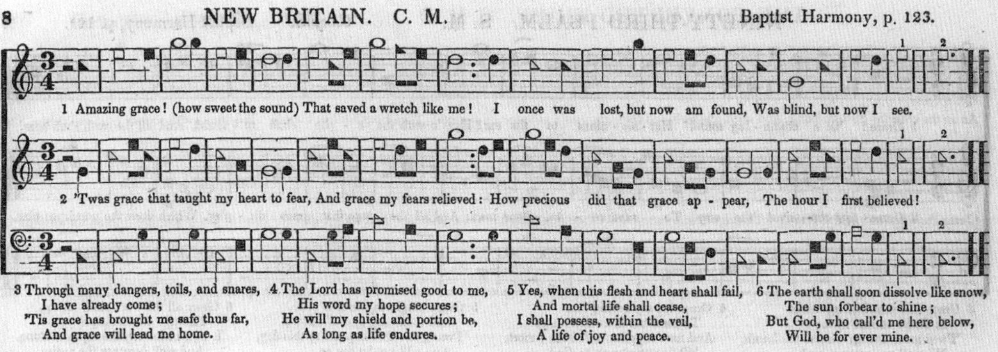

sustain himself. It is fiction, but it is surely exactly what Luther had hoped to achieve. A poorly educated man, alone and in distress, finds through music the words that strengthen his faith and give him hope – words familiar to him from singing in church, and so words that he knows he shares with a large community of which he is still a part. It is indeed amazing. Beecher Stowe's novel was a worldwide best-seller, and 'Amazing Grace' became one of the anthems of emancipation, included in hymn books given to Northern soldiers in the American Civil War.

From at least the 1940s it was performed in concert by black civil rights singers like Mahalia Jackson, and it was sung as an assertion of shared purpose by thousands, of all faiths, as they marched protesting for civil rights in the Southern states in the 1950s and 1960s. This may seem a long way from sixteenth-century Germany, but the name of one of the leaders of those civil rights protests was, not coincidentally, Dr Martin Luther King. Today, 'Amazing Grace' is one of the few songs whose words Americans of all generations are likely to know by heart. In Charleston, South Carolina, in 2015, the Reverend Clementa Pinckney, who had trained in a Lutheran seminary, was killed in a racially motivated mass shooting. Delivering the oration at his funeral, President Obama startled the huge crowd by beginning to sing – alone – 'Amazing Grace'. The response was immediate: within a minute, everybody was singing with him. Neither Martin Luther nor the man who wore our *Kirchenpelz* in nineteenth-century Transylvania would have been surprised.

The popularity of the Lutheran model of communal music-making shows no sign of abating. In countries where traditional church attendance is declining – rapidly in Europe, and at a slower rate in the US – many communities based on music are thriving, especially those that draw on African-American models. Everywhere, singing together seems to play a central part in some of the fastest-growing Christian movements. The Hillsong Pentecostal

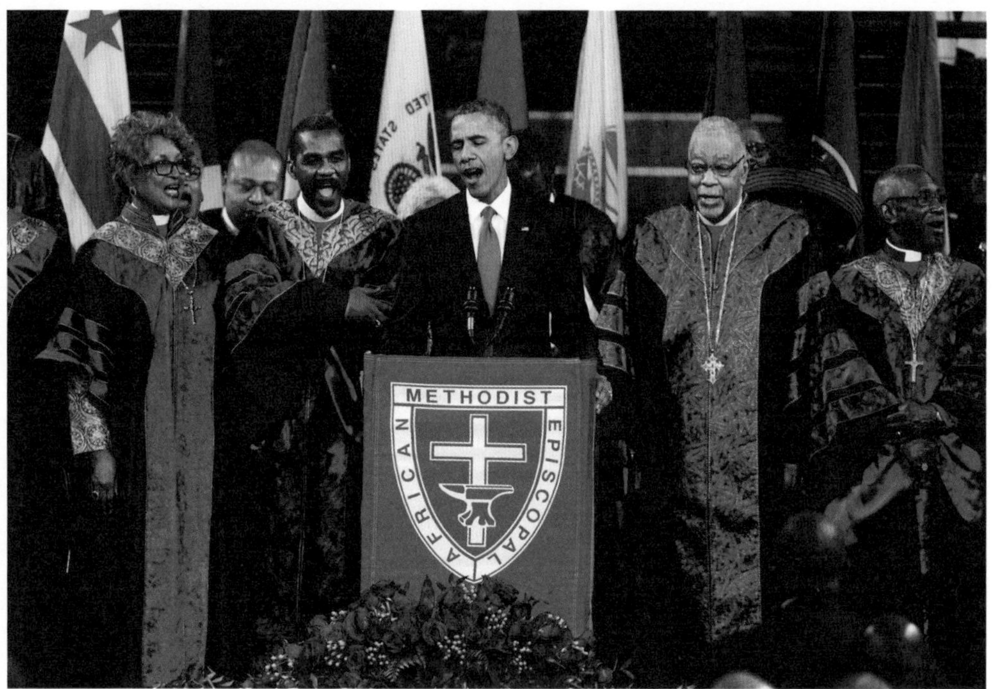

President Obama leads the congregation in 'Amazing Grace' at the funeral of the Reverend Clementa Pinckney in Charleston, 2015.

church in Sydney, Australia, now has affiliated churches around the world: the New York branch, for example, attracts over 6,000 people every Sunday for a service where all can join in the exuberant singing, cheering and (not always perfectly synchronized) whooping.

In the Lutheran pattern of Sunday worship, says John Butt, highly trained professional performers no longer have the monopoly of making music, but they are by no means excluded – in fact they remain a central part of the service:

Luther seems to have maintained a sense of the value to congregations of hearing as well as performing music. Lutheranism has always been very flexible in allowing congregational participation, but also not throwing away the more specialist, more complex forms of musical devotion. If you have a good choir, for instance, you will have a special piece for that choir to which the congregation merely listens.

But they will, John Butt argues, listen differently. This characteristically Lutheran approach changes the way in which a congregation hears music, precisely because they are also involved in making it. And that created the conditions for some of the greatest of all European music – J. S. Bach's settings of the Passion:

If you think of the liturgy for which Bach was writing his Passions, the fact that the congregation sings a chorale at the beginning, in the middle and at the end gets them into a particular mental posture, a resonating space, a receptive space; so that even if they're not singing at all during the Passion itself, a kind of active contemplation has been made possible, because they have all played a part in that communal framing of the entire event.

It is a pattern of mixed listening and participation which in the Protestant world has flourished over the centuries at every level of musical sophistication – a Lutheran legacy which is easily recognizable today in choral societies, congregational choirs and the humblest carol services everywhere. John Butt sees another, much wider and entirely secular resonance of this tradition too:

At least in British-American cultures it seems to have moved into the pop concert arena, where people listen to the performers, but also sing along with remarkable gusto. They know the words and the actions, and it is clear that there is a sense of community created. Protestant cultures do have an innate tradition of coming together in song.

It is a beguiling thought – Woodstock and Glastonbury as the unexpected late flowerings of the Protestant Sunday.

PART THREE

Theatres of Faith

All religious traditions attach great importance to the public, ritual enactment of the spiritual life. In such ceremonies, the members of the community are simultaneously participants and spectators, a dual role that is central to the creation of spiritual and social cohesion.

In this public realm of faith, the political and the religious are necessarily closely entwined. In sacred buildings and in ritual acts of sacrifice and offering, societies articulate a view of the proper ordering of the world. And in festivals, repeated over the generations, they define and re-imagine the spiritual community and enable it to continue beyond the single life of the believer.

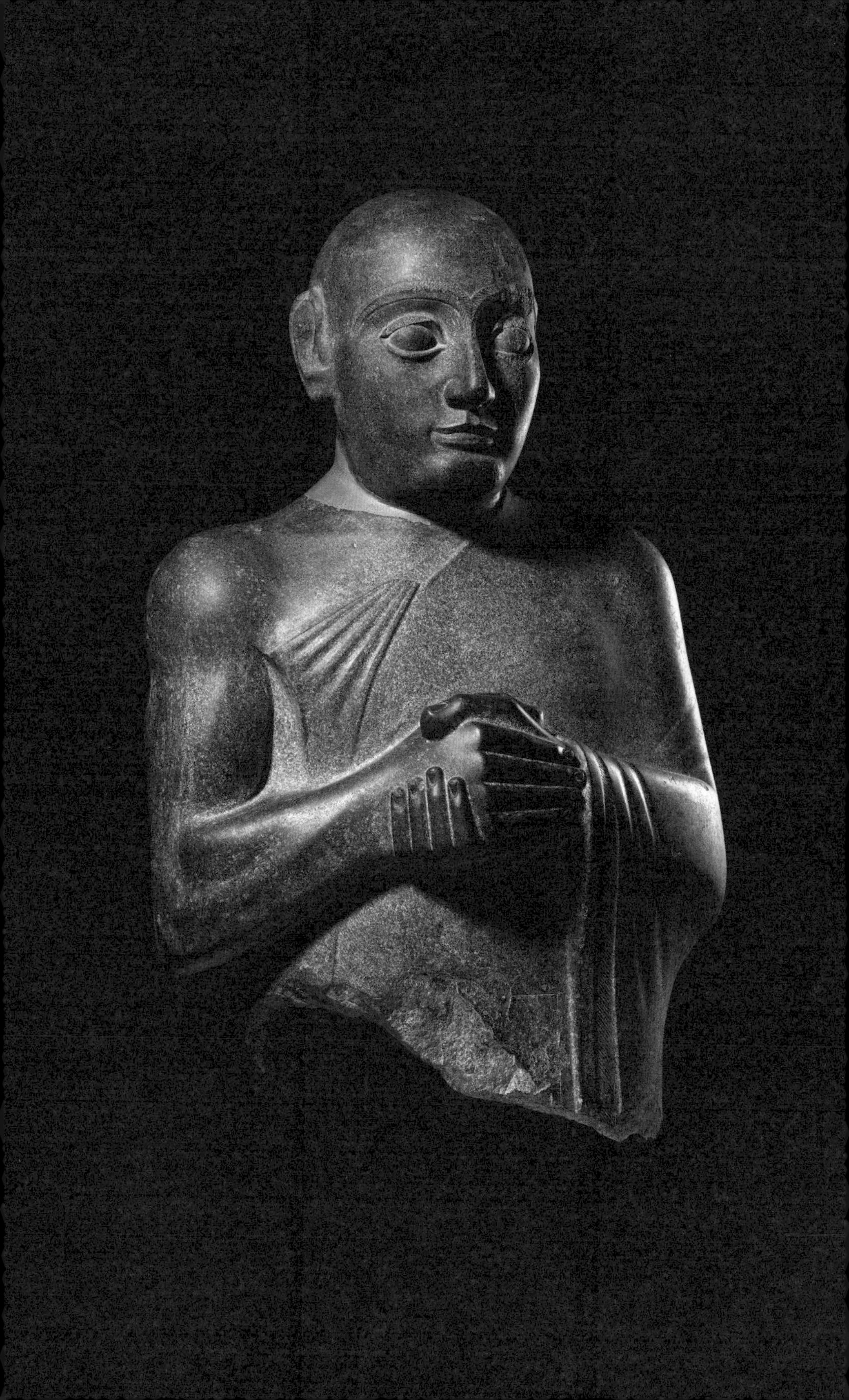

11

THE HOUSE OF GOD

The site of Göbekli Tepe is little known outside archaeological circles: yet it holds a central, perhaps the prime, place in the history of religious building. The name means Potbelly Hill, and it is in south-eastern Turkey, near the border with Syria. It is not much of a hill – only about fifteen metres high. The land around it is now barren scrub; but excavations begun in 1996 indicate that here, between 11,000 and 12,000 years ago, a society of hunter-gatherers came together to build an enormous stone monument. It contains at least 200 megalithic pillars, some nearly six metres tall, and most are arranged within circular enclosures. Some are decorated with relief sculptures of animals – generally not of the deer on which the local population fed, but of dangerous beasts such as lions, snakes and vultures. What was it for?

Most of the site remains to be excavated, but the archaeologist Klaus Schmidt, who led the digs in the late 1990s, contended that this huge, mysterious construction was not a settlement, but a sanctuary – a place of periodic gatherings, probably dedicated to cults focused on the dead. He found animal bones which suggested large occasional feasts held over several centuries, but not

King Gudea of Lagash, founder of the temple at Girsu (in modern Iraq), worshipping the god Ningirsu, *c.*2130 BCE

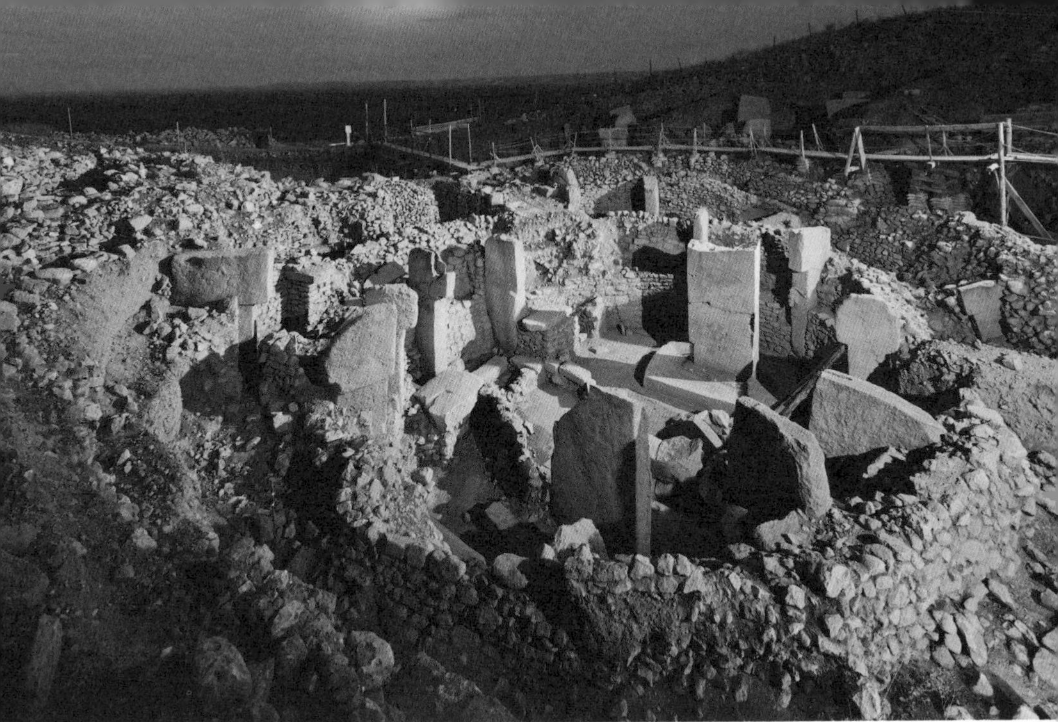

Excavations at Göbekli Tepe in south-east Turkey, believed to be the oldest religious site in the world

continuous habitation. Schmidt concluded that Göbekli Tepe, erected a full 6,000 years before Stonehenge, is the oldest large-scale religious construction anywhere in the world.

If he is correct, this site represents that pivotal moment in history when human beings for the first time created a colossal structure to accommodate rituals of faith. Like Newgrange, it was evidently a place built at great cost by a large community with a shared set of beliefs. In that sense it was a development, on a massive scale, of what we think we can discern at the mouth of the Lion Man cave in Chapter 1, a place where people from a wide area gathered for ritual celebrations.

Schmidt suggested that Göbekli Tepe might be even more significant: that a shared belief system not only drew scattered people to assemble here, but enabled its makers to collaborate on a greater scale than ever before. He argued that it was because hunter-gatherers first learnt how to co-operate in making a site like this for religious ceremonies that they were later able to live and work together in cities. Planning and building a great sacred space was the necessary trial run for urban civilization – or, as he strikingly put it, reversing the traditional sequence, 'First came the temple, then came the city.' In other words, we lived with the gods before we lived at close quarters with each other.

In the last two chapters we looked at how people try to engage with the divine, how strategies have been devised – contemplation, prayer and singing – to help us move away from everyday concerns, and focus instead on a world beyond immediate cares. But just as important as *how* we encounter the divine has always been *where.* In most cities and civilizations, the sacred structures are the grandest, the costliest and the most enduring, often the culmination of communal as well as spiritual life. This is true of the temple of Artemis at Ephesus (Chapter 16), of the great stupa at Sarnath (Chapter 14) or of the cathedral at Cologne (Chapter 14). But how do you design such buildings – places where gods may come to their people, and the people to their gods?

We can only speculate what ideas or politics lay behind the complex shapes and sculptures of Göbekli Tepe, though we may learn more as the excavations proceed. The oldest sacred spaces about which written texts survive – where we can be fairly confident that we know what people were thinking, and how the building process was directed – are just a few hundred miles south of Göbekli Tepe, in Mesopotamia. They were built about eight millennia later, shortly before 2000 BCE. The British Museum holds both texts and objects from one of these sacred sites, a temple in a city just north of where the Tigris and Euphrates meet. It was then called Girsu, and is now Telloh in Iraq.

Girsu was the religious centre of Lagash, a small state of about 600 square miles, containing several important and, by the standards of the time, large cities. Lagash had grown rich on agriculture and trade, importing gold from Sinai, copper from Arabia, and

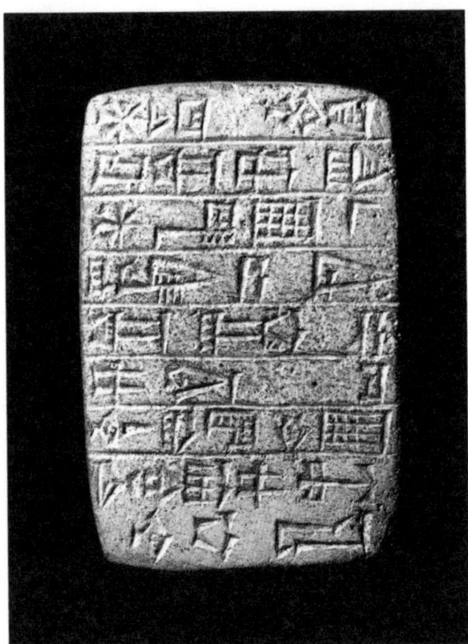

Left: Stone tablet recording King Gudea's renovation of the temple at Girsu: 'Gudea, ruler of Lagash, made things function as they should'

Opposite: Four copper gods plant foundation pegs for the temple at Girsu

cedar wood from Lebanon; and it had successfully fought off its neighbours under the protection of its principal god, Ningirsu, who governed rain and thunder, agriculture and war. His main temple, in Girsu, was the most important religious building in Lagash.

The first step in the creation of this sacred space, according to a poem preserved in a cuneiform text in the Louvre, was a visit by a god to Gudea, king of Lagash, in his dreams. The god instructed him to turn a piece of ordinary ground into the site for a temple to Ningirsu. Gudea was of course obedient, and had wealth at his command, but was uncertain how to proceed: 'Ningirsu, I am to build your house, but I don't know how! Warrior, you have called for the "proper thing", but lord Ningirsu, son of Enlil, the heart of the matter I cannot know.' He clearly soon found somebody who did know, because in the British Museum is the evidence of what happened next: four copper alloy figurines of bearded men about fifteen or twenty centimetres high, each down on one knee, holding in his hand a copper nail more than half the size of his body. As Sébastien Rey, the curator at the British Museum who is

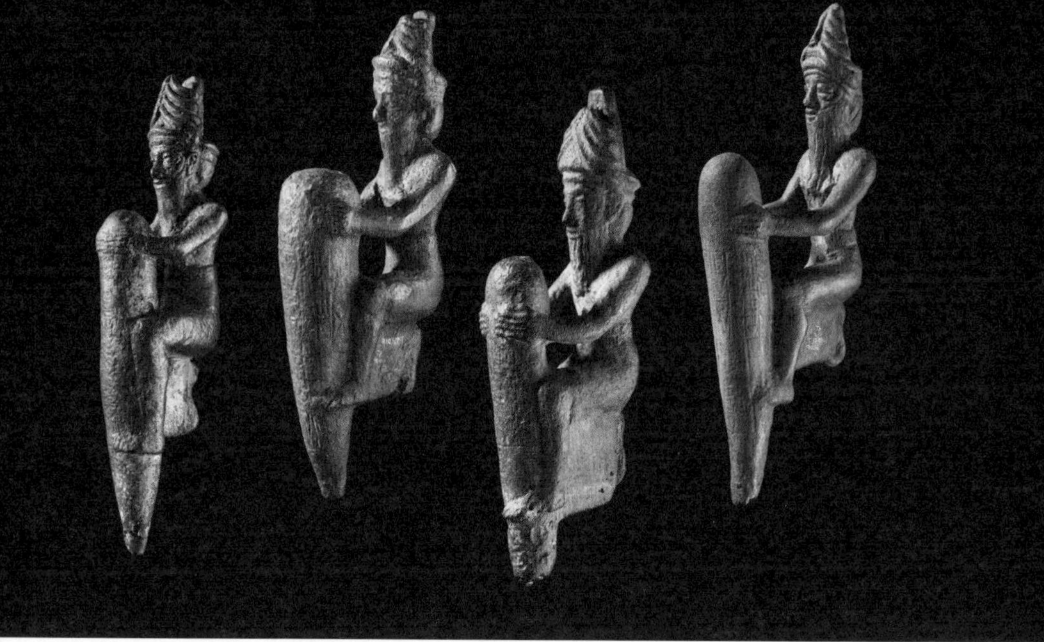

currently excavating the site, explains, they are not your average Bronze Age construction workers:

These people are gods: they are wearing tiaras with four horns, the symbol of divinity. They are carrying foundation pegs. Their role is to consecrate the ground, and they were buried to mark the boundary of the sacred space of the temple. Tablets placed in the foundations told the gods – and so ultimately us – that this temple was called Eninnu, which means 'House-fifty'. It seems a strange name, but fifty was the secret number of Enlil, the supreme god of the Lagash pantheon and the father of Ningirsu. Inside the sacred space of the temple were lots of different artefacts – statues, plaques and inscribed vessels – all dedicated to the god.

There would certainly have been statues of Ningirsu himself in his human form, but not one of these remains: they were made from composites of wood and precious metals – silver and gold, which were probably later melted down. But the British Museum also contains a copper alloy relief from a neighbouring temple, where

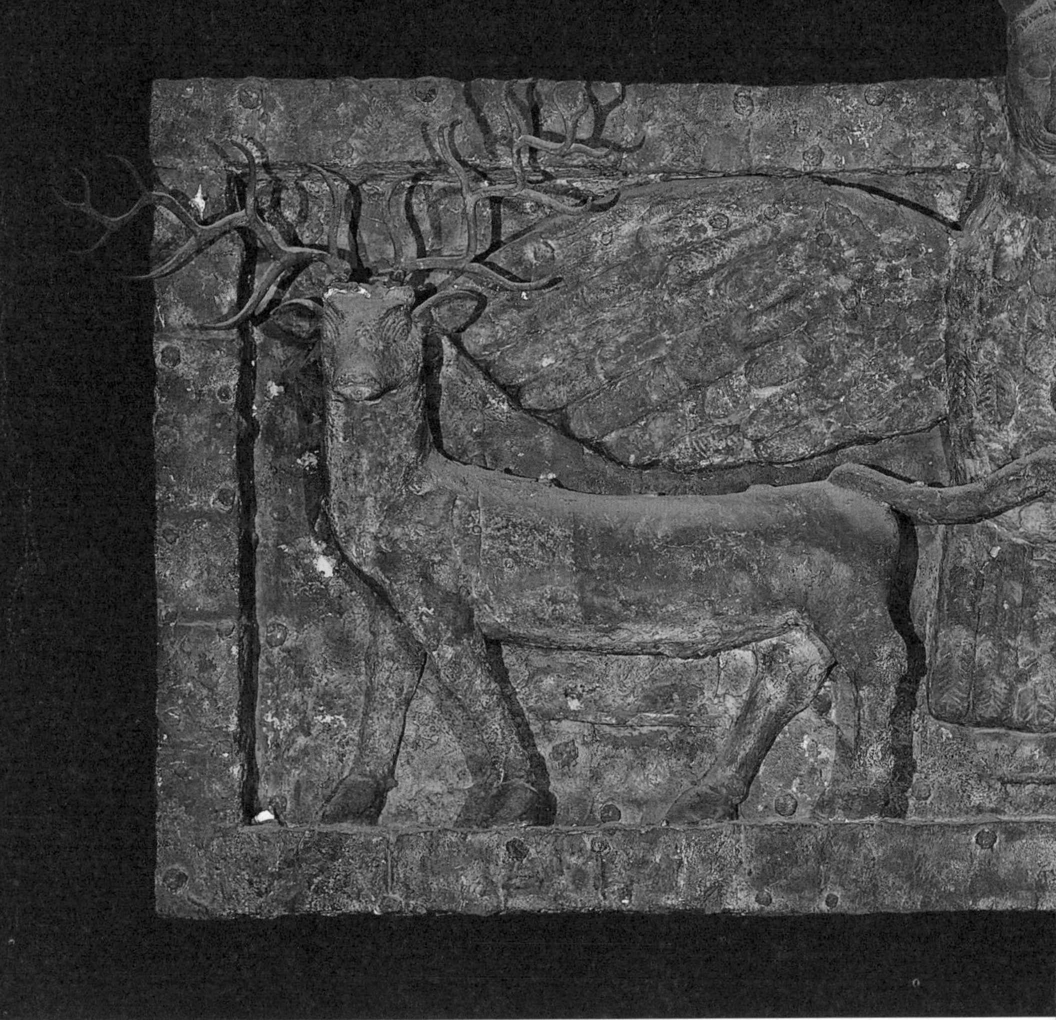

we can see Ningirsu in his non-human form – as the flashing tempest bird, a lion-headed eagle. He is the master of the wilderness, sinking his talons into a pair of aggressively antlered stags. He is so powerful that his head bursts out of the top of the frame into the space of the spectator. When he flaps his wings, he creates storms. He holds the forces of the natural world within bounds. He is the defender of Lagash.

The statues of Ningirsu in his human form would have been at the very centre of the temple, in an enclosed space, beside statues of

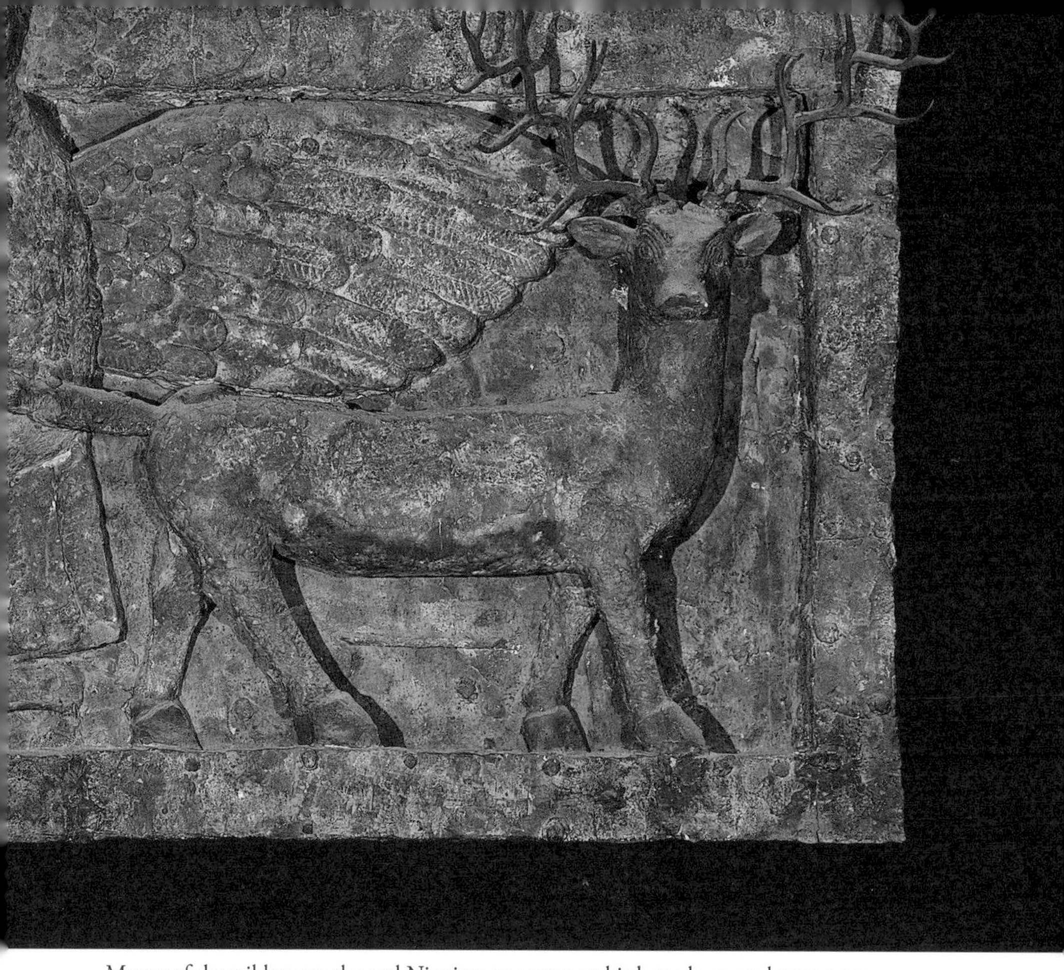

Master of the wilderness: the god Ningirsu as a tempest bird, made around 2500 BCE

King Gudea: god and builder side by side. We know what Gudea looked like, because he was a particularly enthusiastic temple-builder and many statues of him have survived. One of these statues is now in the British Museum (p. 154). Standing face to face with him is a disconcerting experience. The statue is virtually life-size, carved in dolerite, a hard green-black stone, so the features are boldly schematized. His head is completely shaved, his eyebrows are one great dipping bow over his eyes. He is wearing a robe that leaves one shoulder bare and his folded hands visible. This is a representation of a powerful man unconcerned about who might be looking at him, focused entirely on prayer. Sébastien Rey explains:

Gudea's statue was placed within the holy of holies, the most sacred place in the temple, so that he could gaze upon the god Ningirsu and worship him for eternity, even after his own death. His eyes are big, because he sees Ningirsu; he has large ears, because he can hear the voice and the message of Ningirsu. And as the ruler worships the god, the spectators worship both the god and the ruler.

Not all worshippers had access to all parts of the temple. There were gradations of sacred space within it: thresholds, marked by colossal stone door sockets and large corridors, through and across which only some were permitted to pass. Status would determine who could use which entrance, and how far towards the inner sanctum – how close to Ningirsu himself – they could go. The temple was, for the inhabitants of Lagash, the god's palace, and just as in a royal palace, most of the population would be kept outside, in the forecourt. Our word 'basilica', which derives from the Greek for a royal court of justice, shows how deeply this equation of the divine with the kingly has shaped later, Christian religious building. But in Girsu the temple was in a literal sense the god's home, with private spaces crafted to meet his every need, including kitchens and dining rooms, family rooms and spaces for guests. Here and in temples like it, the gods had their own beds, and there is evidence dating back to the first millennium BC of complex priestly rituals by which meals and clothes, vessels and other objects, were laid before them. Sébastien Rey continues:

A newly fashioned statue of a god was turned into something animated – a living entity – by means of a ritual to wash its mouth. After that, these cult statues received the attention of priests as though they were human beings. They were awakened in the morning, they were clothed, and they received two meals a day.

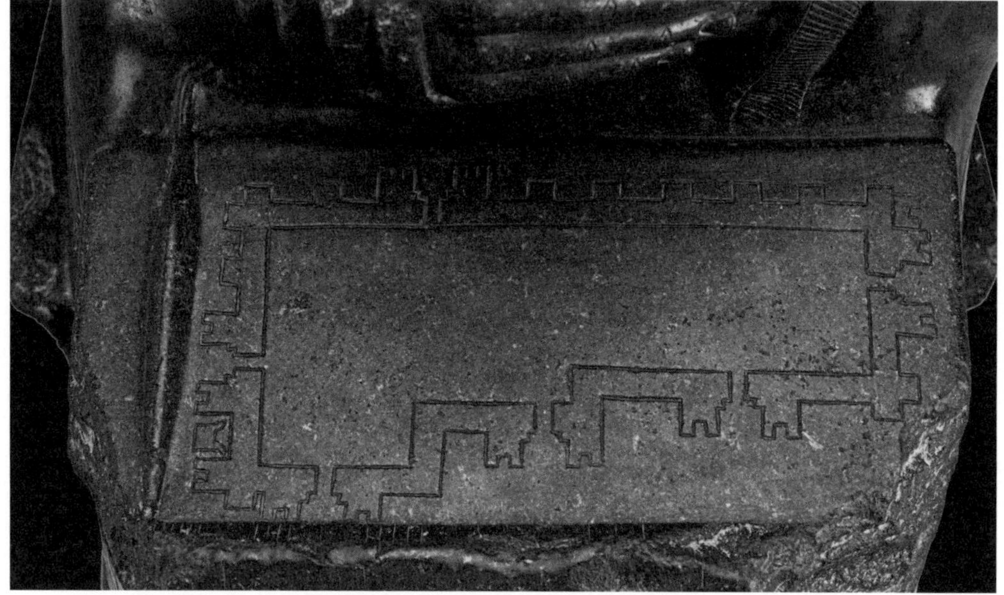

On the lap of a statue of King Gudea in the Louvre is a groundplan of the shrine of the god Ningirsu. It clearly shows the enclosure of sacred space where Ningirsu dwells and is worshipped, separated from the city by thick buttressed walls and gates flanked by towers.

At the end of the day, they were put to bed in their own chambers within the temple.

So it was not simply a case of human beings aspiring to live with the gods, but of the gods coming to live with us. And they were not confined to their temples. They owned the land of Lagash, so several times a year the statues would be taken out of the temples and carried around in chariots, or boats, touring the fields, leading grand processions. The statue of a god like Ningirsu would also set out to visit other divinities, especially his relatives, whose temple-homes were in other cities of Lagash: his sister, Nanshe, in Nigen (present-day Zurghul), his wife, Bau, close at hand in the same complex at Girsu, and so on. These processions of gods and people played an important part in what we would now describe as state-building. They reminded the inhabitants of Lagash that, although they lived in different cities, they were part of one state, subjects of the same ruler and united in their worship of the same gods.

The temple of Ningirsu was built, furnished and inhabited over 4,000 years ago. Yet the patterns and the ideas that shaped the sacred space in ancient Lagash are surprisingly familiar today across the whole of Eurasia. The doors of St Paul's Cathedral in London carry an inscription to remind the visitor that 'This is none other than the House of God', suggesting, at least metaphorically, that it too is a residence as much as a sanctuary. Inside are monuments erected in gratitude to God for battles won and a state preserved: the link between secular and divine power could hardly be clearer. In Hindu temples all round the world, the gods rest, and are wakened and tended at the appropriate hours of the day. A Roman Catholic church will usually have an image of the saint to whom it is dedicated, as images of Ningirsu presided in his temple – and in Southern Europe and Latin America statues of those saints sometimes visit other saints in churches throughout the city, as Ningirsu visited his family millennia ago.

The hierarchy of access which is already clear in the Mesopotamian temples at such an early stage is later replicated across the rest of Eurasia too. In Girsu most were excluded from the inner

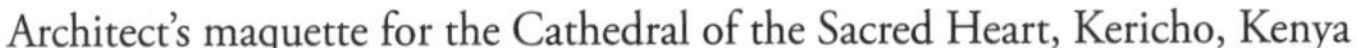

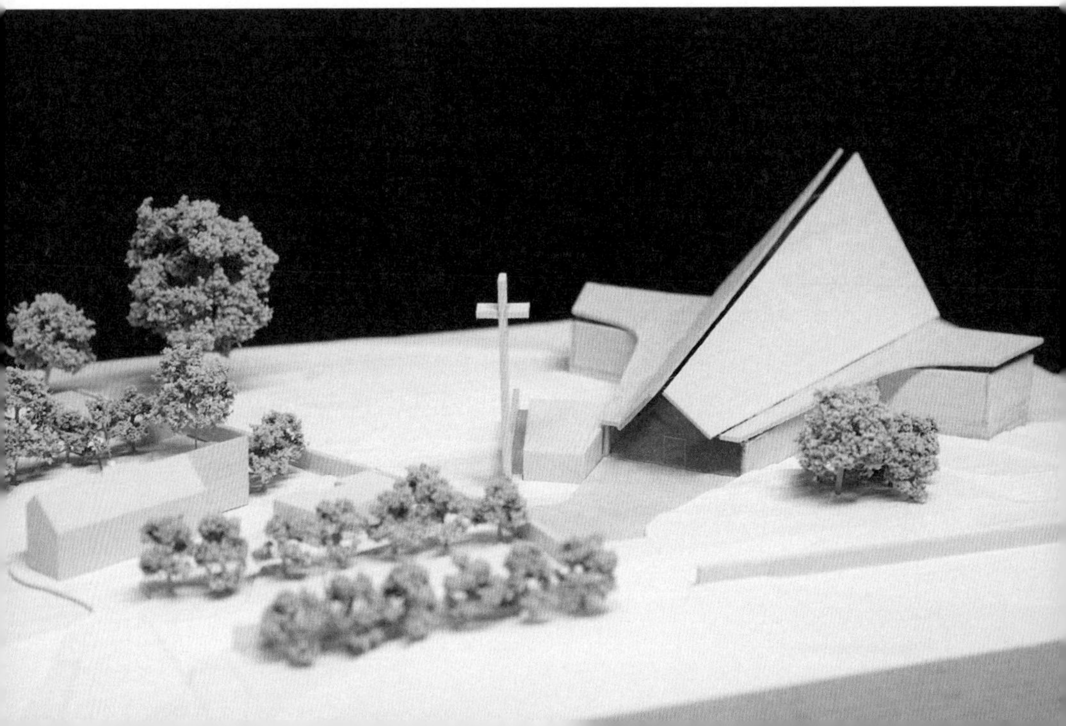

Architect's maquette for the Cathedral of the Sacred Heart, Kericho, Kenya

sanctum, where the god was housed, and remained in the forecourt. At the Temple in Jerusalem, over 1,000 years later, there was a comparable system of strict gradation, for gentiles, women, men and priests. In Zoroastrian temples only priests may approach and tend the sacred fire (Chapter 2). For much of Christian history altars have been similarly screened off and the space around them reserved for clergy. Even today, during the liturgy in Greek and Russian Orthodox churches, the laity cannot enter or see inside the holy of holies, to which priests alone have access. Across the millennia, statues of builders and benefactors have been set nearest to the sanctuary in Christian churches and cathedrals, where, as in Girsu, they are shown praying not just in perpetuity but in privileged proximity to the god they worship. The Mesopotamian tablets and sculptures in the British Museum show the beginnings of patterns of astonishing longevity, patterns where power secures access – and access further reinforces power.

At the opposite end of the documented time scale to King Gudea's dream, and gods carrying foundation pegs, are the designs and models prepared by the British architects John McAslan + Partners in 2012 for a new cathedral in Kericho in Kenya, about 125 miles north-west of Nairobi. Here every assumption about space seems to be different. The hierarchy of access, the fencing-off of particular areas, the rigid division between inner and outer space have all disappeared. Where Ningirsu's temple replicates many features of Royal palace architecture, the design here speaks of a desire for transparency and democratic openness. This society meets its god on a quite different footing.

The cathedral at Kericho stands high on a hill, with broad views over extensive tea plantations, on the edge of the Rift Valley. Its red-tiled roof can be seen from miles around. Consecrated in May 2015, it is a landmark for its region. It illustrates some of the issues architects today must confront as they take on the

An expanding cathedral: Kericho Cathedral reaches its greatest extent at the altar

millennia-old challenge of building sacred spaces for large communities, in this case a diocese of around 250,000 people. The simple lines of the architect's model show how inside there are no internal thresholds, no reserved spaces: the interior steadily expands, getting wider and higher as visitors move from the west door to the altar at the east end. It is entirely shaped and contained by ten exposed concrete ribs, in the shape of inverted Vs, lined with slats of wood, which filter the strong African light. Funding was provided by a foreign benefactor. But where the great temple builders of antiquity – Gudea in Lagash or Solomon in Jerusalem – brought exotic woods and metals from afar, the architects here were clear that this should be an African, in fact a Kenyan, building. Aidan Potter, one of the architects, explains their thinking:

We didn't want to import any materials. It's a grand building in its scale and size, but we didn't want it to feel as if it was imposing a European or American act of generosity, helicoptered onto this site. The floors are of Kenyan granite and bluestone, and the sculptures of local soapstone. The timber slats, the doors and furniture are of Kericho-grown cypress. And the red-pantile roof is a local material. Although it was funded by an act of generous philanthropy, we did want to make sure that the building had a certain frugal quality.

Once the materials had been chosen, the design was discussed with the Bishop of Kericho, Emmanuel Okombo, and the decision taken to dissolve the divisions of space often found in traditional churches:

The bishop was very keen to promote a greater engagement of the congregation in the celebration of the Mass. So the cathedral departs from the classic Latin cross configuration. The space and the volume get bigger the nearer you get to the altar: the idea of that was to make sure that there was the largest possible number of people around a very wide altar – to maximize the visual and social engagement of the entire community in the focus on the Mass.

Remarkably, Aidan Potter found that one of the most important considerations in designing the new building was exactly the one that had preoccupied the builders of Newgrange 5,000 years ago (Chapter 4): how the light gets in.

How do you make a sacred space? A lot of it is to do with the careful admission of light. The great mysterious spaces always pay very careful attention to light. In our cathedral, we used a roof light to cast a line of light down the central aisle of the church, coming to a focus on the altar. We wanted the perimeter of the building to be slightly gloomy, slightly darker, to enhance the dramatic effect of the light. The result was a gentle, serene space with a wonderful glow given off by local timber. It helps create an interesting dynamic of sacred space: it can comfortably accommodate two people, or fifteen hundred people – and no one is short-changed, experientially, anywhere in between.

As well as the architects and the bishop, the congregation played a major part in the planning process. The choice of local materials reflected the tastes of the community, just as the design reflected the way they come to church. Although it is contained by solid walls, which carry sculptures showing the Stations of the Cross, the perimeter of this sacred space is extravagantly porous. Aidan Potter explains:

The bishop had a beautiful idea, which was that down either side of the cathedral we would have multiple doors and at the end of the service all of them would be flung open. The idea was that, after Mass, everybody would go forth, as though sent, like the apostles, by Christ himself into the world outside. The numbers wanting to use the cathedral are so great in Kericho that the next congregation is always stacking up outside the cathedral, waiting to get into the next service. When they open all the doors and the first congregation leaves, there's a mêlée of people from the service meeting friends outside, and it's a marvellous moment – a very African phenomenon, which the building enables and encourages. It lets the building breathe socially and environmentally. At the same time, it creates an extra-communal community and a lot of social and sacred activities actually happen outside. It's a lesson that we can learn from Africa: that faith can be practised and celebrated outside the conventional enclosures that we design.

The cathedral at Kericho could hardly be further removed in conception as well as in time from the temple at Girsu, and it exemplifies a radical shift in Christian architecture world-wide in recent decades. This cathedral is still conceived as a house of God, but it is very much a house of God where all people are equal. There are no internal divisions of space to assert hierarchy or to separate the different parts of the community. It is a space from which the sacred can spill out into the landscape around it. Like the temple at Girsu, like all religious buildings, the cathedral at

Kericho, in its plan and in its materials, reflects aspirations and ideals that are as much political as religious.

The way in which sacred spaces operate may be changing, but much of the experience within them remains as it always has been. These spaces are hallowed by the presence and prayers of previous generations, sometimes stretching over centuries – an atmosphere of holiness, impossible to define, but not difficult to sense, which allows believers to feel closer to the divine. This may explain the striking increase in recent years in attendance at English cathedral services – even those whose beliefs may be uncertain are drawn by the music, the beauty of building and the sense of an enduring pattern and community in which they have a place.

This is one reason why abandoning sacred spaces is often so problematic. Although many countries in the West are increasingly secular, there are frequently mixed feelings, publicly voiced, about using deconsecrated churches for housing and simple commercial purposes. Many of them have become community centres, art galleries or concert halls, so remaining places of refuge from the worries of the outside world, where people come together to encounter something beyond themselves – a kind of secular sacred space.

This enduring respect for sacred spaces is clearest when a place of worship – mosque, temple, synagogue or church – is desecrated. Even if nobody is hurt, it is universally read as an attack not just on a building, but on a community. From the destruction of the Temple in Jerusalem in 70 CE (Chapter 27), to the demolition of the Huguenot church in Charenton in 1685 (Chapter 28), the mosque at Ayodhya in 1992 (Chapter 28) and the Orthodox churches and mosques in the Balkans in the same decade, such attacks shock and threaten as few assaults on property can: people, beliefs and buildings are instinctively understood to be one.

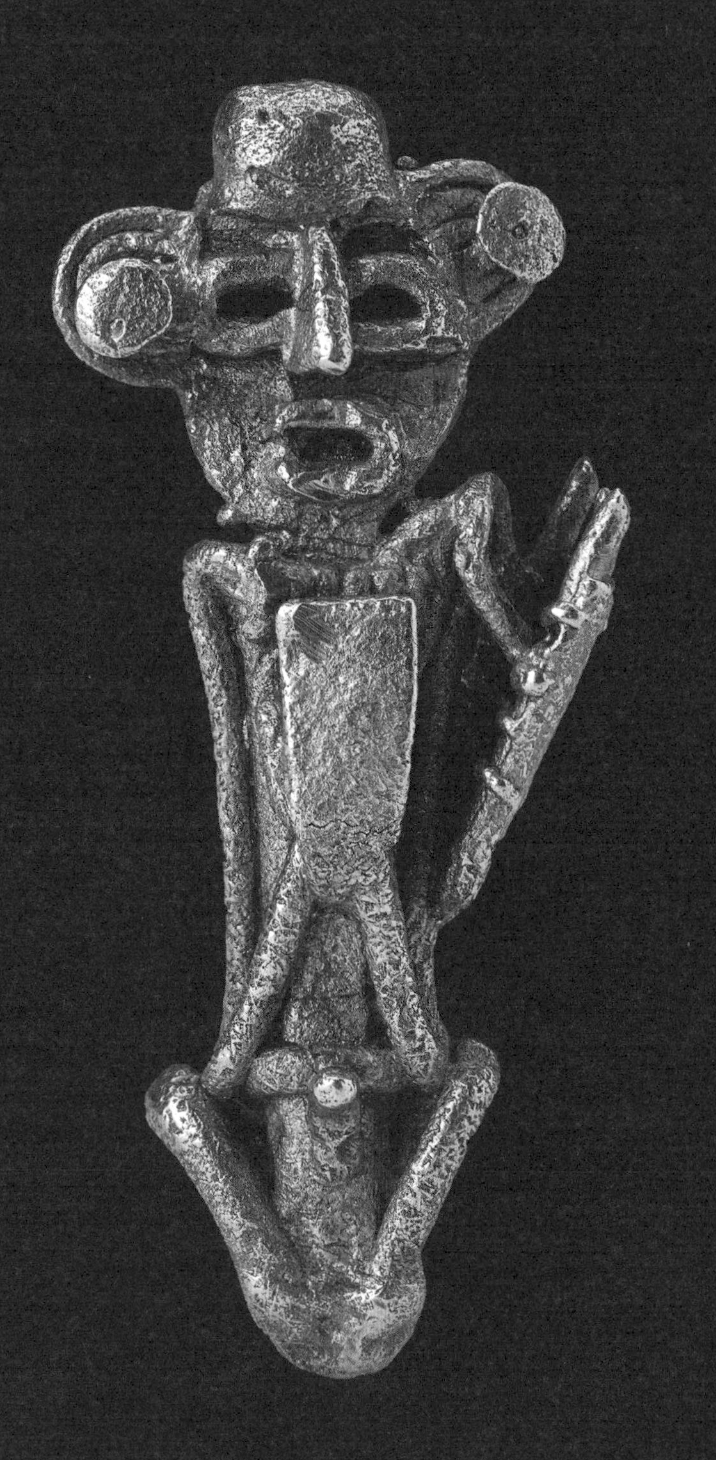

12
GIFTS TO THE GODS

Every now and then in the British Museum after hours, the cleaning staff find little offerings of fruit or flowers placed carefully in front of a statue – generally a Hindu statue, Ganesh a particular favourite. They are moving evidence of a habit of making regular small gifts – offerings of thanks or simply of reverence – that is deeply embedded in Hindu practice. It is of course a habit by no means limited to Hinduism: in most religions daily living with gods is inseparable from regular giving to gods – or giving to charity in the name of gods. This pattern of giving affirms a continuing relationship of reciprocal generosity and obligation.

The museum is full of such offerings, expressions simple or extravagant of human hopes, needs and generosity, over millennia and from all over the world. Most of these gifts to the gods were clearly offered by individuals, and some of the most poignant are small models of body parts, cheaply made in clay, metal or wax, presented in the hope of cure, or more often in thanksgiving for health restored. They are moving, but for the most part resolutely anonymous. Behind them lie cults which are often obscure, and lives and stories which we can never know.

The treasure of Lake Guatavita: a Muisca gold figure ritually cast into the lake around 1500 CE

We do, however, have much more evidence about how whole societies made gifts to the gods, and why as communities they chose to do it. This seems also to be a universal phenomenon, and this chapter is about two particularly striking examples, both played out in spectacular settings, that may truly be described as theatres of faith – Lake Guatavita, high in the Colombian Andes, and the Parthenon in Athens. They tell us much about the gods that were worshipped there, and, unsurprisingly, even more about those who worshipped them.

During the ceremony, which took place at the lagoon, they made a raft of rushes, embellishing and decorating it with the most attractive things they had.

At this time, they stripped the heir to his skin, and anointed him with a sticky earth on which they placed gold dust so that he was completely covered with this material. They placed him on the raft, on which he remained motionless, and at his feet they placed a great heap of gold and emeralds for him to offer to his god. On the raft with him went four principal subject chiefs, decked in plumes, crowns, bracelets, pendants and earrings all of gold. They, too, were naked, and each one carried his offering. As the raft left the shore music began, with trumpets, flutes and other instruments, and with singing which shook the mountains and valleys, until, when the raft reached the centre of the lagoon, they raised a banner as a signal for silence.

The gilded Indian then made his offering, throwing out all the pile of gold into the middle of the lake, and the chiefs who had accompanied him did the same on their own accounts. After this they lowered the flag, which had remained up during the whole time of offering, and, as the raft moved towards the shore, the shouting began again, with pipes, flutes, and large teams of singers and dancers. With this ceremony the new ruler was received, and was recognized as lord and king. From this

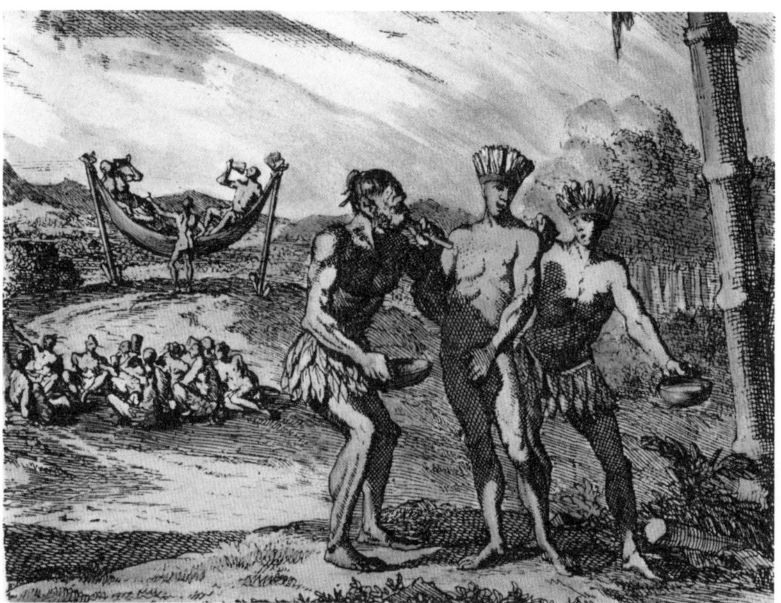

The Golden Man being covered in gold dust in preparation for his 'coronation' ceremony on Lake Guatavita, from Freyle's account of El Dorado

ceremony came the celebrated name of El Dorado, which has cost so many lives.

This is the famous account by Juan Rodríguez Freyle, written around 1636, of the 'coronation' ceremony of the ruler of the Muisca people, who lived in the north of what is now Colombia and who had been conquered a hundred years earlier by the Spanish invaders. By the time of Freyle's writing, *El Dorado*, the gilded man, was already well known to Europeans, the emblem of a fantastical world of wealth, which, if only they could reach it, they would be able to plunder at will. Attempts to do so had, as Freyle said, cost many lives, overwhelmingly indigenous ones, but also of hundreds of European adventurers, among them Sir Walter Raleigh, who in 1595 and again in 1617 attempted unsuccessfully to reach and to rob the kingdom of gold. Returning empty-handed twice, and having against orders attacked the occupying Spaniards, Raleigh was executed at the Tower of London in 1618.

What drew him, and fascinated all Europeans, was the gigantic quantity of gold reportedly possessed by the Muisca. What bewildered those who eventually got there was that the Muisca saw gold not at all in terms of monetary value, but as part of a cosmic choreography of equilibrium and exchange – as something which might properly, and best, be given to the gods.

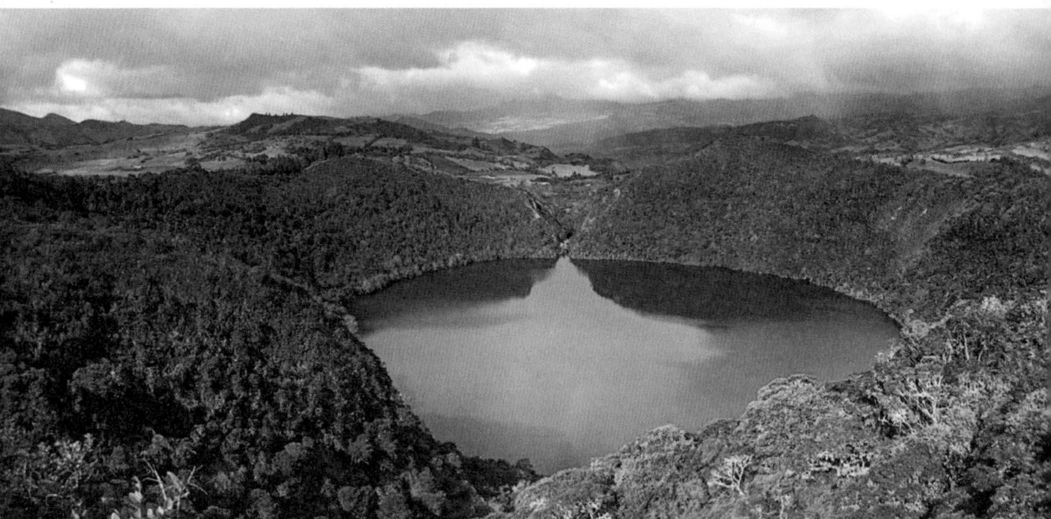

Lake Guatavita in the Colombian Andes, scene of the *El Dorado* ceremony. Clearly visible is the wedge cut in the rim of the lake in 1580 in an attempt to drain it and recover its gold.

In the British Museum is a small selection of objects once ritually thrown into the lake by *El Dorado* or his followers, and much later recovered by acquisitive Europeans: they include a few bells (as mentioned by Freyle) made of stone or slate, and some highly wrought figurines of clay and gold. Jago Cooper is head of the Americas section at the British Museum:

Lake Guatavita is one of the most beautiful lakes in the world. It is a small crucible lake in the high cordillera of the Andes of eastern Colombia, at the heart of the area inhabited by the Muisca: an indigenous community who thrived between 600 ce and their first contact with Europeans around the 1530s, and who were some of the finest gold-workers in the world.

You can see the quality of that work in a flat, almost two-dimensional figure of a man, two or three inches high, found at the bottom of Lake Guatavita in the early twentieth century (p. 170). Made from an alloy of gold with some copper, probably around 1500, he looks as though he is wearing a crown, has elaborate earrings and in one hand is holding a gourd used to hold coca leaves for chewing. Slight roughnesses at the edge of the figure, the remains of tiny tubes to carry the metal while it was still in its molten state, show that it was made by the lost-wax technique: a figure is finely modelled in beeswax, left to harden, and then coated in clay; when the clay is heated, the wax melts and runs out, leaving a void into which liquid metal can be poured. When that cools and hardens, the golden statue has been made.

It is a technique of which the Muisca were masters. Indeed we know that in order to have waxes with varying degrees of malleability, which would allow them to achieve the greatest possible precision in modelling, they kept several different varieties of bees. The making of the gold sculpture was not, however, just a feat of skilled craftsmanship: as Jago Cooper recounts, it was also in some measure seen and practised as a religious act:

The Muisca believed that humans are an integral part of an ecology of different relationships in a dualistic world – male/female, dark/light, liquid/solid, wet/dry and so on. They had individual deities, but these deities were essentially just part of a great system of cosmic equilibrium; they represented opposites that had to be brought together by humans, who had the power to mediate with this spiritual world. You could say that balance itself was the ultimate deity of the Muisca and of many other indigenous groups throughout South America.

When in any area of life that balance seemed to get out of kilter – if, for instance, there had been a long drought – offerings could be made in order to restore it. The process of making a little gold figure like this one played out the pervasive dualistic idea: wax melted and disappeared, liquid metal became solid, and a quite new object emerged. It was a process seen as a ritual of transformation and replacement, and the wax-/metal-worker would usually be part priest. The object created was thus by its very nature an ideal offering to help restore the equilibrium of the world, by being gifted to the gods at the portals to their world – buried in caves or under stones, or deposited in lakes.

Although the Muisca did use gold objects and ornaments for themselves, archaeologists estimate that about half of the gold-work they created was made to be offered to the gods, to be buried or placed in water, designed to disappear for ever. So it is perfectly possible that the visible lifetime of these gold objects, some of them complex works of art, might have been just a matter of hours. Our little figurine was probably made in order to be almost immediately consigned to the waters of the lake where, centuries later, it was found. Individuals might privately make gifts of single objects, but in a 'coronation' ceremony the act of offering fell to the new leader. Jago Cooper explains what happened:

When a 'Zipa', a new chief, rose up, he would be put on a balsa raft, and go out on to Lake Guatavita. This was a very special place for the Muisca, as it was the home of Bachué, mother goddess of all humanity. There the Zipa would immerse himself in a ritual purification, and throw objects like those now in the British Museum into the lake, the ceremony being witnessed by thousands of people. This enormous public offering, probably including objects given by people of all classes, was the trigger for a new equilibrium: to a gift like this, the gods would surely respond by making gifts in return, to the benefit of the Muisca and their new leader.

The most famous piece of Muisca goldwork to have survived, now in the Gold Museum in Bogotá, may well illustrate this ceremony (pp. 178 and 179). On a raft about twenty centimetres long stands a large, sumptuously dressed figure. Around him are twelve smaller characters wearing jaguar masks, and carrying banners and canes. Some may be rowers, ferrying the Zipa to the centre of the lake, where even pieces as impressive as this could be consigned to the water.

As far as historians can judge, the Muisca had no material economic metric by which produce and commodities were exchanged. This was a society without currency: value resided supremely in the creation of peaceful equilibrium between heaven and earth, by surrendering for ever things so glimmeringly attractive and so painstakingly made. Jago Cooper describes the contrast with the invaders:

Europeans, whose religious and economic assumptions were of course radically other, almost immediately began trying to recover for themselves what the Muisca had given to the gods. In 1580 a Spaniard cut a great wedge out of the side of the lake, drained it by about twenty metres, and found huge amounts of gold, which he sent back to the king of Spain. In the 1890s a British company spent twenty years planning and building a large tunnel through which they drained the lake down to the mud. They immediately began excavating, finding many things, but the next day the mud had baked solid as concrete and they couldn't get anything more out of it. Some of the objects they did recover were sold at auction – our little golden figure among them – and bought by the British Museum in 1910.

Lake Guatavita is now protected by law from future treasure-hunters.

*

Over: The most spectacular surviving piece of Muisca goldwork, thought to show the *El Dorado* ceremony. The large figure is probably the Zipa.

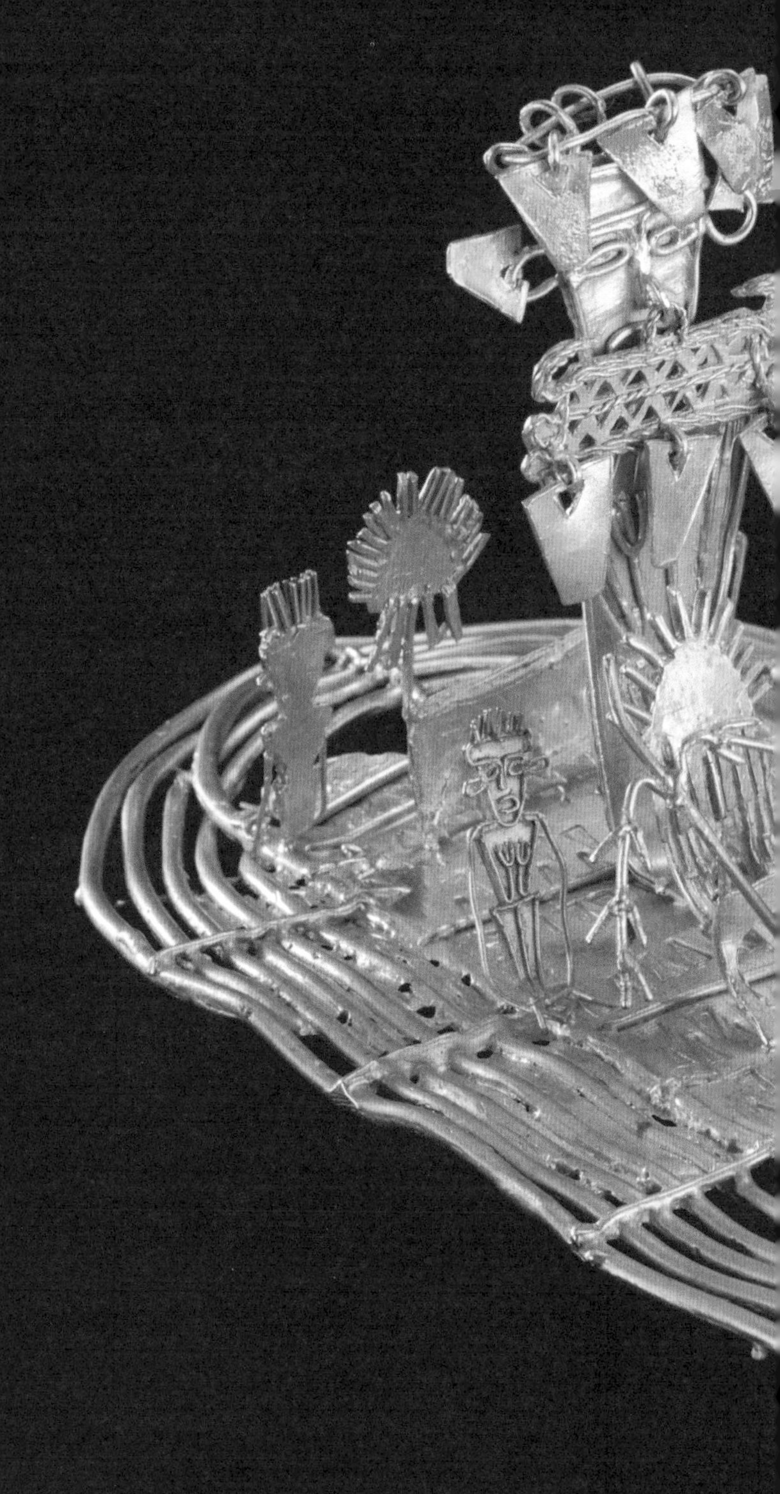

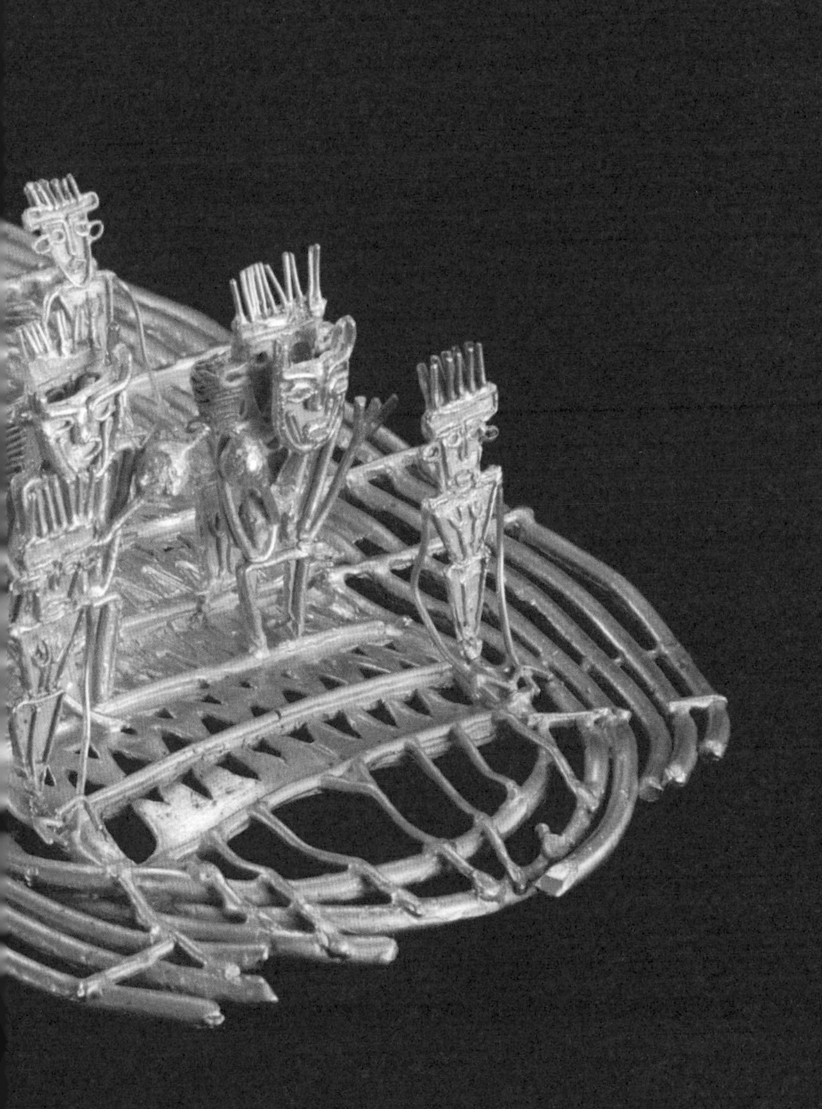

Europe too has a long history of offering precious objects to the gods, and, like the Muisca, of depositing valuable metal in water. Swords, shields and helmets are found in rivers or bogs across the continent, clearly put there deliberately as offerings. The custom mysteriously survives in the modern habit of throwing coins into fountains, wells and rivers, with an unspecified expectation that good fortune will somehow result. In Rome, the Trevi Fountain receives thousands of euros every day (the money is gathered and used for charitable purposes). But Europe has no real equivalent of Lake Guatavita. The great communal acts of giving have mostly taken place in cities, focused on the temples of the gods.

In the British Museum stand four large blocks of white marble. They are all roughly the same size, about eighty centimetres high, forty-five across and fifteen deep; they date from around 400 BCE, and are inscribed with neatly chiselled lines of Greek script. They are ledgers, literally carved in stone, created by ancient Athenian 'accountants'. Their client was effectively the goddess Athena herself, after whom the city had taken its name – an unusual act of homage in the ancient world – and these are records of the treasures kept in her temple, the religious centre of the city, the Parthenon.

These inventories were updated annually. They list objects such as wine bowls, silver cups and drinking horns, incense-burners and trays for offerings, a golden statue of Victory along with its wings, bracelet and crown, and so on. In the Parthenon frieze you can see figures carrying things very like these, as the citizens bring their offerings to Athena. Some objects, the inventories tell us, were gifts of individuals, others of cities, but all were intended to ensure that the goddess was properly, lavishly reverenced in the ceremonies held in her honour. Rather as Lake Guatavita held a particular significance for the Muisca, Athenians had a peculiarly close connection to the Parthenon: so one might imagine that these two acts of giving, on the face of it similar, are in essence the same. But there are significant differences, not least that objects given to the

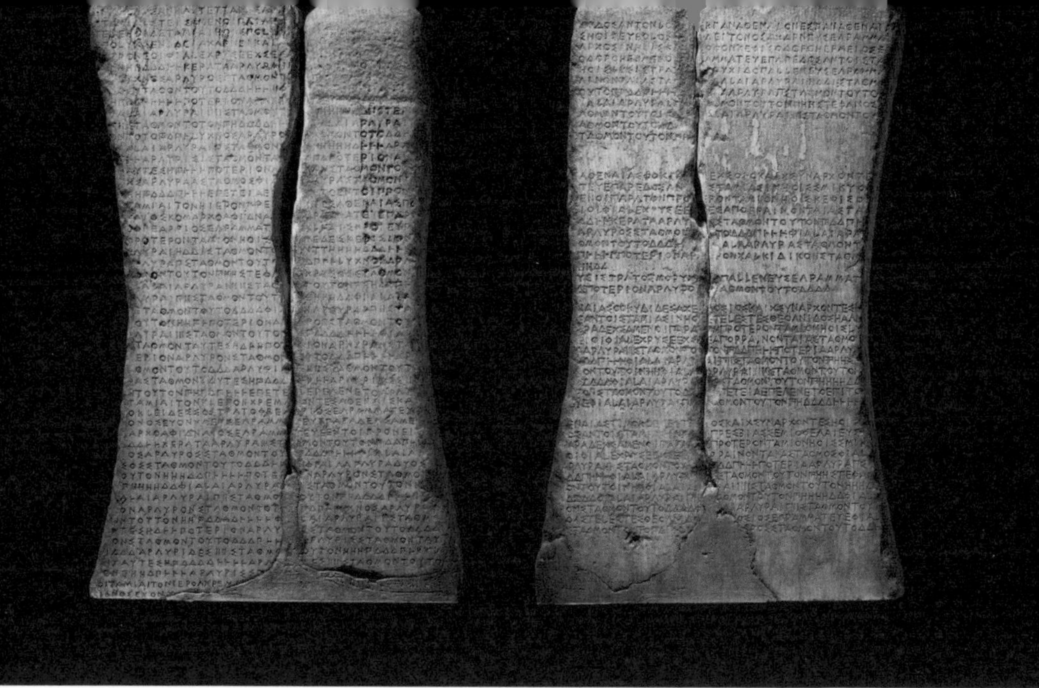

The marble inventories of the Parthenon for 426–412 BCE

Parthenon could be put on show, and – just as important – they could be removed at a later date. Athenian gifts to the gods were an altogether more tentative – and negotiable – business.

Tim Whitmarsh, Leventis Professor of Greek Culture at Cambridge University, describes the process:

The Parthenon was a very unusual temple: it was really an instrument of state. In the modern world we tend to think of the distinction between the sacred and the public/political as absolutely clear-cut. Phrases like 'offerings' or 'votive dedications' make sense to us as religious phenomena. But what is fascinating about the Parthenon and its contents is how they swing between those two categories of the religious and the political.

The inscriptions in the British Museum were part of the rhetoric of officialdom: uniform in size, and employing formulaic phrases that tell us who the officials in charge were at the time, who the treasurers and secretaries were, etc. But alongside their pragmatic function, which is to inventory the sacred possessions of Athena, these inscriptions also served as the projection of Athenian statehood.

Statehood in Greek terms is actually about centralized finance, about the way in which you organize taxation, bringing it together into a central spot. The Parthenon is the product not just of local taxation, but also of taxation of the Athenian Empire, and what is stored in it is really an expression of Athenian wealth and power. Some of the objects listed in the inventory could be used in ritual activities – knives and bowls, for example – but there is little evidence that the Parthenon was actually used for ritual practices. Instead, it was designed, around 438 bce, as the treasury of the Athenian Empire: a huge store of wealth, which was under the ownership and overview of the goddess Athena, but which was capable of being repurposed as state finance.

The Athenians are apparently making their offerings for a very different purpose from the Muisca; there seems to be little thought here of irrevocable gifts to restore a cosmic balance. In the Parthenon, the surrounding of the goddess with ostentatious splendour was no doubt in part so that she would continue to protect them, but it was also a demonstration of the Athenians' own remarkable achievements – and power.

Inventories like these reflect only a small proportion of the vast wealth that was held inside the Parthenon. But they are useful, because they allow us to track particular objects year by year. We can see when they were taken away and presumably melted down – with a rapid rise in withdrawals during periods of crisis and danger for the state. Tim Whitmarsh suggests that tablets like those in the British Museum may provide an example:

The Parthenon, dominating ancient Athens, was not just a temple but a storehouse of offerings and a demonstration of Athenian wealth

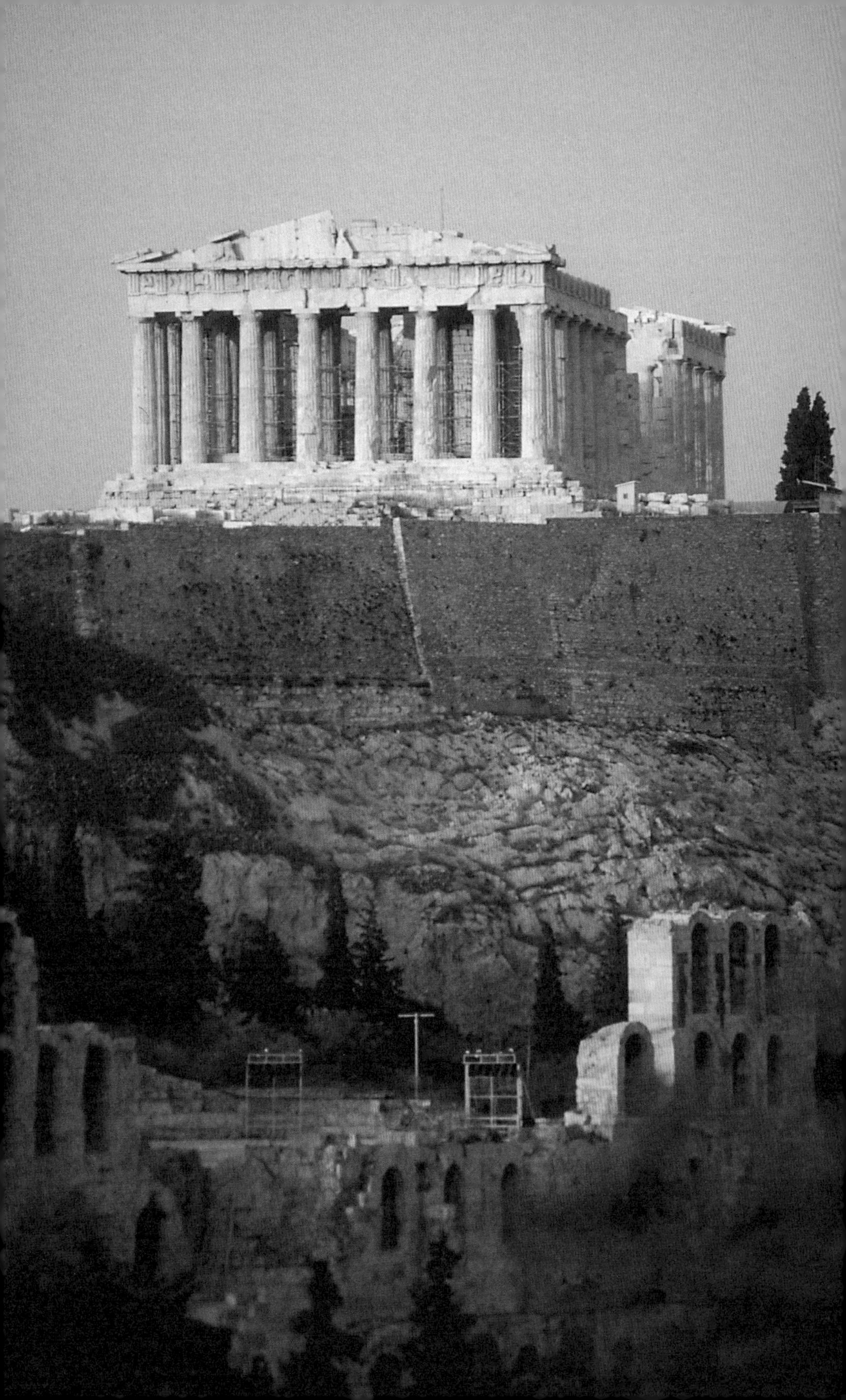

There is a very interesting moment in one of these inscriptions, where we have catalogues for two successive years: one is from 414 bce, the other from 413 bce. They are almost identical – except that in 413 there's a missing lustral bowl, a silver bowl used for water that would then be sprinkled out in ritual acts. Why this lustral bowl is missing is not clear. No one says it was sold off or it was melted down or anything like that. But this was a very significant date, because it is the time of a catastrophic Athenian expedition to Sicily and the decimation of the Athenian population, a time when the Spartans were fortifying and occupying a key Athenian site. So it was a period of severe loss and great financial insecurity in Athens. This one missing silver lustral bowl may well be the tip of a huge iceberg of objects removed.

This is perhaps the key difference between these two patterns of offering. The gifts to Athena came from a world of money, in which bronze, silver and gold had a real commercial value, which they never entirely lost. In an emergency, gifts made by the community could be taken back from the goddess and used for money, to secure the interests of her city – temporarily at any rate. But Tim Whitmarsh explains that there was a hitch:

The Athenians did draw lines between state finance and sacred finance. And though these lines could be transgressed, there was an understanding that if you took religious items and repurposed them as state finance, that was not a gift on the part of Athena to the state. The Parthenon was the sacred hub of the city, and you could not just take things as freebies. You had to give them back. The goddess had to be repaid.

To make an anachronistic comparison, we might say that the Parthenon was allowed to function in part as a central bank, or the International Monetary Fund – able to use its holdings to make loans in times of crisis, but on the strict condition of repayment in due course. Whereas the Muisca gift was ostensibly irrecoverable

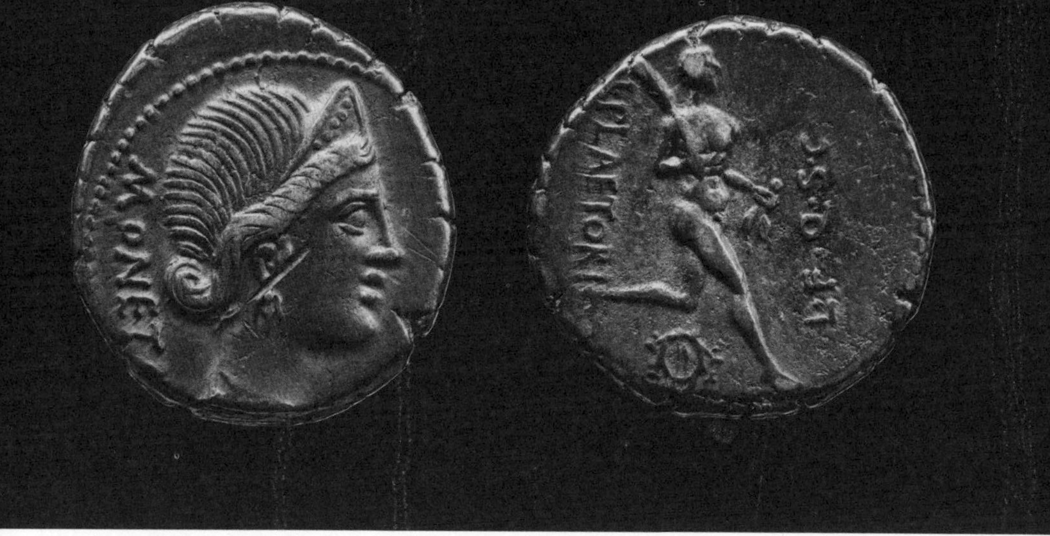

A Roman silver denarius of 74 BCE showing the goddess Juno Moneta, whose name gives us the word 'money'

and – they thought – for all time, the ancient Greek offering was continually provisional.

The intimate connection between the temple of a goddess and the finance of the state was by no means unique to Athens. The public treasury was located in a temple in many cities of the ancient world. In Rome, the temple of Juno Moneta on the Capitol was the place where the city's weights and measures, and many significant archives, were lodged. This was not just for safe keeping: in the realms of both history and commerce, the goddess was thought to provide the ultimate seal of authenticity. It was only appropriate therefore that her temple should become the site of the Roman mint. *Moneta* is today the Italian word for small change. And in English every time we use the word 'money' we acknowledge that the sacred and the financial have a long shared history.

In the next chapter, we shall be looking at another important role for the classical temple – this time not as a bank, but as an abattoir.

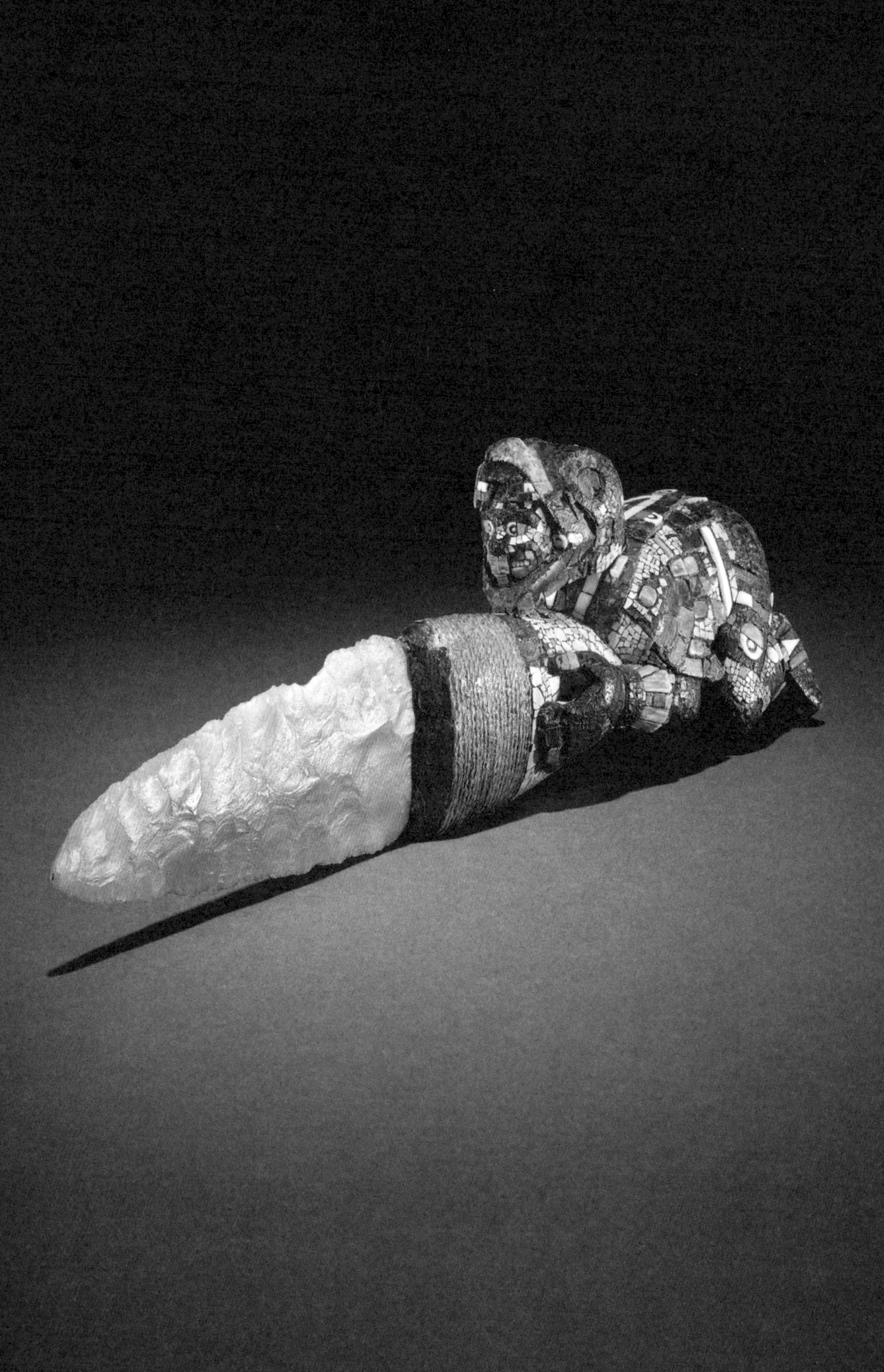

Fairport Public Library
(585) 223-9091
www.fairportlibrary.org

6/6/2019 5:51:51 PM

Customer Number: 29077009496709

Items Borrowed:

1: Living with the gods : on beliefs and p
Item #: 39077086301531
Due Date: 6/27/2019

Some Items May Renew - Call 223-9091

Cost of buying these items:
$40.00
Cost of using the library:
Priceless!

--Please retain this slip as your receipt--

13
HOLY KILLING

In the Mexican room in the British Museum there is a knife, about thirty centimetres long, with a handle made from *cedro* wood and a stone chalcedony blade, sharp-tipped and with carefully serrated edges. The handle is magnificent: the dark, sweet-smelling wood (prized in Mexico because it is particularly resistant to termites) is inlaid with a mosaic of pale turquoise and dark-green malachite, and enlivened by three different types of shell – mother of pearl, white conch and scarlet thorny oyster. As you admire the patterning and the contrast of colour, it can take a moment to realize that this is in fact a crouching Aztec. His face peers out from the open beak of an eagle head-dress, demonstrating that he is a high-ranking 'eagle warrior'; his chin rests near to where the terrifying blade begins, his teeth are bared and his eyes stare with great intensity down towards the tip of the blade.

The virtuoso craftsmanship of this object, and the cool, serene galleries in which it is displayed, give almost no clue at all as to where this knife has been or what it was for. To understand its purpose, move your gaze from the handle – so finely worked that each of the warrior's individual teeth is visible – to the blade itself.

A fifteenth-century Aztec stone knife used for the ritual removal of the hearts of sacrificial victims

The reason for this crouching man's eager anticipation becomes clear: he is waiting for blood – human blood.

In the years around 1500, knives like these – possibly this very knife – were used to pierce the skin on a human abdomen, working downwards from the bottom of the ribcage into the muscle fibres of the diaphragm. A temple priest would then insert his hand with swift efficiency into the newly formed cavity, reach

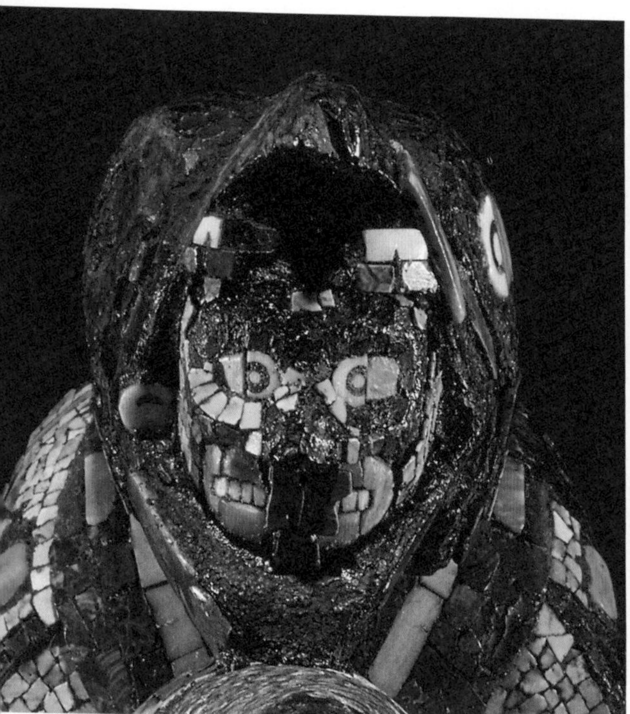

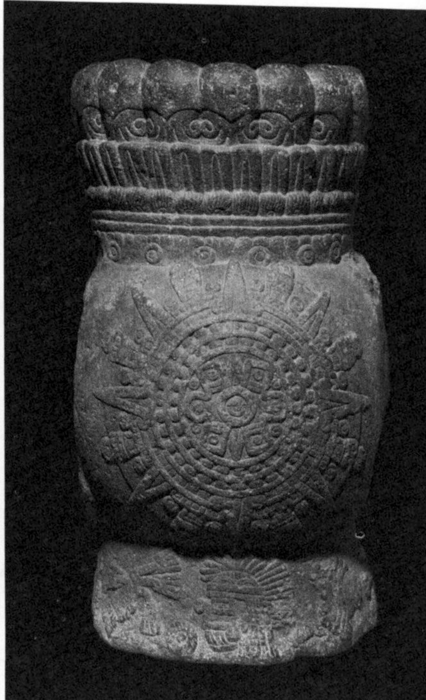

Left: Aztec warrior wearing an eagle mask on the handle of the sacrificial knife. *Right*: Offering vessel made of basalt, decorated with a sunburst on the front and human hearts at the rim, into which the victims' hearts would be placed

upwards and tear the heart from its moorings. He would then deposit it, still beating, in a shallow bowl carved into a basalt stand, specially decorated for just this purpose with a sunburst and a rim of sculpted human hearts. The dying body of the victim would then be thrown down the steps of the temple.

This spectacle of blood and pain would be watched by a cheering, festive audience of thousands, while percussion orchestras played and dance troupes performed; for a sacrifice of this sort would usually be the result of a military campaign. It served as an imperial victory parade, affirming through the killing of the victim the Aztecs' right to expand their empire under the protection of the god of sun and war, Huitzilopochtli.

Sacrifice. The Latin origins of the word mean nothing more than doing a sacred or a holy thing. It says a great deal about the religious traditions of the ancient Mediterranean, and how deeply they have shaped our habits of thought, that this 'holy thing' goes far beyond the idea of a mere offering or gift. Sacrifice implies not just putting something highly prized for ever beyond our reach, like the Muisca gold, but effectively destroying it, in the belief that we can propitiate a higher power and that a greater purpose can thus be served. The pouring of wine into the earth as a libation or the burning of precious incense are obvious examples – they can never again be used. But sacrifice can, and frequently does, go further: destruction can mean the spilling of blood and the taking of life.

If our – English – word, sacrifice, derives from Roman traditions and practices, the idea itself appears to be almost universal. Few topics have more exercised historians of religion over recent decades than sacrifice, and especially the public, ritual killing of animals or humans. Some scholars have seen in these practices a means of acknowledging the violence inherent in human existence, of limiting it, and assuaging or exorcising the collective guilt that results. Others have focused on the role sacrifices play in building community and solidarity. Understandably, few topics raise more uncomfortable questions about what it means to be human: few touch deeper emotions.

*

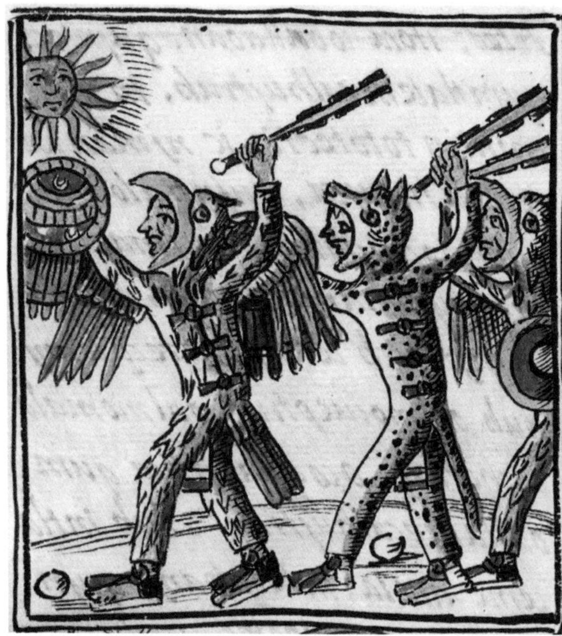

Left: A sixteenth-century Spanish view of Aztec eagle and jaguar warriors

Opposite: Tezcatlipoca, the Aztec god of change through conflict, takes the heart of a sacrificial victim, in a fourteenth-century Aztec codex.

Jago Cooper, head of the Americas section at the British Museum, believes that to enter into the thought-world that lies behind the Aztec stone knife, and the sacrificial killings for which it was made, you have first to understand what war meant to the Aztecs:

The Aztec Empire was relatively fleeting, lasting barely a hundred years: it arose around 1428, and always had warfare at the centre of its being. It flourished and expanded, covering much of modern Mexico and parts of the southern United States, until the arrival of the Spanish conquistador Hernán Cortés in 1521, who quickly overwhelmed it and effectively brought it to an end. In this highly militarized state, the rank of 'eagle warrior' was one of the highest positions in the official hierarchy. To become an 'eagle warrior' you had to capture a victim in battle and bring him back to be held as a prisoner or a slave – or to be publicly sacrificed.

While the Aztec Empire was expanding, England was engaged in the Wars of the Roses. European warfare at this date

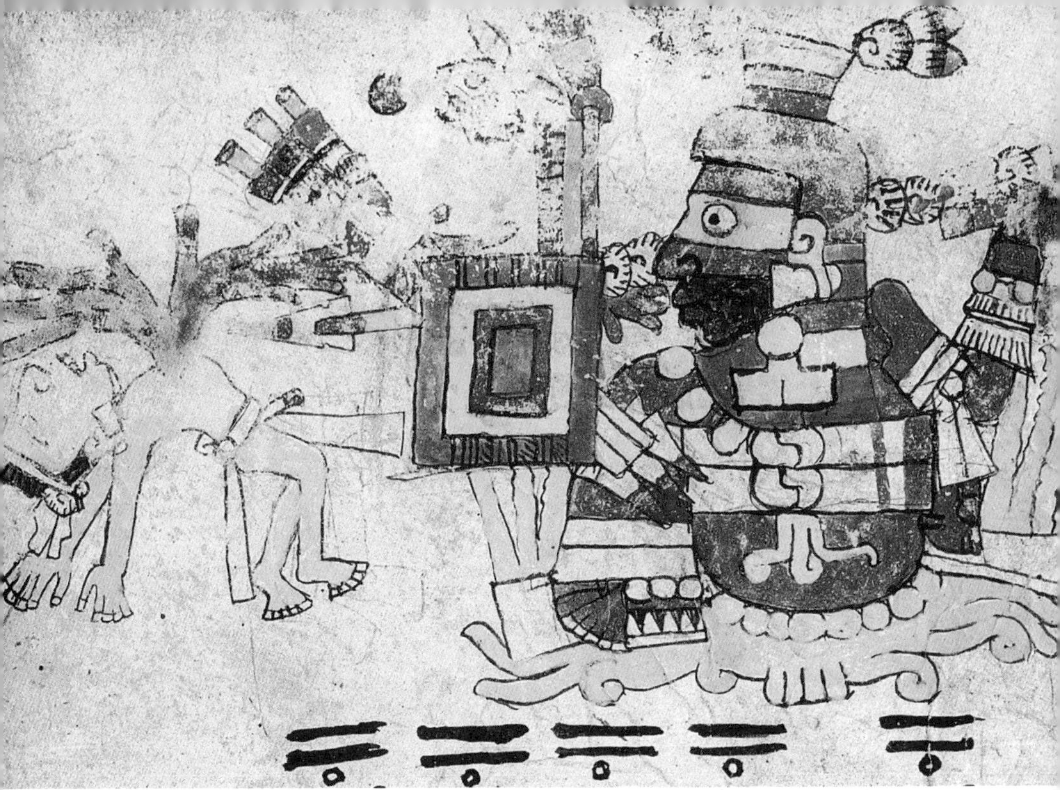

generally involved very heavy casualties: deadly volleys of arrows, thousands of armed men attacking each other with sharp metal weapons, attempting to hack each other to death. Whatever the outcome, hundreds on both sides would be left wounded or mutilated, painfully dying on the battlefield. Aztec warfare was profoundly different. The brutality of European warfare and the massacring of large numbers of people on the battlefield would have been abhorrent to them. The Aztec aim was not to kill, but to conquer – and to capture. Often a group of warriors would seize one victim and bring him back to the capital city. To do otherwise would have made no sense: the Aztecs relied on tribute from the people they had subjected, tribute produced by those who came home from the war. They were taking a sample of the opposing army, rather than trying to wipe it out. The person whose heart might have been removed with this knife was most likely a prisoner of war: that was the most common form of sacrificial victim within the Aztec world.

It is easy to imagine what a deterrent effect on potential opponents of the Aztec state witnessing a sacrificial murder like this might have had. And it is an intriguing, if counter-intuitive, thought that this wilfully bloodthirsty ritual may have been specifically designed to limit the killing and suffering inherent in warfare. What we can be certain of is that it suited the Spaniards to make much of the brutalities of the people they were slaughtering, and of the empire they were plundering.

The knife both dramatically symbolizes and physically embodies the two central aspects of Aztec warfare: the sacrifice of their selected victims and the tribute system they then imposed on their subject peoples. The different components of its decoration – turquoise and malachite, thorny oyster and mother of pearl – were all highly prized materials. They come from sites in different parts of the empire, many hundreds of miles apart, and they feature regularly in surviving tribute lists. Collected locally, they were transported to the capital, and there the wealth of the whole empire was combined and fashioned into magnificent ceremonial objects.

Alongside the sound psychology and economics of this way of making war, Jago Cooper describes, there was also powerful religious significance for the Aztecs in sacrificing human life.

The Aztec deity Huitzilopochtli, god of war, was associated with the burning sun. Aztecs believed that the gods had once sacrificed themselves, letting out their own blood in order to create human life. The human heart was held to represent a drop of the essence of the power of the sun here on earth. So by removing the heart from a human body, Aztec priests were offering it up to the gods, in part payment of an enormous debt owed by all humanity. It was a payment that would also help keep the sun moving through its appointed cycles – hence the sunburst on the stand to receive the recently removed hearts. To die as a sacrificial victim was therefore considered a good and useful death, in a society where the manner of one's dying mattered a great deal.

As we saw in the previous chapter, gifts to the gods are often given to elicit benefits in return. For the Aztecs, the outcome hoped for was the maintenance of order in both the empire and the cosmos, secured through the spilling of human blood.

The Nereid Monument is an enormous sculptured tomb from Xanthos, in what is now western Turkey, so named because of the many dancing figures of sea-nymphs, Nereids, which adorn it. It was built in the early fourth century BCE as a tomb for Erbinna,

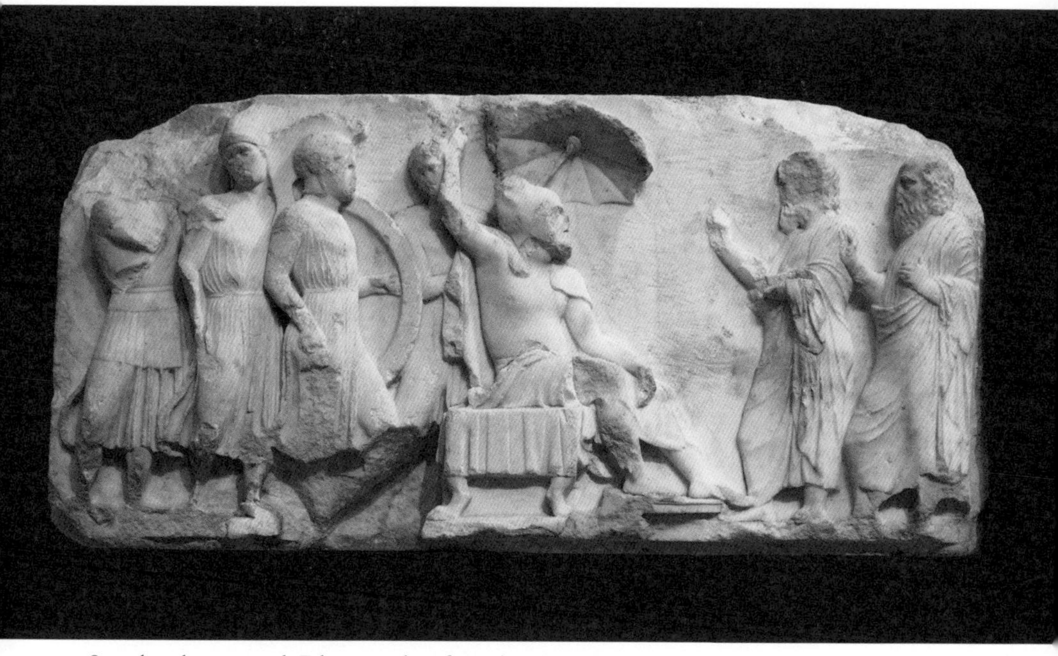

Seated under a parasol, Erbinna, ruler of Xanthos in western Turkey, greets arriving ambassadors. From the Nereid Monument, *c.*390–380 BCE

the local dynast, in the form of a Greek Ionic temple, and was richly decorated with many sculptured panels, now pale grey, but originally brightly coloured. They show Erbinna in various political and military roles, greeting ambassadors, banqueting and so on; and two of them show another key aspect of the kingdom's public life – the sacrifice of animals.

After the spectacular ritual murders of the Aztecs, we might think that the Nereid Monument returns us to the reassuringly calm embrace of the Greeks: classical robes and tunics and a lucid, chiselled aesthetic. But we find there is brutal violence here as well. One of the figures is trying to drag a goat by its horns, which the

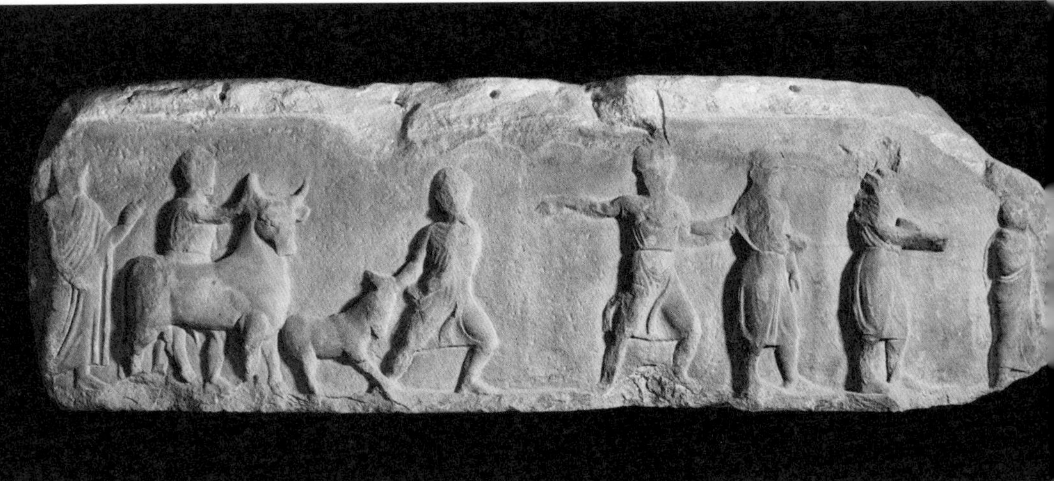

Beasts to the slaughter: animals are dragged to the sacrificial altar. From the Nereid Monument, *c.*390–380 BCE

animal resists with all its strength, digging in its hooves and leaning back as the man tries to haul it forward. A bull is being led along just behind. In the second panel it becomes clear what is in store for them both: a sacrificial altar. A priestly figure stands on one side; on the other is a man who has taken off his top to keep it clean. We are seconds away here from the screams of animals as the ritual unfolds: the shredding of flesh; the blood spurting and flies swarming; the reek of animal entrails publicly exposed. The precinct of a Greek temple could often be a sacred public slaughterhouse.

Sacrifices like this, involving the regular killing of domestic animals, were common everywhere in the ancient Mediterranean – among Greeks, Romans and Phoenicians, and in the Temple at Jerusalem for the Jews. It was clearly a nasty business, inevitably smelly with much animal waste, but it was at the heart of serious religious activity, domestic or public. Esther Eidinow, Professor of Ancient History at Bristol University, explains:

This is a key ritual, through which you communicate with the gods, whom you cannot see: it is through animal sacrifices that you worship and thank them. Through the entrails of the animals, you find out whether they are on your side, and you ask them for things.

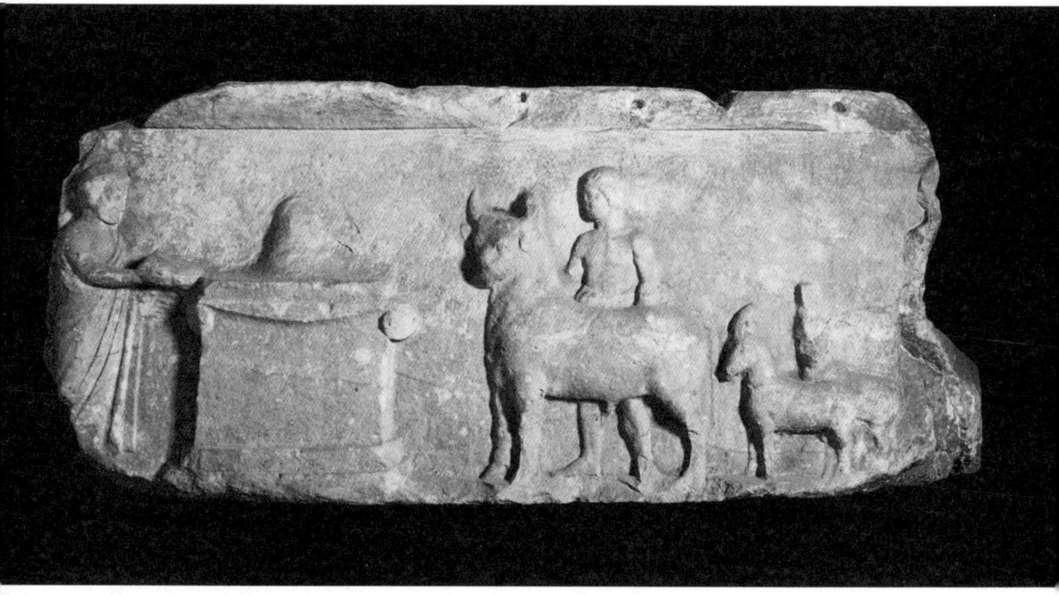

Preparing to kill the sacrificial beasts. From the Nereid Monument, *c.*390–380 BCE

In other words, animal sacrifice in some ways performed for the classical world the same function as prayer in the Christian tradition: it is the ritual language in which you may speak to, and listen to, the deity. In the Roman world, before battle, the livers of sacrificed animals were examined by experts to discover the intentions of the gods. Sacrifices could be conducted individually in the family home, or in small groups, but the great civic celebrations of course took place at the temple.

You would know that a sacrifice was going on at the temple because you would smell it. There would be a procession, leading a garlanded animal towards an altar. The animal was always carefully chosen, because it had to be a fine specimen, beautiful, valuable and pleasing to the gods. The altar was usually placed just in front of the temple – outside it, in the open air, so that the gods would be able to see and smell the sacrifice. The priest would normally be facing east, towards the rising sun. The overall effect was of a great technicolour stage set, designed for a large public.

The gods were expected to be part of the audience. A divine presence at sacrifice was always assumed – to hear and answer prayers, to smell the smoke of the incense and the burning animal remains, and to listen to the accompanying music. In theory the animals had to consent to being sacrificed (rather as the seals in Chapter 5): water was splashed on the heads of the bigger beasts to make them nod before they were killed. Esther Eidinow:

If it was a large animal like an ox, it would be stunned first and then its throat cut; if a smaller beast, its throat was simply cut very quickly with a long knife. At the point where the animal was slaughtered, the women in the audience would ululate – a kind of ritual screaming – which would have added yet another layer to the general sensory experience of the sacrifice.

Some scholars argue that elaborate rituals of this sort may have been an acknowledgement of the shocking nature of killing. If blood is to be shed, then it must be done publicly, solemnly, with the community gathered in the face of the gods. The animal killed must be honoured as it gives itself for the benefit of all within the ritual framework of the moral order. Sacralized slaughter accepts the guilt everybody should and must feel at the enormity of taking life; but it finds a way of expiating, or at least containing, it. As with Aztec ritual murder, a ceremony that seems to us brutal may carry a deep ethical charge.

In the Greek temple, once the animal had been ceremonially killed, a new element joined the assault on the senses: the sound, and the smell, of meat roasting. A sacrifice to the gods was usually followed by a feast for everyone, in which the gods were invited to join. In Book One of the *Iliad*, Homer gives a memorable description of a sacrificial banquet for Apollo offered by Odysseus and his fellow warriors. In Esther Eidinow's words:

They drew back the victims' heads, slit their throats, and flayed them. Then they cut slices from the thighs, wrapped them in layers of fat, and laid raw meat on top. These the old man burnt on the fire, sprinkling over them a libation of red wine, while the young men stood by, five-pronged forks in their hands.

Roasting the sacrificial meat for distribution to the people. The horn of an ox can be seen on the burning altar for the gods. An Attic vase made around 450–430 BCE

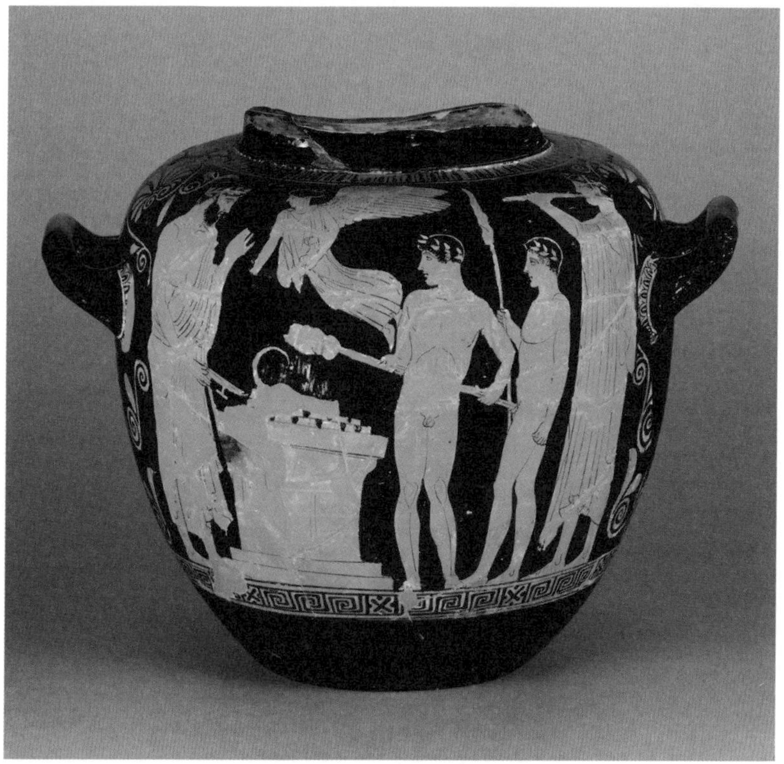

The sacrifice panels and the banquet scenes that accompany them on the Nereid Monument express the hope that its builder will for ever be able to take part in just such heroic celebrations, where the ruler himself often also assumed the role of priest. Viewed like this, sacrifice is not just about giving up a domestic animal for the good fortune of everyone else: it brings the community together, in political and religious solidarity, to share food with each other and with the gods. For many Greeks, this might be the only time they ever ate meat. Esther Eidinow tells how, here too, there were strict rules to be followed:

The carcass was divided up – some for the gods and some for the people. The thigh bones, sacrum and tail were taken out and burned for the gods, who consumed the smoke. The entrails were examined for signs of whether the gods had approved of the sacrifice, and then they were put on spits and barbecued. The body was carved up, and might be cooked and eaten there and then. There were sometimes dining rooms at a little distance from the main part of the sanctuary, where people could go and eat, or the meat might be taken home and eaten there. It was distributed fairly – the meat offered in sacrifice became part of how the society fed itself.

The 'liturgy' of animal sacrifice in the Greek world was then a process which simultaneously strengthened people's relationships with the gods and with each other. People went together through an intensely emotional and sensually heavily laden experience. Then they ate together. They were eating in the presence of the gods, but as the gods consumed only smoke, this was a reminder that they inhabited a different cosmological realm. The order of the world, human, animal and divine – separate, yet interconnected and interdependent – had again been reaffirmed.

The enduring influence of this great Greek civic and religious ritual, later taken over by the Romans, and practised throughout

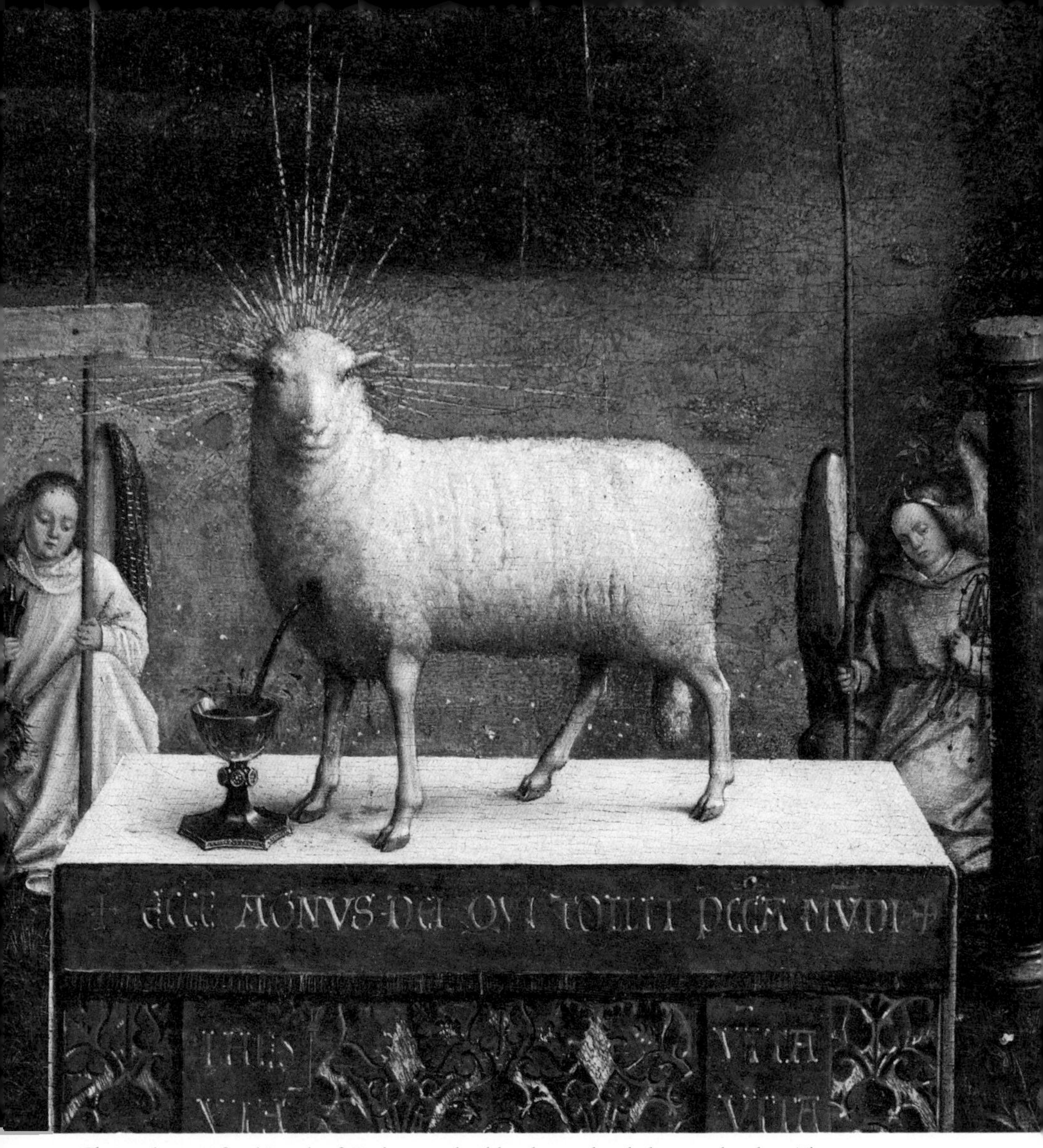

Christ, the sacrificial Lamb of God, pours his blood into the chalice on the altar. The central detail from the Ghent altarpiece by Hubert and Jan van Eyck, 1432

their empire, can hardly be over-emphasized. A ritual sacrifice is offered by a priest, a sacrifice which the people hope may be found acceptable. The smoke of incense rises. The blood of the victim is drunk, and the body shared and eaten by the community, which is united and strengthened by the process. The Christians who emerged from this classical world described the central ritual of their new faith as the sacrifice, and the supper, of the Lamb.

Quod this Somonour / and I bishrewe me
But if I telle tales / two or thre
Of freres / er I come to Sidyngborne
That I shal make / thyn herte for to morne
ffor wel I woot / thy pacience is gon
Oure hoost cride pees / and that anon
And seyde lat the womman telle hir tale
Ye fare as folk / that dronken were of ale
Do dame / telle forth youre tale / and that is best /
Al redy sire quod she / right as yow lest
If I haue licence / of this worthy frere
Yis dame quod he / tel forth / and I wol heere

Heere endeth the wyf of Bathe hir prologe / And
bigynneth hir tale

In tholde dayes / of kyng Arthour
Of which that Britons / speken greet honour
Al was this land / fulfild of ffayerye
The elf queene / with hir ioly compaignye
Daunced ful ofte / in many a grene mede
This was the olde opinion as I rede
I speke / of manye hundred yeres ago
But now kan no man / se none elues mo
ffor now the grete charitee / and prayeres
Of lymytours / and othere holy freres
That serchen / euery lond / and euery streem
As thikke as motes / in the sonne beem
Blessynge halles / chambres / kichenes boures
Citees / Burghes / Castels / hye toures
Thropes / Bernes / Shipnes / Dayeryes
This maketh that ther been no ffayeryes
ffor ther as wont to walken was an elf
Ther walketh now the lymytour hym self
In vndermeles / and in morwenynges
And seyth his matyns / and his holy thynges
As he gooth in his lymytacioun
Wommen may go saufly vp and doun
In euery bussh / or vnder euery tree
Ther is noon oother Incubus / but he
And he ne wol doon hem / but dishonour
And so bifel / that this kyng Arthour
Hadde in hous / a lusty bacheler
That on a day / cam ridynge fro ryuer
And happed that allone / as he was born
He saugh a mayde walkynge hym biforn

14

TO BE A PILGRIM

Bold was her face, and fair, and red of hue.
She was a worthy woman all her life,
Husbands at the church door had she five,

Thrice had she been at Jerusalem;
She hadde passed many a strange stream
At Rome she had been, and at Bologne,
In Galice at Saint James, and at Cologne;
She coude much of wand'ring by the Way.

Of all the pilgrims in Chaucer's *Canterbury Tales*, the Wife of Bath is surely the liveliest, and would probably have been the best company. Most of them have a fund of bawdy stories, but she is much the raunchiest, boasting hilariously of her ability to exhaust one husband after another with her insatiable demands in bed – and able to justify her behaviour with agile, entirely apposite, quotations from Old and New Testaments. She is also certainly the most widely travelled of the company. The list of places she had visited 'wand'ring by the Way' gives us a map of the world as imagined by the (prosperous) pious European at the end of the fourteenth

Chaucer's raunchy Wife of Bath rides in the margin of the Ellesmere Manuscript of the *Canterbury Tales*.

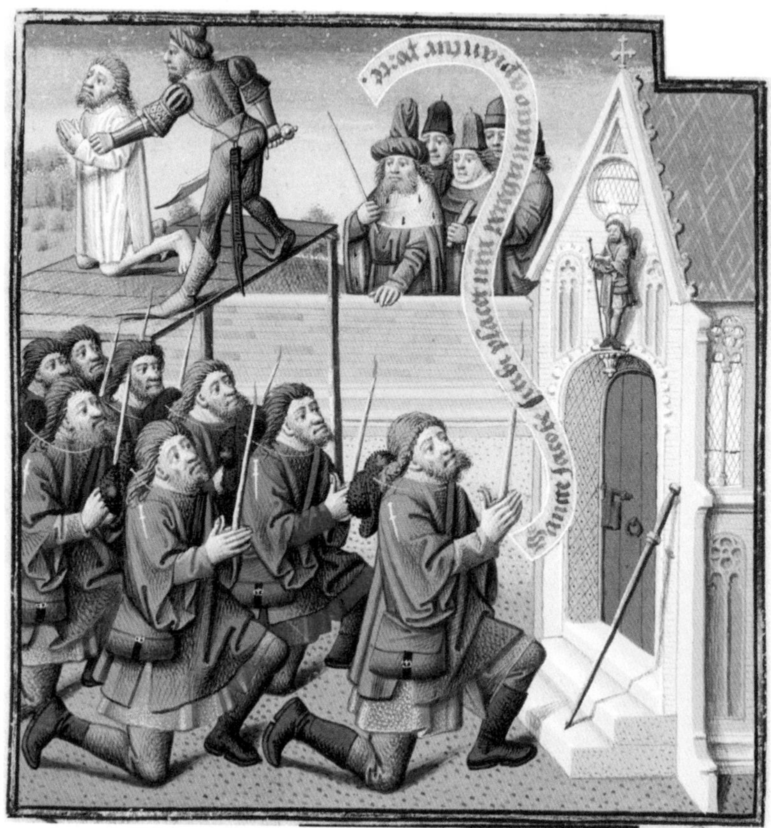

Pilgrims wearing scallop shell badges on their hats worshipping the statue of Saint James of Compostela. The saint is being beheaded in the background.

century – a spiritual geography determined almost entirely by relics and pilgrimage. These were the great sights and sites of the known world, the sacred places *par excellence*.

Boulogne was easily reachable for English travellers as they headed for the continent: it held a much-venerated statue of the Virgin Mary, with crown and sceptre, carrying the Christ child, which had arrived by boat, unaccompanied, some unknown time before and then began to work miracles and attract followers. A large number of English pilgrims went further and made the long journey to Rome, particularly at times when the Pope was offering special indulgences. At Santiago de Compostela, the relics of Saint James the Apostle were a major international attraction and

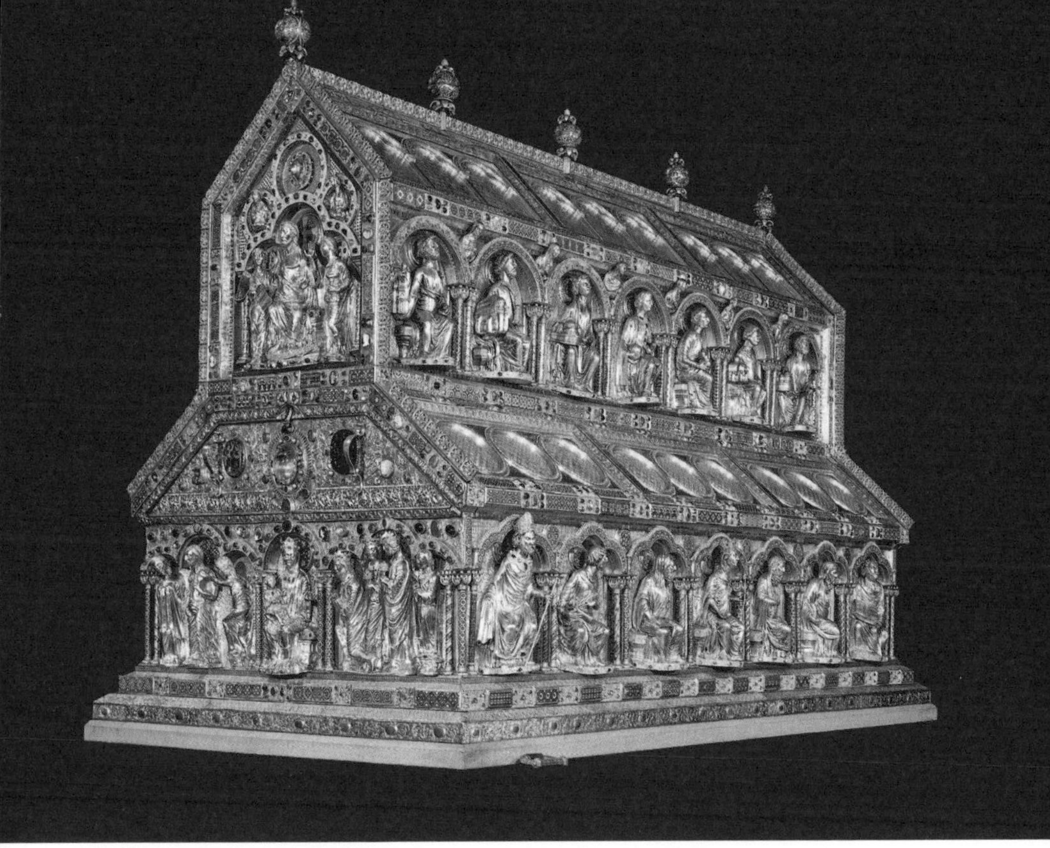

The golden shrine containing the relics of the Three Kings, in Cologne Cathedral, which was rebuilt to house them

in Cologne were the bones of the Three Kings who came to worship the Christ child. In both these places, you could be physically close to, almost in contact with, the remains of people who had seen and touched Jesus. In the Holy Land you could be in the very places where Jesus had been born, lived, taught, died and risen. To have visited Boulogne, Cologne, Compostela and Rome was rare, to visit Jerusalem more than once exceptional; but the Wife of Bath, affluent thanks to her skills as a cloth-maker (and to her many deceased husbands) was clearly one of the great frequent flyers of medieval pilgrimage. She had been to Jerusalem no fewer than three times, and was now on her way to the most popular shrine in England, the tomb and relics of Saint Thomas Becket, in the cathedral where the martyr-archbishop was murdered, in Canterbury.

She may have been rich, but she was also brave. Most of these pilgrim journeys were long and expensive, and they were always arduous and risky. Many who set out were robbed or died on the journey. (You were advised to make your will before you left home.) Yet we know that large numbers of people undertook them, both from contemporary accounts, and more directly from the many surviving badges or other objects that they brought back to England from the great centres of pilgrimage. These are on the whole cheap souvenirs, just an inch or so high: intimate little mementos of a great religious journey. They are of course demonstrations to friends and neighbours that you have travelled, but perhaps also a reminder of a closer approach to the divine, a moment of grace which your souvenir helps you relive.

In the British Museum are many such souvenirs, the sort of thing which the Wife of Bath might well have bought on her travels and either sewn to her hat (which Chaucer says was splendid), or carried with her to show to her companions. From Jerusalem a small lead bottle – an ampulla – designed to be worn round the neck, to hold water or oil that had been poured over holy relics and so had absorbed some of their sanctity; a cap badge from Rome with the papal keys and Saints Peter and Paul, whose tombs were the focus of intense devotion; another from Boulogne showing the miraculous statue arriving in its boat; a cockle shell coarsely made of lead, to signal that you had walked or ridden along the path to Compostela; and many souvenirs from Canterbury, among them one showing Becket in his archbishop's mitre, as he appeared on his reliquary in the cathedral.

Souvenirs the Wife of Bath might have bought: (*clockwise from top left*) a lead flask for holy oil or water from the Church of the Holy Sepulchre, Jerusalem; badge showing the heads of Saint Peter and Saint Paul from Rome; badge showing the head of Thomas Becket in Canterbury; badge of the Boulogne statue of the Virgin and Child in a boat

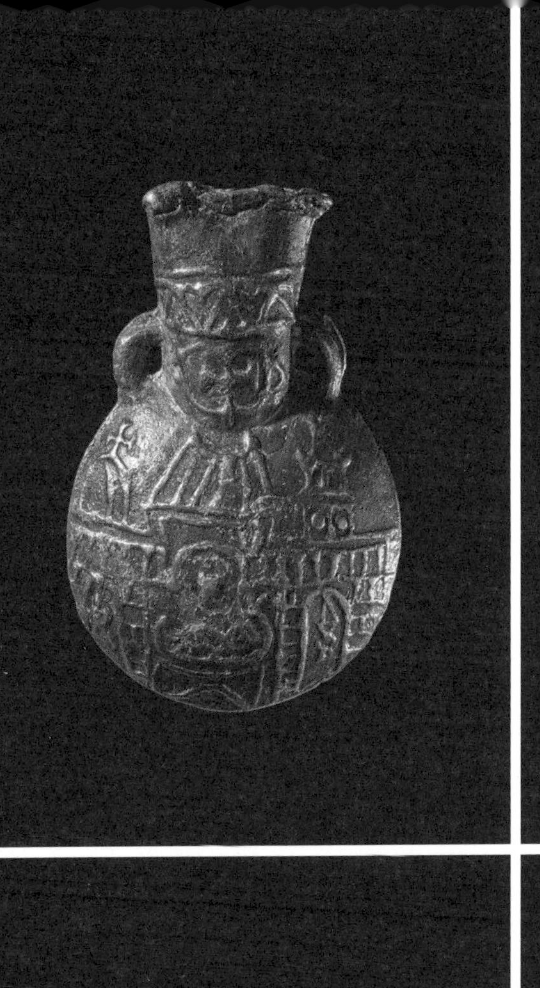
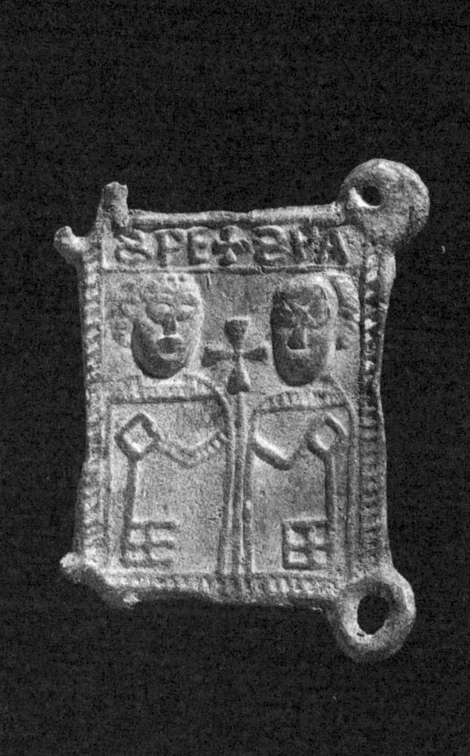
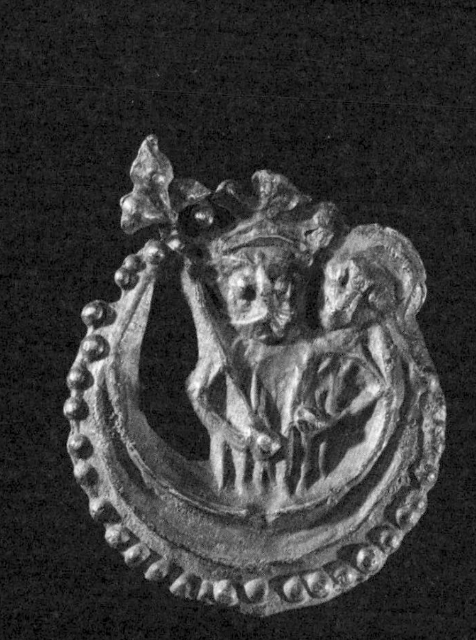
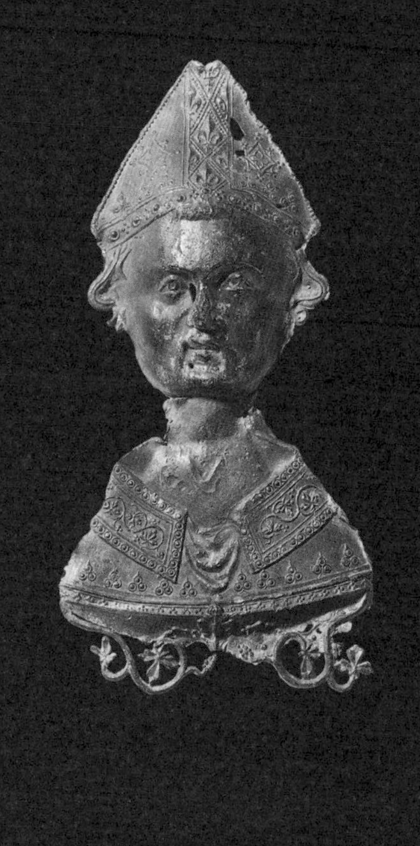

Looking at these little metal objects, which were presumably laid out on stalls for pilgrims to buy, evocative and temptingly tactile, it is easy to understand why a spurious sequel to the *Canterbury Tales*, entitled the *Tale of Beryn*, reports that while most of Chaucer's company bought some souvenirs, two of them – the Miller and the Pardoner – simply shoplifted them. It was clearly a common practice, and some of the badges in the British Museum were probably pilfered. But we do know for certain the history of some of these mementos, and they tell a more sobering story.

Many of the badges now in museums, especially those in the Museum of London, were found in the mud of the Thames. When pilgrims arrived safely back at the dock, they might drop a pilgrimage badge into the water as a thank-offering for their safe return after a perilous journey. What was it that led people of all classes in such numbers to incur the expense, hardships and risks involved in going on pilgrimage? What was the point?

Eamon Duffy is Professor of the History of Christianity at the University of Cambridge:

The basic motivation is to go to a place of special holiness and pray there.

Christianity is a materialist religion. It emphasizes the material world and the human body as vehicles of the divine. So people may find it helpful to follow in the footsteps of Jesus, to see the places where he lived and died and to pray there.

At a very early stage, Christians began putting the tombs of the martyrs in great churches, often under the altar. So an association develops between the body of Christ and the body of the martyr. People go to be near it, to touch it, to kiss it, to have contact in some way with relics.

The most frequently venerated relic of Becket at Canterbury was the water in which his brains and blood were said to have been washed. This was endlessly diluted, and little drops were put into lead capsules, which were sealed and would have on them an emblem of Canterbury. In this way, you could take away some of the holiness.

The intensity of the desire to be near the saints and martyrs made relics by far the most valuable moveable objects in medieval Europe. Competition to own them was fierce. Possession of them brought prestige, attracted pilgrims, and gave rise to some of the finest metalwork and the greatest buildings. The Sainte-Chapelle in Paris, a gothic masterpiece built in the 1240s by Saint Louis to house the Crown of Thorns, cost 40,000 *livres*: the relic itself, believed to have been on Jesus' head during the crucifixion, cost him over three times that.

If relics could not be bought, they might be stolen or taken by force. St Mark's in Venice was built to receive with appropriate magnificence the body of the saint, which Venetian merchants stole from Alexandria on the orders of the Doge, in 828. And when the German emperor Frederick Barbarossa conquered Milan in 1162, he removed the city's most precious possession – the bones of the Three Kings who had worshipped the Christ child – and took them to Cologne. There they were housed in a golden reliquary of incomparable splendour, and a new cathedral was built in their honour – the largest gothic cathedral in Northern Europe. It is that reliquary in that new cathedral which the Wife of Bath travelled to see, and it can still be seen there today.

The euphoric climax of the pilgrimage was of course the sight of the shrine itself, and pilgrims would often make the final approach on their knees. What all such places, far or near, offered was the possibility of drawing closer to the divine, of praying more effectively, perhaps with the help of a particular saint, of seeking healing or forgiveness. What it always required was leaving your home and your daily routines, and setting off, usually in a group, with a clear spiritual focus in view. Eamon Duffy describes the importance of travelling:

The journey itself is part of the point. The metaphor of life as a journey is a very old one. The technical term for the Last Rites, the final communion you receive as you are dying, is viaticum, 'journey money'. Both life and death have long been thought about as journeys – into the unknown.

The danger and discomfort were also part of the point – pilgrims knew that they would end up footsore and weary:

A lot of pilgrimages were penitential. Those who had done bad things were given, as a penance, the instruction to make a journey. So people go on pilgrimage at life-changing moments, essentially to sort their heads out. Walking or travelling can be a way of separating yourself from the world in which you are usually enmeshed, enabling you to see life with a new kind of radical simplicity, experiencing danger and discomfort.

In other words, the place where things change is not necessarily the shrine or sanctuary: it is often on the journey itself. There, without the support of familiar structures and daily routines, without many possessions, you are dependent on your companions or on strangers. And when you return to your old patterns, you should be able to see them, yourself and God more clearly.

Pilgrimage plays a large part in many faiths and, strikingly, most of them see it as functioning in very much the same way. It is felt that in some places the divine is more immediately present, especially places where the foundational figures of the faith were active on earth. Christians visiting the Holy Land hope to see Bethlehem and Nazareth, the Sea of Galilee and Calvary. Sikhs make the journey to Amritsar, where the *Guru Granth Sahib*, the holy scriptures that are a perpetual guide to the faithful, are preserved in the Golden Temple (Chapter 25).

Four great sites of pilgrimage are recommended to followers of the Buddha, all clustered in the north-east of the Indian

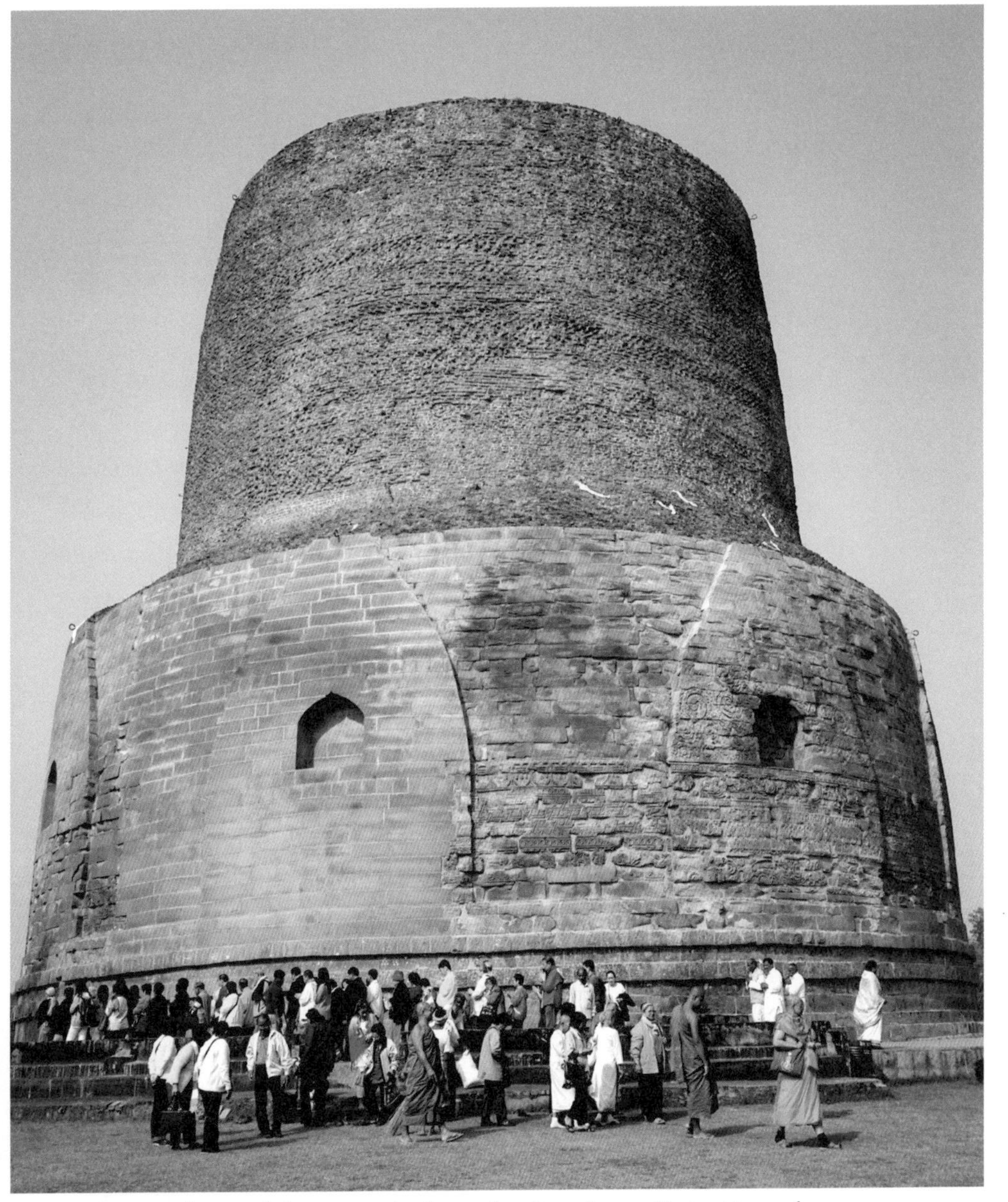

Pilgrims walk around the stupa in the deer park at Sarnath, near Varanasi in northern India, where the Buddha preached his first sermon.

sub-continent: Lumbini in Nepal, where the Buddha was born; Kushinagar, in the Indian state of Uttar Pradesh, where he died; Bodh Gaya, in India's Bihar state, home to the Bodhi tree under which he attained enlightenment; and finally, just a few kilometres north-east of the great Hindu pilgrimage city of Varanasi, lies the deer park at Sarnath, where the enlightened Buddha gave his first teachings (Chapter 19), the spot now marked by an enormous circular stupa on which – in spite of signs forbidding it – pilgrims stick small sheets of gold leaf. Devdutt Pattanaik, who writes on Indian religious life, strikes a note very close to Eamon Duffy's:

I think that by walking this trail you connect yourself with the Buddha. Human beings are not comfortable just with ideas. We need something tangible. We need to link ideas to things we can touch and feel, or to a place or time. A river or a mountain or a deer park is a physical reality, the very place where the Buddha lived and walked and breathed. We need that tangibility to come into touch with the divine.

Near the stupa in Sarnath are hostels and temples built in the styles of the different countries from which pilgrims come – there are temples from Japan and Myanmar, Tibet and Sri Lanka, Thailand and China – so that walking round the town is like a whirlwind tour of the religious architecture of eastern Asia. Sarnath thus becomes more than a place of individual pilgrimage: here the whole Buddhist world is gathered in prayer.

There is, however, one great pilgrimage that stands out among all the others: Hajj, the annual Muslim pilgrimage to Mecca. It was here that according to the Qur'an Abraham built the Kaaba, the granite structure which is the holiest site in Islam, here that water sprang at the Zamzam well to refresh Abraham's slave-girl Hagar and their son Ishmael, and here that Muhammad was born and cleansed the Kaaba of idols. Islam has five 'pillars', five elements that the faithful must make central to their lives. The first four are faith, prayer, charity and fasting. The fifth stipulates that every able-bodied Muslim, if they can afford it, should at least once in their life make the pilgrimage to Mecca during the month of Dhu al-Hijjah. Such a journey was, for most of history, and for most Muslims, especially women, simply out of the question. Thanks to air travel, however, millions every year now can and do make Hajj, visiting the great mosques at Mecca and Medina, and posing enormous logistic challenges to the authorities. Keeping the pilgrims safe is the supreme responsibility and honour of the kings of Saudi Arabia. It is a duty which must be performed whatever the political tensions or divisions within the Islamic world, and it brings them an incomparable prestige: their proudest title is 'Custodian of the two holy mosques'.

Batool Al-Toma is director of the New Muslims Project, a UK-based service that supports converts to Islam. While it would be inappropriate to compare her in any other respect to the Wife of Bath, she has gone on Hajj a remarkable thirteen times:

Any pilgrimage is good for the soul. People who go on pilgrimage are in search of something to regenerate themselves, to fulfil their spiritual needs, to reconnect with God. And they have to prepare

Millions of pilgrims come to Mecca every year and turn to pray towards the black cube of the Kaaba, visible here in the centre of the great mosque complex

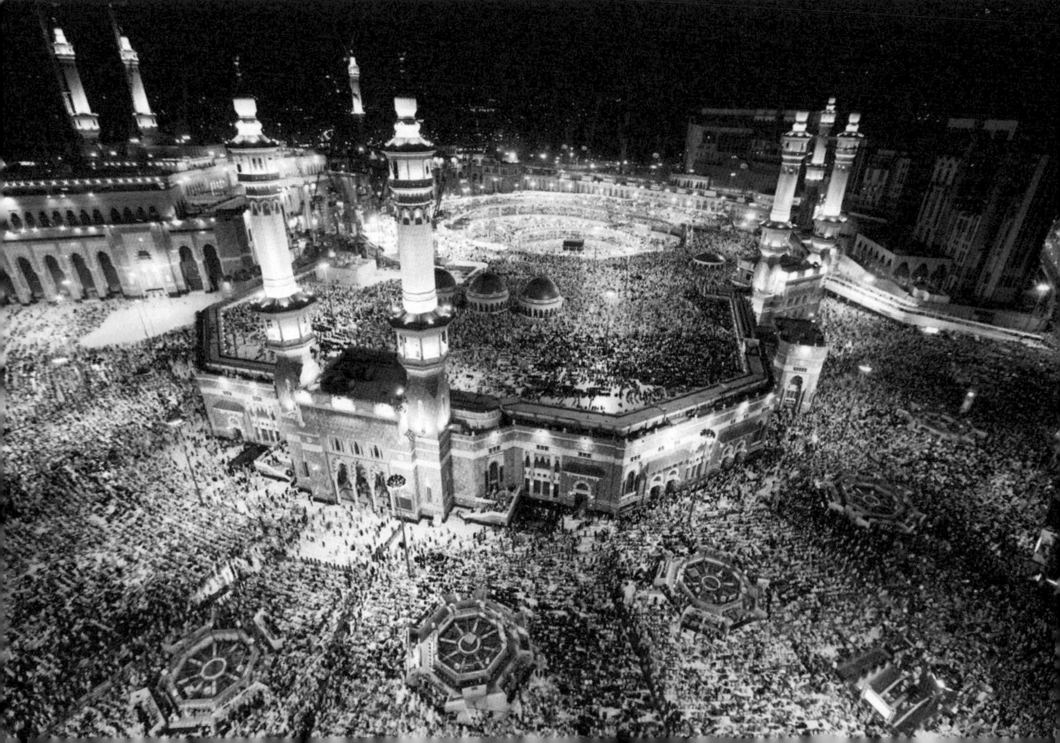

well. You need to be able to leave your family in safe hands while you are away, to make sure that they are sustained and looked after. It's not something that you take lightly. Then you prepare yourself. The practical side is really important, because being 'a guest of God', as we call pilgrimage, can be daunting. You depend on strangers. But people are so warm and hospitable and generous. They will give you prayer beads that they have just bought or been using, and ask you to remember them in your prayers.

A pilgrim, or 'Hajji', is called to make a movement from their everyday community and to embark on a journey that may last months or longer. They are to become for a time part of a much larger community, focused only on God, one where wealth and status should mean nothing, and then they are to bring something of that experience back into their everyday life. Batool Al-Toma continues:

There is a sense that when you go on Hajj, you all become equal, because our attire is kept modest. Men wear two items of cover,

The equalizing humility of the Hajj: three present and future kings of Saudi Arabia in the simple robes of the pilgrim: (*left to right*) Kings Abdullah, Fahd and Faisal

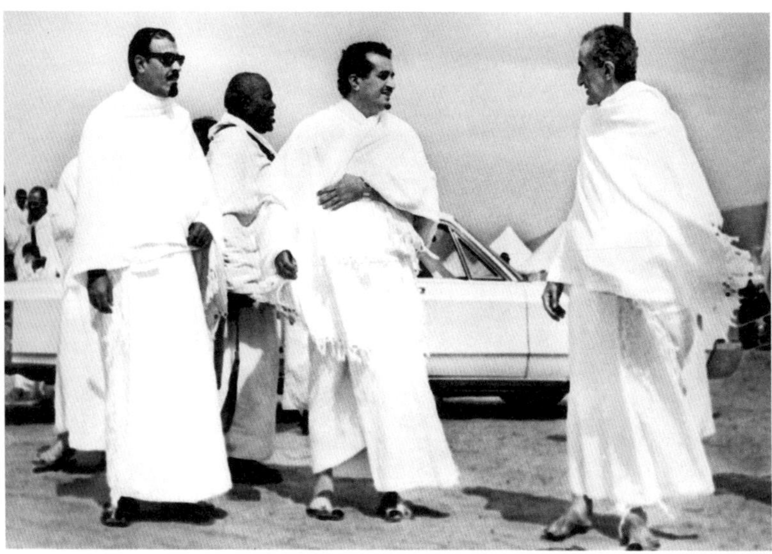

rather like two very large bath sheets. They are made from towelling material, unsewn, and one is wrapped around from the waist down probably to mid-shin, while the other is just thrown around the shoulders like any kind of a shawl or cover. They will begin and end their Hajj with just these two pieces of cloth. Women are encouraged to wear a dress. A lot of women like to choose white, because the men wear white, but it can be a dress of any colour as long as it is clean and comfortable and respectful.

Dressed like this, it is not possible to see whether people are rich or poor. They are all pilgrims. When you arrive, you see people coming from all over the world, and it puts the little discussions that we have back home about our faith into new perspective. It helps us get beyond those small, hair-splitting issues. Life begins to become quite real to you. You start to think, 'What do I really need? What do I really want in this world?'

In Islam, as in Christianity, this question is itself one of the reasons to undertake this difficult and expensive journey. But whereas the aim of Christian pilgrimage is essentially to see or touch the holy object, or be in the sacred place, Hajj requires action. The pilgrims, the men all dressed identically, will walk seven times round the Kaaba, then walk to the site where Satan must be symbolically stoned, will spend the night in the desert, run like Hagar looking for water and then return to the Kaaba. Performed together with hundreds of thousands of others, often in great heat, this experience is exhausting and exhilarating, purifying and equalizing.

When hajjis return home from this transformative journey, like all pilgrims they want to take with them mementos or gifts from the holy places. These of course have fewer images than Christian souvenirs, medieval or modern, and are more often objects linked to practical aspects of devotion: a *qibla* compass to find the direction of Mecca, mats, caps and beads to use while praying. Some will bring bottles of water from the Zamzam well, which will refresh the faithful in moments of spiritual need (Chapter 3). But

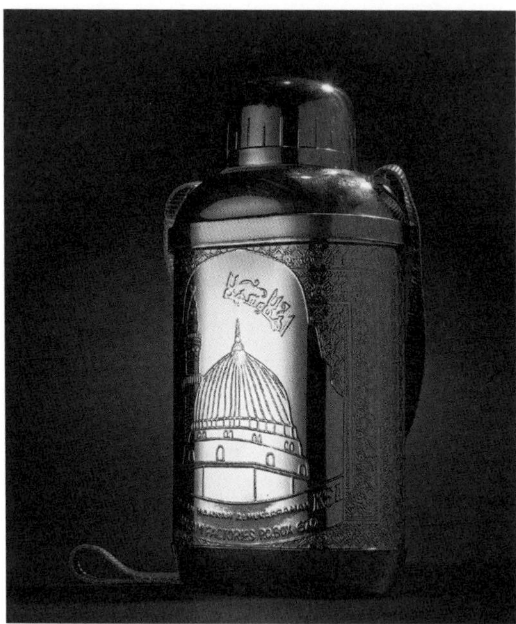

A golden plastic souvenir flask in which Hajjis carry Zamzam water home from Mecca. The Qur'an tells that the Zamzam well sprang up when Hagar in the desert was looking for water for her son Ishmael.

the purpose of all these objects is the same as the medieval tokens at the beginning of this chapter: to remind the pilgrim of a place and a moment of intense devotion, when they were close to God and part of a greater whole.

Because Hajj every year brings Muslims from all over the world to Mecca over the same short period, it affirms with peculiar power the idea of Islam as a global community, equal before God, diverse in every way, but united in prayer. It is hard to think of any mechanism other than pilgrimage which could so effectively achieve that purpose.

Today, pilgrimage is booming as never before. It is not just Mecca which has to cater for ever vaster crowds. In India improved transport now allows millions at a time to take part in the Hindu ritual bathing in the Ganges at the Kumbh Mela (Chapters 3 and 30), while the sites connected to the life of the Buddha attract more and more air-borne religious tourists from all over east Asia. Since the 1990s, Christian pilgrimage has been on the increase too, although its focus over the last century and a half has been moving from the tangible to the intangible: in place of the relics and sites that attracted Chaucer's pilgrims, people now travel to the scenes of visions and divine epiphanies. For Roman Catholics, apparitions of the Virgin Mary have come to take centre-stage, at sites like Lourdes (which quickly became famous for miraculous cures), Fatima, Knock and Međjugorje in Europe; Guadalupe in Mexico (Chapter 16); Velankanni in Tamil Nadu in south India; and Manaoag in the Philippines. In every case, these apparitions were to poorly educated youngsters, and although not all have been approved by the Vatican – Međjugorje and Velankanni are still under discussion – all now draw enormous numbers of pilgrims every year, moved by the hope that simple piety may open the way to transformative contact with the divine. In France, only Paris has more hotel rooms than Lourdes: there are more than six million visitors annually.

There has always been a contentious side to pilgrimage. In every tradition and in every century there have been criticisms of the bad behaviour of pilgrims, the greed of those who cater for them and the commercialization of the holy places. Many, especially in the monotheisms, are uneasy about any implied suggestion that god is nearer humankind in some places than others. Most Protestants from the sixteenth century onwards held that there was simply no need for any of this: it was wastefully expensive, even idolatrous, and, most important of all, nowhere in the Bible is it clearly required. Pilgrimage for them was the daily struggle to live a godly life, a struggle requiring just as much courage and endurance as physical journeying. The 'pilgrim's progress' was the surmounting of spiritual obstacles and difficulties, whether 'Vanity Fair' or the 'Slough of Despond', to find the true path to God. But, as Eamon Duffy points out, just because pilgrimage is not explicitly discussed in the Bible, that does not mean it is absent:

The practices of faith are determined as much by the imagery of the scriptures as anything else, and that imagery is saturated with pilgrimage: the wanderings of Abraham in search of the Holy Land, the wanderings of Moses and the Israelites in the desert after they left Egypt. Right from the Old Testament onwards, there are very profound images of pilgrimage.

Both Judaism and Christianity understand these images of Abraham and of Moses, leading their people into the wilderness, as journeys of transformation, pilgrimages towards places where the people can live closer to god. A new kind of godly community can emerge. It is an idea expounded in eloquent detail in Saint Paul's Epistle to the Hebrews: 'By faith Abraham … obeyed and went, even though he did not know where he was going.' These biblical journeys are, however, pilgrimages of a very particular sort. The purpose is not to return, changed, to the point of departure, but rather to reach in the right spirit the place where God may be worshipped in the proper way and a new society will be possible. When, at Passover or on the Day of Atonement, Jews say, 'Next year in Jerusalem', the hope being expressed is not just of a limited visit, but that all Jews may be able to return, and remain, to witness the coming of the Messiah.

This kind of spiritual journey is a key part of the foundation myth of the United States. When a group of dissenting Puritans sailed from Plymouth in 1620 to establish a colony in New England where they could worship as they believed right, they saw themselves as the successors of Abraham and Moses, journeying by faith to establish a new community in a godly place, a 'city on a hill'. William Bradford, who sailed on the *Mayflower*, later governed the colony that the emigrants established and wrote its history, expressed it unambiguously: 'They knew they were pilgrims, and … lifted up their eyes to the heavens, their dearest country'. It is in this biblical sense that they are honoured to this day by the whole of the United States as the Pilgrim Fathers.

15
FESTIVAL TIME

Pilgrimage asks individuals to travel in faith to a particular place, perhaps only once in their life. Festivals invite whole communities to renew themselves every year in the same place, as the generations pass. But, whereas pilgrimage generally implies hardship and risk, most festivals contrive to combine reverence for the divine with throwing a great party: not just living with the gods, but celebrating with them. The Yup'ik Bladder Festival, which we looked at in Chapter 5, was the traditional expression of a deep spiritual interdependence between the human and the animal worlds. The festivals in this chapter by contrast, as they change over time, tell us almost as much about politics as they do about religion.

At festival time, our ordinary lives, our everyday schedules, our plans for the future – all these are put to one side. In their place, for a few short, intense hours or days, we think about – and indeed come to feel – much larger patterns of life which contain us, but which also stretch far beyond us. And because each festival is a re-enactment of all its predecessors, we come to a powerful appreciation that life, both communitarian and cosmic, is not a lonely, one-act story with a beginning and an end, but a grand

Over: Mid-nineteenth-century model, made of prehistoric mammoth ivory, of the Ysyakh festival, celebrating midsummer in eastern Siberia

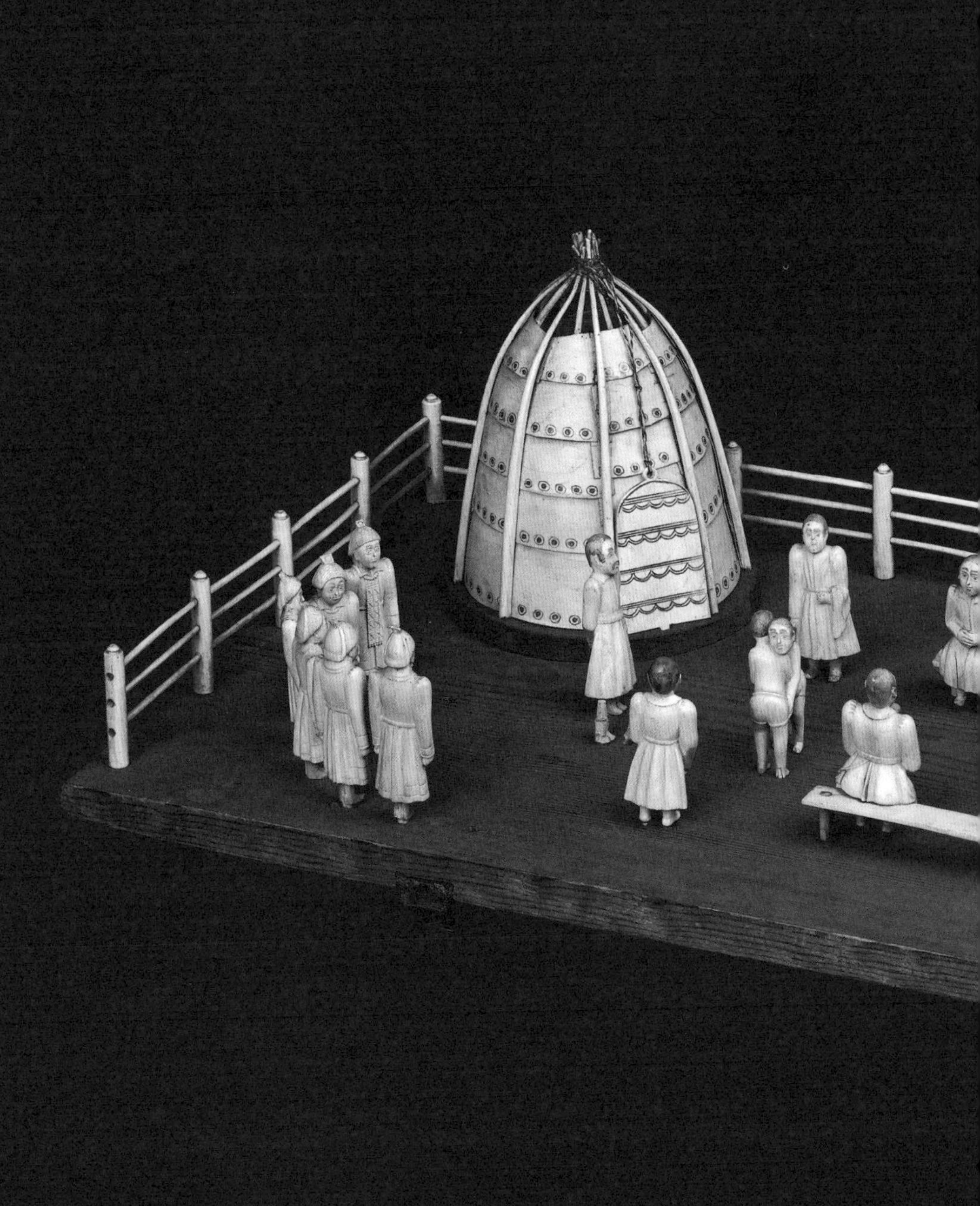

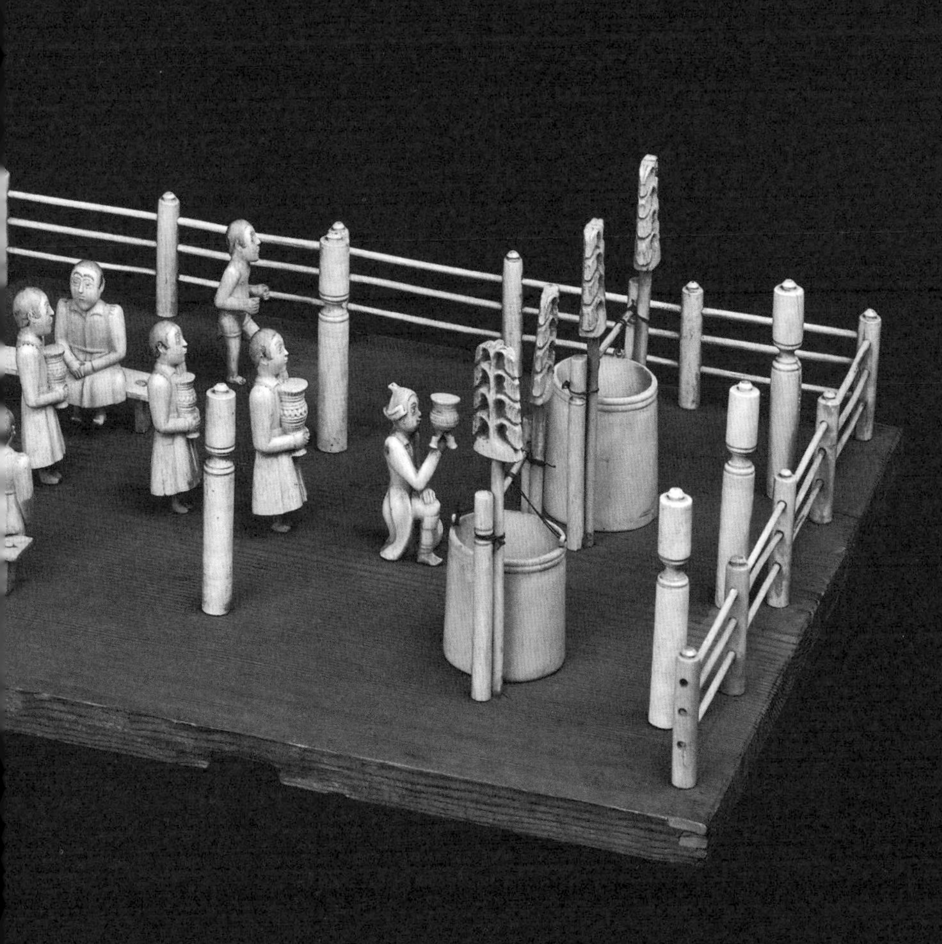

dramatic cycle, whose end – if it has one – lies beyond our own lifetime.

Almost every religious tradition has festivals, most tied to the movements of the sun, moon and seasons, and in the northern latitudes, where variation in daylight is pronounced over the year, most cultures find a way to mark the longest and shortest days (Chapter 3). In the British Museum, you can be a privileged spectator at one that few outsiders visit. At first sight, it seems like a festival in Lilliput. Mounted on a simple board of unpainted conifer wood is a group of around twenty small, finely worked, part-coloured ivory sculptures of people assembled to take part in some kind of ceremony. It is a modest work of art, but also a rare record of a moment of great significance for the Sakha people, one of Siberia's largest indigenous populations. It shows the traditional summer solstice celebration of Ysyakh, still today the Sakhas' most important annual festival. Essentially a ritual to honour the spirits of the landscape, Ysyakh is a remarkable example of what a religious festival can be, and can do. Like most festivals it has survived and changed over the centuries, offering an annual moment for giving thanks to the gods, celebrating with friends and affirming – despite exceptional levels of political, economic and cultural disruption over the last 150 years – the capacity of a community to sustain and to adapt both itself and its beliefs.

Some time around 1300 the nomadic Sakha, who speak a Turkic language, moved north from Lake Baikal, and settled around the River Lena, in a region that has the coldest winters in the northern hemisphere: temperatures below –50°C are not uncommon. According to tradition, when they reached a particularly attractive spot, they appealed to the spirits, who answered their call, sending birds for them to eat, and providing luscious grass for their horses. Ever since then, when the new growing season has begun, the Sakha gather, coming from great distances (the modern Republic of Sakha Yakutia, part of the Russian Federation, is almost the size of India) to commemorate the founding of their homeland. Led by their shamans, who have privileged access in ecstatic trances to the world of the spirits, they celebrate with food and drink, dances, songs and horse races. They make offerings to thank the deities for surviving the winter, and ask their help for the future. One could almost say that this festival is to the Sakha people what Thanksgiving is in the United States.

Tatiana Argounova-Low of the University of Aberdeen is a native Sakha, born in Yakutsk, the capital city of Sakha Yakutia, about 3,000 miles east of Moscow:

There are records of the Ysyakh festival going back to the seventeenth or eighteenth century. It may be even older, dating from the time the Sakha people first travelled north and settled in what seemed to them a perfect place on the banks of the Lena River.

Although the written sources for the festival go back further, our model, made around 1860, is of particular interest, as it is the oldest visual record:

People at that date lived in very harsh conditions. Sakha have always been pastoralists, their main occupation horse- and cattle-breeding, so getting the animals through the six months of deep frost was always a challenge. Horses were the most important livestock: the Sakha relied on them for transport – and for food. Even in minus forty, minus fifty in winter, horses were able to dig the grass out of snow to feed themselves. Yet it was often touch and go whether the people would survive.

In early June the grass starts growing vigorously and fruits begin to ripen. In July, August and September all energies had to be devoted to hay-making and fruit-harvesting, to gather enough for the next winter. The summer solstice, when the ground was passable and the weather warm, was therefore the moment when the Sakha could come together before the months of intense labour began:

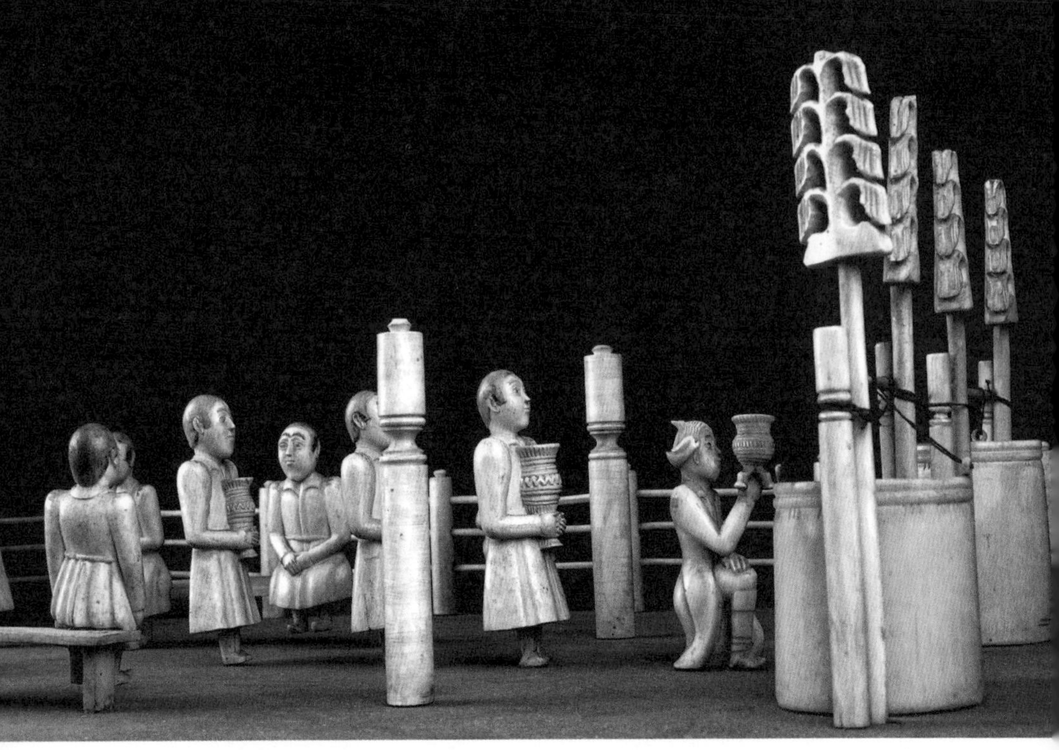

The kneeling shaman leads a procession offering fermented mare's milk during the Ysyakh festival.

They were in the mood to celebrate life before the beginning of a new economic season. They would gather together at the festival, normally organized by a rich landlord. He would invite everyone, primarily his relatives but also poor people who did not have very much, to enjoy and share food together. It is about enjoying companionship and music, about the joy of life.

You can see some of this joy of life even in the stiffly carved figures of our model. The patrons of the festival – presumably the local landowners – are seated on the two benches in the middle. The five tall hitching posts are for tethering the horses on which people would come from afar to the celebration. At one end is a conical yurt, a portable tent made out of birch bark attached to flexible poles, with a decorated door flap; at the other end are two large vats for *kumys*, a slightly alcoholic drink of fermented mare's milk, set between severely stylized trees. Beside the yurt a group of men and women are singing, others are watching a wrestling match. In the centre, figures walk in line carrying drinking vessels for mare's milk, while the leader of the procession goes down on one knee, singing a prayer-poem of supplication to Urung Aiyy Toyon, the most important of the deities: the 'white lord creator', 'father of the light', whom the Sakha people identify with the sun itself. In Tatiana Argounova-Low's words:

People thanked the deities for their protection. You can see in the model that the master of ceremonies, probably close to being a shaman, is leading the boys and girls in the special ritual of feeding the fire. This is basically a way of talking to the gods and spirits, and making them a thank-offering of mare's milk, butter, meat and pancakes. They are also asking for continued protection and guardianship in the years to come.

It is extremely important that Ysyakh is held outside and with as many people as possible, because for the Sakha every single element of nature and of landscape is spirited, is animated, is sentient. The whole environment is a spiritual, living thing.

Our model was exhibited at, and may even have been made for, the enormous Exposition Universelle in Paris in 1867, at which the countries of the world were invited to display the products of their new industries. They were also encouraged to present some of their folk traditions, which were in many cases being destroyed by the very advances in transport, communication and technology which made such great international exhibitions possible. It was a Europe-wide phenomenon at the time. In Britain the first National Eistedfodd of Wales had been held in Aberdare in 1861, and in Scotland the Royal National Mòd would follow a few decades later – yet, at the same time, both Welsh and Gaelic were in steep decline as communications improved, the role of central government increased, and English everywhere came to dominate. Our little model of the Ysyakh festival may be part of a comparable phenomenon. As Tsarist Russia tightened its political grip on eastern Siberia, the officially sponsored spread of the Russian language and Orthodox Christianity began to weaken indigenous traditions and beliefs; the model exhibited in Paris, 'the capital of the nineteenth century', was a demonstration that modern, west-facing Russia still had its rural, picturesque, Asian past. The message seemed to be that this Turkic, non-Christian, Siberian religious ceremony would soon either die out or be consigned to the charming but harmless realm of folklore.

As Tatiana Argounova-Low explains, Ysyakh very nearly did die out. Sakha culture suffered even more under the centralizing atheism of the Soviets than it had under the Tsars. Its modern revival began only after the collapse of the Soviet Union in the early 1990s:

I never went to an Ysyakh until I was in my late thirties. I missed out, and so did a whole generation of Soviet children. There is so much knowledge about our community that our parents meant to pass on to us, but could not because of Soviet ideology, which created a sanitized environment where ethnic minority cultures were concerned. Ysyakh was probably celebrated in small villages during this period, but not on the previous scale, nor in the same spiritual way: it would have been all about Soviet ideology – thanking Lenin and Marx.

For this reason, the revived Ysyakh festival, since the 1990s, is a celebration of ethnic belonging: the beauty of songs and storytelling, traditional costume, jewellery and silverware, dances and horse-riding – but also fashion shows and pop concerts. It occasionally reminds me of the opening ceremony of the London Olympics in 2012. People from all over the region will come to this annual celebration. We are talking about tens of thousands of people, arriving by car and plane, just to be together to celebrate.

It is surely not just by chance that this Sakha recovery – and re-invention – of their almost extinguished traditions has occurred at the same time as the revival of Celtic culture and language – and political confidence – in Scotland and Wales:

At the same time, however, Ysyakh has never lost its spiritual and religious dimension: it is still about addressing the deities and spirits that help people to survive the winter – not even Soviet ideology could change the climate.

It is to the climate that we owe the ivory in which the figures of our model were carved: it comes not from elephants, but from the tusk of a mammoth – and so, astonishingly, from the same material as was used to carve the Lion Man in Chapter 1. Mammoths became extinct in Siberia at least 5,000 years ago, but their bodies and tusks, preserved in the permafrost, are still found when floods wash away the banks of the Lena. That ancient material, carved in the 1860s, is now playing a small part in the continuing development of Ysyakh.

Since the end of the Soviet era, Ysyakh celebrations have revived. The yurts at the 2016 festival clearly echo the one in the nineteenth-century model.

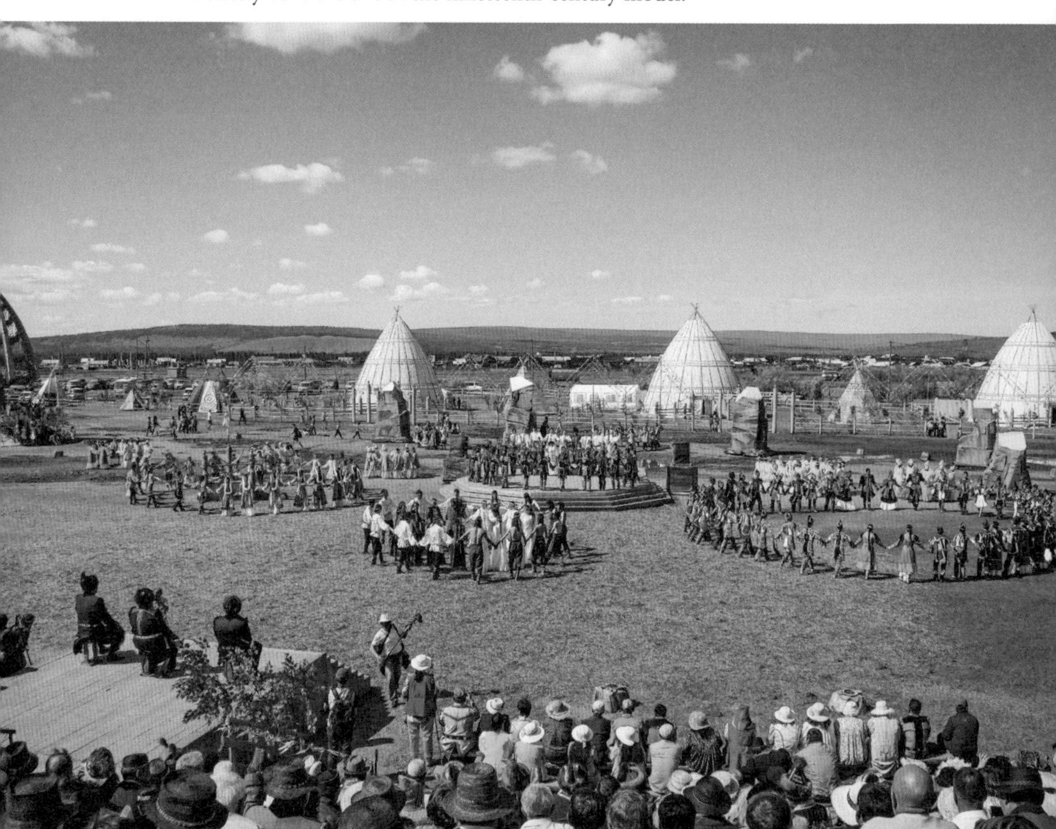

In 2015 the British Museum model travelled to Yakutsk. There it was closely studied, seen as a valuable document that can help to plan and authenticate future festivals. Unexpectedly, it turned out in Yakutsk that the model had originally been larger, with more figures and more activities: the missing parts are now being reconstructed, using the existing figures as guides. It is a striking reversal of fortune. Made to mark the ceremony's decline into picturesque folklore, the model is now being used, like the festival itself, to strengthen the traditional system of belief in an animate landscape, to tie people, gods and land together, and to reclaim a Sakha identity in the modern world.

In spite of strong Russian immigration, intense Christianization in the nineteenth century and atheist indoctrination in the twentieth, a 2012 survey found that nearly 150,000 out of Sakha Yakutia's population of less than a million gave their religion as traditional Yakut Shaman. One of the world's smaller religions appears to be flourishing.

Compared with a multi-figured model carved out of ancient Siberian mammoth tusk, a commercial Christmas card showing Santa Claus bringing presents is a pretty unprepossessing object; but it documents just as clearly the extraordinary power of religious festivals to renew themselves, and to adapt to political and economic developments.

In the Gospel narratives, we are not told whether the birth of Christ happened in summer or winter, and it is not until the wise men arrive from the east, at an unspecified later date, bringing gold, frankincense and myrrh, that there is any mention of presents. So it has long been a matter of speculation as to how and why the Christian world came to celebrate on 25 December.

The slaves will become the masters, the masters the slaves. This is not some radical religious or political credo, but one of the central features of the Roman festival of Saturnalia, in honour of the

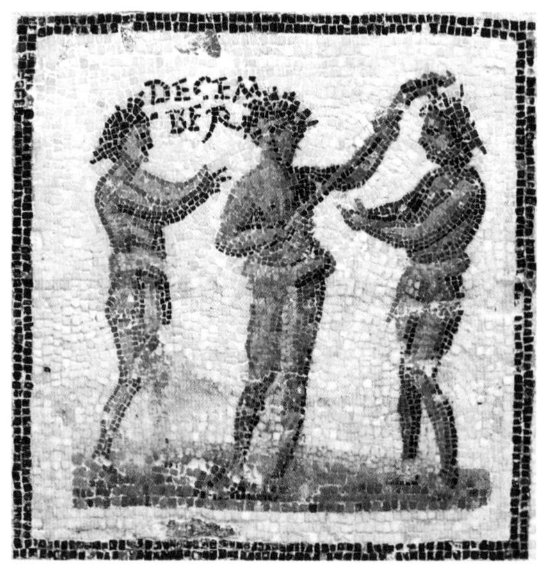

Leaf-crowned slaves celebrating the Roman mid-winter Saturnalia festivities in a third-century calendar mosaic from El Djem in modern Tunisia

god Saturn. Held each year, from 17 December to around the 23rd, this was the most anticipated of Roman holidays – the poet Catullus called these 'the best of days'. The Roman Republic, and later the Empire, would ring to the sound of '*Io Saturnalia!*' 'It's Saturnalia! Hurray!' Households would come together, feast, exchange gifts – often pottery or wax figurines. Slaves could expect their masters to serve them food, or even to share their dining table with them. As Saturn himself put it, his words formed for him by the satirist Lucian:

During my week the serious is barred: no business allowed. Drinking and being drunk, noise and games of dice, appointing of kings and feasting of slaves, singing naked, clapping ... an occasional ducking of corked faces in icy water – such are the functions over which I preside.

A much-anticipated, much-loved, late-December Roman festival. Gifts and games. Work suspended in favour of family time. Alcoholic drinks on hand to lubricate conversations and to help people put up with their relatives. As we would now say – *Merry Christmas!*

Such a simple appropriation of one religion's festival by another would be an elegant explanation – one often advanced – of the date and the habits of Christmas, but it is by no means the whole story. Diarmaid MacCulloch, Professor of the History of the Church at Oxford, points out that the origins of Christmas, and when people first began to celebrate it, are both pretty confused:

We don't know when Jesus was born. Christianity has put it in the darkest season of the year, and naturally one thinks that's probably because there were lots of festivals around at that time, one of which would be the Roman Saturnalia – about which we don't know very much either. There is also the festival of Sol Invictus, the Unconquered Sun. But it could be that as Christianity spread, and became a threat, anxious Roman emperors actually encouraged non-Christian festivals that could balance out what the Christians were doing.

Christmas is probably third century in its origins: so it is ancient, but definitely not biblical. Later, some Protestant Christians would point that out and try to get rid of Christmas altogether. You could have a proper Protestant celebration of Easter for instance, because its date is calculated by biblical means, but Christmas is an intruder. And of course technically they were right: it was not a festival in the very early church.

After the Reformation, most Protestant churches continued, like the Roman Catholics, to celebrate Christmas as a major festival. But the Puritan dislike of a feast without scriptural authority was intense, and for 200 years – surprisingly, when we think of its modern popularity in all parts of society – Christmas remained a bone of bitter religious, and political, contention. The Pilgrim Fathers, arriving in America in 1620, made a point of working

A composite Christmas: a pagan Christmas tree from Germany, Arctic reindeer, a Gothic church, and a Turkish saint from New York and the Netherlands

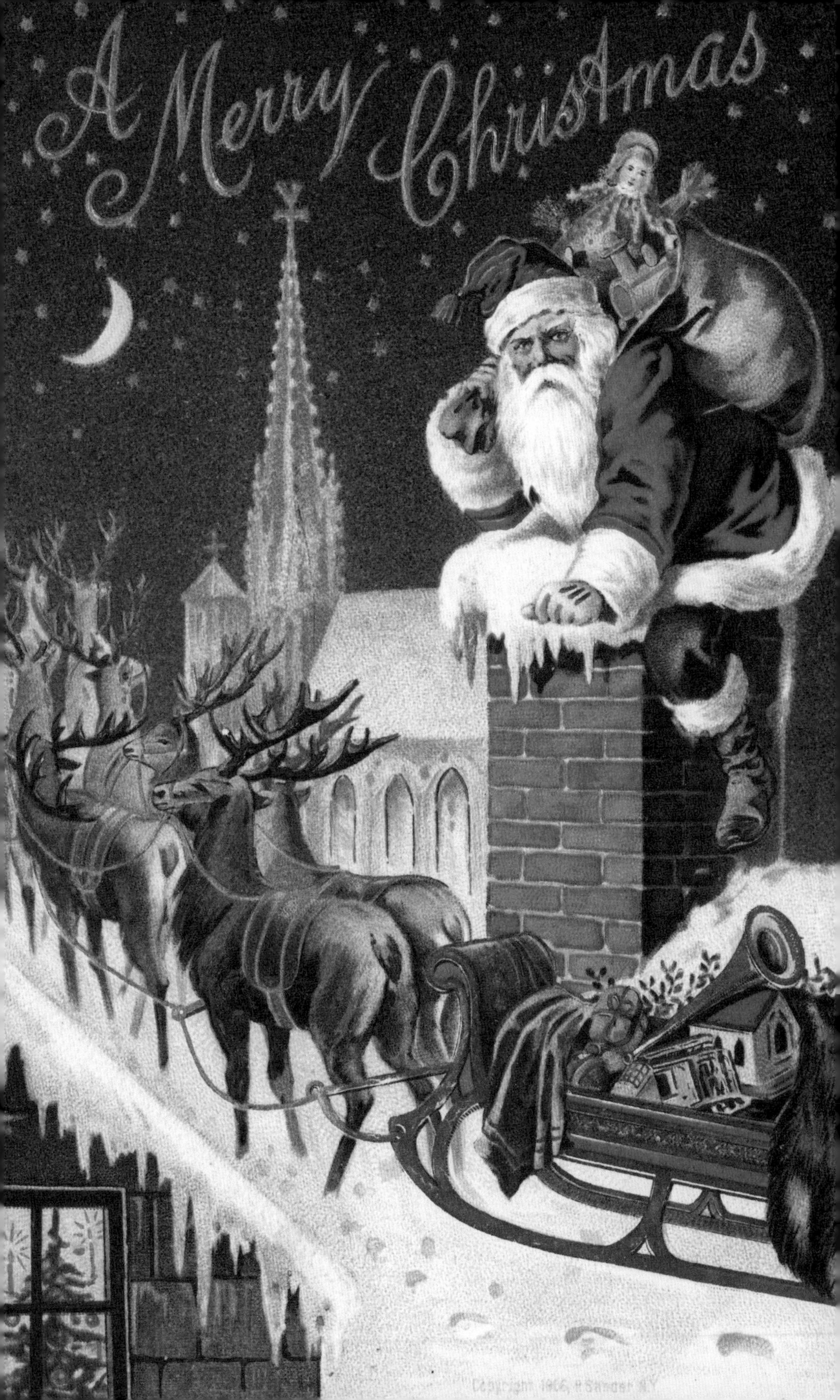
A Merry Christmas

on Christmas Day, as there was no biblical reason to do otherwise. Under Cromwell, the holiday was banned in England by the Puritan majority in Parliament (to great public protest), and was restored along with the monarchy in 1660. The Scottish Parliament abolished all celebration of what was considered a dangerously Papist feast – the Christ Mass – in 1640, and the main midwinter celebration moved to New Year, where for many Scots it still remains. As late as 1958 Christmas Day was a normal working day in Scotland.

So how did we arrive at our all-embracing modern Christmas with its familiar imagery? Because the laity usually play almost as important a role as the clergy in shaping them, religious festivals are wonderfully malleable, and can reflect almost immediately shifts in popular taste, adding and absorbing new elements from widely disparate sources (as we shall see with Durga Puja in Chapter 17). That is of course what enables them to survive, and to go on fulfilling their central function in society. Under the influence of the writings of Saint Bridget, the Middle Ages had radically reimagined Western European Christmas to meet its changing spiritual concerns (as we shall see in Chapter 18). Our modern version of the festival also owes a great deal to popular writers, as well as to political and economic changes: it is, as Diarmaid MacCulloch explains, essentially a nineteenth-century invention, and many aspects of it – the Pilgrim Fathers would surely have been surprised – begin in New York:

Early North American Protestantism effectively lost Christmas, because it was a Puritan culture. But after the War of Independence, when Americans were trying to create a festival calendar

The many translations of Saint Nicholas: (*left to right, top to bottom*) the Orthodox saint at the church in Myra, southern Turkey, twelfth century; the fifteenth-century benefactor of destitute young women in the Netherlands; galloping over Dutch rooftops and dropping presents through the chimneys with his assistant, Black Peter, 1850; bringing Christmas cheer to Bengal, 2016

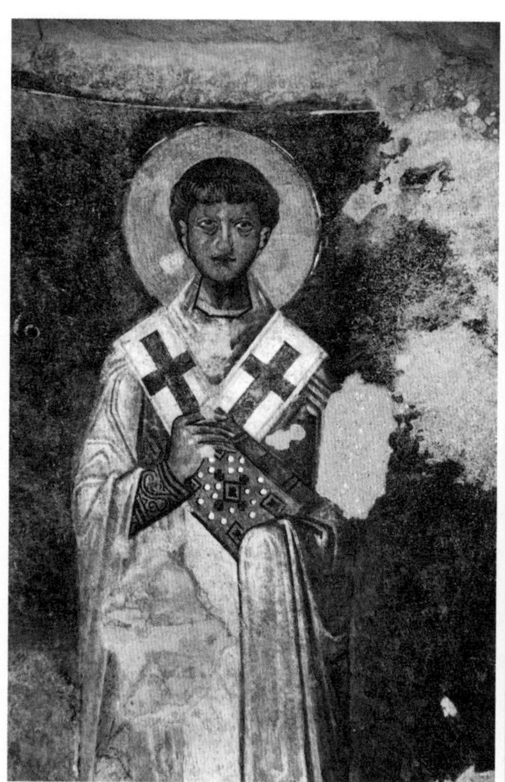

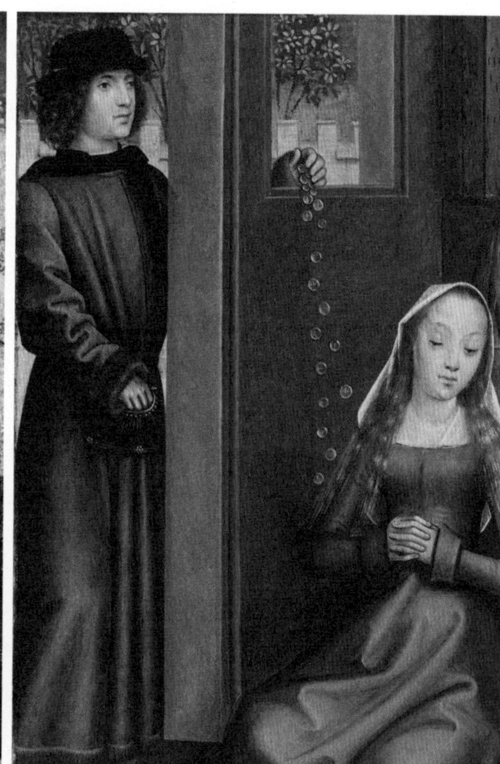

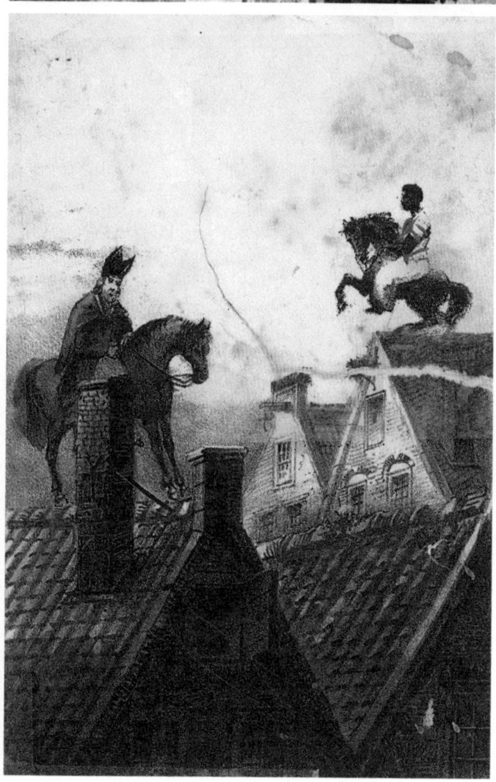

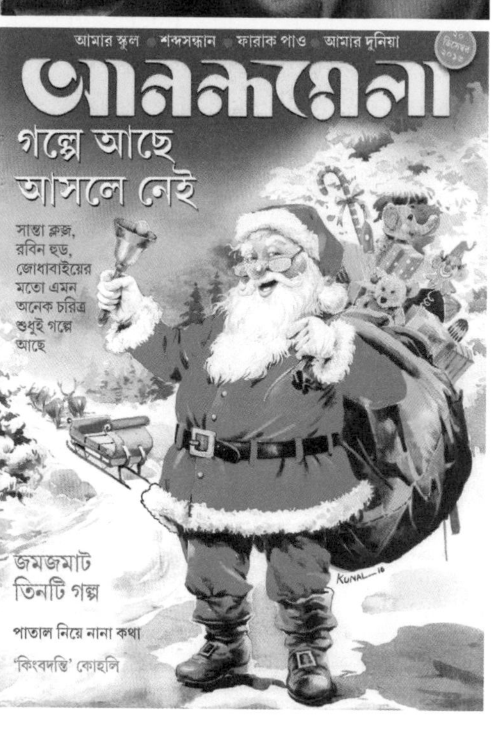
আমার স্কুল • শব্দসন্ধান • ফারাক পাও • আমার দুনিয়া
আনন্দমেলা
গল্পে আছে
আসলে নেই
সান্তা ক্লজ,
রবিন হুড,
জোধাবাইয়ের
মতো এমন
অনেক চরিত্র
শুধুই গল্পে
আছে
জমজমাট
তিনটি গল্প
পাতাল নিয়ে নানা কথা
'কিংবদন্তি' কোহলি
KUNAL

for themselves in the new republic, one or two groups majored on bits of the old European traditions. As New York rediscovered its Dutch roots, in opposition to English colonialism, the Dutch tradition of Saint Nicholas – originally Bishop of Myra in southern Turkey – whose name had morphed into Sinterklaas – was taken up. This bishop of the early church had survived in the Netherlands as a popular figure in spite of the Reformation, and now became a feature of the American Christmas. Gradually he became less bishop-like, turning instead into a jolly old man, and his name morphing once more. Santa Claus is really a globalizing interloper from the United States.

In Dutch tradition, Saint Nicholas visits every house on the eve of his feast-day on 6 December, to bring presents for every (good) child. In North America around 1800, his gift-giving habit, which now had the added charm of being an anti-British gesture, was moved a few weeks later, to coincide with Christmas – a festival which in Protestant North America (except of course among Puritans) would be celebrated as much in the home as in the church. The Dutch Saint Nicholas/Santa Claus traditionally arrived on horseback, with one helper, Black Peter. But the Americans changed all that too. They decided to combine him with a completely different Northern European midwinter tradition, and so the ancient Mediterranean bishop startlingly acquired a team of Arctic reindeer.

All this might have remained just a quaint bit of New England tradition–invention, until in 1823 a professor of theology in New York, Clement Clarke Moore, turned this farrago of religious odds and ends into a poem:

T'was the Night before Christmas, when all through the house
Not a creature was stirring, not even a mouse;
The stockings were hung by the chimney with care,
In hopes that Saint Nicholas soon would be there.

It was nonsense, but rhythmic and memorable nonsense, and it quickly became a bestseller on both sides of the Atlantic:

When, what to my wondering eyes should appear,
But a miniature sleigh, and eight tiny reindeer,
With a little old driver, so lively and quick,
I knew in a moment it must be Saint Nick.

English-speaking Christmas has been marked by it ever since. On both sides of the Atlantic, the focus of the feast now shifted to children. Saint Nicholas distributing presents from his sleigh (his eight reindeer each given a name by Moore – Prancer, Dancer, Vixen, etc.), became a central part of a festival which was now also about gifts: Christmas shopping had begun. And it was Christmas shopping that a century later brought the ninth and most famous of all the reindeer into the story: in 1939 the Montgomery Ward department stores in the United States published a promotional ditty to encourage Christmas customers – and Rudolph's red nose has been shining ever since.

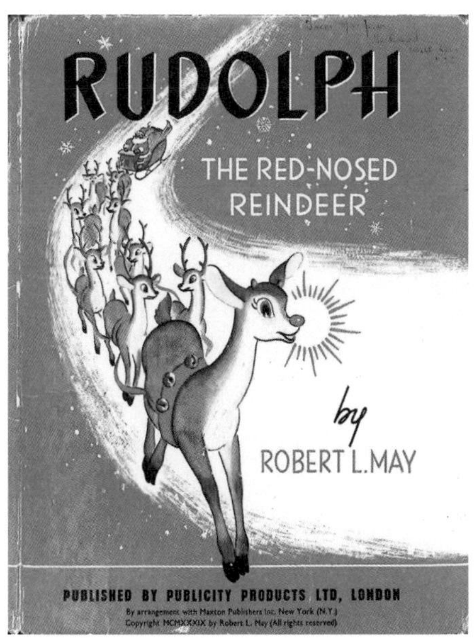

Rudolph the Red-Nosed Reindeer arrived in 1939 to lead his eight fellows from the 1820s.

The American reinvention of Christmas in the 1820s was enthusiastically taken up in Britain – and then developed further in equally surprising directions, above all as a result of Charles Dickens's *A Christmas Carol*, published in 1843. The short story about the miser Scrooge was an instant success, selling out thirteen editions in its first year. It has influenced almost every aspect of British Christmas since. The highlight of the traditional Christmas meal, for example, had long been goose; but the first act of the reformed Scrooge was to buy a huge turkey to send to his poor clerk, Bob Cratchit. Turkey swiftly became the bird of choice for the whole family, and its reluctance to vote for Christmas passed into proverb.

Much more important, Dickens insisted that Christmas was the moment of the year when the rich ought to remember their obligations to the poor, or, as Scrooge's generous nephew puts it, 'when men and women seem by one consent to open their shut-up hearts freely, and to think of people below them as if they really were fellow-passengers to the grave, and not another race of creatures bound on other journeys'. As much as a religious celebration, Dickens suggests, Christmas should be a festival of social harmony, a moment for generosity, for solidarity across the classes. It was an idea that struck a deep chord in Victorian Britain, especially in the industrial cities. It is still felt strongly. Today all British charities concerned with social deprivation record peak donations at Christmas.

Like all festivals, Christmas evolves as it is repeated over the years, each individual celebration resonating consciously or unconsciously with every other, and all calling for reflection. As Scrooge is visited by the spirits of Christmas past, present and future, he and the reader are left in no doubt of the part they both must play in the cycle that shapes each individual life and continues far beyond it, binding the generations together. When he awakes, transformed, on Christmas morning, he announces the

The Ghost of Christmas Yet to Come. An illustration to Dickens's bestseller *A Christmas Carol*

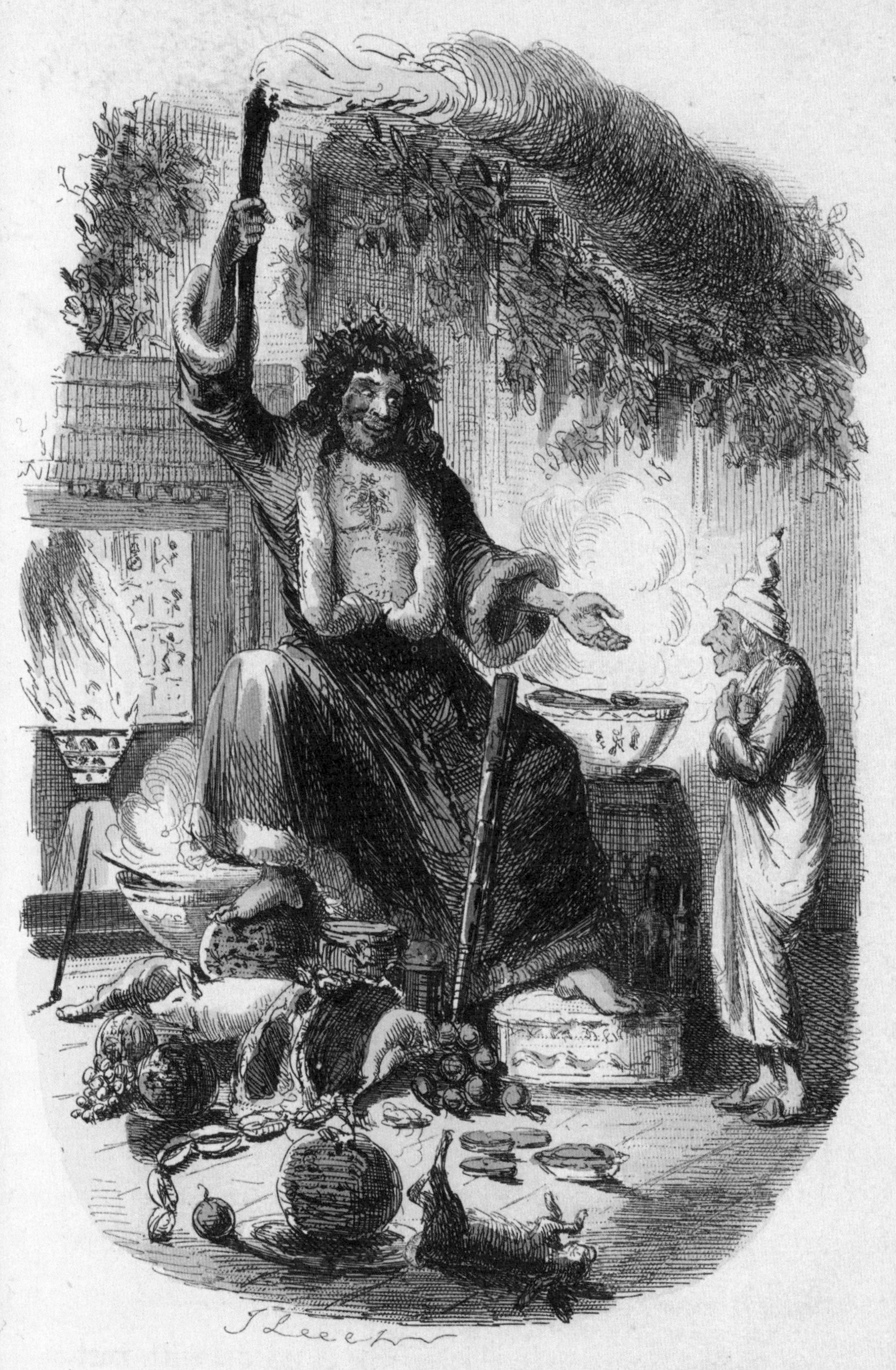

Scrooge's third Visitor.

basis of his new warm-hearted wisdom: 'I will live in the Past, the Present and the Future.' That is precisely the point of a festival.

There is one nineteenth-century addition to the modern Christmas which links our celebrations to the world of the Ysyakh festival in Siberia. In many traditional religions of northern Eurasia, the ever-green conifer, through its roots, trunk and branches, is thought to connect the underworld with this world and the heavens. On its branches are hung shiny totemic objects, originally representing spiritual forces in the landscape. In Scandinavia and Germany there is a Christmas habit of carrying an evergreen tree – part of the primal forest – into the house. It was popularized in Britain by Queen Victoria and Prince Albert, who brought the tradition with him from Coburg: the image of the royal couple peacefully gathered, with their children, round the Christmas tree at Windsor published in the *Illustrated London News* in 1848 had an impact across the whole country. This was the year when revolution had shaken Europe and finally toppled the French monarchy. The print presented the British royal family in a consciously unmonarchical light, close to the lives of their subjects, almost members of the respectable middle classes: their Christmas tree was copied everywhere by those who could afford it, a familial affirmation of harmonious social cohesion.

It was also the last step in the long process of conflation which leads ultimately to our Christmas cards and the modern Christmas experience: the most popular festival of a Middle Eastern religion, which overlapped with an ancient Roman holiday, absorbed nature worship imported from Germany, was reshaped and set to lyrics in New York, and eventually leads to trees in bedecked department stores all over the world, next to escalators taking children to Santa's grotto. (When did he first get *that*?)

The Puritans objected to Christmas because the feast lacked a

While revolutions shook the European continent in 1848, the British royal family gathered around their Christmas tree at Windsor.

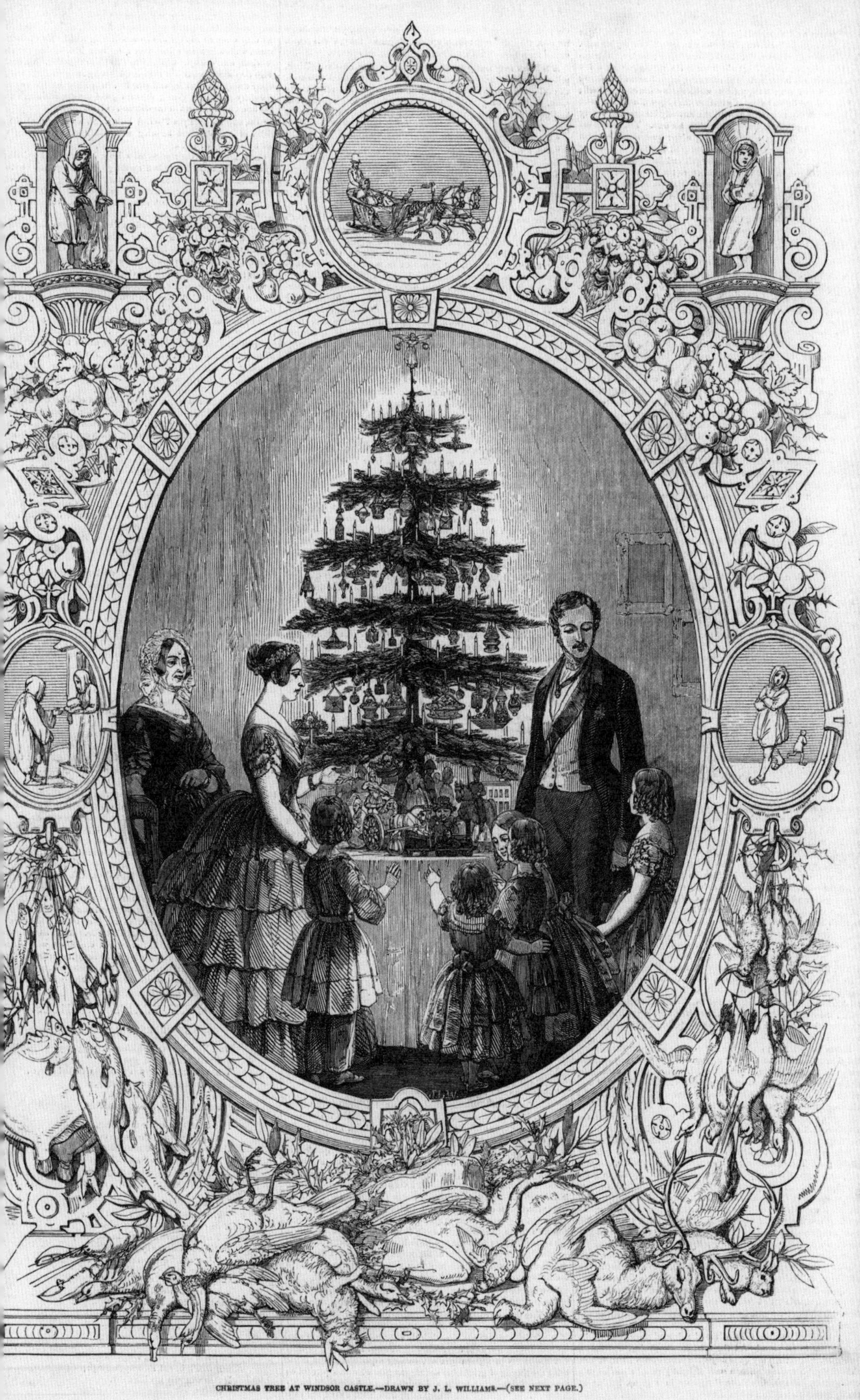

CHRISTMAS TREE AT WINDSOR CASTLE.—DRAWN BY J. L. WILLIAMS.—(SEE NEXT PAGE.)

biblical basis. Modern critics focus on self-indulgence and commercial excess, but Diarmaid MacCulloch thinks this is to miss an essential point:

Christmas has always been pretty materialistic, in the sense that it is about good cheer, and that has always caused trouble – medieval church moralists were always inveighing against lascivious dancing and the like. That's the problem with celebration: it will always have a double character. Festivals have a sacred character, if they claim to be a religious festival. But if they are any good, they will always penetrate into ordinary life too. People have a good time – that's why they remember them, and continue to observe them.

Christmas at the present day is surprisingly religious. An enormous number of people who would not normally think of going to church do so. They connect with an idea which is very compelling – a helpless baby, who has profound significance for us all – and they love the things that the church does with that. It is noticeable that the churches are much fuller at Christmas than they are on Good Friday, the celebration of Christ's crucifixion, or even at Easter, his resurrection. Those are much more difficult concepts for those on the edge of the church to feel empathy with. Christmas works because it says something profound which we cannot escape: we are all born helpless, and a new birth is a moment of enormous joy and celebration.

Religious festivals, whether in midwinter Britain or midsummer Siberia, are constantly reshaped, not by the authorities but by the people. They allow us to consider ourselves and those around us at the same point of every passing year. Most of us remember the Christmases (or Eids, Diwalis or Hannukahs) of our childhood, and those, now dead, with whom we celebrated them; and we assume that our children and grandchildren will still be celebrating them long after we too are dead, reaffirming both the inheritance that we share and our own transient place in the pattern of time.

PART FOUR

The Power of Images

Previous sections have examined communities of faith. In this section we explore the idea of a community of the image. God-given images inspire extraordinary devotion and can come to represent the entire nation, effectively playing the role of Head of State. But manmade images, made, re-made and endlessly reproduced, can be just as powerful a means of binding people together. They unite those who make them in a shared sense of belonging, or those who look at them across the centuries in a common conviction that they will be guided and protected. Sculpture and painting can carry us to worlds beyond words and beyond ourselves, worlds normally accessible only to poets and prophets, mystics and shamans. The ambiguities and contradictions of belief, with which language struggles, can be accommodated or even dissolved. Images which carry different kinds of truth and different levels of reality have for most societies been a key part of living with the gods.

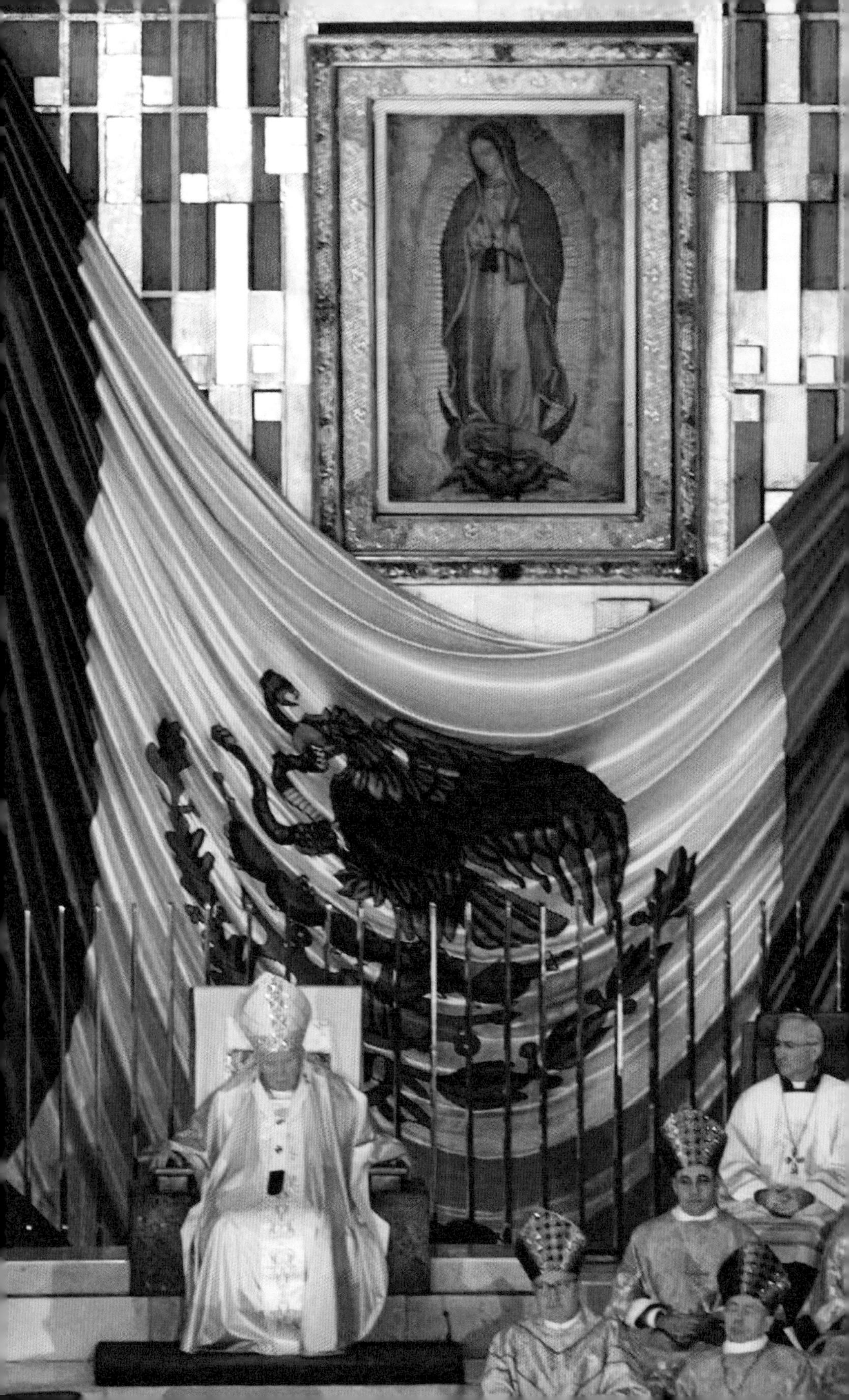

16

THE PROTECTORESSES

In 1568 an English traveller, Miles Philips, described what struck him as an idiosyncratic, but noteworthy, bit of behaviour in colonial Mexico:

There is an image of our Lady of silver and gilt, being as high, and as large as a tall woman ... Whensoever any Spaniards passe by this church, although they be on horse backe, they will alight, come into the church, and kneele before the image and pray to our Lady to defend them from all evil ... which image they call in the Spanish tongue, Nuestra sennora de Guadalupe: Our Lady of Guadalupe.

A little over thirty years earlier (so the story goes) a young man of native Mexican birth, called Juan Diego, had been walking near the outskirts of the new Spanish capital city of Mexico when a strange young woman appeared, speaking to him in his native tongue, Nahuatl – the language of the Aztecs. Introducing herself as the Virgin Mary, she made a request: that Juan Diego should have a church built for her on that very spot, near the hill of Tepeyac in Guadalupe.

Pope John Paul II sits under 'the Queen of Mexico' and in front of an outsize Mexican flag showing the Aztec eagle during Mass at the Basilica of Our Lady of Guadalupe, 23 January 1999.

Confronted with a sceptical local archbishop, Juan Diego eventually asked her for a sign to prove who she was. He was told that flowers would bloom miraculously on the barren hillside (it was the 12th of December) which he should gather in his *tilma* – a native cloak or apron – and then take to the archbishop. As Juan Diego presented the unseasonal flowers, there appeared, clearly imprinted on the *tilma*, a sublime image of the Virgin Mary, standing on a crescent moon held by a cherub, clothed in a gold robe and a blue mantle spangled with stars. News of the miraculous image, and of the Virgin's repeated appearances with words of encouragement and comfort, spread. A shrine was quickly erected with Juan Diego's divinely transformed *tilma* as its centrepiece, no longer a humble garment, but mounted and presented like a painted altarpiece.

Through all Mexico's political vicissitudes, and despite a bomb attack by an anti-clerical revolutionary in the 1920s, it has hung there ever since. Pilgrims, who now come not like Miles Philips's on horseback but in tourist buses, still pray to the Virgin of Guadalupe to 'defend them from all evil', but it is harder now for them to kneel in front of her: the crowds are so great that they have to pass slowly in front of the image, all gently carried forward on a moving walkway.

As the cultural historian Marina Warner observes, you can see from the souvenirs the pilgrims take away with them that this image, in many ways a conventional Catholic representation of the period, had one striking peculiarity:

An important part of this image is her dark skin. There are black virgins in Europe dating back to the Middle Ages, but they don't resemble black people, and even less local people. Our Lady of Guadalupe, by contrast, actually looks like an indigenous Mexican woman – an 'Indian', to use the terminology of the day. So this is a miraculous image of the Virgin Mary in which she appears not as a European, like the new colonial masters, but as an indigenous Mexican. She speaks to Juan Diego in Nahuatl. It is part of asserting the 'Indian-ness' of the church in Mexico, important to the Catholic policy of extending its embrace to all peoples.

The ethnically inclusive aspect of the Virgin of Guadalupe remains powerful. Where many representations of Mary in Catholic churches worldwide still show a young, clearly Caucasian, woman, the Mary encountered here, although wearing European-style clothes, is clearly from the region. This is an image of the church that crosses an ethnic barrier and actively embraces all Mexicans, whatever their origins. In a popular ceremony, where boys are brought to the basilica wearing a miniature copy of Juan Diego's *tilma*, even those of entirely European descent are dressed in Mexican-Indian costume, and proudly photographed in their new role as *dieguitos* – little Juan Diegos. This is truly the Virgin of Guadalupe – and also of Mexico as a whole. Marina Warner describes how:

She has become the embodiment of the nation, well beyond the purely religious. The cult of Our Lady of Guadalupe is followed by Mexicans everywhere, including in the United States. It is an assertion of identity, often by people who feel themselves to be discriminated against. She gives them comfort and strength.

As Marina Warner points out, the political repercussions of this image have been profound – and unpredictable. A vision, seen only a dozen years after the conquering Spaniards imposed their faith, became first the symbol of an indigenous American Catholicism, and in the nineteenth century a means of defining Mexican national identity in opposition to Spanish power. This 'patriotic' aspect of the cult has been fostered and developed over the centuries by both the secular and the religious authorities. After the rebellion against the Spanish crown from which Mexico emerged around 1820 as an independent republic, the first president of the new state marked his triumph and declared his true allegiance by changing his name from José Miguel Fernández y Félix to – Guadalupe Victoria.

After independence came further wars against the rapidly expanding United States and, later, the invading French. Throughout, those fighting for national freedom – across the political spectrum – continued to invoke the protection of the Virgin of Guadalupe. Looking back around 1870, after the French had been expelled, the radical campaigner Ignacio Manuel Altamirano stated simply:

The day in which the Virgin of Tepayac (Guadalupe) is not adored in this land, it is certain that there shall have disappeared, not only Mexican nationality, but also the very memory of the dwellers of Mexico today.

Astonishingly, not even the violently anti-clerical governments of the 1920s and 1930s could seriously undermine the popular habit, in moments of personal crisis or political oppression, of trusting to the Virgin of Guadalupe. In 1945 Pius XII proclaimed her Queen of Mexico and Empress of the Americas. Her basilica, which can hold over 10,000 people, is now said to be the most visited Roman

Mexican farm workers on strike in California, in 1966, march under the banner of Our Lady of Guadalupe, the protectoress of poor Mexicans everywhere.

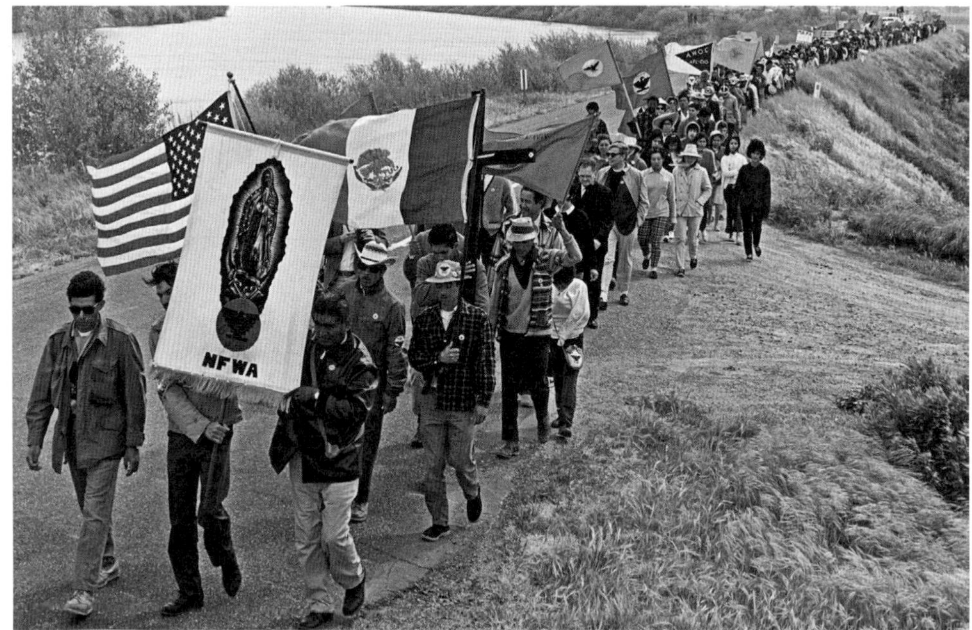

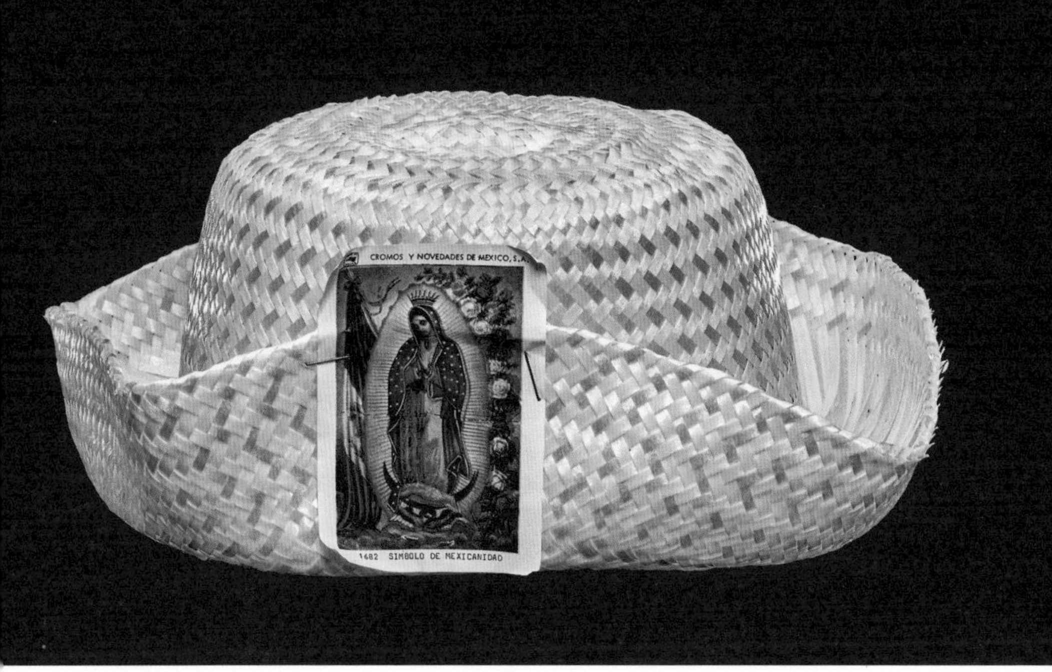

A simple souvenir: a Virgin Mary with indigenous Mexican features and who speaks Nahuatl

Catholic pilgrimage site in the world. Millions of Mexicans in the United States invoke her regularly.

This long politico-religious process can perhaps be summed up in one simple Mexican souvenir now in the British Museum – a girl's bright-yellow straw hat. Stapled to the side, like a medieval pilgrim's badge, is a small, crude colour-printed card showing an immediately recognizable Virgin of Guadalupe. Below it is printed not a blessing or a religious text, but the words *Simbolo de Mexicanidad* – the symbol of Mexican-ness. The Virgin of Guadalupe distils the essence of her people.

Just as the Mexican shrine is reportedly the supreme destination for Catholic pilgrims in the modern world, the sanctuary of Artemis/Diana in the great trading city of Ephesus, now in western Turkey, was by far the most celebrated temple of the antique Mediterranean. There is evidence for a cult of an Ephesian goddess as far back as the Bronze Age. The first known temple to Artemis appeared in the eighth century BCE. Sometime in the

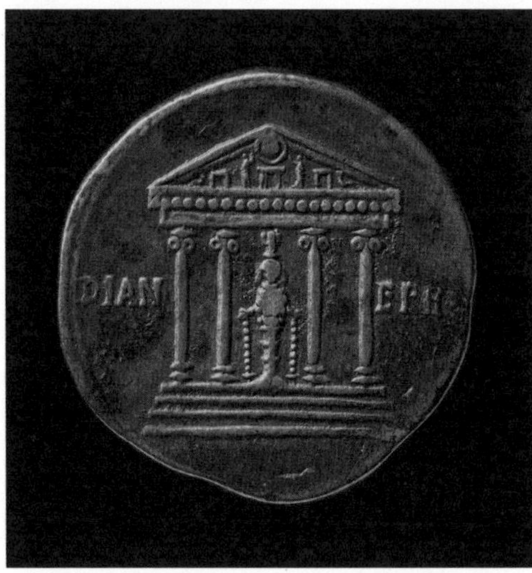

Left: Artemis dominates her Temple at Ephesus on this silver Roman coin *c.* 50 CE.

Opposite: Across the ancient world everybody would have recognized the unmistakable, many-breasted Artemis/Diana, protectoress of Ephesus and the Ephesians, standing between her two fawns.

sixth century, a new building was erected that was later declared one of the Seven Wonders of the World – it was the only temple among them and three times the size of the Parthenon. Stephanie Lynn Budin has made a special study of it:

This was a gigantic, absolutely stunning temple, and enormously rich: whole cities as well as private individuals, from humble folk to foreign ambassadors, brought offerings to this goddess. The wealth of the world was gathered here.

From her temple, Artemis looked over the city, protecting it and its residents. She provided blessings of peace and fertility, and general beneficence to the people of Ephesus, and to all who worshipped her.

Like the Virgin of Guadalupe on Juan Diego's *tilma*, the image of Artemis that presided over Ephesus was inherently sacred, because – crucially – it had not been made by any human hand: it was said to have fallen, at Zeus's command, direct from heaven. And, like the Mexican image of Mary, the Ephesian Artemis was like no other: so she was instantly recognizable when copied, a protectoress who retained her local identity as she went global.

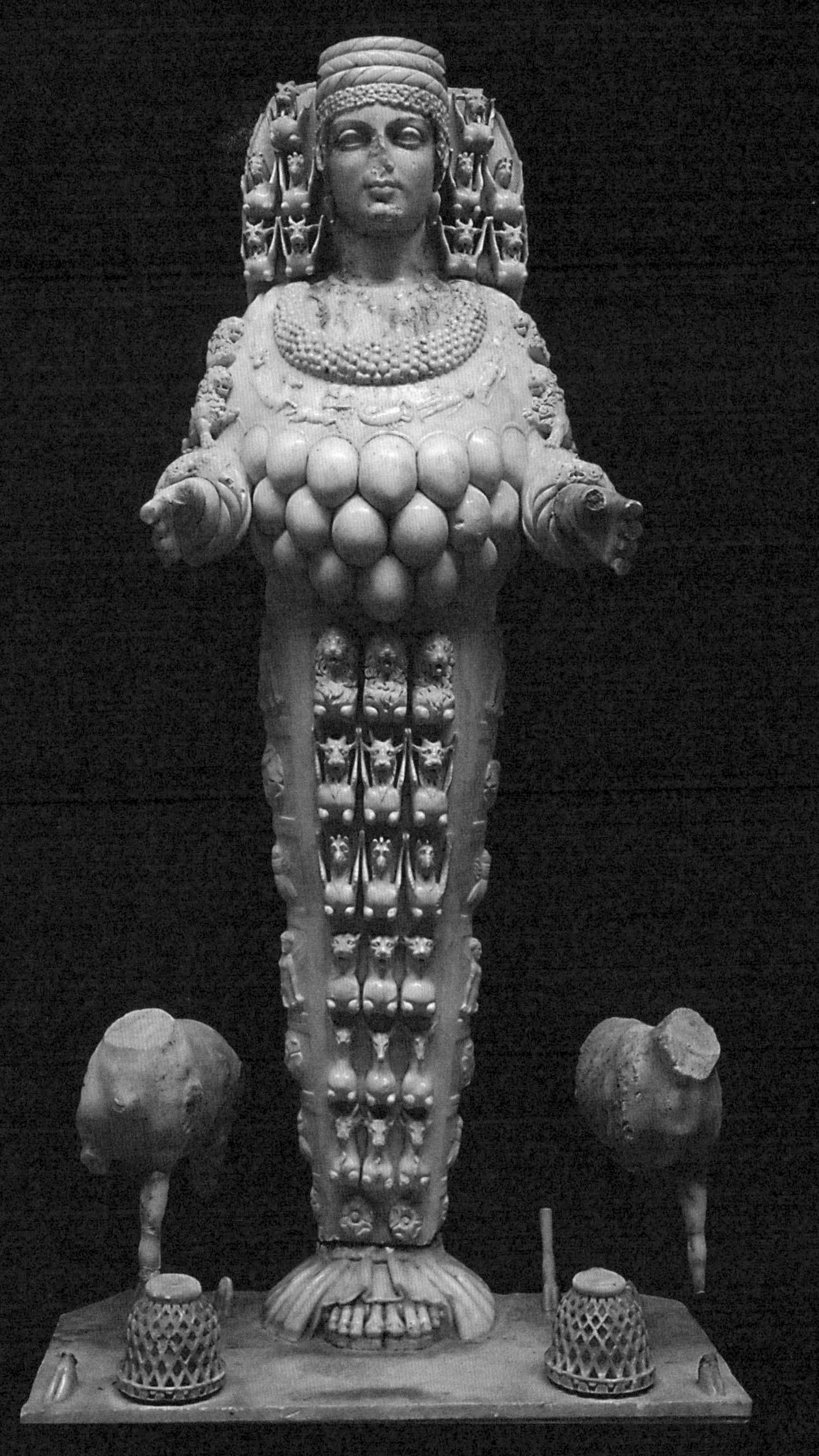

As Stephanie Lynn Budin points out, Artemis, goddess of nature and hunting, here takes on other, surprising characteristics:

She generally has fawns to either side of her and wears a 'polos' crown, indicative of her divinity. But strikingly her upper body is covered with what have been interpreted variously as multiple breasts, or bull's testicles, possibly offered in sacrifice. There's even a third possibility: these protuberances, which are her hallmark, may be bags, sometimes found on deities in Anatolia (modern Turkey), designed to contain gifts for human beings, ranging from food and drink to the blessings of wealth and children.

Thanks largely to centuries of sea-trading and colonization, the cult of Artemis of Ephesus spread eastwards into the Black Sea, and westwards to Spain. This particular – and peculiar – version of the goddess was copied everywhere, not least in her temple in Rome. Whenever you find a statue looking like this, it is very specifically Ephesian Artemis, with all the associations connected to that cult; it is distinctively Artemis with the power and prestige of this rich and important city.

Those associations were carried not just by the large statues erected in temples across the ancient world, most of which have perished. They were also present in small portable versions of Ephesian Artemis, made in ceramic or metal, gifts to be offered at her shrine, or souvenirs to be taken home, and which have survived in great quantities, all immediately recognizable. The original divine statue, said to be of wood, probably perished in a great fire in 356 BCE. Most of the surviving images are made of relatively inexpensive materials – more precious statuettes would have been melted down at various times and the metal reused. But we know from the Acts of the Apostles that there was a thriving luxury trade in such objects for prosperous pilgrims.

Saint Paul, preaching against pagan gods and their temples as he travelled, understandably caused particular alarm in Ephesus,

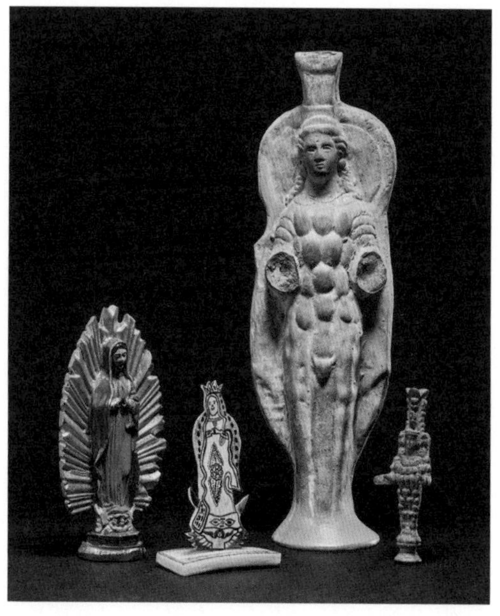

Portable images of Our Lady of Guadalupe and Artemis of the Ephesians made in different materials for pious pilgrims

which had the greatest temple of all. There he provoked a riot, led, the Bible tells us, by 'Demetrius, a silversmith, who made silver shrines for Artemis, which brought no small gain to the craftsmen'. He and his fellows could see that, if the new Christian teaching took hold, 'not only this our craft is in danger to be set at nought; but also that the temple of the great goddess Artemis should be despised, and her magnificence should be destroyed, whom all Asia and the world worshippeth'. The economic argument is swiftly submerged by the political, and an angry crowd gathers.

For about two hours all of them shouted in unison: 'Great is Artemis of the Ephesians!' And when the town clerk had quieted the crowd, he said, 'Citizens of Ephesus, who is there that does not know that the city of the Ephesians worships the great goddess Artemis, and the statue that fell down from heaven?'

The threat of riot passed: the cult and the temple are just too famous and too big for anybody even to imagine that they could be closed down.

The short biblical account leaves no doubt about the fervour of the citizens. Artemis had become the embodiment of the community, the very identity of the city, and any challenge to that idea would be violently opposed. Ancient Ephesus, like modern Mexico, clearly could not conceive of itself without its divine protectoress, worshipped there but revered throughout the world.

What did the Ephesian Artemis, through her image sent to earth by Zeus himself, actually do for the worshippers who showed her such devotion? In Stephanie Budin's words:

Artemis and her brother Apollo never grow up. They are always teenagers, so Artemis is the nubile teenager who is always at the edge of sexuality. And because she never passes over that threshold, she harnesses that fertility within herself without using it. That gives her control over her own body. She is the goddess of wild animals, and in Greek ideology unmarried girls were also wild. It was claimed that they were tamed by marriage: but the goddess of wild animals can never be tamed. She is a universal deity, protecting women as well as men, and in particular she oversees dangerous transitions – women in childbirth, the move from childhood into adulthood, and so on.

As Marina Warner explains, Artemis's virginity is an important element of her cult – though not necessarily because virginity as such is especially highly valued:

The interesting thing is that this idea of the virgin really relates less to the idea of being sexually chaste than to the idea of being single and powerful, which is more the essence of the classical Greek or Roman idea of the virgo. *The word is actually related to* vir *– the Latin for a man, a strong man – as well as to* virtus, *the word for virtue.*

It is this reserve of strength which allows Artemis in Ephesus, in direct contact with heaven, to protect the vulnerable at their moments of greatest personal danger. Marina Warner sees this most clearly expressed in the small bronze statuette of Artemis which reminds her of an Italian Renaissance Madonna della Misericordia (p. 249):

She has her arms in a receiving, open gesture. Her hands are open, her palms are spread and she is offering an embrace. So here the tutelary goddess of the city is welcoming the citizens, welcoming the people under her protection. She's extending her arms to shelter them.

It is an idea that recalls in many ways the words spoken to an apprehensive Juan Diego by the Virgin in one of her appearances to him, as his faith appeared to waver:

Am I not here who am your Mother? Are you not under my shadow and protection? Am I not your fountain of life? Are you not in the folds of my mantle, in the crossing of my arms? Is there anything else you need?

It is surely the power of that promise of protection that explains the number of souvenirs which are sold today in Guadalupe and which survive from Ephesus. The holy image, in its particular, hallowed place, offers unusually intimate contact with the divine. As we saw with the pilgrims in Chapter 14, a small copy, a reminder of that contact, can be with you anywhere, a presiding presence and a comfort in your daily life.

One striking aspect of the cult of these protective figures is how deeply rooted they are in popular affection. The people of Ephesus rioted to defend Artemis against Paul's criticisms, and her cult continued to thrive there for centuries more. In 1990, when Pope John Paul II decided to beatify Juan Diego, the Abbot of Guadalupe protested on the grounds that there was insufficient historical evidence to prove that he had even existed. In the face of great popular anger at this, the abbot resigned, the beatification

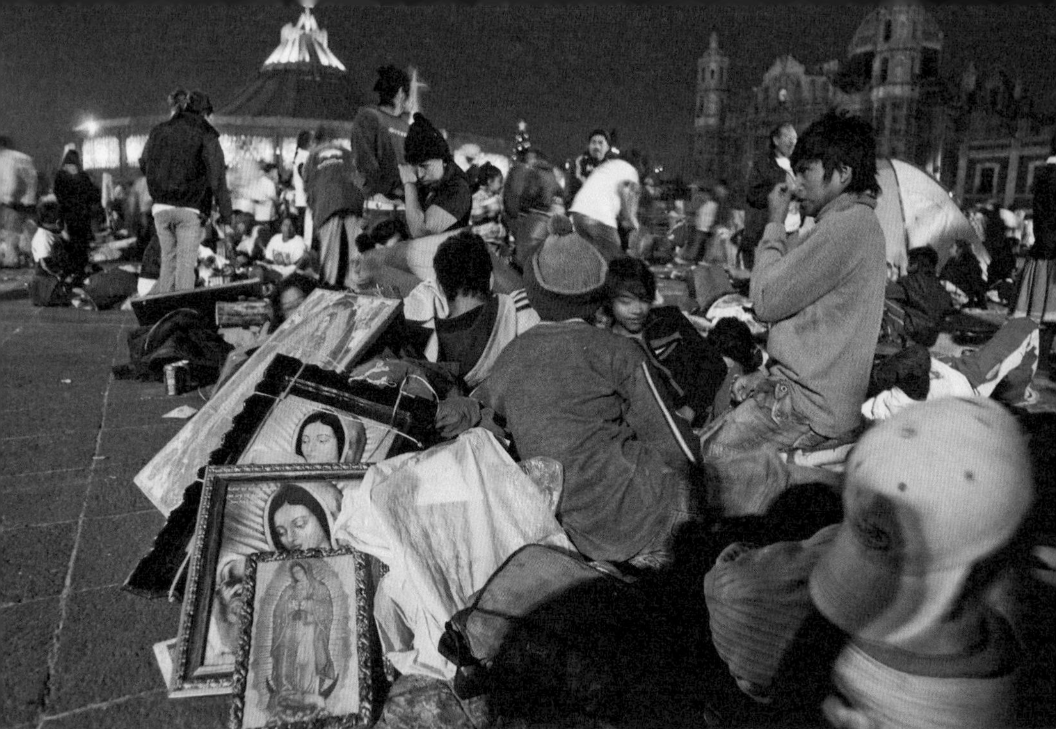

Countless images of the Virgin of Guadalupe are sold every year to the pilgrims that come to her shrine. The Basilica of Guadalupe is the most visited Christian pilgrimage site in the world

went ahead, and twelve years later, in 2002, the Pope declared Juan Diego the first indigenous American saint.

Marina Warner believes that the recent child abuse scandals in the church, which all round the world have undermined trust in male clergy, have strengthened the desire for the motherly divine protection offered by the Virgin Mary, leading to a flourishing of particular cults like Our Lady of Guadalupe. In secular, modern Europe is there any figure that might seem able to provide a comparable sense of communal belonging and individual protection?

Princess Diana came very close to it. That outpouring of flowers when she died, and the astonishing wave of grief, arose from the sense that by looking after the victims of Aids and of landmines, she had taken on that special role of protector and comforter to the vulnerable, especially the young.

Marina Warner points out that you can see this very clearly in

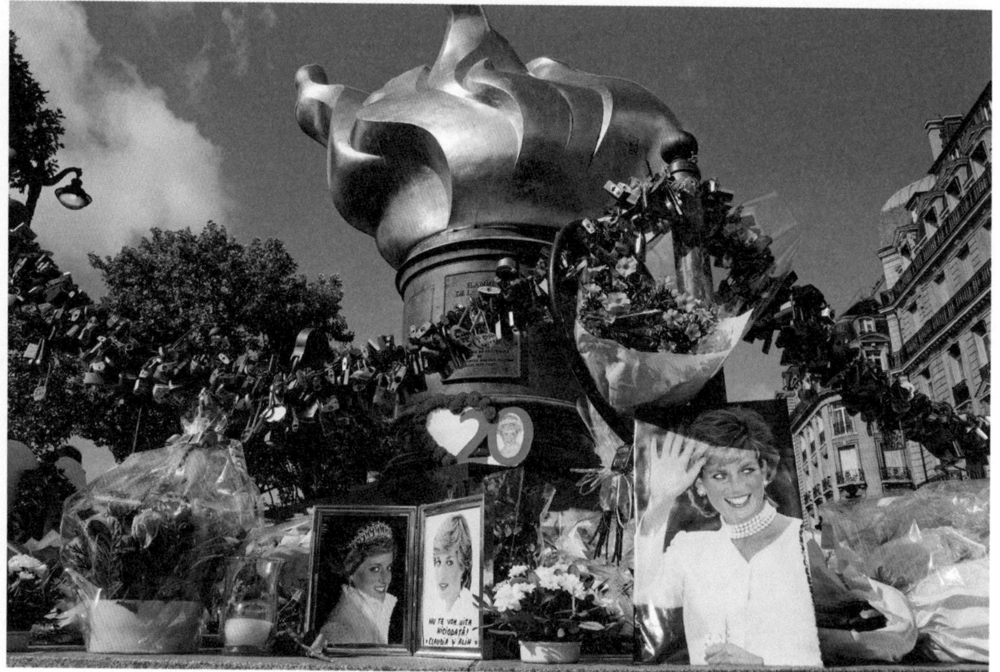

A replica in Paris of the flame of the Statue of Liberty appropriated as a shrine to Princess Diana. This photograph was taken in August 2017, on the twentieth anniversary of her death.

Paris, just a few yards from the Seine, at a spot above the tunnel where the Princess had her fatal car crash. In 1989, a monument to Franco-American friendship was erected there – a gilt bronze flame about ten feet high, a replica of the flame held by the Statue of Liberty. In 1997, when Princess Diana died, the public appropriated this monument, completely ignored its original meaning, and transformed it into a shrine to her.

Twenty years after her death, the bronze flame is still surrounded by photographs of the Princess. Offerings of flowers, and handwritten messages of affection written in many languages, expressing thanks or asking for help, are placed there regularly by people who could, I think, be described as pilgrims. The authorities clear the offerings away, but they return. There could hardly be a clearer demonstration of just how deeply people want a mother figure, a being from another sphere, to inspire, guide and protect them.

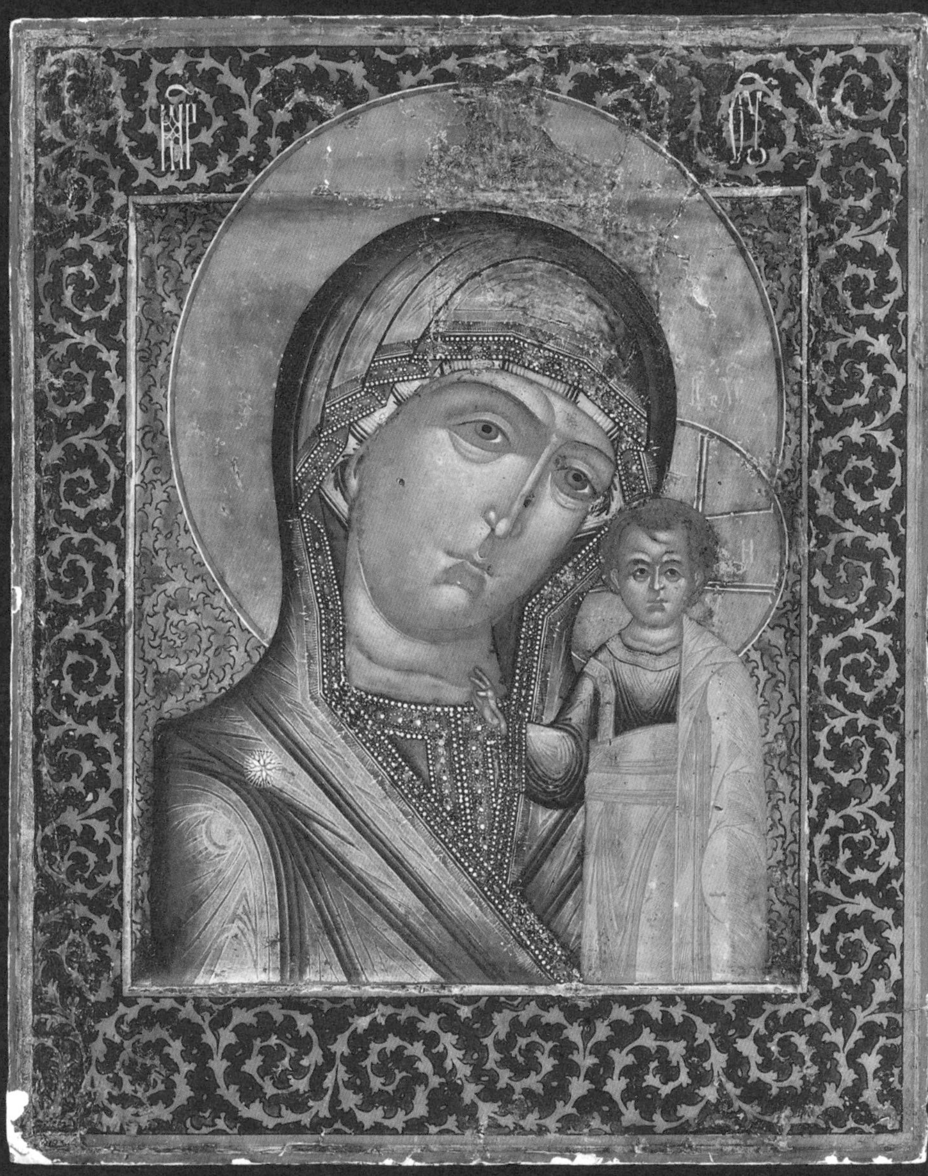

17

THE WORK OF ART IN TIMES OF SPIRITUAL REPRODUCTION

Images sent directly from heaven clearly have a particular authority. The divine force believed to have shaped both Artemis of the Ephesians and Our Lady of Guadalupe made them not just rallying-points for a whole society, but effectively idealized heads of state. Yet images unquestionably made on earth and also many times reproduced can play a central role in the life of a modern nation too and can also be appropriated to political ends. Made by human hands specifically to bring the divine into the daily lives of individuals, the icons and statues in this chapter also foster a deep sense of community, transcending social divisions and the passing generations. Their capacity to do this depends not on the aesthetic quality of their execution but much more on the particular way in which they are made, and how they are then used and venerated.

Images like these, significant to millions, exist entirely outside our familiar Western European categories of art or art history, which are based above all on the idea of a unique work, the creation of a great genius with a particular vision and style. Most of those looking at Piero della Francesca's *Baptism of Christ* in the

Icon of Our Lady of Kazan in a version made in Yaroslavl around 1850. The Christ-child stands to teach the spectator the lessons of child-like humility.

National Gallery in London, for instance, are more likely to be interested in what it tells us about Piero than in the theology of the event he depicted. For most of the thousands of visitors who see it every day, Leonardo's *Last Supper* in Santa Maria delle Grazie in Milan is just that: Leonardo's. The original work, even if severely damaged, gives us access to the insights of a supreme artist, the subject itself often little more than a backdrop which allows us to enter their individual world and to admire their skill in rendering emotion, capturing the fall of light, or manipulating space, texture and depth. The original spiritual purpose of the work has been overwhelmed by the cult of the artist who produced it.

That is emphatically not the point of these two Russian icons in the British Museum. We often talk about a great work of art as 'transcendent', or as possessing the power to 'transport' us. But such definitions of 'artistry' do not apply in this case, and in a narrowly aesthetic sense these two objects could safely be described as undistinguished. They are small in scale, and probably made to be used at home. There is nothing in the handling of the paint to excite our attention, far less our admiration. The aim of the artists here was not to realize on panel their own particular vision of the world, but to open a gateway to the divine by repeating a composition immediately recognizable to everybody who would look at it, and as familiar as a prayer or a song learnt in childhood.

In both icons, Mary holds her infant son on her left arm, and bends her head gently towards him. He stands erect in tunic and golden robe, and solemnly holds up his right hand in a gesture that both guides us and blesses us. There is little sense of any natural source of light, but there is celestial light: both mother and son have haloes, the Virgin's breaking the inner frame. There is virtually no moulding or suggestion of depth. Nothing disturbs the perception that this is merely paint on a flat surface, and one

Icon of Our Lady of Kazan, in a version made in Moscow in the seventeenth century

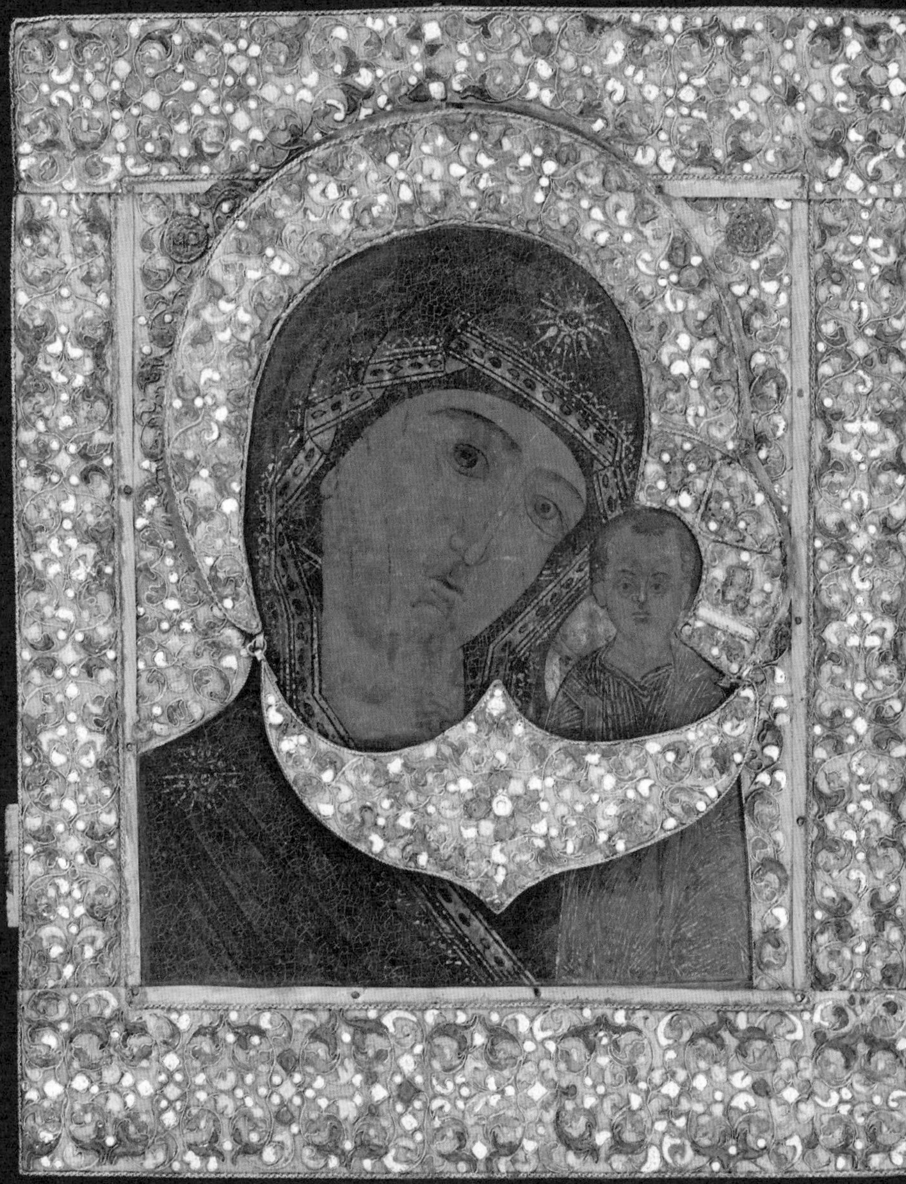

image has a protective enamel revetment which allows that surface to be kissed in devotion without being too much damaged. (It is a major conservation hazard of Russian icons that they are on occasion kissed into extinction.)

The two images were painted in different cities roughly 200 years apart – the silver-gilt version made in Moscow in the seventeenth century, the golden in Yaroslavl in the first half of the nineteenth. Yet in the two centuries that separate them very little has changed – the placing in the frame, the expression and modelling, pose, gesture, glance and mood are all essentially identical. And that is because both are copies – and designed to be instantly recognizable as such – of one of the most celebrated and holiest icons in the history of Russia: Our Lady of Kazan.

The original icon that lies behind both our versions was said to have come, a little after 1200, from Constantinople to Kazan, a great citadel on the Volga some 500 miles east of Moscow. In the fifteenth century, when Tartar invaders captured Kazan, the icon was hidden, and then lost. But after Ivan the Terrible had driven the enemy armies out in 1552, the Virgin Mary appeared in a dream to a young girl and revealed its whereabouts. Since then, the image, quickly found to have miracle-working properties, has been invoked against other invaders of Russian soil – against Poles in the seventeenth century, Swedes in the eighteenth and French in the nineteenth, in every case with triumphant results. The icon was soon venerated as the Holy Protectoress of Russia, and many copies were made and distributed. A cathedral was built in Kazan itself to house it, and further cathedrals dedicated to this image, Our Lady of Kazan, were erected in Moscow and St Petersburg, both of them, of course, holding copies. In 1904 the original was stolen: a sacrilege to which the pious attributed the calamities of the country's defeat in the Russo-Japanese War and of the failed Revolution of 1905. It has never been recovered. The original work of art, with whatever aesthetic qualities it may have had, is lost,

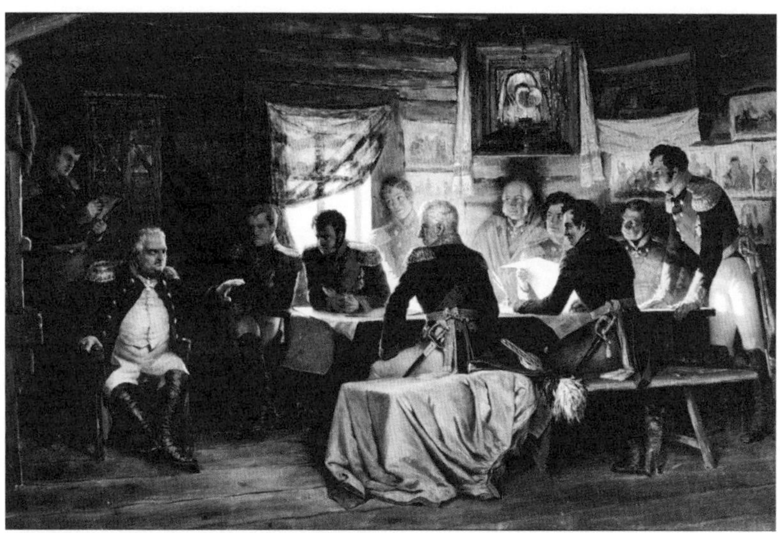

How Our Lady of Kazan saved Russia: in a painting from the 1880s, Kutuzov, commander of the Russian armies, confers with his generals during the struggle against Napoleon, 1812. Our Lady of Kazan presides over the conference.

but the celestial vision it embodied lives on in countless copies, its help still invoked daily by millions. The two icons in the British Museum are a tiny part of a large, widely scattered family.

Rowan Williams, formerly Archbishop of Canterbury, explains how the spectator is intended to use images like these, many times multiplied, and so far removed from our familiar conventions of realism in representation, or our ideas of artistic creativity. What can we hope to get from them?

The main point of the icon is that it is a vehicle of the divine presence – and action. It carries that action by depicting literally the act of god. So when you stand prayerfully in front of an icon, the idea is that you are actually in some sense opening up to the action of god. In this case, with an icon of Our Lady of Kazan, you are invited to look at particular dimensions, or aspects, of the relation of Christ to his mother – and therefore of Christ's relation to the believer, represented here by the Virgin. Different icon traditions explore different aspects of that relationship.

So, for example, in the tradition of Our Lady of Vladimir, you see the child nestling up very closely to the face of Mary with one arm round her neck: and that is often called the Virgin of Loving Kindness. In the Kazan tradition, you have the child indicating with his hand the way of the faithful, engaged in teaching us, and the Virgin is a witness to his action. The way in which her inclined head and eyes are depicted is a way of suggesting how the believer might look towards – and move towards – the figure of Christ.

It's a rather unexpected depiction in the sense that he is really behaving as an adult might, whereas, in Vladimir icons, the child is behaving like a child, cuddling up to his mother. In the 'Kazan' image, he is obviously a foreshadowing of the great teacher he will later become as an adult, but he is also reminding us that even as an infant Christ teaches us something: that the humility or vulnerability of the child is part of the divine action.

If that is their purpose for the viewer, what is the task of their creator? Making an image like this, which is about perpetual relationships rather than fleeting appearances, requires particular training and skills that go beyond the ability merely to make and manage materials. Manuals of guidance for icon painters stress the importance of mastering long-agreed conventions for representing the saints. The task of the painter is not to invent but to 'transcribe' these holy images of the Church, already revealed and revered. To do so the artist should prepare himself spiritually, through prayer or fasting, so that his hand will be guided by God.

Some icon painters are of course more gifted than others, and some have a style which can be recognized as their own – Andrei Rublev is the paramount example. Yet the principal purpose is the continuation of a tradition, a long sequence of transmitting an honoured image, in which the painter seeks only to take his proper place. His own achievement is secondary in a centuries-old relationship between worshippers and god. Rowan Williams explains the power of this self-effacing view of the artist:

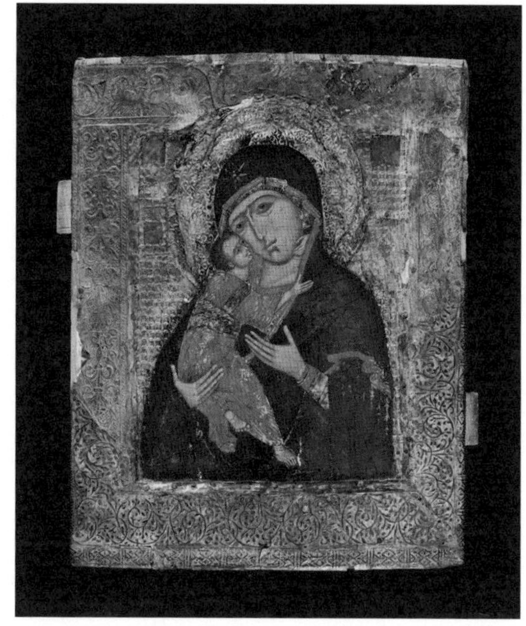

Icon of Our Lady of Vladimir, in a version made in Moscow in the nineteenth century. The Christ-child cuddles lovingly up to his ever-protective mother.

It is part of the general Eastern, Orthodox, Christian attitude which says that originality is not what you prize. What you look for and value is reliability, for a way of entering into the on-going stream of a common life.

In other words, icons like this affirm the belief that looking at them makes you part of a huge community, living and dead, who like you have prayed before an image that looked very like this one – the 'on-going stream of a common life'. For Rowan Williams there is another sense in which these images, although generally intended for individual contemplation, or use at home, create a sense of community:

As far back as I can remember, for decades and decades, I have tended to say daily prayers in front of an icon. If you want to sit in silence, if you want to be acted upon in prayer, and be open to something, then the icon is the ideal vehicle.

Yet every icon has its true home in the church where it's part of a whole system of decoration: there you are surrounded by images, other icons, each of them embodying or conveying different aspects of the divine action in one mode or another. As I sometimes rather irreverently put it, there's a sort of jacuzzi effect if you are in church. The energy of the images is coming at you from all around. And so even when you're praying at home, on your own in front of an icon, you will be aware that it has its place within that wider scheme, just as you have your place within the wider praying body. So an icon is never just a little amulet in your pocket. It represents the entire praying, contemplating, reflecting work of the church. It represents the way in which the church transmits to you and to everybody the energy, the action of god.

*

Our Lady of Kazan is mostly prayed to at home or in church, often in solitude. Durga, on the other hand, is a goddess of the streets, who moves happily through the crowds – above all the crowds of the city of Kolkata:

She descends from her divine abode, but she doesn't come into a temple: she actually comes into the streets, so that people can carry her, hold her, see her – and so that she can see them.

Sunil Khilnani, the historian of modern India, is describing what happens across Bengal every year in the popular festival of Durga Puja.

Durga is a powerful warrior goddess, a fearful mixture of the martial and the maternal. She is a being with one central purpose: to destroy evil. The Hindu scriptures tell how, after performing a number of heroic acts, the warrior Mahishasura was granted a boon by the gods: no man would be able to defeat him. This enabled him to win many victories, until at last he turned his power against the gods themselves, who at that point were all male, in an attempt to usurp their strength for his own evil ends. Alarmed, the gods held an assembly. Their anger and frustration that, as males, they could do nothing to stop Mahishasura turned into a burst of light and energy, which was transformed into a woman: Durga.

Each of the male gods gave her a weapon, and she was equipped with a lion to ride on. Thus armed and mounted, she set out to do battle with Mahishasura, who sometimes took the form of a buffalo. Undaunted, she defeated him by cutting off his head, thus restoring the authority of the gods and the moral order of the world. This is Durga, the warrior goddess, who conquers evil, and who once a year comes to visit. Sunil Khilnani portrays the scene:

It's usually late in September or early October – it depends on the moon. The gods and goddesses are busy people. They have a lot of matters to attend to, so they only turn up from time to time and there's a lot of preparation that goes into getting ready for the goddess. Houses are painted, sweets are prepared, new clothes are bought. This is a real moment of welcoming the goddess as she passes through. But first there is the building of the image which she comes to inhabit during the time of the festival.

Across Bengal these images, painted clay representations of the goddess, are made not by a solitary artist, but effectively (like the Parsi fire in Chapter 3) by the whole community, and according to well-established conventions. Supported by a wicker frame, the bulk of the body is composed of earth. Great efforts are made to incorporate at least a bit of earth from all parts of the locality, and there should always be some from the banks of the Ganges, as Durga has a close connection to the river. A priest must also beg for some from a prostitute's house to be added to the final mix. Durga is shown at the moment of her triumph, with long arms and large hands, vanquishing with her spear the evil Mahishasura – represented either as a man or as a buffalo. Her face is rounded like a betel leaf; her mouth is small, but her large eyes are elongated, stretched almost to her ears. The last stage of the making is the painting-in of these eyes, which are added either by

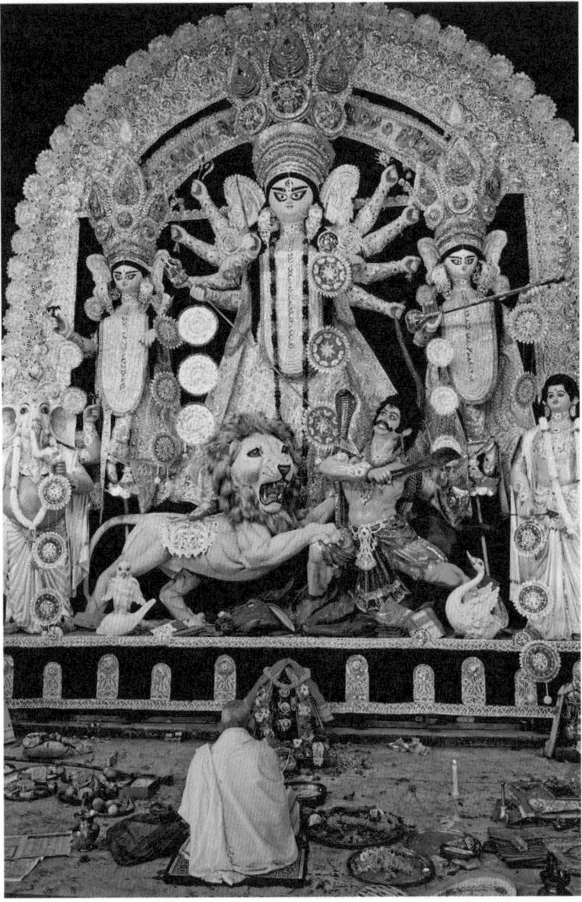

Worshipper in front of Durga in her splendour during the Durga Puja festival, Kolkata, 2013

a priest himself or by an artist whose arm the priest guides. From that moment, the image is fit for Durga to inhabit. The huge eyes are an essential point of contact between her and the people. Her gaze, which seems to have no particular object of focus, enables her to return the glance of her devotees from any angle – and this exchange of glances, this seeing the goddess face to face, is a profoundly important aspect of spiritual engagement.

Because of the way in which the materials for the statue are collected and combined, the image which Durga comes to inhabit has within it the whole place and the whole community, physically and symbolically present. In Sunil Khilnani's interpretation:

What's striking about the Durga image is that it is made of very simple materials, with nothing valuable. There are no jewels, no gold or silver as you might see in an icon. It's clay, wood, straw and oil paint and its power is partly the ordinariness of it, the fact that these are everyday materials, which then are endowed with a special and transcendental character for those temporary moments when attention is focused on the image.

Everyone in the community contributes to the making of it – if not actually making it or giving the materials, then by contributing some money. Each neighbourhood will have its own Durga image and people feel very strong allegiance to that particular image, because they've seen it being built, or they have paid for it to be built.

The strength of that community allegiance can be seen in the intense rivalry between different neighbourhoods of Kolkata to produce the most impressive temporary housing – or *pandal* – for the images of the goddess during her stay. Some of them are colossal and truly spectacular. People go from one *pandal* to another, comparing and competing. And to these *pandals*, in the days of festival, the concerns of the city and the world will be brought to be put in front of Durga. The war with China in the Himalayas, strikes in the Tata car factory, worries about pollution, floods and tsunamis, episodes from *Harry Potter* – even the death of Princess Diana – over the years, all have been represented in miniature and found their place in the *pandal* under the gaze of the goddess.

As Sunil Khilnani points out, this political aspect of the Durga Puja as a focus for communal identity is by no means new:

These sorts of popular religious festivals have of course been going on for a very long time, but I think you can see that from the late nineteenth century they came to have a particular importance as a way of establishing identity vis-à-vis the British. In Bombay, there were popular, city-wide pujas in honour of Ganesh which also became very political. And this dimension was certainly present in the Durga Puja in Calcutta. They became a way of affirming a certain kind of Hindu identity in the face of British rule. Today politicians still seek to be involved in the festival. In Kolkata, for instance, Mamata Banerjee, the chief minister of West Bengal, has composed songs for the Durga Puja.

Just as Our Lady of Kazan became a focus of Russian resistance to foreign invasion, Durga assumed a political role in opposition to the British Raj. As an emblem of Bengali identity it is a role she has continued to perform since independence.

The British Museum has many icons in its collection besides these two of Our Lady of Kazan. But it has not a single large-scale painted image of Durga, although over the centuries thousands of them have been made and discarded. The reason is simple and surprising: at the climactic end of the festival, Durga returns to her home in the Himalayas. The *pandals* are dismantled. The clay statues are taken not to a temple, to be reverently stored, but carried, with great fanfares and accompanied by dancers, to the banks of the Ganges. There they are consigned to the sacred river, to dissolve into it and be carried by it out into the Bay of Bengal. It is estimated that over the festival's closing nights as many as 1,500 immersions take place in Kolkata alone – at peak times one every five minutes, so many that they have become an environmental problem for authorities across the region. The statues are no longer venerated, because they are no longer inhabited by the goddess. They have served their purpose and have once again become what they always were: earth, straw and paint. Sunil Khilnani recounts how the unmaking of these images is in every way as significant as their making:

This is a very social moment. As many people as possible will be involved in the immersion of the image at the end of the festival, which is when Durga really departs. By the immersion of this

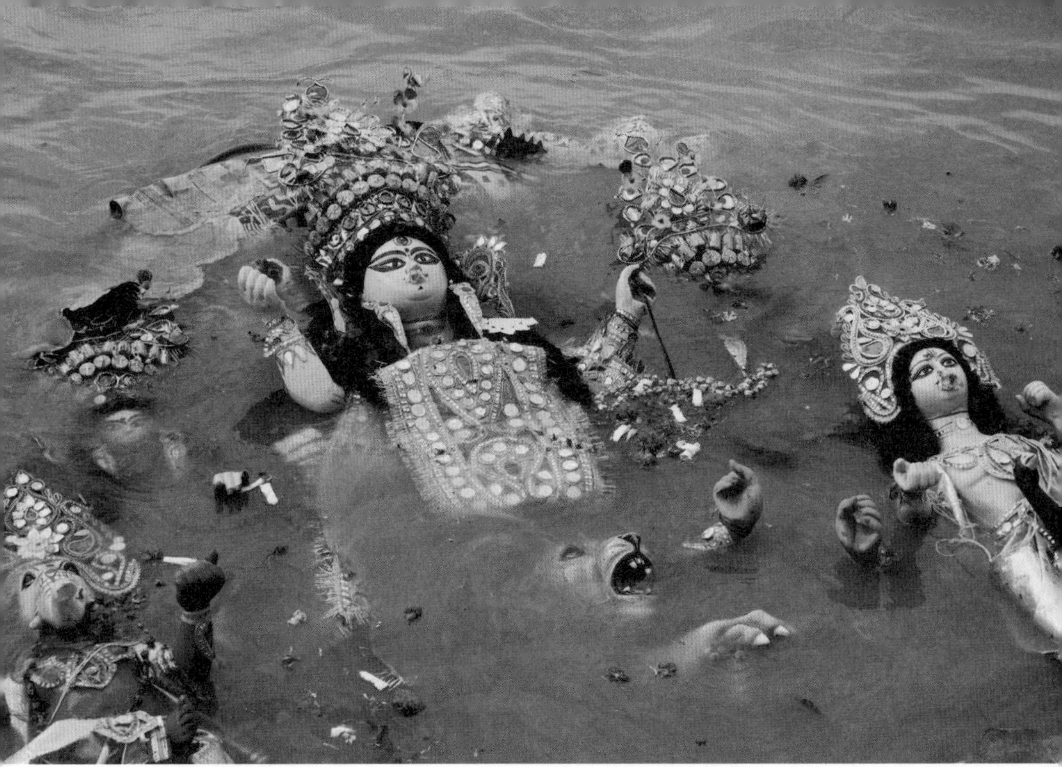

The statue of Durga dissolves in the Ganges and floats away towards the Bay of Bengal.

painted mud in water, the statue returns to its component earthly elements. Everybody gathers as she is lowered into the water and sent off until her next visit the following year.

*

The making of the image of Durga, in which all the community is symbolically present, and her material dissolution, assert through rituals as powerful as they are popular that she is a goddess not for an individual, but for a society. The icons of Our Lady of Kazan make the same point. They are painted to remind viewers that when they look at this Virgin and Child, they do so in the company of millions who have prayed before an image almost identical. In both cases the images themselves are of little inherent value. They are made and they are remade. But that continuous remaking provides a pattern in which all can find their place – a pattern of enduring connection between human and divine, and one that shapes and sustains a society over centuries.

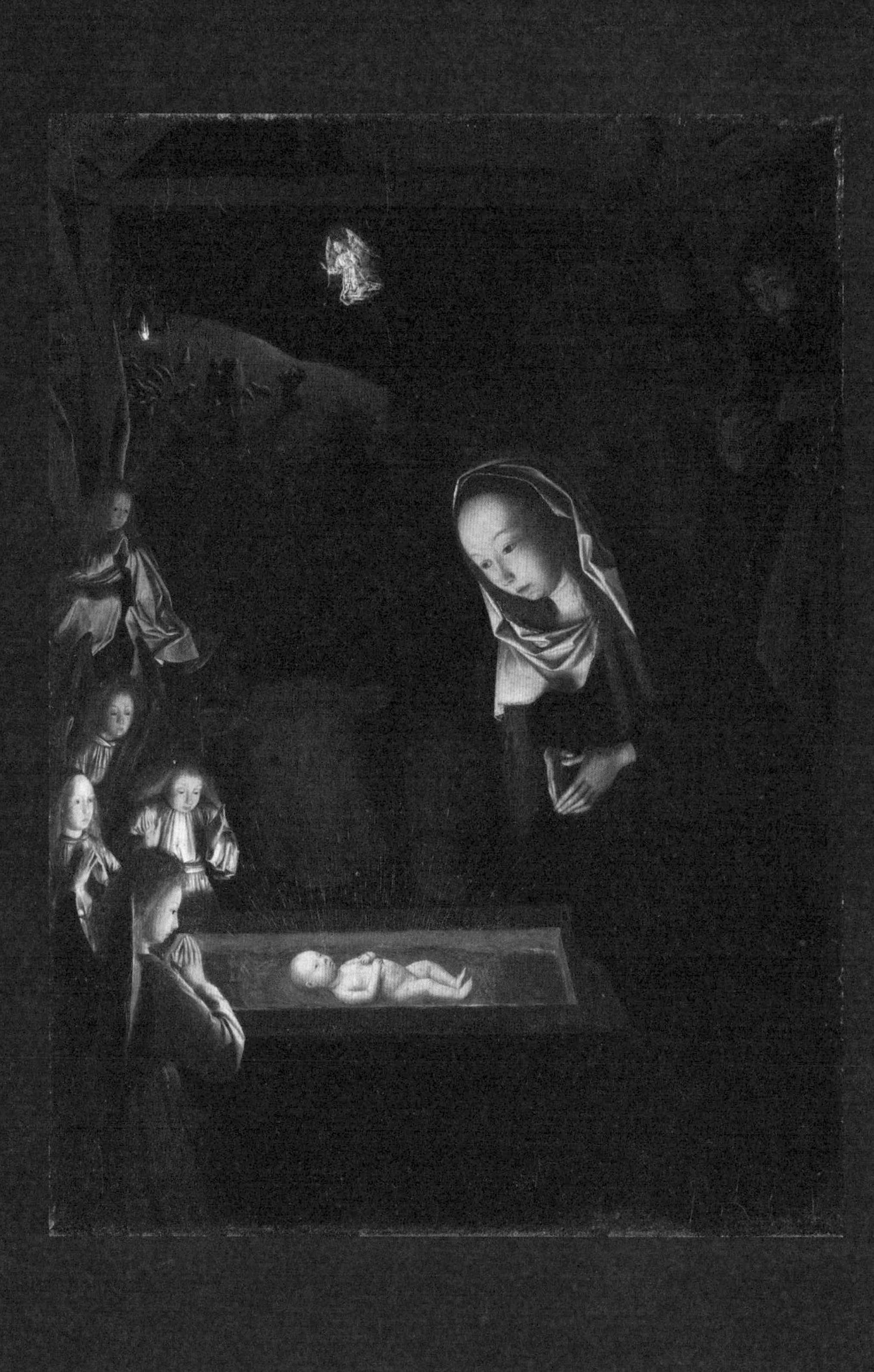

18
THE ACCRETION OF MEANING

One of the most popular Christmas cards sold by the National Gallery in London is the *Nativity*, painted around 1490 by the Netherlandish artist Geertgen tot Sint Jans. In the darkness of the stable, Mary is joined by angels to worship the newborn child who illuminates the scene, radiating light. Behind the manger, the ox and the ass look on. In the far distance, an angel is telling the shepherds what has just happened.

It is a scene so familiar to most of us that it is easy to overlook its complexity. Not for the first time in this book, we see the frontier between heaven and earth miraculously dissolved. Here, angels pass easily from one to the other. Most people, if asked, would say that Geertgen is illustrating the Gospel narrative. But he does far more than that. This Nativity combines three very different kinds of stories – historic, prophetic and mystic – into one powerful image.

Saint Luke's account of Christ's birth seems to report a historical event which occurred when Caesar Augustus ordered a census. Neither ox nor ass, however, appears in the Gospel. Hundreds of years earlier the Hebrew prophet Isaiah had foretold that those

Nativity by Geertgen tot Sint Jans, *c.* 1490: the birth of Jesus as Saint Bridget of Sweden saw it in her vision

animals would one day recognize the future master of Israel, the Messiah. So they have been led from the Old Testament to the New, and into the stable at Bethlehem to acknowledge the Christ child: an obscure prophetic utterance, turned into beasts that every western child today recognizes – a much loved, but very imperfectly understood, addition to Saint Luke's story.

The shining, luminous body of the newborn baby, giving out rays of light like the sun, is also not to be found in the Gospel: this detail was provided by Saint Bridget of Sweden, a fourteenth-century mystic who in a vision had found herself present at the Nativity. Her published 'eye-witness' account of what she saw there – the stable made dark by the brilliance coming from the child, Mary worshipping her son, angels singing – was hugely popular in Northern Europe around 1500. That is what is shown here, as we are allowed to join Bridget on her mystic journey back in time, seeing what she saw, while also sharing Isaiah's looking forward to the coming of the Messiah. The brisk Gospel narrative of the first century – 'she laid him in a manger, because there was no room at the inn' – is fused with dreams and visions written down at nearly 2,000 years' distance from each other, which we now overlay with our own memories of childhood and the strains of 'Silent Night'. Like most religious pictures, this one tells not one story, but several – and allows us to add ours.

This capacity of images seamlessly to combine the seen and imagined worlds has been exploited wherever humans have tried to convey spiritual experience. Across Southern Africa, we find art ranging over many centuries, painted on the rock in thousands of caves and shelters, by the people long misleadingly described by Europeans as 'Bushmen'. Although there are many different linguistic groups and there is no one name on which all agree, they are now most commonly referred to as San|Bushmen. They are considered to be autochthonous: in other words, they are

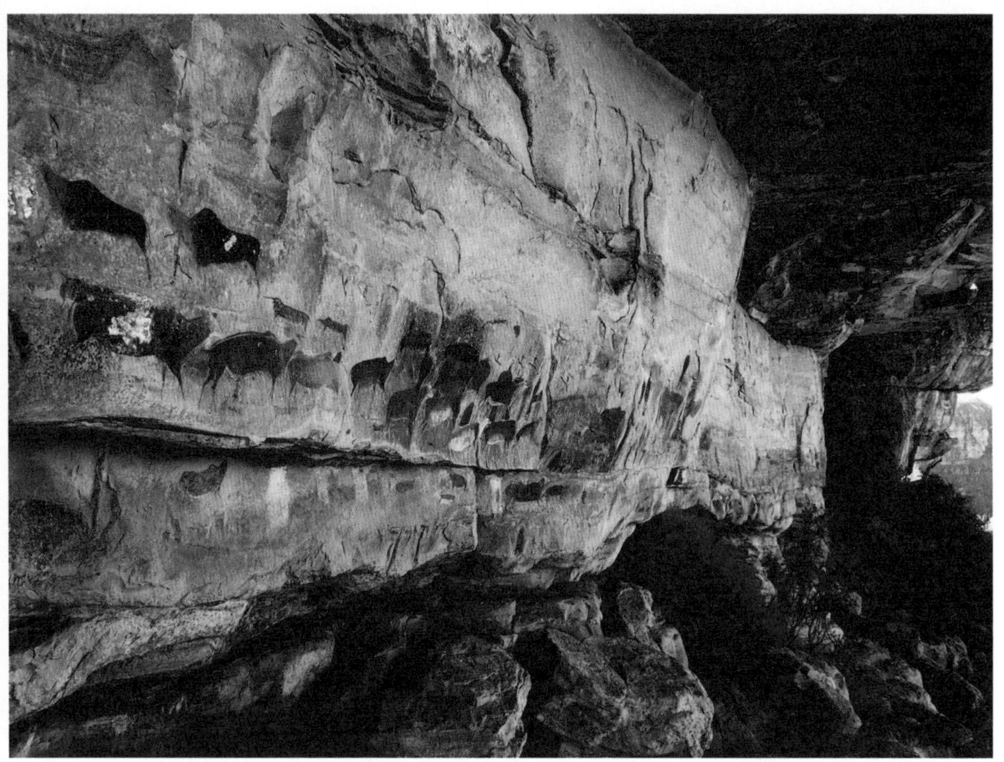

The Game Pass shelter at Drakensberg, South Africa, one of the most celebrated examples of San|Bushman rock art painting

still living in the same region as they did over 70,000 years ago, when their ancestors (like all our ancestors) evolved into modern humans. Until relatively recently, they were essentially hunter-gatherers (and to some extent still are). Their hunters pursued eland, a kind of antelope. Outsiders have long been fascinated by their languages, characterized by a system of clicks, which to non-San speakers are bewilderingly difficult to mimic, and which combine to make more distinctly different consonants than any other known language.

Their rock art paintings are equally intriguing. Human figures, often tall and wispy, some with animal heads, seem to be progressing across a landscape. Many have in their hands implements of some sort, perhaps tools or weapons. Others are flying or jumping, not always clearly distinguishable from animals doing the same.

For the uninitiated viewer there is wonderment and frustration

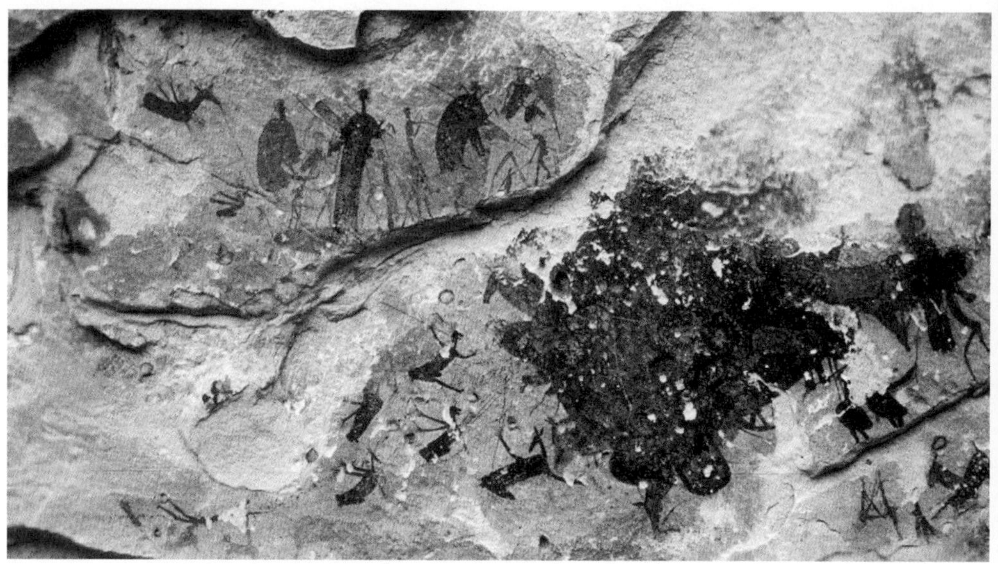

In this San|Bushman rock painting in the Free State Province of South Africa, eland and shamans move across the surface of the rock on a journey into the world of the spirits.

in almost equal measure. We know that this art was made by people with brains like our own. We know that there must be meaning encoded here, which we ought to be able to understand if only we had the key. Recovering the meaning of an image like this is a little like deciphering a lost language, or trying to work out what is going on in a game of cricket if you do not know the rules: the allure of discovering significance and coherence is tempered by a profound sense of being an ignorant interloper into somebody else's thought world.

David Lewis-Williams, of the University of Witwatersrand in Johannesburg, knows a great deal about these sorts of frustrations with San art, and also about the fruits of long effort trying to enter its imagery and thought:

There are many forms of rock art around the world for which we have no corresponding verbal record telling us about the beliefs and practices of the people who created them. With San art, we do have such records. For many years it was a matter of gaze and guess: if you gaze long enough, your guess will take you close to what it's all about. But I'm afraid that's not how it works. We need more than that. And here, luckily, we have it. Back in the 1870s, at around the time that the last rock paintings were being made, a German linguist called Wilhelm Bleek came to South Africa, conversed extensively with the San – in a San language which is no longer spoken – and developed a phonetic script for writing down everything they said. His sister-in-law, Lucy Lloyd, compiled the results: a vast collection of biographies, and many accounts of rituals and myths.

The result of this timely nineteenth-century fieldwork is that we are able to match what we know of the San world of thought and practice with what we see in their rock art, in much the same way as we can with European art. As David Lewis-Williams points out, if you look at a Renaissance painting and see a man having water poured over his head, with a dove depicted above, we know that this is not just a record of a man who was having a shower one day when a bird flew by. We understand that in this tradition the dove represents the Holy Spirit, that water is used for ritual purification, and that this scene must therefore be the baptism of Christ. The same applies to the rich symbolism of San rock art:

There are crucial details in this image [p. 274], *which once you understand them immediately transform it from something mundane into an account of a journey into the spirit world. A fly whisk, drawn as a straight line with a thicker piece hanging down – an antelope tail – indicates a shaman, a medicine man. The San people who made these paintings used fly whisks only in their medicine dance – they didn't use them in daily life, to bat away flies. And our records tell us that when people went into an altered state of consciousness, to visit the spirit world, they suffered a nasal haemorrhage. They then smeared the blood on people, in the belief that the power of the blood and the smell of the blood – because smell and power are much the same thing – would keep the evil spirits away. So there are many reasons to regard this*

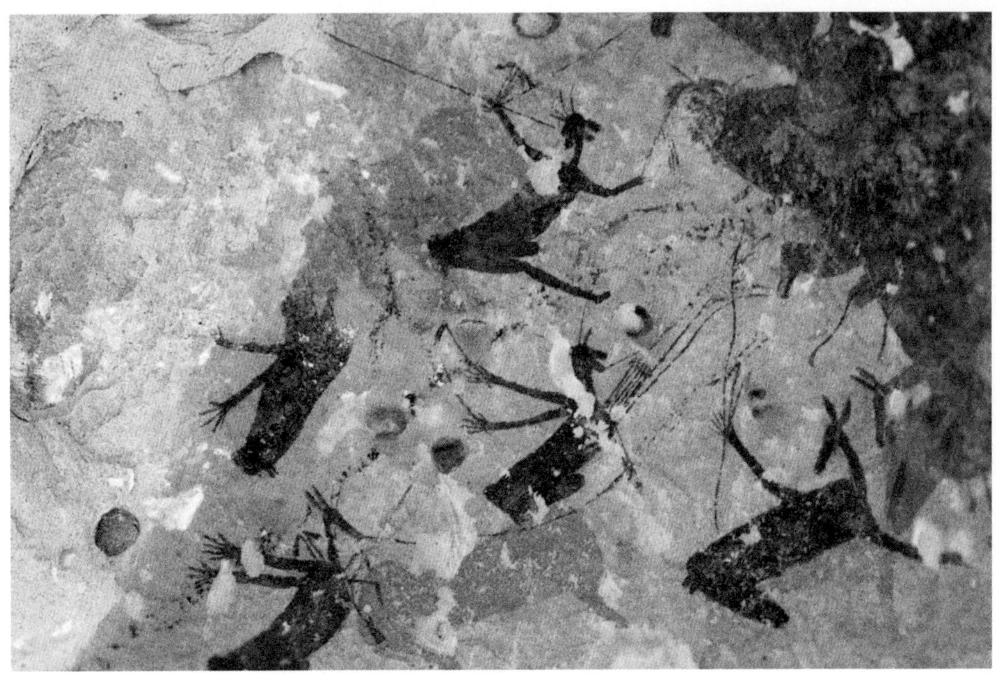

Detail of San|Bushman rock painting (p. 272) showing figures with their arms stretched out behind them

image as representing the experience of a shaman going into the spirit world while being watched by others.

The posture of one of these figures on the left confirms this hypothesis. His arms are sticking out behind his shoulders, a posture painted all over Southern Africa, which puzzled us for a long time. And then, many years ago, I was in the Kalahari talking to the medicine people – who had never seen copies of rock paintings. During a lull in the conversation, one of the men stood up and put his arms into just such a backward position. He told us that some people dance like this when they're asking god to put more potency into their bodies, so that they can go to the spirit world and cure people. After all those decades of puzzling, there was the answer. 'Why didn't you tell us before?' I said. 'You never asked,' was the reply.

Bit by bit, we begin to see that there are different levels of meaning here. What had looked like a simple hunting scene becomes a record of a spiritual journey into another realm of experience as well. The hybrid human–animal images are shamans in some kind of trance, absorbing the power of animals to help them gain access to the spirit world. On their return, they may well have created art like this as a way of explaining to people where they had been and what they had seen and done. David Lewis Williams goes even further: he suggests that when the shamans enter an altered state of consciousness, a wall painting like this would allow the rest of the group, who are not in a trance, to share in the shamans' heightened spiritual experience – in some measure, to accompany them on their journey to a different world:

in rather the same way that the whole congregation in a cathedral might experience a sense of being uplifted, transported, when music by Tallis is being sung by the choir. I think that the paintings helped spread the experience of the spirit world so that ordinary people could share vicariously in what the shamans experienced.

If this is so, then the rock paintings of the San are not so different in function from the National Gallery *Nativity*, which allows ordinary spectators to share Saint Bridget's vision on her mystical visit to the stable in Bethlehem.

The work of the artist Grayson Perry is frequently based on narratives, many about his own imaginative experience, which viewers have to decipher for themselves. Asking him to comment on the San|Bushmen rock paintings, with no prior knowledge of their beliefs and practices, it was striking how much he was able to intuit. At first, unsurprisingly, he thought that these were hunting scenes of some sort. Then he noticed that animal and human figures were becoming mixed, and that the scene including the arms-back posture has the ecstatic quality of a ritual dance. He speculated on its purpose:

I imagine these people were living very harsh lives. The animals were not only their food source, the people would also probably be under threat from wild beasts – as potential prey themselves.

I wonder whether these people were almost literally trying to get into the heads of the animals, so that they would understand better how they could either kill them, or not be killed by them. Holding your arms stretched out behind you makes you very vulnerable: you are entering a space with your head and your face. You don't have your arms to protect you, and that means that you're giving yourself up to whatever you encounter.

There is a rare keenness and imagination to Grayson Perry's insights here: the mark, perhaps, of the accomplished artist used to inviting people into his own imagined world. He finds it unsurprising that religious experience should often be closely connected to deep engagement with works of art:

Significance and beauty in art are communally agreed things. People construct their own narratives based on my work – or any work – a real investment of themselves. Religion, to begin with, is bound up with society's emotional needs, and art is about emotional investment in the thing itself, not about the facts that may or may not surround it. We all bring our own life story and experience to bear on every image that we ever contemplate. So religion and art are both negotiations. Some people want to know exactly how they are meant to feel. They want to be drawn along by a narrative, so that their emotions are manipulated by the story and they feel like they're doing it right. Other people are happy just to have a spontaneous amorphous reaction – a sensory response. Art, for me, is about making meaning. It's about trying to offer some fragile foothold in the moment, amidst the chaos of life.

*

In that chaos, images allow people to make, and to convey, meanings of almost infinitely fluid complexity which words would struggle to carry. The San|Bushmen rock painting seems to take a community of hunter-gatherers on a journey into the world of the spirits. We can witness the reverse phenomenon in a small nineteenth-century Japanese shrine where the spirits come to visit a long-settled agricultural society (p. 279). The curved doors of a small wooden box about a foot high open to reveal, inside, a shimmering world of carved gilded wood. On a decorated pedestal is a group of three foxes, arranged symmetrically. To left and right a fox sits with its tail proudly up, together looking out at us like heraldic beasts. One of them is holding a key in its jaws. The third fox, placed higher and in the middle, carries on its back a large, plump, female figure holding a sword in one hand, a heart in the other. Her garment has strips of bright red, the only colour amidst all the gold.

Set to work on the shrine – an object also totally new to him – Grayson Perry quickly devised a narrative:

It's about survival and comfort and good things and the continuation of a healthy happy life, yet, with the sword and the heart, death is hovering. It's always hovering there isn't it, death? Even within the bounty of the earth and the natural world. Maybe without the anger of that goddess, we might be a bit smug.

It is surely a testament to our abilities as human beings to both shape and appropriate other people's stories that an artist is able here to take an unfamiliar image and tradition and construct, out of three foxes, a lady and a sword, a coherent narrative about death, life, abundance and violence – or, in his words, to make meaning amidst the chaos of life.

This is, in fact, an image that most people in Japan would be able to read immediately – although they would not all read it the same way. The fox on the left, with the key, tells a Japanese viewer that the figure in the centre must be Inari, the important Shinto deity, or *kami*. The deity appears in this image in an early role, as protector of agriculture in general and the rice harvest in particular: the key in the fox's mouth is the key to a rice storehouse, and one of the possible sources for the name 'Inari' is the Japanese phrase *ine-nari*, meaning 'rice is growing'. Inari is often depicted as coming to earth from heaven riding on a fox. Some claim this was because foxes' tails can look like sheaves of rice, others that foxes are often seen around rice fields, possibly feeding on birds and animals that might eat the crop. However that may be, around a third of all the Shinto shrines in Japan today – over 30,000 of them – are dedicated to Inari. Those in shrines in the countryside regularly provide nourishment for the local foxes – fried tofu is traditionally their food of choice. So far, so simple: this little sculpture seems to be as easy for a Japanese to read as the *Nativity* for a European.

Then it gets more complicated. Beyond rice, Inari has a range of further associations, including tea, saké, human fertility, industry, wealth and success in commerce. The deity has a wide, apparently constantly expanding portfolio, and a presence in everything from ancient tales to contemporary manga and anime: on the roof of the Tokyo headquarters of the huge Shiseido cosmetics company is a famous shrine to Inari, who can protect corporate profits as well as rice harvests. More confusingly, Inari is not always necessarily female, and can occasionally take the form of an old man carrying rice on his back. Because of Inari's immense popularity, there are many additional meanings – complementary or competing – bound up in an image like this one, which different viewers would invest with different significance.

Some would see the foxes here as messengers, others as deities in their own right. And some might see, conjoined in the central figure, a second quite different deity. As Buddhism spread from the Asian mainland to Japan, from the sixth century onwards, the deities brought by the incoming religion were slowly – and deliberately – equated with deities in the indigenous Shinto tradition. It was a remarkable feat of assimilation, comparable in some ways to the fusion of Greek and Roman gods. New patterns of belief were

The fox and the key: in this Japanese house shrine, the fox of Inari holding the key to the rice store flanks the figure of Dakini in a complex merging of spiritual narratives.

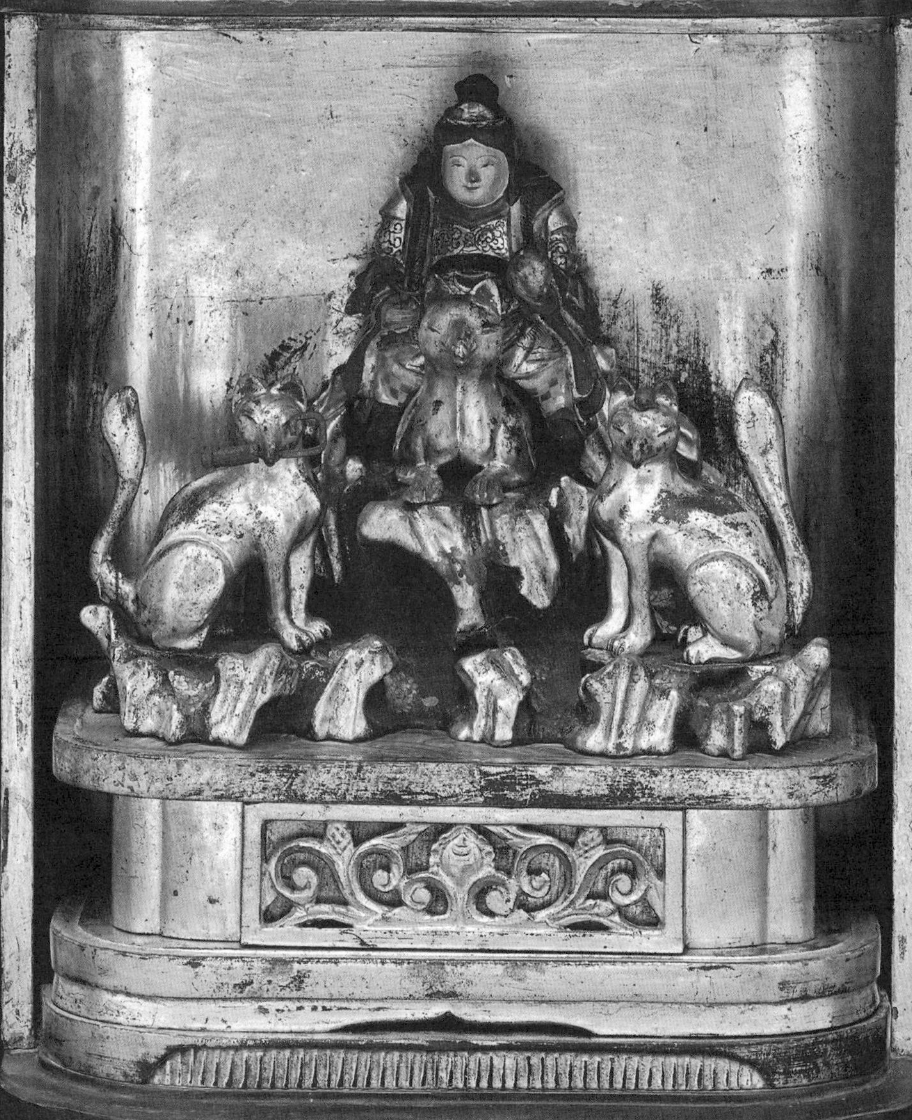

superimposed on the old, supplementing but not supplanting them. As part of this process one Buddhist deity, Dakini, originally Indian, who is both protective and destructive, who sometimes cherishes human hearts and sometimes eats them, came to be identified, indeed to co-exist, with the Shinto Inari. It is that amalgamated deity that we see so imposingly here: the central figure is carrying a heart and a sword, the emblem of Dakini, who is now surprisingly appearing in – in fact reshaping – Inari's story. One might compare Dakini's presence in Inari's world with the intrusion of Santa Claus, originally Saint Nicholas, a bishop from southern Turkey, and reindeer from the North Pole into the biblical narrative of Christmas (Chapter 15). Something of the same sort goes on in the floating, ever-widening range of Inari's meanings.

This shrine, which is at once Inari *and* Dakini, shows the extraordinary power of an image to combine narratives that are on the surface irreconcilable. It also demonstrates the capacity of Japan's religious culture to absorb new elements, most notably in its sustained adoption of incoming Buddhist beliefs and practices. Only when it was confronted with a religion which refused all such negotiation – Christianity – did the Japanese spirit harden, as we shall see in Chapter 28. In the Japanese tradition, there is space for several truths, which may be incompatible yet are co-existent. The Inari shrine exemplifies what happens when stories of belief are allowed to grow in complexity and the images of those stories change to meet the new understandings. As the philosopher John Gray writes, 'Religions seem substantial and enduring only because they are always invisibly changing.'

The current coat of arms of South Africa, introduced in 2000, bears an image of a standing man, taken from a San rock painting, accompanied by a motto (roughly 'Diverse people unite') in a San|Bushmen language that was recorded by Bleek in the 1870s, and which is now extinct. An image and a language equally distant

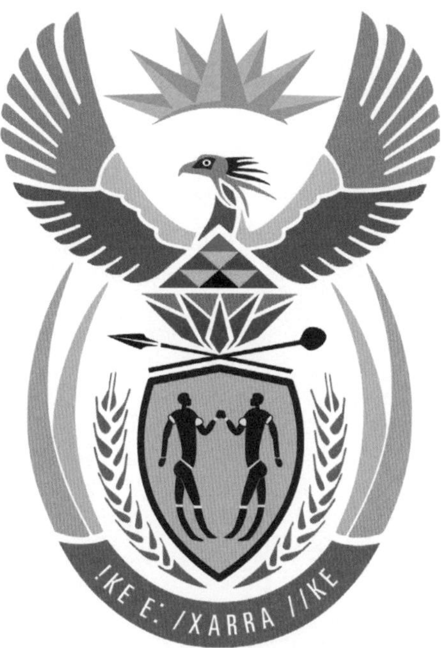

The coat of arms of modern South Africa. Figures derived from San|Bushman rock art, with the motto 'Diverse people unite' written in Khosan, a now extinct San|Bushman language

from all modern South Africans allow them to travel together to a world of harmonious unity – a political, secular transposition of a San shamanic journey.

Both rock painting and shrine demonstrate the ability of images to take those who look on them into areas of meaning well beyond the bounds of language and obvious rationality. In this potent but unstable mix nobody can ever be certain what meaning will be taken away. It is then no surprise that, over the millennia, religions have both exploited and rejected, with equal vigour, images as a means of guiding the people. That is the subject of the next two chapters.

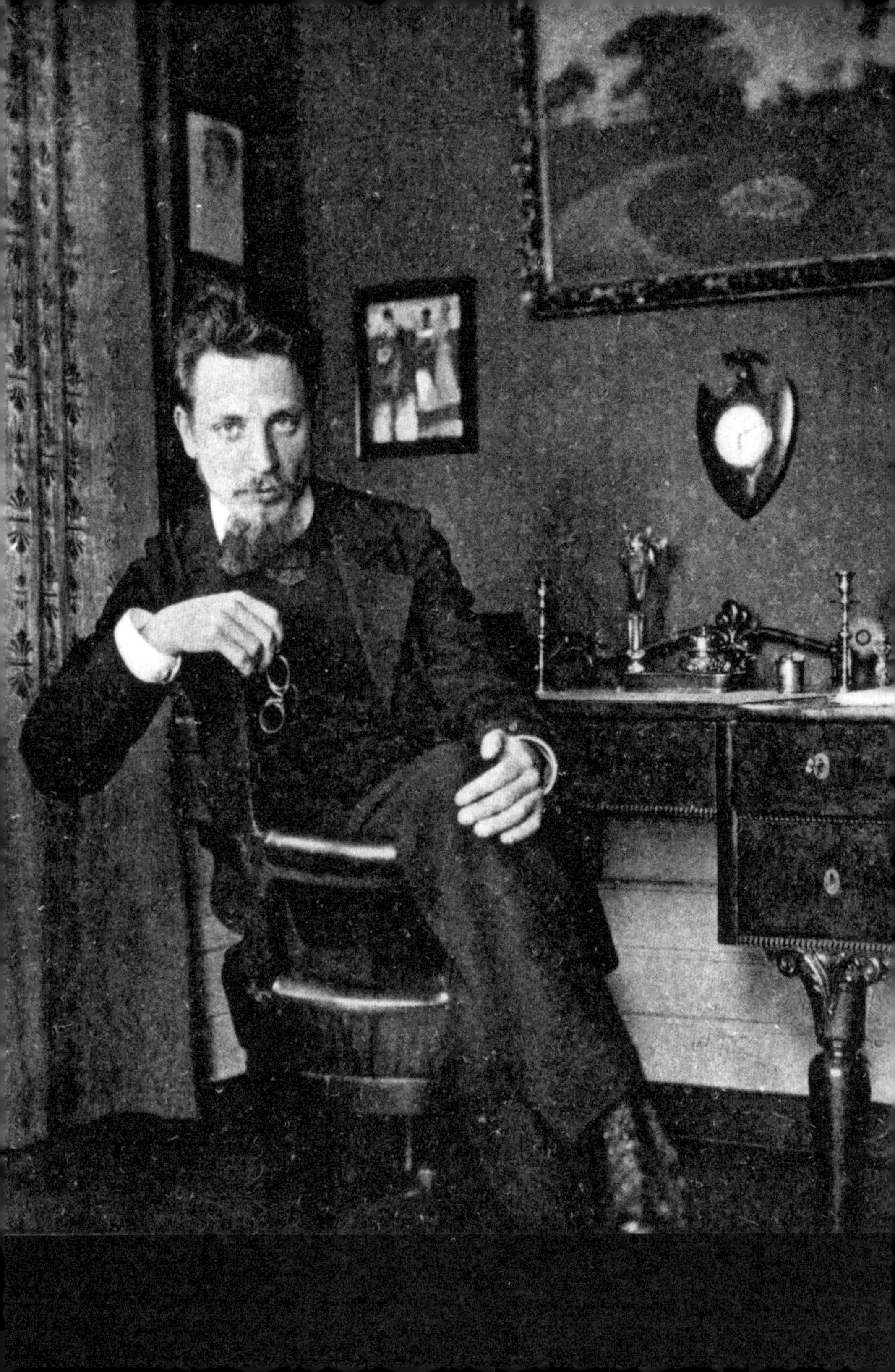

19
CHANGE YOUR LIFE

In a sonnet published in 1908, the German poet Rainer Maria Rilke wrote of being overwhelmed by the intense contemplation of an archaic Greek torso of Apollo:

Yet still
his torso glows, like candles lit
in which his gaze, though dimmed,
persists and shines

The sculpted stone body, although headless, was so filled with assured and joyous energy that the usual roles of sculpture and spectator seemed to Rilke to be reversed. Rather than him looking at it, every part of it seemed to be looking at him, and giving him the clear, invigorating and disconcerting instruction: '*Du musst dein Leben ändern*' – 'You must change your life'.

That is in fact the central purpose of many religious images. They are designed to move, fascinate or unsettle us to the point where we will want to change our life. After looking at one of these images, we should, if they have done their job, never be the same again.

*

The challenging gaze: Rainer Maria Rilke in 1902

O, My people, what have I done to you?
How have I offended you? Answer me!
I led you out of Egypt,
from slavery to freedom,
but you led your Saviour to the Cross.
O, My people, what have I done to you?
How have I offended you? Answer me!
What more could I have done for you?
I planted you as my fairest vine,
but you yielded only bitterness:
when I was thirsty you gave me vinegar to drink,
and you pierced your Saviour with a lance.

These are the *Improperia*, or *Reproaches*, part of the liturgy used in Catholic churches on Good Friday, in which God rebukes his people for continually failing to respond to his loving guidance over the generations. They remind us of the extraordinary centrality in Western Christianity of a single, highly charged image: Christ hanging, dying or dead, on the Cross, and of the idea that we, sinful humanity, are responsible for his anguish. The agony he is enduring, the Good Friday *Reproaches* tell us, is the consequence of what we have done.

A small coloured woodcut in the British Museum, created in the Netherlands around 1500, offers a particularly gruesome rendering of this response to Christ's Passion. We are outside Jerusalem, at Golgotha, 'the place of the skull' – hence the skulls and bones at the foot of the Cross – where, according to the Gospels, Christ was crucified. Christ is pictured with blood pouring from his torso, his head, his legs and his outstretched arms. These are not realistically arranged droplets but a flurry of vertical red strokes, tightly packed together and evenly spaced. It is almost the way a child might draw a rainy day, but here is clearly a notation for unbearable pain. The emotional register is high. In the background, two of the city gates are shown blood red. Around

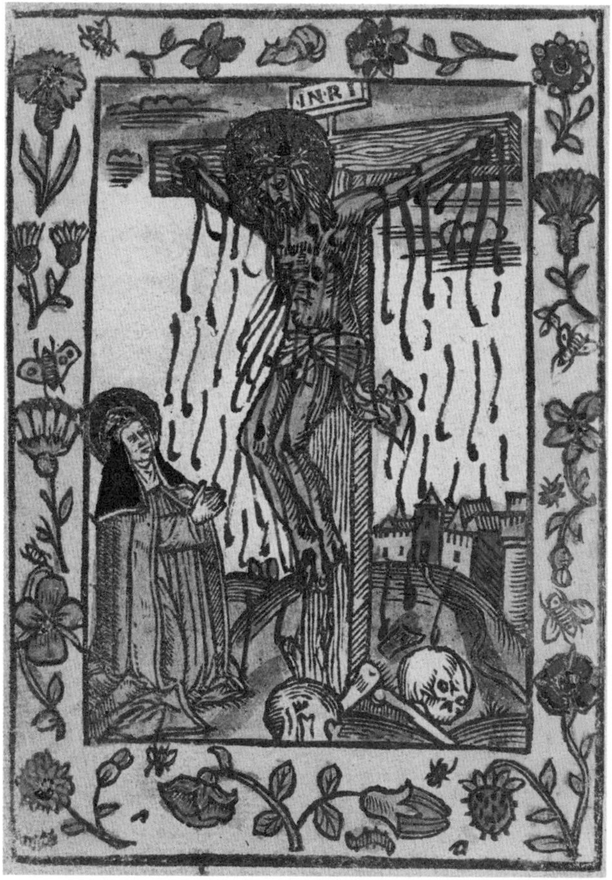

Saint Bridget's vision of the agony of the Crucifixion: in a sixteenth-century Netherlandish woodcut, she kneels before the suffering Christ

the edges of the image, however, we find something unexpected: a gaily coloured, almost whimsical border telling of spring and early summer, where roses, pinks and strawberries are clearly recognizable. The image of suffering is joyfully framed with flowers. What is going on? The message seems to be clear: you and I did this to Christ, by our sins. In the words of the Good Friday *Reproaches*: 'you led your Saviour to the Cross'. How are we meant to use an image like this, one cheap enough for many to have at home? And what is it, and the surrounding flowers, meant to do to us?

Karen Armstrong, a historian of religion who was for some years a Roman Catholic nun, finds this print very difficult to use in any constructive way:

Abelard, the twelfth-century philosopher, said that when we look at the crucifix we should be filled with pity and it would be that act of compassion that saves us, that breaking of our heart as we look at an image like this. But this particular image is to me so horrendous that it's hard even to feel pity. It makes it seem as though God is behind this terrible violence and torture, that God is somehow condoning it to save the world. It seems to me a perversion of the Christian message.

Nor is it an image that would be recognized by the artists who first represented the crucifixion, sometime around 400. They would wonder what had happened to Christ's triumph over death which the Cross is supposed to represent. Where is the divine power? Where is any notion of love? Early images of the crucifixion made all these things clear, showing Jesus standing tall and proud atop the Cross at the moment of his greatest victory – and ours. Yet here he hangs limply from it, half obscured by a blizzard of crimson. As Karen Armstrong points out, other Christian traditions continued with the early view, while Western, Catholic Christianity took its own road:

The image of Christ bleeding profusely on the Cross is not one that you would find in the Greek Orthodox or Russian Orthodox churches. For them the dominant image is not of Christ suffering on the Cross, but of Christ transfigured – and humanity transfigured with him. The Orthodox especially value the account of Jesus going up the mountain with his disciples and his humanity being glorified before them, his face shining, his garments shining, so that you have a glimpse of what a human being can be. We can all be like him, they say, even in this life – if we get rid of the self-seeking and violence and hatred that so often mar our humanity.

The Western church, dominated by the crucifix, has instead over the centuries filled us with terrible, endless guilt, so that we are mired in the self and the very imperfections that we are trying

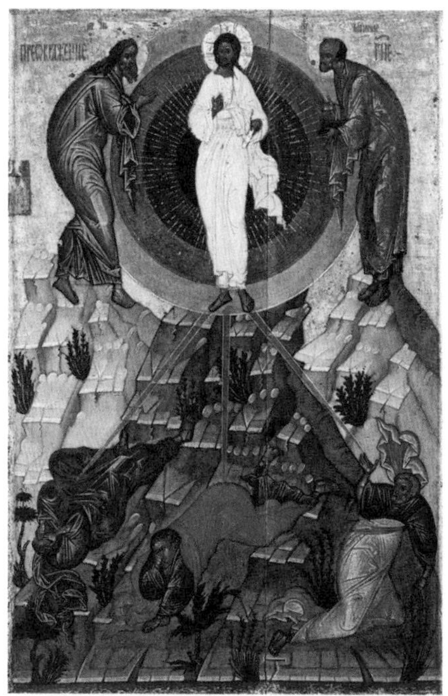

The Orthodox tradition emphasizes not Christ's suffering, but his triumph and his transfiguration. In this fifteenth-century Russian icon, he stands in shining white between Moses and Elijah.

to transcend. We constantly feel burdened. Somehow we believe we have to torture the body so that we can identify with Christ.

Karen Armstrong's revulsion is shared by many people today, whenever a print like this is exhibited. Insofar as it affects their actions at all, it is usually to make them turn away and think of something else. Yet this was certainly not the response that its maker intended – and it is probably not how the print would have affected those who first used it for their private devotions.

The clue lies, or rather kneels, in the bottom left-hand corner. A woman, dressed as a nun and marked by a halo, is on her knees, gazing in adoration at the crucified Christ. She is the fourteenth-century saint Bridget of Sweden. In the last chapter we saw how Bridget's visions changed the imagery of Christ's birth. The prayers to Christ on the Cross, attributed to her, and famous across Northern Europe, similarly changed the way many people visualized his death. In the *Nativity* we saw only her vision, but at the Cross she herself is present. So we are not meant to look at this image on our own, but are being asked to join Bridget in her vision and prayers. She is here not to pray for us as an intercessor, but to guide us to the true meaning of what we see. And if we see with her eyes and pray with her understanding, then we shall both grasp our responsibility for causing this unbearable suffering, and also acknowledge the blessings it brings us: this is not just the execution of a man, but the redemption of mankind.

If this original meaning can be recovered, we can overcome our instinctive revulsion at the brutal depiction of such suffering. For Eamon Duffy, it is very much an image of its time and must be understood in this light:

In thirteenth- and fourteenth-century Europe there is a new kind of spiritual interiority, not just in religion but in love poetry too. People become more interested in what we would now call human psychology. This brings with it an emphasis on the emotional element in religion, cultivated particularly by the Franciscan order but drawing also on people like Saint Anselm and the Cistercians. That approach to faith moves out into the lay world, where people explore a wider range of emotions in their religious experience. This is the beginning of the age of the Christmas carol, for example, when you think tenderly about the baby in the crib. There is none of that in the first millennium. And, in the same way, you think sorrowfully about the sufferings of the god-man on the Cross.

Images like this become a spiritual tool, helping people to come to their senses about what life is for. Powerful emotion, whether it is sweetness, tenderness or the savagery with which Christ was treated, all contribute to our waking up. A hymn like the 'Stabat Mater', for example, about Mary standing by the Cross and sharing her son's sufferings, was intended to make the people who sang it borrow some of her emotion so that they could respond adequately to what was going on.

Bridget of Sweden was one of a number of mystics of this era whose visions and writings contributed to this deepening of European spirituality. Because she was a courtier and a mother, who had played an active part in the world, her appeal went far beyond those living in religious houses, and her supposed prayers to the crucified Christ were widely used by the laity. Eamon Duffy develops this theme:

At the end of the Middle Ages, one popular form of Christian piety was devotion to the details of the Passion, to the wounds of Jesus, to the drops of his blood. There are very large numbers of images of Jesus covered in blood or bleeding, not just from the five major wounds – of the nails on hands and feet, and the side pierced by the lance – but also from the wounds in his forehead from the crown of thorns, and all across his body, from his scourging.

A number of late-medieval visionaries, particularly Bridget of Sweden, enumerated the holes in Jesus' body, the wounds from which blood proceeded, and reflected on their meaning. The best English examples of this are the revelations of Julian of Norwich, a woman who had a series of visions in the 1370s.

Julian doesn't experience the sight of the Passion as merely gruesome. For her, it is both dreadful and beautiful. She is aware that this is a human being bleeding to death, but behind that she sees the love of God overflowing, like a mighty river or a sea. She compares the blood in her vision flowing from Christ's wounded head to the rain streaming off the eaves of a house in a rain storm. For her, this kind of image is one of the copiousness of God's love and mercy.

If most people looking at our woodcut around 1500 would have seen in the blood of Christ not gore but grace, then it is entirely appropriate that it should be gaily surrounded by early-summer flowers. However surprising to us, this image is a celebration of love – and as such it has the capacity to change our life. We join Saint Bridget and pray with her to Jesus through his wounds – ideally in the words of her widely popular prayers. In them, gratitude for Jesus' loving willingness to bear those wounds leads directly to the plea that 'tears of penitence and love may be my bread both night and day: and convert me wholly to you, that my heart may ever be a dwelling-place for you, and my behaviour may be always pleasing and acceptable to you'. Contemplation of the pain of crucifixion should lead to new and joyful life.

This response would have been reinforced by the many other images which the faithful would have had in their heads, each one complementing and deepening the others. Eamon Duffy describes how:

Medieval churches were jam-packed with images. The most important single image was the crucifix, but next to that, there would usually have been up to three or four images of the Virgin Mary: most commonly with her child as an image of tender nurture, but perhaps also with her dead son at the foot of the Cross. There would have been many images of cheerful-looking saints, too. So one needs to put these fairly gruesome images into a much wider visual world.

In that context, this kind of vivid evocation of the Passion would make you realize the extent of the suffering that the Son of God had freely embraced for you. But, crucially, this is about guilt that is forgiven, and that is very different from just making people feel bad about themselves. It is not the pointless generation of guilt. This blood does not call for vengeance, it brings forgiveness. The message is: your sin is great, but God's love is greater.

Eamon Duffy and Karen Armstrong, both trained in Catholic theology and both deeply thoughtful historians of Christianity, agree about the power of this image but radically disagree about where that power is directing us.

*

You see the Buddha sitting in the yogic position, his face expressing tranquillity. This is what a human being can become. Unlike

Western Christianity, which has tended to belittle the body, early Buddhist texts revel in the glory of the Buddha's body. People who converted to Buddhism early on probably did so in part because of the beauty, tranquil demeanour and grace of Buddhists who had mastered the self.

Most people would agree with Karen Armstrong's view that this serene figure in grey schist (p. 293), made probably in the third century CE in the Indic kingdom of Gandhara (now north-west Pakistan), is a more approachable and reassuring image than the suffering, deeply unsettling Christ. Yet its purpose is essentially the same, and it too requires of the viewer both knowledge and imaginative engagement if it is to achieve its aim.

Clothed in drapery clearly influenced by Greek and Roman models, the Buddha is shown here in mid-career, a halo behind his head, already in his enlightened state. The turban crown is an attribute of wisdom and generosity. He sits cross-legged on a cushion, the toes of his left foot just showing. Eyes half shut, he looks calmly into the beyond. His earlobes have been elongated by the weight of the princely jewellery, now absent, which in his early life hung heavy from them, but he has renounced wealth. His left thumb and forefinger are joined just below the little finger of the right hand. The folds of the garment are simple and broad, almost symmetrically arranged, and its hem spills into the scene below, where another seated figure is surrounded by two men and two women. The whole statue is about a metre high.

How would people have responded to this sculpture when they encountered it in the temple, where it would originally have sat? Sarah Shaw is an honorary fellow at the Oxford Centre for Buddhist Studies:

They might offer flowers, incense or butter lamps, to show their reverence and respect. They might put their hands together in greeting, and perhaps chant or prostrate themselves. They would see the straight back and would remember to straighten their own backs. They would try to find in themselves some of the qualities that they could see in front of them, trying to arouse them in their own being, in their own body, as part of their devotion.

But they wouldn't try too hard. In Buddhism, there is a state of consciousness said to be experienced only by those who have achieved awakening. And that consciousness produces the sort of smile you often see in Buddhist statues like this one. Anybody sitting in the presence of this smiling figure would experience it as a kind of reassurance, offering stability, teaching and a model for meditation.

We can see something of this here. Below the cushion on which the Buddha is seated we find a group of people depicted in miniature. At the centre is a seated, haloed and turbaned Bodhisattva: a human being who has achieved enlightenment, but who has deferred passage into nirvana, the supremely desired state of nothingness, in order to teach and encourage enlightenment in others. The Bodhisattva is flanked by four figures, very possibly donors who paid for this statue and for the shrine in which it was originally set, much as donors also appear in later, Christian, art. As Saint Bridget guided those who looked at the crucifixion print to its true meaning, so the Bodhisattva here leads the figures around him – and us – in prayerful instruction. Sarah Shaw explains how this is entirely appropriate, for the statue is above all about teaching, or rather about following a teacher:

The Buddha's hands are performing the dharmachakra pavatna mudra: the hand gesture that implies the turning of the wheel. This refers to a specific point in the Buddha's life. He had rejected the path of extreme asceticism, and through meditation

The seated Buddha preaching his first sermon at Sarnath. The hem of his garment flows into the space below where his precepts are being taught. From Gandhara, Pakistan, second to third century CE

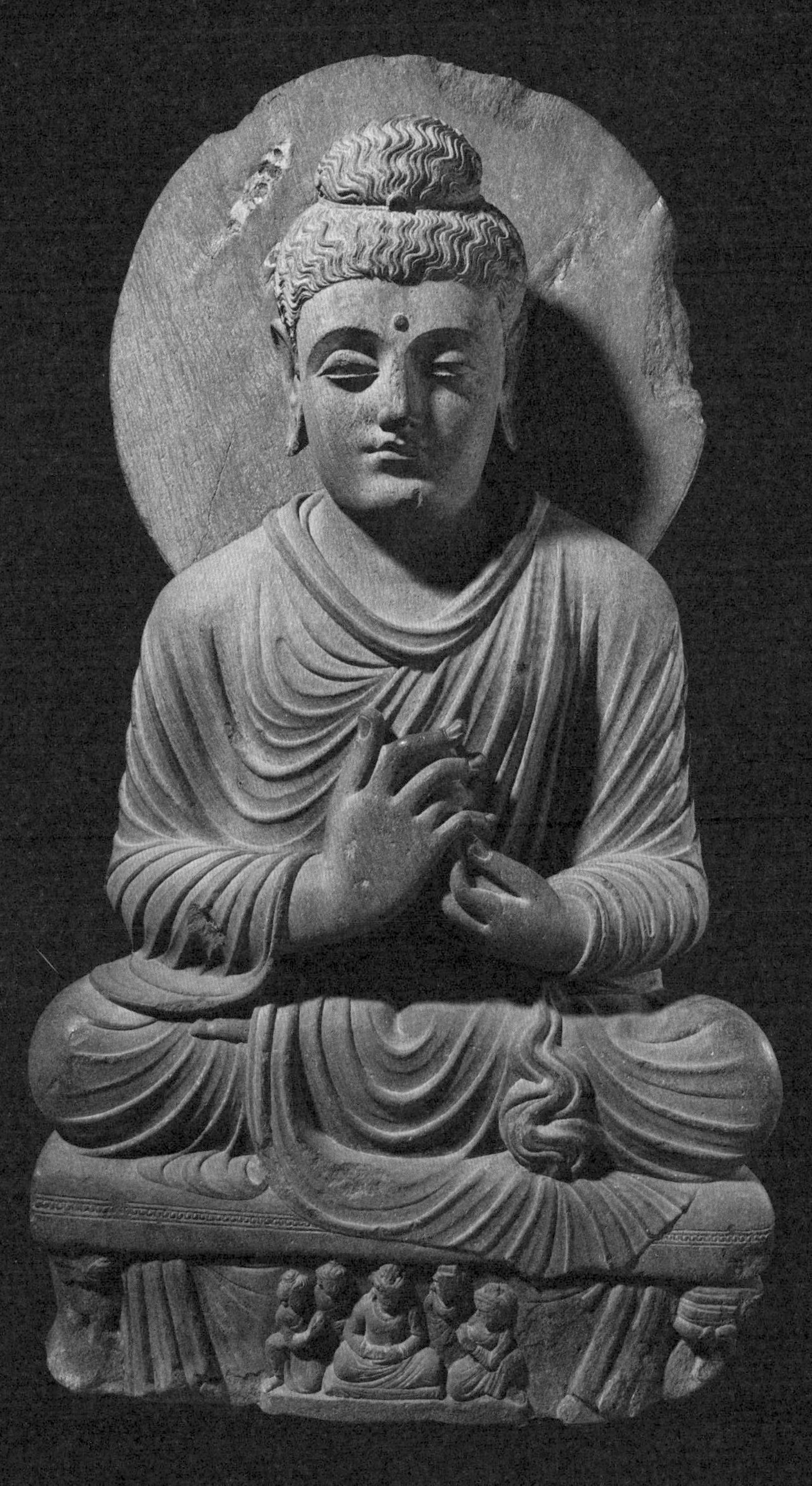

and the practice of the Middle Way between self-indulgence and self-punishment he had found freedom from suffering, and liberation of spirit. His first teaching on the Middle Way was delivered to five ascetics, who had been practising extreme mortification. They were so impressed by his radiance and beauty that they realized something extraordinary had happened: he had become awakened. So they asked him to teach them.

That is the moment we see in this statue. Buddha is preaching his first sermon, delivered, tradition has it, in the deer park at Sarnath, near the Ganges at Varanasi. The spot is now marked by a huge stupa, and has become one of the most visited of all Buddhist pilgrimage sites (see Chapter 14). It is one of the key moments in the history of world religions, the point at which Buddhism, as a set of teachings and practices, begins: and the wheel here being set in motion symbolizes, among other things, the rapidity with which it can effect spiritual change in those who decide to follow it. It transformed the lives of the five ascetics who heard the Buddha's teaching and were soon joined in a new community by many more disciples. It challenges us, the beholders, to follow the example of those five – and of the small figures in the base – to embark on the demanding discipline of the Middle Way. The falling hem encouragingly shows us that the world of our endeavours is always connected to the enlightening presence of the Buddha himself. The tone is much less shrill, the emotional pitch less intense than in the print of the Crucifixion; there is no suggestion here of value in suffering. Yet the aim of the two images is the same: to make us want to be different, better people, and to lead wiser, better lives.

Images challenging us to behave differently are still very much with us. In secular Europe or America much charitable fundraising has remained firmly in the Franciscan tradition of high emotion. Especially in appeals for victims of famine or war, images of almost unbearable human suffering are used to arouse compassion and generosity; and

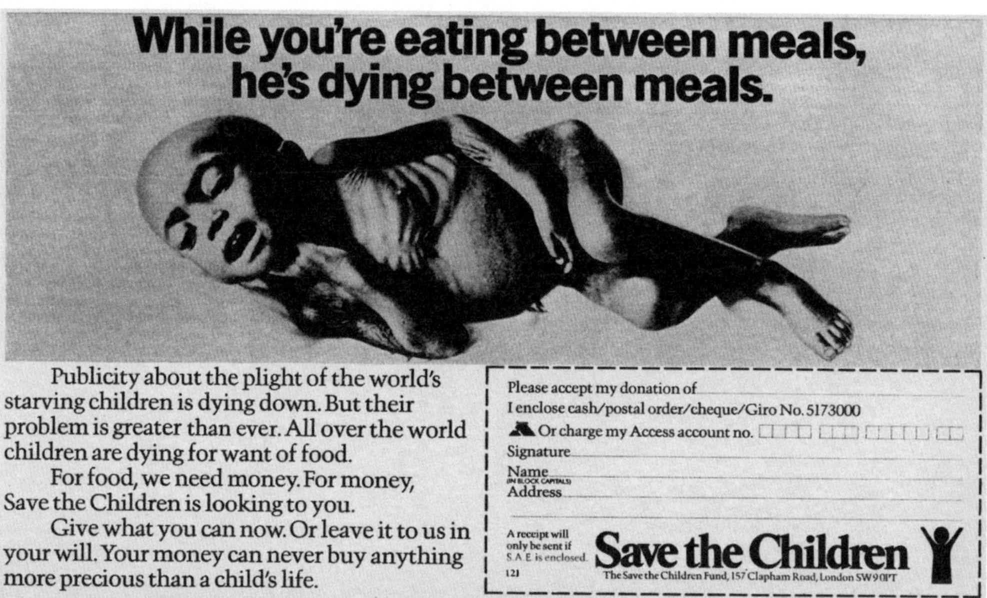

While you're eating between meals,
he's dying between meals.
Publicity about the plight of the world's starving children is dying down. But their problem is greater than ever. All over the world children are dying for want of food.
For food, we need money. For money, Save the Children is looking to you.
Give what you can now. Or leave it to us in your will. Your money can never buy anything more precious than a child's life.
Please accept my donation of
I enclose cash/postal order/cheque/Giro No. 5173000
Or charge my Access account no.
Signature
Name
(IN BLOCK CAPITALS)
Address
A receipt will only be sent if S.A.E. is enclosed.
121
Save the Children
The Save the Children Fund, 157 Clapham Road, London SW9 0PT

The sight of extreme suffering in the modern world, designed to distress viewers and shock them into changed behaviour. A 1970s newspaper advertisement for famine relief

they are often just as effective in doing so as were once the images of Saint Bridget praying to the wounds of Christ. The idea of divine redemption may have been largely lost in the post-Christian West, but the sight of suffering is still deployed to move us to action.

Like the San|Bushmen rock painting and the Inari shrine, both the images we have been looking at in this chapter are almost incomprehensible in distant cultural worlds. Left to our own devices, few of us would guess the effortful renunciation and detachment to which we are summoned by the tranquil Buddha's hand gesture, and even fewer read the Crucifixion print as a prayer to divine love. But objects like these raise another, graver difficulty: because we can read them in different ways, and the emotions they can arouse are highly charged, they can lead those who look at them in directions which religious authorities can neither predict nor control. The life-changing image is a very loose cannon. It was partly for this reason that most Protestant reformers were profoundly hostile to them. Like many religious movements, they believed that the only reliable way of communicating the truths of religion was by the word: the image was a danger to true faith and best destroyed.

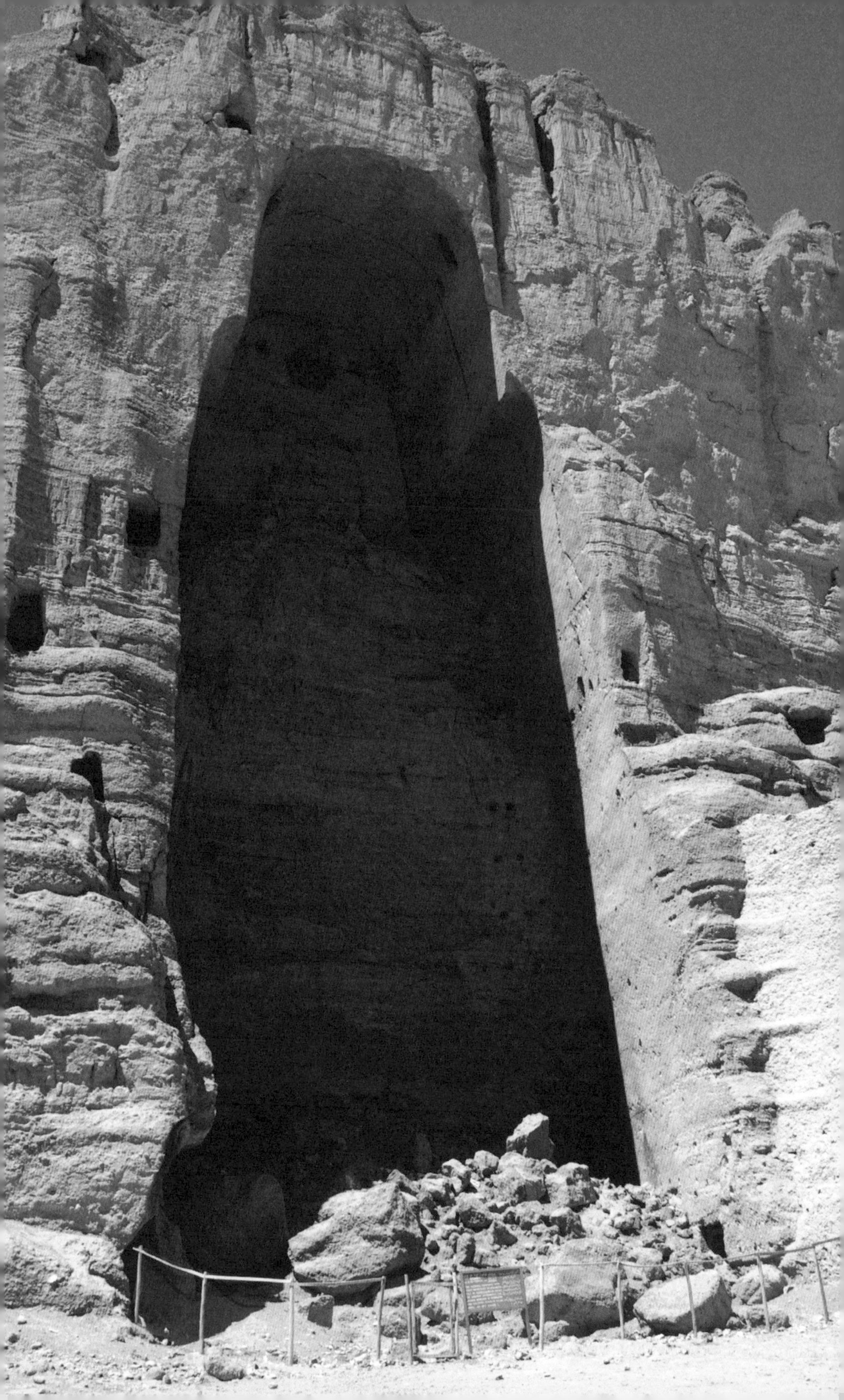

20
REJECTING THE IMAGE, REVERING THE WORD

In March 2001, the Islamic fundamentalist Taliban government in Afghanistan blew up the Bamiyan Buddhas. Two monumental images made in the sixth century, one fifty-three, the other thirty-five metres tall, the largest representations of a standing Buddha anywhere in the world, were systematically reduced to rubble. Their destruction was a gesture designed to proclaim a particular notion of religious purity, attract attention to Afghanistan and provoke political enemies. It was entirely successful on every count. Photographs of the empty niches were reproduced around the globe, eliciting outraged condemnation. Iconoclasm had once again returned to world politics. It is still very much present. In the years since 2001, other pre-Islamic images have been deliberately destroyed in Syria and Iraq by the so-called Islamic State to similar effect. In all these cases, religion and politics have been inextricably mixed, but they nonetheless afford the most violent demonstration possible that there have always been many who believe that images are effectively idolatry, and that only the word can lead to God.

You do not of course have to look to Islam, or go to Afghanistan, to witness the destruction of religious sculptures. There

The emptied spiritual space: after the destruction of the Bamiyan Buddhas, only rubble remains. Afghanistan, March 2001

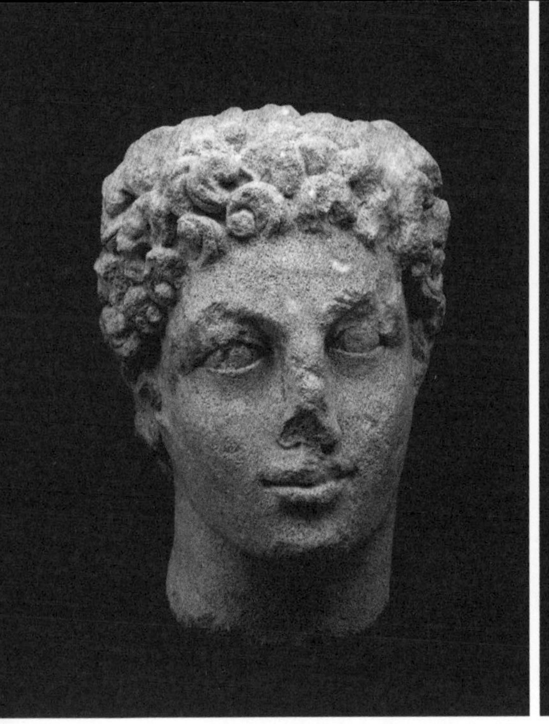
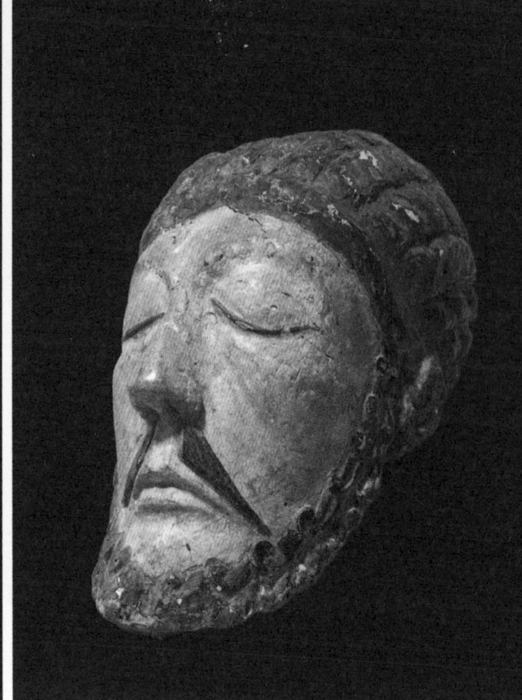

The heads of two gods, Mercury (*left*) and Christ (*right*), severed in Gloucestershire more than a millennium apart

have been casualties even in the Cotswolds, as can be seen in two severed heads discovered in Gloucestershire. The first, magnificently carved in coarse Cotswold limestone during the second century CE, shows Mercury, the Roman god of commerce and communication – life-size, curly-haired, alert, youthful. What was once a full-scale standing statue of Mercury, housed in the Roman temple at Uley, was destroyed around 400, almost certainly by early Christians, in this respect like the Islamic fundamentalists, determined to smash pagan idols. But the head survived. It was reverently buried by people who must have retained an affectionate allegiance to their familiar, handsome Mercury, and may have been apprehensive about the continuing power of a slighted god.

Over a thousand years later, a strikingly similar story of destruction – and preservation – was repeated, this time by Christians against other Christians, only a few miles away. The second head, much smaller in scale, once belonged to a painted wooden crucifix, made in England around 1100, which hung in the church of All Hallows, South Cerney. It is a study of suffering serenely endured. Christ's hair and moustache are heavily stylized, the elongated face thin and drawn. The eyes are closed, either in pain or in death. During the sixteenth and seventeenth centuries, Protestant reformers, in an attempt to return to the 'purity' of the early Christians, smashed sculptures like this, which to them were as idolatrous as the gods of pagan Rome. All across Northern Europe, paintings, stained glass and statues were destroyed. But in South Cerney this little statue seems to have been taken down, carefully hidden in a cavity in the church wall, and preserved. It looks like a moving reprise of what probably happened to the severed head of Mercury. Presumably some parishioners of the old tradition, who had worshipped in front of it, wanted to save it from desecration, and perhaps one day restore it to its original place. In the damp of the church wall most of the sculpture eventually rotted, but the head and a few fragments survived.

These two heads, from a single English county, speak of a universal phenomenon. They are poignant evidence of the devotion and affection which images can inspire, and how difficult it is for those who have grown used to them to worship without them. It was a question which led to bloody division and battles over iconoclasm in the Byzantine Orthodox Church for nearly a century. Yet worshipping without images appears to be exactly what is ordered by the second commandment, which God gave to Moses in the Book of Exodus: 'Thou shalt not make unto thee any graven image, or any likeness of any thing that is in heaven above or that is in the earth beneath, or that is in the water under the earth.' In spite of such unequivocal words, most branches of Christianity make great use of images in worship and prayer. The other two Abrahamic faiths, however, have rarely wavered. The Hebrew scriptures have many virulent condemnations of those who worship statues: Muhammad himself is recorded as removing all idols in Mecca. In Judaism and Islam it is the word alone which is to be revered as the path to God: that reverence has produced supreme works of art in Islam, and had profound social consequences in both faiths.

The British Museum has only a small collection of Judaica, as books and manuscripts are now held in the British Library. But it does have a little hand, a right hand with a pointing index finger, crafted in silver and mounted on a round silver shaft about thirty centimetres long. This is a *yad* (which in Hebrew simply means 'hand') and, although small, it plays an important role at the centre of Jewish religious life. It helps you read the scriptures in the synagogue.

As Rabbi Julia Neuberger explains, after the Temple in Jerusalem was destroyed in 70 CE (cf. Chapter 27), the focus of devotion and religious practice moved away from ritual and sacrifice to concentrate instead on the scriptures, and on a rabbinic tradition of reading and listening, pondering and interpreting the meaning of the Jewish law:

Different ways of worshipping had already predated the destruction of the Temple, because Judaism was already a worldwide religion – or at least a Roman Empire-wide religion. We know that at various times the Roman Empire might have been around 10 per cent Jewish. But with the destruction of the Temple the particular rituals focused on Jerusalem ended and people became synagogue-goers or house-of-study goers: synagogue is simply the Greek word for 'coming together'. The extent to which this was about worship as opposed to study is very hard to know at this distance, but certainly people would have read from the Torah – the first five books of the Hebrew scriptures, what Christians call the Old Testament, with the commentaries on them.

It is said that this is why there are so many Jewish lawyers, because they're very good at arguing over texts. The old joke about two Jews having three opinions is not really a joke at all. It's bound up with the way that we bat words around and talk about meaning. And we focus on words because of the prohibition on using images. We approach God through the word.

The central concern, of course, is with idolatry, the worship of idols, rather than the worship of the one true God. I come from a family that on one side is very Orthodox. My grandfather or great-grandfather was supposedly given a bust of the composer Rossini, and in the Orthodox spirit of not keeping images of the human body he knocked off his nose. I don't know if that quite counts as iconoclasm.

The synagogue in Plymouth, built in the 1760s, gives a powerful impression of the particular kind of sacred space that can be created by a religion that values words over images. The Jews had been allowed to return to England only a century earlier, following their persecution and expulsion at the end of the thirteenth century. Like Catholics, they were tolerated rather than welcome, so newly built synagogues like this one were designed to be discreet and unobtrusive. It is a simple rectangular building that looks from the outside like a Nonconformist chapel or a Quaker meeting house, and it is thought to be the oldest Ashkenazi synagogue in the English-speaking world in continuous use. It comes as a surprise, when you go inside, that the first thing you see, under the east window, is a magnificent two-storey carved and columned classical structure, with elaborate urns and gilded capitals. Anyone from a Christian tradition might think it was a baroque altarpiece, strayed into Devon from a continental Catholic church, but where you would expect to find an image is a red curtain instead, and crowning the whole edifice are words written in Hebrew script. It was made in the Netherlands, through which many Ashkenazi Jews had passed on their way from Germany and Eastern Europe to England; to use an anachronistic term, it was then flat-packed, shipped to Plymouth and reassembled. In contrast to the exterior, this focal point of the synagogue is anything

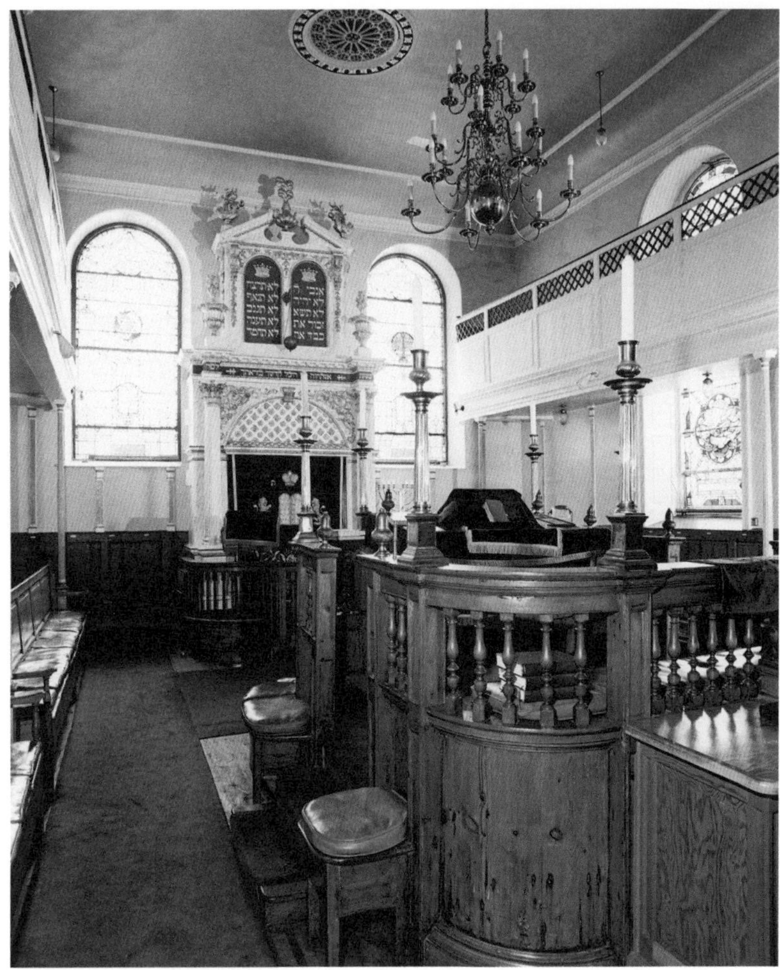

The Baroque splendour of the Plymouth Synagogue: between the windows facing Jerusalem, the Torah scrolls are housed in a gilded ark made in the Netherlands.

but unobtrusive. And that is as it should be: for this is the storage place of the Torah – the ark, where the word itself is housed. Julia Neuberger describes its significance:

The ark is 'Aron Kodesh' or 'holy cupboard', the cupboard in which you keep the scrolls of the law. All arks would be located in such a way that as you face the ark you are facing towards Jerusalem. It's very common to have the Ten Commandments written either on the ark itself, on the sides, or, as in Plymouth, above. Interestingly, the ark in Plymouth was probably made by Christian craftsmen in the Netherlands, which is why it looks very much like a high altar.

Unlike a Catholic church, where seeing the celebration of Mass at the altar is central, the main purpose of a synagogue, as of most Protestant churches, is to let the congregation hear the word of God read and expounded (see Chapter 28). In Plymouth, as in all synagogues, an elaborate ritual accompanies the removal of the scrolls of the law from the ark for their ceremonial reading. Julia Neuberger explains:

In our synagogue, we read the Torah only on Sabbath morning, and it is the central part of the service. The Torah is first processed around the synagogue, giving people a chance to touch its velvet mantel with their prayerbooks. And then it gets 'undressed' by the children, or somebody else who has been given that honour. Its bells and breastplate are taken off, then the silk tie that holds it together is removed. It is unrolled on the reading desk, and people are called up to read; usually one of the rabbis, but barmitzvah or batmitzvah youngsters will read the Torah too, or we will ask a member of the congregation.

It is at this point that the *yad* comes in:

When we read from the Torah scroll, we don't touch it. Some people think that this is because it is holy, but actually it's in order not to damage it. It is written on parchment, animal skin, and is coated – powdered, almost – and then inked, so it is extremely delicate. That makes the Hebrew script even more difficult to read: it is beautifully written by a scribe, but it does not show any vowels, so you have to be reasonably knowledgeable in the language to be able to read it aloud. Using this little silver hand, with the index finger pointing out, you can keep track of where you are. I don't think I would be very comfortable reading the Torah without a yad.

This is why a *yad* is known as a *hidur mitzvah*, an 'embellishment

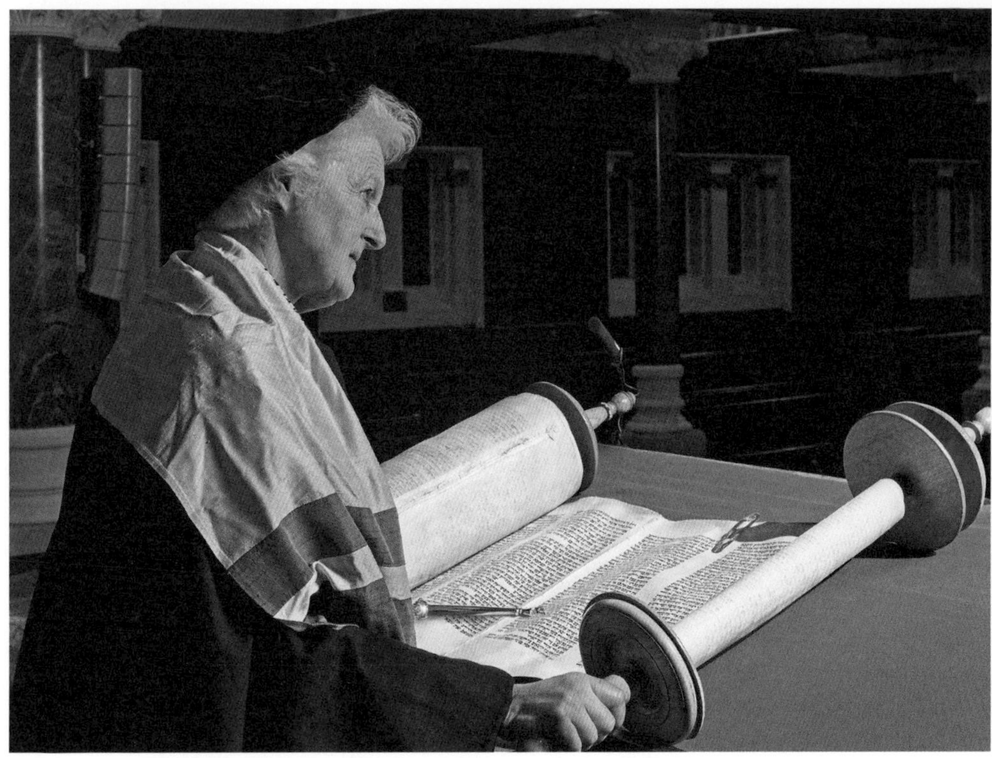

The *yad* given by Joseph Yakov to the Plymouth Synagogue in 1745 (*opposite*) and Rabbi Julia Neuberger, with her *yad*, reading the Torah (*above*)

of the commandment' to read the Torah; and, as this is such a central part of Jewish life, many people have their own. The *yad* in the British Museum comes from the earliest years of the Plymouth Jewish community. It has a silver chain and a square handle, with the inscription: 'this *yad* belongs to Joseph, son of Yahuda Yakov from Schermbeck, here in Plymouth in the year 1745'. Schermbeck is a town just north of Düsseldorf in western Germany, and Yakov had clearly been living in Plymouth for over fifteen years before the synagogue was built. Another *yad*, also in the British Museum, lists on its octagonal handle the names, German or Polish, of eight of the synagogue's founders – a gift proclaiming that in their new country, as in the old, they were going to do what Jews everywhere had always done: read and reverence the word. Jerusalem was out of reach and the Temple destroyed, but the Torah was in Plymouth.

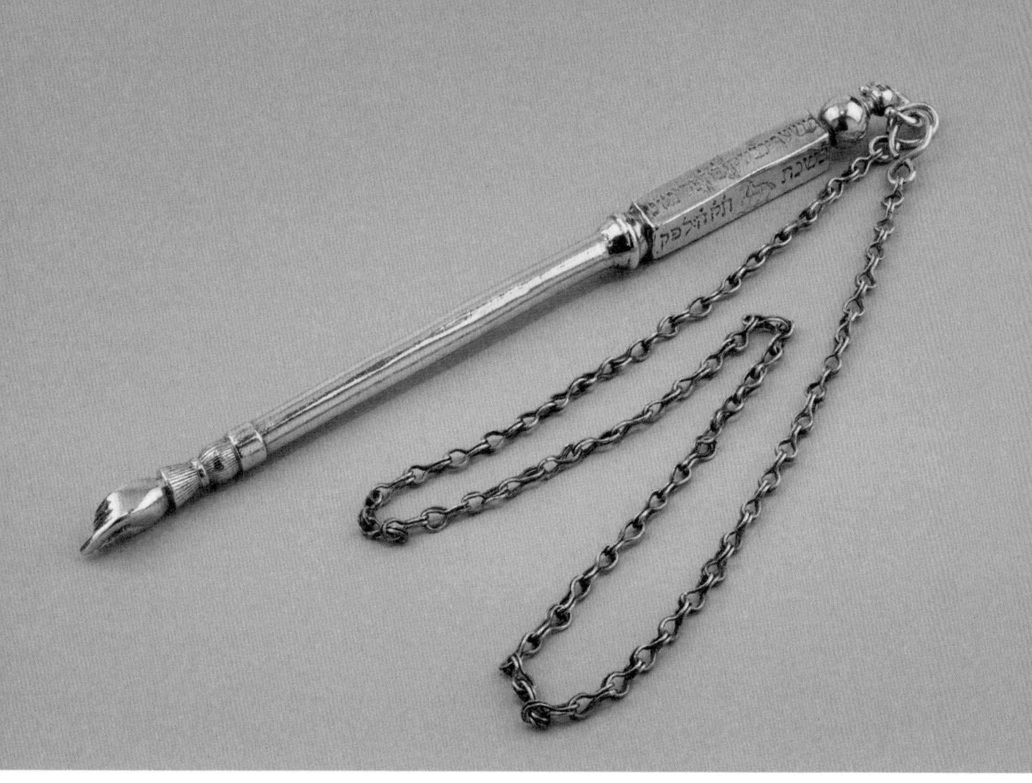

Julia Neuberger points out that in all synagogues, in front of the ark:

you have the eternal light, which is kept burning all the time, usually an oil lamp. It is to remind you of God's eternal presence in and around you. We put the light in front of the ark, because the word of God in the shape of the Torah is that abiding presence.

*

Exactly the same idea lies behind the Islamic practice of decorating lamps with verses from the Qur'an: hanging in the mosque, they remind everybody that they are in the presence of God, not mediated through an image, but approachable and perceptible as both light and word.

One of the most beautiful mosque lamps in the British Museum dates to 1570–75, during the reign of the Ottoman sultan Suleiman the Magnificent. Made not far from Istanbul, its ceramic waisted body is coloured a striking cobalt blue, enlivened here and there with dashes of turquoise and red. Its three looped handles were used to suspend it from the ceiling, so that everybody in the mosque would be able to admire its inscription, bold white against the deep blue, and many would be able to read it: on the lower part is a verse from the Qur'an, 'Praise and thanks be to God; there is no might or power except in God', and around the neck the Shahada, the Islamic profession of faith: 'There is no God but God and Muhammad is his prophet'.

Reading Hebrew is regarded as essential for a full understanding of the Jewish law. In Islam to read the Qur'an in Arabic is to draw close, perhaps as close as possible, to the divine: you are hearing the very words that, in a number of revelations over more than twenty years, Allah used to address the Prophet Muhammad through the mediation of the angel Gabriel. The Prophet then recited what he had heard to his followers, and they were later written down and collected as the 'Qur'an' – which itself translates as 'read' or 'recitation'. Not surprisingly therefore the Qur'an is very clear about the importance of recording and reciting words: 'Recite in the name of thy Lord, who created all things ... He has taught the use of the pen. He has taught man that which he knew not' (Qur'an, XCVI, 1–5). The word, written and spoken – the very words of God – is at the heart of Islam.

This makes the Qur'an an essentially different kind of text from Christian scripture. The Gospels, as they have come down to us, report in ancient demotic Greek what Jesus had said a generation earlier in Aramaic. They are translations of recollections, and most people now read them in a second translation, from the Greek – and thus at an even further remove from the words originally spoken. Christians do of course reverence the Bible. But because Jews and Muslims believe that in their sacred texts are words directly communicated by God, physical copies of the Torah and the Qur'an are treated with extreme respect. The Torah, as we have seen, is

The word of God lighting the world. Sixteenth-century mosque lamp from Iznik

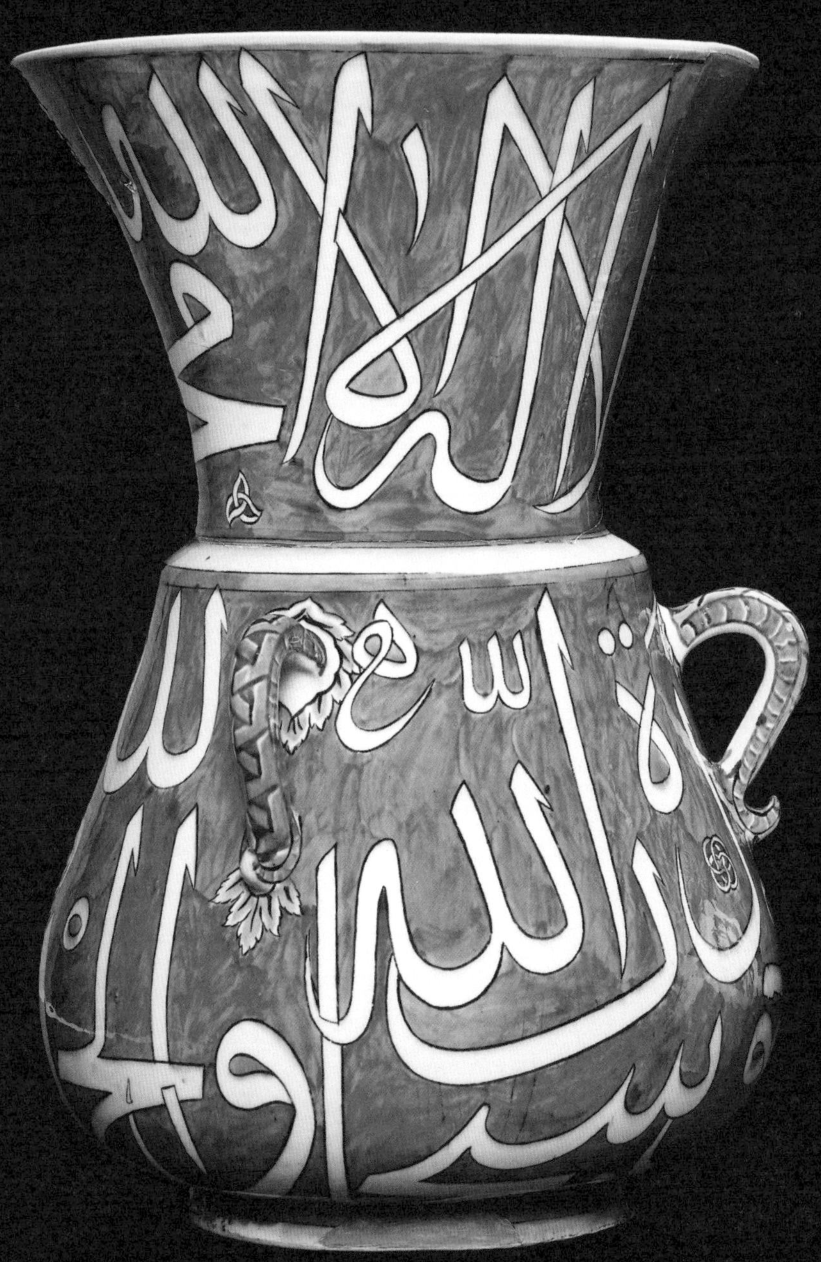

housed and transported and read with the utmost care. According to Dr Afifi al-Akiti, of the Oxford Centre of Islamic Studies:

One of the striking things to the non-Muslim world is the extraordinary reverence of the printed word of God, of the book itself. This runs so deep that people have sometimes been attacked because they are thought to have been disrespectful to the Qur'an. There is an irony here, because in the Muslim legal tradition one of the ways in which it is permitted to dispose of a copy of the Qur'an, for example if it is infested or damaged, is to burn it. But of course if someone burns the Qur'an with a different intention, Muslims feel deeply slighted, perhaps in the same way that Christians who venerate the Cross would feel if it were trampled underfoot.

This comparison gains further power when we think about the Japanese authorities' decision in the seventeenth century to force suspect Christians to do just that, as incontrovertible proof that they had abandoned their faith (Chapter 28). And it explains the care Muslims take, and expect others to take, to ensure that the Qur'an is never placed on the floor, or otherwise subjected to casual indignity. In the home, it is a book to be treated as an honoured guest. Some Muslims will not sit with their back to it.

Our lamp shows one particular, and particularly Islamic, way of doing honour to the text: calligraphy. The letters have been shaped and placed not just to fill completely the space they occupy, as the word of God fills the created world, but to dance in pleasing rhythmic patterns over the round forms of the lamp. The Prophet Muhammad is recorded as saying that 'Good writing makes the truth stand out.' This is why, over time, calligraphy became by far the most important means of visual expression in Islam: a sacramental art, the creation of beauty and in time the defining visual language of Islamic civilization. Afifi al-Akiti describes this impulse:

Around the eighth and ninth Christian centuries (the second Muslim century), there is a flowering of the calligraphic tradition in

Islam, initially in mosques but increasingly outside mosques, too – on domestic objects of all sorts. Since originally these words were held to reflect the divine, it was very natural, very human, to try to reflect it – in something that would be a delight to the eyes. It is not something that was planned. It just came as a result of that convergence between the divine and the finite.

But, as so often, beauty came at a cost:

It's often quite difficult to read very beautiful calligraphy. When I was much younger, I helped to catalogue some of the Arabic manuscripts in the Bodleian Library here at the University of Oxford. It took quite some time to learn the trade, and I spent a while in Morocco learning from various masters how to read the different scripts. Still today, lots of Arabic manuscripts are not decipherable until you find a master who can read them.

In many mosques calligraphy goes far beyond objects like our lamp, or decorations on wood, metal or tile. In the Sheikh Lutfallah mosque in Isfahan, for example, it decorates pillars, walls and dome, sustaining and filling the entire building with the lively word of the Qur'an and other holy texts. Even if unable to read the writing, when you pray in a mosque like this, you can feel yourself being surrounded by – immersed in, embraced by – the presence of God, through God's word made manifest to ears and eyes alike, at the same time. It is the equivalent in words to the immersion in images which Rowan Williams describes in an Orthodox church (Chapter 17).

Julia Neuberger tells how this focus on the word in both faiths has necessarily encouraged learning and literacy:

Literacy amongst Jewish women developed comparatively early. Children, particularly boys, were also taught to read at a very

Over: The Sheikh Lutfallah Mosque, in Isfahan, Iran, built around 1610: the word of God surrounds believers, sustaining both them and the building

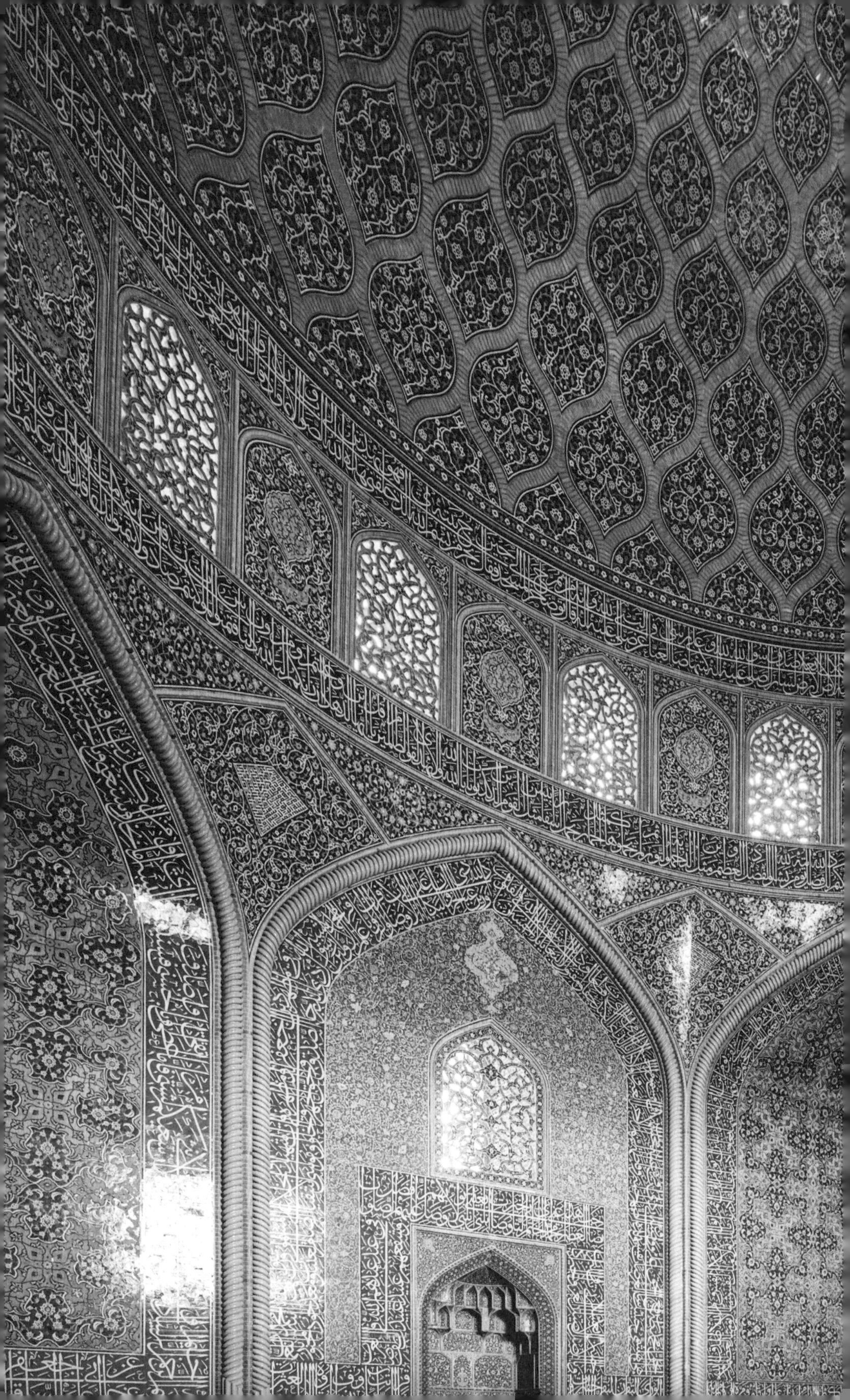

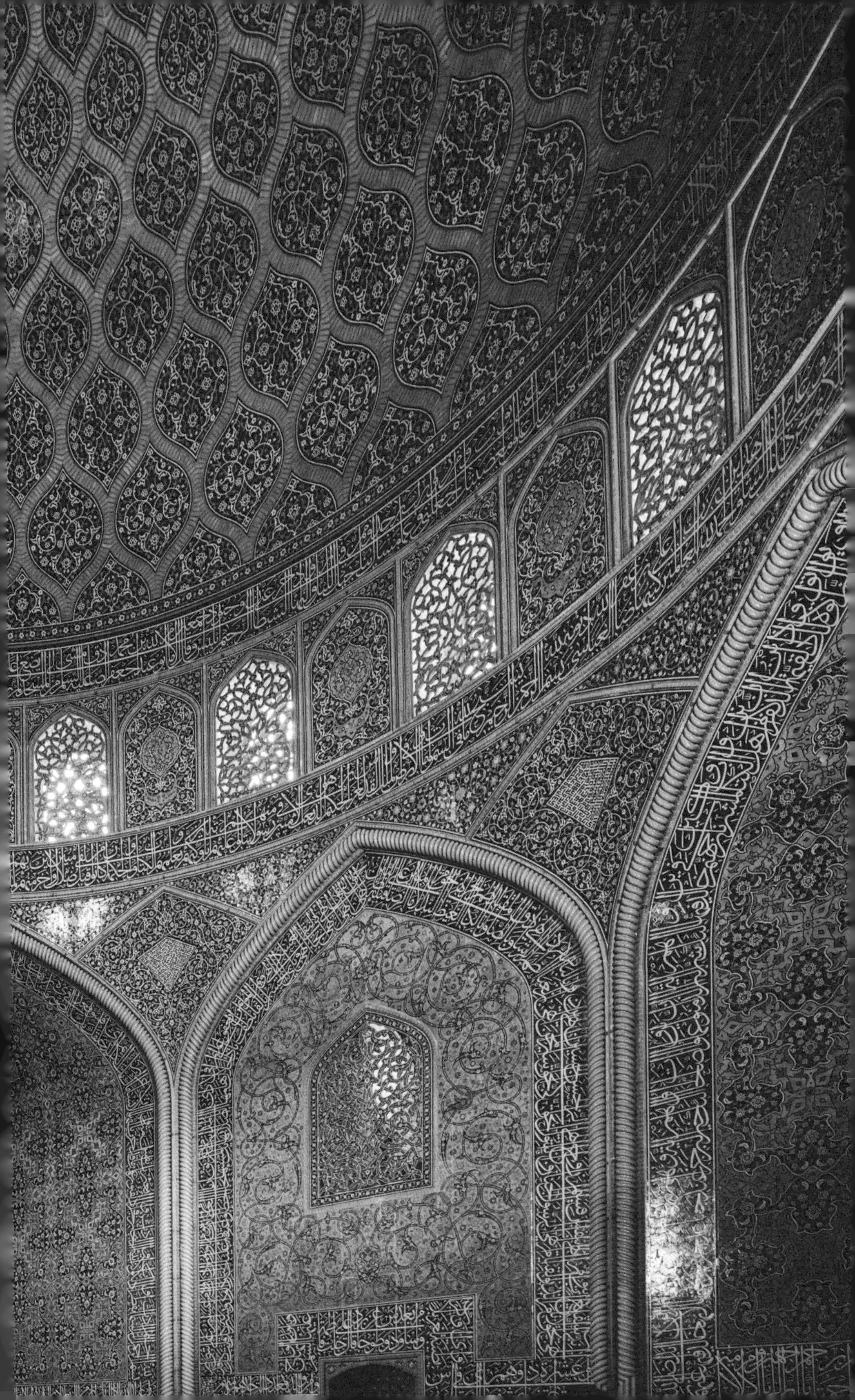

early age – and often just taught to read holy texts. There are wonderful stories about children gathered round a Torah scroll because there were not enough copies for everyone. Some of them only learned to read upside down.

Afifi al-Akiti talks of a comparable yearning for literacy in parts of the Islamic world:

In the pre-modern period, we find cases of farmers who perhaps in another cultural setting might not be able to read, in fact being literate. They buy books, manuscripts, starting with the Qur'an and then other sorts of devotional literature.

In a world where there were no printed books, and manuscripts were rare and expensive, for many communities there was only one way to share and study the sacred text, as Afifi al-Akiti explains:

That is why there are strong traditions of memorizing and reciting the Qur'an. In a typical madrasa, you would probably take about six to nine years to complete learning it, but some have virtually memorized it in as little as three. Even today, when printed books are cheap, an astonishing number of people can recite the entire Qur'an by heart.

The seventeenth day of Ramadan is marked by Muslims as the day when the Qur'an was first revealed to the Prophet Muhammad. So Muslims all over the world today try, during the month of Ramadan, to recite the Qur'an in full, and to complete it by the seventeenth if they can. In various Muslim seminaries and Islamic schools, for example in Malaysia and Singapore, there are competitions for reciting the Qur'an. There are international competitions, too – a World Cup for Qur'an recitation.

But this deep personal appropriation of the text brings with it many challenges. Afifi al-Akiti details how, like the ancient

Hebrew of the Torah, the seventh-century Arabic of the Qur'an is open to many different interpretations:

Whereas in the Christian tradition the word of God is made flesh in the person of Christ, for Muslims God came into the world as word. And just as Christians have to grapple with the problem of incarnation, Muslims have to grapple with the problem of 'inverbation' – God becoming word. It is difficult, because although Muslims believe that the Qur'an is the sublime literal word of God, that doesn't mean that they can read the Qur'an literally. These are two different things. You need qualified scholarship, proper guidance, to make sure that you do not misunderstand the Qur'an. Scholars, jurists, theologians, Sufis: you need such people to interpret this sublime divine word of God for earthly understanding.

But even Muslim scholars acknowledge that no one can fathom completely the word of God. There has to be humility and we have to acknowledge our fallibility. Nobody has a monopoly on knowing fully, except of course, as Muslims believe, the prophets. This is where we run into challenges today, as young Muslims

Boys compete to learn and recite the Qur'an in a madrasa in Malaysia

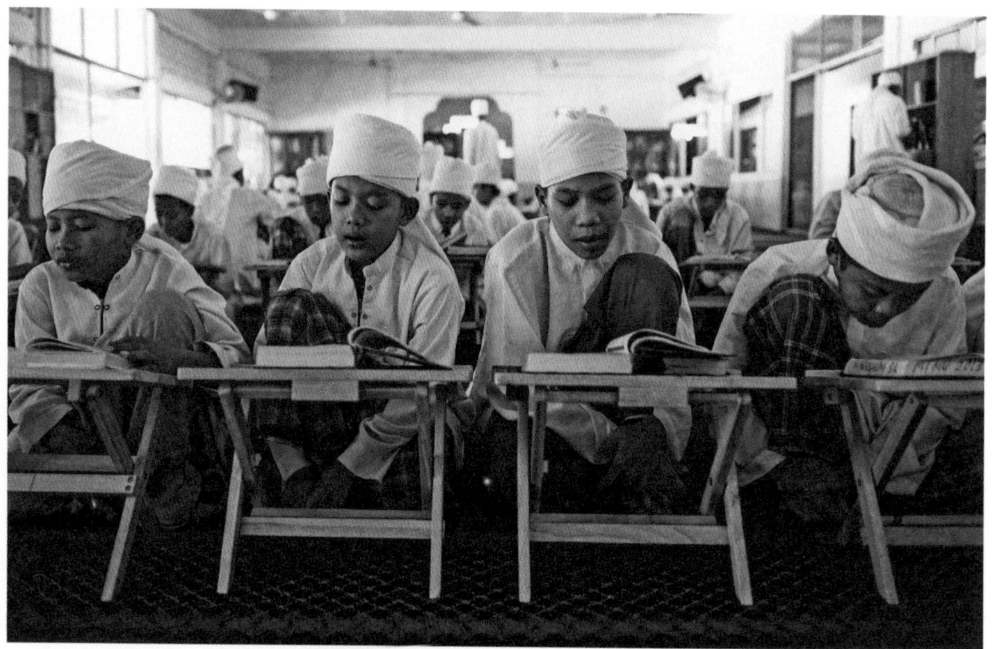

grow up not realizing this, and approach the word of God without those filters of informed debate. It can be poisonous if one is not careful.

Afifi al-Akiti is of course referring to bitter disagreements within modern Islam about the proper interpretation of holy texts, especially those concerning images – back to the Bamiyan Buddhas – and to the justifications for violence produced by extreme Islamist movements. Judaism is also sharply divided by different schools of interpreting the Torah, some of them with far-reaching political repercussions for the Middle East too. One can see why both faiths have always handled the text with such care and apprehension. It was one of the saddest ironies of the Reformation that the word for which the reformers claimed such authority turned out to be as ambiguous and divisive as the images they destroyed. The proper interpretation of Christian texts has been just as acrimonious and at least as bloody as any disagreements in Islam and Judaism.

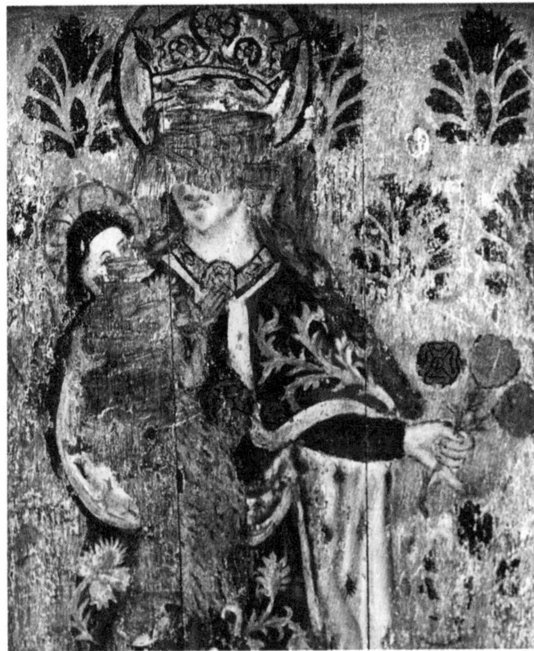

The destruction of images during the European Reformation: the faces of the Virgin and Christ-child are scratched away at Great Snoring in Norfolk.

PART FIVE

One God or Many

Some societies acknowledge only one god, some live comfortably with many, and for others even the idea of gods in the plural is offensive. For most Europeans the notion of multiple gods suggests the mythologies of Greece and Rome, where each god or goddess has a clearly defined role. Many communities, however, both ancient and modern, do not think in such terms at all: they share the world around them with local spirits, shape-shifting supernatural beings that inhabit particular places and which are certainly not gods in that classical Mediterranean sense. Whether the society is monotheistic or polytheistic, the political consequences are far-reaching – especially when, as in ancient Rome or modern India, the key question is how to live not only with your own gods, but with the gods of others.

21
THE BLESSINGS OF MANY GODS

In 1844, a Roman earthenware jar, that looks like a small round cooking pot, was dug up in a sand-hill near Felmingham Hall in Norfolk. Made of reddish-brown clay with two rings as handles, it is an ordinary, everyday pot, but a handsome one: inside, you might expect to find a good soup or stew. What the 1840s excavators in fact found in it was a belief system – or rather several belief systems, all mixed up together: a jumble of small bronze gods, deities of different kinds and from different traditions. Together, they let us form some idea of how the inhabitants of the Roman Empire, or at least Roman north Norfolk around the year 250 CE, lived with quite a large number of gods.

The Felmingham deities now sit together in a case at the British Museum. There are three bronze heads, probably designed to fit on to wooden bodies. Largest and most imposing among them is – appropriately – Jupiter, god of sky and thunder, chief among the gods of Rome, with hair and beard elaborately styled and combed. The eyes have been removed from their sockets, which gives a ghostly air to his commanding presence, and the hole at his throat suggests that he certainly was once attached to a body. Near him is a female head, with tightly pursed lips and wearing a magnificently crested helmet – she is his daughter, Minerva, goddess of wisdom and military strategy. Between these two is a younger, handsome god, Sol or Helios, who wears a crescent moon set among the rays of the sun, which he represents. So far, so conventionally Roman: but then it gets more complicated, as Mary Beard, Professor of Classics at Cambridge University, explains:

Some of the pieces in the hoard stand out to me as absolute trad Roman religious images. There's one very lovely figurine of a Lar, a so-called household god. He looks after the home. He is wearing bootees and a little skirt and carries an offering dish in his hand: you can find statues like this wherever the Romans go.

Then there is the nice Minerva: whenever you see a lady with a helmet on, it always means a goddess, and if you're Roman you'd say this is the goddess Minerva. If you're Greek you'd call her Athena. So there are gods and goddesses here in Felmingham that would be recognizable all over the Roman world – but referred to by different names and given slightly different roles. But very interestingly here they are mixed up with things that are certainly pre-Roman, though I wouldn't necessarily call them Celtic – religious bits and bobs. There's a tiny bronze model of a wheel, which is often associated with one of the pre-Roman gods in Britain. This hoard is a lovely mixture.

In front of the Roman household god are two miniature bronze birds, perhaps a raven and a dove, each holding in its beak what looks like a small round stone. Birds like these are found in settlements from Ireland to Central Europe, part of an earlier tradition that embraced much of the Continent, and in Britain long predated the arrival of the Romans. They clearly had a symbolic or ritual significance, but we can only guess at what that might be. Then there is the little wheel, about six centimetres in diameter. Spoked wheels like this one were connected with a major Celtic

(*Over*) Religious objects from the Felmingham hoard, with the clay pot in which they were buried in Norfolk around 260 CE

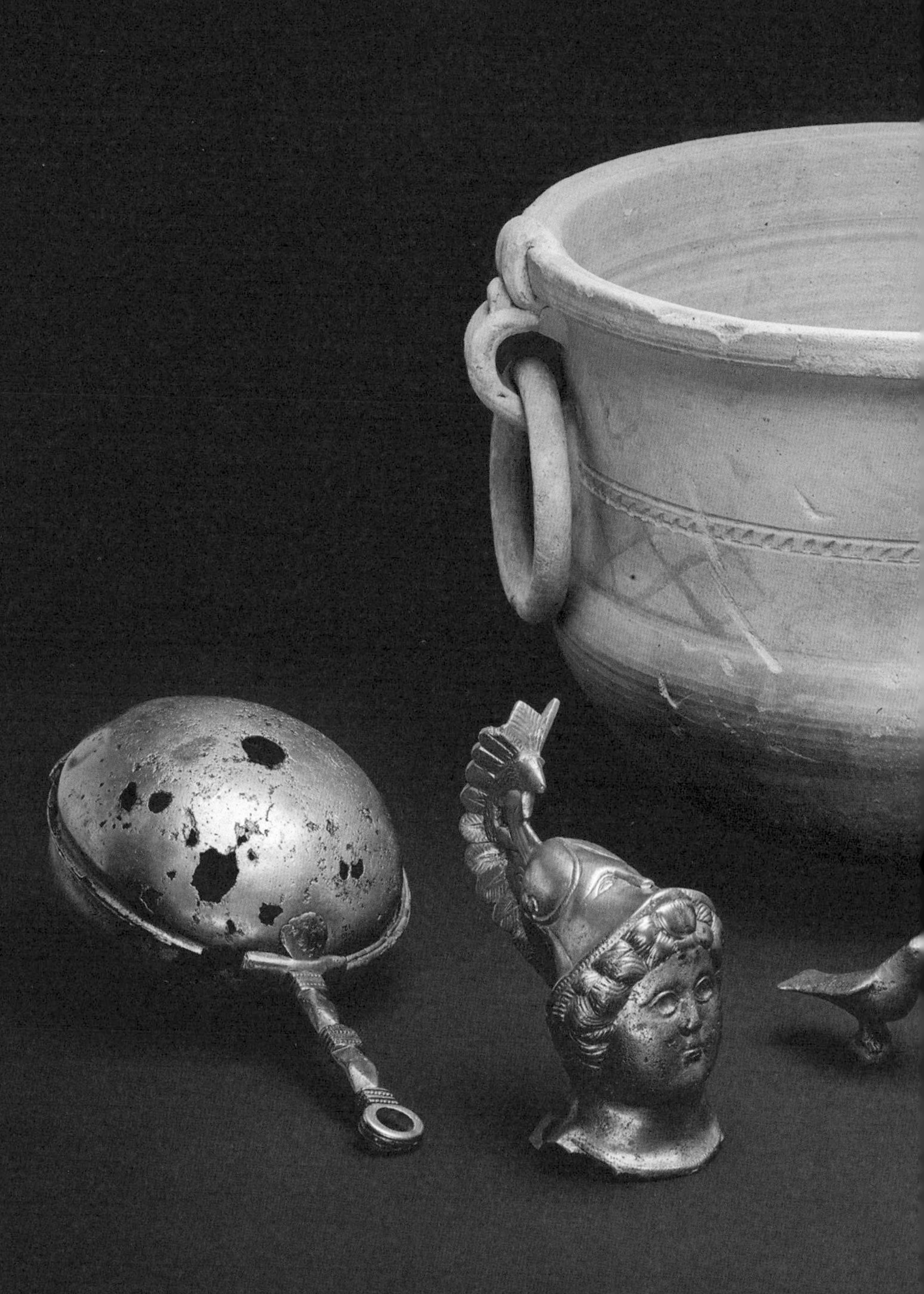

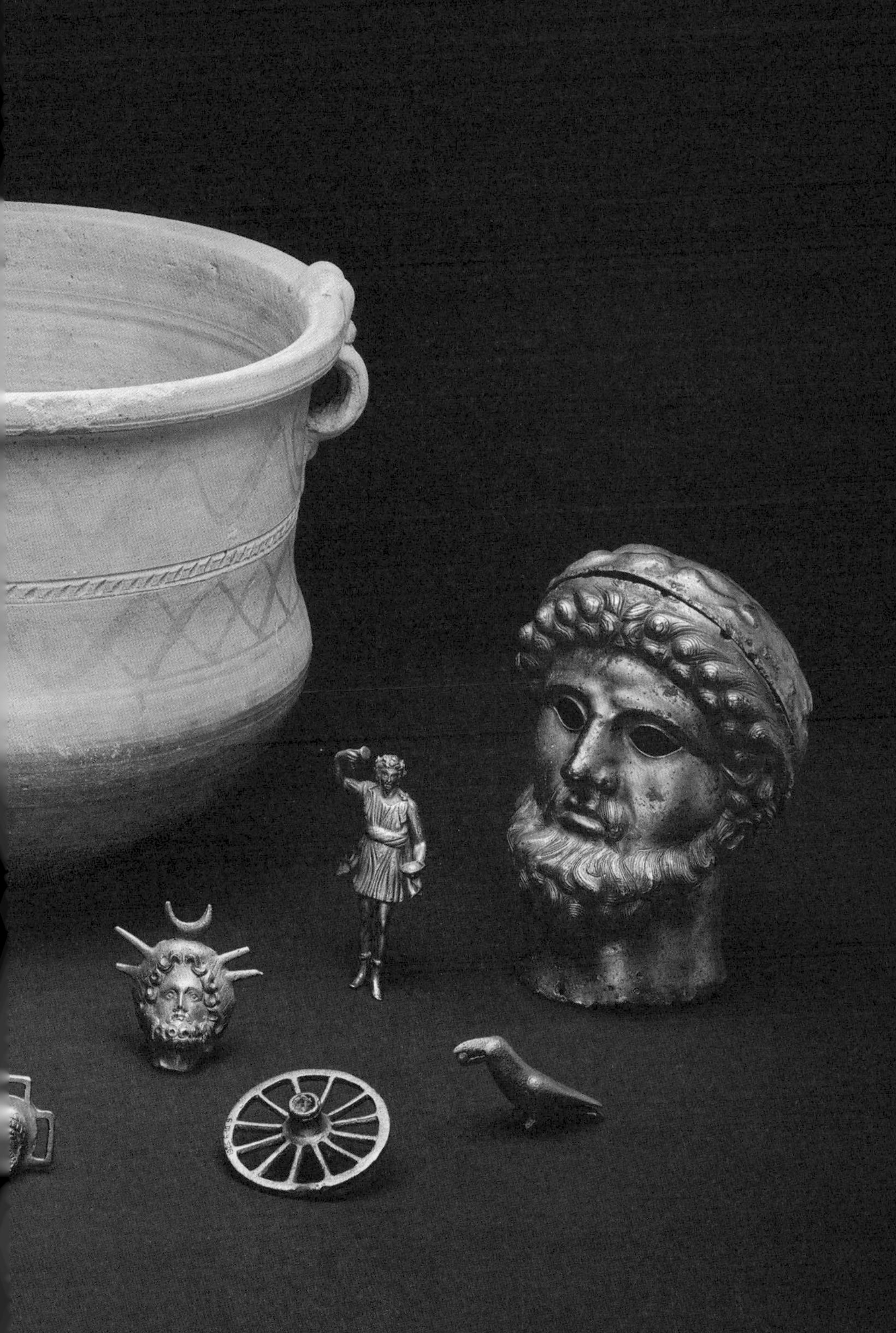

deity known as Taranis: the name means 'thunder-clap' in Welsh. By the time our hoard was buried, the Celtic Taranis, or Tanarus, had become associated, indeed almost conflated, with the Roman Jupiter – the two gods of thunder had almost become a composite deity, who could be worshipped in two forms, which may be why they are both present in this hoard. (We saw a very similar conflation in Japan in Chapter 18.) At around the time the Felmingham pot was buried about 250 CE, an altar near Chester was dedicated to Jupiter Optimus Maximus Tanarus. It is a typical Roman situation, replicated across the empire: two gods, one of the victors, one of the vanquished, had become neighbours, found common ground, and not just co-existed but intermingled.

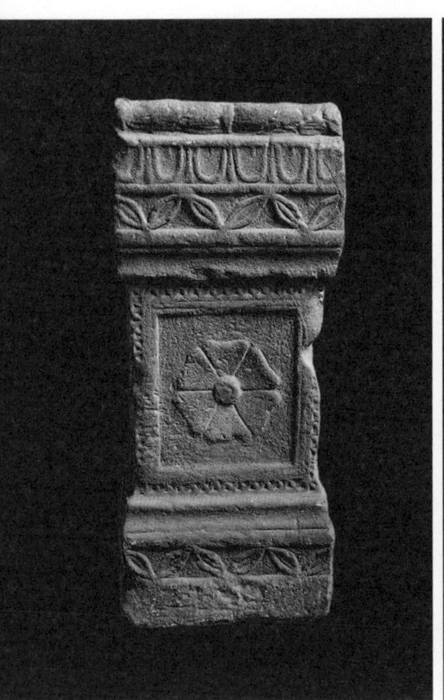

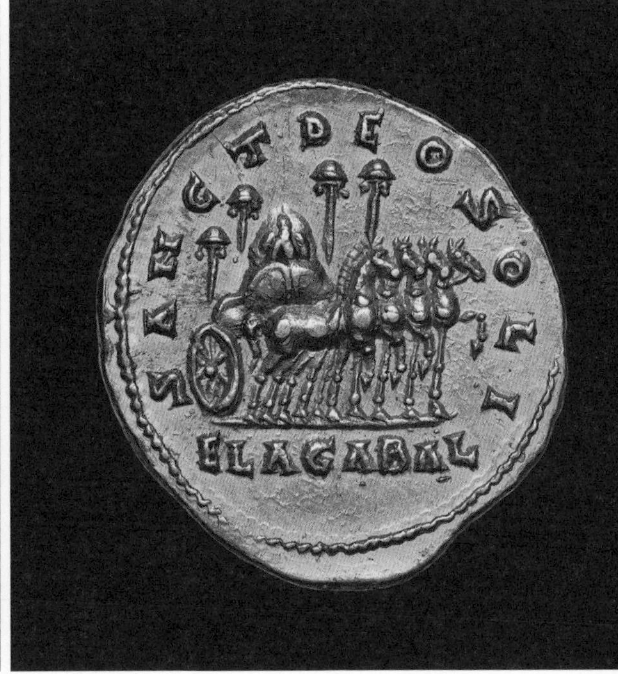

This altar near Chester, dedicated to Jupiter Optimus Maximus Tanarus at around the time the Felmingham pot was buried, shows the fusion of Imperial Roman and indigenous British beliefs (*left*); and (*right*) the conical stone representing the Levantine god Baal is brought in triumph to Rome on this gold coin of 218–19 CE. He was venerated there under his Roman name, Elagabalus.

We do not know why the Felmingham pot was buried, but it appears to have been done with great care. Perhaps there was a temporary breakdown of order, with a fear of looting. Or it may be that a temple, perhaps one dedicated to Jupiter/Tanarus, was closing down. Or it may have been a more permanent arrangement – a long-term deposit in the earth at a holy spot, an offering to all the gods who were worshipped in that place. But whatever the reason, these objects taken together tell the story of one of the world's great polytheistic societies: Rome.

As the empire grew, Roman gods were exported to its new provinces, and temples built for them, so that sacrifices could be offered to them there. But these were not jealous gods, and this was in no sense a missionary campaign to convert the infidel. The gods of the defeated regions, far from being displaced, continued to be honoured and worshipped locally: they might be 'invited' to take their place in the Roman pantheon, and some – the Levantine Baal (frequently mentioned in the Hebrew bible) or the Anatolian goddess Cybele – might even have a temple built for them in Rome. That practice had started early, with the adopting and co-opting of gods from neighbouring towns as Rome began to expand its territory. It embraced the deities of the defeated Etruscans to the north, and then the Greek colonies in southern Italy. Centuries before the thundering Roman Jupiter met the British Tanarus, he had been equated and conflated with the Greek thunder god, Zeus, just as Minerva had merged with the Greek goddess of wisdom, Athena. When they arrived in Felmingham, both gods therefore already had dual nationality. When Egypt was conquered, major temples to its gods – including Isis and Osiris – were similarly erected in Rome, reflecting the way the Romans absorbed and integrated the territories, people and customs of their growing empire. This allowed them constantly to readjust themselves geographically and culturally, and to engage mentally with almost every part of the Roman world. Once conquest was secure, politics and religion, effectively inseparable, marched in step – and a tolerant, all-embracing step it usually was. (The major exception, as we shall see in Chapter 27, was with the single god of the Jews.) As Mary Beard explains, the Romans awarded citizenship not just to conquered peoples, but to conquered gods:

Romans treated their gods and goddesses as they did their citizens. When they conquered another place, they regularly gave the conquered people some form of Roman citizenship – they incorporated them. Partly that demonstrated Roman power, but it also showed Rome's fluidity in thinking about who was entitled to belong in Rome. And in many ways it was the same with the gods. They treated the conquered gods a little like they treated the conquered people. They were welcome, but there was never any doubt who was in charge.

They were a hospitable crew, the Roman gods. I suspect that Jupiter and Minerva sitting in their comfortable home on the Capitoline Hill in Rome knew for certain that they were the people who really ruled the roost there. It didn't matter in some ways that the new gods were slightly odd: part of the point of granting them a temple in Rome was to erode that oddity. It was a step in the process of them becoming you.

Them becoming you: it was a way of thinking, perhaps more a habit than a strategy, that allowed the Roman Empire to become an outstandingly successful – and long-lasting – multi-racial, multi-faith state. If you honour other people's gods, you acknowledge them, and the people who worship them, as a legitimate part of your community. They and their gods become less strange: in the process, you and they both change. It was an approach endorsed in Rome at the highest level: in 173 BCE a decree of the Senate commented, *iidem ubique di immortales*: 'the immortal gods are the same everywhere'. You cannot imagine the government of any later European colonial empire ever putting it quite like that.

'Polytheism' has in many ways become part of a rogues'

gallery of disparaging words – like 'pagans', 'heathens', 'idolatry'. Hovering around the worship of many gods is a distinct whiff of European Enlightenment disapproval. It has been an influential disapproval, stoked by the economic and cultural power of modern monotheisms, and the conviction of all three Abrahamic faiths that they are in a favoured relationship with the one and only god, and that each possesses in a uniquely sacred text the supreme, perhaps the sole, truth. That can make co-existence hard and often makes it impossible. Mary Beard concludes:

Rome was in many ways a really typical polytheism and I think one of the big advantages of having lots of gods is that you can have more or fewer as you decide. So that there isn't the kind of head-to-head clash that you get when monotheistic cultures meet.

Living with many different gods allowed the Romans to live on good terms with many different peoples.

If we go back in time 1,500 years before the Roman Empire, and a little further east, ancient Mesopotamia shows us other benefits of having several gods – and how useful it can be if they do not always agree.

A man receives a divine command to build a boat. His god gives precise specifications, right down to sealing the boat with pitch. This has to be a big vessel – in fact, an ark. And aboard this ark, a man, his family and many animals will survive a great storm and flood, in which all others will perish. But this is not the story of Noah (Chapter 5) in the Book of Genesis. It is the tale of a man called Utnapishtim, a character in one of the oldest poems that we know, the Mesopotamian *Epic of Gilgamesh*. This section of the poem, the story of the flood and the ark, is written on a broken clay tablet that was baked in Assyria, modern Iraq, in the seventh century BCE, and is now in the British Museum.

Fifteen centimetres long by thirteen wide, the Flood Tablet, as it is known, is one of the most famous cuneiform texts in the world. On it are two tightly packed columns of wedge-shaped letters, scratched with a reed pen into the wet clay. They present a narrative with striking similarities to, but important differences from, the Noah story. Both tell of a divinely ordained deluge and of one family being chosen to survive it. And yet the divine role in these two accounts could hardly be more different. In the Hebrew Bible, Noah is told to build his boat by the one and only god, who alone has created all things, and is now about to flood the world and destroy all its disappointingly sinful human inhabitants. The god who speaks to Utnapishtim, by contrast, is one of many.

The *Epic of Gilgamesh,* a poem composed and recited in the city states of Mesopotamia some time before 2000 BCE (and written down much later) also contains the first description in literature of a council of gods. Individual deities in Mesopotamia were closely associated with particular cities (Chapter 11), where they were effectively local landlords, or sometimes landladies, their temples sustained by agricultural surplus. But although the gods each had their separate cities, they had family connections and worked together in governing a wide area, under a kind of federal arrangement. No one city – so no one god – was allowed to dominate. There was always discussion and, inevitably, disagreement. It was a process that inherently had its confusions, but it seems that the Mesopotamians found it preferable to having just one authoritarian, centralizing, all-deciding god.

Andrew George, Professor of Babylonian at the School of Oriental and African Studies, outlines the politics of the key debate in the council of the gods:

The gods had held a council and determined to bring a flood to wipe out humankind. The reason isn't explained in Gilgamesh,

Seventh-century BCE clay tablet of the *Epic of Gilgamesh,* inscribed with the Babylonian account of the Flood, composed over a thousand years earlier

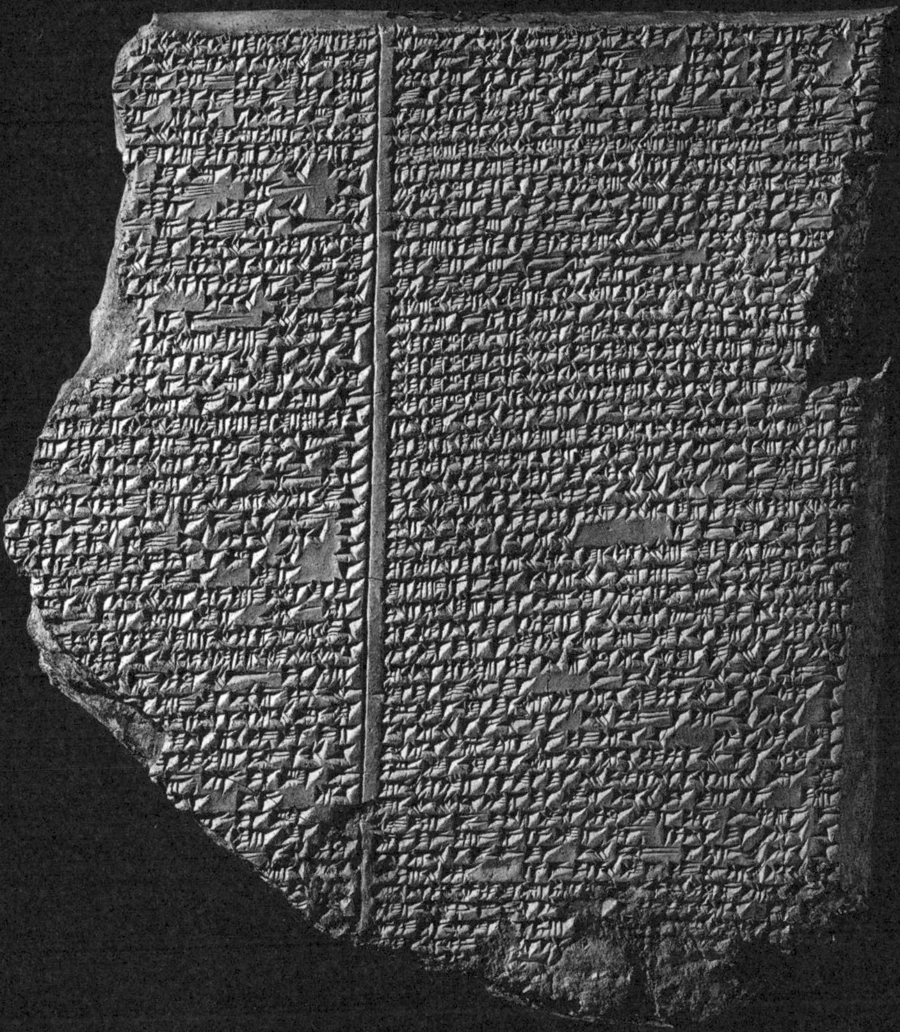

but it is given in other narrative poems: there are too many humans – at this stage, they are immortal and they keep breeding – and they make so much noise that they are annoying the gods, who can't get to sleep. In particular, Enlil, the king of the gods, can't sleep. He says: 'This is no good, we have to get rid of these pests and then we can have peace again.'

He tries plague, but clearly more is needed. So the council meets and they all surrender to the wishes of Enlil, rather as if he were a dictator. But later in the poem, after the flood, Enlil is accused of wielding power without restraint. I think Babylonian poets recognized that such excessive power, in the hands of one person, was dangerous, and was likely to lead to problems: dictators can take countries into all sorts of nasty places, with disastrous results. Rather as in the American Constitution, the Babylonians saw the need to curtail power with checks and balances. The flood story is used, I think, as an example of what can happen when people fall in behind absolute power.

But one god – Enlil's younger brother – does not agree with Enlil's dictatorial decision : if humans are exterminated, who is going to worship the gods, and grow food for their temples? So he decides to be a whistle-blower, and subvert what he thinks is a false step by the misguided gods. He finds a way to warn one man – Utnapishtim, the man in our Flood Tablet –– and tells him how to save his family and the animals by building his ark.

It is thought that both *Gilgamesh* and the later Noah story may draw on a shared legend about a great flood that had devastated much of the modern Middle East, perhaps as sea levels rose at the end of the last Ice Age. After the waters settled came the question: why had it happened? And why had some – but only some – people and animals survived? The answer: there must be an element of divine discretion involved. In Genesis, that takes the form of a single, wise god deciding to condemn the wicked to death by drowning, and to save the one good man and his family. In

Gilgamesh, a group of dysfunctional insomniac gods fortuitously has a dissenting member, who rescues the one person he can. As Andrew George points out, Mesopotamian society's religion, and its politics, was marked by profound scepticism about the wisdom of its rulers, both on earth and in heaven:

The problem with the gods in assembly is that they often have beer to drink, and therefore their decisions are not always thought out properly. They make mistakes, and one of those had been to produce a human race that was both immortal and capable of reproducing itself unchecked.

In the end, the Mesopotamian council of gods recognized that the flood was not the answer to their insomnia – or to all the other problems they had with the ever more numerous and noisy humans. Instead, they created death, which would in future limit the population and so allow them to get some sleep. They saw that their decision to unleash the flood had been a wrong one, which a dissenter had put right, allowing them to change their collective mind. It is a model of governance that is possible only if you have many gods, and only if they are, and know themselves to be, fallible.

Placed side by side, the two stories – Hebrew and Babylonian – raise the same fundamental question about natural disasters, but offer radically different narratives and moral answers. For the Babylonians, a lethal flood could be the result of drunken, misguided gods. But Andrew George explains how that answer is not open to Jews and Christians, with a single God both omnipotent and invariably just:

The Babylonians recognized that there was in the world a kind of arbitrary bad, which arose sometimes from the actions of the gods, but often just arose, and had to be pushed back and defeated by the gods. But if you have a monotheism, then of course you have to work out a different explanation of why that one god decides to do harm to the human race. This is the question and

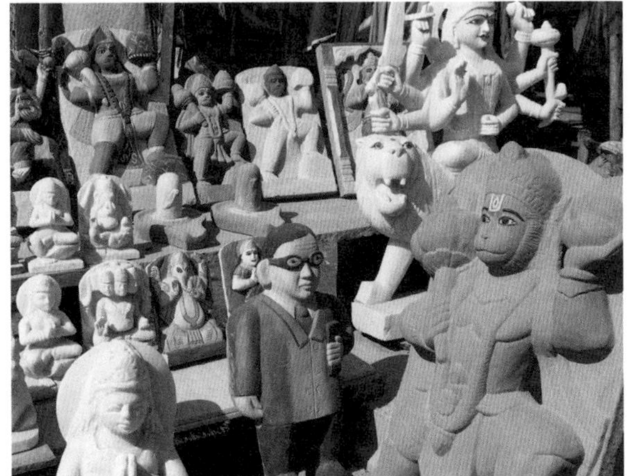

Dr Ambedkar, the author of the Indian Constitution, takes his place in the portable pantheon of Indian gods at a roadside stall in Uttar Pradesh, 2017.

the narrative that you find throughout the Old Testament: how is it that our god can do us damage, do us harm? And the answer is of course – because we sin.

In the book of Genesis, Noah is saved because Noah alone is righteous. Those who drown are wicked: the victims are to blame for their own suffering. In the *Epic of Gilgamesh* you could say – to borrow language from a more modern disaster in Mesopotamia/Iraq – that people die simply because 'stuff happens'; and that 3,000 years ago 'unknown unknowns' were already around. Did Donald Rumsfeld know in 2003 that he was standing in the rich tradition of Mesopotamian theology?

The squabbles in Olympus that provoked and prolonged the Trojan War have more than a passing similarity to the disagreements in *Gilgamesh*. Polytheism may lack what we think of as intellectual coherence or moral clarity, but coherence and clarity are perhaps not the supreme, and are certainly not the only, virtues in a system of belief. Living with many gods allowed the Romans to absorb an astounding range of new peoples, from Egypt to Norfolk, into a highly successful state, of which all could be citizens; and it offered the Mesopotamians a world view in which natural disaster – not infrequent in a region of earthquakes and floods – was not the fault of those who suffered it.

Polytheism, porous, adaptable and tolerant, is of course by no means restricted to the ancient world. A frequent sight in India today is the wayside stall selling religious images. Cheek by jowl, small statues of the Buddha, Shiva lingams and figures of different Hindu gods wait to be bought and taken home. Some stalls include more recent arrivals in the august company. Here, flanked by the elephant-headed Ganesha, the monkey-god Hanuman and the many-armed Durga (Chapter 17), is a man in a suit wearing spectacles. He is Dr Ambedkar, principal author of the Indian Constitution, a leading figure in the independence movement, and the hero of the *dalits*, the lowest group in the Hindu caste system, once known as Untouchables. A *dalit* himself, he studied at the London School of Economics, became a lawyer (he always wore his trademark lawyerly suit), worked with Gandhi and Nehru in the struggle for independence, and campaigned indomitably for the abolition of the caste system. Disappointed by the failure of the Congress party to implement his proposals, in the 1950s he led his followers to escape its constraints by converting *en masse* to Buddhism. The Neo-Buddhists are today a powerful political force, and, in a way Ambedkar would have abhorred, his devotees (now in the literal sense of that word) have begun to revere him as far more than just a politician: he is seen as almost divine, an enlightened being, who, like other gods, can help them through the difficulties of life. Hence his presence on the stall. Without texts, without priests, and most certainly without the help of central government, the people have added him to their pantheon.

The politics of faith in societies with many gods – today, as in the ancient world – are necessarily pluralist. Far from being primitive, as they were long considered, they can clearly be sophisticated, welcoming and admirably humane. But as we shall see in Chapter 25, polytheism, no less than monotheism, can in the modern world also provide a vehicle for exclusion and political intolerance.

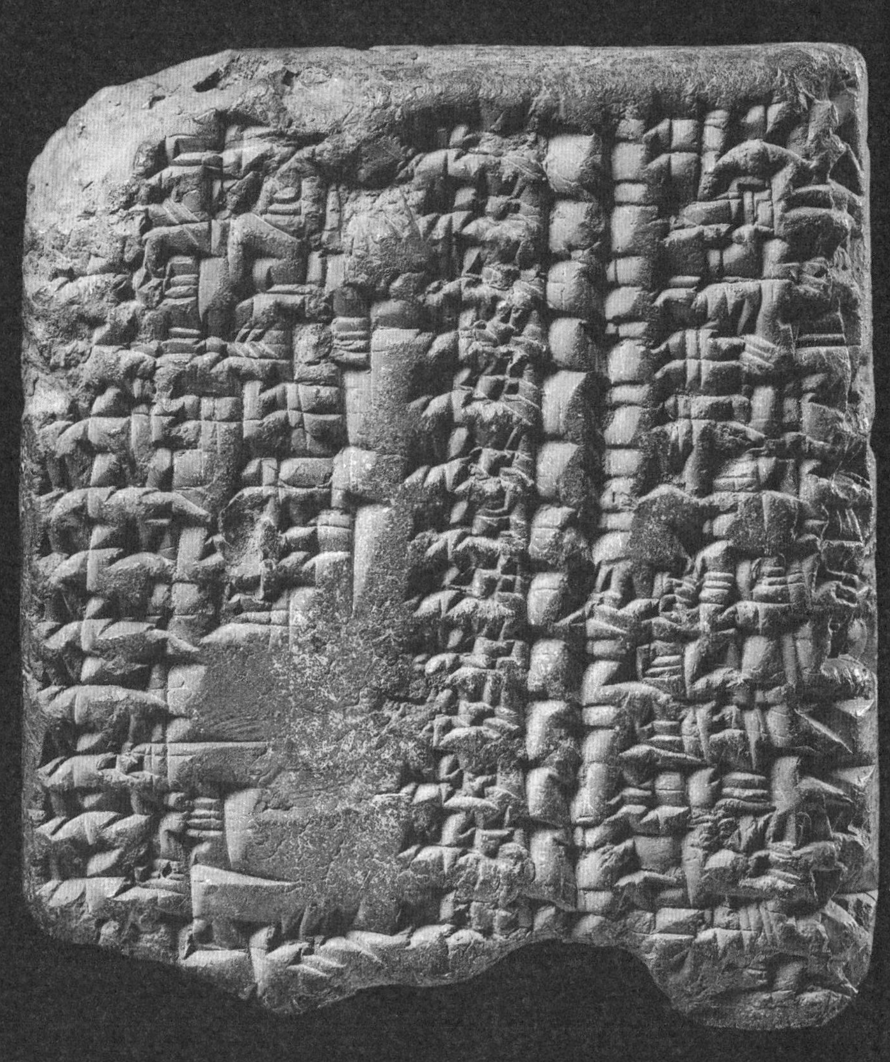

22

THE POWER OF ONE

In the last chapter, the Flood Tablet showed the workings of a sophisticated polytheism. On another Mesopotamian tablet, one that sits comfortably in the palm of the hand, it may just be that we can see the beginnings of monotheism.

Ninurta is Marduk of the plough
Nergal is Marduk of war
Nabu is Marduk of accounting
Sin is Marduk as illuminator of the night
Shamash is Marduk of justice
Adad is Marduk of rain
Tishpak is Marduk of troops
[—–] is Marduk of everything

In this small tablet, a revolution is perhaps taking place: many gods are, it seems, becoming one. This little lump of earth, baked dry in the Babylonian sun over 2,500 years ago, is a kind of thought experiment, and it has a rare immediacy. In dense lines of tiny script, we can watch a Babylonian priest or scholar of the time of Nebuchadnezzar, about 580 BCE, jotting down an idea – as it

The Mesopotamian Marduk tablet, around 580 BCE: in the left-hand column are the names of fourteen major male gods, with Marduk's name repeated on every line on the right.

were on a cuneiform post-it note. He is wondering whether the many and mighty gods of Mesopotamia, whose names he lists, and each of whom controls a crucial aspect of life – agriculture, weather, war – might not in fact be separate gods, but actually all merely aspects of one god: Marduk, the patron deity of Babylon. Infuriatingly, the name of the last god, who might already have an overarching role, is no longer legible.

At the end of the nineteenth century this little tablet in the British Museum played a significant role in a heated international debate: where did monotheism begin? Who first got the idea that there was only one god? Was it the Egyptians, the Babylonians or the Jews? It was part of a wider questioning of the uniqueness and historical reliability of the Hebrew Bible, in which the Flood Tablet also played a major part. Unsurprisingly, given the many close connections across the ancient Middle East, the answer seems to be that many people had the same idea at roughly the same time.

Jonathan Stökl, of the Theology Department of King's College London, believes that this tablet is not, as its nineteenth-century champions hoped, a clear statement of faith in one god, but more probably notes from a brain-storming session with a group of Babylonian intellectuals :

It looks as if this theological author was trying out ideas. 'What if the moon god Sin isn't actually an independent deity, but simply Marduk, our chief deity who shines and lights the night for us? He simply asks that question, and answers in the affirmative – but he doesn't go on to say what would happen if that were the case. These are highly trained specialist thinkers, trying to understand how their world worked: the idea of there possibly being a category of the divine which is larger than any individual god – that might have been quite exciting to them.

This little tablet proposes a new answer to the never-ending human quest, with which this book began, to understand our place in the universe. And it raises questions as contentious today as they were in ancient Babylon. Are the complexities of our world the result of different forces in conflict with each other, or is there one, controlling, force? And if there is, how should we humans engage with it? Is it male or female, both or neither? Is it a moral force? Or is the idea of one god in command of everything part of a political exercise to legitimize authoritarian rule?

We saw in Chapter 11 how in Mesopotamia, each major god protected the city that had its principal temple but was worshipped across a much wider area. The structures of the pantheon – the council of gods – in large measure reflected the balance of political and economic power among the cities. When our tablet was written – around 580 BCE – that balance was shifting. Babylon now had a population larger than any of its neighbours and Nebuchadnezzar, celebrated as the king who conquered Jerusalem and carried the Jews into captivity (Chapter 27), was equally effective as a military campaigner nearer home. Jonathan Stökl explains:

Most theology is political, and in the ancient world most politics are religious: it's our Western post-Enlightenment view that makes us want to distinguish sharply between the two. In ancient Mesopotamia that would certainly not have been as clear-cut.

For the first time in a very long period, Nebuchadnezzar had again made Babylon not just a cultural centre, but the major political power in the region. It was now the city where all political and all religious power were concentrated. So it's maybe not surprising that our scribe suggests that all the gods might be unified in Marduk, the god of Babylon.

Our tablet may in fact show less a speculative scholar boldly edging towards a hypothesis of monotheism, than a politically driven suggestion that Babylon's new dominant status on earth might be mirrored in the order of heaven. In that sense it is perhaps a little like the nineteenth-century notion of the United States' Manifest Destiny: a theological construct devised to confirm a political ambition. It is an idea that would of course have been energetically resisted by Babylon's neighbours, the cities and temples of all the other gods, whose priests would understandably be opposed to a forced merger with – or into – Marduk. Whatever the case, it looks as though nothing actually happened. However radical the thoughts on our tablet were, they remained just that – thoughts on clay. The worship of all the deities listed seems to have continued unchanged, with the vested interests of their priests and temples undiminished. The people, uninterested in theological speculation, remained loyal to their traditional gods.

But Jonathan Stökl sees in this tablet the outlines of another idea, with similar potential for divisive debate:

It's perhaps telling that this tablet mentions only male deities. It does not mention a single female deity, of which there were hundreds. So some people have thought that this tablet is actually preparing the way for a divine couple. I think that is simplifying things, but the text could lend itself to that sort of interpretation – so you would have all female deities on one tablet and all male deities on another.

Was there another tablet, listing the names and roles of the female gods, and suggesting that they too were essentially one? If there was, it has not yet been found. But it points us to the unavoidable and, for many, uncomfortable question of the gender of a single god.

About 800 years before our Babylonian tablet was written, an Egyptian pharaoh had already tried to give political effect to its central idea. He decided to abandon the cults of the many traditional gods of Egypt, like Osiris (Chapter 5) and Amun, and replace them instead with the worship of one supreme god, whose praise would be constantly sung:

How numerous are your works, though hidden from sight.
Unique god, there is none beside him.
You mould the earth to your wish, you and you alone.
All people, herds and flocks,
All on earth that walk on legs,
All on high that fly with their wings.

The words translate a text written around 1340 BCE, by the pharaoh Akhenaten. They are part of a long hymn to the glory of Aten, the sun god, who, Akhenaten believed, alone created and sustained all living things: 'Thou, sole god, there is no other like thee.' These words from the hymn, and the ideas in it, are strikingly similar to those of the Hebrew Psalms, especially Psalm 104, written down many centuries later:

O, Lord how manifold are thy works: in wisdom hast thou made them all. The earth is full of thy riches

The hymn to Aten provided yet more fodder for the nineteenth-century debate about the origins of belief in a single god. But as in Babylon, it also coincided with a political shift: in this instance, a revolution in Egyptian politics and the introduction of a new, monotheistic state religion.

Words from the hymn appear on a small white limestone slab, carved in low relief, now in the British Museum – or, at least, on the right-hand half of a slab, as the left side is missing. It shows Akhenaten seated on a cushioned throne, looking to the left, where almost certainly his wife Nefertiti was sitting – both their names appear in the hieroglyphic inscriptions. Akhenaten's arms and upper body are bare, but he wears a blue crown and the long white ceremonial linen kilt of the pharaohs. He is basking in rays of sunlight, each one clearly and sharply cut into the stone. They belong to and extend from the sun god, Aten, and appear to be reaching out protectively towards the pharaoh. The bright paint with which the scene was originally coloured has faded a little across 3,500 years, but as Neal Spencer, Keeper of Ancient Egypt and Sudan at the British Museum, explains, the fragment retains a dazzling significance, because what seems to be happening here is a radical reimagining of the relationship between the pharaoh, the Egyptian people and the divine:

In traditional Egyptian religion, the king was the intermediary between the people and the gods. The pharaoh protects and expands the borders of Egypt, and in return the gods ensure an eternal life and a prosperous reign. What we have here is a much closer relationship between one god, Aten, and the pharaoh, Akhenaten. This is expressed elsewhere in Akhenaten's hymn: 'You are in my heart, there is none other who knows you besides your son. You instruct him in your plans, in your strength.'

It is a simple statement of the link between the powers of heaven and earth: there is only one god, Aten, and his son, Akhenaten, is the only person who truly knows him. The rays of sunlight in our sculpture perfectly match the tenderness in the words of the hymn – each sunbeam has at its end a small hand, which reaches out as though to caress the pharaoh on his throne, or to pat him on the head like a beloved child.

Jonathan Stökl describes how:

Already in the reign of Akhenaten's father there had been an increasing emphasis on the role of the sun god. But Akhenaten was a rebel, and took the idea much further than ever before: here he is breaking completely with traditional Egyptian religion. He decided not just to build new temples for the sun god, but to found

The pharaoh Akhenaten seated on his throne is touched by the rays of his father, the sun god Aten, *c.*1350 BCE.

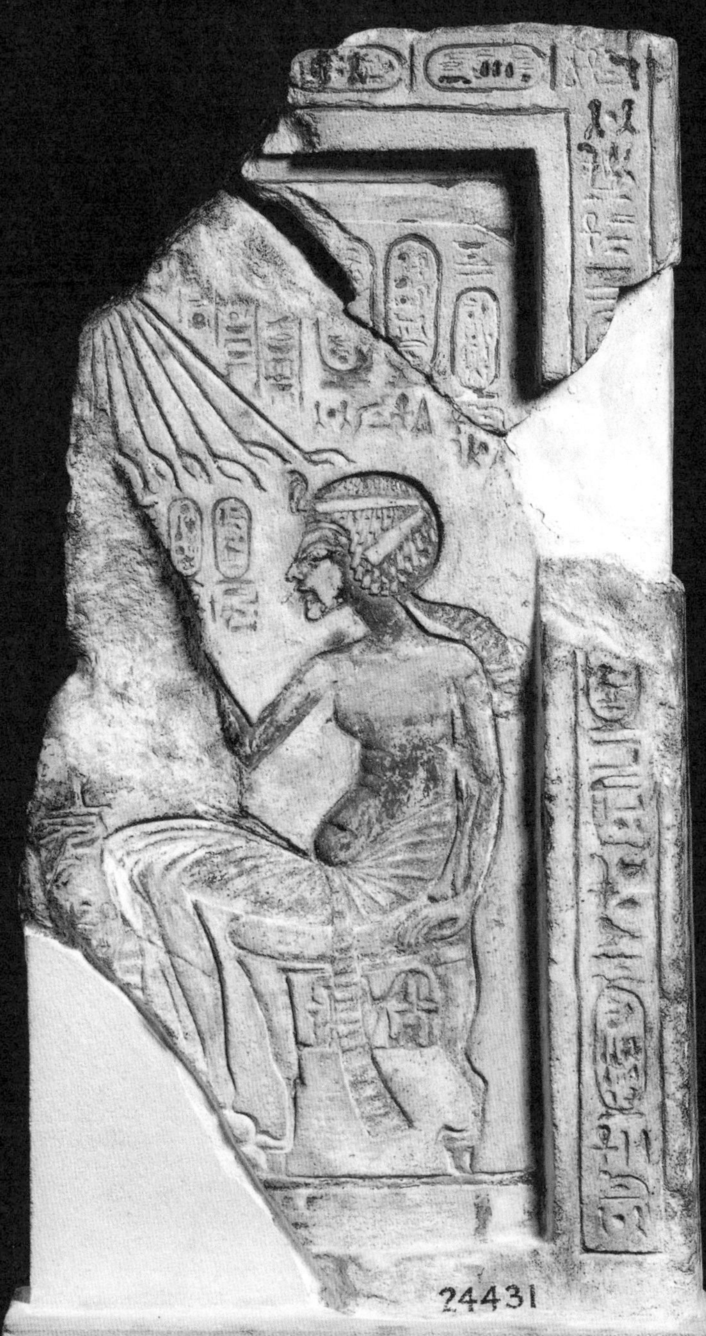
24431

a completely new city, Amarna, to provide an appropriate setting for his belief in Aten.

The young Pharaoh had, after a few years on the throne, made an extraordinary declaration of his new faith, by changing his name from Amenhotep ('Amun is satisfied') to Akhenaten ('effective for Aten'). Fired by the conviction that there was only one, single, god, he turned away from the temples and the rituals established and endowed over centuries by his predecessors. The old religious centres of Thebes and Karnak, along with their privileged priests, were neglected. Inscriptions referring to gods in the plural were changed to the singular. All resources and energy were focused on the city being built at Amarna. There was to be a new religious order in Egypt.

But the experiment with monotheism was short-lived. Akhenaten had no real disciples able to continue what he had begun. As seems to have been the case later in Mesopotamia, the people preferred to stay with their familiar gods in their familiar temples, and the priests of those gods were of course unremittingly hostile. After Akhenaten's death, the elites of Egypt quickly returned to the old order. The ancient temples were restored, familiar cults re-endowed. Statues of Akhenaten on the other hand were destroyed, his tomb savagely smashed, and his name removed from inscriptions. The powers of polytheism had prevailed. Akhenaten, the only pharaoh to proclaim his belief in one and only one god, was written out of official Egyptian history, and until Amarna was excavated in the mid-nineteenth century, he effectively disappeared.

Akhenaten named his son Tutankhaten, meaning 'the living image of Aten'. But, after only a year on the throne, Tutankhaten reverted to worshipping the chief of the traditional gods, Amun, and he, like his father, changed his name. So we know him as Tutankhamun, whose tomb was spectacularly discovered in 1922.

A closer look at our relief shows that something else may have been going on, just as revolutionary as the uniquely close relationship between Akhenaten and his heavenly father. It takes us

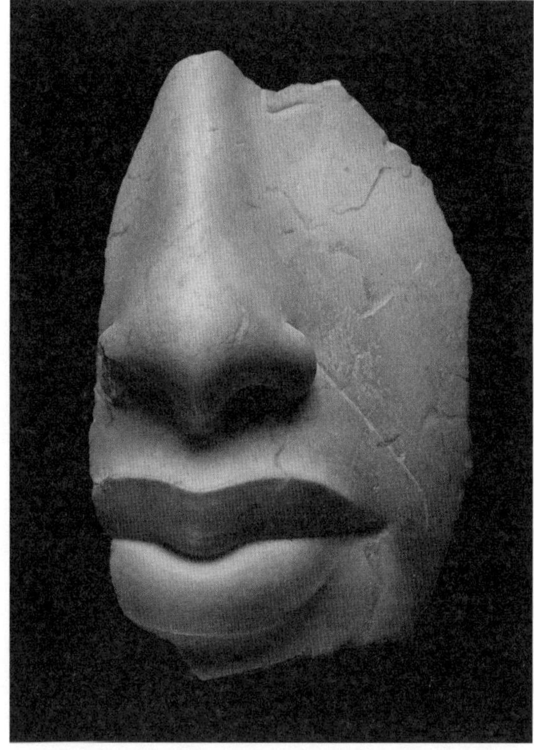
The lips of Akhenaten from the Sanctuary of the Great Aten Temple, Amarna, 1353–1336 BCE

back to one of the questions raised by the Marduk tablet – what could be the gender of a single creator god? As in other images of Akhenaten, he is depicted here in a manner unparalleled in Egyptian royal imagery, whether in painting or sculpture. Unlike the normal, physically powerful pharaoh, he is shown with a slender upper body, delicate features, and a round female breast – a startling image of androgynous beauty. Some scholars see here a hermaphrodite pharaoh, and hail it as a pioneering piece of iconography, expressing the universality of Aten as both the 'mother and father of all humankind', a duality embodied in his earthly son. This single creator god cannot be reduced to a single gender.

These two early manifestations show us some of the difficulties inherent in the idea and the imposition of monotheism. Yet the notion that there is only one, almighty, god has great intellectual and emotional attractions. If there is a single will, a single intellect that created and sustains the universe, then everything must ultimately be organized on coherent, comprehensible principles. There is security, and enormous strength, in believing that the apparently random events of the world, not least the persistence

The Power of One: William Blake's 'Ancient of Days' creates an ordered universe, mathematically measured by a pair of dividers like rays of light.

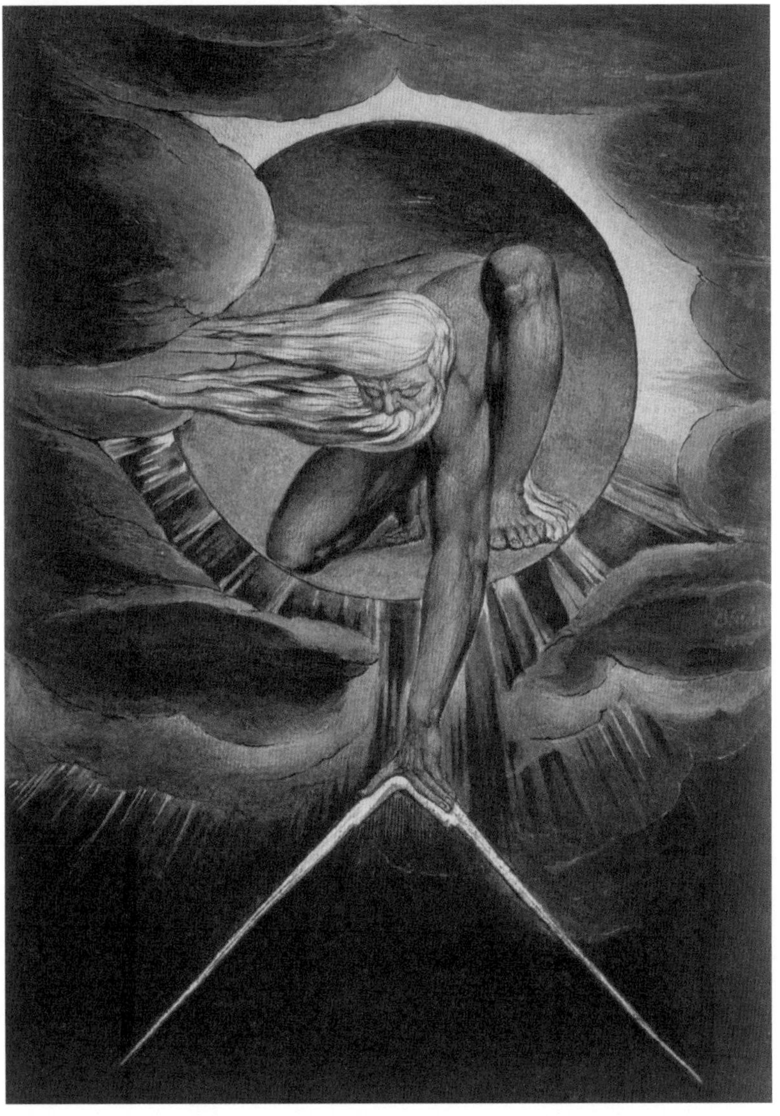

of evil and suffering, are not simply stuff that happens (as in the polytheistic world of the last chapter), but must in fact be part of a – divine – plan.

It is this idea which lies behind the beginnings of modern science and which clearly informed the work of Copernicus, Galileo and Newton. Whether innately or as the result of long training, the children of monotheism have a strong sense that unity is the ultimate, indeed the only, satisfactory end-point to any quest for explanation, and that resolution can in principle be reached. Rowan Williams, former Archbishop of Canterbury, argues that this is both the attraction and the achievement of monotheism:

It guarantees a coherence and stability in the world we inhabit, and in how we understand human well-being. You don't have a god of this group and that group, who may or may not get on with each other. You don't have a god who looks after this bit of the universe and a different god looking after another bit of the universe, which may or may not hang together. You have a single purpose: an eternal consistency, always working itself out through imperfect and limited agencies, therefore never perfectly realized inside the universe and yet on which the universe always depends for its continued intelligible movement and growth. It is that sense of deep ultimate coherence that is one of the most significant things about monotheism.

It is this dream of an ultimate, all-embracing harmony, as beguiling morally as intellectually, that inspired Joseph Addison's hymn to the great patterns of the cosmos, recently uncovered by Isaac Newton. As sun, moon, planets and stars revolve according to one universal law of gravitation:

In reason's ear, they all rejoice
And utter forth a glorious voice,
Forever singing as they shine,
'The hand that made us is divine'.

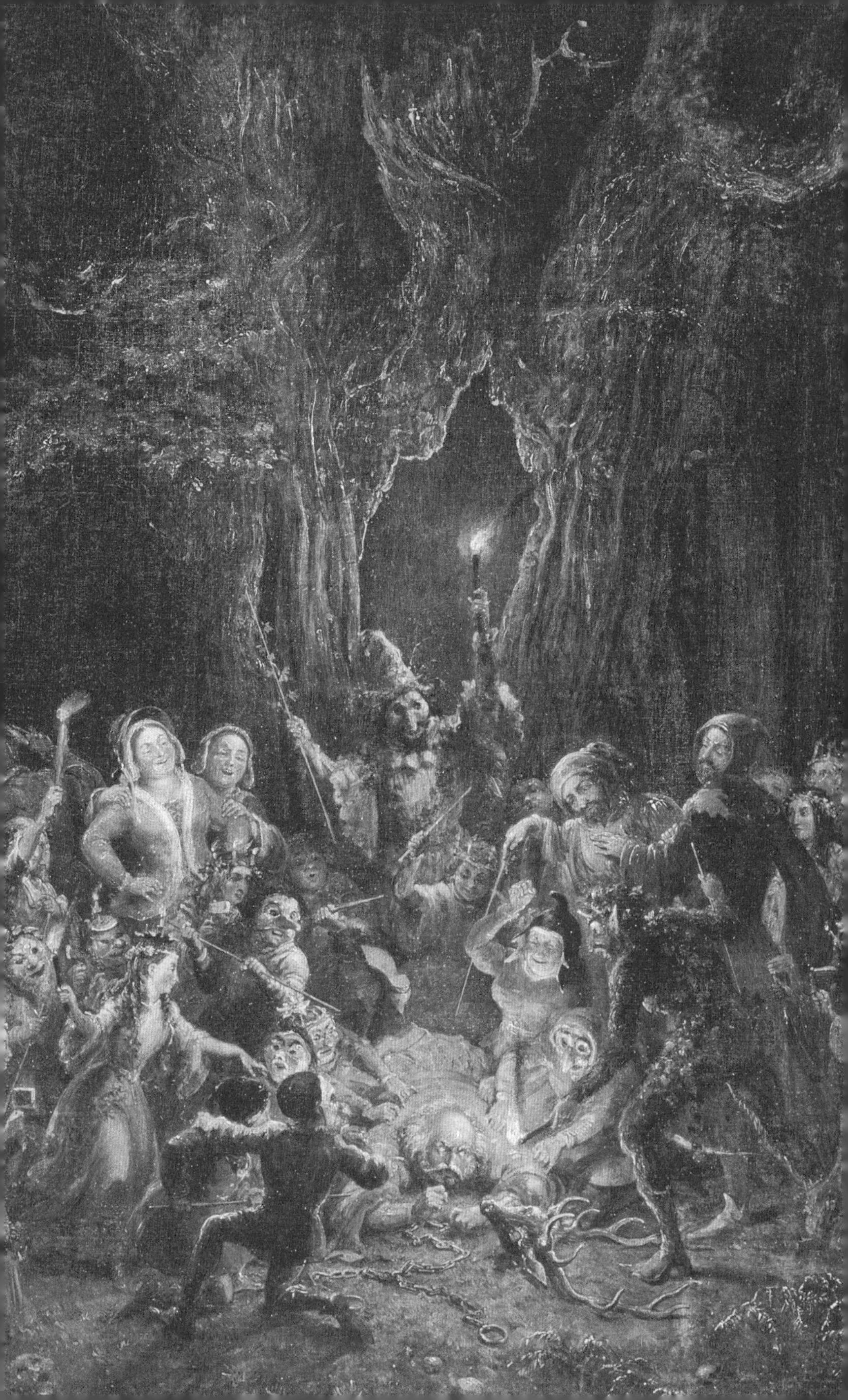

23
SPIRITS OF PLACE

Elves or sprites, gnomes, goblins or fairies: they are slight and quick, darting around and never caught or clearly seen, frequently doing very unpleasant things, and usually appearing close to a particular place that everybody knows. In Shakespeare's *Merry Wives of Windsor*, that spot is Herne's Oak:

> *There is an old tale goes that Herne the Hunter,*
> *Sometime a keeper here in Windsor Forest,*
> *Doth all the winter-time, at still midnight,*
> *Walk round about an oak, with great ragg'd horns:*
> *And there he blasts the tree, and takes the cattle,*
> *And makes milch-kine yield blood, and shakes a chain*
> *In a most hideous and dreadful manner.*
> *You have heard of such a spirit ...*

Stories of such figures are passed down through the generations by word of mouth. In the popular song, the fairies' kingdom is at the bottom of the garden. Playful, tricky and dangerous, they are usually 'not so very, very far away', but just out of sight, and a constant near-presence in English folklore and literature from

Herne's Oak in Windsor Forest where Falstaff is teased by the spirit of Herne the Hunter and his fairy companions. By George Cruikshank, *c.*1857

Chaucer to Tolkien. Until quite recently, along with their cousins the leprechauns and the trolls, they were everywhere in rural Europe, from Ireland to Siberia – survivals of ancient beliefs about landscapes thought to be animated and inhabited. For centuries they co-existed edgily with official Christianity and predictably often attracted extreme church disapproval. They did not move with us to the cities in the nineteenth century, and for most Europeans these flickering traces of much older beliefs today sit, divertingly, somewhere between superstition, whimsy and Middle Earth.

But the lives of millions across the world, particularly those who spend most of their existence in one familiar landscape, are still shaped by the intuition of forces and beings who also inhabit our world. They live with us, and interact with us, even if we only intermittently see them. These intuitions are shared by only a small group in a specific landscape. As once in Europe, they are handed on within the family and the community, but rarely written down. They are taken very seriously: the spirits of place.

Where more precisely do such invisible spirits live? That of course depends on which country, which culture, you – and they – are in. In the British Museum there is a small wooden house built as a residence for the spirits of place in Thailand. These spirits are disembodied entities, ranging from village guardians to bringers of disease; they may be household spirits or men and women who have met with violent or unjust ends. Spirit-houses like this one are built to appease malevolent spirits, or to encourage a protective guardian to live locally – or sometimes both – and to provide spaces for people to make offerings to them.This particular spirit-house would once have made a fine spirit-home. At first sight, it looks like a miniature Buddhist temple from Northern Thailand, carved from wood, inset with glass, and finished with red lacquer and flashes of gold. Over a metre high, it has one central hall, covered by a steep pitched roof, that is decorated with

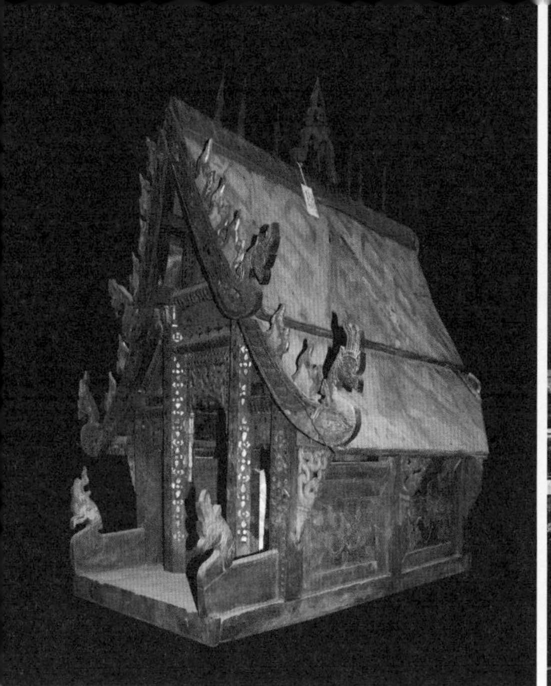
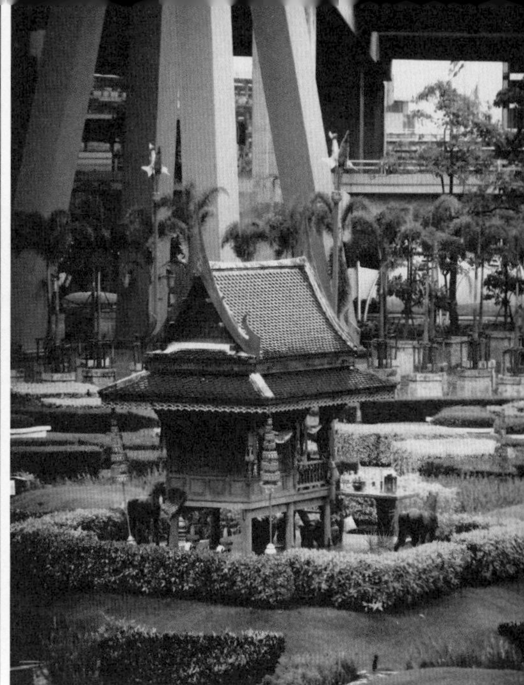

Left: A nineteenth-century Thai spirit-house, in the form of a miniature Buddhist temple. *Right*: Spirit-houses are very much part of modern Thailand, and are often seen in public spaces.

imagery representing the centre of the Buddhist universe and with mythical serpents, guardians of water and prosperity, who link the earthly and spiritual worlds. The spirit-house would have been elevated on a pillar, and people would have festooned it with flowers, placed food and drinks for the spirits around it, and burned incense in front of it. In spite of modern Thailand's rapid urbanization, spirit-houses like this are still very common: you find them in airports, shopping centres and schools, and along particularly dangerous stretches of highways. Unlike many of the supernatural beings that we look at in this book, the spirits in Thailand were never 'gods' of any sort: they are other kinds of living beings. Most important, they have not come from somewhere else – they are not tourists in the human realm. This is their home. It is where they live – alongside us, in a world that we co-inhabit.

This is an area of belief and behaviour for which we often in English do not have the right words. Our language and our thoughts have been so shaped by Christianity and the classical world that we struggle to find a vocabulary to discuss sufficiently precisely or seriously beings that are very definitely neither gods nor demons. Almost all the words available to us when considering the idea of an animated landscape have belittling connotations of childish fantasy, missionary disparagement, or spiritualist trickery.

Yet most people have places that are for them inhabited by collective or individual memories, sometimes very powerful ones. For those who live in large and mobile modern communities, these are just a faint echo of experiencing a landscape where you and all your family have lived for generations. In this kind of society, which included much of Europe until at least the eighteenth century, almost everything that is meaningful in life is linked to this one landscape, and to the beings – living, dead or non-human – that populate it.

In Pacific island communities today the landscape still determines not just how people think about the world, but even the language in which they can describe it. Lissant Bolton, keeper of the Pacific collections in the British Museum, has worked over many years in the Pacific island nation of Vanuatu:

In the languages in north Vanuatu, which all belong to the Austronesian language family, you cannot speak without doing so in relation to the landscape. So you don't say: 'This glass is in front of this cup.' Rather, you say: 'This glass is on the sea-side of this cup', or 'further from the sea than this cup', because all your sense of position is oriented to where the sea is. Your very way of speaking is intimately embedded in the landscape. Your life is so deeply bound up with it that it's very hard to disconnect from it.

To walk through this kind of landscape is to walk through an inherited web of shared stories. As Lissant Bolton points out, we ought not to find this such an unfamiliar idea:

When you live in the same landscape all your life, you have both your own experiences in it and also those from the stories of your people that have been passed down to you. You know that this is the cave where a particular character went and hid for ever, or this is the path that another took to go up to the volcano. The landscape is built up of the history of your own life and also the lives of the people who were in that landscape before you.

In Vanuatu, people have generally not worshipped gods. But they have been aware that they were not the sole inhabitants of a landscape, that other beings were in the landscape with them. In north Vanuatu, on the island of Ambae, people understand there to be mwai or vavi living with them. They know where their villages are, where their dancing grounds are, and they interact with them. Similar beings in the landscape on the nearby island of Pentecost in north Vanuatu are so close that they are 'just the other side of the leaf' from human beings. Some might need to be avoided, like you might avoid a slightly crazy neighbour – people who are a little hazardous, a little risky, people you don't want to pass in the street on a dark night, because they are capable of malevolence of some kind or another.

If you go to a place where you know there is a spirit or another non-human being, you may take the time to stop and address them and say 'I've just come here to pick the mangoes off this tree; that is why I'm here, and then I'm going back'. It may be as simple as that.

In Thailand, the spirits of place, who lodge in the houses built specially to accommodate them, are kept close so that they can protect the locality and be easily honoured and propitiated. In Vanuatu, the relationship between the human and non-human members of the community is, as we have seen, much closer, sharing the landscape and occasionally directly interacting – the spirits living, in that memorable phrase, just on the other side of the leaf.

In many Aboriginal Australian societies, the link between the spirits of the landscape and the members of a community, both living and dead, is even more intimate and intense. Here, the landscape is not just the terrain that ancestors once walked, and which their spirits still inhabit: it is made by and from those ancestors. The original ancestral beings created and empowered the landscape, and those who understand this can see and read their deeds in every detail of it: rivers and hills, trees and plants; the sharpness of the pebbles in a creek and the touch of the wind. And when a person in the community dies, they return to the land – 'country' as they call it – and become part of its physical form. As far as we know, this has been going on for 60,000 years since *Homo sapiens* first reached Australia. For all we know, the men and women who handled the Lion Man, on the other side of the world, may have had similar patterns of belief.

The reciprocal relationship between people, country and the ancestors starts before birth, is strengthened throughout life and continues after death. People are born into country and acquire names associated with particular places – for example, the place where their unborn spirit first announced itself to its parents. Throughout life they acquire a growing spiritual identity that links them to other locations; and after death the dead person's spirit returns to its home in the clan's territory. Their memory then becomes for all time a resonance in that place.

We find this clearly illustrated in the rites for the dead practised by the Yolngu people from Arnhem Land, in Northern Australia. When a member of the community died, their remains were placed into a *larrakitj*. These are tall poles made from the trunks of a particular eucalyptus tree called stringybark, which have been hollowed out by termites and fire. They are cut down and the bark is stripped away to reveal the sapwood, which is then sanded and decorated with intricate painted clan designs.

The dead body was for a time exposed to the elements on a raised platform. When only the bones were left, they were placed inside the *larrakitj*, which was placed beside others already standing at a significant spiritual site. Then the third and final part of

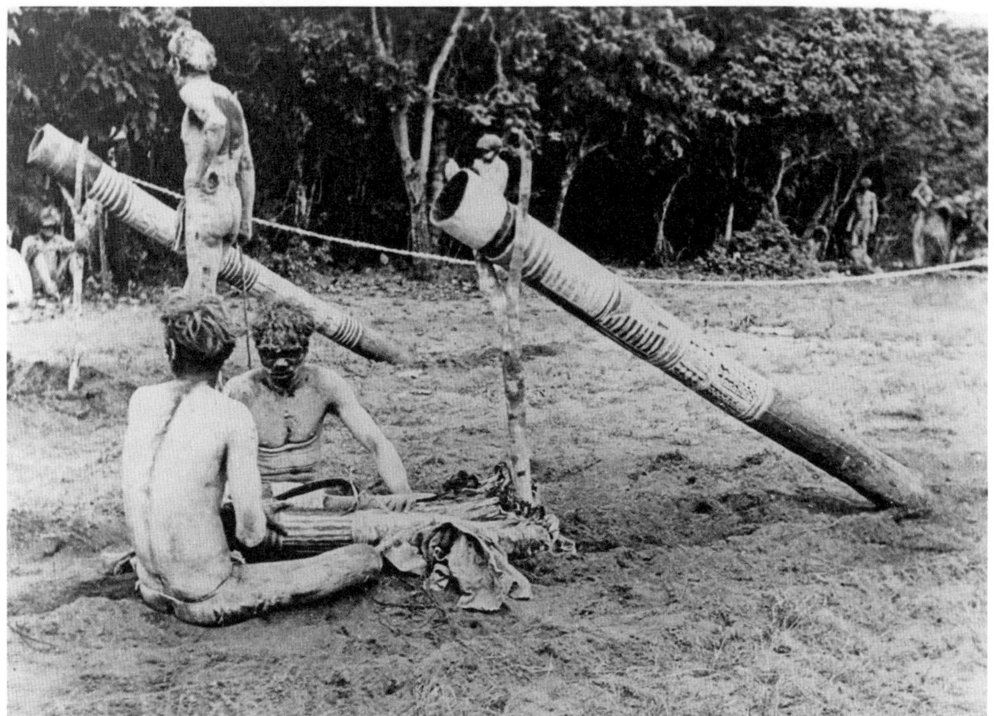

Preparations for a *larrakitj* ceremony in Yirrkala, Northern Territory, 1946

the person is cared for. Together with rituals, music and dancing, the *larrakitj*'s painted designs will help guide the soul as it rejoins the communal spirit, which resides in sacred springs or rivers.

As Wukun Wanambi, a Yolngu artist, puts it:

In Yolngu, we understand the life of the spirit as a circle. We believe that the spirit travels through the water and returns to its source and then is born anew. The body dissolves and the bones return to the land as the larrakitj decays.

In the British Museum is a *larrakitj* created by Wukun Wanambi, as an art piece. Unlike most traditional *larrakitj*, Wukun's creations are not perfect cylinders of wood. They take a less regular form, as he leaves the trees with splits and holes in the trunk, to evoke the unevenness and complexity of the landscape. The painted designs on this *larrakitj* refer to a specific place, Bamurrunu, a sacred, solitary rock in Trial Bay.

The entire surface of the two poles is covered in a dense network

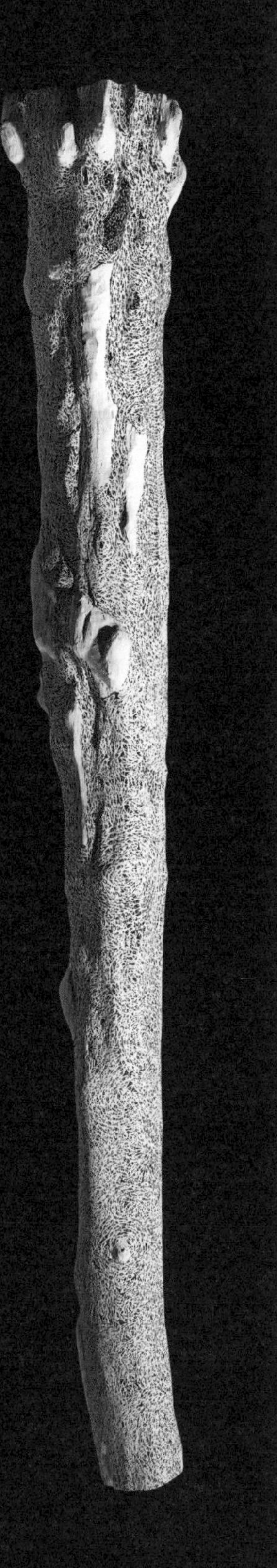

of painted lines – white, red and black. From a distance it looks as if a fine mesh has been wrapped round the trees and is clinging closely to them. But, as you get nearer, you can see that in fact around the trunks are swimming thousands and thousands of tiny fish, swirling around the bumps and the protuberances, many different shoals moving in different directions. These painted fish refer to sacred places in Trial Bay, a landscape made up of Wukun's ancestors. The teeming, ceaseless energy of the fish on his *larrakitj* conveys his sense of the flow of ancestral power beneath the waters of the bay.

Listening to Wukun, it becomes clear that, for him and the Yolngu, 'ancestors' are more than just a list of the people who make up the family tree. They reach outwards, on and on, to the point where each person has a connection to every animate, and indeed inanimate, part of the landscape, all of which are inhabited by the ubiquitous life force.

This is perhaps a uniquely coherent view of existence, locating each individ-ual life in an enduring framework of both time and space. In Chapter 5 we looked at how the Yup'ik people in Alaska affirmed their connection with the animals and plants that sustained them; and in Chapter 6 at how the Peruvians and the Chinese contrive to remain in

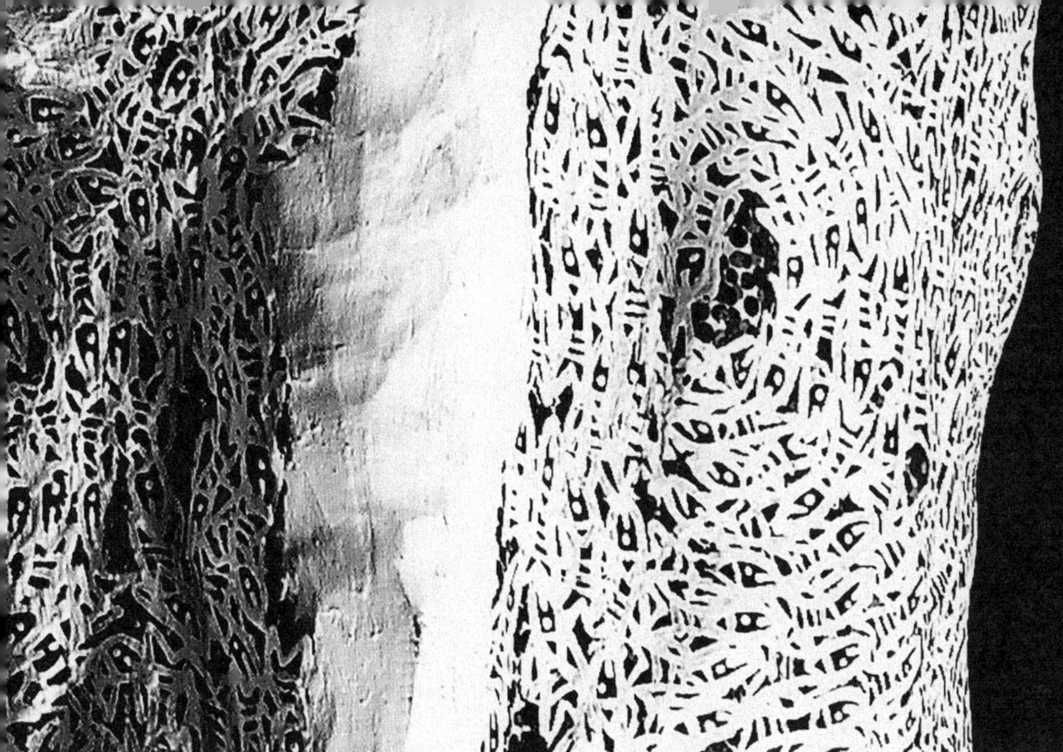

Detail (*above*) of a *larrakitj* memorial pole (*opposite*), made from the trunk of a eucalyptus tree, by Wukun Wanambi, 2014. Small fish are swarming in great numbers.

dialogue with their ancestors over many generations. The Yolngu have found a way of doing both these things and more. They have developed what one might call a theology of place. It holds the whole society in a world view which is inscribed and enacted entirely in *their* landscape, the place which – unborn, living or dead – they perpetually inhabit. The community and the place are, if not exactly the same thing, then certainly inseparable. To societies like this, the arrival of commercial miners, farmers or loggers means not just social and economic disruption: it rends the very fabric of the world. The direct, sacred, quickening link with the land is irrecoverably broken.

Only around 4 per cent of the global population now lives like this. These are not belief systems that can move to the nearby city, or accommodate much disruption. It is not easy to see what their future will be.

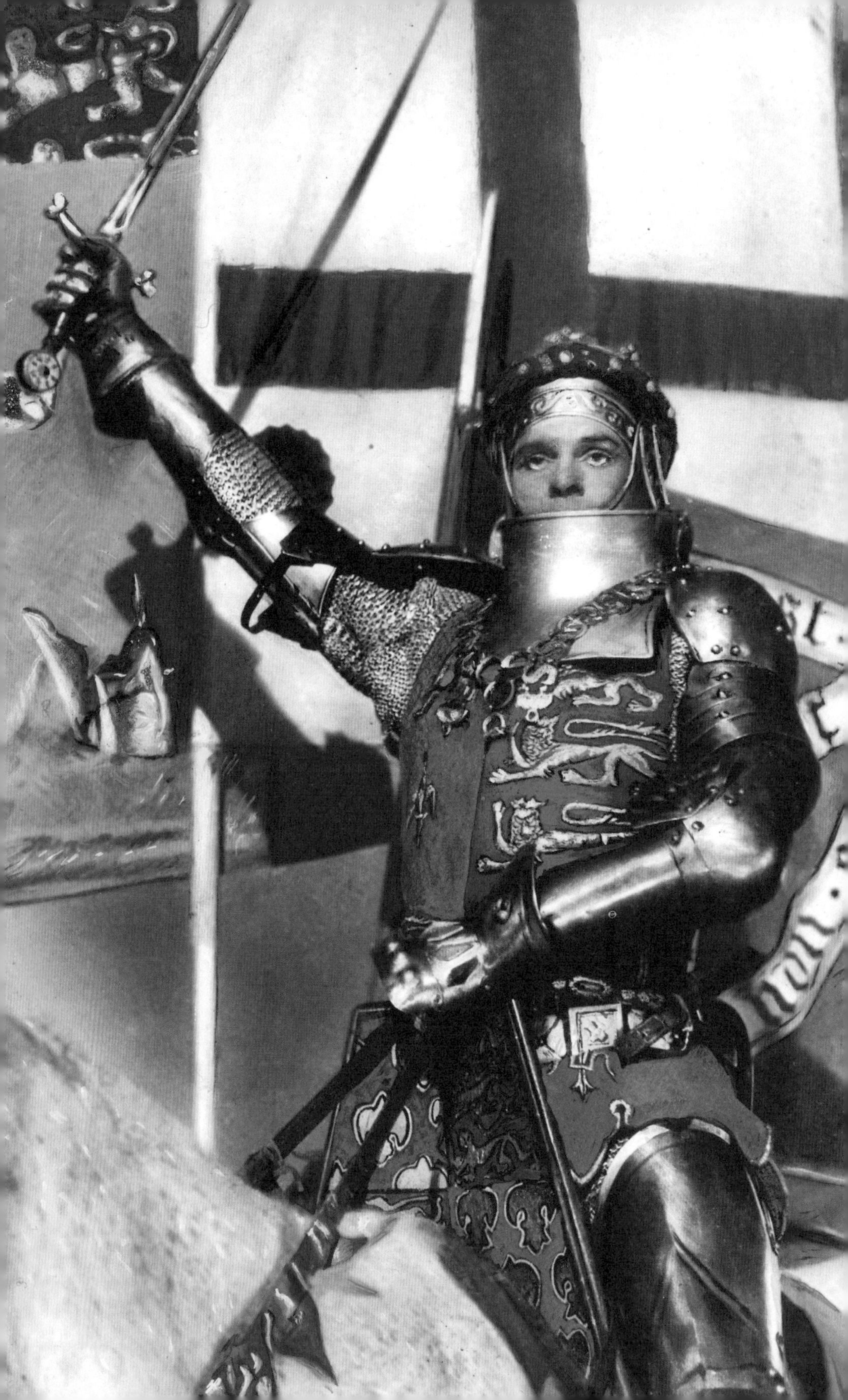

24
IF GOD BE WITH US

I see you stand like greyhounds in the slips,
Straining upon the start. The game's afoot.
Follow your spirit, and upon this charge
Cry 'God for Harry, England and Saint George!'

With spine-tingling rhetoric, Shakespeare's Henry V leads his troops into battle at Harfleur. Saint George wins the day, and the English go on to victory over the French at Agincourt. Shakespeare's Henry and his soldiers, the 'happy few', become a central element of English national identity, the foundation myth patriotically revived at the Battle of Britain, and celebrated in the famous Laurence Olivier film of 1944.

Shakespeare knew exactly what he was about, when he offered his audience the rousing spectacle of a small, embattled England, struggling against huge odds, but with God very definitely on its side. It had little to do with the actual history of Henry, everything to do with the new self-image of Elizabeth's England in the 1590s. What now defined the country above all else was that it was Protestant, bravely fighting against the might of Catholic Spain – or, in later centuries, Catholic France – confident that God would

Cry 'God for Harry, England and Saint George!': Laurence Olivier as Henry V, 1944

protect it, as he had in 1588 when he sent his winds to scatter the Armada. Religious difference had become the bedrock of the state. It was and remains to this day a potent force for building national unity. At around the time that the English state became Protestant, Iran became Shia – thus setting it apart from the surrounding Sunni states, and forging a new sense of what it meant to be Persian. Like England's distinctive Protestantism, that shaped Iran's history for centuries. Remarkable things happen when you live with a god who is not your neighbour's – especially if the god of a nation state is also the god of battles.

Harfleur and Agincourt in 1415 are by no means Saint George's only military campaigns. On 2 March 1896, he was in the field again, this time fighting not for the English, but for another isolated and embattled people, the Ethiopians, of whom he is also the patron saint, and whom he was helping – with similar success – in their struggle against the invading Italians at the Battle of Adwa.

In a painting in the British Museum, you can see Saint George in the sky, mounted on his prancing white horse, spear poised to strike not the dragon, but the Italian colonial aggressor. It is a wonderfully straightforward battle picture, with no confusion possible. On either side, lined up in straight rows on the yellow desert sand, are soldiers manning field guns or carrying rifles – Italians on the right facing Ethiopians on the left, with a space in the middle where there is some hand-to-hand fighting and a few dead bodies. The Italians, wearing khaki, are all shown in profile – a convention in Ethiopian painting to denote the wicked. The good are always shown full face, and so everybody on the Ethiopian side, dressed in colourful stripes, looks straight out at us, even as they take aim with their rifles against the enemy opposite. The only Italians shown full face – so the only good ones – are the dead ones in the middle. Needless to say, the picture was painted by an Ethiopian.

At the back, the emperor Menelik, wearing crown and velvet cape, stands under the imperial umbrella and watches the battle. But his wife, the Empress Taytu, is at the front of the painting, riding side-saddle, shown full face, looking out at us, while pointing an enormous revolver at the Italians. The message of the painting is clear: 'God for Menelik, Ethiopia and Saint George!'

The Battle of Adwa was a total victory for the Ethiopians. Internal divisions were put aside, women fought alongside men, different tribes united against the foe (the variety of skin tones in the painting is striking), and 2 March is still celebrated in Ethiopia as a national holiday. The Italians lost thousands of men and almost all their equipment, and were forced to retreat ignominiously back to Eritrea. An African country, under African leadership, had utterly vanquished a European army. The world was astonished. Africa was energized. Nine years later, the Japanese defeat of the Russian navy had something of the same effect in Asia, but at Adwa in 1896 Ethiopia had shown – for the first time in centuries – that Europeans did not always win. They could be driven out. In the struggle for independence against colonial rule throughout the next century, Ethiopia was the model and inspiration for the whole of Africa.

We shall never know how much Saint George actually contributed to it, but I think it may be said that one reason for the Ethiopians' victory was their Christian faith, or, more precisely, their distinctive African version of it, which not only set them apart from their mostly Muslim neighbours, but from every other Christian tradition. In spite of strong and divisive tribal loyalties, the Ethiopian church had, over many centuries, helped build a confident national identity. By the time of the Battle of Adwa, Ethiopia had been a Christian state – if a very particular one – for well over 1,500 years.

Over: The Battle of Adwa, 2 March 1896, where Ethiopia defeated the Italian invaders. This painting was made in the 1940s when Ethiopia was at war with Mussolini's Italy.

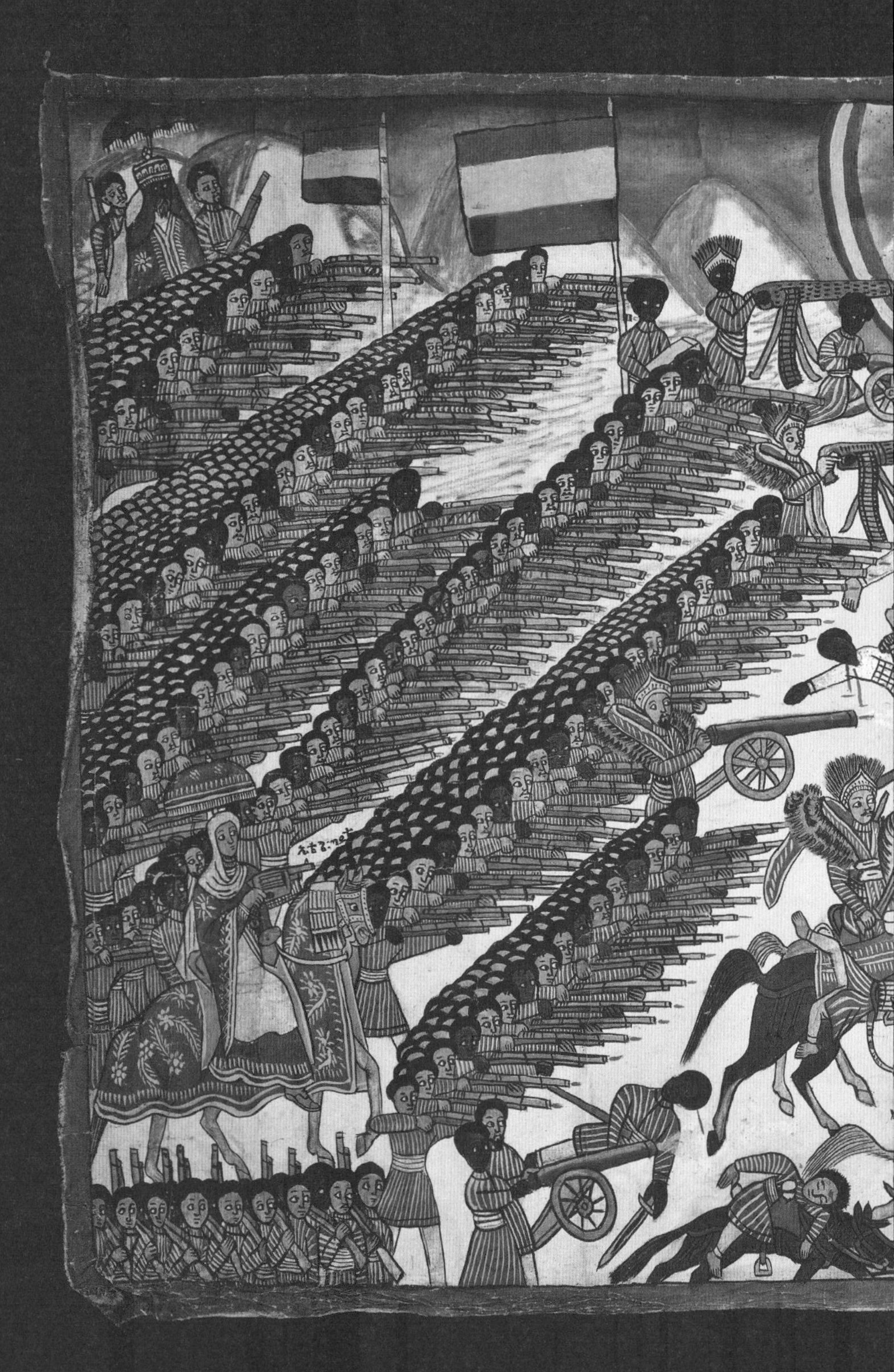
እቴጌ፡ጣይቱ

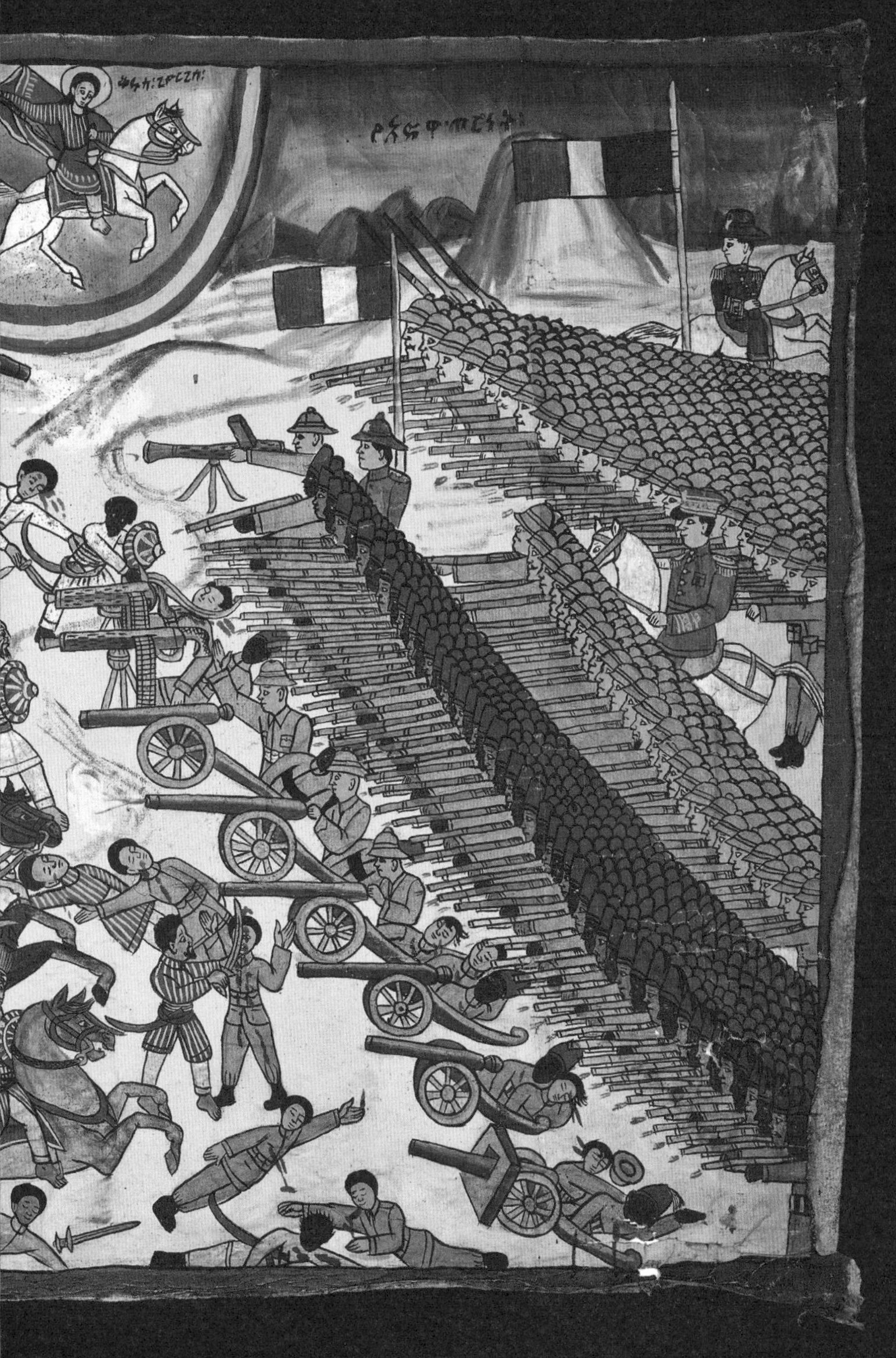
ቅዱስ፡ጊዮርጊስ፡
የአድዋ፡ጦርነት፡

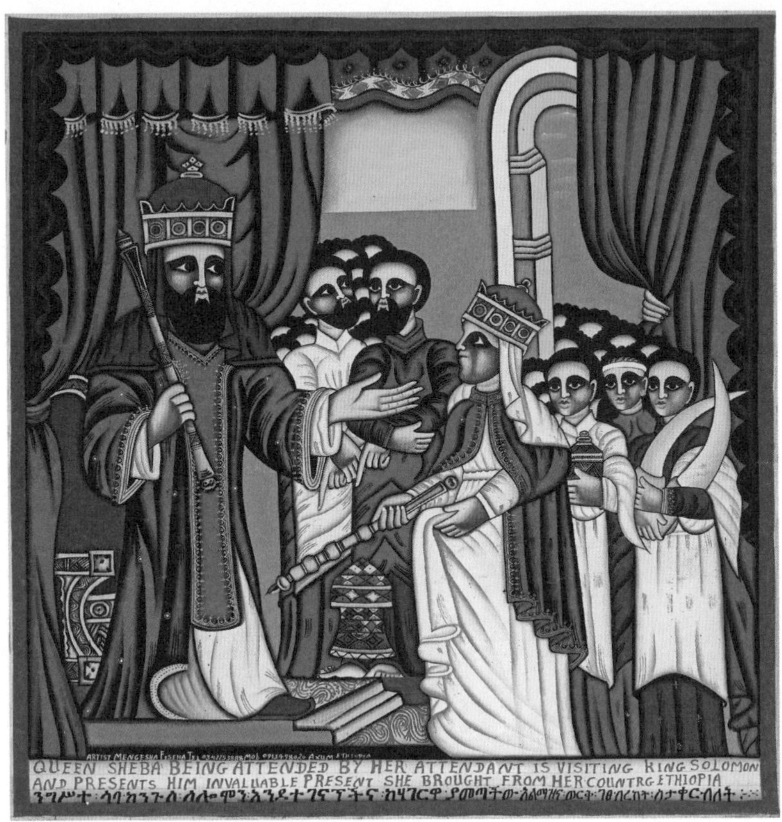

King Solomon welcomes the Queen of Sheba. Their son will become the emperor of Ethiopia. The foundation myth of Ethiopian identity is still alive in this painting, 2008

Diarmaid MacCulloch, Professor of the History of the Church at the University of Oxford, explains:

Christianity reached Ethiopia pretty early, and, as so often in early Christian expansion, through trade routes. Although Ethiopian Christianity has become profoundly African, its sources were in Syria, because the main trade routes were not along the Nile, but eastwards out of Ethiopia towards the Fertile Crescent and up into the Middle East. It was a Middle Eastern Christianity which arrived in the fourth century.

By about 330, only slightly later than the Roman Empire, Christianity had become the state religion. From then on, thanks to

Ethiopia's geographical remoteness, it developed there independently of the imperial churches of Rome and Constantinople, remaining true to its ancient roots in the Jewish Middle East. There is a legend that the Queen of Sheba, who in the Hebrew scriptures came from the south to visit King Solomon in Jerusalem, had in fact been Ethiopian; and that she had not just visited Solomon, but had a son by him. From that son of Solomon and Sheba, all Ethiopian emperors claimed to be descended. Perhaps in consequence, this is the most Jewish of Christian churches, with the Old Testament almost as much in evidence as the New: Saturday is observed as a Sabbath, as well as Sunday; pork is not eaten; and prayer shawls are often worn during worship. The emperor bore the imperial title of Lion of Judah, the biblical Jewish kingdom which had Jerusalem – Zion – as its capital. And through his ancestor King Solomon, the emperor of Ethiopia was, like Jesus himself, of the royal house of David.

Ethiopian Christians, wearing prayer shawls derived from Jewish tradition, celebrate Easter in Addis Ababa in 2015.

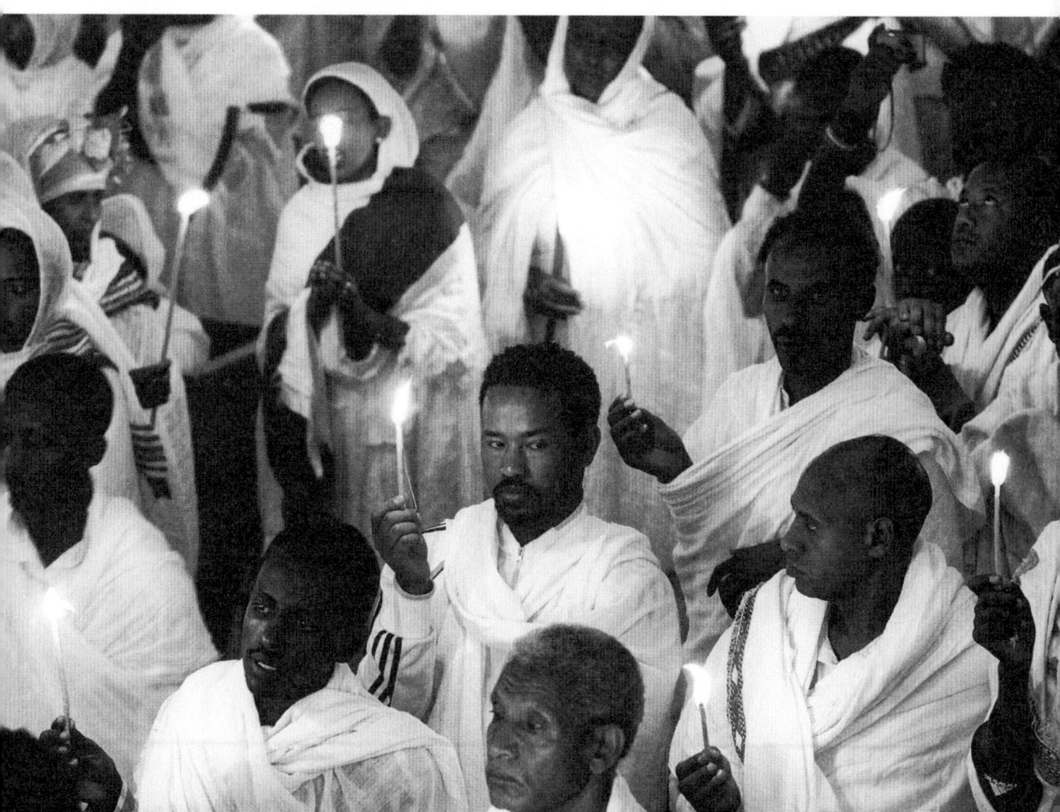

But, as Diarmaid MacCulloch points out, this 'Jewish' Christian church has been shaped by local circumstances:

People do most of their worshipping in the open air, and that means a possibility of movement – it means dance, it means processions. For many centuries the Ethiopian church was usually preoccupied simply with surviving against external enemies, particularly Muslim enemies. So it's never been a missionary faith. It's simply been there as the faith of Ethiopia, the celebration of Ethiopia.

The church's role in uniting the kingdom against its Muslim neighbours gave Ethiopia a distinctive national identity. Paradoxically, this became even more important when, from the middle of the nineteenth century, Ethiopia had to confront as its key enemies not Muslims, but aggressive Christians – the predatory European colonial powers. First came the Protestant British, who carried out a punitive raid in 1868, and then in 1895 the Catholic Italians, intent on permanent conquest. Our painting of the Battle of Adwa was made (like Olivier's *Henry V*) during the Second World War, when Ethiopians were once again fighting the Italians. It reminded them of their glorious past, and reassured them that heaven would be on their side: Saint George and his white horse are circled by a great halo of the green, gold and red of the Ethiopian flag. Diarmaid MacCulloch comments further:

Ethiopian Christianity was African, and it had been African for a very long time. So it was an alternative way of expressing a Christian identity to all those imported by Western Europeans – Catholic ones, and all sorts of different Protestant ones. Here was something which was both Christian and African.

In this African Christian tradition, so marked by its Jewish inheritance, the world looks wonderfully strange to anybody used

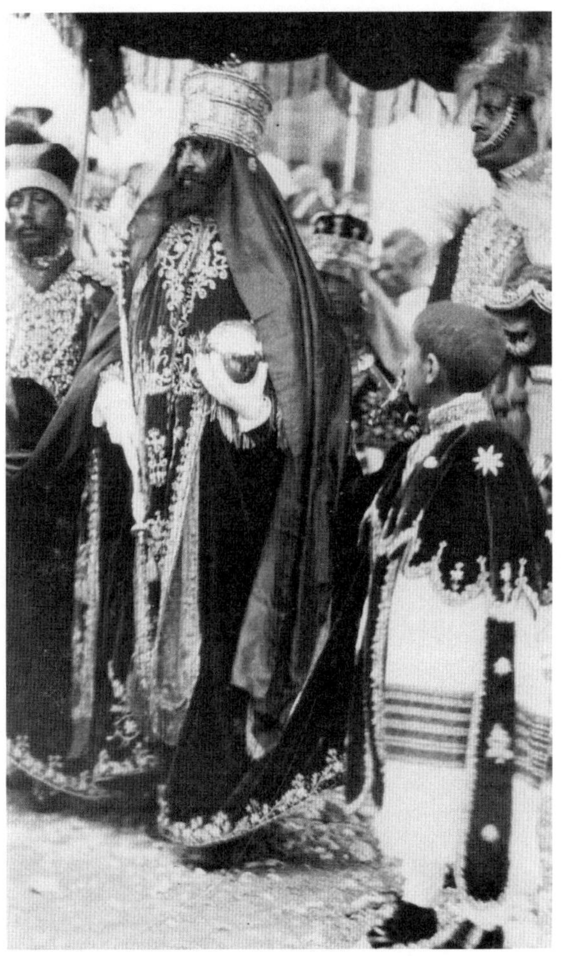
Haile Selassie on the day of his coronation, 2 November 1930, a day of pride for the African diaspora across the world

to Catholic altarpieces or Orthodox icons – as is very evident in another painting at the British Museum. It is a celebration of the coronation in Addis Ababa in 1930 of Emperor Haile Selassie, where he was invested with the orb and sceptre of a Christian monarch, in the presence of international VIPs. But this is not what our painting shows. It looks instead like a Last Supper, with the participants sitting round a circular table. Presiding over the meal, in the centre of the painting, sits not Jesus but a lion, and

Over: The Lion of Judah brings peace to Africa and Christian truth overcomes evil: the coronation of Haile Selassie in an Ethiopian painting of 1930

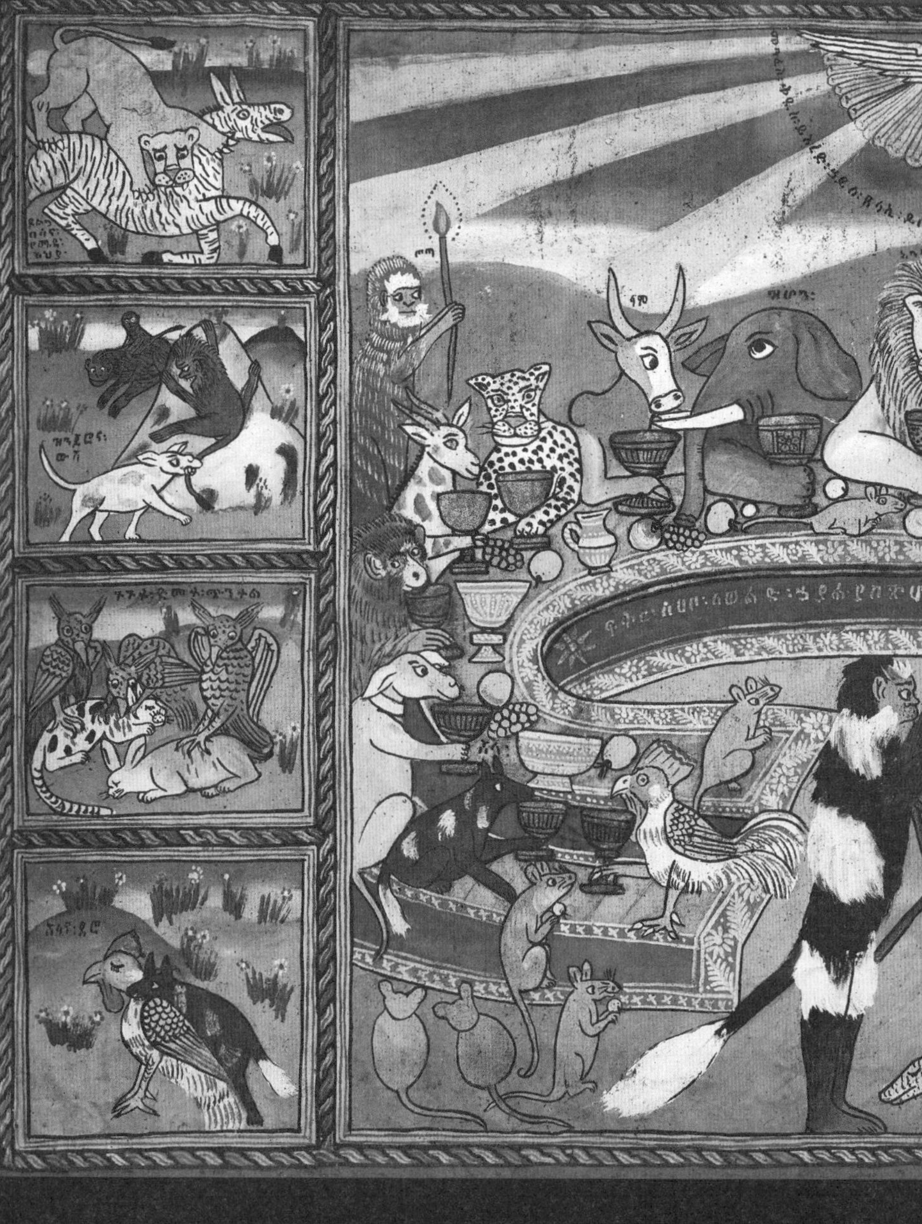

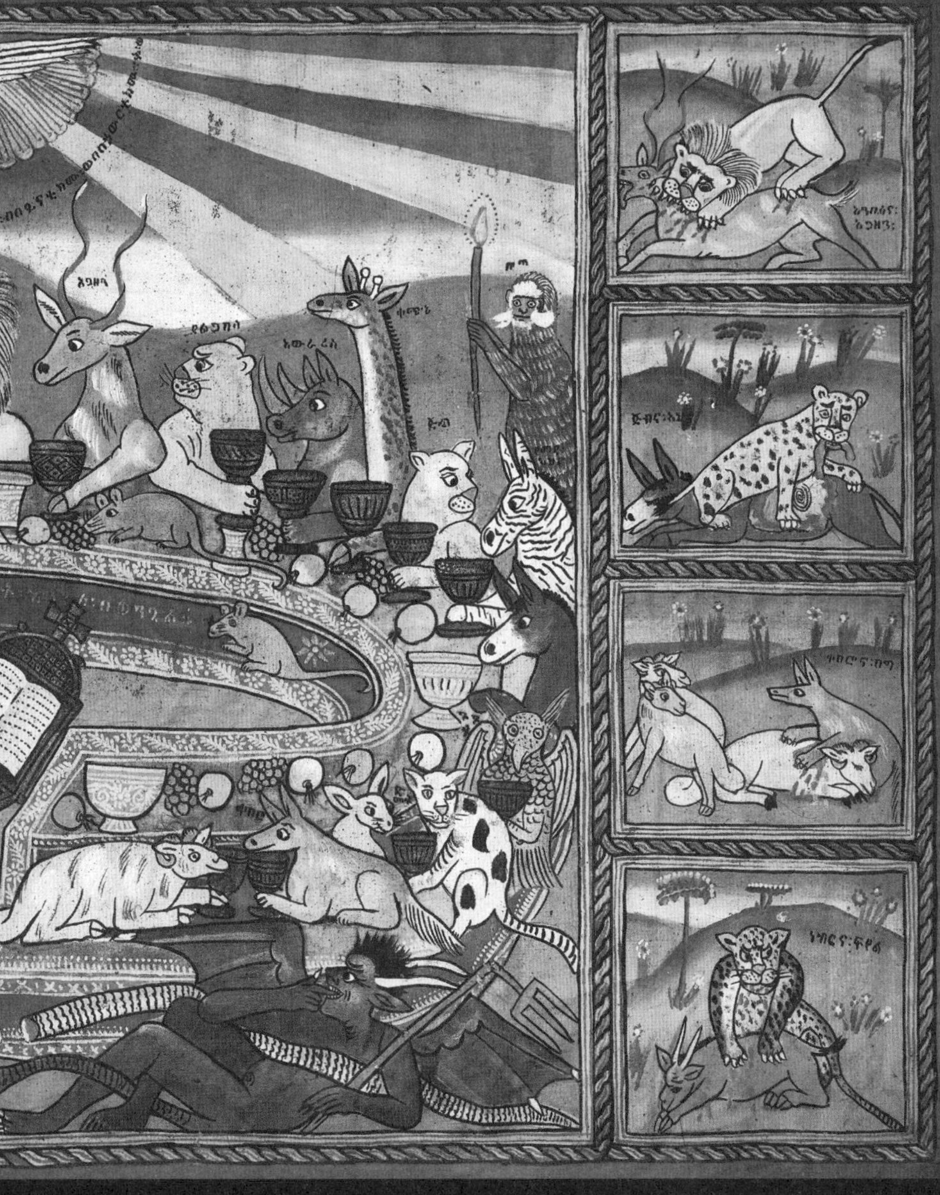

round the table are gathered not the disciples, but the animals of Africa – elephant and giraffe, rhinoceros and leopard, gazelle and zebra – each with a goblet in its hand, amiably talking and drinking. The birds and the smaller animals sip from their glasses while the rats prepare to eat the leftover food. But this is not happy hour at the zoo, or the carnival of the animals. It is a serious, and very political, interpretation of scripture. A tall black and white monkey reads the Bible from a lectern, and at the front of the painting lies the figure of the devil, holding a serpent whose head has been severed, defeated by the word of God.

It is an image that could have been produced only in the Ethiopian church. The artist has taken from the Hebrew prophet Isaiah his messianic vision of the peaceable kingdom of God, where, under a ruler from King David's family, strife will cease, and all animals will live in harmony together. He has then fused this with an image of the Christian Last Supper, with its promise of redemption through suffering and of ultimate peace. The Old and New Testaments are thus combined – in a uniquely African way. On either side of the painting are small scenes showing the animals at the table attacking each other in the state of nature. But above the head of the presiding lion is the dove of the Holy Spirit, whose rays illuminate the scene. The lion is – of course – the Lion of Judah, the new emperor, Haile Selassie, blessed and guided by God and sitting in the place of Jesus. He will bring peace not just to his kingdom and to the warring animals, but to the world.

That is not how things turned out. Five years after the coronation, in 1935, Ethiopia was once again attacked by Italian forces – this time the fascist regime of Mussolini. It was conquered and brutally occupied. Ethiopian culture was suppressed. Local churches were destroyed and Catholic ones built. Haile Selassie had to flee. As the Lion of Judah he naturally – and symbolically – went first to his ancient capital of Jerusalem, before continuing to Europe. Diarmaid MacCulloch describes how:

Famously he made an appeal in the League of Nations, putting an uncomfortable world on the spot. Many African Christians especially were very angry – a Nigerian Christian newspaper, for example, attacked the Pope for not criticizing Mussolini, one Italian not prepared to take a moral stance against another.

Although he had been defeated and exiled, Haile Selassie's moral authority remained intact in the quiet dignity with which he bore his humiliation. European Christianity appeared indifferent to African suffering, and did little for Ethiopia's plight, until East Africa was caught up in the wider conflict of the Second World War. In 1941, a combination of Ethiopian and British Empire troops, many of them African, drove out the Italians, and the monarch was able to return to Addis Ababa in triumph. As after the Battle of Adwa, the event resounded throughout the continent, this time with an additional religious inflection. In Diarmaid MacCulloch's analysis, it was not just that God had upheld the right, and helped the faithful Ethiopians to victory:

Haile Selassie, dignified and charismatic, became a sort of emblem of Christian suffering. This suffering saviour, as you might almost call him, was restored to the Ethiopian throne. It was a great moment for Africa and it had an enormous impact abroad. You could say that the Ethiopians had now defeated Europeans twice. So here was a model in the 1950s and 1960s for what black Africa – and colonized peoples everywhere – wanted to do.

Haile Selassie's name before he became emperor had been Tafari – Ras Tafari, or Prince Tafari, and this name, Rastafari, became very important as far away as Jamaica. The Rastafarian movement looked to the dignity of African Christianity as embodied in Ethiopia. Jamaica was a colonial, former slave state where many were reaching for an alternative, non-colonial Christian identity. What could be more Christian – and also African – than the story of Ras Tafari, the emperor Haile Selassie?

The Rastafari movement, which had begun to take shape in Jamaica in the 1930s shortly after Haile Selassie's coronation, saw Ethiopia as the unconquered homeland of all black Africans, and the emperor as their ruler and saviour. According to Dr William Henry of the University of West London, himself of Jamaican descent, both strands are already clearly visible in the coronation painting:

His Majesty is depicted as a lion, because he's regarded as the conquering lion of the tribe of Judah, the elect of God, earth's rightful ruler. That's what Rastafari say about him. All the other kings of the world can be at the table, but the supreme ruler, the King of Kings, is His Majesty, Emperor Haile Selassie. His lineage is longer than any other king presently sitting on a throne – and he's a black African. Suddenly, everything that you've been taught about yourself as an African person, all of that goes out of the window, because here is a living example of kingship that is older than anything in Europe.

In Jamaica the Jewish-African Christianity of Ethiopia had taken a new turn. The traditions of this national church were now appropriated by people thousands of miles away, and with no previous connection to it. Ethiopia, divinely delivered from European aggression, came to be seen as a black Zion (Chapter 28). Africans from all over the continent had been led away into slavery and captivity, as the Jews had been deported to Babylon. And, like the Jews, they would one day be able to return, leaving the Babylon of Europe and America for the Zion of Ethiopia. The Lion of Judah himself, Haile Selassie, had been in exile, and been restored. All Africans, says William Henry, might follow him:

There was always this notion that there was one place in Africa that had never been colonized or totally dominated by Europeans. So for Rastafari that would be the focal point. We would return to that place.

Rastafari belief has few formal structures, so it allows a wide range of views on key questions: is Haile Selassie a prophet or is he the saviour? And is it only black Africans who may enjoy the peaceable kingdom that will follow the return to Zion? For William Henry, it is a faith that now embraces the dispossessed everywhere:

When I was younger, you had to be black African and oppressed by white people to embrace Rastafari, but it's always in flux. If you see your suffering represented in what it suggests, then you can embrace Rastafari. It has become a global voice for anybody who thinks that they are oppressed or down pressed, a universal voice for the voice-less.

In other words anybody – no longer just Africans – may now become Rastafari, and they do. This is an extraordinary development. In the last chapter, we looked at a system of belief that cannot be separated from the landscape in which it is embedded – and which cannot travel. But in this case, a church which had developed as an exclusively Ethiopian national institution, shaped by and for local circumstances and defining local, national identity, has given people with completely different histories, and living

Rastafari button badges of the 1980s celebrating Haile Selassie and Ethiopia/Africa as the promised land

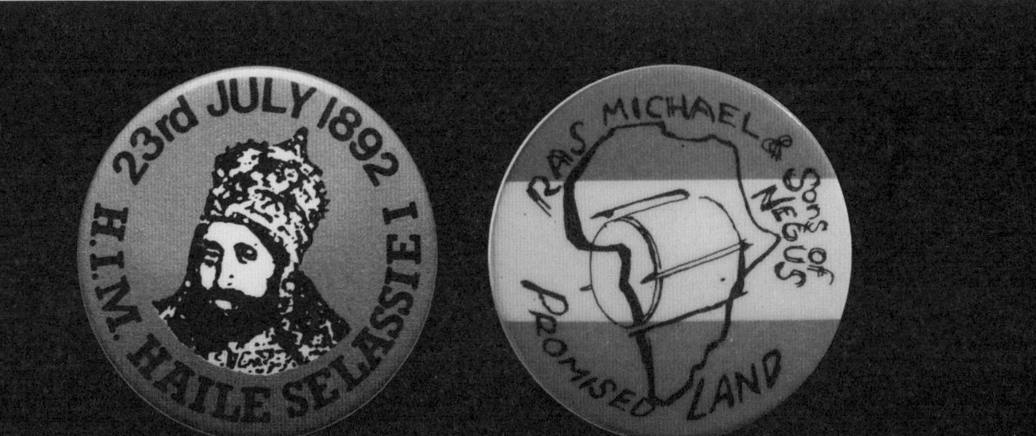

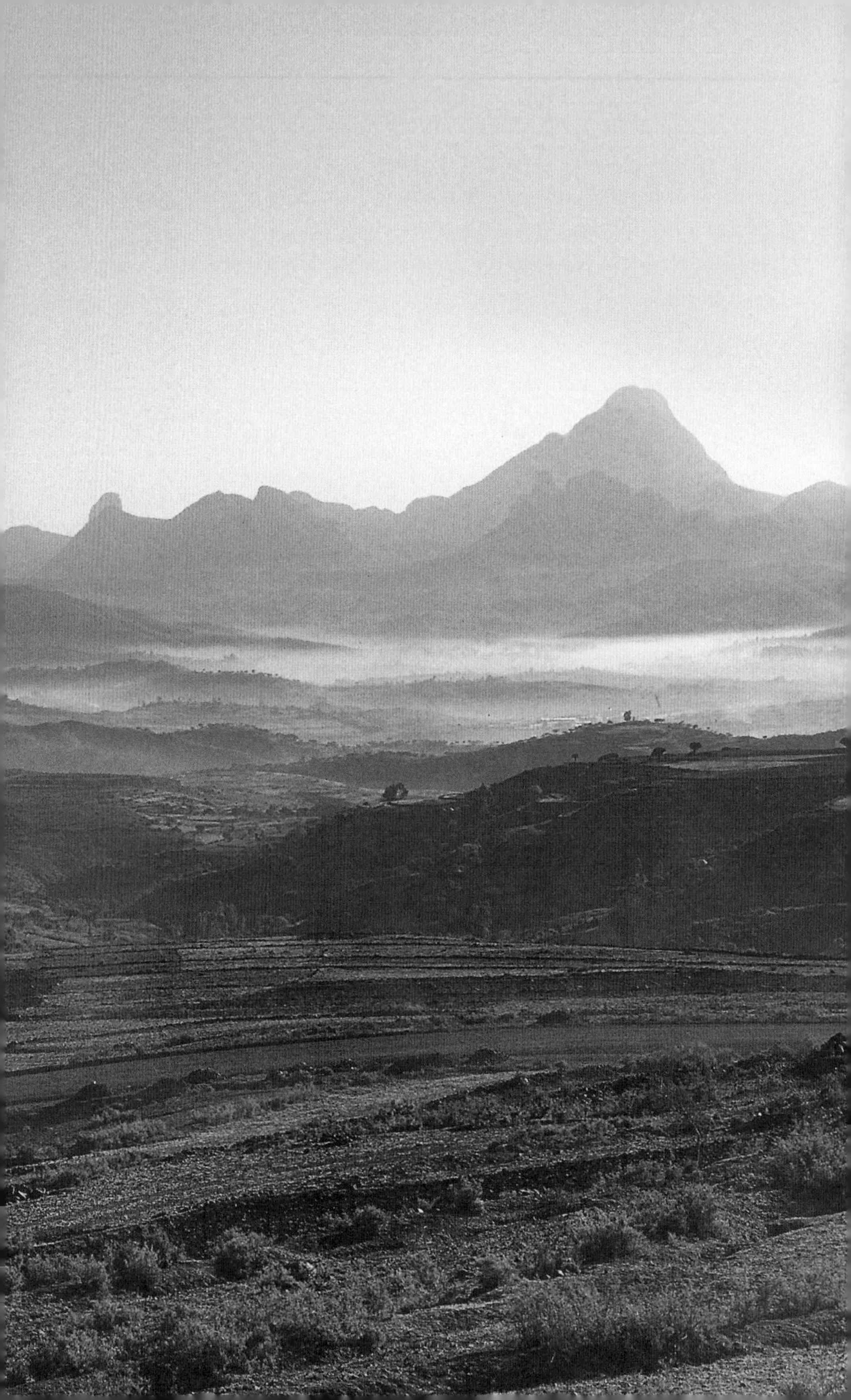

in a different continent, a tradition and a figure which they have made their own. Ras Tafari, Haile Selassie, has become a symbol of hope to many across the world as much because of his defeat, as because of his later triumph. His ignominious death in 1975, imprisoned and humiliated by rebels, did little to diminish his stature: one of the few Rastafari objects in the British Museum is a portrait of Ras Tafari himself, wearing the imperial crown, and inscribed 'H. I. M. – His Imperial Majesty – Haile Selassie'. But it is not another oil painting: it is a mass-produced button badge bought in London, among Afro-Caribbean celebrations at the Notting Hill Carnival in 1983, eight years after his death. From Ethiopia to Jamaica, and now back to one of the old imperial capitals of Europe, the cult had moved again.

How has this happened? Europeans at different times have used military power, economic supremacy and organized mission to spread their versions of Christianity. By contrast, says William Henry, Rastafari has used none of these, but has spread its beliefs around the world in a much gentler way:

Music is central to Rastafari. It is the vehicle, it is the main medium for getting out that message, because if you think about it most people in the world know of Rastafari through music, most often through Bob Marley. Reggae music is the foremost global voice for the oppressed.

The reach of that global voice has been enormous. It sings of Ethiopia as Zion, but not as a familiar place to which exiles may return, as the Jews sang of Jerusalem in Babylon (Chapter 28). The Ethiopia of the Rastafari is no longer a nation state defined by its religion, but a homeland of the suffering spirit, which all may enter, and where they will at last find God on their side.

Ethiopia, the Zion of the Rastafarians. The site of the Battle of Adwa, where Ethiopians defeated Italians on 2 March 1896

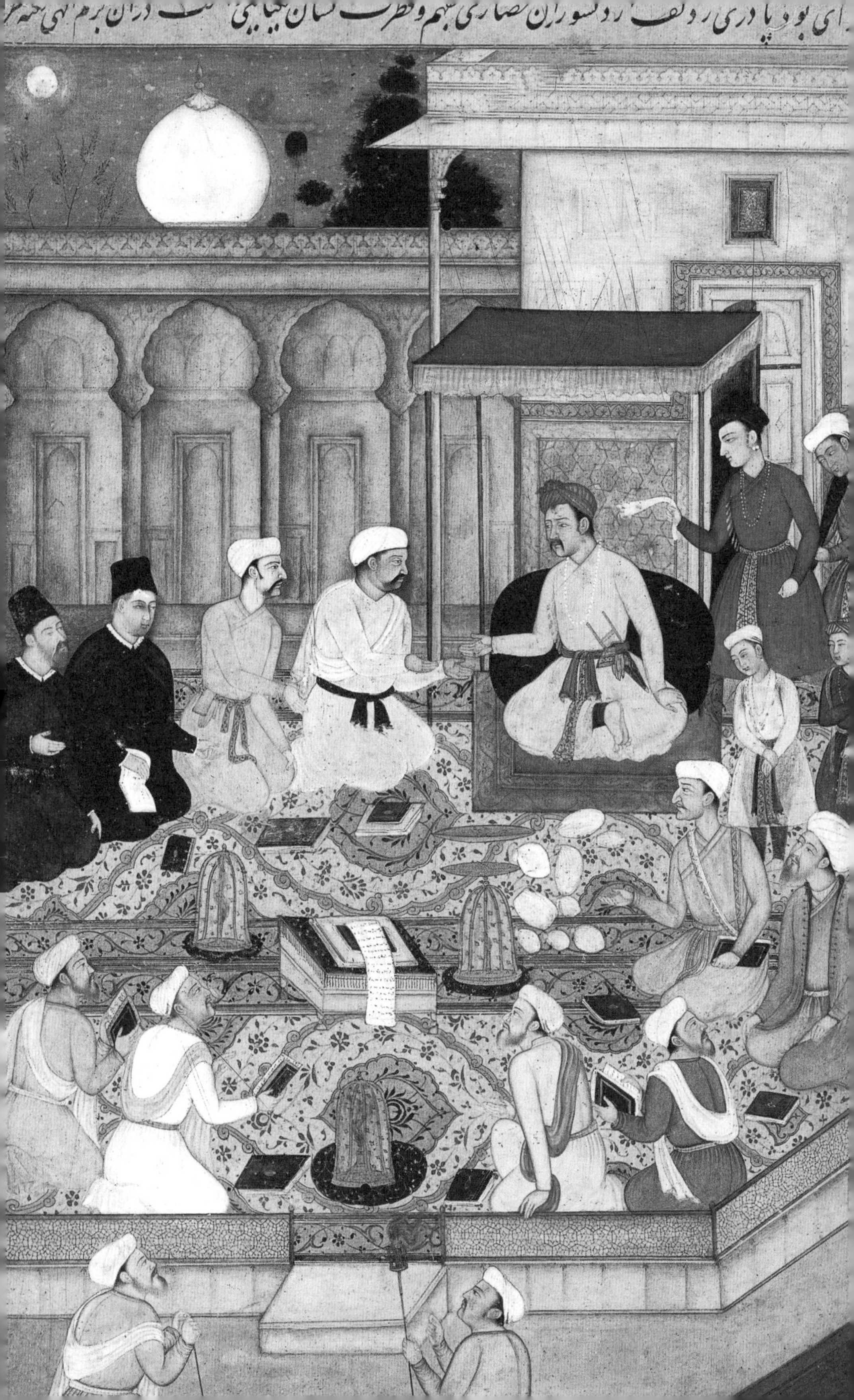

25

TOLERATING AND NOT TOLERATING

Our Lady of Glory in Mumbai is a tall, brick Roman Catholic church built in the best mid-nineteenth-century English Gothic style. As you stand on its steps, you can see on the other side of the road a bright-green mosque, whose walls in turn butt up against the orange and yellow of a temple to Hanuman, the Hindu monkey god. A few hundred yards to the left is a synagogue, while the same distance in the other direction stands a Zoroastrian fire temple. Just a little further on are a Jain sanctuary and a Buddhist temple.

It may sound like a theme park for world religions, but this is the real Mumbai, the cosmopolitan commercial capital of modern India. It is a multi-lingual, multi-racial and multi-faith metropolis built up over the last 300 years by Christians and Hindus, Parsis and Jews, Muslims and Jains, all living cheek by jowl in what has been, for most of that period, harmonious co-existence.

The previous chapter examined how a single shared religion can define and strengthen a state, setting it apart from its neighbours. In India, the world's major faiths are practised side by side in greater numbers than anywhere else in the world. But many would argue that this state too is held together by a single shared

The Muslim emperor Akbar regularly engaged with adherents of other faiths. In this late-sixteenth-century painting he is in discussions with Jesuit missionaries.

belief – a civic faith in a pluralist society. This is not only the result of a long habit of tolerance: it is a positive belief in a very Indian form of secularism. Where much European secularism is essentially anti-clerical, often the result of long struggles against the political power of the Catholic church (Chapters 26 and 28), the Indian version is not grounded in hostility towards the institutions of religion. For the Indian economist and philosopher Amartya Sen this secularism is based rather on the principle of 'equidistance':

All religions have to be tolerated and treated with respect. So secularism in the Indian form means not 'no religion in government matters', but 'no favouritism of any religion over any other'.

It is perhaps the only way that so large a country with so many religions can be peacefully governed.

It is an idea with a long history, as you can see from a manuscript illumination in the British Museum. Painted in bright watercolours in 1598, it shows a scene from the Hindu epic poem the *Mahabharata*. In the centre, dying from his wounds and surrounded by kneeling attendants, is Bhishma, a heroic warrior renowned for his virtue. He is saying his last words to the god Krishna, while warriors and horsemen stand behind, dismayed, in a fantasy rocky landscape.

This illustration of a Hindu tale was made not, however, for a Hindu patron, but for the Muslim emperor, Akbar, a rough contemporary of Elizabeth I, whose huge empire included most of the sub-continent north of the River Godavari. Whereas Elizabeth's English state was forged through the adoption of an exclusive Protestantism, Akbar's political priority was to foster an informed religious pluralism. In 1574 he set up a special office of state to translate the most important Hindu scriptures and poems

The death of Bhishma: a Hindu tale illustrated in 1598 for the Muslim emperor Akbar

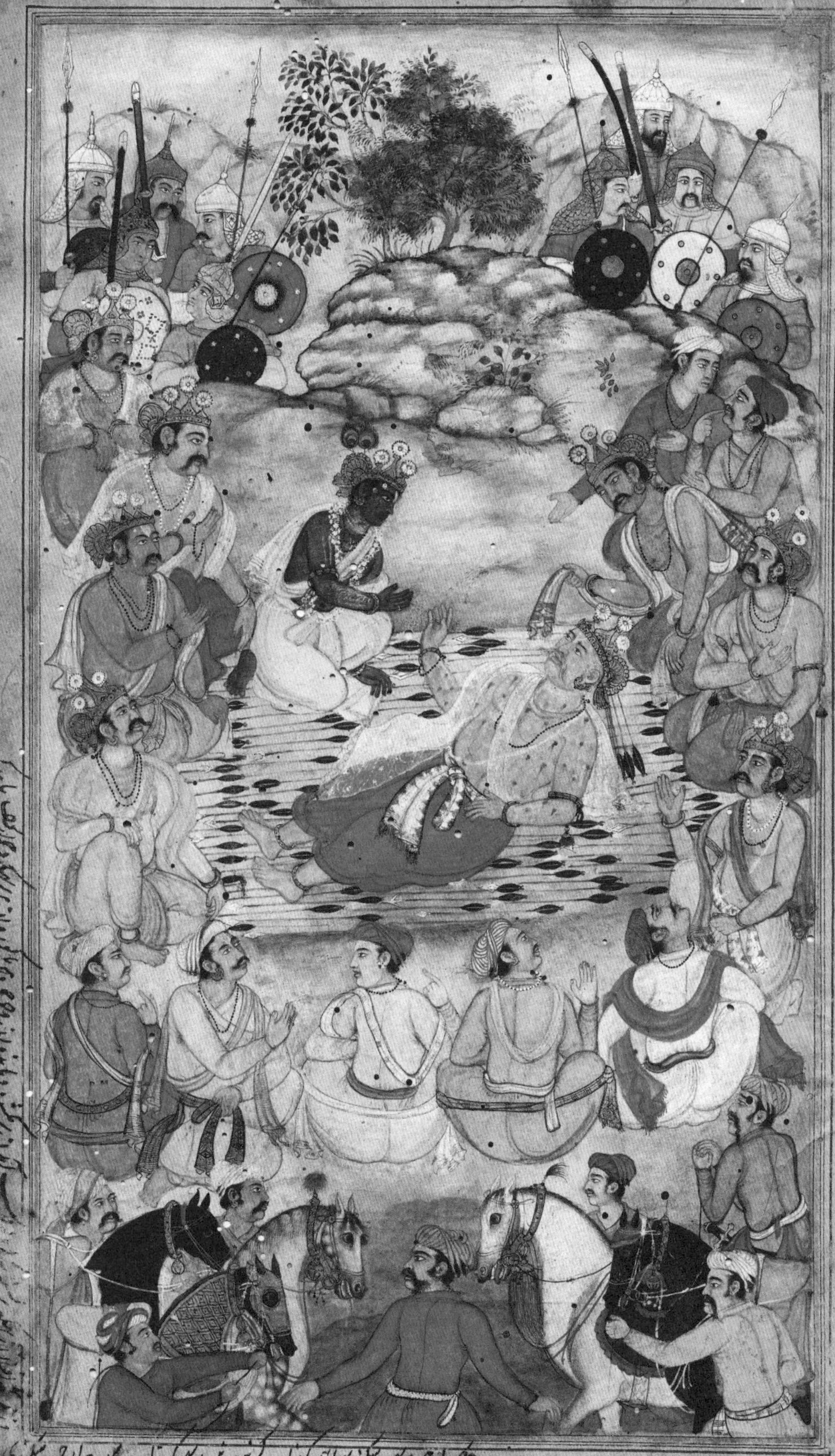

into Persian, the language of Mughal court administration, specifically so that Muslims would be able to understand better the wisdom in Hindu religion. Our beautiful painting is a small but telling part of Akbar's pluralist project.

Akbar's tolerance ran deep – and wide. His son Jahangir (whose own openness in matters of religion later amazed English visitors) reported that under his father's reign 'The road to altercation was closed. Sunnis and Shias met in one mosque, and Christians and Jews in one church, and observed their form of worship.' It is the last part of that sentence which is perhaps the most significant. Nobody abandoned their own beliefs: they practised them peaceably side by side, in a way then unthinkable in Christian Europe. And it seemed to many that Akbar's commitment to understanding other faiths was driven not only by political calculation. Abdul-Qadir Bada'uni, a court historian, claimed that the emperor operated out of a 'conviction in his heart that there were sensible men in all religions ... If some true knowledge was thus everywhere to be found, why should truth be confined to one religion?'

Akbar's prudent refusal (mostly) to try to impose his own Muslim faith on his subjects, like his equidistant respect for all the other religions practised in his realms, was nothing new in India. It had first been articulated, and widely promulgated, in the edicts carved in stone by the Buddhist emperor Ashoka, who had ruled most of northern India 1,800 years earlier, in the third century BCE, and who could claim, truthfully, that 'I have honoured all religious sects with various offerings.'

This capacious approach to the government of India was duly followed even by the devoutly Christian Queen Victoria. In 1858, eighteen years before she was declared Empress of India, the proclamation of British rule insisted that there was to be no 'interference with the religious belief or worship of any of our subjects'. Missionary activity (Chapter 4) might be tolerated, but it was certainly not to be endorsed or encouraged by the state. After independence in 1947, this ancient principle of the secular, equidistant state was enshrined in the constitution of the Republic of India.

One of the sub-continent's many achievements in religious tolerance can be seen on a more intimate scale in a circular silver temple token, three centimetres in diameter, struck in 1898. One side bears an inscription in Punjabi:

There is but one God. True is his name, creative his personality and immortal his form. He is without fear, without enmity, unborn and self-illuminated. By the Guru's grace, he is obtained.

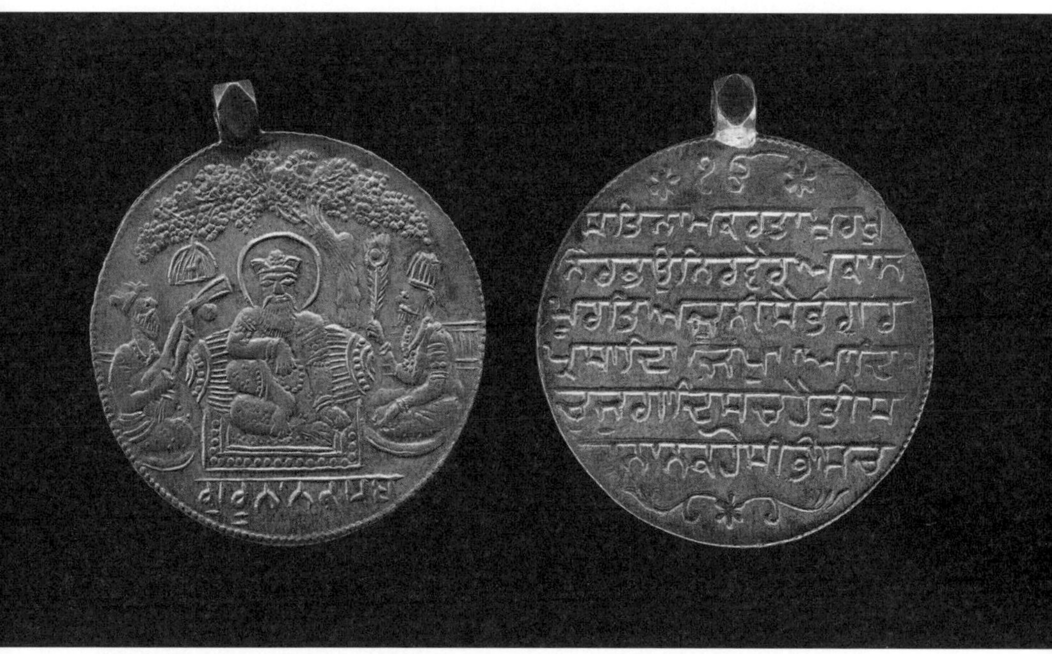

Silver token from the Golden Temple at Amritsar: Guru Nanak, founder of the Sikh faith, sits between Hindu and Muslim friends

The Guru whose grace might help us to reach this one God is Guru Nanak, the founder of the Sikh faith, who lived and taught around 1500. And these words are the opening lines of Sikhism's most important text, the *Guru Granth Sahib*, which guides the thinking of the faithful. On the other side of the token is a scene familiar to all Sikhs: we see Guru Nanak himself, with a crown and a halo, seated between his two close friends on a carpet under a tree. On the left, Mardana, a Muslim musician, sits playing an instrument like a lute with a very long neck, a gift from Guru Nanak. On the right is Bala Sindhu, a Hindu, holding a fly whisk. As well as listening to music, they are clearly conversing.

This single image takes us to the heart of Guru Nanak's teachings. After experiencing a religious vision at the age of about thirty, he is said to have exclaimed: 'There is no Hindu, no Muslim' – taken to mean that true faith transcends the different traditions and wisdoms of any particular religion. He sits here, literally equidistant from both his friends, setting out his central ideas of generosity to the less fortunate, service to others, and the equality of all before the one God.

Temple tokens like these would be handed out to pilgrims visiting the centre of the Sikh faith: the Sri Harmandir Sahib, or Golden Temple, in Amritsar, in India's north-western state of Punjab, a serene masterpiece of symbolic religious architecture. The main building stands surrounded by water: in Sikh tradition this pool is the nectar of immortality. Unlike most religious structures, which stand high so that you have to climb up to them, here the faithful must go down steps as a sign of their humility in the face of the divine. The Sri Harmandir Sahib itself is a temple of the word. No images are worshipped here. Instead, every day at dawn, the sacred text, the *Guru Granth Sahib*, which Sikhs regard as a living Guru, is carried into the temple, where (in a manner not unlike the Torah or the Qur'an, see Chapter 20) it is revered, its verses read and chanted until dusk, and broadcast around the whole temple precinct. Instead of one main entrance, there are four, open to all points of the compass, welcoming the whole of humanity, all who choose to enter. And very large numbers do enter: not far from the Golden Temple stands the Langar, a huge

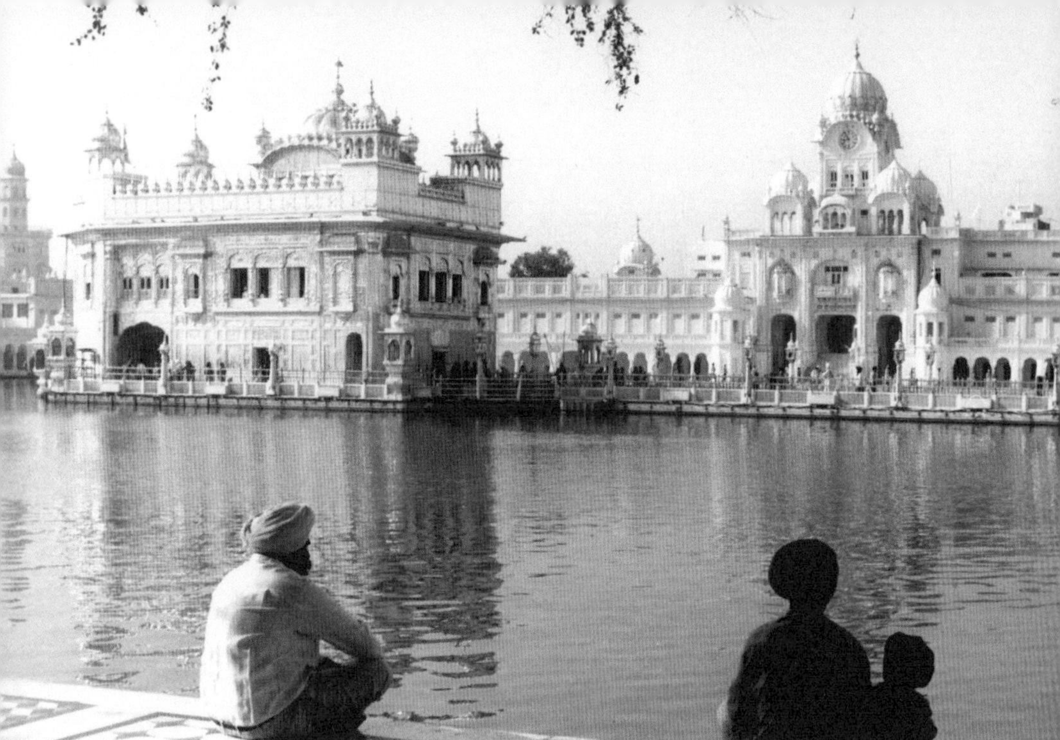

The Golden Temple at Amritsar

dining hall that offers free food to everybody with no distinction of caste or race and sometimes serves as many as 100,000 people a day. This holy place strikes the visitor as a tranquil tribute to the values of Guru Nanak in particular, and the Indian tradition of pluralism more broadly: openness, generosity, tolerance, oneness.

Professor Gurharpal Singh, of the School of Oriental and African Studies in London, explains the precinct's significance for pilgrims:

The Golden Temple is the main place of worship for Sikhs, but it's much more. It symbolizes the faith, the beginnings of the Sikh community and its emergence as a powerful force in northern India. The Golden Temple is the holiest of holies. But it is also a complex that embodies the cultural, spiritual and physical dimensions of the community's history over the last 400 years.

A significant, painful chapter of that history was written here in 1984, when a bloody pitched battle took place between the Indian army and militant champions of a Sikh national homeland. Under British colonial rule in the nineteenth and early twentieth centuries, India's supple religious diversity hardened into interest groups competing for government recognition and favours, or into potential voting blocs as the British embarked on limited experiments with democracy. Leaders on all sides, not least the British, advanced the (very European) notion that communities of faith might be reflected in political groupings, might indeed require particular political, even territorial, guarantees: 'Pakistan' for the sub-continent's Muslims, or 'Khalistan' for the Sikhs – both names meaning 'land of the pure', in Urdu and Punjabi respectively.

Pakistan was eventually born in the murderous violence of Partition in 1947, which split the Sikh heartlands of the Punjab in two. Sikh calls for their own Khalistan went unanswered. Yet the Sikh separatist movement did not die out. Over the following decades, rival Sikh religious parties squabbled, while the government in Delhi appeared indecisive and inconsistent. By June 1984 a militant Sikh leader, Jarnail Singh Bhindranwale, previously supported by the Prime Minister, Indira Gandhi, but now actively opposed to her and by her, was calling for the establishment of a separate Sikh state, and, with seeming impunity, had defiantly taken up residence inside the Golden Temple. As the government, alarmed by separatist claims, finally turned against him, Bhindranwale began preparing the Golden Temple against possible military attack. Mark Tully, a journalist and broadcaster who has lived much of his life in India, was a witness to what happened next:

Journalists could see Bhindranwale's fortification of the Golden Temple taking place. People were terrified of him by this point, and so the Sikh clergy, particularly the clergy of the temple, allowed this to happen. When the Indian army arrived to put a stop to it, they mistakenly thought that when Bhindranwale saw

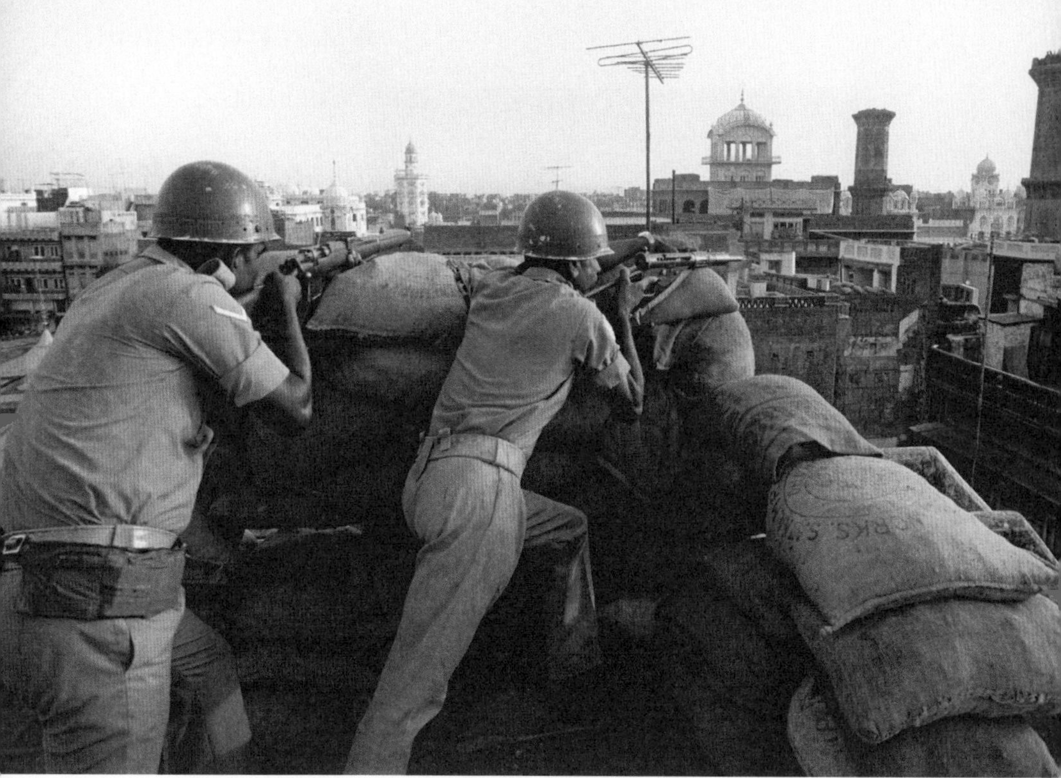

Indian troops preparing for the assault on the Golden Temple, June 1984

them coming, he would collapse and surrender. But he resisted, and eventually the army had to bring in tanks, firing at the Akal Takht, the second most sacred building in the compound.

In the conflict that ensued, Bhindranwale and hundreds of his supporters were killed, along with Indian army soldiers and Sikh pilgrims who were visiting at the time of the attack. The traces of the battle are still very evident in the precinct today. There is an impressive memorial to those Sikhs who died in the fighting. On the walls of the Golden Temple are bullet holes, now framed with metal discs. On nearby buildings you can see the damage inflicted by the tanks.

The Golden Temple was eventually taken by the army, and peace returned. Talk of 'Khalistan' died down. But the events of Operation Blue Star, as the government's offensive against Bhindranwale in the Golden Temple was known, left a bitter legacy.

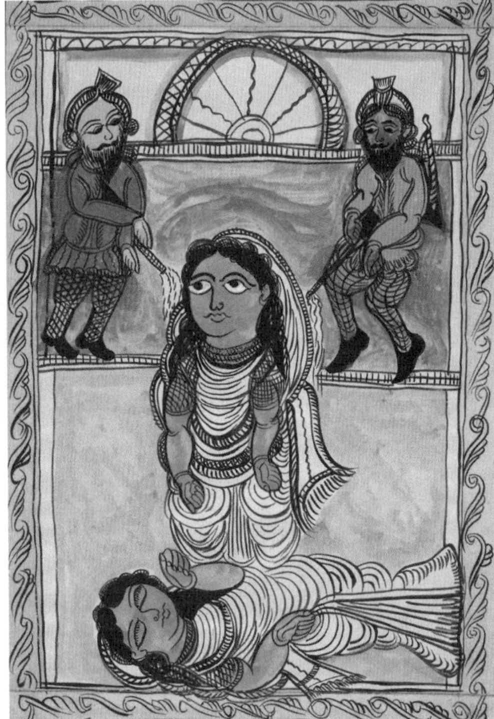

Indira Gandhi's assassination, 31 October 1984: scroll-painting for an itinerant Bengali story-teller

Both sides were accused of desecrating this holy place. A few months afterwards, Indira Gandhi was assassinated by two of her Sikh bodyguards. A frenzy of anti-Sikh violence erupted across Delhi, and by the time order was belatedly restored, thousands of Sikhs had been killed, and tens of thousands more had fled Delhi for the relative safety of Punjab.

In the very fabric of the Golden Temple you can see what happened when the humane ideals of Guru Nanak were overwhelmed by the politics of religious identity. The contrast between the serene and peaceful scene depicted on the Temple token, and the scars still visible on the Temple's walls, speaks of the tensions that arise when the strong sense of belonging which comes from shared beliefs is redirected to a political end – and when the central state feels compelled to intervene.

*

If the Sikhs have been caught up in politically driven violence, so also have the two other faiths represented on our silver temple token. The image there of Guru Nanak with Mardana and Bala Sindhu shows an ideal of peaceful Hindu–Muslim co-existence, which, in spite of Partition, constant tension and even war between India and Pakistan, was never entirely lost in India after independence. In recent years, however, it has come under growing strain, nowhere more so than in the city of Ayodhya, a few hundred miles south-east of Delhi. According to Hindu scriptures, Ayodhya is where God was made man. Many devoutly believe that the great god Vishnu there became incarnate as Lord Ram (the protagonist of the epic poem the *Ramayana*), thus making it a supremely holy place for Hindus, and one which should house a major temple in his honour.

As Amartya Sen argues, the situation is, however, more complex, and texts like the *Ramayana* should be read with caution:

There is very little evidence as to whether historically there ever was a person called Ram exactly as described in the epic Ramayana, *or where he was born. The connection with modern Ayodhya is very tenuous.*

Until the early 1990s Ayodhya's most celebrated building was a majestic domed mosque, the Babri Masjid, said on somewhat flimsy evidence to have been built by Babur, grandfather of Emperor Akbar. But today there is no mosque, just a heap of rubble standing on some of the most contested ground in India. The mosque of 'Babur' was built on the site of an earlier, presumably Hindu, temple (although archaeologists are unable to say with certainty which god was worshipped there), which had probably been demolished for the purpose.

After the mosque was built, the local Hindu population continued worshipping in its grounds, and the site was increasingly venerated as the birthplace of Ram. Tension between the Muslim and Hindu communities simmered for centuries, occasionally flaring, and leading the British authorities in 1859 to impose a compromise under which Muslims continued to worship in the mosque, while Hindus venerated Ram's birthplace in a fenced-off area within the precinct. But the conflict persisted, and in 1949 the local state government closed the entire complex to both Muslims and Hindus. Three decades later, after much political manoeuvring, the mosque was reopened for worship. It, and the ground around it, quickly became the focus of ever more violent clashes, until on 6 December 1992 Hindu activists stormed the site.

Once again, Mark Tully was there:

The whole thing climaxed when large numbers of people gathered in Ayodhya for a Hindu religious ceremony. The situation got out of control, and huge crowds swarmed towards the mosque, breaking through the police barriers. The police initially did very little to prevent it, and then just disappeared altogether. I was watching when the security broke down. I left to telephone a report. When I returned I found a scene of utter chaos, people shouting obscene slogans against Muslims – clearly an act designed to provoke Muslims and also to provoke Hindus to appear angry about Muslims. People had started to pull the mosque down, while others were beating up journalists.

In less than twenty-four hours, the crowd, using sticks, pikes and pickaxes, demolished the mosque completely. Almost nothing remains.

Visiting the site today is a disconcerting experience. The whole area is fenced off with three distinct barriers, one behind the other, punctuated by watchtowers – a combination disturbingly reminiscent of the old frontier between West and East Germany. Visitors have to leave behind watches, mobile phones and any

Hindu activists storming the Babri Masjid mosque at Ayodhya on 6 December 1992

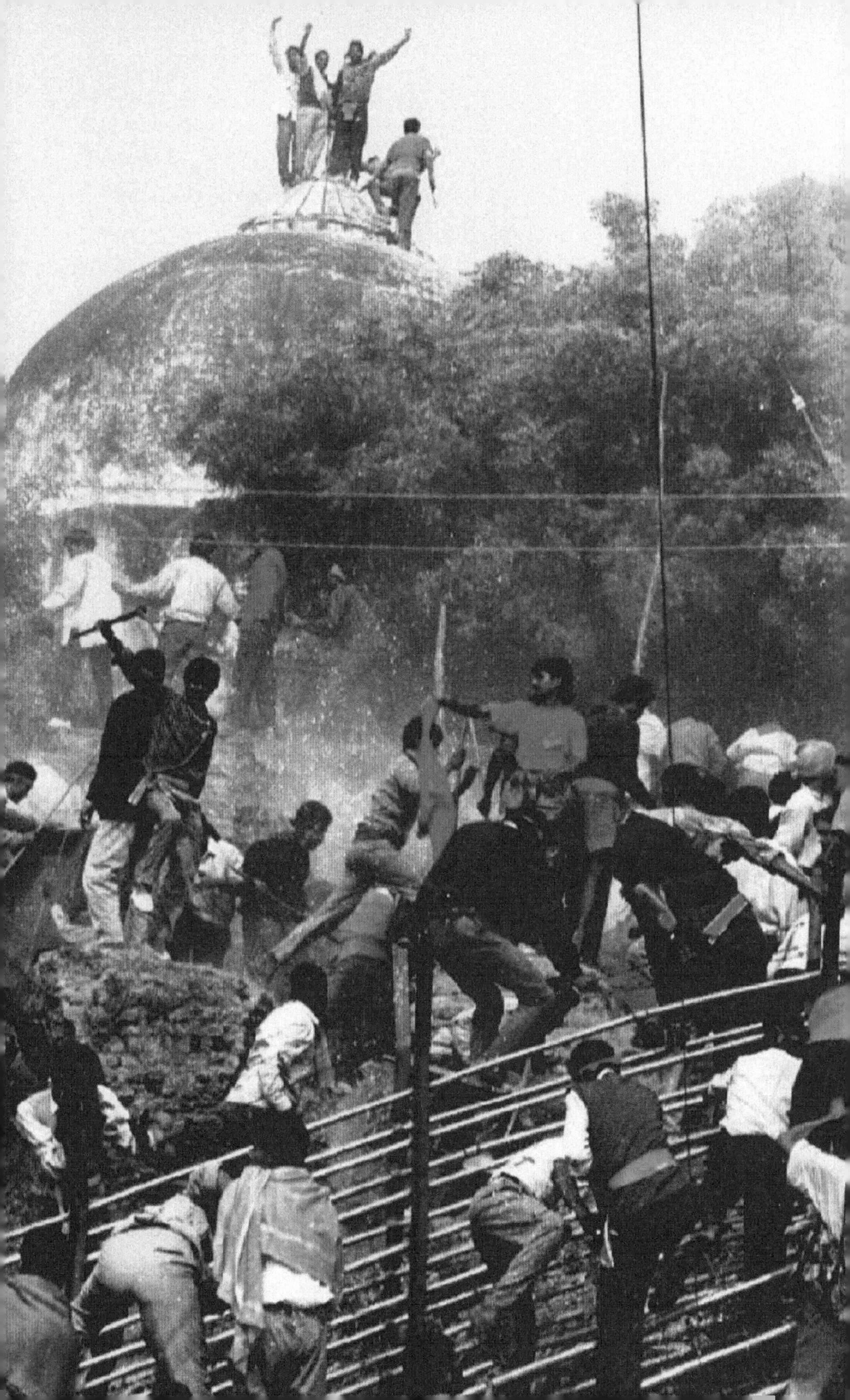

other electronic equipment, and pass through two metal detectors and three separate body searches before entering a caged walkway flanked on either side by soldiers, which twists and turns until it reaches the site of the demolished mosque. There, in a temporary structure, effectively a large tent, is a shrine of Ram, marking the supposed place of his birth. The pilgrims in the caged walkway can pause briefly for *darshan* – a direct view of a modern statue of the god – and make an offering. As they leave this militarized shrine, visitors are given holy water and *prasad*, an offering of temple sweets. At no point would anybody know that there had ever been a mosque here.

The continuing and increasingly bitter dispute in Ayodhya – to which group should the site belong? – has become one of national importance, running all the way to the Supreme Court in Delhi. After more than twenty years of litigation, that question is still not definitively settled, but in 2017 local politicians campaigned – and won great support – for building a Hindu temple on the site of the mosque. The future is uncertain, but few things could better demonstrate how difficult it is for modern nation states to manage conflicting religious beliefs when they become markers of communal identity, articulated with ever fiercer conviction. It is a phenomenon growing in intensity all around the world.

Many are concerned that India's ideals of respectful co-existence, a beacon of enlightened thinking that long predates any European Enlightenment, are not being upheld with the commitment which the Constitution requires. Gurharpal Singh sets out his worries:

I think we are going through a very difficult time, where the relationship of the state with societal religious pluralism is very problematic. There is a concerted effort to impose a particular kind of identity on Indians through the power of the state and this sits very oddly with the religious pluralism and diversity that

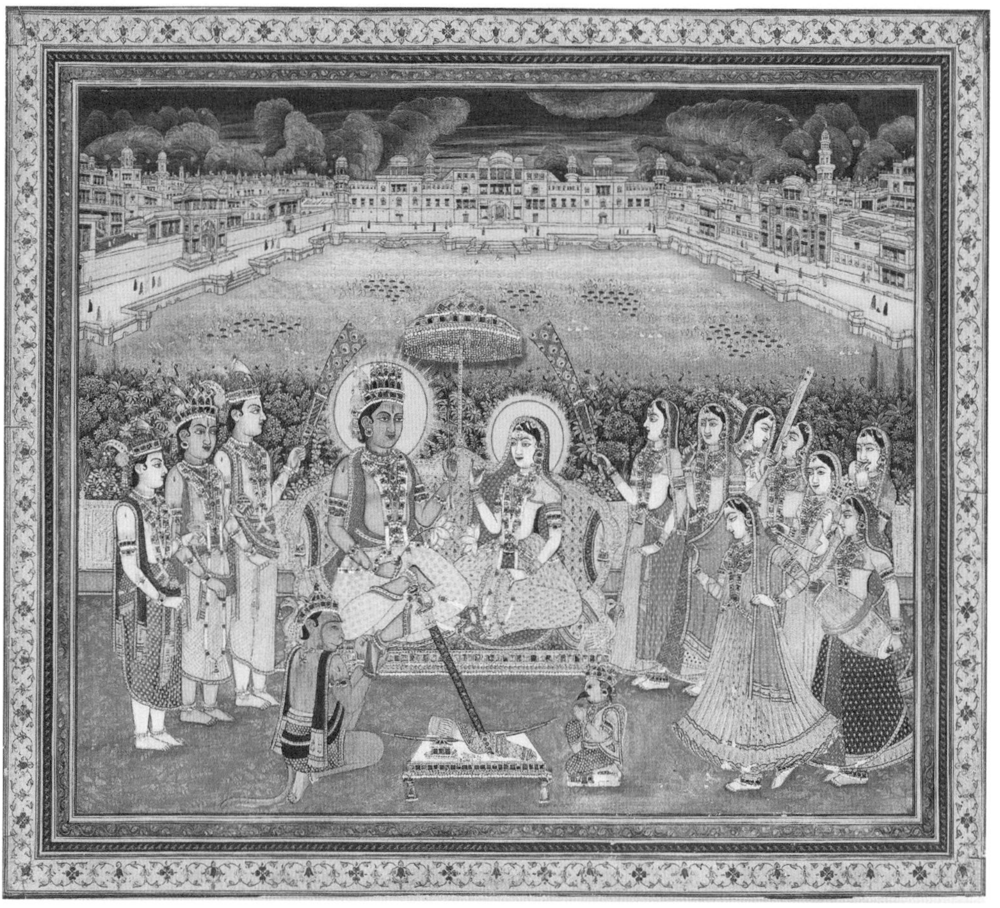

Ram and Sita on golden thrones in front of the Ayodhya imagined by a painter around 1800

make up India. It remains to be seen which force will be triumphant. The only hope is, Mahatma Gandhi said, in the religious pluralism and diversity of India itself.

For Amartya Sen, one of the factors behind the Ayodhya episode is a confusion of myth with historic fact, a willingness to take poetic texts like the *Ramayana* as literally true. It is perhaps the Hindu equivalent of the growing trend towards literalist readings of holy texts that was discussed in a Jewish and Muslim context in Chapter 20. Amartya Sen:

What is very important is to recognize that we should not take the richness of Indian literature – poetry with stories in it – as history.

And the Ram story is part of Indian culture, not just of Hindu culture: it's a story which has also had an enormous impact in India among Buddhists, among Sikhs and also among Christians and Jews who read the story.

The Indian historian Sunil Khilnani of King's College, London, sees a similar danger, and also worries that as a consequence the ancient traditions of Ashoka and Akbar are being undermined:

I think what you have seen in recent years in India is the territorialization of the imagination, the attempt to pin it down to specific places. It began of course with the drawing of borders, the partition of India, and suddenly language belonged to one or another religion. That became the motivating factor in thinking about religion for some people. The Ayodhya dispute is, I think, very closely linked to the creation of the modern nation state on the European model. That's to say, a land or a territory belongs to a culture or a language or a religion, and therefore one group has the priority in defining what gets built where. The model that India tried to build was a very different model of the nation state, in many ways a unique model. I think it's much more based on a deeper history of the relationship between political power and belief in India, which extends much further back than the nation state.

At the beginning of this chapter, we compared Elizabethan England with Akbar's India. Western Europe has now, after centuries of conflict, almost entirely abandoned the notion of a state being defined by one shared faith, and has, since the eighteenth century, moved steadily towards Ashoka's inclusive principles. It would be a bitter irony if at this moment India were to move in the opposite direction.

PART SIX
Powers Earthly and Divine

'Thy kingdom come': the words have become so familiar we have almost forgotten that they call for nothing less than a world governed directly by God. In this section, we look at attempts to usher in such a kingdom. But before that day comes, how do communities of faith flourish in societies inevitably run by politicians? Religious teachings can underpin the authority of rulers, but can also be used to hold them to account. Strengthening the nation state by imposing one national faith – or even a national atheism – has always had great appeal, but also brought great problems. In spite of all difficulties, the dream of a heavenly city, somehow to be achieved on earth, endures.

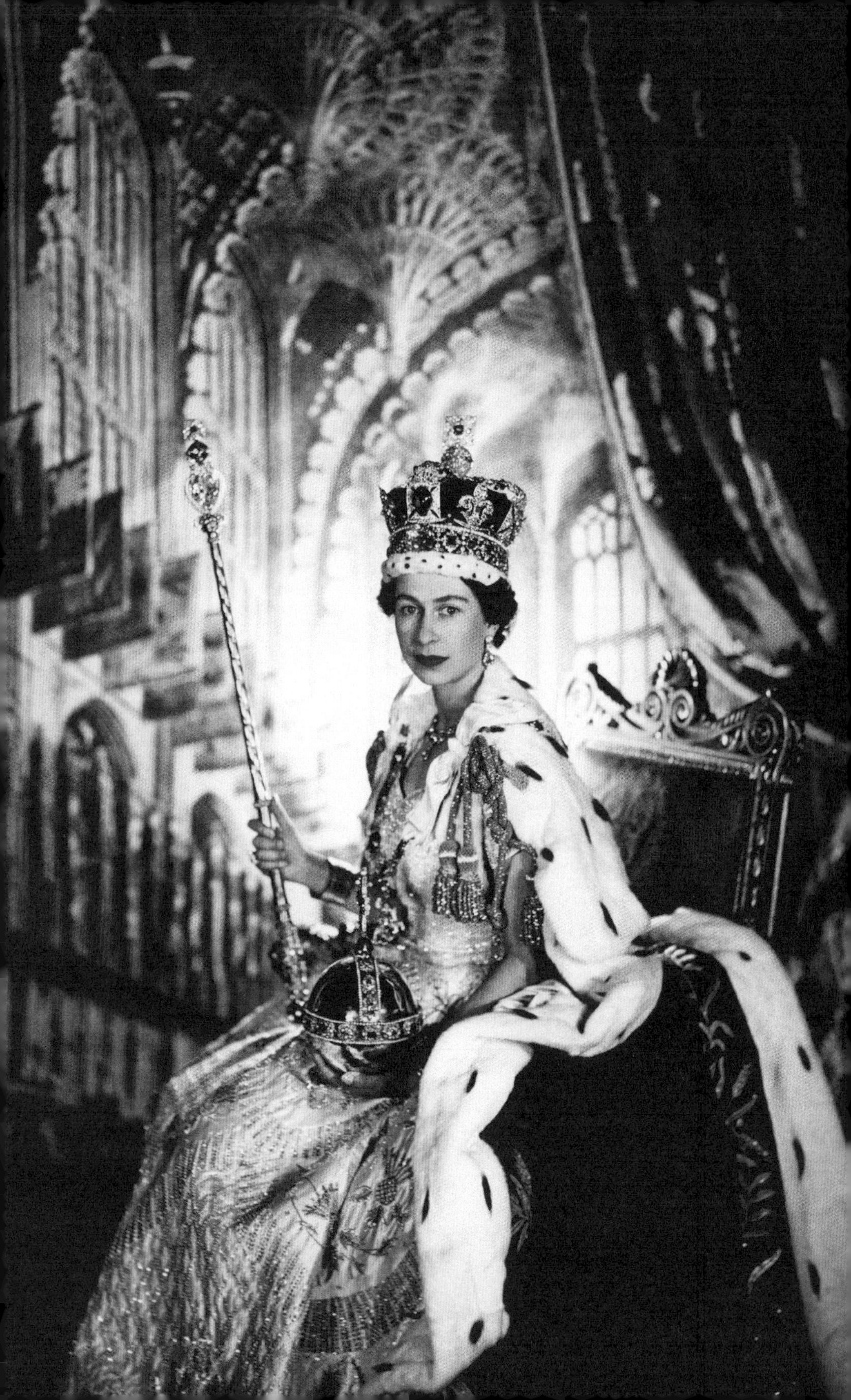

26
THE MANDATE OF HEAVEN

And as Solomon was anointed king
by Zadok the priest and Nathan the prophet,
so be thou anointed, blessed, and consecrated Queen
over the Peoples, whom the Lord thy God
hath given thee to rule and govern,
in the name of the Father, and of the Son, and of the
Holy Ghost. Amen

Westminster Abbey, 2 June 1953. The Archbishop of Canterbury pours holy oil over Elizabeth II during her coronation. Like the biblical kings of Israel, but unique now among European monarchs, she is the Anointed of the Lord. Nobody watching that ceremony could fail to be moved by the idea of the sovereign, wearing a simple tunic, being invested with all temporal power by the Almighty, and anointed in his name. The choir sings Handel's 'Zadok the Priest', as at every coronation since George II's in 1727, for which the anthem was composed. The archbishop invokes Solomon, wisest of all monarchs, but he also mentions Nathan – the Hebrew prophet who, in the Book of Samuel,

Queen Elizabeth II after her coronation in 1953, holding the orb and sceptre, photographed by Cecil Beaton

rebuked and publicly humiliated Solomon's father, the great King David, and called him to repentance for abusing his power. To be a leader in the eyes of a people, it has in most societies, and for most of history, been necessary to be their leader in the eyes of God. Divine endorsement has usually been central to the idea of monarchy, but divine right comes with a no less divinely sanctioned duty to your people: authority is matched with a penalty for breach of trust. As Nathan reminded David, a king – or queen – must make, and must keep, an oath made before God.

The defining image of the Queen's coronation is of the young monarch, fresh from taking her oath, sitting beneath the weight of her new crown and holding the orb and sceptre – the symbols of power spiritual and temporal. Both are kept with the Crown Jewels in the Tower of London. But in the British Museum you can find these two forms of sovereignty combined in one *single* sceptre – or, more accurately, staff of office. Around a metre long, cast in brass and about 200 years old, the staff swells at three key points along its length to form figures representing separate dimensions of the sovereign's authority. Each figure is decorated with intricate patterns, the brass expertly cast to suggest a wide variety of textures. Together, the three figures show what it means to be a divinely ordained monarch in Africa. At the top is the king, holding a leopard in either hand, and with a pair of mudfish that issue from his nostrils. Below his feet is a frog, set between two small severed human heads. The king we see here is a stylized likeness of the Oba of Benin, ruler of a mighty kingdom in what is today southern Nigeria and which had its capital in Edo, now Benin City, about 300 miles east of Lagos. At its height in the sixteenth century, Benin controlled a large, rich and tightly organized empire, and it remained a significant power until the early twentieth.

Osaren Ogbomo, a brass-caster from Benin City, explains the significance of the different figures shown on the staff:

All this symbolizes the weight of the land (the leopards) and the sea (the fish). The Oba is in charge of all these things, because we believe that the Oba of Benin is the earthly god. Every Benin man or Benin woman knows that the Oba is a representative of god on earth.

The figure in the centre of the staff, a little below the Oba, is disconcerting: it is a man without a torso – a human head with arms protruding from his scalp, and legs from his jowls.

In Benin, in my language we call him 'Ofoe nuku Ogiuwu', the messenger of death. When you are against the Oba, if you are against his laws, Ofoe nuku Ogiuwu will visit you. To go against the laws of the land is to play with your life.

The third figure, towards the base of the staff, is a head modelled with full lips, which are pursed as though about to speak; and this figure too has mud-fish emanating from its nostrils:

This is the chief priest of the Osun shrine, dedicated to a deity that helps the Oba in controlling the entire

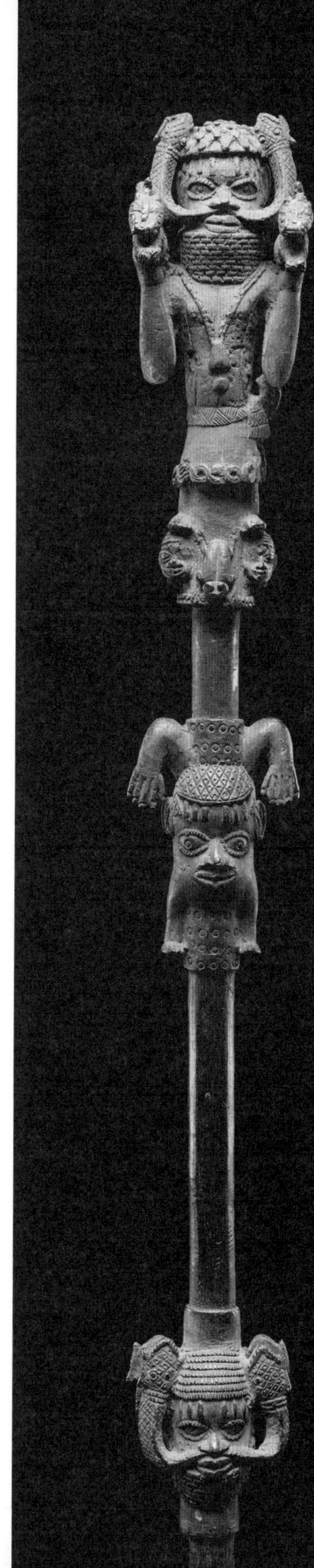

The brass staff of office of the Oba of Benin, showing him as ruler of all, and lord of life and death. Eighteenth or nineteenth century

community. All the deities have their own priest. And each priest receives his power from the Oba.

We have no written records from Benin itself that tell us exactly what the Oba did with this staff, but we do know from European visitors' accounts that he was, just as it shows, both a religious and a political leader. Portuguese travellers in the mid-sixteenth century, for example, reported that the Oba would never eat in public, because his subjects believed him to be a god, and so he could survive without food. It was crucial to his authority to maintain that belief.

The Oba's authority was extensive, running across trade and tribute, tax and justice. In so far as we can reconstruct the role without written sources, the Oba seems to have begun essentially as a warrior-leader, becoming in later centuries a more secluded performer of religious rites, the guarantor of the safe and prosperous interaction of the human and spiritual worlds. In the later nineteenth century European traders and colonizers – above all the British – encroached ever more aggressively upon Benin territory. Finally, in 1897, there was a bloody showdown. A British delegation was attacked on its way to Benin City, and in retaliation London ordered a 'punitive expedition'. The territory was occupied, and much of Benin City destroyed. The British army carried away great quantities of art, including many exquisitely worked brass sculptures, which became widely, if inaccurately, known as the Benin bronzes. These were mostly sold off at auction and are now dispersed in museums around the world. Before 1897 export of brass objects had been forbidden – which is why the sculptures seized and sold by the British troops attracted great attention from scholars when they reached the outside world.

The kingdom of Benin was incorporated into what became a British colony, and later the republic of Nigeria. But the office of Oba survives to this day, and he still plays a significant role in the ritual and spiritual life of his people.

As the animals on this staff of office imply, the fusion of the natural and the supernatural in the person of the Oba is a central aspect of his kingship. He is thought to understand better than anybody else the deities and forces that govern the world and to be able to channel them in order to protect the community from

The Oba of Benin with fish and leopards, spiritually in control of land and sea. This sixteenth-/seventeenth-century plaque, used to decorate his palace, was taken by the British army in the raid of 1897.

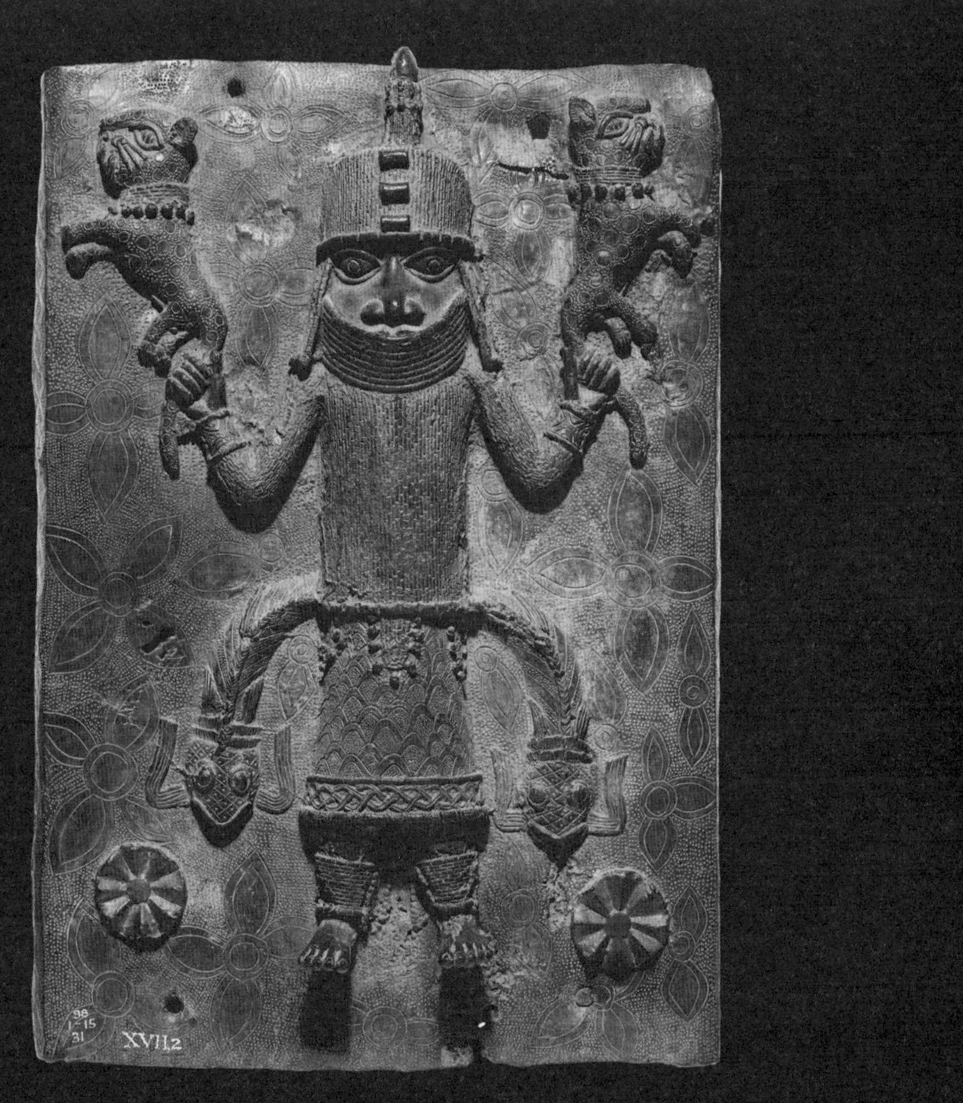

harm. One purpose of the Oba's staff is to assert those claims in a public context, symbolically linking the ruler to animals with particular significance. Mudfish, for example, can live for a long time on land as well as in water, so they suggest that the Oba also can move between elements, with power over land and sea.

In each hand the Oba holds a leopard. Dr Charles Gore of the School of Oriental and African Studies in London explains:

The leopard of the bush is the most powerful animal in the forest and can kill any other animal. Likewise, the Oba of Benin is the political and spiritual head of the kingdom, and he is the one person who has the right of life and death over his subjects. Humans cannot oppose the king because he is not human in the way that his subjects are. He is part of the natural world.

Then there are the two severed heads and a frog. Prior to 1897, an important part of activating metaphysical energies in the world was the sacrifice of animals, in certain circumstances humans. The fact that human heads are being sacrificed represents the capacity and power of the king, rearticulating the idea that the king alone has the right of life and death over his communities.

The very material of the staff is in itself a statement of royal power. Charles Gore continues:

Leaded brass, bronze, ivory and coral don't disintegrate in a tropical climate, which for 90 per cent of the year is very humid and is home to insects that will eat and destroy a piece of wood within only a few years. The use of these materials is making an iconic statement about kingship: that it's permanent. It will last as long as these materials last. Any visitor to the Oba's palace would be dazzled by an array of objects made from materials that are resistant to change, that endure.

The monarchy of Benin has indeed, like brass, endured. On 20 October 2016 the coronation of the current Oba drew huge and enthusiastic crowds. He no longer has the power of life and death, and most of his subjects are now Christian or Muslim, but the Oba, ritually initiated into his ancient office, is still profoundly revered as the father of his people.

The Oba's staff was designed to assert the absolute authority inherent in him from his divine nature: he ruled as a god and with the gods, because he was in some sense one of them. There is another grand metal object in the British Museum which offers a radically different view of the terms on which a ruler holds office under heaven – one that insists that royal authority is not absolute, but is exercised subject to stringent conditions, and is very much dependent on performance.

Made in China between 1000 and 800 BCE, this magnificent *gui*, a round-bodied cooking pot about forty centimetres across, is cast in bronze. It would probably have been used to prepare ritual meals for the dead – an important part of Chinese ceremonies designed to honour the ancestors (Chapter 6). It has four large handles, which divide the outside of the pot into separate sections. On each of these, cast in low relief, is a fabulous creature, a schematized, playful, geometric elephant, with just a hint of dragon in it. These are superb feats of technical metalwork that at this date could have been made nowhere in the world but China.

But for our purposes it is the inside of this beautifully crafted vessel that matters most; for there we find an inscription that records a marquess being granted certain rights by a king of the relatively new Zhou dynasty. After talking of the ritual observances due to the ancestors, it notes the unimpeachable source of the king's authority – he is described as the son of heaven. At first sight, this seems very close to the divine endorsement enjoyed by both Elizabeth II and the Oba of Benin. But there follows what is to Europeans an unexpected thought:

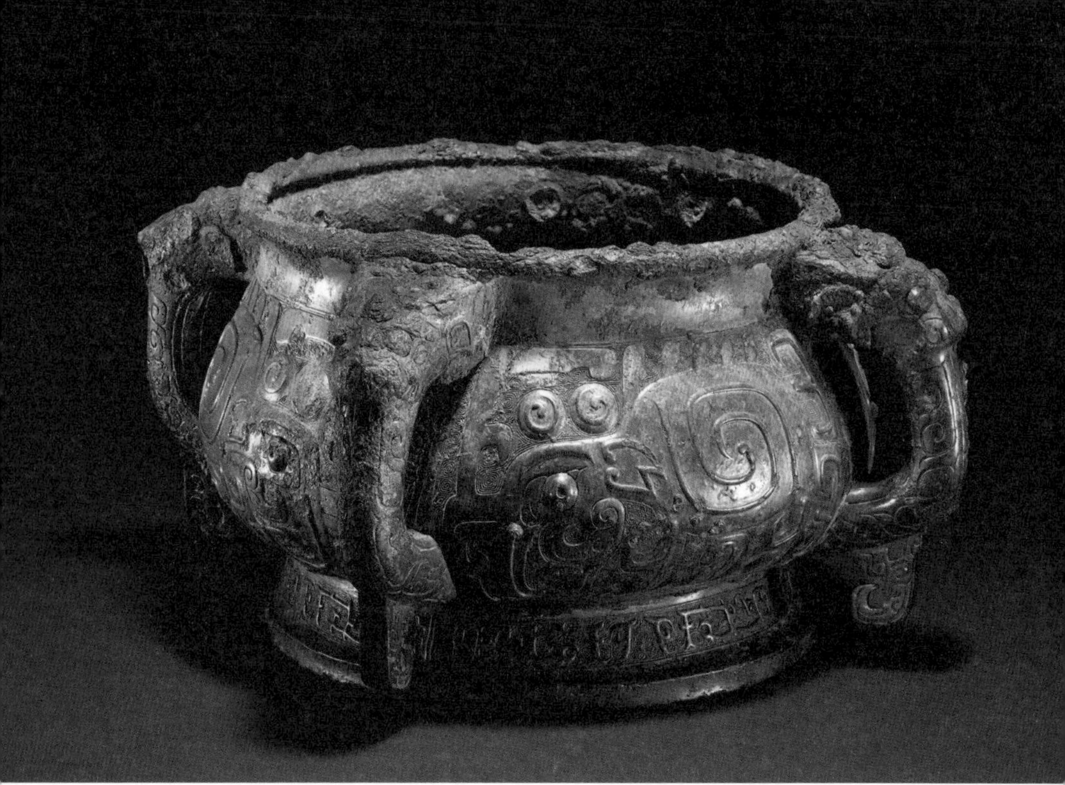

We cross our hands and lower our heads to praise the son of heaven for effecting this favour and blessing. May the High Ancestor not end the mandate for the existence of the Zhou.

This *gui* is the earliest evidence we have of a concept of leadership that has held sway in China for 3,000 years. The Zhou dynasty had overthrown their rivals and come to power around 1050 BCE. They had been able to do so, they claimed, not just because they had, like so many new Chinese rulers, conquered in battle, but because they had what came to be called a Mandate of Heaven. And, strikingly, in our pot, they feel the need to pray that this mandate will not be taken from them.

For Yuri Pines, Professor of Asian Studies at the Hebrew University of Jerusalem, this is a very unusual view of a monarch's divine right:

The right to govern can be removed. If our descendants misbehave, inscriptions like this are saying, if they oppress the people

A ceremonial bronze pot cast in China between 1000 and 800 BCE (*left*). Inside is an inscription describing the king as the son of heaven, ruling by – revocable – divine mandate (*right*).

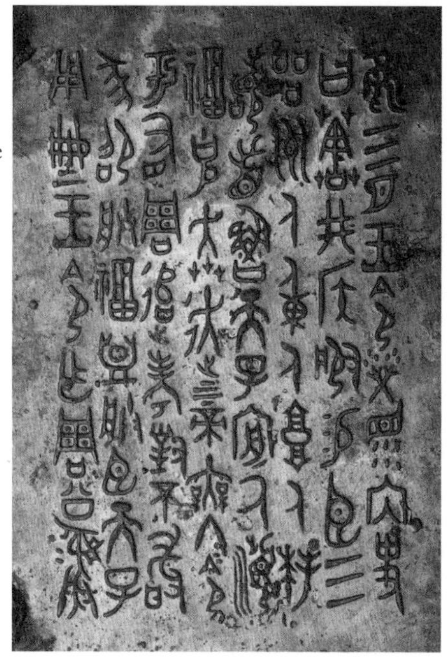

or fail to maintain a good political system, then heaven will replace us and give the mandate to somebody else. This is the real novelty: the Zhou are saying that heaven's grace cannot be taken for granted.

European Christian monarchs, ruling 'by the grace of God', understood their authority as rulers to come from the same God whom their people worshipped. The Chinese Mandate of Heaven was very different:

In China, the religion which sanctifies the role of the son of heaven (the emperor) is not a popular religion, the religion of the masses, but rather the private religion of the emperor and his immediate entourage. There are no priests who claim to speak on behalf of heaven. There is no such collision of the sort that we find in Abrahamic religions, where prophets (like Nathan) tell kings: 'Sorry, God has told me that you're wrong.' Instead, in China, heaven usually manifests its will either through omens and potions, which are then interpreted, or through popular rebellion or discontent.

This particularly Chinese notion of divine right, inscribed on the inside of our *gui*, attached great significance to such popular manifestations. It did not mean that every uprising would be sympathetically listened to. But there were scholars at the imperial court whose job it was to know the will of the people – and through them the will of heaven. If enough people expressed sufficient discontent over a lengthy period of time, the scholars might suggest that the ruler's time was up, that heaven had turned away in displeasure – or, to use the words of the inscription tucked away inside the *gui*, that the High Ancestor had brought the Mandate to an end.

One might expect that an idea like the Mandate of Heaven would be anathema to the atheist principles of China's Communist regime. But not so. The Mandate has always been as much a political philosophy as a religious ideal: it recognizes that a restive population will in the end be able to topple even those whose power appears unassailable.

According to Yuri Pines, this is an idea that Communist teaching has failed to dislodge, and which perhaps lies behind Western misunderstandings of contemporary China, and of the differences between Russian and Chinese communism:

The idea that popular discontent indicates a lack of legitimacy of the government remains very powerful. If the people are strongly dissatisfied, then the government must reflect on it and somehow modify its ways. The consequence of this way of thinking is a system that is much more flexible and attentive to the people's opinion than we would normally expect with authoritarian political systems.

The idea of the Mandate of Heaven may actually be more important now than in the past, because theoretically the Communist Party is the party of the people. To put it mildly, elections in China are not very significant. But the people's level of satisfaction with the government is. In China, people don't have any real possibility of voting you out, but they have a much more potent weapon: if they rebel, it will mean disaster for the entire political system. So it is much better that you pay attention every day to what the people want, thinking all the time that the Mandate of Heaven is not for ever – even though, of course, officially now nobody uses this term.

Mao's successors saw that some of the most destructive aspects of his rule – the famines of the Great Leap Forward, or the chaotic violence of the Cultural Revolution – had brought the country to the brink of yet another uprising. So, on this reading, in the decades following Mao's death they stepped back and took a radically different direction, thus preserving not just their power but their Mandate to rule.

In Britain today the Queen's anointing and the sacramental dimension of her constitutional role are often forgotten. But in Russia and the United States the Christian God now plays a conspicuous part in politics. Both Vladimir Putin and Donald Trump offer themselves to their people as strongmen enjoying the favour of divine power. Putin's supremacy has gone hand in hand with the revival of the Russian Orthodox church, which co-operates with his regime, and of which he is an ostentatious supporter (p. 453). President Trump's inauguration in 2017 was almost a religious festival, with church choirs and multi-religious prayer. 'There should be no fear,' the new American president told the nation. 'We are protected and we will always be protected … by the great men and women of our military and law enforcement. And, most importantly, we will be protected by God.'

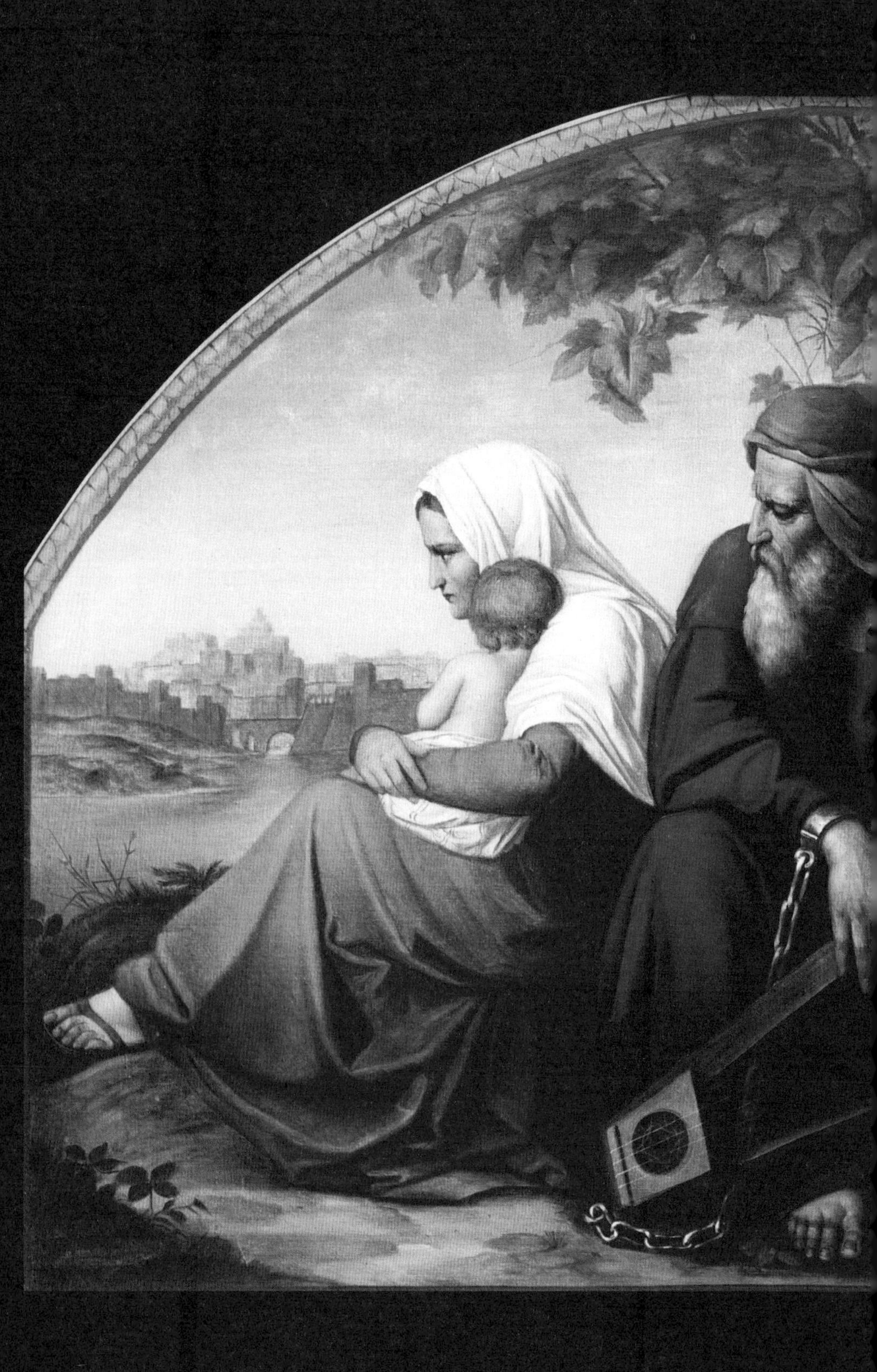

27
THY KINGDOM COME

By the rivers of Babylon –
there we sat down; and there we wept
when we remembered Zion.

Of all the hits in modern pop music, the verses of Psalm 137 must surely be among the most improbable. In 1970 a Jamaican reggae band, the Melodians, turned the lament of the Jews, sighing in captivity for Zion – their lost Jerusalem – into a Rastafarian song of hope. In the process they created one of the most popular of all black spirituals. Initially banned as dangerously subversive by the Jamaican government – until it was pointed out that most of the words came straight from the Bible – its popularity spread, and in 1978 the song, performed by the German group Boney M, topped the charts across Europe. But the concern of the Jamaican government was well founded: religious belief is often subversive, and scripture is rarely about preserving the status quo. Remembering Zion has been a subject not just of song but of political action for over 2,500 years.

In 587 BCE, Nebuchadnezzar, king of Babylon, conquered Jerusalem. He destroyed and plundered the Temple, the supreme

'How shall we sing the Lord's song in a strange land?' The German-Jewish artist Eduard Bendemann paints the exiled, captive Jews by the rivers of Babylon, 1832.

focus of Jewish worship and ritual sacrifice, which had been built and embellished around 400 years earlier by King Solomon. Many thousands of Jews were deported to Babylon, by whose rivers – the canals of the Euphrates – they dreamt of the day when they might return to the land of their fathers and worship in a rebuilt Temple. Until then, they would endure their exile, and repeat the plaintive question of the psalmist: 'How shall we sing the Lord's song in a strange land?' The idea of Zion, a place remembered or imagined where the people of God could properly worship their God free from the tyranny of the powerful, became an enduring strand of Jewish thought, and later of all three Abrahamic faiths.

The songs of the Jews deported to Babylon naturally resonated strongly with African-Caribbean and African-American Christians, themselves descendants of slaves who had been forcibly carried into distant exile, and the black spiritual tradition is profoundly marked by the Hebrew psalms of lament and deliverance (Chapter 10). From the 1930s onwards, Rastafarians went further – they hoped to escape from what they saw as the 'Babylon' of white colonial oppression in ex-slave societies like Jamaica, in order to build a just society in an African Zion more imagined than remembered (Chapter 24).

The hopes of the Jews in exile were fulfilled from an unexpected quarter. In 539 BCE Cyrus, King of Persia, conquered Babylon. He allowed the deported Jews to return in joy to Jerusalem, to rebuild the city, and – even more important – the Temple, where worship and sacrifice resumed. It seemed a miraculous deliverance. Yet the experience of exile left a deep mark, spiritual as well as scriptural. Over millennia Muslims and Christians, like Jews, have continued to dream of living in a land where they can give political expression to their hopes and ideals, where the will of God, as revealed in scripture, will shape society. Most have been content to watch and pray until, in the fullness of time, the kingdom of God arrives on earth. But some have tried to hasten its coming by taking up arms; and in almost every case the attempt has ended in slaughter. That ought not to come as a surprise: imposing the kingdom of God inevitably requires the overthrow of existing structures of power, which are well equipped to fight back. And the last lines of Psalm 137 are chilling reminders that those who seek to establish Zion are often alarmingly eager to see dreadful vengeance visited on those who stand in the way:

O daughter of Babylon, wasted with misery; yea, happy shall he be that rewardeth thee as thou hast served us.

Blessed shall be he that taketh thy children: and throweth them against the stones.

Such blood-curdling violence in the name of faith has been witnessed many times in European history, above all during the Reformation, as zealots on all sides tried to usher in their idea of the kingdom of God. In Geneva and Zurich the radical Reformation sought to turn those cities into new Jerusalems, compelling everyone to be their citizens. In Münster, where the charismatic leader of the Reformers compared himself to King David in Jerusalem, the brutal imposition of a religious and social revolution in anticipation of the Last Days was bloodily put down by the established powers.

As the Jamaican government in 1970 suspected, in such dreams of Zion politics, religion and violence are inseparable. Two objects in the British Museum, one Jewish, one Islamic, tell the human cost of pursuing the kingdom of heaven on earth.

Jerusalem itself, the Zion of song and of longing in Babylon, is perhaps the single most bitterly contested patch of land in human history. The tragic conflicts of today are only the latest phase of a continuum that stretches back over thousands of years and includes British and Babylonians, Arabs, Crusaders, Persians, Egyptians and, most systematically brutal of all, Romans.

By around the year 60 BCE, the Romans had effectively taken control of the area around Jerusalem, a strategic crossroads between Egypt and Persia, and quickly reached an accommodation with the local Jewish authorities, civil and religious. The result was that a puppet Jewish king and the local elite enjoyed wealth and power under a Roman occupation that taxed the people and imposed order; and in the Jewish Temple there were sacrifices and prayers not just to the God of Israel, but for the good of Rome and later for the deified Roman emperors. The Jews were not required actually to worship the emperor, or even to accept his statue in the Temple, but the taxes were of course resented, and some among the Jews felt the purity of their faith had been sullied. Nonetheless, for a hundred years or so, it worked. This is the accommodation explained and defended by Jesus in the gospels, when

The palimpsest of faith: the Temple Mount, Jerusalem, site of the Jewish Temple destroyed by the Romans in 70 CE, with the Dome of the Rock and the Western Wall

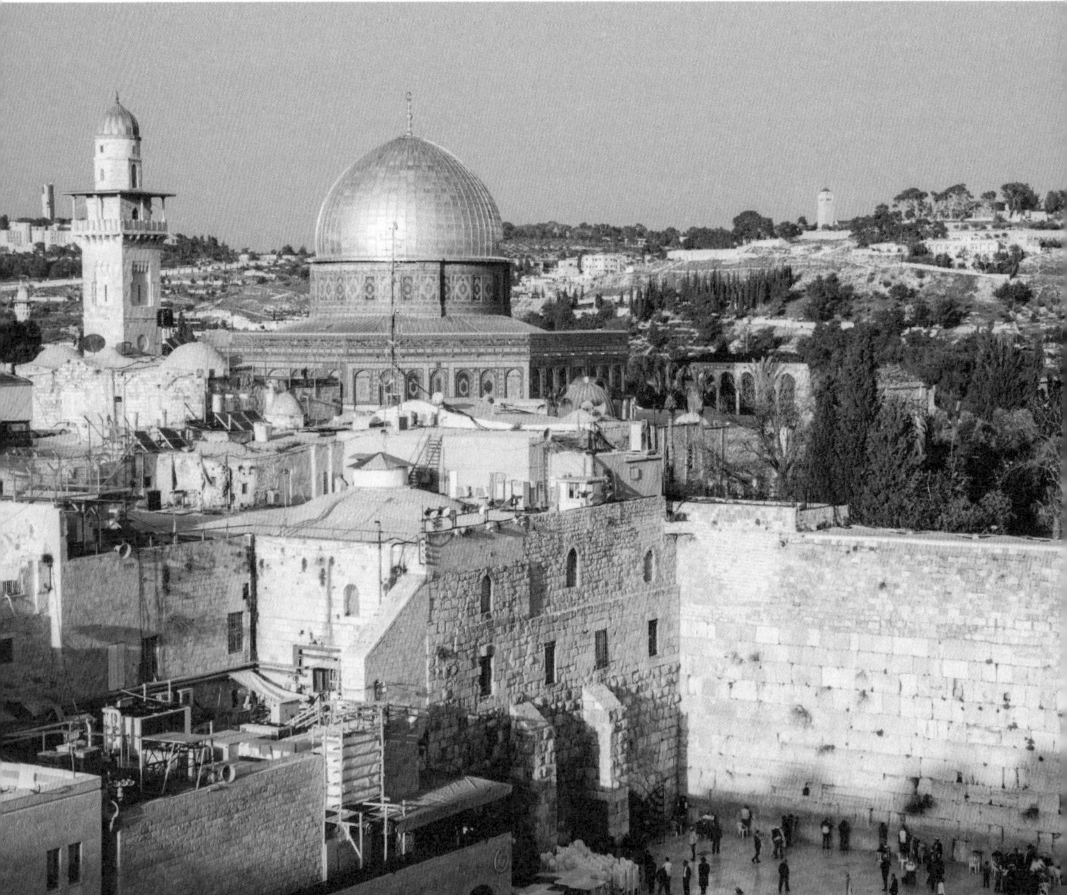

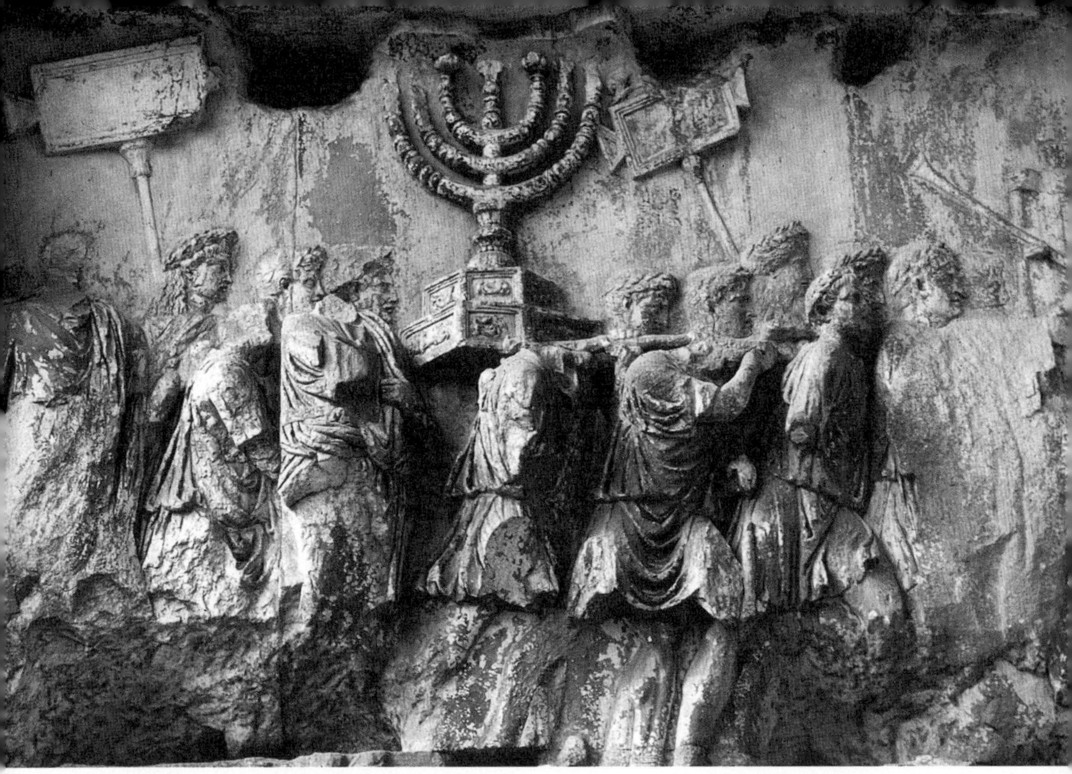

On the Arch of Titus in Rome, Roman soldiers carry the golden menorah plundered from the Temple of Jerusalem, destroyed by the emperor Titus in 70 CE.

he took a Roman coin, showed the emperor's head on it, and told his antagonists to 'render unto Caesar the things that are Caesar's and to God the things that are God's'. In the decades after Jesus' death, thanks largely to incompetent Roman governors and intransigent Jewish leaders, that compromise collapsed.

Another coin, now in the British Museum, tells the tragic consequence of that breakdown. It is a silver shekel, about the size of a ten-pence piece, dating from the 130s CE, which originally also carried the head of Caesar. About seventy years earlier, in 66 CE, a great revolt against Roman military occupation had broken out. It culminated not just in defeat for the Jews, but in what became the defining disaster of their history: the total destruction in the year 70 of the Temple in Jerusalem. Rome's victory over the Jews became for decades a central part of imperial propaganda, an example to all of how effectively the emperor could impose his will on rebellious peoples anywhere.

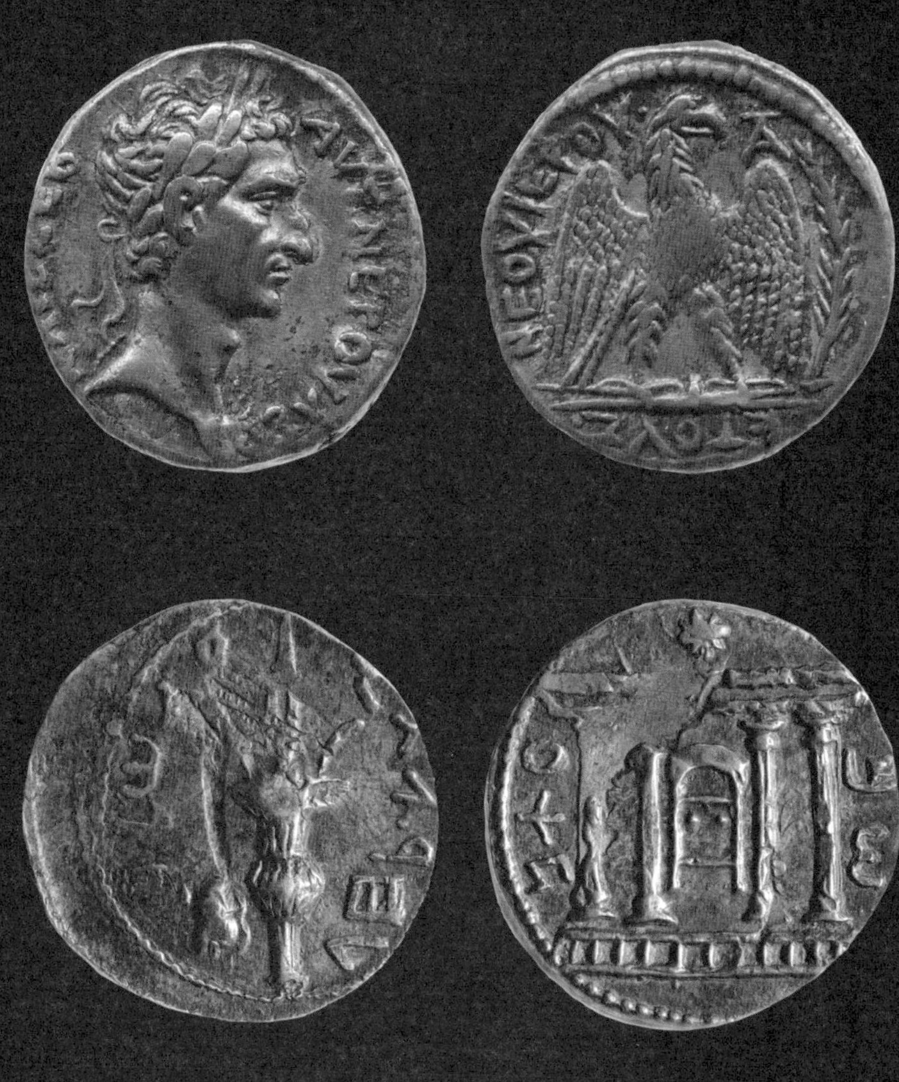

Peace in the province was restored, but the Romans punitively refused to allow the Jews to rebuild the ruined Temple. Instead, they were forced to pay a special tax to expand the temple of Jupiter in Rome. Not surprisingly, hatred for the occupiers simmered on. The last straw was a visit to Judaea in 131 by the emperor Hadrian, who planned to rebuild Jerusalem as a Roman city, and, it was reported, to erect on the desolate ruins of the Jewish Temple a new Roman temple. A second war broke out. The rebel cry went up for an independent state, where Jews could freely worship with the sacrifices and rituals that their scriptures and traditions required. Our coin was struck – clumsily – by the Jewish rebels around 132. It is a rough, powerful statement of the strength of that desire, as Mary Beard, Professor of Classics at the University of Cambridge, explains:

On one side, you have what is clearly an image of the Temple that had been destroyed in the first Jewish revolt. Around the edge you can read the name, written in an early form of Hebrew, of 'Shimon' – one of the revolt's leaders, Simon bar Kokhba.

On the other side we have palm branches in a sort of ceremonial vase, and in the same kind of Hebrew script the words: 'For the liberation of Jerusalem'. So this is a heavily loaded, aggressively propagandist coin, minted by the rebels of that second great revolt.

Aggressively propagandist it may be, but this coin is also a brilliant synthesis of different aspects of Jewish religious and political history, and an inspiring expression of hope. It concentrates all attention on one great symbol: the lost Temple. In between the columns can be seen the stand on which loaves of bread – the 'showbread' – are constantly displayed in the presence of God, as

Stamping out the imperial power: a silver tetradrachm of the Roman emperor Nerva, 97–8 CE (*above*), is transformed by Simon bar Kokhba and the Jewish rebels into a coin for a new Jewish state, *c.*132 CE (*below*)

prescribed in the book of Exodus, reminders of his strengthening presence in his Temple. Here his people would find the sustenance to do his will on earth.

Every Jew handling this coin would know that the building they saw on it, the Temple which in 70 CE the Romans had reduced to rubble, was the second Temple, the one rebuilt after the return from Babylon. And that was in fact the coin's key message: the miracle of deliverance from oppression, and of restoring worship in the Temple, had happened before. The hope of the psalm sung by the rivers of Babylon had been fulfilled for the Jews once: the promise of 'Shimon' – Simon bar Kokhba – and his coin was that it could happen again. The occupier could be driven out. Zion could be restored.

Our rebel shekel is in itself a material assertion that it could be done, for it has been struck over what was originally a Roman coin, a silver tetradrachm. But here there is no head of the emperor. It has been removed. It is just possible to see, under the Temple, traces of the profile of the emperor Nerva. But that too has been obliterated, and replaced by another – 'Shimon'. On the other side the palm branches, which were for the Romans the symbol of their province of Judaea, ringed with the words that convey their new sense: 'For the liberation of Jerusalem'. Defacing the emperor's currency, and inscribing a new political reality on his piece of silver, is a wonderfully public rewriting of the rules. There is no longer a Caesar to whom to render anything. Everybody using the coin could see that Jewish faith had supplanted Roman power.

Dr Guy Stiebel, an archaeologist at Tel Aviv University, points out that the coin offers a prospect which is both distant yet close, in space and in time:

Hadrian had forbidden Jews even to approach the vicinity of Jerusalem, so they could look at the site of the Temple only from a distance. They were close to the core of the nation, but unable to reach it. By the time coins like this were produced, it had been nearly three generations since the destruction of the Temple. What you find on them is people's hopes for redemption, and the resurrection of this holy place.

On the other side of the coin you can see palm branches, which for the Jews symbolized and celebrated their journey from being slaves in Egypt to the promised land of Israel. So, this is not just about the Temple. This is our way back to freedom, back to the Promised Land.

The Jews' escape from slavery in Egypt merges with their return from captivity in Babylon, and is combined with a significant new element: above the Temple is a star. It has been suggested that this might represent a comet sighted in the year 132, and taken by some as an omen of divine support for the rebellion. It seems more likely that it is a reference to its leader: Simon 'bar Kokhba' means 'Son of the Star' in Aramaic, and is a reference to a prophecy in the Book of Numbers, 'there shall come a star out of Jacob'. Many came to regard this charismatic leader and skilled military commander as the Messiah. By all reports he was a devout and ruthless leader. He is alleged to have asked his soldiers to cut off a finger to demonstrate their commitment to the cause, and he showed no mercy to opponents. But bar Kokhba was able for a few short years to give his followers what they dreamt of, a Jewish state, as Guy Stiebel describes:

It was a very, very small state called Beth Israel, which means 'the house of Israel'. And for three and a half years there was an independent, functioning administration. Bar Kokhba authorized and issued his own coins and weights. He controlled the distribution of land. We see him sending letters, ordering people to pay money or dues, threatening to punish them if they do not. He was a strong, competent leader.

Although bar Kokhba and his troops never succeeded in taking Jerusalem, their little state of Beth Israel held out for an astonishing three years against the encircling Roman armies. It is estimated that several hundred thousand died in the course of the war. But the weight of Roman arms and resources proved impossible to resist. After a heroic last stand at the fort of Betar in 135, the revolt was over and bar Kokhba dead.

Hadrian took a coolly calculated revenge. This time, it was not just a single building but a whole culture and its memories that were to be wiped off the map. The Roman province of Judaea, the ancient Jewish kingdom of Judah, was renamed Syria Palestina, suggesting that the land belonged properly to the long-standing enemies of the Jews, the Philistines. 'Jerusalem' simply ceased to exist. The newly built, newly named city, Aelia Capitolina, took its place; and where the Jewish people had once worshipped Jehovah in his Temple, the cult of Jupiter and the Roman emperor was now celebrated. For Romans as for Jews, it had become impossible to separate politics and religion.

Turning the oppressors' coinage into your own propaganda machine is a powerfully symbolic form of rebellion. Creating a flag for the state you hope to found, and then inviting others to fight with you beneath it, is an even more overt challenge to the status quo. Just such a confrontational flag is kept in the African collections of the British Museum: like Simon bar Kokhba's coin, it bears the name of the leader of the revolt, and is a relic of a holy war, waged by a small group of fervent idealists against the superpower of the day – this time, the British.

The flag was designed to lead those struggling in the 1880s to create a pure Islamic state in the area around Khartoum in present-day Sudan. Those who fought under it were inspired and led by Muhammad Ahmad, a leader both religious and political, whom they called the Mahdi, meaning 'the rightly guided one'. Framed in a pale-blue border, this fine white cotton flag carries four lines of boldly appliquéed Arabic script.

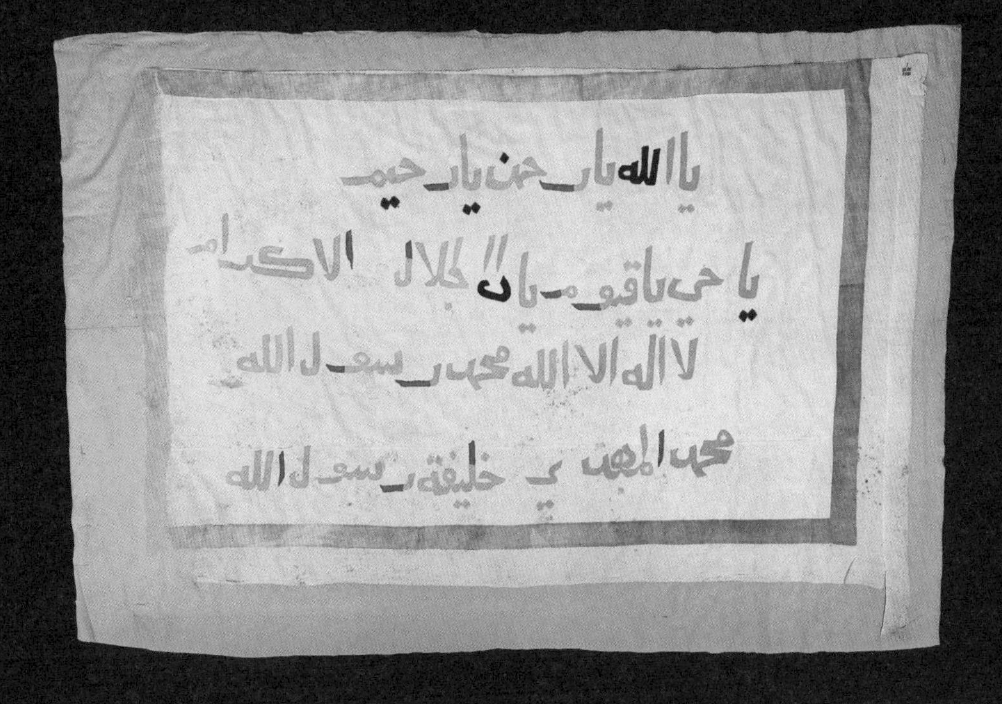

The flag which led the Mahdi's followers in the 1880s, captured by the British at the Battle of Atbara, 1896

Robert Kramer, Professor of History at St Norbert College, Wisconsin, explains:

There are many flags like this still in existence. The words on it are essentially the Mahdist testament of faith. The first line invokes Allah, the Merciful, the Compassionate. The next lines proclaim the second pillar of Islam: 'there is no God but God and Muhammad is his prophet'. And then the followers of the Mahdi have added to that the very significant claim: 'Muhammad Ahmad is the successor to the messenger of God'.

It was as successor to the Prophet himself that Muhammad Ahmad, the Mahdi, son of a boat-builder, mystic and ascetic, led his people in a great insurgency.

By the late nineteenth century, the Sudan had become a flash-point in international power politics. The north was ruled from

Egypt, technically part of the Turkish Ottoman Empire. But in 1882 Egypt had been occupied by the British, who along with the French were determined to protect their interests in the Suez Canal, opened in 1869 and already a key artery in the imperial economic system. The two European powers imposed their will, and their cosmopolitan values, not just on a complaisant Egyptian government, but on the whole society, from Alexandria to Khartoum, with the result described by Robert Kramer:

Muhammad Ahmad was so convincing and compelling because he appeared at a time when Sudan was under a very corrupt and inefficient form of rule by the Turko-Egyptians, who were also imposing a more legalistic and less ascetic form of Islam than the Sudanese were used to. To make matters worse, the Egyptian government was employing to act on its behalf a number of Christian administrators from Europe, who were frankly regarded as infidels.

The Sudanese saw corrupt cosmopolitan or foreign authorities taxing them unjustly, and undermining the traditional practice of their faith. Like the Jews of second-century Jerusalem, they longed for a messiah. And, like them, they were offered one. Robert Kramer continues:

Among the Hadiths, the oral traditions of the prophet Muhammad, is one that says that after him there would be twelve reformers of the faith; then a thirteenth, who would be the man sent by God to prepare the world for the end times. Muhammad Ahmad made his claim exactly when the thirteenth century of the Islamic calendar came to an end. His timing was impeccable, and he was in exactly the right place in terms of the conditions in the Sudan.

On 29 June 1881 in our calendar, Muhammad Ahmad proclaimed himself the Mahdi, the messianic redeemer of Islam, appointed by an assembly of the prophets to restore unity to the faithful across the world, and to bring in the end of time. He called his followers to an austere life of Qur'anic study and prayer – and summoned them to battle against the infidel.

The uniform of this people's army was itself a symbol of the values for which they were fighting: it was based on the jubba, a beggar's tunic, made of rags and patches, which had been for centuries the dress of Sufi religious orders – ascetic mystics – and signified their contempt for worldly goods. One such jubba is also in the British Museum. It is made of pale cotton, in a simple kaftan shape, with blue and red squares stitched on to it that at first sight look like mending. But the air of poverty is an affectation. The expensive cotton is of very high quality, and the squares have been

The jubba that belonged to Uthman Diqna, a beggar's tunic reinvented as an elegant uniform

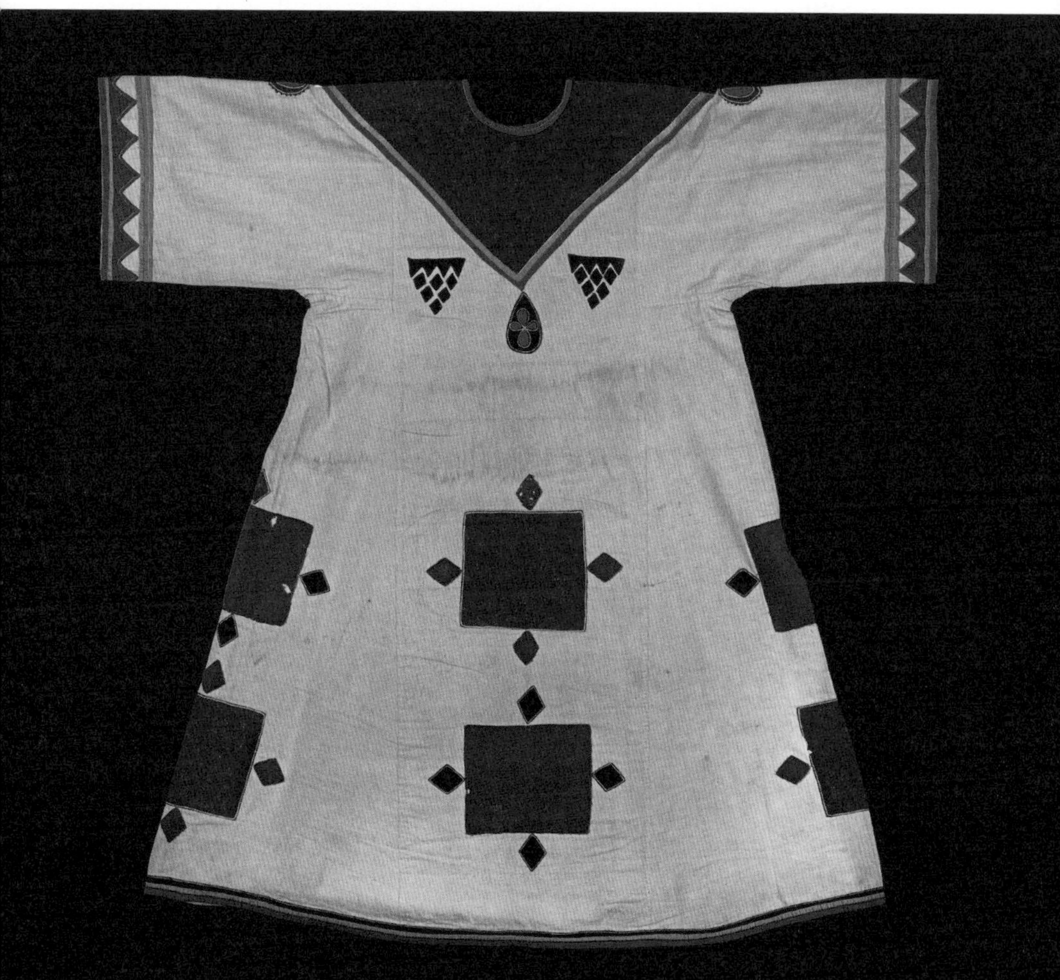

sewn on meticulously with almost invisible stitching. Round the edges, however, have been added crude, black stitches, designed to make the trim squares look like rough patches. This is no beggar's garment, but an expertly made uniform: it belonged to one of the Mahdi's commanders, Uthman Diqna, who fought in north-east Sudan. In the Mahdi's army, everybody strove to look alike – a statement of shared commitment to the cause, and of equality before God. So a powerful officer dressed like a wandering religious beggar – though, in this case, a distinctly elegant one.

It was this army of beggars poor and rich, and which also contained many slaves, that in 1885 startled the world by taking Khartoum. They inflicted a resounding and humiliating defeat not just on the Turkish-Egyptians but on their British allies led by General Gordon, who died as the city fell, quickly becoming a martyr hero to the British public. The Mahdi and his army had triumphed over the foreign infidel. Muhammad Ahmad was soon hard at work preparing for the worldwide triumph of Islam, at which point all conflict would cease. Among other things, he wrote to Queen Victoria, inviting her to convert and become one of his followers. Her reaction is alas lost to history.

Six months later the Mahdi unexpectedly died. He was forty years old. For thirteen years, his successor, Abdallahi ibn Muhammad, who called himself the Khalifa – the Caliph – managed to forge and to rule a Sudanese state which sought to return to a pure form of Islam. The global messianic dream had become a local political reality – but it was a closely controlled and heavily militarized one, because the new state was under constant threat from the colonial powers that surrounded it. An offer from the emperor of Ethiopia of an alliance against the European aggressors was rejected – the Islamic state would not fight with Christian allies (Chapter 24). In 1896 an Anglo-Egyptian force, armed with modern machine guns and led by General Kitchener, marched south from Egypt. On 2 September 1898 at the Battle of Omdurman, just north of Khartoum, over 12,000 Mahdists were killed and 13,000 wounded. Kitchener's better-armed forces (which included the young Winston Churchill) lost only forty-seven men. Our cotton flag had already been captured in battle in 1896 by Captain Goyede Smith, commanding the 45th Sikhs of the Indian Army. The jubba was acquired by a British official some time after Omdurman as a souvenir. The dream of the Mahdi and his followers was over. The Khalifa's state was dismantled and from 1898 until 1956 the Sudan was administered by the British.

Nevertheless, the Mahdi's descendants and those of his closest followers are today among the most influential families in Sudanese society and politics. Robert Kramer describes what the legacy of Muhammad Ahmad now means:

In Omdurman the Mahdi's tomb has been a focal point for Sudanese Muslims for over a hundred years and continues to be a place

Battle of Omdurman, 2 September 1898, where British troops defeated the Mahdist army on the Nile near Khartoum

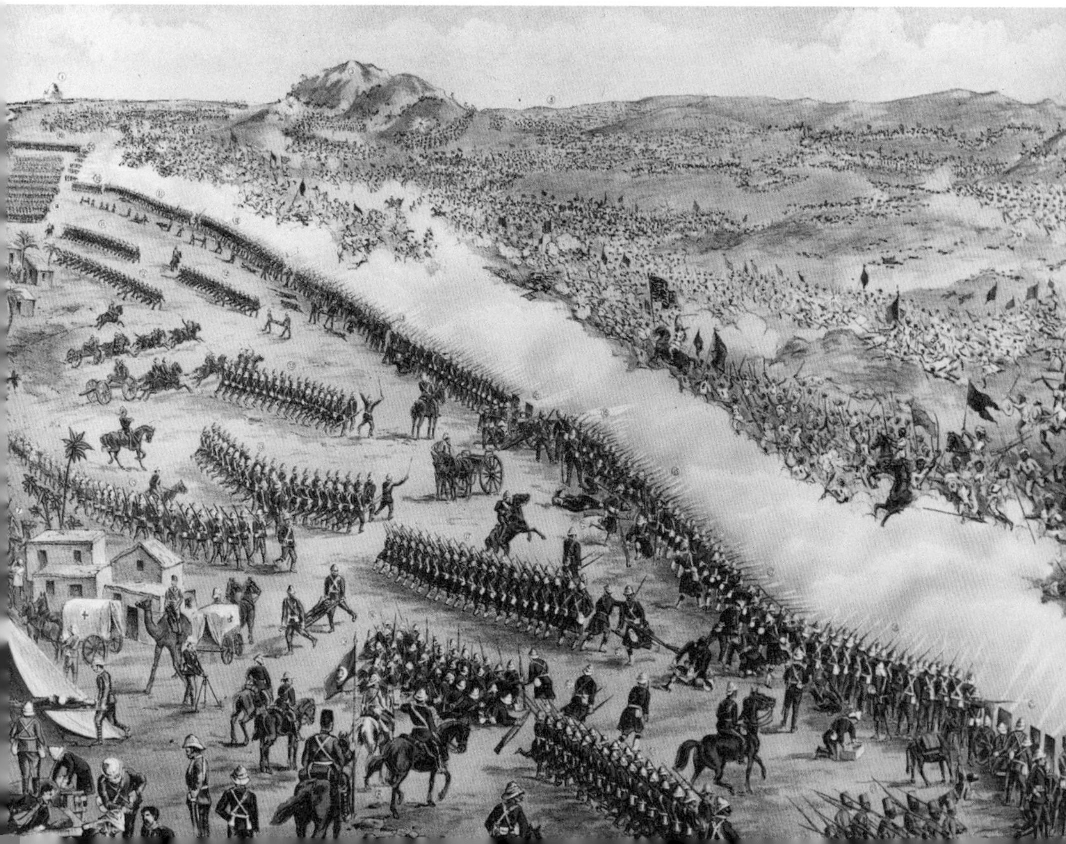

of pilgrimage and worship for Sudanese Muslims. Whether they believe that he really was the divinely guided one, sent by God to prepare the world for Judgement Day is almost irrelevant. His legacy has been resolved into something else. He is a guide to correct Islamic practice and a source of blessedness for Sudanese people.

The idea of an inherently Islamic Sudanese state, realized for thirteen years, has never disappeared: it underlay much of the civil war that plagued Sudan from 1956 until the ultimate secession of

The tomb of the Mahdi at Omdurman, severely damaged by shelling during the campaign of 1898, is now a place of pilgrimage for Sudanese Muslims.

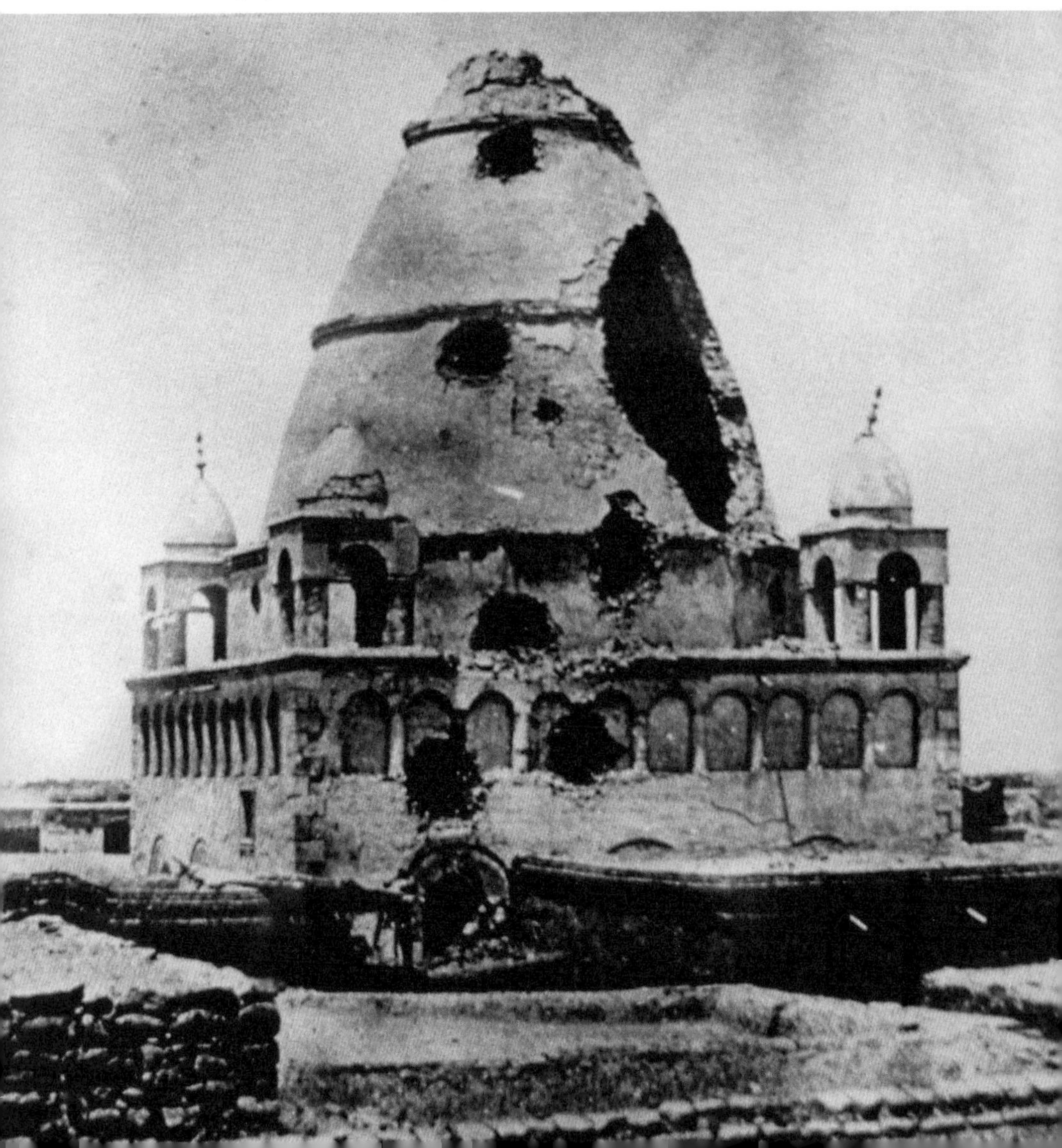

South Sudan in 2011, and still drives much of Sudanese politics today. The rhetoric of the Mahdi and his followers and their call to arms against Western infidels corrupting the purity of Islam has resonated in recent years with deadly effect across much of the Middle East.

Bar Kokhba's revolt has also cast a long shadow. Betar, the fort at which he made his last stand, was the name taken by young Latvian Zionists in Riga in 1923, when they founded a new militant movement. Betar played a key part in recruiting forces first to fight against the Nazis, and then, emulating bar Kokhba's soldiers, to wage a guerrilla war against British and Arabs in Palestine, in the struggle to establish an independent state of Israel. After 1948, Simon bar Kokhba was adopted by many in the new state as the model of a strong leader prepared to fight even a superpower.

Both the revolts we have looked at in this chapter were fuelled by local, religious anger at the behaviour of a corrupt elite working with a foreign occupying force, and both fused religion and politics to great military effect. Both speak to the unique power of the appeal of building an ideal state, where all can lead a godly life and fulfil the promises of scripture. Both also exemplify the violence and suffering to which those endeavours seem inescapably to lead.

In Chapter 30, we shall look at a different narrative of destruction and renewal, based not on achieving an enduring state of ideal purity, but on embracing a cycle of endless transience.

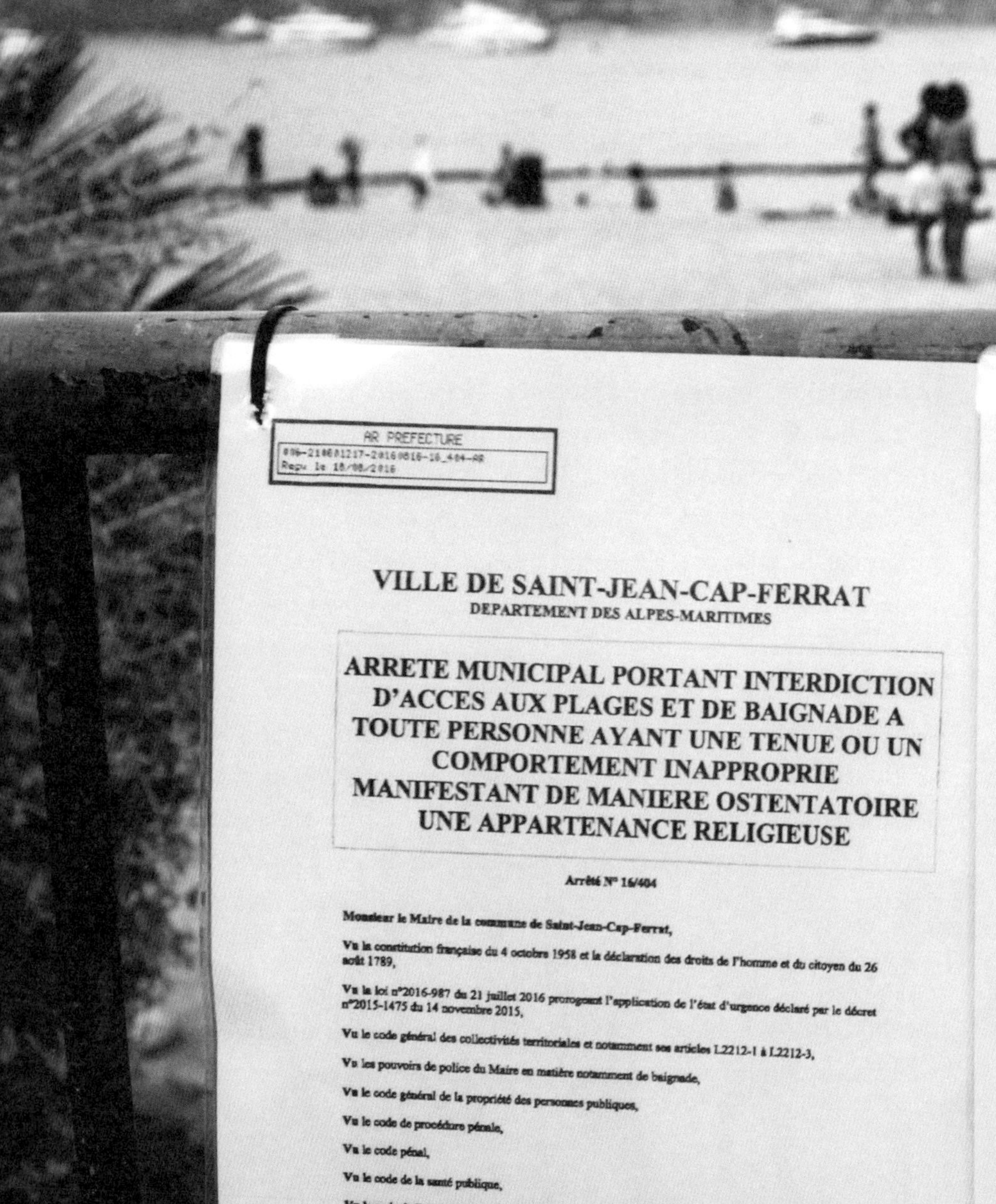

AR PREFECTURE

VILLE DE SAINT-JEAN-CAP-FERRAT

DEPARTEMENT DES ALPES-MARITIMES

ARRETE MUNICIPAL PORTANT INTERDICTION D'ACCES AUX PLAGES ET DE BAIGNADE A TOUTE PERSONNE AYANT UNE TENUE OU UN COMPORTEMENT INAPPROPRIE MANIFESTANT DE MANIERE OSTENTATOIRE UNE APPARTENANCE RELIGIEUSE

Arrêté N° 16/404

Monsieur le Maire de la commune de Saint-Jean-Cap-Ferrat,

Vu la constitution française du 4 octobre 1958 et la déclaration des droits de l'homme et du citoyen du 26 août 1789,

Vu la loi n°2016-987 du 21 juillet 2016 prorogeant l'application de l'état d'urgence déclaré par le décret n°2015-1475 du 14 novembre 2015,

Vu le code général des collectivités territoriales et notamment ses articles L2212-1 à L2212-3,

Vu les pouvoirs de police du Maire en matière notamment de baignade,

Vu le code général de la propriété des personnes publiques,

Vu le code de procédure pénale,

Vu le code pénal,

Vu le code de la santé publique,

Vu le code de l'environnement,

Vu l'arrêté préfectoral du 24 avril 1997 réglementant l'organisation de la sécurité des plages, baignades et activités nautiques sur le littoral des Alpes-Maritimes et ses annexes,

Vu les arrêtés préfectoraux du 6 août 2013 portant attribution de la concession des plages naturelles et artificielles à la commune de Saint-Jean-Cap-Ferrat,

Considérant la forte fréquentation des plages de la ville de Saint-Jean-Cap-Ferrat durant la période estivale,

1

28

TURNING THE SCREW

For over a hundred years, fashionable sun lovers have flocked to the beaches of the French Riviera. Over those hundred years bathing costumes have become steadily skimpier, sometimes disappearing altogether, to the delight – or disapproval – of others on the beach. Every now and then, though ever less frequently, the police have intervened, declaring that 'Un outrage aux bonnes moeurs', an affront to decency, has occurred. But if, in the summer of 2016, you had risked wearing a particular kind of swimsuit on a number of Riviera beaches, including Cannes, St-Jean-Cap-Ferrat or Villeneuve-Loubet, you might well have found the state stepping in to stop you – police warning you against the disrespect you were showing not just towards the 'bonnes moeurs' of proper behaviour, but also towards *laïcité* – the principle of secularism enshrined in the French constitution since the early twentieth century.

All this, not because you were wearing too little – because you were wearing *too much*. The bathing costumes causing the fuss were burkinis – full-body swimsuits, intended for women who want to observe Islamic modesty codes while on the beach or in

Banned from the beach: the municipal authorities forbid on the beach any behaviour or clothing which demonstrates religious allegiance, French Riviera, 2016.

the sea. They were originally designed in Australia, but rapidly became popular among Islamic women in Europe. In most countries, they attracted little attention. But in August 2016, when France was struggling to come to terms with several terrorist attacks, a number of towns on the Côte d'Azur invoked the law to prevent women – they were of course all Muslim women – from wearing them on local beaches. It quickly became much more than a local issue: French national politicians queued up to support the restriction and to insist that, beyond the bathing costume, a fundamental constitutional principle was at stake. Wearing the burkini, it was declared, was not compatible with French values. In the words of the then Prime Minister: 'The burkini is not a fashion – it is the expression of a political project, a counter-society.'

The rest of Europe was bewildered. How could wearing a supremely modest swimsuit, designed in Australia, be seriously considered a step towards a 'counter-society', or cause such a constitutional storm? The answer, of course, is that – as the Prime Minister said – it had little to do with clothes, and really was about politics; more specifically, it was about the collision of politics with faith. The point at issue was the public demonstration of religious allegiance in a French state which has for over a hundred years defined itself as exclusively and uniformly secular.

Behind that, however, lies another more general question: how do states with a clear view of what constitutes national identity accommodate – or oppress – a minority faith seeking publicly to assert its distinctiveness? To look at that question, I want to start not on the beaches of the French Riviera in 2016, but in seventeenth-century Japan.

*

Christianity has been forbidden for many years.
If you see someone suspicious, you must report them.
Rewards will be given as follows:

For handing over a priest – 500 pieces of silver
For handing over a monk – 300 pieces of silver
For someone who has returned to their Christian faith – 100 pieces of silver
For reporting someone who shelters Christians, or is an ordinary believer, you may be paid up to 500 pieces of silver, depending on their importance

The Magistrate, 1st day, 5th month, Tenna 2.
It is hereby ordered and must be strictly observed in this territory.

These chilling words, written in Japanese, are painted in black ink on a crudely made wooden noticeboard, almost a metre wide, with a little gabled 'roof' to protect the writing from the rain. The era of 'Tenna', or Heavenly Imperial Peace, began in Japan in September 1681, so this inscription dates from early 1682. As Tim Clark, Head of the Japanese section at the British Museum, explains:

It is a typical public noticeboard of the period, called a kusatsu in Japanese, and it is part of a system that had been used by the central government – or Shogunate – since the early seventeenth century to enforce its regulations throughout the whole country. There were hundreds of such noticeboards all over Japan, typically located at the approaches to bridges and along public highways, where large numbers would see them – rather like hoardings beside a modern motorway. They carry prohibitions against behaviour deemed to be a threat to the state, such as counterfeiting

Over: Japanese noticeboard offering substantial rewards to anybody denouncing or turning in Christians, 1682

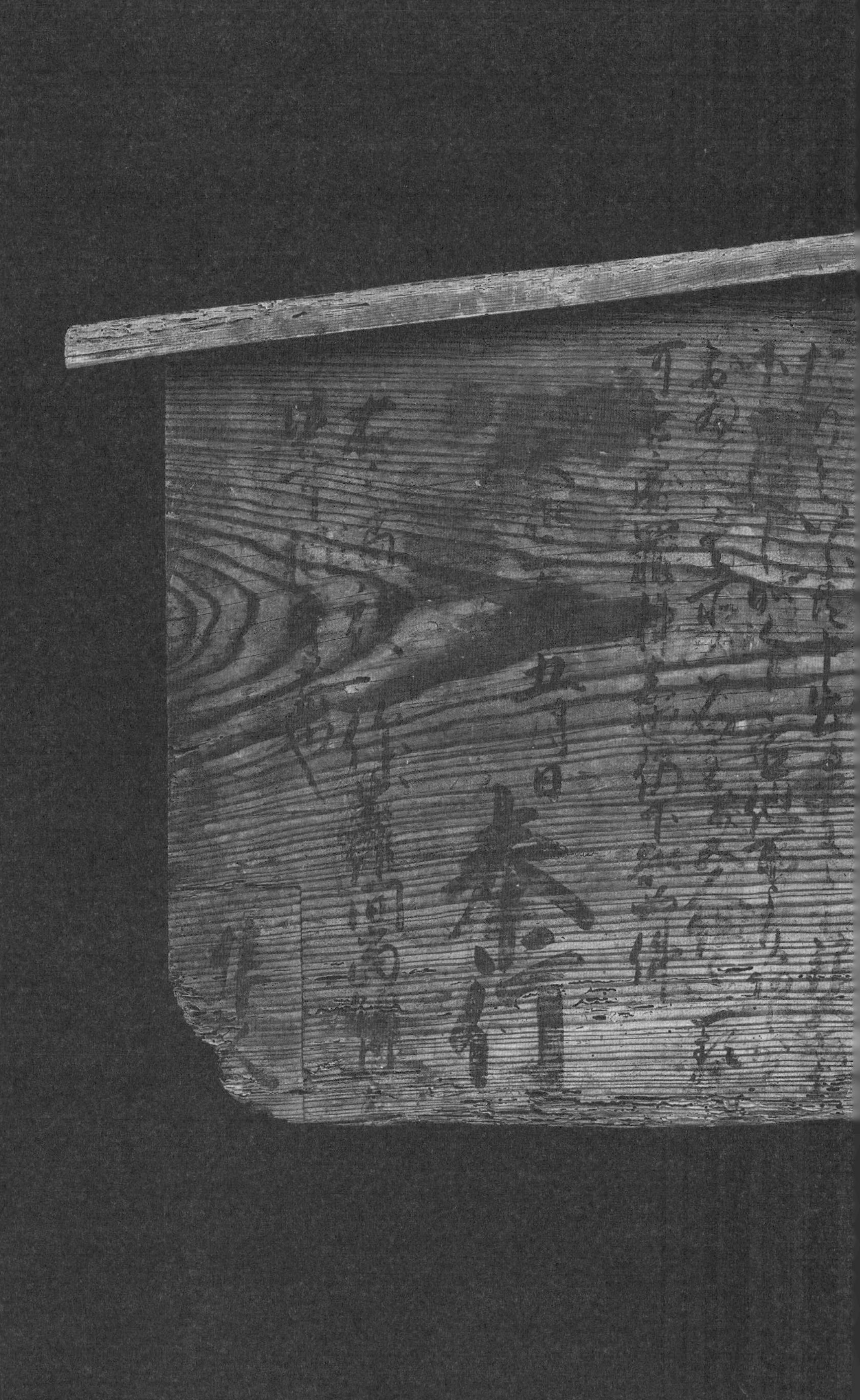
奉行

currency, peddling fake medicines or poisons, and so on – or, as here, against sheltering anyone connected to Christianity.

What was it about Christians that led the Japanese state to see them as a dangerous 'counter-society', a threat to the state that could properly be condemned alongside poisons and counterfeit currency?

By 1600, Japan was home to a surprisingly large number of Christians: around 300,000, out of a total population estimated to be 12 million, the great majority of whom practised a particularly Japanese mixture of Buddhism and traditional Shintoism (Chapter 18). The increasing number of Christians worried the state authorities, but the 'threat' from Christianity went much deeper.

Christianity had entered Japan in 1543 with a group of Jesuit missionaries led by Francis Xavier, travelling on Portuguese trading ships carrying all kinds of European goods, not least guns. The Portuguese merchant venturers and Christian missionaries arrived at a critical time in Japanese history, when the country was in the grip of civil war, split between rival regional rulers. Tim Clark

On a Japanese seventeenth-century folding screen, a Portuguese trade ship arrives in Nagasaki, carrying European goods and Jesuit missionaries. After unloading, the Europeans are taken to kneel before the local ruler (*top right*).

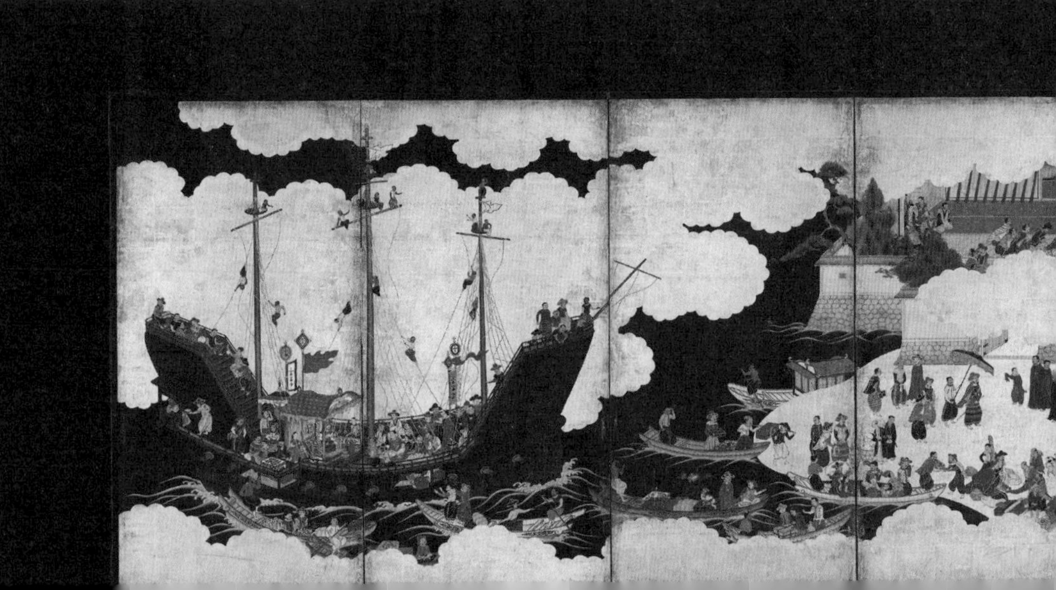

describes how eventually, towards the end of the century, Japan was once again united under a strong central government. Portuguese rifles, and Japanese copies of them, had played a significant part in making that happen:

Nagasaki, the main port in south-west Japan, became the centre of Portuguese trade, in guns and much else, and also of Catholic missionary activity. In due course the entire city was effectively ceded to the Jesuits. Many rulers in the area converted to Christianity, sometimes for their own personal pious reasons, sometimes with an eye to the profits of trading with the Portuguese. They would normally then ensure that all their subjects also became Christian, through mass baptisms, with tens of thousands of people converting at the same time. For the newly established central government, still uncertain of its authority, these territories, controlled by prosperous Christian convert rulers, came to be seen as an alternative, and very dangerous, power base, a threat which simply could not be tolerated.

By the end of the 1500s the Jesuits based in Nagasaki had also become a force to be reckoned with. They were setting up schools and preaching persuasively to the powerful. Disturbingly, they clearly looked for ultimate authority not to any person or system inside Japan, but across water and land all the way to Rome – and from there to a God apparently hostile to the traditional deities of Japanese Buddhism and Shinto. This alien allegiance had dramatic local consequences, especially in the region around Nagasaki. One prominent Christian ruler, for example, Ômura Sumitada, who took the name Dom Bartolomeu on his conversion in 1563, a few years later ordered the destruction of all the Buddhist temples and Shinto shrines within the area over which he held sway.

Two years later, in 1565, a large group of islands south-west of Japan was invaded and claimed in the name of the Spanish king. The fate of the 'Philippines' seemed to offer the Japanese a disturbing warning, says Tim Clark: the Christian Bible is likely to be followed by the Spanish sword:

Christianity posed a complex threat to the Japanese leaders, concerned above all to hold the state together. They were working on a knife-edge. Native Japanese religion, initially Shinto (the worship of the traditional kami gods of Japan) and then latterly Buddhist, had by this point been well established in Japan for at least a thousand years, a major unifying force. The two traditions had managed to co-exist by finding equivalent deities in each other's pantheons, leading to a kind of syncretic belief in both religions at once (see Chapter 18). *To the Japanese way of thinking, Christianity was very intransigent. Unsurprisingly to us, but shockingly to the Japanese, it would not accept the Buddhist or the Shinto deities as being equivalents – or avatars – of the Christian god and saints: instead, it declared itself in possession of the only truth. I think ultimately this meant that Christianity was in a philosophical way seen as incompatible with Japanese culture.*

Soon enough, these twin worries, about aggressively intransigent missionaries and the uncertain allegiances of their Japanese Christian converts, combined to inspire acts of repressive violence. Hideyoshi, the general who in 1590 had effectively made himself supreme in a unified Japan, crushed local opposition, banished Christian missionaries from his territories, and described Japan as 'the land of the gods', meaning the 'national' gods of the Shinto and Buddhist tradition.

In 1597 twenty-six Christians were put to death in Nagasaki, all crucified, in a macabre and brilliantly stage-managed public spectacle, whose attention to detail included piercing their sides with spears. The massacre was widely publicized in Europe, where

The Franciscan Martyrs of Nagasaki. On 5 February 1597, twenty-six Christians were publicly crucified by the Japanese authorities. This engraving by Jacques Callot, 1627, shows only the twenty-three Franciscans: the Jesuits are not included.

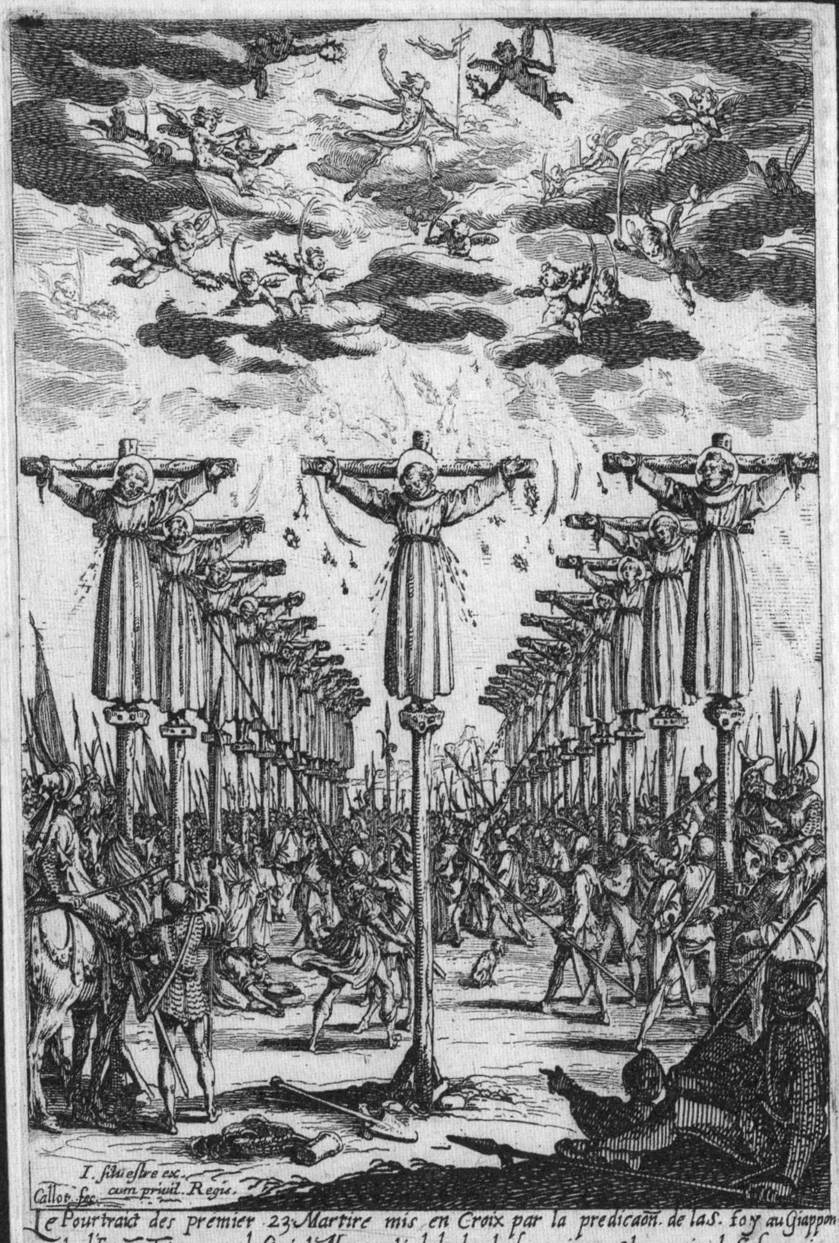
I. silvestre ex.
Callot fec. cum privil. Regis.
Le Pourtraict des premier 23 Martire mis en Croix par la predicaon. de la S. foy au Giappon
soubs l'Empe. Taicosam en la Cite de Mongasachi, de lordre des freres mineurs Obseruantin de S. Francois.

Jesuits and Franciscans were engaged in bitter conflict with the Protestants, and proudly proclaimed the courage and faith of Catholic martyrs on the far side of the world.

Thereafter, the pace of prosecution quickened. In 1614 Christianity was officially prohibited in Japan. Churches were demolished or converted into temples. In 1639 the Portuguese – and with them the Catholic clergy they protected – were expelled. The exclusive right to trade with Europe was given instead to the Protestant Dutch, who were delighted to see Catholic Spaniards and Portuguese discomfited, and were happy to trade (extremely profitably) without meddling in matters religious. Nagasaki became Japan's only point of contact with the world beyond Asia. All other ports were closed to foreign ships.

The Catholic priests had gone. The church, as a church, no longer existed. But to ensure the complete eradication of the alien faith, the state went even further. Anybody suspected of being a secret Christian was obliged – on pain of death – to appear in a nearby Buddhist temple. There, in order to demonstrate that they

Left: Stamping out the foreign faith: painting on silk showing the annual *fumi-e* loyalty test. Nagasaki, Japan, 1820s. *Right*: Bronze *fumi-e* with an image of the Crucifixion, worn away by those who trod on it to prove they had renounced Christianity

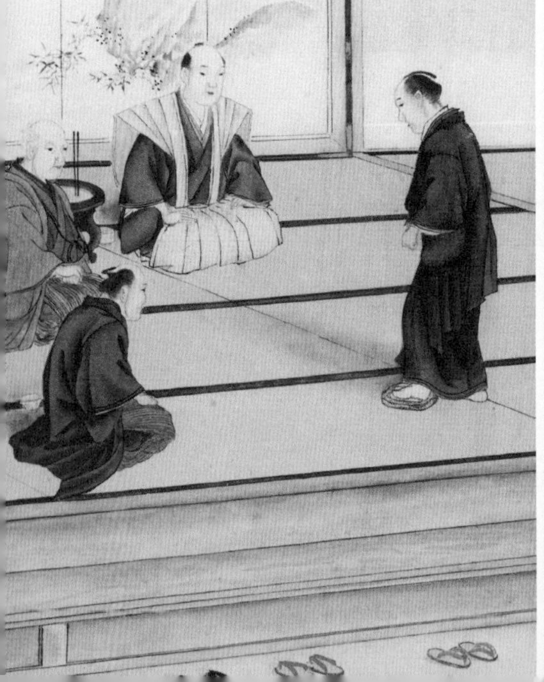

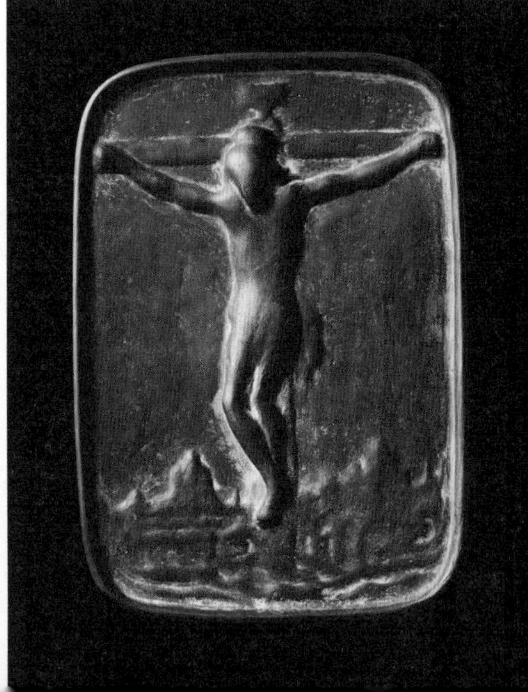

were no longer part of the forbidden sect, they had publicly to abjure their faith, and stamp on a small plaque carrying the sculpted image of Christ or the Virgin Mary. Some of these *fumi-e*, literally 'stamp-images', have survived. They are, I think, inexpressibly poignant. In the history of art, they form an almost unique category: images of real quality made explicitly to be humiliated and destroyed. Based on Flemish or Italian engravings, frequently sculpted by Japanese artists, they show scenes of Christ's life and Passion, still just legible, but almost worn away by the feet of those forced to desecrate them: faint remains of a faith wiped out.

This systematic persecution was, not surprisingly, extremely effective. By the 1660s there were virtually no publicly practising Christians left in the main part of Japan; and those who continued to pray in secret hardly posed even a notional threat. So when in 1682 the state issued the edicts painted on our noticeboard, they were aiming at a foe already long vanquished. Why? Tim Clark explains:

Christianity remained a useful symbolic enemy, a hypothetical danger which the central government could deploy to its advantage as an instrument of social control. Even though there were in effect no Christians left in the country, it was important for the authorities to insist that they had to inspect all books coming into Japan, so that they could excise any references or imagery associated with the Christian faith. This justified a censorship system and a tight grip on all overseas contacts, which served very well to keep control over many other aspects of society.

So the creation and posting of boards like this was not really about banning something – it was about demonstrating the *power* to ban something. These edict-boards doubled as propaganda for a new, centralized Japanese state and its rulers. You now live in a country – says this board – that possesses the legitimacy and the manpower to banish foreigners from its shores. It is in a position to keep a very close eye on you and everything you do.

This, in other words, was a state not so much protecting itself against outside threat, as asserting its control over its own people by doubling down on the already defeated. This was now the natural order, social, spiritual and political. To be Japanese was to live in the land of the traditional gods, and there was no room in it for a deviant sect like Christianity, which originated from abroad.

The edicts stayed in force and were regularly reissued for nearly 200 years, and the assumptions behind them have continued to influence Japanese habits of thought down to the present. People were still being punished, and indeed executed, for being Christian when Commander Matthew Perry arrived in the Bay of Tokyo in a US warship in 1853 and forced, this time with American guns, the opening of Japanese ports, and minds, to the world.

In the 1690s, a few years after the edicts urging the Japanese to denounce fellow citizens whom they suspected of still being Christian, Sébastien Leclerc, the most celebrated engraver of his day in Paris, began work on a print of the *Destruction of the Huguenot Temple* (or church) at Charenton, a few miles east of Paris. The church, erected in the 1620s, was the work of Salomon de Brosse, architect of the Luxembourg Palace in Paris. It was the most prominent Protestant church in France, renowned across Europe for its generous congregational space, perfectly shaped for preaching. It had been widely admired by Jewish and Protestant architects, and among other buildings had inspired two great synagogues in Amsterdam and Christopher Wren's church of St James's, Piccadilly, in London. In October 1685, on the orders of Louis XIV, de Brosse's sober masterpiece was razed to the ground.

Leclerc's engraving is a disturbing work of art. He animates and agitates his composition with abrupt shifts from bright, blank white to heavily hatched darkness. The ordered classical columns and galleries on the left are reduced to a dense heap of rubble in the centre. Large numbers of workmen hack and haul with

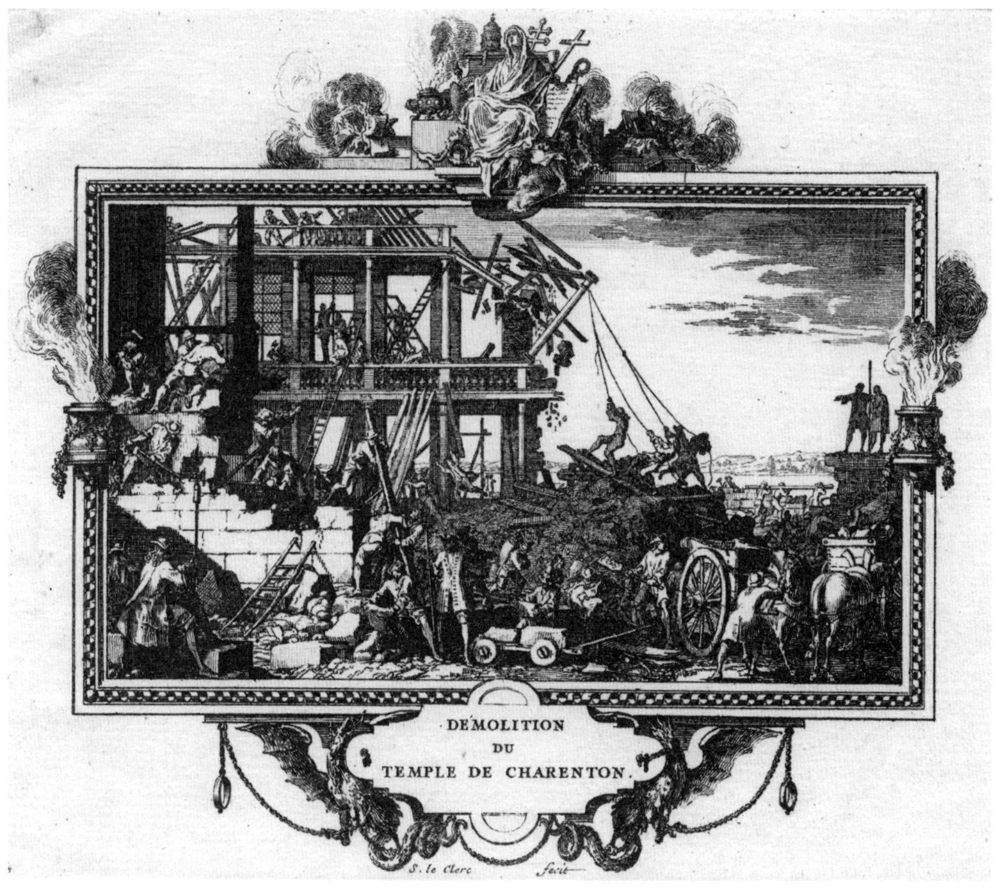

One of the King's Little Conquests: Sébastien Leclerc's engraving of the destruction of the Protestant church at Charenton after the Revocation of the Edict of Nantes in 1685

brio: walls are demolished, beams brought down, and columns and window frames carried off as spoil. The detail of this work of boisterous destruction is eerily legible – frenzy recorded with precision. At bottom left a soldier holding a halberd calmly monitors progress, while, on the right, two figures in silhouette point to a brightening sky. With consummate mastery a great engraver celebrates the destruction of a great piece of architecture.

Like the Japanese noticeboard, this engraving is part of a series. It is one of Leclerc's *Petites Conquêtes du Roi*, the 'Little Conquests of the King', a series of eight engravings produced around 1690 to celebrate the achievements of Louis XIV. As you might expect, there is also a larger-format series called *Les Grandes Conquêtes du*

Roi, showing the king's many victories over the enemies of France. The years around 1690 were the military and diplomatic high point of Louis XIV's reign, the culmination of twenty-five years of almost constant aggressive warfare against the Habsburgs and their allies. For the first time in over a century, France was now secure against attack, and militarily supreme in Europe. These two magnificent series of prints are effectively state propaganda – we know that Leclerc was paid by the royal household while producing the *Grandes Conquêtes*. Every image is clearly labelled to identify the event being celebrated, and framed with abundant allegorical detail reflecting on the action. Leclerc's engravings allow the viewer fortunate enough to own them (they were expensive collectors' items) to look with informed wonder and visual delight at the feats of the self-styled Sun King.

Six of the *Petites Conquêtes* are what you would expect: scenes of battles, mostly against Austrians, Spaniards and Dutch, on the northern and eastern frontiers of France. But two celebrate other kinds of victories. One is the reception at Versailles in 1686 of the ambassadors of Siam, a great diplomatic coup, which opened a new avenue for French foreign policy in the Far East. The other is the demolition of the temple at Charenton, a 'victory' a few miles from the capital, this time over the king's own loyal Protestant subjects.

The religious Reformations of the sixteenth century had transformed Western and Central Europe from a region of broadly uniform belief and practice into one of shifting and competing denominations. And that led to a profound, indeed existential political question: could any European state, for centuries structured and sustained by shared Catholic religious practice, continue to function when people within it believed radically different things and could no longer worship together? Could a house divided against itself stand? In France that tension led to a generation of civil war between Roman Catholics and Calvinist Protestants, which by the 1590s had cost countless lives and devastated the country. France had to find an answer. That answer finally came when Henry IV issued the Edict of Nantes in 1598.

France's Protestants – the Huguenots – were allowed to practise their faith, subject to many restrictions, and were given guarantees to protect their rights. The Edict of Nantes brought peace, and with it a stability that allowed the French crown to start rebuilding the state. In a process strikingly similar to Japan's, the bloody civil wars of the sixteenth century were followed in the seventeenth by the establishment of an ever more authoritarian centralized power, insistently claiming to defend the traditional faith. And, in both countries, in the 1680s that power was asserted against a small and weak religious minority.

The Edict of Nantes was toleration of a sort, but it left Huguenots essentially with the status of unwelcome guests – or guests who would, if one waited long enough, eventually come round to the right way of thinking and return to the Catholic fold. By the early 1680s Louis XIV was prepared to wait no longer. He showed the Huguenots what it was like to have unwelcome guests, by billeting his troops in their homes. The soldiers terrorized and impoverished the Huguenot families and wrecked their houses. The only way to avoid ruin was to convert to Catholicism. It was the culmination of a long campaign of harassment over decades. The civil rights of Huguenots had been steadily eroded, professions closed to them and pensions withheld. Large numbers abandoned their faith or emigrated.

In consequence, the Protestants had effectively been broken as any kind of coherent force by the time that Louis took the final step on 22 October 1685 and revoked the Edict altogether. By that act, the practice of the Protestant faith was declared illegal, all Huguenot civil rights were withdrawn, their clergy were to be subject to the death penalty, and their churches demolished.

The destruction of the Charenton temple began the next day. The Revocation of the Edict of Nantes was one of the most popular decisions of Louis's long reign.

Professor Robert Tombs of the University of Cambridge thinks this explains the number of people to be seen at work in Leclerc's engraving:

It is as if this is in a sense not an act of the state, but an act of the people, who have been permitted by the king's revocation of the decree to vent their hatred of Protestantism. There was widespread popular participation in wrecking Huguenot churches, and in desecrating Protestant cemeteries: the king in this sense was giving free rein to the sectarianism within the kingdom, an absolute monarch playing the populist card.

If this reading is right, there is a disturbing echo here of the destruction of the mosque at Ayodhya (Chapter 25), where the state also appears to have stepped aside and left the people to carry out the work of destruction. And as in India, says Robert Tombs, the French decision was made with an eye to international politics.

Louis is claiming to be the Rex Christianissimus, 'le roi très chrétien', the title always assumed by the French monarchy to demonstrate that it – and France – were, in another famous phrase, the 'eldest daughter of the church': it was an assertion that Catholicism was the hallmark of the French monarchy, the basis of its claim not only to legitimacy at home, but to primacy in Europe. In 1685 Louis was particularly eager to repeat that claim, as he had been widely criticized for allying France with the Muslim Turks against the Habsburgs, and was on exceedingly bad terms with the Papacy.

The final suppression of Protestantism was intended to substantiate the claim that the French monarchy was, in spite of supporting the Turks and opposing the political interests of the Pope,

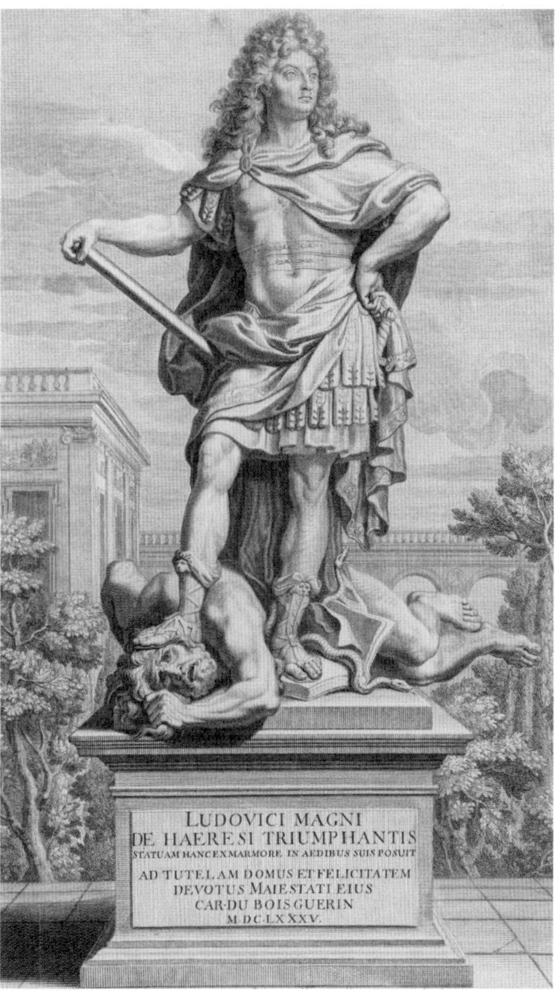

Louis XIV triumphing over heresy, 1685 – the year of the Revocation of the Edict of Nantes

the faithful 'eldest daughter' of the church of Rome. Which explains why, presiding over the print's frame, is the allegorical figure of the 'Catholic Church Triumphant', adorned with crosses, incense-burners and the papal tiara. On either side books, presumably heretical Protestant books, are burning. From the bottom of the frame hang chains of the sort used to shackle prisoners condemned, as many Huguenots were, to serve in the royal galleys. The viewer can be in no doubt that the king of France, in persecuting the Protestants, is doing the work of God's holy church.

And yet the Huguenots to the end insisted that they were the most loyal of Louis's subjects, firm believers in the king's divine right to make what decisions he thought proper. Like the Christians in Japan at the same date, they were in no way a threat to an ever more assertive central state. So why, other than to cut a Catholic dash in front of a disaffected Papacy and a sceptical Europe, did Louis regard their crushing as a conquest to be celebrated? Robert Tombs sees here the beginning of a pattern of political thought which is still very much alive:

The Edict of Nantes had given Protestants considerable political and military rights, and I think, without being too fanciful, that one can see in the Revocation the origins of the strong, and now very long-lived, French dislike of anything that might be seen as a state within the state. That was the charge against the Protestants under Louis XIV. It was said to be true of them still in the nineteenth century; and later said to be true of Jews, a debate that shaped much of the argument about national identity around 1900; and today of course, in remarkably similar terms, it is said about Muslims.

There was a very interesting debate in the National Assembly in 1789, discussing the status of Jews in France. A famous speech laid down that one should give everything to the Jews as individuals, but give nothing to the Jews as a community. The idea is that a religion, let us say Islam today, is to be seen not as a number of individuals who hold a particular set of beliefs, but as an organized group who claim some sort of separate identity.

If one doesn't believe too readily in historical coincidences, then one would think that there must be some continuity of attitude here, a certain way of understanding what it means to be French.

Leclerc's engraving should no longer surprise. Seen in this light, the challenge posed by the mere existence of the Huguenots to this new unitary notion of Frenchness was as dangerous and insidious as any external military threat. And now, thanks to the king, it had been removed: cause for celebration. From this point on, France was to be defined not by blood or language, but by uniform acceptance of its rules and norms. It is, Tombs suggests, the startling strength and longevity of this political attitude which explains the intensity of French reaction to the burkini on the beach with which this chapter began:

The revolution of 1789 tries to create a new kind of unity, based not on the uniformity of Catholicism but on a uniformity of secularism which later came to be called laïcité. It insists that religious belief and practice have no role in the public life of the state. They should remain a private matter, in which case no one will be troubled. But when people start to display their religious beliefs in public, and start claiming for their religious status something that marks them off from other citizens, then neither republicanism nor traditional French royalism can accept it.

For Republicans, who are at the forefront of the moves to ban the burka and the burkini, it goes much further. Secularism is seen by hardline Republicans as a fundamental part of what it means to be French. Without secularism, many would say, there cannot be true equality between men and women, there cannot be true democracy.

If we follow this line of argument, the existence of the temple at Charenton, like the wearing of the burka or the burkini, is to the authorities a provocative refusal to accept what it means to be a true citizen of France. They may in consequence take 'appropriate measures'.

Christianity never really recovered from its persecution at the hands of the state in seventeenth-century Japan. When the regime was overthrown in the middle of the nineteenth century, Japan's new leaders restored to the centre of national life an emperor declared to be divine (Chapter 4). Jealously protective of this most potent of symbols, these leaders understandably continued the ban on Christianity, until after Commodore Perry's show of force richer and better-armed Christian states forced them to drop it. 'There is no room in Japan,' one Japanese official had proudly declared, 'for two sons of God.' Although returning missionaries had found small groups of Japanese still using rosaries, Christianity continued to be regarded as a foreign and therefore suspect faith. The sense of a Japanese identity long preserved by restricting contact with foreigners is thought by many to explain modern Japan's great reluctance, in spite of a strong economy and a major demographic crisis, to accept foreign immigrants. On the basis of public-opinion polls, it is sometimes joked that most Japanese would prefer to see their aged parents looked after by a robot than by a Filipino.

On 26 August 2016, the Conseil d'Etat in Paris, France's supreme administrative court, eventually decided that wearing a burkini on a beach did not constitute a threat to public order, and so should not be forbidden. But that other marker of Islamic identity, the full face-covering burka, remains forbidden in the French street. For nearly 350 years, the notion that one can be fully a French citizen, and also visibly a member of a minority religious community – Protestant, Jewish or Muslim – has been thought to threaten the identity of the French state.

29

'THERE IS NO GOD!'

Faith makes people kill other people, set off bombs, start wars and de-humanise others who disagree: that is a serious problem. In the core sense of faith as religious commitment, I think one would always want to try to confront and challenge it with reason.

Anthony Grayling, philosopher and powerful advocate of secular humanism, is saying what many think: that religion in the modern world is essentially bigoted mumbo-jumbo, in the name of which people blow each other up. And evidence to support that view is not hard to find. Almost every day there are reports of oppression, cruelty and killing in the name of one god or another – a pattern which, as we saw in the last chapter, has a long and bloody history. A key task for governments all over the world is now to 'de-radicalize' religious extremists both within their borders and beyond.

Grayling, a distinguished teacher, proposes his solution: patient rational argument, the best method of exposing what he sees as the fallacies of faith. This should in due course persuade individuals away from a pattern of belief which leads to violence towards a reasoned understanding of the world which does not

Over: On 20 Brumaire, Year 2 (10 November 1793), the Festival of Reason was celebrated in 'the former church of Notre-Dame' in Paris

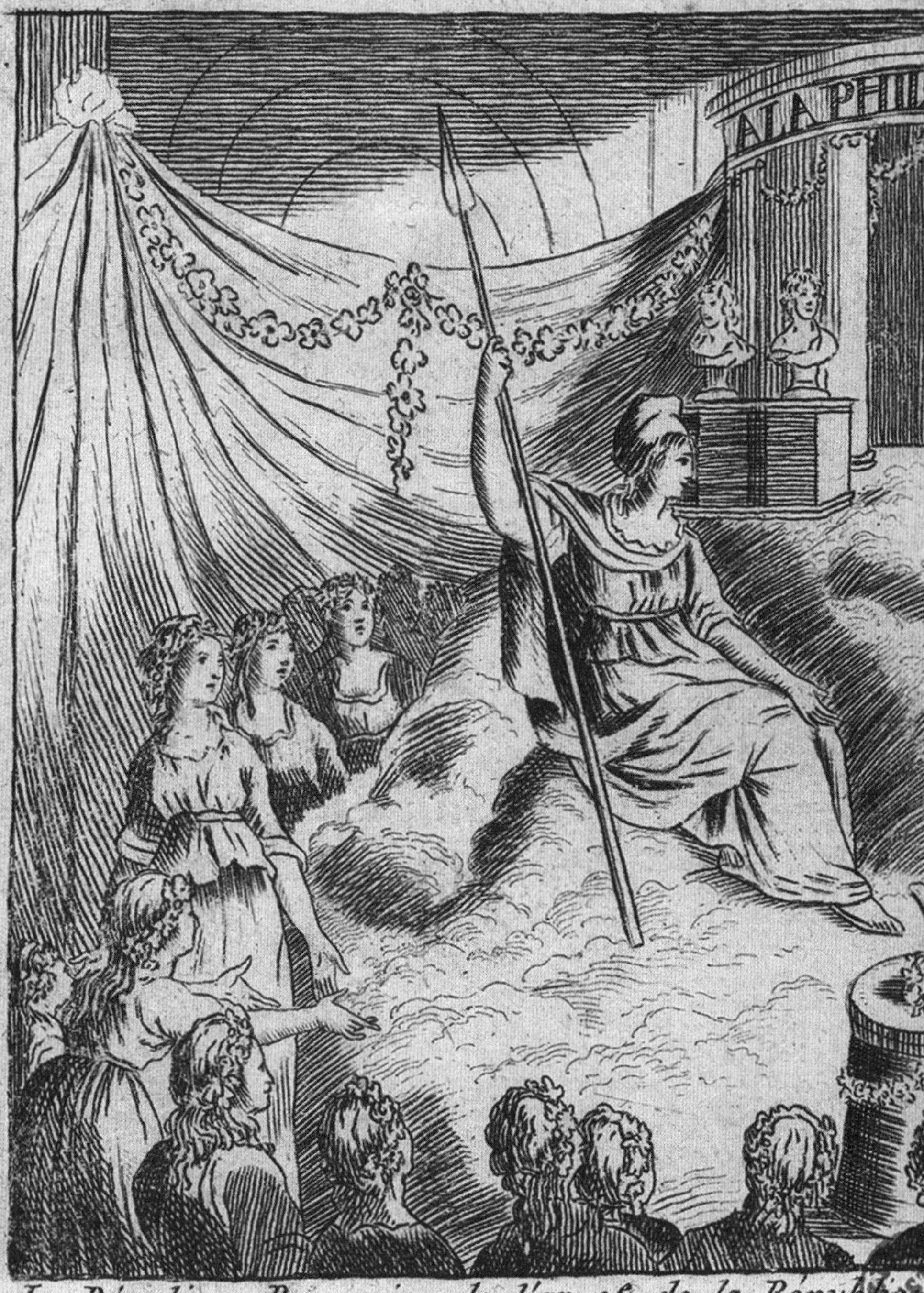

Le Décadi 20 Brumaire de l'an 2e. de la Républiq
a été Célébrée dans la Cidevant Eglise de Notre

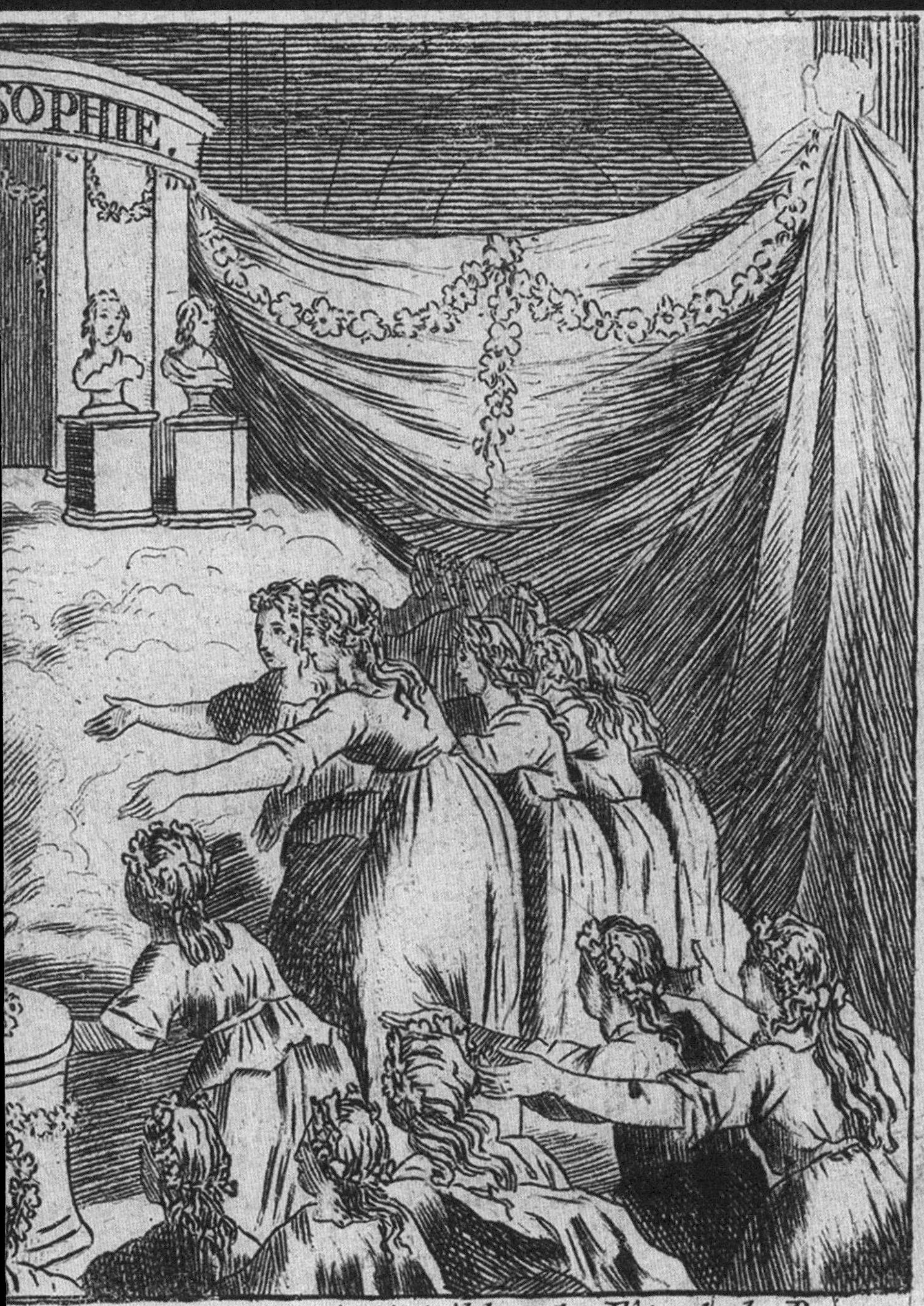

française une et indivisible, la Fête de la Raison
me.

require faith at all. The hope is that a society without irrational faith structures should be able to avoid the suffering that religious intolerance often brings. However, atheists regretfully concede that even the best-conducted of such debates take time. This chapter looks at the attempts by two governments – two states – to move much faster: to abolish faith in the public realm without slow public deliberations, and to instal reason as the guiding principle of political life.

In Chapter 26 we looked at the coronation of the British monarch in Westminster Abbey, where, through the bishops of the established church, the sovereign receives all power from God. Those present in Notre-Dame in Paris on Sunday, 10 November 1793, witnessed a very different kind of coronation. In a building that had recently ceased to be a Catholic cathedral, modern Europe's first officially godless state – the French Republic, One and Indivisible – inaugurated in splendour the Cult of Reason.

Ten months earlier, the revolutionaries had guillotined the king, and abolished the monarchy. They also abolished the Catholic church as the official religion of France: in its place they installed a new guiding Spirit by whose rules the state would now be governed: Reason. At Notre-Dame, they beheaded the statues of the saints – the aristocrats of the Christian faith – and redesignated the cathedral, along with those of Chartres and Rheims (where French monarchs, like their English counterparts, were anointed and consecrated at their coronation), as the Temple of Reason. On that November Sunday in 1793, to music specially composed by François-Joseph Gossec, the French nation celebrated the first *Fête de la Raison*, the Festival of Reason.

The moment was recorded in a simple print. Inside the former cathedral, maidens in loosely Roman-style tunics with *tricolore* sashes surrounded the Goddess of Reason herself, represented by the wife of the leading revolutionary politician who had promoted the idea of the cult. Sophie Momoro, racily draped, carrying a spear, and wearing the red cap of liberty, solemnly took her place on an artificial mound which had replaced the altar of the de-Christianized Notre-Dame. Once enthroned, she looked towards a temple dedicated to Philosophy, beckoning all to follow the path that led to wisdom. It was a tribute to the great *philosophes* – Voltaire, Diderot, Rousseau and their colleagues, the secular saints of the French Revolution – who over the previous fifty years had argued for political freedoms, and had attacked and ruthlessly satirized the dogmas and political privileges of the Catholic church. Thanks to the *philosophes*, there were many in Notre-Dame that day who would have regarded God as – at most – the Divine Clock-Maker, one-off designer of a rationally ordered universe.

In the *ancien régime* the fusion of church and state had run very deep. The king had been 'His Most Christian Majesty' and France 'the eldest daughter of the Catholic church' (Chapter 28). As the French Republic celebrated the apotheosis of Reason, it was trying to abolish 1,500 years of political Christianity, which had begun in Rome with the conversion of the emperor Constantine, probably in 312, and had shaped the history of Europe.

Even at this distance, it is easy to feel how astonishing and unsettling such a radical innovation must have been. But it was only part of a much wider disorientation, for the congregation in (the ex-) Notre-Dame that day would have said that they were celebrating the Festival of Reason not on Sunday, 10 November 1793, but on Décadi, 20 Brumaire, Year Two. Reason and the revolution had abolished not just God – they had reordered time. Paris was exhilarated by its own daring. The rest of Europe was appalled.

Christianity and Islam both begin their calendars with the event that marks the foundation of their faith and so, they believe, a new era for all humanity: the birth of Christ in the one case, in the other the Prophet's flight from Mecca to Medina. On 22 September 1792, the French Republic had been proclaimed – and an entirely new world was born, again for the benefit of all humanity.

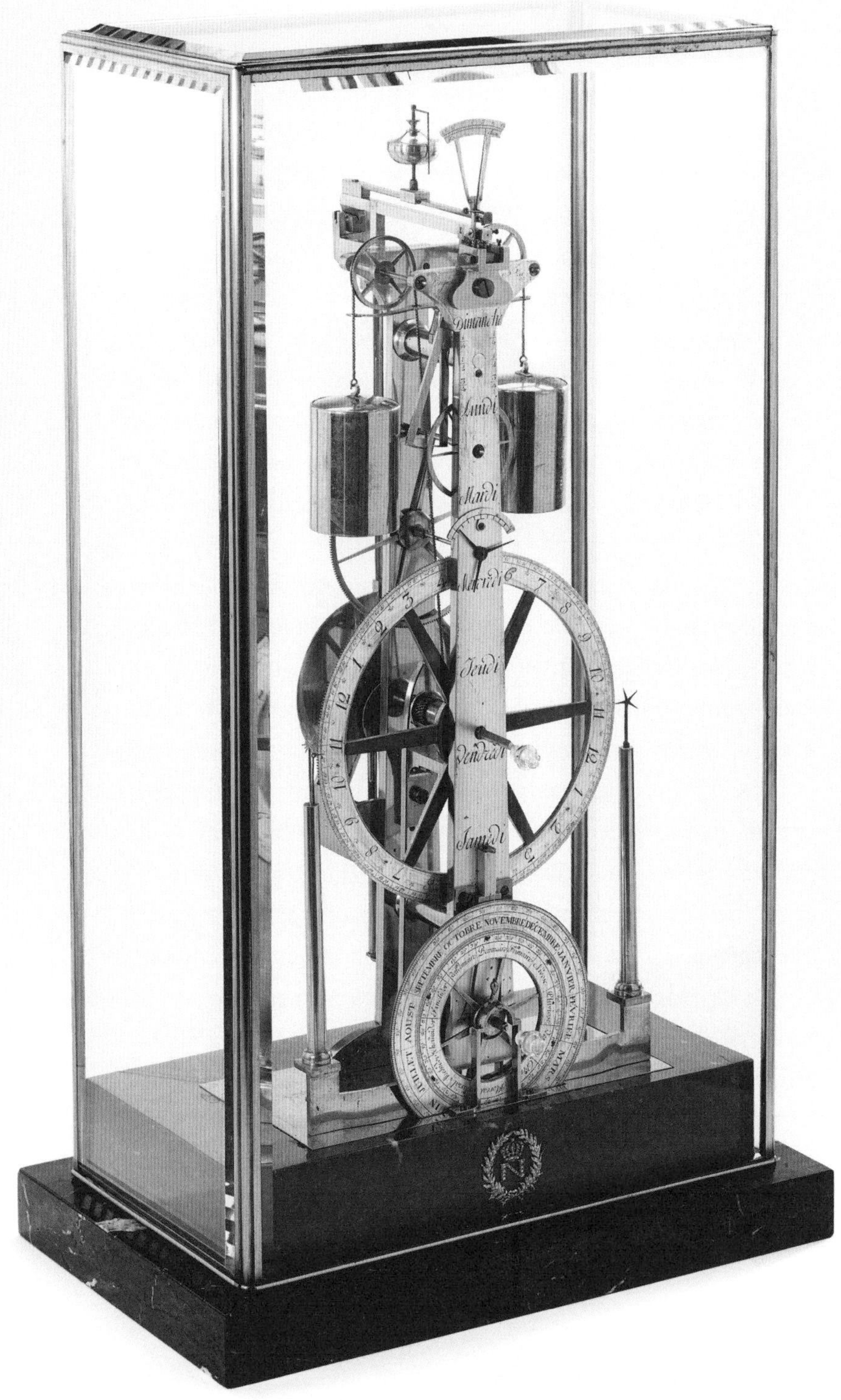

Dimanche
Lundi
Mardi
Mercredi
Jeudi
Vendredi
Samedi
JUILLET AOUST SEPTEMBRE OCTOBRE NOVEMBRE DECEMBRE JANVIER FEVRIER MARS

So on that day the calendar too began anew: no longer the year of Our Lord 1792, but Year One of the French Republic, in which the people would rule, the obfuscating hocus-pocus of religion would be banished, and reason alone would measure and determine every area of life. In due course, the old complex systems of distances, weights and measures, many of which varied from one city to another, were all abolished. Life would be lived in the uniform lucidity of the decimal system – a system 'for all people for all time'.

You can see – and hear – this new rational world in a clock now in the British Museum, created by the Swiss-born Abraham-Louis Breguet, around Year 3 – that is, 1795. Mounted on a base of red marble, and standing about sixty centimetres high, the mechanism sits, entirely visible, inside a glass box. There is no wooden casing, no ornament: just the machine.

But what a machine it is. Weights and pendulum are in shining gilded brass. The parts that tell you the time are in grey polished steel. A tall vertical rod, inscribed with the days of the week, supports two dials, the upper one a twenty-four-hour clock, the smaller, lower, one showing the months. There is no decoration; complexity is presented in absolute simplicity. This is an object designed to inspire trust – one is even tempted to say 'faith' – in mechanical reason. It aspires quite simply to show the very workings of time itself. In contrast to the elaborate and enclosed timepieces of the *ancien régime*, it insists that there is nothing mysterious or miraculous about the world we inhabit, that all aspects of it are clear and regular, measurable and visible. This clock is a Festival of Reason on a domestic scale.

The dial carries the traditional, familiar names of the months. But these had recently been abolished by the new government: they were inconsistent in length, and some – January, June – were named

Time transparent and transformed. Breguet's skeleton regulator clock, made in Paris around 1795, carries both the traditional Gregorian and the new French republican calendar. It may later have belonged to Napoleon.

after false Roman gods, while others – July, August – worse still, commemorated the tyrannical Roman emperors who had overthrown the Republic. In consequence, the clock also shows the new, rational and politically correct names of the months of the Revolutionary calendar. All now were the same length – thirty days – divided not into four weeks, but into three *décadis*, each of ten numbered days (there were a further five special days at the turn of the year). The months were named in almost-rhyming triads after the natural cycle of agriculture and the seasons: Vendémiaire – 'wine-making', Brumaire – 'misty', Frimaire – 'frosty', and so on. Or, as a sceptical commentator from across the English Channel put it in the *Sporting Magazine* in 1800: 'Wheezy, Sneezy, Freezy', etc.

Breguet's clock is a transitional object, showing time both old and new. The Revolution would be truly secure when French citizens – no longer subjects – needed no help to translate between the old era and its successor. But that proved much harder and took much longer than the revolutionaries expected, and above all where religion was concerned. It turned out that while people had disliked the wealth and power of the church, they had not been unduly concerned by the irrational aspects of its teaching so mocked by the *philosophes*. Above all, at local level, they cherished its role in gathering them together, and as the organizer of festivals that punctuated the year, in which all knew their traditional place. The Cult of Reason seemed abstract and remote, and it was rapidly replaced by festivals of Liberty or of the Supreme Being, an undefined, but generally benevolent divine creative force. But they were just not the same. It was the practices as much as the beliefs of the church that had shaped society, and the loss of that familiarity was widely resented: in a world without a church, when did people get together? Who was going to bless a child arriving in the world, minister to the dying, or bury the dead?

The Perpetual Calendar of the French Republic, which from 1793 to 1805 renumbered years, and renamed months and days of the week

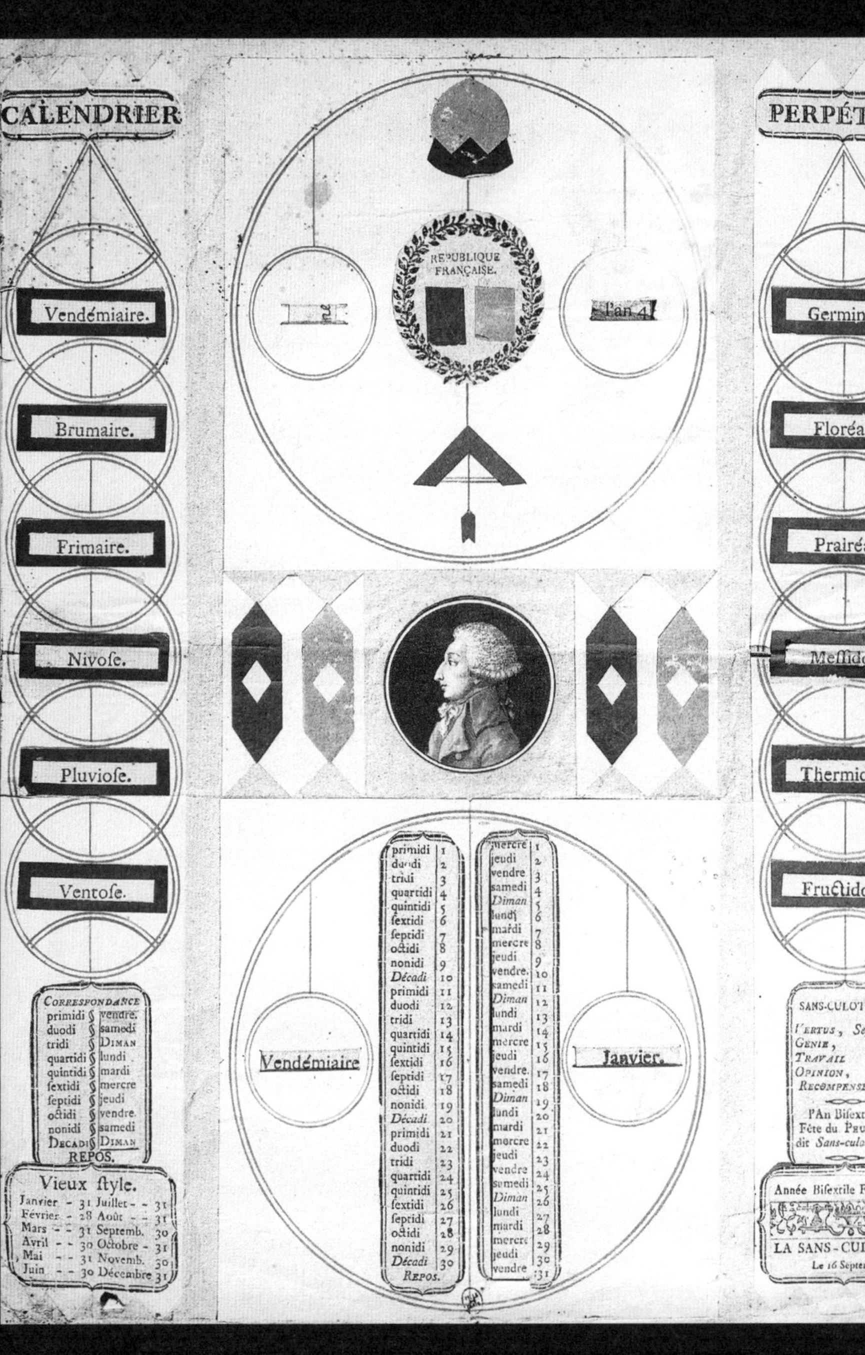

CALENDRIER
PERPÉTUEL.
RÉPUBLIQUE FRANÇAISE.
l'an 4
Vendémiaire.
Brumaire.
Frimaire.
Nivoſe.
Pluvioſe.
Ventoſe.
Germinal.
Floréal.
Prairéal.
Meſſidor.
Thermidor.
Fructidor.
primidi 1 duodi 2 tridi 3 quartidi 4 quintidi 5 ſextidi 6 ſeptidi 7 octidi 8 nonidi 9 Décadi 10 primidi 11 duodi 12 tridi 13 quartidi 14 quintidi 15 ſextidi 16 ſeptidi 17 octidi 18 nonidi 19 Décadi 20 primidi 21 duodi 22 tridi 23 quartidi 24 quintidi 25 ſextidi 26 ſeptidi 27 octidi 28 nonidi 29 Décadi 30
REPOS.
mercre 1 jeudi 2 vendre 3 samedi 4 Diman 5 lundi 6 mardi 7 mercre 8 jeudi 9 vendre. 10 samedi 11 Diman 12 lundi 13 mardi 14 mercre 15 jeudi 16 vendre. 17 samedi 18 Diman 19 lundi 20 mardi 21 mercre 22 jeudi 23 vendre 24 samedi 25 Diman 26 lundi 27 mardi 28 mercre 29 jeudi 30 vendre 31
Vendémiaire
Janvier.
CORRESPONDANCE
primidi § vendre.
duodi § samedi
tridi § DIMAN
quartidi § lundi
quintidi § mardi
ſextidi § mercre
ſeptidi § jeudi
octidi § vendre.
nonidi § samedi
DECADI § DIMAN
REPOS.
Vieux ſtyle.
Janvier - 31 Juillet - - 31
Février - 28 Août - - 31
Mars - - 31 Septemb. 30
Avril - - 30 Octobre - 31
Mai - - 31 Novemb. 30
Juin - - 30 Décembre 31
SANS-CULOTIDES
Vertus, Sept. 17
Genie, 18
Travail 19
Opinion, 20
Recompenses, 21
l'An Biſextile la Fête du Peuple, dit Sans-culotide.
Année Biſextile Février 29 j
LA SANS-CULOTIDE,
Le 16 Septembre.

The Revolution itself was rapidly becoming less benevolent, adopting many of the habits of the regime and the church it so detested: those who did not share its views were exiled or guillotined, those who died defending it were revered as martyrs. In November 1793, while the Festival of Reason was being celebrated at Notre-Dame, 'enemies of the people' – who could be aristocrats or priests, or virtually anybody who opposed the revolutionary authorities – were being summarily condemned in ever-growing numbers. The Terror, as it came to be known, was in full swing: dozens were being publicly executed every day.

Ten years later, it was all over. On 18 Germinal, Year 10 (8 April 1802), the Cult of Reason was abolished. The church had been chastened and weakened but it had unquestionably survived. The base of our clock shows how, just as in ancient Rome, the story of the Republic ended in Empire: it bears a silver capital letter 'N', studded with sparkling stones, celebrating Napoleon, to whom it may well have belonged.

Within a few years of Napoleon's coming to power, most of the symbols of the Triumph of Reason had disappeared. The revolutionary calendar had been abandoned, and a new agreement, a Concordat with the Papacy, re-established the official role of the church in France. On 2 December 1804 (though some zealous reformers still referred to it as 11 Frimaire, Year 13), in a Notre-Dame that was once again a Catholic cathedral with a proper altar, visitors watched not the enthronement of Reason, but Napoleon crowning himself emperor of France. The Pope, forcibly brought from Rome, had to sit in humiliating attendance and provide the useful blessing of the reinstated Christian god.

Just over a hundred years later, Russian revolutionaries embarked on a course strikingly similar to the French. All citizens were to be equal in the new republic. The monarchy was abolished, and the monarch killed, and the state set about dismantling a rich,

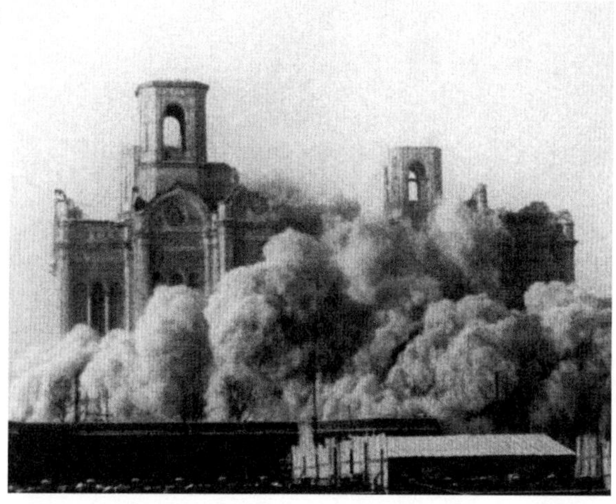
On Stalin's orders, the Cathedral of Christ the Saviour, Moscow, was dynamited in 1931.

politically powerful church. It sought to suppress all traces of the practice of religion, replacing it with a rational, scientific approach to the world. As in France, the new state found it was obliged to murder its enemies. 'It is necessary,' Lenin wrote in 1918, 'to conduct a merciless mass terror campaign against ... priests.'

Geoffrey Hosking, Emeritus Professor of Russian History at University College London, explains what happened:

Originally Lenin and the leaders of the Soviet state wanted to destroy established religion of all kinds. They set out to destroy in particular the Russian Orthodox church as the principal church of the Soviet Union. They plundered churches, or they turned them into warehouses, cinemas, all kinds of public, non-religious institutions. A huge number of priests and bishops were arrested, and many of them died in labour camps. By 1939 there were only four out of about 150 bishops still alive and actually practising in their dioceses. So, over the course of the first twenty years or so, the Communist Party very nearly did destroy the Orthodox church. This applies to other established faiths as well.

In the Soviet Union as in France, the move against religion was accompanied by a devout belief in the power of rationality to

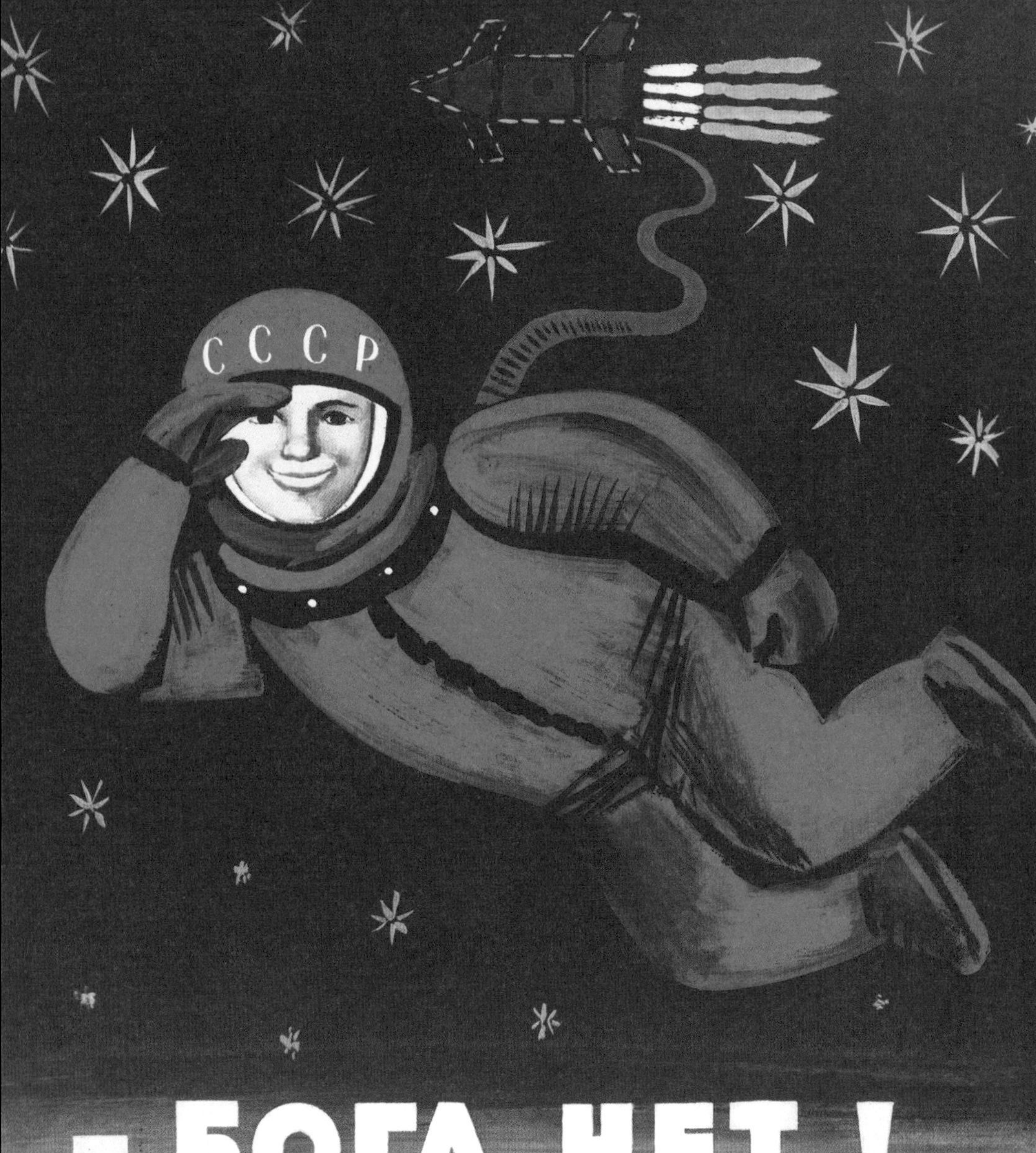
СССР
— БОГА НЕТ !
Боевой карандаш
Художник В. МЕНЬШИКОВ
БЕЗ БОГА ШИРЕ ДОРОГА
Издательство «Художник РСФСР»
Изд. № 504074. Тираж 5000. Зак. 8253. Цена плаката 8 коп.
Ордена Трудового Красного Знамени
типография им. Володарского Лениздата,
191023. Ленинград, Фонтанка, 57
А 80202—224 / М173(03)—75 —75
© Издательство «Художник РСФСР». 1975

refashion the world. Breguet's clock shows the French attempt to reorder time. The Soviets wanted to conquer space. On 12 April 1961, Yuri Gagarin became the first man to orbit the earth: at last humans had entered heaven, and it was the result not of faith, but science. What it was like in heaven we can see in a poster designed to celebrate both the triumph of the Soviet space programme (which had stolen a march on that of the United States) and the vindication of rational atheism. It shows the youthful Gagarin floating among the stars. He wears a space suit in brilliant Communist red, and beams engagingly out at us from above two bold words: *Boga Nyet* – 'There is no God!'. The heavens are empty of divine beings; full, instead, of starry promise. The only true paradise is the earthly one, and Gagarin is its emissary. 'CCCP' says his helmet: Сою́з Сове́тских Социалисти́ческих Респу́блик, the Union of Soviet Socialist Republics. He floats over the domes and crosses of Orthodox churches, and a mosque crowned with a crescent moon. Thanks to the Soviet system man has literally transcended religion.

The prominent presence of these churches in the poster – the fact that so long after the Revolution they were still there at all – is explained by the events of twenty years earlier. The dream of a secular, rational Soviet state, free from the shackles of religion and superstition, was brutally disrupted by Germany's invasion of the Soviet Union in June 1941. It was essential for the government to win the people's support in the Great Patriotic War. As a desperate measure, religious restrictions were eased, and parish churches reopened. It is a stark demonstration of how strong a force for social cohesion the church's practices had been – and, in spite of twenty years of repression, still were. As in France, people had found nothing that could take the place of the church-based rituals of everyday local life. As Geoffrey Hosking describes, after victory had been secured, Stalin left some of this renewed church presence in place,

The Soviet Union goes to heaven: the first man in space, Yuri Gagarin, floats over churches and mosques and announces: 'There is no God!' Print by Vladimir Menshikov, 1975

and set out to reinstate the Orthodox church as a tool for internal control and for his postwar diplomacy – particularly useful in parts of the world with large Orthodox Christian populations:

He took the remarkable step of re-establishing the patriarchate. The patriarchs and the entire church hierarchy were appointed with the agreement of the party and the state. The state also appointed a special committee to monitor them, and many of the bishops and some of the priests became agents reporting to the security police on possible subversion. Believers were required to register with the authorities.

Observers of contemporary Russia see Vladimir Putin pursuing a rather similar policy, and even more enthusiastically. Churches have not only been reopened, but rebuilt. Unlike Stalin decades before, however, Putin claims to be a believer, baptized by a grandmother who brought him up in the traditional practices of the faith. According to Geoffrey Hosking, Putin has understood that the Orthodox church, almost as much as being a system of belief, is the hallmark and the guardian of key aspects of the Russian national identity which he is eager to reassert:

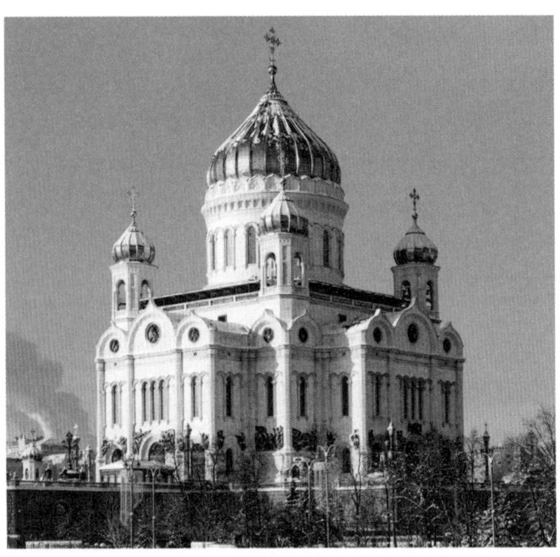

The Cathedral of Christ the Saviour in Moscow, demolished on Stalin's orders, reconstructed in the 1990s as the Soviet Union collapsed

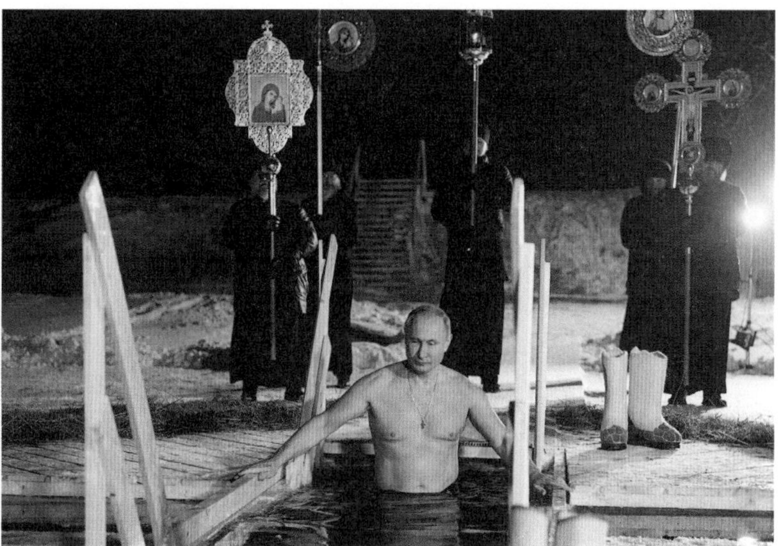

Beneath an image of Our Lady of Kazan (Chapter 17), and wearing a cross round his neck, President Putin celebrates Epiphany in the Orthodox tradition by ritual immersion through a hole in the ice, at Lake Seliger, north of Moscow, January 2018.

Putin regularly quotes biblical texts, he visits church quite often, he maintains a very good relationship with the patriarch, Kirill, so it is a way of encouraging Russian patriotism, the idea that Russia is separate and valuable because the Orthodox church is distinctive. It's a national church.

The transformation is profound. The museum which originally acquired our Gagarin poster was the Leningrad Museum of the History of Religion and Atheism in Leningrad: it is now the State Museum of the History of Religion in St Petersburg. In Moscow, the reconstruction of the Cathedral of Christ the Saviour (p. 452) was completed in 2000 and the headquarters of the dreaded KGB (renamed the Federal Security Service) today has a church dedicated to Sophia, the Divine Wisdom, with icons blessed by the Patriarch of all Russia. Atheism has been officially discarded.

Whatever political history it may encapsulate, our clock, made of stone, metal and glass, is surely the ultimate rational timepiece: it forms a lucid transparent world, without mystery, where the workings of the mechanism are designed to be utterly graspable. The passage of time is not just to be measured: it is to be revealed. Anthony Grayling locates the origins of, and the need for, religion in pre-scientific attempts to reach a comparable understanding of the world:

Human beings love narrative. We want a beginning a middle and an end. And we want an explanation. In the very earliest phases of human history, people used their own experience of agency as a starting point. I can pick up a stone and throw it into a pond: it will make a splash. I did that. From here, the wind, the growth of the plants, the movement of the trees, the rolling of a rock down a mountainside were all attributed to agency in nature: to nymphs, dryads and sylphs.

As we got more acquainted with nature, so these agencies withdrew. They went to the tops of mountains, which were regarded as sacred, holy places: Mount Olympus, or the burning bush on the mountain top encountered by Moses. When people eventually got to the tops of mountains, and didn't find any supernatural agencies, they put them into the sky. The further these agencies removed themselves from the immediate proximity of human beings, the fewer in number they became. They're now down to one or three, depending upon your arithmetic. And they are no longer in space and time. The less that people understand about science, the bigger the gap between their disciplined empirical investigation of the world and their incomprehension of it, the easier it is for them to reach for a faith-based explanation.

According to this view, modern science answers the questions and solves the problems that have long lain at the roots of the religious impulse, thus removing the need for faith. As our knowledge of the physical world advances, so our need for religion to explain it recedes.

It is certainly true that most people no longer try to explain natural phenomena in supernatural terms. But this leaves unexplained the reaction of the bulk of the population in both France and in Russia when the state abolished religion. In both instances it became clear that the key issue was not the truth or otherwise of the propositions that the churches taught, and perhaps not even the evident greed and corruption at the heart of both institutions: it was the social engagement which accompanied the practice of the faith, and the need for a notion of existence – for meaning – beyond the individual and the individual life. Eamon Duffy has charted a comparable popular, local reaction during the English Reformation – the anger and distress at the destruction of patterns of communal life that had been hallowed by time.

Anthony Grayling believes that we have come so far in our knowledge of the universe that we can – and do – now manage our moral lives without such structures:

In most of the advanced democracies of the world today we witness the functioning of societies which are not predicated on a particular doctrinal framework. And we don't seem to be collapsing morally, we don't have people out in the street murdering one another or spending all day drunk in the gutter. People are getting on with their lives and their relationships – indeed, even to some extent thinking a bit more carefully about them.

But here too there is another dimension to the argument. It may well be that without God citizens behave no worse than before. Governments, however, are another matter. State Christianity frequently legitimized the oppression of the subject; but it also allowed that subject to assert that there was an even higher power, and that earthly rulers could and would be called to account. In both France and Russia, the power of the absolute monarchs was both given and restrained by God, and brought with it the responsibility to govern justly. Failure to do so would legitimize revolt. There was an agreed vocabulary of moral resistance. When God was abolished, there was no longer even an abstract restraint on state power, and in Russia and in France, murder followed in the name of reason.

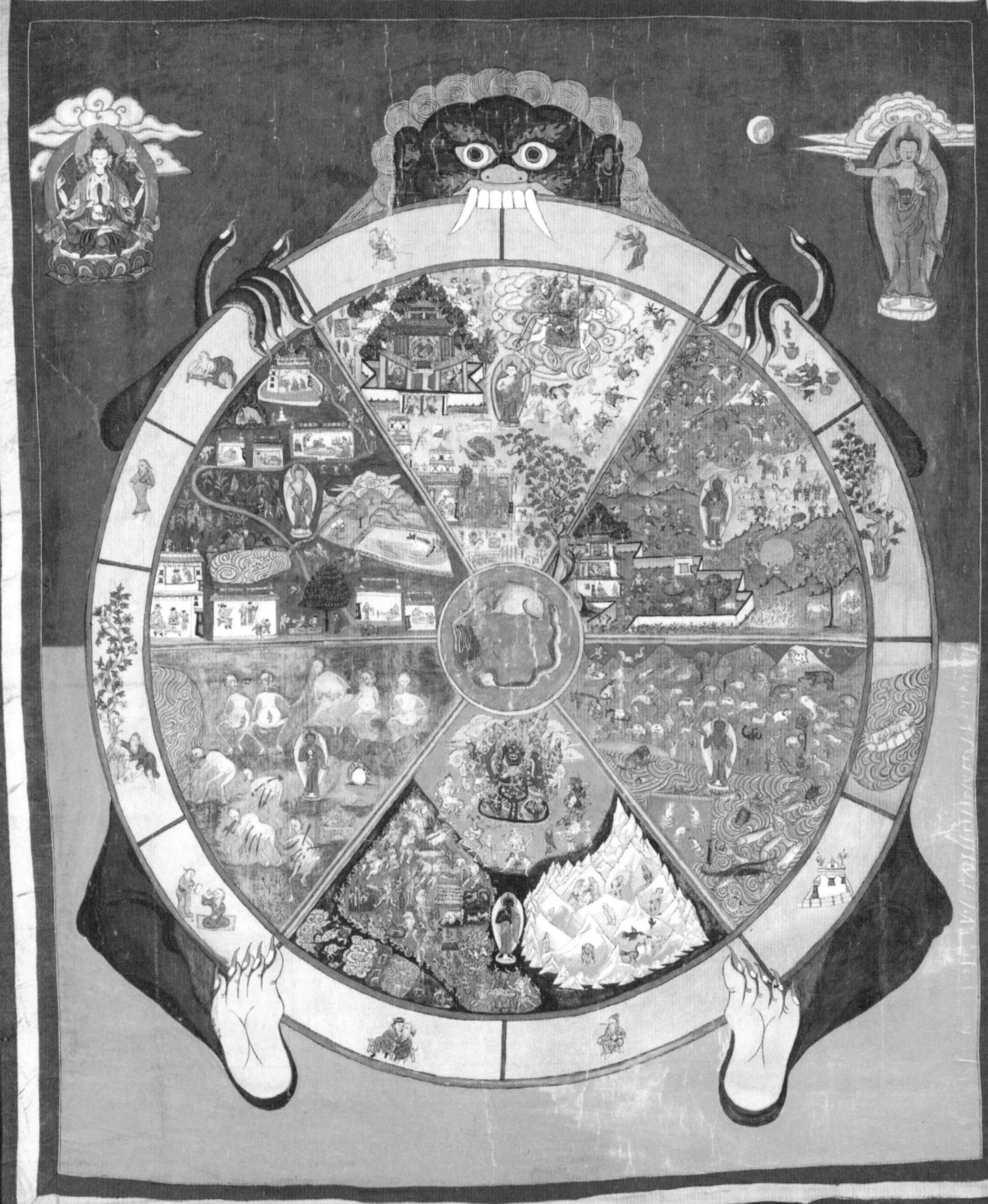

30
LIVING WITH EACH OTHER

It is the human predicament; it is the story of each one of us; it is the history of the world so far, and for ever – all in a single brilliantly coloured painting which shows the endlessly turning wheel of our life and our lives. This *thangka*, a nineteenth-century Tibetan Buddhist painting on textile, mounted on blue cotton with loops for rods at top and bottom, was made to hang on the walls of a temple in Tibet or India. It is about the size of a very big home television screen, and it has the same high-definition intensity of colour and detail. Designed for slow meditation, especially for those unable to read, it offers a guide to the terrain of everyday life, and how to move beyond it.

All the way through this book, from the Ice Age to the present, we have been looking at how societies first imagine and then enact their place in a world that is constantly changing, and often dangerous. In conveying the Buddhist view of the universe, this *thangka* does what all religions have to do: it tells a story – one that connects our individual lives to the community and to the world of which we are, fleetingly, a part. And it tells it in a wheel, because

Life determined and devoured by transience. The Buddhist Wheel of Life shows the cycle of rebirth and different aspects of the human condition. A nineteenth-century Tibetan *thangka*

though our lives are finite, the tale of the world that it presents has neither beginning nor end.

The rim of the wheel is pistachio green, and its spokes divide it into six sections, each with landscape and figures. At the very centre, in the red hub, are the three driving forces which govern our lives, keep turning the wheel and make the world go round: greed in the form of a green snake, ignorance, shown as a pig, and a proudly plumed cockerel for hatred. Each of these destroying habits feeds off the others: so in an inspired visual metaphor they are shown here spinning round and round, biting one another's tails. There is only one way we can be freed from them and their cycle of destruction: following the path and teachings of the Buddha – detachment from desire, and compassion for all living things. If we are left to our own unenlightened devices, these three ravening beasts will inform all our actions, shape our lives, and take us through a sequence of births and rebirths into six different realms in the cycle of existence, each shown in one of the large segments of our wheel.

In this *thangka* we can see, set out for tranquil contemplation, the essence of the Buddha's first sermon, on the wheel of the law, which he preached to his followers in the deer park at Sarnath (Chapters 14 and 19): how we choose to behave to each other has consequences that resonate not just through society but across time, as the cosmic wheel endlessly turns. Morality is destiny.

In the centre at the top, as you might expect, is the golden realm of the gods, a world of abundance and ease. But this is not eternal paradise as Europeans usually think of it: these gods are mortal. Because they have so much, they are distracted by meaningless pleasures, and so fail in compassion and self-discipline. Greed, ignorance and hatred drive even them forward. When the wheel turns, they will die and be reborn into a lower realm. And so the story goes on, clockwise around the wheel, our progress determined by our behaviour: self-indulgent gods who become squabbling and discontented demi-gods, or animals living in constant fear of violence, or even descending, right at the bottom, to the many torments of hell itself.

To the left of hell are nine oddly shaped naked human figures. Every other segment of the wheel, even hell, has a bright abundant landscape, but these figures, known in Buddhism as the hungry ghosts, are in an almost featureless realm of dull grey. Madeleine Bunting, a writer and religious commentator, shaped by both Catholic and Buddhist traditions, finds them especially worth pondering:

They have huge pot-bellied tummies and, famously, pinhole mouths. The point about the hungry ghosts – and I feel I see them every day of my life – is that these are people who would love to experience a depth and richness of life, but cannot. They are hungry, hungry, hungry, but they don't know how to absorb the joys of existence. They seem to me to embody the T. S. Eliot line: 'We had the experience and missed the meaning'. The question this section of the wheel asks is: how do you open your mouths so that you can take in the nourishment that a life can bring – connection to other people, sheer gratitude for the astonishing beauty of the world, and compassion for others, to help wherever and whenever you can?

Our realm, the human realm, is the scene just above the hungry ghosts, and we are clearly doing a little better – but only a little. There is a lush fertile landscape, and winding through it is the path which leads us all from birth towards old age, sickness and finally death. It will not be an easy journey. On either side of the path, we see extremes of heat and cold, hard work, suffering, hunger and thirst. Everywhere there is separation from loved ones and the frustration of desire.

Despite this unvarnished depiction of the human journey, the point of the painting is emphatically not to cast us into gloom over our condition, but to give us hope. This great image of the cosmos declares in its circularity that everything the world contains – pleasure and pain, love and loss – is always changing and turning. Nothing is for ever. It is perhaps similar to the idea of the ancient Greek philosopher Heraclitus that 'we cannot step into the same river twice'. In our *thangka* the wheel of life is being held, is possibly about to be devoured, by a fearsomely fanged bear-like monster, the embodiment of transience. Our human world, as we see it here, and as we ought to understand it, is caught in the claws and the jaws of impermanence.

And that gives us hope. For, as the world must change, so must we, but the simple message of this complex painting is that it is possible to escape from the three base passions of greed, ignorance and hatred. By practising the teachings of the Buddha, by exercising detachment from the things and affections of the world, and showing compassion to everybody, all may be well. And we are not asked to struggle alone. As you can see in the *thangka*, Madeleine Bunting tells us, the Buddha is always within sight, to counsel and to guide:

The key thing is that in each of the realms there is an image of the Buddha. You may be in hell or you may be amongst the gods or the hungry ghosts. But, wherever you are, there is the potential for enlightenment and for Buddhahood. We all have a Buddha nature. It is close to the Christian idea of the God within. We can all reach enlightenment, no matter where we are, whatever our life stories are. That is the radical hope and promise that this painting and this teaching offer.

*

Every year on the banks of the Ganges, a drama of transience and renewal, comparable to the one we see in our *thangka*, is played out on a massive scale, with a similar focus on the redeeming virtues of detachment and compassion. As we saw in Chapter 3, the waters of the goddess Ganga – waters which in a spiritual sense may be found in many rivers of India – link earth to heaven, and play a central role in the Hindu understanding of life and death.

In Chapter 3 we looked at the virtues of dying and being cremated on the Ganges at Varanasi, and so being freed from the endless cycle of reincarnation. But Hindus believe that to bathe in the Ganges at Allahabad, at the point where it is joined by the River Yamuna, confers outstanding spiritual benefit on the living, especially on certain days in January and February. So every year, in the dry autumn months after the monsoon rains, a great city is built in the riverbed at Allahabad, to allow many millions of pilgrims to come to bathe over fifty-five days, and to celebrate the Magh Mela – the festival (*mela*) that begins in *Magh* (the Hindu month that straddles January and February). Every twelve years it is even more than usually auspicious to immerse yourself in the life-renewing Ganges here, when an even greater celebration, called the Kumbh Mela, takes place (*kumbh* means a water-pitcher). In 2013 it is estimated that an astonishing 120 million people – twice the population of the UK – took part in the Kumbh Mela over the two-month period.

Every year, in order to house the Magh or the Kumbh Mela, a transient metropolis, a mobile megacity, is built in the riverbed of the Ganges. There is literally nothing like it in the world. Rahul Mehrotra is an architect in Mumbai, and also teaches at Harvard. He has made an exhaustive study of the ephemeral city that accommodated the Kumbh Mela in 2013:

There are about seven million people who live there for the entire festival, so it's essentially a megacity where people settle for fifty-five days. For the annual Magh Mela the numbers are slightly smaller, but still several millions. At both there are some specially sacred days, when there are large influxes of people, so on each of

Over: A transient city. Thousands of Hindu pilgrims crossing pontoon bridges over the Ganges at Allahabad, during the Kumbh Mela, 2013. On the most auspicious days, around twenty million bathe in the river.

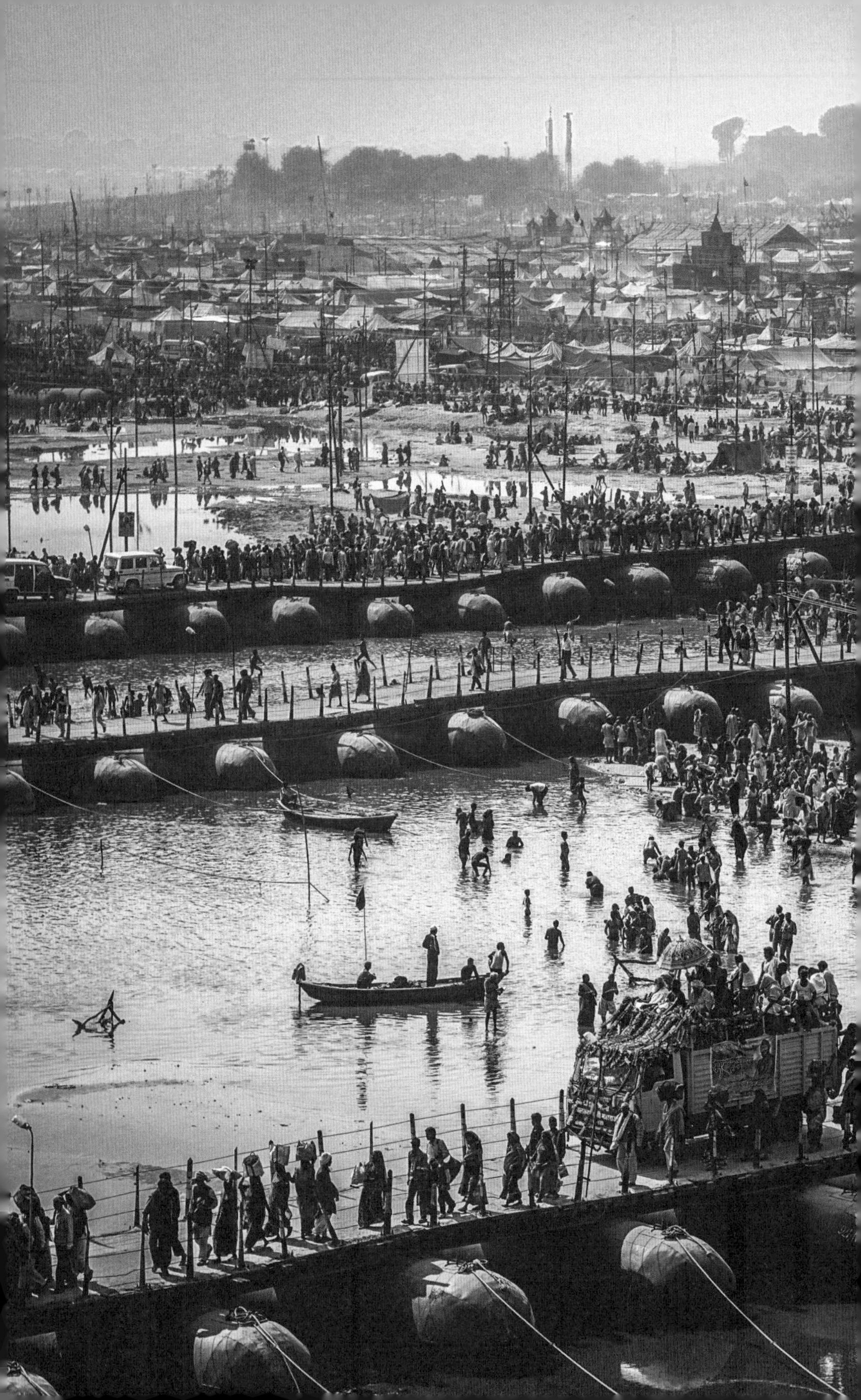

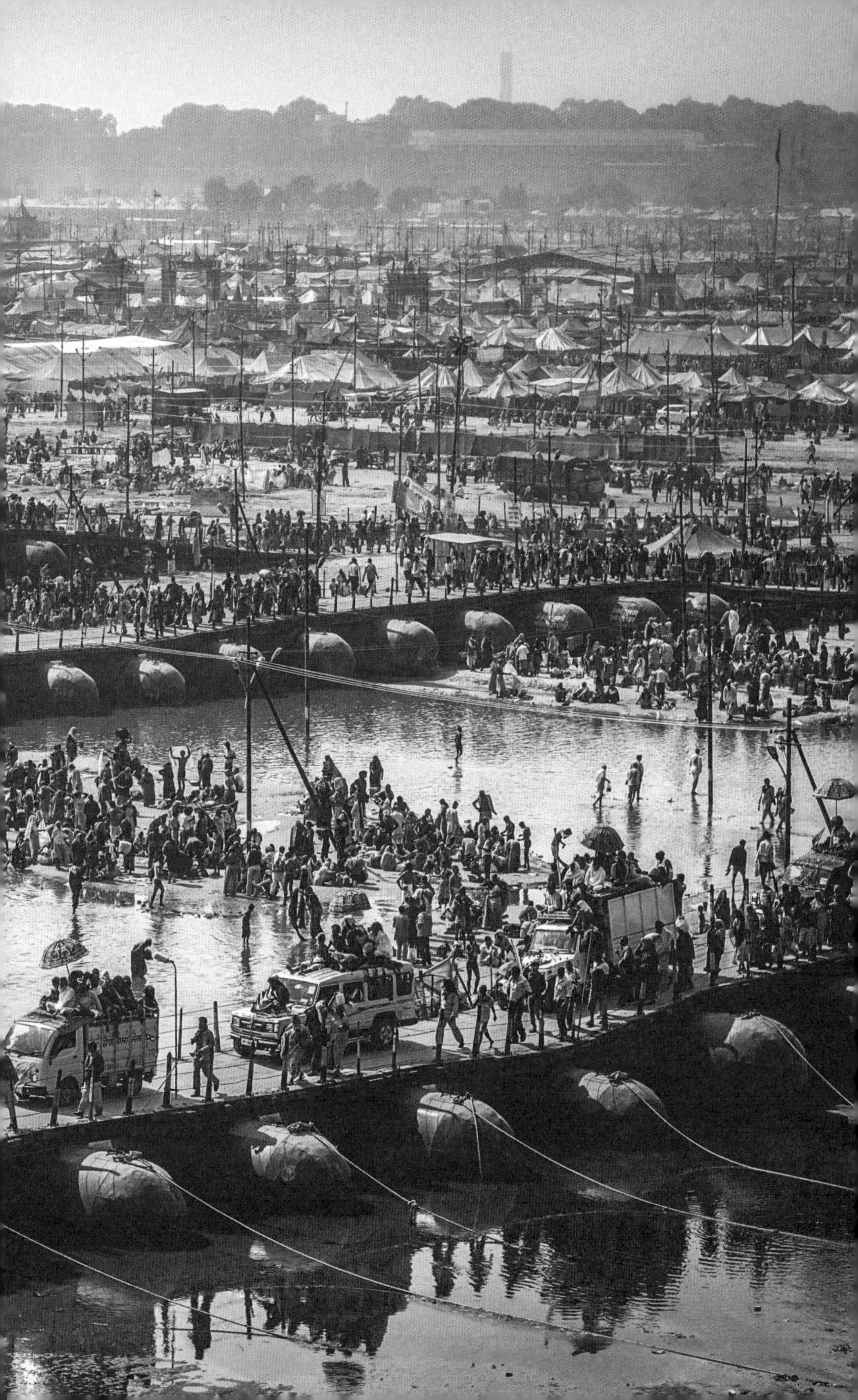

the three particularly auspicious bathing days there are influxes of over twenty million people.

The site on which the city must be built emerges after the monsoon rains, when the rivers recede and the sand banks are revealed, some time between the end of September and the middle of October. So essentially the government has about two months to erect a megacity for seven million people, who will start arriving in January. The striking thing about it is that it emerges from an undefined landscape which is virtually a sandbank. Equally compelling and beautiful is that it completely disappears again when the rivers flood in the next monsoon.

The logistics of such an event are more challenging even than those for Hajj, where there is a large permanent infrastructure and a well-established system of quotas to manage the huge influx (Chapter 14). But as with Hajj everybody here has come with the same purpose: to focus for a time on the essentials of their existence, to pray, to worship and to be freed from the weight of their wrongdoing. It is a holy city, but, unlike Zion, here there is no thought of permanence, and it can be regularly – briefly – attained.

Visiting this huge but temporary city is an unforgettable experience. The population on any given day is likely to be larger than any European capital except perhaps London. It has street lighting and sanitation, its own hospitals and its own police force (mostly to manage crowds and reunite people who are lost – very few crimes are reported). Walking in the streets you are conscious of a gentle serenity that would be surprising anywhere, a quiet sense of shared purpose which grows stronger as you approach the bathing places.

There are no hotels. The city is laid out on a grid plan, with the city blocks made up not of buildings but of large tents. These are big enough to house 700 or 800 people, who bring rugs and bedding on which to sit and sleep. In the centre of the tents are spaces kept free for spiritual instruction by a wide range of gurus, for religious services and private meditation. It is never a quiet environment, but many people seem surprisingly able to find a space to focus on their own inner meditations.

The pilgrims come from all over India and stay, free of charge, for as long as they like. They bring few possessions. Most will bathe several times. The tents – there are many thousands of them – provide a safe environment for pilgrims, many of whom are unused to travelling outside their village. Within them, religious organizations ensure that everybody is not just lodged but fed at no cost. Everything is provided. This is charity on an extraordinary scale, and with another unusual feature, as Rahul Mehrotra recounts:

One of the most interesting things about the Kumbh Mela – and the Magh Mela – is that it has the scale of any contemporary megacity, but just one, single purpose. And, crucially, it does not function as a commercial space. Food and shelter for everybody are provided. That for me symbolizes the bigger idea of the whole city – that it is about producing something with real commitment but then accepting its disappearance just as easily.

You are all the time aware that this great metropolis, laboriously built, is no abiding city. In a few weeks, if it were not dismantled, then the very river which offers pilgrims a new spiritual life would destroy it completely. But next year there will be a new city, new pilgrims, and the same river will be flowing with different water.

The Kumbh Mela is by far the largest religious event – indeed by far the largest human gathering – anywhere on earth. But the millions of bathers in the Ganges are, I think, doing something similar to other groups whom we have looked at in the course of this book – the farmers who built the great tomb at Newgrange to link the living and the dead at the moment of the winter solstice, the festivals that mark summer in Siberia or honour the slaughtered seals in Alaska, the congregations singing in Lutheran churches, or the pilgrims to Canterbury or Guadalupe or Mecca.

All are taking part in complex and demanding rituals by which they understand their place in the world and in time. Participation brings the hope of a new beginning, and strengthens the community that enacts them.

This book began in a cave near the river Danube, where 40,000 years ago a small, portable sculpture of the Lion Man played a central part in what we can reasonably describe as a religious ceremony. It is an imagined reshaping of the world, a magnificent work of art, in which the destructive, threatening power of the lion has been transformed by imagination and great skill into a source of strength that can be shared by everyone. I want to end in another echoing space, St Paul's Cathedral in London, with another small sculpture, which was also designed to be held in the hand, this one made in our modern world in an attempt to turn destruction into an emblem of hope. It is a small cross, simply made of two pieces of wood fitted together, which in Refugee Week 2016 stood on the high altar of the cathedral.

Francesco Tuccio is a carpenter on Lampedusa, the tiny Italian island between Sicily and the coast of Tunisia. It has become the goal for tens of thousands of migrants and asylum-seekers from Africa, desperate to reach a Europe which does not want to receive them. Thousands have drowned in small, overloaded boats that sank during the short sea crossing. Most of those who do reach Lampedusa are destitute and many are traumatized. Tuccio, wanting to give something to the migrants as a token of welcome and compassion, began fashioning crosses like this one from the wreckage of migrant boats that had been washed ashore, from wood that, as he said, smelt of salt, sea and suffering.

We have talked many times in this book of objects where the material itself is part of the message. Of none is that more

The Lampedusa Cross on the High Altar of St Paul's Cathedral, June 2016

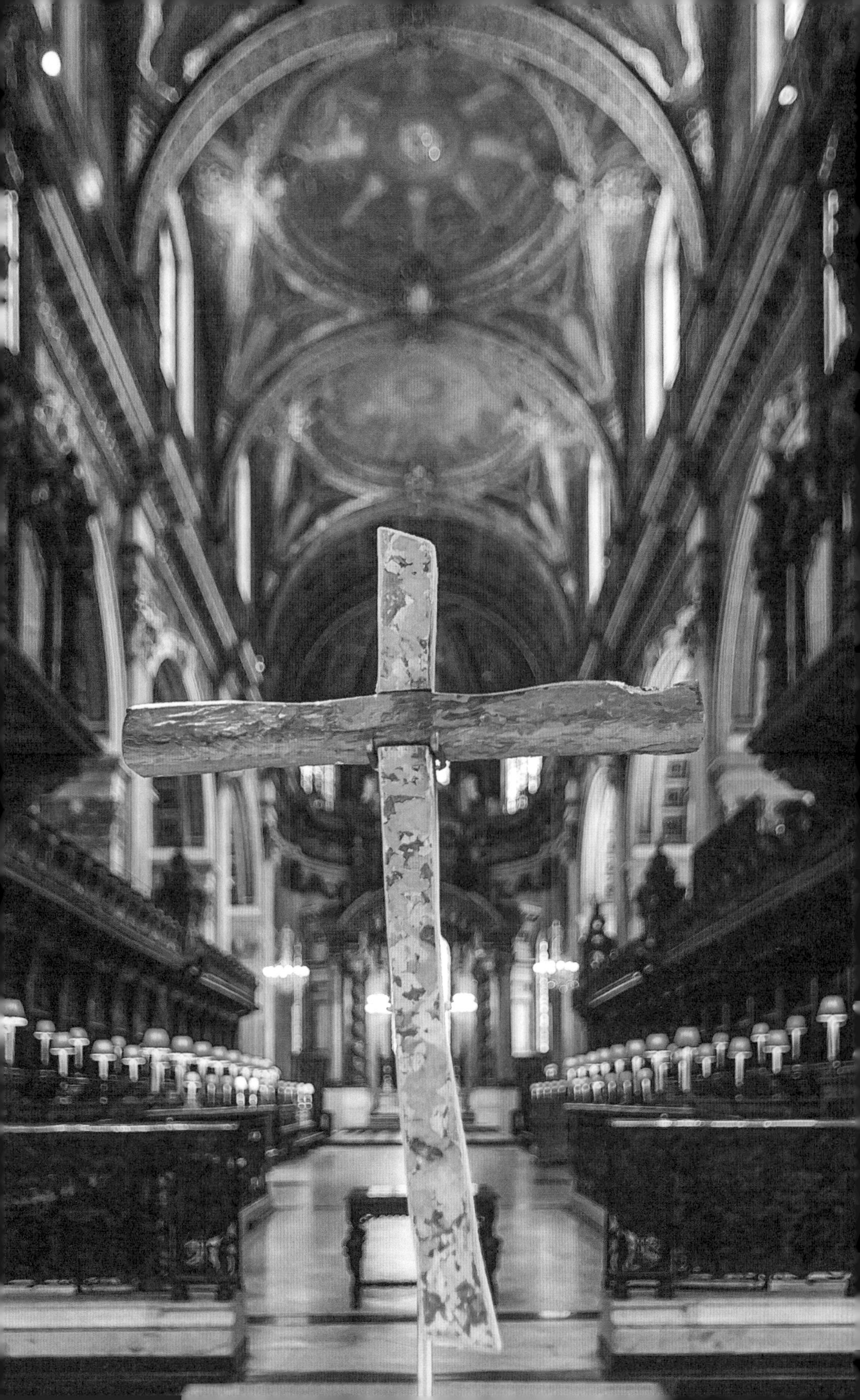

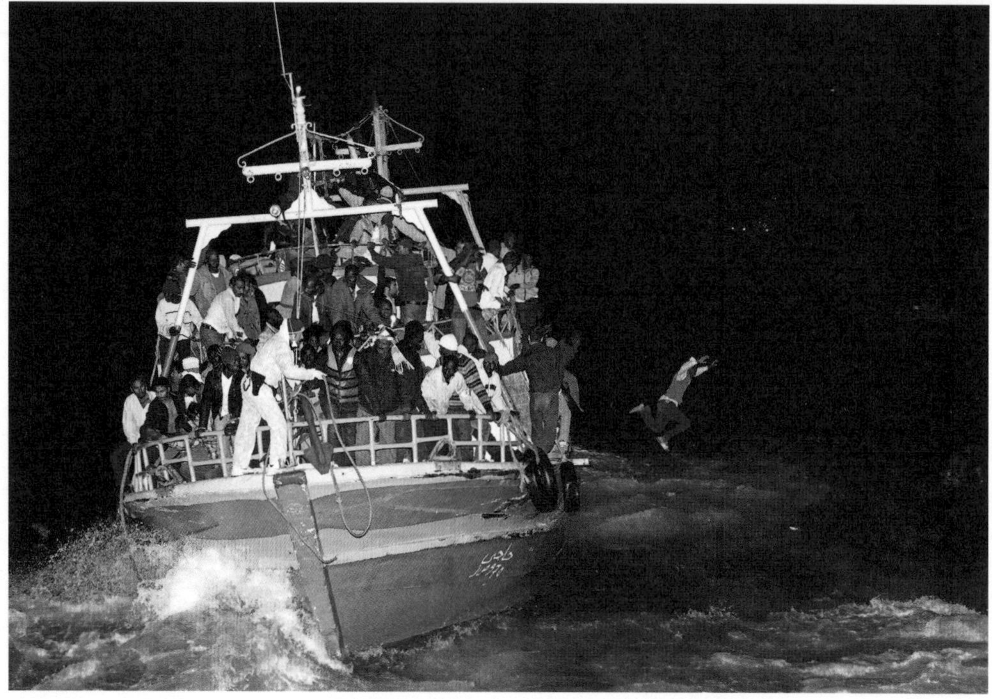

Refugees arriving by boat at the island of Lampedusa, between Sicily and Tunisia

powerfully true than of this cross, made from the wreckage of a boat which foundered off Lampedusa on 11 October 2013 – 311 Somali and Eritrean migrants drowned. The inhabitants of Lampedusa managed to save 155 others. On the horizontal bar you can see the remains of the scuffed blue paint of the shipwrecked boat, with the bare wood beneath; on the upright, many layers of paint, time and again damaged, scraped back and renewed, remind us of the shattered human lives which the boat once carried. In 2015, Francesco Tuccio gave the cross to the British Museum. It is an object which in its simplicity and in the directness of its message humbles even the great museum that houses it.

The teachings of the Buddha, represented in the *thangka*, offer reconciliation and release to those who follow them. The Lampedusa cross is a statement, Christian and also universal, that out of destruction and suffering can come redemption and new life. Tuccio intended it as a plea that our idea of community should be able to embrace not just those who share our beliefs, but all those who share our world. He gave a similar cross to Pope Francis, who carried it in a penitential Mass held on Lampedusa on 8 July 2013, in memory of the migrants who had lost their lives trying to cross the Mediterranean. In his homily the Pope called on all to consider their responsibility for, and their response to, the moral danger that he described as 'the globalization of indifference'.

The objects we have looked at in this book have been connected to many faiths, some long dead, others that today shape the lives of millions. We have encountered a wealth of different stories about the world and our place in it, but we have looked less at what individuals believe, and more at what communities do as ways of giving expression to those shared beliefs. And all those practices seem to me to assert essentially the same thing: that we are each part of a narrative much bigger than ourselves, members of a continuing community in which there is a shared companionship of purpose. Practices like these mark identity and strengthen cohesion – which is why societies from the Ice Age onwards have been willing to pour such enormous resources into them. That heightened sense of identity can of course be exclusive and confrontational, as we saw in Ayodhya, Jerusalem, Nagasaki, Paris and Khartoum; but it will also enable societies to survive against enormous odds, as when the Parsis were forced to leave Iran for Gujarat, the Ethiopians resisted Italian invasion, African-American slaves struggled for freedom, or the Siberian Sakha preserved their traditions in the face of Russian encroachment over centuries.

The decline of Christian religious observance in Europe began with the rejection on rationalist grounds of the dogmas of the church and hostility to its political power. It has continued through growing indifference, until for many people it is now little more than a folk memory. In the eighteenth and nineteenth centuries, many believed that governments used religion to maintain control of their potentially criminal or rebellious subjects. There appears to be no connection today between levels of secularity of particular states and their levels of criminality – or rebelliousness. But the declining role of institutional religion has, I think, led to a serious loss of community, as the religious participant has given way to the ever more atomized consumer. All the traditions we have looked at affirm that the life of the individual can best be lived in a community, and all of them offer ways of making that affirmation a reality. Jean-Paul Sartre famously observed that 'Hell is other people.' The narratives and practices we have looked at in this book argue precisely the contrary: that living properly with other people, living with each other, is the nearest we can get to heaven.

One sculpture, more than any other object that I know, gives physical form to this idea. It comes inevitably from a particular tradition – the Christian – and from a particular time – around 1480. But it embodies the universal phenomenon of a sustaining community of belief. It closes the circle of this book, for it was made in south Germany, in the neighbourhood of Ulm, not many miles from where the Lion Man was found. It shows, slightly smaller than life size, what Germans call a 'Schutzmantel-Maria': the Virgin Mary spreading her protective cloak. Beneath its sheltering folds are ten small figures, representatives of a whole society: men and women of different ages and types, all either praying or looking anxiously out. But Mary, who by tradition represents the Church, is serene. Splendid in gold and blue, she gathers the community of the faithful, holds them together and shields them from harm. On a different scale from those she protects, she is the continuing story in which they are mere episodes, an enduring institution which embraces them all, and will outlive them all. She looks steadfastly to the future and strikingly, she – and they – are moving forwards.

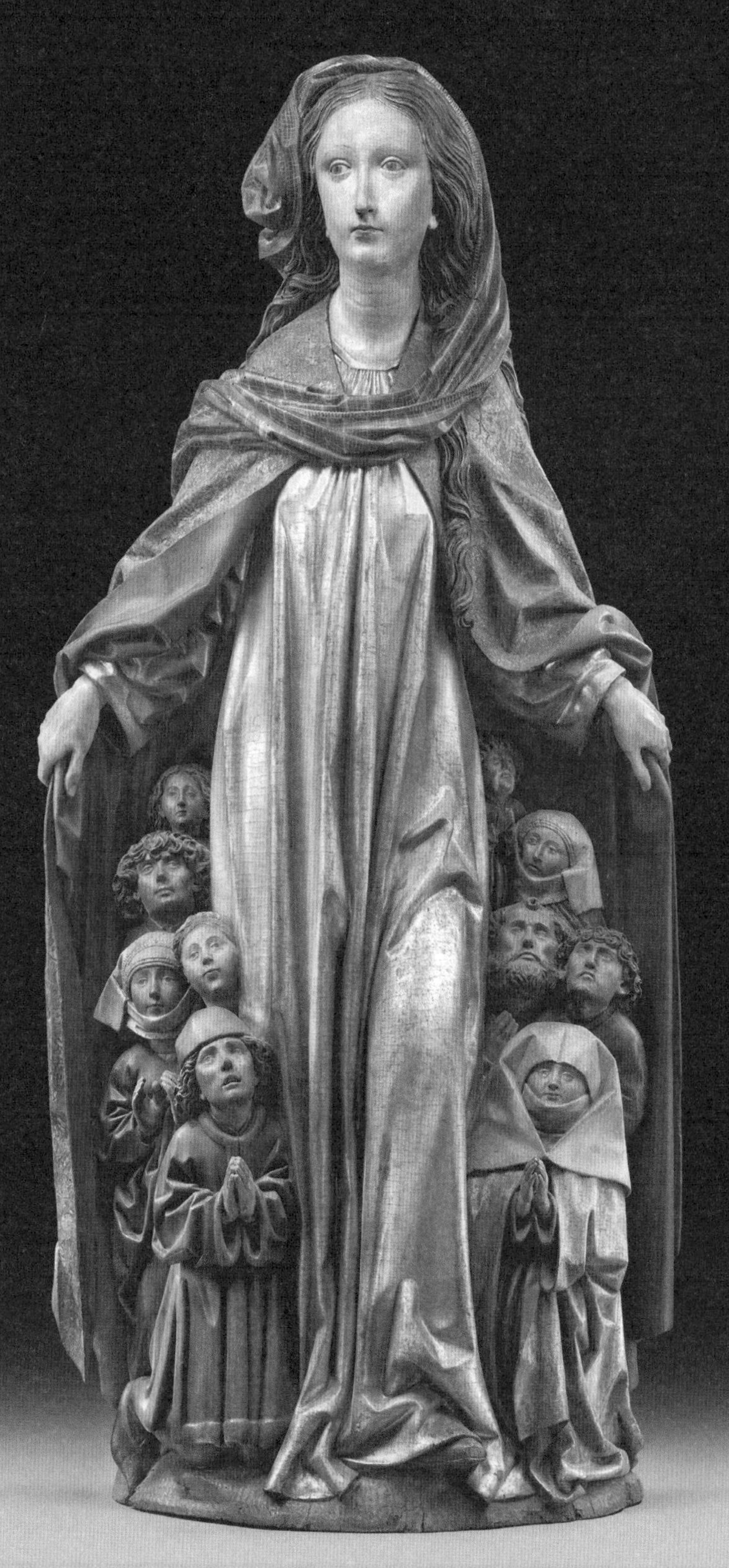

LIST OF ILLUSTRATIONS

Every effort has been made to contact all copyright holders. The publishers will be pleased to amend in future editions any errors or omissions brought to their attention.

203. Shrine of the Three Kings, *c.*1225. Cologne Cathedral. *Interfoto/akg-images*
205 (*top left*). Ampulla, twelfth/thirteenth century. © *The Trustees of the British Museum (1876,1214.18)*
205 (*top right*). Pilgrim badge, thirteenth century. © *The Trustees of the British Museum (1921,0216.69)*
205 (*bottom left*). Pilgrim badge, thirteenth century. © *The Trustees of the British Museum (1856,0701.2053)*
205 (*bottom right*). Fragment of a pilgrim souvenir, *c.*1320–75. © *The Trustees of the British Museum (2001,0702.1)*
209. Dhamekh stupa, Sarnath. *Alamy*
211. Pilgrims on the Hajj, Mecca. *Muhammad Hamed/Reuters*
212. Three rulers on the Hajj, 1960s. *King Fahd National Library, Riyadh*
214. Zamzam flask, twenty-first century. © *The Trustees of the British Museum (2011,6043.75)*
218-219. Model of Ysyakh festival, mid-nineteenth century. © *The Trustees of the British Museum (As.5068.a)*
222. Detail of kneeling priest from the model of the Ysyakh festival. © *The Trustees of the British Museum (As.5068.a)*
225. Ysyakh festival, Tuimaada, 2016. © YSIA.*ru*
227. Mosaic depicting the month of December, early third century, from El Jem. *Archaeological Museum, Sousse, Tunisia*
229. English Christmas card, early twentieth century. © *Look and Learn/Valerie Jackson Harris Collection/Bridgeman Images*
231 (*top left*). Fresco, fourth century, at Church of St Nicholas, Myra, Turkey. *Alamy*
231 (*top right*). The Charity of St Nicholas (detail) by Master of Leg of St Lucy, 15th century. Groeningemuseum, Bruges. *Lukas - Art in Flanders* VZW / *Bridgeman Images*
231 (*bottom left*). Illustration from Jan Schenkman, *St. Nikolaas en zijn knecht*, 1850. *Koninklijke Bibliotheek, The Hague*
231 (*bottom right*). Front cover of the Bengali magazine *Anandamela*, 2016.
233. Front cover of *Rudolph the Red-Nosed Reindeer*, by Robert L. May, New York, 1939.
235. Scrooge's third visitor, illustration by John Leech from Charles Dickens, *A Christmas Carol*, 1843. © *British Library Board. All Rights Reserved/Bridgeman Images*
237. Christmas tree at Windsor Castle, 1848. © *Look and Learn/ Illustrated Papers Collection/Bridgeman Images*
240. Pope John Paul II at the Basilica of Our Lady of Guadalupe, 1999. *M. Sambucetti/* AFP / *Getty Images*
244. Farm workers on strike, San Joaquin valley, California, March 1966. *Photo courtesy Estuary Press* © *The Harvey Richards Media Archive*
245. Straw hat, 1980s. © *The Trustees of the British Museum (Am1988,08.204)*
246. Roman coin, *c.*41–54 CE. © *The Trustees of the British Museum (1844,0425.460.A)*
247. Artemis as the mother goddess of fertility, Ephesus, second century. Archaeological Museum, Ephesus. *Werner Forman Archive/Bridgeman Images*
249. Our Lady of Guadalupe and Diana of Ephesus figurines, 1980s, 1970s, second–first century BCE, first–second century CE. © *The Trustees of the British Museum (Am1990,08.316.a, Am1978,15.913.a, 1883,0724.1, 1909,0620.2)*
252. Pilgrims at the Basilica of Guadalupe, Mexico, 2008. *A. Estrella/* AFP / *Getty Images*
253. Dedications to Diana, Princess of Wales, Paris, 1997. *Thierry Chesnot/Getty Images*
254. The Mother of God Kazanskaya icon from Yaroslavl, 1800–1850. © *The Trustees of the British Museum (1998,0605.30)*
257. The Mother of God Kazanskaya icon from Moscow, seventeenth to nineteenth century. © *The Trustees of the British Museum (1895,1224.1)*
259. *Council of War in Fili in 1812*, by Aleksei Danilovich Kivshenko, 1882. Tretyakov Gallery, Moscow. *Bridgeman Images*
261. The Mother of God Vladimirskaya icon, nineteenth century. © *The Trustees of the British Museum (1998,0605.8)*
264. Temporary *pandal* built for Durga Puja, Kolkata, 2013. *Tuul and Bruno Morandi/Alamy*
267. Durga Puja, Kolkata. © *A. Abbas/Magnum Photos*
268. *Nativity*, by Geertgen tot Sint Jans, *c.*1490. National Gallery, London. *Bridgeman Images*
271. Game Pass shelter, Drakensberg, Kwazulu Natal. *Ariadne Van Zandbergen/Alamy*
272. San rock art (MUN1 36). *Rock Art Research Institute/* SARADA, *University of the Witwatersrand*
274. Detail of San rock art (MUN1 36). *Rock Art Research Institute/* SARADA, *University of the Witwatersrand*
279. Japanese house shrine. © *The Trustees of the British Museum (1893,1101.22)*
281. Coat of arms of South Africa.
282. Rainer Maria Rilke, 1902. *akg-images*
285. Crucifixion with St Bridget in adoration, sixteenth century, Netherlandish school. © *The Trustees of the British Museum (1856,0209.81)*
287. Icon depicting the transfiguration, fifteenth century, Novgorod School. Museum of Art, Novgorod. *Bridgeman Images*
293. Seated Buddha, second or third century, Gandhara, Pakistan. © *The Trustees of the British Museum (1895,1026.1)*
295. Save the Children advertisement, 1970s. *The Advertising Archives*
296. Remains of Bamiyan Buddhas, third and fifth centuries, Afghanistan. © *World Religions Photo Library/Bridgeman Images*
298 (*left*). Head of Hermes/Mercury, second century. © *The Trustees of the British Museum (1978,0102.1)*
298 (*right*). Head of Christ, *c.*1130. © *The Trustees of the British Museum (1994,1008.1)*
302. Torah Ark, Plymouth Synagogue. © *Historic England Archive*
304. Rabbi Julia Neuberger. © *Suki Dhanda*
305. Torah *yad* (pointer), *c.*1745. © *The Trustees of the British Museum (2010,8002.1)*
307. Mosque lamp, *c.*1570–75, Turkey. © *The Trustees of the British Museum (G.143)*
310–11. Shaikh Lutfallah Mosque, Isfahan, Iran. *B. O'Kane/ Alamy*
313. Reading the Koran, Hulu Langat, Malaysia. *M. Rasfan/* AFP / *Getty Images*
314. Mary and the Infant Christ, fifteenth century. Great Snoring, Norfolk. *Holmes Garden Photos/Alamy*
318–19. The Felmingham Hall hoard, second–third century. © *The Trustees of the British Museum (1925,0610.32)*
320 (*left*). Altar dedicated to Jupiter Optimus Maximus Tanarus found near Chester. © *Ashmolean Museum, University of Oxford* (ANC*handler.3.1)*
320 (*right*). Gold coin, 218–19 CE. © *The Trustees of the British Museum (1922,0909.4)*
325. The Gilgamesh tablet, seventh century BCE. © *The Trustees of the British Museum (K.3375)*
328. Dr Ambedkar statue. © *Paul Kobrak*

FURTHER READING

Further information on all the British Museum objects is available on the British Museum website (www.britishmuseum.org) and these bibliographies are regularly updated. Only literature in English is listed here. Comprehensive bibliographies will be found in the books listed for the individual chapters and in the Oxford Handbooks of *Ancient Greek Religion* (eds. Esther Eidinow and Julia Kindt, 2015), *The Archaeology of Ritual and Religion* (ed. Timothy Insoll, 2011), *Contemporary Buddhism* (ed. Michael Jerryson, 2016), *Indian Philosophy* (ed. Jonardon Ganeri, 2017), *Islamic Theology* (ed. Sabine Schmidtke, 2016), *Jewish Studies* (ed. Martin Goodman, 2002) and *Medieval Christianity* (ed. John H. Arnold, 2014).

GENERAL READING

Armstrong, Karen. *Islam: A Short History*, 2000
Beard, Mary, John North and Simon Price. *Religions of Rome*, 1998
Fisher, Mary Pat. *Living Religions*, 2011
Goodman, Martin. *A History of Judaism*, 2017
Gray, John. *Seven Kinds of Atheism*, 2018
Grayling, A. C. *The God Argument: The Case Against Religion and for Humanism*, 2013
MacCulloch, Diarmaid. *A History of Christianity: The First Three Thousand Years*, 2009
McLeod, Hew. *Sikhism*, 1997
Neuberger, Julia. *On Being Jewish*, 1995
Pattanaik, Devdutt. *Myth=Mithya: A Handbook of Hindu Mythology*, 2014
Praet, Istvan, ed. *Animism and the Question of Life*, 2014
Quirke, Stephen. *Ancient Egyptian Religion*, 1992
Sengupta, Arputha Rani. *Buddhist Art and Culture: Symbols and Significance*, 2013
Woodhead, Linda, and Andrew Brown. *That Was the Church That Was: How the Church of England Lost the English People*, 2017
Woodhead, Linda, and Rebecca Catto, eds. *Religion and Change in Modern Britain*, 2012

1. THE BEGINNINGS OF BELIEF

Cook, Jill. *Ice Age Art: Arrival of the Modern Mind*, 2013
Gamble, Clive. *Settling the Earth: The Archaeology of Deep Human History*, 2013
Harari, Yuval Noah. *Sapiens: A Brief History of Humankind*, 2014
Wehrberger, Kurt, ed. *The Return of the Lion Man: History, Myth, Magic*, 2013

2. FIRE AND STATE

Kaliff, Anders. 'Fire', in Insoll, ed. *Ritual and Religion*, 51–62
Pyne, Stephen J. *Vestal Fire: An Environmental History, Told through Fire, of Europe and Europe's Encounter with the World*, 1997
Stewart, Sarah, ed. *The Everlasting Flame: Zoroastrianism in History and Imagination*, 2013
Wildfang, Robin Lorsch. *Rome's Vestal Virgins: A Study of Rome's Vestal Priestesses in the Late Republic and Early Empire*, 2006

3. WATER OF LIFE AND DEATH

Darian, Steven G. *The Ganges in Myth and History*, 1978
Eck, Diana L. *Banaras: City of Light*, 1982
Eck, Diana L. *India: A Sacred Geography*, 2012
Fagan, Brian. *Elixir: A History of Water and Humankind*, 2011
Reinhart, A. Kevin. 'Impurity/No Danger', *History of Religions* 30:1 (1990), 1–24

4. THE RETURN OF THE LIGHT

Dowd, Marion, and Robert Hensey, eds. *The Archaeology of Darkness*, 2016
Hensey, Robert. *First Light: The Origins of Newgrange*, 2015
Kirkland, Russell. 'The Sun and the Throne: The Origins of the Royal Descent Myth in Ancient Japan', *Numen* 44:2 (1997), 109–52
Stout, Geraldine, and Matthew Stout. *Newgrange*, 2008

5. HARVEST AND HOMAGE

King, J. C. H. *First Peoples, First Contacts: Native Peoples of North America*, 1999
Laugrand, Frédéric, and Jarich Oosten. *Hunters, Predators and Prey: Inuit Perceptions of Animals*, 2015
Lincoln, Amber, with John Goodwin et al. *Living with Old Things: Inupiaq Stories, Bering Strait Histories*, 2010
Mojsov, Bojana. *Osiris: Death and Afterlife of a God*, 2005
Taylor, John. *Death and the Afterlife in Ancient Egypt*, 2001

6. LIVING WITH THE DEAD

Besom, Thomas. *Of Summits and Sacrifice: An Ethnohistoric Study of Inka Religious Practices*, 2009
Isbell, William H. *Mummies and Mortuary Monuments: A Postprocessual Prehistory of Central Andean Social Organization*, 1997
Ruitenbeek, Klaas, ed. *Faces of China: Portrait Painting of the Ming and Qing Dynasties*, 2017
Scott, Janet Lee. *For Gods, Ghosts and Ancestors: The Chinese Tradition of Paper Offerings*, 2007
Stuart, Jan, and Evelyn S. Rawski. *Worshiping the Ancestors: Chinese Commemorative Portraits*, 2001

7. BIRTH AND THE BODY

Dresvina, Juliana. *A Maid with a Dragon: The Cult of St Margaret of Antioch in Medieval England*, 2016
Reader, Ian, and George J. Tanabe, *Practically Religious: Worldly Benefits and the Common Religion of Japan*, 1998

8. A PLACE IN TRADITION

Bolton, Lissant. 'Teaching the Next Generation: A Lock of Hair from Tanna', in L. Bolton et al, *Melanesia: Art and Encounter*, 2013, 285–6
Eis, Ruth. *Torah Binders of the Judah L. Magnes Museum*, 1979
van Gennep, Arnold. *The Rites of Passage*, trans. Monkia B. Vizedom and Gabrielle L. Caffee, 1960
Grimes, Ronald L. *Deeply into the Bone: Re-Inventing Rites of Passage*, 2002

Shaw, Sarah. *The Spirit of Buddhist Meditation*, 2014
Sperber, Daniel. *The Jewish Life Cycle: Custom, Lore and Iconography*, 2008

9. LET US PRAY

Ettinghausen, Richard, ed. *Prayer Rugs*, 1974
Mauss, Marcel. *On Prayer*, trans. W. S. F. Pickering and Howard Morphy, 2003
Winston-Allen, Anne. *Stories of the Rose: The Making of the Rosary in the Middle Ages*, 1997

10. THE POWER OF SONG

Butt, John. *The Cambridge Companion to Bach*, 1997
Gardiner, John Eliot. *Music in the Castle of Heaven*, 2013
Joseph, Jordania. *Choral Singing in Human Culture and Evolution*, 2015
Troeger, Thomas H. *Music as Prayer: The Theology and Practice of Church Music*, 2013
Wild, Beate. 'Fur Within, Flowers Without: A Transylvanian Fur Coat Worn to Church', in eds. Elisabeth Tietmeyer and Irene Ziehe. *Discover Europe!*, 2008, 26–34

11. THE HOUSE OF GOD

Cohen, Michael, ed. *Sacred Gardens and Landscape: Ritual and Agency*, 2007
Luckert, Karl W. *Stone Age Religion at Göbekli Tepe: From Hunting to Domestication, Warfare and Civilization*, 2013
McNeill, William H. *Keeping Together in Time: Dance and Drill in Human History*, 1997
Morris, Colin. *The Sepulchre of Christ and the Medieval West: From the Beginning to 1600*, 2005
Rey, Sébastien. *For the Gods of Girsu: City-State Formation in Ancient Sumer*, 2016
Suter, Claudia E. *Gudea's Temple Building: The Representation of an Early Mesopotamian Ruler in Text and Image*, 2000

12. GIFTS TO THE GODS

Cooper, Jago. *Lost Kingdoms of South America*, BBC 4, 2014
Harris, Diane. *The Treasures of the Parthenon and Erechtheion*, 1995
Llonch, Elisenda Vila. *Beyond El Dorado: Power and Gold in Ancient Colombia*, 2013
Whitmarsh, Tim. *Battling the Gods: Atheism in the Ancient World*, 2016

13. HOLY KILLING

Bremmer, Jan N., ed. *The Strange World of Human Sacrifice*, 2007
Burkert, Walter. *Homo Necans: The Anthropology of Ancient Greek Sacrificial Ritual and Myth*, trans. Peter Bing, 1983
Cooper, Jago. *The Inca: Masters of the Clouds*, BBC 4, 2015
Girard, René. *Violence and the Sacred*, trans. Patrick Gregory, 1977
James, E. O. *Sacrifice and Sacrament*, 1962
McClymond, Kathryn. *Beyond Sacred Violence: A Comparative Study of Sacrifice*, 2008
McEwan, Colin, and Leonardo López Luján. *Moctezuma: Aztec Ruler*, 2009
Naiden, Fred. 'Sacrifice', in Eidinow and Kindt, eds. *Ancient Greek Religion*, 463–76

14. TO BE A PILGRIM

Duffy, Eamon. *The Heart in Pilgrimage: A Prayerbook for Catholic Christians*, 2014
Porter, Venetia, ed. *Hajj: Journey to the Heart of Islam*, 2012
Spencer, Brian. *Pilgrim Souvenirs and Secular Badges*, 2017
Sumption, Jonathan. *Pilgrimage: An Image of Medieval Religion*, 1975
Webb, Diana. *Pilgrimage in Medieval England*, 2000

15. FESTIVAL TIME

Falassi, Alessandro, ed. *Time Out of Time: Essays on the Festival*, 1987
Leach, Edmund. 'Time and False Noses', in *The Essential Edmund Leach I: Anthropology and Society*, eds. Stephen Hugh-Jones and James Laidlaw, 2000, 182–5
Restad, Penne L. *Christmas in America: A History*, 1996
Whiteley, Sheila, ed. *Christmas, Ideology and Popular Culture*, 2008

16. THE PROTECTORESSES

Brading, D. A. *Mexican Phoenix: Our Lady of Guadalupe*, 2001
Budin, Stephanie. *Artemis*, 2015
MacLean Rogers, Guy. *The Mysteries of Artemis of Ephesos: Cult, Polis, and Change in the Graeco-Roman World*, 2013
Rietveld, James D. *Artemis of the Ephesians: Mystery, Magic and Her Sacred Landscape*, 2014
Warner, Marina. *Alone of All Her Sex: Cult of the Virgin Mary*, 1976

17. THE WORK OF ART IN TIMES OF SPIRITUAL REPRODUCTION

Banerjee, Sudeshna. *Durga Puja: Celebrating the Goddess*, 2006
Bobrov, Yury. *A Catalogue of the Russian Icons in the British Museum*, ed. Chris Entwistle, 2008
Cormack, Robin. *Icons*, 2007
Guha-Thakurta, Tapati. *In the Name of the Goddess: The Durga Pujas of Contemporary Kolkata*, 2015
Khilnani, Sunil. *The Idea of India*, 1997
Williams, Rowan. *The Dwelling of the Light: Praying with Icons of Christ*, 2003

18. THE ACCRETION OF MEANING

Lewis-Williams, David, and Sam Challis. *Deciphering Ancient Minds: The Mystery of San Bushman Rock Art*, 2011
Perry, Grayson. *The Tomb of the Unknown Craftsman*, 2011
Smyers, Karen A. *The Fox and the Jewel: Shared and Private Meanings of Contemporary Japanese Inari Worship*, 1999

19. CHANGE YOUR LIFE

Armstrong, Karen. *A History of God: From Abraham to the Present*, 1999
Beguin, Giles. *Buddhist Art: An Historical and Cultural Journey*, 2009
Bynum, C. *Wonderful Blood: Theology and Practice in Late Medieval Northern Germany and Beyond*, 2007
Diamond, Debra. *Paths to Perfection: Buddhist Art at the Freer|Sackler*, 2017
Duffy, Eamon. *The Stripping of the Altars: Traditional Religion in England, 1400–1580*, 1992
MacGregor, Neil, with Erika Langmuir. *Seeing Salvation: Images of Christ in Art*, 2000

20. REJECTING THE IMAGE, REVERING THE WORD

Al-Akiti, Afifi, and Joshua Hordern. 'New Conversations in Islamic and Christian Thought', *Muslim World* 106:2 (2016), 219–25
Freedberg, David. *The Power of Images: Studies in the History and Theory of Response*, 1989
Kolrud, Kristine, and Marina Prusac, eds. *Iconoclasm from Antiquity to Modernity*, 2014

Neuberger, Julia. *On Being Jewish*, 1995
Noyes, James. *The Politics of Iconoclasm: Religion, Violence and the Culture of Image-Breaking in Christianity and Islam*, 2013
Porter, Venetia, and Heba Nayel Barakat, eds. *Mightier than the Sword: Arabic Script*, 2004

21. THE BLESSINGS OF MANY GODS

George, A. R. *The Babylonian Gilgamesh Epic: Introduction, Critical Edition and Cuneiform Texts*, 2003
Haeussler, Ralph, and Anthony King, eds. *Celtic Religions in the Roman Period: Personal, Local, and Global*, 2017
Henig, Martin. *Religion in Roman Britain*, 1984

22. THE POWER OF ONE

Crouch, C. L., Jonathan Stökl and Anna Louise Zernecke, eds. *Mediating Between Heaven and Earth: Communication with the Divine in the Ancient Near East*, 2012
Hoffmeier, James K. *Akhenaten and the Origins of Monotheism*, 2015
Kemp, Barry. *The City of Akhenaten and Nefertiti: Amarna and its People*, 2013
Mitchell, Stephen, and Peter Van Nuffelen, eds. *One God: Pagan Monotheism in the Roman Empire*, 2010

23. SPIRITS OF PLACE

Bell, Michael Mayerfeld. 'The Ghosts of Place', *Theory and Society* 26:6 (1997), 813–36
Bolton, Lissant. 'Dressing for Transition: Weddings, Clothing and Change in Vanuatu', in Susanne Küechler and Graeme Were, eds. *The Art of Clothing: A Pacific Experience*, 2005, 19–32
Brody, A. M. *Larrakitj: Kerry Stokes Collection*, 2011
Terwiel, B. J. *Monks and Magic: Revisiting a Classic Study of Religious Ceremonies in Thailand*, 1975

24. IF GOD BE WITH US

Barnett, Michael. *The Rastafari Movement: A North American and Caribbean Perspective*, 2018
Binns, John. *The Orthodox Church of Ethiopia: A History*, 2016
Henry, William 'Lez'. 'Reggae, Rasta and the Role of the Deejay in the Black British Experience', *Contemporary British History* 26:3 (2012), 355–73.
Lee, Hélène. *First Rasta: Leonard Howell and the Rise of Rastafarianism*, trans. Lily Davis, 2003

25. TOLERATING AND NOT TOLERATING

Habib, Irfan, ed. *Akbar and his India*, 1997
Khan, Iqtidar Alam. 'Akbar's Personality Traits and World Outlook: A Critical Reappraisal', *Social Scientist* 20:9/10 (1992), 16–30
Khera, Paramdip Kuar. *Catalogue of Sikh Coins in the British Museum*, 2011
Khilnani, Sunil. *Incarnations: India in 50 Lives*, 2016
Sen, Amartya. *The Argumentative Indian: Writings on Indian History, Culture and Identity*, 2006
Shani, Giorgio. *Sikh Nationalism and Identity in a Global Age*, 2008
Spear, Percival. *A History of India II: From the Sixteenth to the Twentieth Century*, 1965
Tully, Mark. *India: The Road Ahead*, 2012
Wink, André. *Akbar*, 2008

26. THE MANDATE OF HEAVEN

Barley, Nigel. *The Art of Benin*, 2010
Fagg, William. *Divine Kingship in Africa*, 1970
Loewe, Michael. *Divination, Mythology and Monarchy in Han China*, 1994
Pines, Yuri. *The Everlasting Empire: The Political Culture of Ancient China and Its Imperial Legacy*, 2012
Plankensteiner, Barbara, ed. *Benin Kings and Rituals: Court Arts from Nigeria*, 2007

27. THY KINGDOM COME

Abdy, Richard, and Amelia Dowler. *Coins and the Bible*, 2013
Avni, Gideon and Guy D. Stiebel, eds. *Roman Jerusalem: A New Old City*, 2017
Goodman, Martin. *Rome and Jerusalem: The Clash of Ancient Civilizations*, 2007
Kramer, Robert S. *Holy City on the Nile: Omdurman During the Mahdiyya, 1885–1898*, 2010
Menahem, Mor. *The Second Jewish Revolt: The Bar Kokhba War, 132–136 CE*, 2016
Nicoll, Fergus. *Sword of the Prophet: The Mahdi of Sudan and the Death of General Gordon*, 2004
Sebag Montefiore, Simon. *Jerusalem: The Biography*, 2011

28. TURNING THE SCREW

Boxer, C. R. *The Christian Century in Japan 1549–1650*, 1993
Chappell Lougee, Carolyn. *Facing the Revocation: Huguenot Families, Faith, and the King's Will*, 2016
Clark, Tim, ed. *Hokusai: Beyond the Great Wave*, 2017
Hesselink, Reiner H. *The Dream of Christian Nagasaki: World Trade and the Clash of Cultures, 1560–1640*, 2015
Sample Wilson, Christie. *Beyond Belief: Surviving the Revocation of the Edict of Nantes in France*, 2011
Tombs, Robert. *France 1814–1914*, 1996

29. 'THERE IS NO GOD!'

Buck, Paul. 'Revolution in Time', *British Museum Magazine*, 2015
Dawkins, Richard. *The God Delusion*, 2006
Grayling, A. C. *The God Argument: The Case Against Religion and for Humanism*, 2013
Hosking, Geoffrey. *The First Socialist Society: A History of the Soviet Union from Within*, 1993
Hosking, Geoffrey. *Russia and the Russians: From Earliest Times to the Present*, 2001
Maier, Hans. 'Political Religion: A Concept and its Limitations', *Totalitarian Movements and Political Religions* 8:1 (2007), 5–16
Pop, Virgiliu. 'Space and Religion in Russia: Cosmonaut Worship to Orthodox Revival', *Astropolitics* 7:2 (2009), 150–163
Shaw, Matthew. *Time and the French Revolution: The Republican Calendar, 1789–Year XIV*, 2011
Symth, Jonathan. *Robespierre and the Festival of the Supreme Being: The Search for a Republican Morality*, 2016

30. LIVING WITH EACH OTHER

Mehrotra, Rahul, and Felipe Vera, eds. *Kumbh Mela: Mapping the Ephemeral Megacity*, 2015
Sopa, Geshe. 'The Tibetan "Wheel of Life": Iconography and Doxography', *Journal of the International Association of Buddhist Studies* 7:1 (1984), 125–46

ACKNOWLEDGEMENTS

This book is the result of a partnership between the British Museum, the BBC and Penguin Books, and all three institutions have contributed greatly to its content and its shape. It is, as the reader will quickly see, a record of many conversations with experts, mostly in the form of interviews for the series of radio programmes of which this book is an expansion and a development. It is impossible to overstate the generosity with which these contributors gave their time, expertise and scholarship: they are acknowledged individually when they are quoted, but my conversations with them have influenced both the discourse and the direction of the book at every stage, and I should like to express here my profound gratitude to them all.

There were of course many other significant conversations and I should like especially to thank Vesta Curtis, Antony Griffiths, Rahul Gumber, Cyrus Guzda, Anna Miller, Catherine Reynolds, Mahrukh Tarapor and Jonathan Williams.

At the heart of most of the chapters are objects from the British Museum, and the book would not have been possible without the patient generosity of that institution and the deep knowledge, always willingly shared, of those who work in it. Many of them – though by no means all – appear in the text. Hartwig Fischer, the Director, and Joanna Mackle, Deputy Director, supported the project from the beginning. The selection of objects from the Museum, and the research into them, was led with erudite calm by Barrie Cook, assisted by Rosie Weetch. Jill Cook conceived and curated the British Museum exhibition associated with the radio programmes, which was, with enormous generosity, sponsored by John Studzinski and the Genesis Foundation. Along with Lissant Bolton, Jill also played a major part in developing both radio series and book, especially in the areas of deep history and small, non-urban societies. Conversations with all these colleagues were as rewarding as they were reliable. Jo Hammond coordinated every aspect of the Museum's engagement, from the moving and photographing of objects to the checking of the smallest details of provenance or condition. How she contrived to do this without a hitch, but with constant good humour, remains a mystery.

In all the museums, sites, buildings and landscapes that we visited, we were welcomed and furnished with whatever access was possible and whatever information was available. I should like particularly to thank Mr Girish Tandon and Mr Alankar Tandon, who arranged for us to be accommodated in the temporary city erected for the Mela in Allahabad, and the District Magistrate and the local authorities of Allahabad for managing the complex logistics of our visit. Mr Ravindra Singh helped organize our visit to Ayodhya, and the High Priest of the Parsi Temple in Udwada took great trouble to ensure that we could see everything which a non-Parsi is allowed to see. In all our journeys in India, I was fortunate to be guided by Mahrukh Tarapor, who provided good counsel and good cheer and steered us smoothly through many perplexing moments.

At the BBC, Radio 4, under the leadership of Gwyneth Williams, was unstinting in its commitment. Mohit Bakaya and Rob Ketteridge oversaw the commissioning and delivery of the series; John Goudie was central to the intellectual structure of the whole and the planning of every individual programme; Anne Smith and Sue Fleming managed the many journeys and guided me through the labyrinths of administration. And Paul Kobrak accompanied me throughout, recorded almost every interview and an astonishing variety of sounds, and then, with a combination of intellect and magic, turned them elegantly into programmes.

In preparing the texts for both the programmes and the book I was greatly assisted by Christopher Harding, who helped enormously with research and with writing, and whose deep knowledge of Japanese culture is evident in several chapters. And I owe a special debt of gratitude to Richard Beresford, who on many occasions rescued me from digital disaster.

At Penguin, Cecilia Mackay has found photographs which have often not just illustrated the text but pointed the argument in new directions. Andrew Barker has designed the interior of the book, as Jim Stoddart has the jacket, with elegance and style. Penelope Vogler has organized the many activities around publication of the book with aplomb. Richard Duguid and Imogen Scott have overseen the whole production process and Ben Sinyor has been tireless in managing the circulation of texts and photographs, endlessly checking and collating — and quietly improving. Stuart Proffitt has gone far beyond what might be expected of any editor, engaging with every argument, challenging propositions, and clarifying every sentence in many hours of happy discussion. His patience and his courtesy never cease to astonish. No author could have been better supported.

Neil MacGregor
June 2018

INDEX